Gale Encyclopedia of
U.S. History:
Government and Politics

Gale Encyclopedia of U.S. History: Government and Politics

VOLUME 2

GALE
CENGAGE Learning

Detroit • New York • San Francisco • New Haven, Conn • Waterville, Maine • London

Gale Encyclopedia of U.S. History: Government and Politics

Paula Kepos and Derek Jacques

Project Editors: Anne Marie Hacht and Dwayne D. Hayes

Editorial: Ira Mark Milne

Rights Acquisition and Management: Margaret Chamberlain-Gaston, Jackie Jones, Jhanay Williams, and Robyn Young

Composition: Evi Abou-El-Seoud

Manufacturing: Wendy Blurton

Imaging: Lezlie Light

Product Design: Jennifer Wahi

For product information and technology assistance, contact us at
Gale Customer Support, 1-800-877-4253.
For permission to use material from this text or product,
submit all requests online at **www.cengage.com/permissions.**
Further permissions questions can be emailed to
permissionrequest@cengage.com

Cover photographs reproduced by permission of Tannen Maury/epa/Corbis (picture of the CNN YouTube Democratic Debate) and Bettmann/Corbis (image of Theodore Roosevelt giving campaign speech).

Library of Congress Cataloging-in-Publication Data

Gale encyclopedia of U.S. history. Government and politics.
   p. cm. --
  Includes bibliographical references and index.
   ISBN 978-1-4144-3118-5 (set) -- ISBN 978-1-4144-3119-2 (vol. 1 hardcover) -- ISBN 978-1-4144-3120-8 (vol. 2 hardcover)
   1. United States--Politics and government--Encyclopedias. 2. Political science--United States--Encyclopedias. I. Gale Group. II. Title: Encyclopedia of U.S. history, government and politics. III. Title: Government and politics.

E183.G235 2008
973.003--dc22
          2007034360

Gale
27500 Drake Rd.
Farmington Hills, MI, 48331-3535

978-1-4144-3118-5 (set)	1-4144-3118-X (set)
978-1-4144-3119-2 (vol. 1)	1-4144-3119-8 (vol. 1)
978-1-4144-3120-8 (vol. 2)	1-4144-3120-1 (vol. 2)

This title is also available as an e-book.
ISBN-13: 978-1-4144-3121-5 ISBN-10: 1-4144-3121-X
Contact your Gale, a part of Cengage Learning sales representative for ordering information.

Printed in the United States of America
1 2 3 4 5 6 7 11 10 09 08

Contents

Contents

Introduction

The *Gale Encyclopedia of U.S. History: Government and Politics* traces the development of the government of the United States from the European powers that explored and colonized the New World beginning in the fifteenth century—and the native people they displaced—to the present day. In eleven chronological chapters, *Gale Encyclopedia of U.S. History: Government and Politics* presents four hundred entries about the people, institutions, laws, and social movements responsible for the evolution of the U.S. government.

Each of the chapters in *Gale Encyclopedia of U.S. History: Government and Politics* covers a specific period in American history and is designed to be compatible with the National Council for Social Studies (NCSS) High School U.S. History Curriculum Standards, as well as textbooks and lesson plans based on those standards.

Each chapter is divided into the following sections:

Introduction: Provides an overview of the historical era and the social changes underway at that time.

How They Were Governed: Describes the institutions, doctrines, and procedures responsible for regulating public life in the Americas throughout its history. From U.S. government agencies to electronic voting machines, the function and origins of each subject is explained, as are its social repercussions.

Important Figures of the Day: Provides biographies of major political figures, social advocates, leaders, lawmakers, and antagonists, with a view to how each inspired social change or government policy.

Political Parties, Platforms, and Key Issues: Focuses on political life, including the ideas, events, and organizations that drive the government and political change. America's political parties and factions lead this section, with major and minor parties described and placed in historical context.

Current Events and Social Movements: Describes events outside of government that had profound repercussions on American politics, including natural disasters, wars, scandals, religious movements, and groups bent on social reform.

Legislation, Court Cases, and Trials: Describes the body of law, including acts of Congress and Supreme Court decisions. Each case, trial, or statute demonstrates the evolution of American lawmaking and reflects the social transformations taking place at the time.

Chronology

1469: Isabella of Castile and Ferdinand of Aragon marry, uniting the Kingdom of Spain under one crown.

1488: Portuguese explorer Bartolomeu Dias sails around the Cape of Good Hope, opening the Asian spice trade to Portugal.

1492: Christopher Columbus, exploring for Spain, makes the first landfall of his voyage to the New World on the island now known as San Salvador in the Bahamas.

1494: The Treaty of Tordesillas establishes a line of demarcation that runs north to south through the Atlantic Ocean, with Spain receiving rights to all newly discovered land to the west of the line and Portugal earning possession of land east of the line.

1497: John Cabot's expedition from England reaches Canada, making Cabot the first European to visit the region since the Vikings.

1519: Spanish conquistador Hernàn Cortés departs on his expedition to Mexico, where he conquers the Aztec Empire for Spain.

1520: Mayan Emperor Moctezuma dies while in the custody of Hernán Cortés.

1521: The expedition of Portuguese explorer Ferdinand Magellan circumnavigates the globe. Magellan himself does not survive the voyage.

1534: Jacques Cartier, exploring for the French, lands in Newfoundland.

King Henry VIII of England forms the Anglican Church, spurring the Reformation in England.

1535: Francisco Pizarro founds the city of Lima near the coast of Peru.

1542: Bartolomé de Las Casa presents to the Spanish royal court *A Short Account of the Destruction of the Indies*, his treatise on the mistreatment of Native Americans by the Spanish.

1570: The Iroquois League adopts a constitution, establishing a participatory democracy.

1584: An expedition from England backed by Sir Walter Raleigh lands in Virginia. Efforts to colonize in Roanoke fail.

1587: A second doomed expedition to settle the Roanoke colony arrives in Virginia.

1588: England defeats the Spanish Armada, curtailing Spain's plans to invade.

1603: Samuel de Champlain of France sets sail for Canada.

1607: The Jamestown colony, the first permanent British settlement in North America, is founded.

1608: Captain John Smith leads the Jamestown colony through early crises with disease and encounters with natives.

1609: Henry Hudson, exploring for the Dutch, navigates the river in the American Northeast that would later bear his name.

1619: Dutch slave traders bring the first African slaves to the Jamestown colony.

The House of Burgesses, the first legislature in the British colonies, is established in Jamestown.

1620: English Puritans embark on a voyage to the New World aboard the *Mayflower*.

1636: Providence becomes the first British settlement in the New World to welcome people of all religious convictions.

1637: Anne Hutchinson is tried for heresy in the Massachusetts Bay Colony.

1660: England's Parliament passes the second Navigation Act, stating that American colonists can only export certain goods to England and imposing duties on those goods.

1675: King Philip's War breaks out between the Wampanoag natives and the colonists of the Plymouth settlement.

1676: Nathaniel Bacon Jr. rebels against the administration of Sir William Berkeley, the governor of Jamestown colony.

1681: William Penn founds the Pennsylvania colony as a "religious experiment."

1686: English King James II forms the Dominion of New England to consolidate authority over the New England colonies by abolishing colonial legislatures.

1688: King James II is deposed—and the Dominion of New England is rescinded—when the Glorious Revolution puts William III and Mary II on the throne.

1691: A new charter is drawn for the Massachusetts colony, reducing Puritan legal authority.

1693: Hysteria over witches in Salem, Massachusetts, leads to more than 185 people being charged with witchcraft, twenty of whom are executed.

1735: Newspaper publisher John Peter Zenger is acquitted of libeling the governor of New York colony, William Cosby.

1754: The French and Indian War begins over a territorial dispute in the Ohio Valley.

1763: The French and Indian War ends with the Treaty of Paris, which cedes all French land east of the Mississippi River to Britain.

1764: The British Parliament passes the Sugar Act, raising penalties for smuggling sugar and other goods.

1765: Parliament passes the Stamp Act, a tax on newspapers, legal documents, and printed materials.

The Quartering Act requires that colonists provide housing and supplies for British soldiers.

1766: On the same day the Stamp Act is repealed, Parliament passes the Declaratory Act, a law asserting Parliament's power to impose statutes and taxes upon the colonies.

1767: Parliament passes the Townshend Acts, a series of taxes levied on products exported to the colonies from England.

1770: British soldiers fire into a crowd of protesters, killing five and wounding six others, in what comes to be known as the Boston Massacre.

1773: England's Parliament passes the Tea Act, giving the British East India Company a monopoly on tea sold in the colonies.

Colonists disguised as Native Americans destroy a tea shipment in Boston Harbor in protest of the Tea Act.

1774: Parliament passes the Coercive Acts, designed to punish Massachusetts after the Boston Tea Party.

The First Continental Congress is held in Philadelphia.

1775: Battles at Lexington and Concord, Massachusetts, mark the beginning of hostilities in the American Revolution.

The Second Continental Congress convenes to discuss issues of war and independence.

The Second Continental Congress selects George Washington to command the Continental Army.

1776: Thomas Paine's pamphlet *Common Sense* is published, calling for independence from Britain and a more democratic system of government.

The Second Continental Congress culminates in the adoption of the Declaration of Independence.

1777: The Marquis de Lafayette of France volunteers to fight with the Continental Army against the British.

1780: General Benedict Arnold's conspiracy to surrender the military fort at West Point is foiled.

1781: The Articles of Confederation are adopted by the Continental Congress.

British forces under General Charles Cornwallis surrender at Yorktown, effectively ending hostilities in the Revolutionary War.

1783: Britain recognizes the independence of the United States by signing the Treaty of Paris, officially ending the Revolutionary War.

1785: The Continental Congress passes the Northwest Ordinance, which allows for expansion of settlements northwest to the Great Lakes.

1786: Daniel Shays leads an armed rebellion in western Massachusetts, protesting taxes imposed by the state legislature.

1787: The Constitutional Convention convenes in Philadelphia for the purpose of replacing the Articles of Confederation.

The series of essays known as the Federalist Papers is published in various New York newspapers.

1789: George Washington is unopposed in the first presidential election.

Alexander Hamilton becomes the first secretary of the Treasury.

1790: Statesman Benjamin Franklin dies in Philadelphia at the age of eighty-four.

1791: The first ten amendments to the U.S. Constitution, called the Bill of Rights, are ratified.

1792: George Washington is reelected president of the United States.

1794: Farmers in western Pennsylvania take up arms against federal excise taxes in the Whiskey Rebellion.

1796: Vice President John Adams defeats Secretary of State Thomas Jefferson in the first contested presidential election in American history.

1797: French agents solicit bribes from American envoys in what comes to be known as the XYZ Affair.

1798: The Federalist-controlled U.S. Congress passes the Sedition Act, granting the president broad powers to suppress criticism of the government.

1799: Congress passes the Logan Act, which prevents private citizens from negotiating with foreign governments.

1800: Thomas Jefferson defeats John Adams in the presidential election of 1800.

1802: Journalist James T. Callender reveals that President Thomas Jefferson fathered children with Sally Hemings, Jefferson's slave.

1803: The U.S. Supreme Court decides the case of *Marbury v. Madison*, which sets forth the doctrine of judicial review.

The Louisiana Purchase treaty is ratified by Congress, nearly doubling the size of the United States for the price of $15 million.

1804: The Twelfth Amendment changes the procedure for presidential elections so the presidential runner-up is no longer awarded the vice presidency.

President Thomas Jefferson sends Meriwether Lewis and William Clark on an expedition of the newly acquired Louisiana Territory.

Alexander Hamilton is killed in a duel with Vice President Aaron Burr.

President Thomas Jefferson wins reelection.

1807: Aaron Burr is arrested for treason for his plot to invade the Louisiana Territory.

1808: James Madison is elected the fourth president of the United States.

1812: The U.S. Congress declares war on Britain, initiating the War of 1812.

1814: New England Federalists gather in Hartford, Connecticut, to protest the War of 1812.

The War of 1812 ends with the signing of the Treaty of Ghent.

1816: James Monroe wins a landslide victory over Federalist Rufus King.

1819: Spain sells Florida to the United States in the Treaty of Adams-Onís.

The U.S. Supreme Court decides the seminal free speech case *Schenck v. United States.*

The U.S. Supreme Court decides the case of *McCulloch v. Maryland*. The decision both defends the power of the federal government to engage in banking and curtails the state's ability to tax a federal entity.

The financial Panic of 1819 is caused by an economic downturn following the end of the Napoleonic Wars and a concurrent increase in loan foreclosures.

1820: Congress negotiates the Missouri Compromise, which allows for territorial expansion of the United States while maintaining the balance of power between northern and southern states.

1823: President James Monroe outlines his foreign policy with regard to Latin America and the Caribbean, later known as the "Monroe Doctrine."

1824: The U.S. Supreme Court decides the landmark case of *Gibbons v. Ogden*, which determines that transportation across state lines cannot be restricted by state laws.

1825: John Quincy Adams wins the contested election of 1824, after the decision is thrown to the House of Representatives due to an electoral college deadlock among four candidates.

1828: Andrew Jackson, the father of the Democratic party, defeats incumbent John Quincy Adams in the presidential election.

John C. Calhoun is reelected as vice president, joining George Clinton as the only vice presidents to serve under two different presidents.

1830: The Indian Removal Act authorizes federal involvement in forced resettlement of Native Americans.

1831: The majority of Andrew Jackson's cabinet, including Vice President John C. Calhoun, resign as a result of the Eaton Affair.

Nat Turner leads a slave rebellion in Virginia that claims the lives of fifty-five white men, women, and children over the course of a single day.

1834: Antonio López de Santa Anna declares himself dictator of Mexico.

1835: John Marshall, the longest sitting and most influential chief justice in U.S. Supreme Court history, dies.

1836: The Republic of Texas declares its independence from Mexico.

William B. Travis, leader of the Texas independence movement, dies during the siege of the Alamo.

The "gag rule" is imposed in the House of Representatives, prohibiting debate or discussion regarding the abolition of slavery.

The Whig Party, dedicated to opposing the political philosophies of Andrew Jackson, participates in its first national election.

Vice President Martin Van Buren, Andrew Jackson's handpicked successor, wins the presidency.

1837: The Panic of 1837 is caused by rampant inflation and a lack of hard currency in circulation.

1840: French aristocrat Alexis de Tocqueville completes his treatise on the American government and politics, *Democracy in America.*

1841: William Henry Harrison dies of pneumonia one month after his inauguration as president, making him the first president to die in office.

John Tyler succeeds William Henry Harrison as president. Within five months, Tyler's Whig cabinet resigns in protest of Tyler's Democratic policies.

1844: Little-known candidate James K. Polk defeats Whig Henry Clay in the presidential election.

1845: Journalist John L. O'Sullivan of the *Democratic Review* coins the term "Manifest Destiny" with regard to the nation's westward expansion.

Narrative of the Life of Frederick Douglass, an American Slave is published.

1848: The Treaty of Guadalupe Hidalgo ends the Mexican-American War.

Women's rights activists Elizabeth Cady Stanton and Lucretia Mott organize the Seneca Falls Convention, which serves as the birthplace of the American women's suffrage movement.

War hero Zachary Taylor defeats Lewis Cass in the presidential election.

1849: Henry David Thoreau's treatise on civil disobedience is published under the name "Resistance to Civil Government."

1850: Vice President Millard Fillmore assumes presidency after Zachary Taylor dies of gastroenteritis.

In order to facilitate California's statehood, a series of laws, collectively known as the Compromise of 1850, is passed to appease both north and south and maintain the balance of power.

1852: Abolitionist Harriet Beecher Stowe's *Uncle Tom's Cabin* is published, galvanizing the U.S. antislavery movement.

Democratic candidate Franklin Pierce decisively defeats Whig Winfield Scott in the presidential election.

1854: The Kansas-Nebraska Act allows residents of Kansas and Nebraska to decide by popular vote whether slavery will be allowed in their territories.

The Republican Party forms in response to the Kansas-Nebraska Act.

1856: Representative Preston Brooks beats Senator Charles Sumner unconscious in the Senate chamber after Sumner insults one of Brooks's relatives, Senator Andrew Butler, during an antislavery speech.

Democrat James Buchanan defeats Republican John C. Fremont in the presidential election.

1857: The U.S. Supreme Court decides the case of *Dred Scott v. Sanford*, which invalidates the Missouri Compromise and maintains that slaves are not U.S. citizens and therefore do not have the right to sue in court.

A variety of factors—the end of the Crimean War, the failure of the Ohio Life Insurance and Trust Company, and the sinking of the merchant ship Central America—spark the Panic of 1857.

1860: The Democratic Party splinters in opposition to Republican Abraham Lincoln, presenting two presidential candidates—southerner John C. Breckenridge and northerner Stephen A. Douglas.

Abraham Lincoln wins the presidential election. By the time of his inauguration, seven states have seceded from the Union in protest.

1861: Seceding states South Carolina, Alabama, Florida, Georgia, Louisiana, and Mississippi establish the Confederate States of America.

Confederate troops attack Fort Sumter, commencing hostilities in the Civil War.

The first U.S. income tax is passed to help pay for the Civil War.

1863: Riots and racial lynching break out in New York City in opposition to the Civil War draft.

1864: Congress passes the National Banking Act to raise money to help fund the Union Army during the Civil War.

1865: General Robert E. Lee surrenders the Army of Northern Virginia, marking the end of major hostilities in the American Civil War.

Vice President Andrew Johnson succeeds Abraham Lincoln after Lincoln's assassination by John Wilkes Booth.

The Thirteenth Amendment, abolishing slavery in the United States, is ratified.

1866: The U.S. Supreme Court decides the case of *Ex parte Milligan*, ruling that civilians cannot be tried by military courts.

1867: The United States purchases Alaska from Russia.

1868: President Andrew Johnson is impeached by Congress over the dismissal of Secretary of War Edwin Stanton. The attempt to remove him from office fails by a single vote.

The Fourteenth Amendment, granting freed slaves U.S. citizenship and overturning a key ruling of *Dred Scott v. Sanford*, is ratified.

Civil War hero Ulysses S. Grant wins the presidential election by a landslide.

1870: The Fifteenth Amendment, granting freed male slaves the right to vote, is ratified.

1872: In an act of civil disobedience in support of women's suffrage, Susan B. Anthony is arrested for attempting to cast a ballot in the presidential election.

1873: The Comstock Act, a piece of federal anti-obscenity legislation, bans the delivery of contraceptives or "lewd and/or lacscivious books" across state lines or by the U.S. Postal Service.

1874: Blanche Bruce becomes the first African-American elected to serve a full term in the U.S. Senate.

1876: Chief Sitting Bull leads the Sioux to victory over the forces of General George Armstrong Custer in the Battle of Little Bighorn.

1877: The contested 1876 election between Rutherford B. Hayes and Samuel Tilden is resolved in Hayes's favor, with an informal compromise that ends Reconstruction in the South.

President Rutherford B. Hayes sends troops to break up a multistate railroad strike.

1880: Republican James A. Garfield wins the presidential election.

1881: James A. Garfield is assassinated by a disappointed office-seeker. Chester A. Arthur succeeds Garfield, whose death draws attention to the evils of the so-called spoils system.

1882: The Chinese Exclusion Act, a law restricting immigration from China and denying citizenship to Chinese residents in the United States, becomes law.

1883: The Civil Service Commission is established to oversee government hiring based on merit rather than the spoils system.

The U.S. Supreme Court rules that the Civil Rights Act of 1875 is unconstitutional, curtailing federal enforcement of the Fourteenth Amendment.

1884: Grover Cleveland becomes the first Democrat to win the presidency since the Civil War.

1887: The Interstate Commerce Commission is established to prevent unfair business practices by railroad companies.

1888: Benjamin Harrison defeats Democratic incumbent Grover Cleveland, despite trailing Cleveland in the popular vote.

1890: The first federal immigration station is established at Ellis Island in New York Harbor.

The Sherman Antitrust Act becomes law.

1892: Grover Cleveland becomes the first president to win nonconsecutive terms of office, defeating incumbent Benjamin Harrison.

1893: The stock market crash known as the Panic of 1893 sends the nation into an economic depression.

1894: Jacob S. Coxey leads a march on Washington by unemployed laborers and farmers, who came to be known as "Coxey's Army."

Grover Cleveland dispatches troops to suppress the Pullman strike in Chicago.

1896: The U.S. Supreme Court decides the case of *Plessy v. Ferguson*, which permitted laws that provided for "separate, but equal" facilities for African-Americans.

Republican William McKinley defeats William Jennings Bryan in the presidential election.

1898: The explosion of the USS *Maine* in Havana harbor triggers the four-month Spanish American War.

1901: The Socialist Party of America is founded.

President William McKinley is assassinated at the Pan-American Exposition in Buffalo, New York. Vice President Theodore Roosevelt succeeds McKinley.

1902: President Theodore Roosevelt announces his corollary to the Monroe Doctrine, proclaiming the United States' right to military intervention in Latin America as "the exercise of an international police power."

1903: President Theodore Roosevelt announces the Square Deal, his platform of social and economic reforms.

After a U.S.-backed revolution grants Panama independence from Colombia, Panama agrees to the Hay-Bunau-Varilla Treaty with the United States, giving the United States control of the Panama Canal Zone in perpetuity.

1904: Incumbent Theodore Roosevelt defeats Democratic candidate Alton B. Parker in the presidential election.

1905: W. E. B. Du Bois and other African-American leaders found the Niagara Movement to pursue an aggressive civil rights agenda.

1906: Theodore Roosevelt is awarded the Nobel Peace Prize for negotiating peace between Japan and Russia.

1908: The Department of Justice's Bureau of Investigation, later renamed the Federal Bureau of Investigation, is established to enforce federal law.

William Howard Taft defeats Democratic candidate William Jennings Bryan in the presidential election.

1909: The National Association for the Advancement of Colored People (NAACP) is founded.

1912: Theodore Roosevelt is denied the Republican nomination and runs for reelection as a third-party candidate, establishing the National Progressive Party, also known as the Bull Moose Party.

Democratic candidate Woodrow Wilson wins the presidential election with only 41 percent of the popular vote, as Theodore Roosevelt and William Howard Taft split Republican support.

1913: The Seventeenth Amendment to the constitution is ratified, requiring direct election of senators and members of Congress.

Alice Paul and Lucy Burns establish the National Woman's Party, dedicated to the passage of a women's suffrage amendment to the federal constitution.

1914: World War I begins in Europe.

The Federal Trade Commission is established to regulate trusts and to prevent deceptive trade practices.

1916: Incumbent Woodrow Wilson wins reelection over Republican Charles Evans Hughes.

1917: The United States enters World War I after months of German attacks on American ships.

1918: The global influenza epidemic reaches the United States, killing 195,000 Americans.

1919: The Eighteenth Amendment is ratified, starting the Prohibition period in the United States.

The League of Nations is formed by the Treaty of Versailles, which ends World War I.

1920: The Nineteenth Amendment, granting women the right to vote, is ratified.

Warren G. Harding defeats James M. Cox in the presidential election.

1921: Former President William Howard Taft is named chief justice of the U.S. Supreme Court.

1923: Vice President Calvin Coolidge becomes president after Warren G. Harding's dies from a sudden illness.

1924: Robert M. La Follette abandons the Republican Party to run for president on the ticket of the new Progressive Party.

Republican incumbent Calvin Coolidge wins the presidential election.

1925: The U.S. Supreme Court decides the case of *Gitlow v. New York*, which extends the protections of the Bill of Rights to the states.

1928: Herbert Hoover wins a landslide presidential victory over New York Governor Alfred E. Smith.

1929: The Black Tuesday stock market crash triggers the Great Depression.

1930: Drought begins in the southeast and spreads over the Great Plains, leading to the Dust Bowl of the 1930s.

1931: The U.S. Supreme Court decides the case of *Near v. Minnesota*, ruling that the government cannot prevent publication of materials by the press.

1932: Approximately twenty thousand World War I veterans march in Washington, D.C., seeking early payment on a cash bonus the government was scheduled to pay them in 1945.

New York Governor Franklin Roosevelt defeats Republican incumbent Herbert Hoover in the presidential election.

The U.S. Supreme Court decides the case of *Powell v. Alabama*, establishing the right to counsel in criminal cases.

1933: Frances Perkins is appointed secretary of labor, becoming the first woman to hold a cabinet-level post.

Prohibition ends with the ratification of the Twenty-First Amendment.

1934: The Federal Communications Commission is established to regulate wire and radio communications.

1935: The Works Progress Administration is established to relieve high unemployment during the Great Depression.

The U.S. Supreme Court decides the case of *Schechter Poultry Corp. v. United States*, invalidating portions of the National Industrial Recovery Act.

The Social Security Administration is created.

1936: Incumbent President Franklin Roosevelt wins reelection by a landslide over Alfred M. Landon.

1937: President Franklin Roosevelt threatens to pack the Supreme Court with new appointees to counteract the court's resistance to the New Deal.

Hugo Black is appointed to the U.S. Supreme Court by Franklin Roosevelt.

1938: The House Un-American Activities Committee (HUAC) is formed.

1940: Franklin Roosevelt becomes the first president to be elected to office three times, defeating Wendell Willkie.

1941: A Japanese attack on the U.S. naval base at Pearl Harbor in Hawaii brings the United States into World War II.

1942: President Franklin Roosevelt signs Executive Order 9066, granting the military the authority to begin the internment of Japanese Americans.

1944: The GI Bill of Rights passes through Congress, providing education, job training, and home loan assistance for American soldiers returning from World War II.

Franklin Roosevelt is elected to his fourth consecutive term as president, defeating Republican Thomas Dewey.

The U.S. Supreme Court decides the case of *Korematsu v. United States*, which upholds the military's authority to intern Japanese Americans.

1945: President Franklin Roosevelt dies of natural causes and is succeeded by Vice President Harry Truman.

President Harry Truman orders atomic bombs to be dropped on the Japanese cities of Hiroshima and Nagasaki. Japan surrenders, ending World War II.

The Senate ratifies the United Nations charter.

1946: Eleanor Roosevelt becomes the first chairperson of the United Nations Commission on Human Rights.

The Employment Act of 1946 is passed amid fears that the return of American soldiers from abroad will cause an economic depression.

1947: The Central Intelligence Agency is created by the National Security Act of 1947.

1948: Executive Order 9981 bans discrimination in the armed forces.

Incumbent Harry Truman defeats Thomas Dewey in the presidential election.

1950: Alger Hiss is found guilty of perjury after having allegedly provided classified documents to *Time* magazine editor Whittaker Chambers.

Senator Joseph McCarthy announces in Wheeling, West Virginia, that he is in possession of a list of communist infiltrators in the U.S. State Department, beginning the period of anticommunist hysteria known as McCarthyism.

North Korea invades South Korea, igniting the Korean War.

1952: General Dwight D. Eisenhower defeats Democratic nominee Adlai Stevenson in the presidential election.

1953: Julius and Ethel Rosenberg are executed for their role in passing nuclear secrets to the Soviet Union.

The Korean War Armistice Agreement is reached, ending the Korean War.

Earl Warren is appointed Chief Justice of the U.S. Supreme Court.

George C. Marshall receives the Nobel Peace Prize for his role in the European Recovery Program, also known as the Marshall Plan.

1954: The U.S. Supreme Court decides the landmark case of *Brown v. Board of Education of Topeka*, requiring the desegregation of public schools.

1955: Rosa Parks is arrested for failing to surrender her seat to a white man on a city bus in Montgomery, Alabama, igniting a series of boycotts and protests.

1956: William Brennan is appointed to the U.S. Supreme Court.

South Vietnam, with military support from the United States, declares independence, setting the stage for the Vietnam War.

Incumbent President Dwight D. Eisenhower wins reelection, again defeating Adlai Stevenson.

1958: The National Aeronautics and Space Administration is created.

Fidel Castro leads a successful revolution against U.S.-backed dictator Fulgencio Batista y Zaldívar in Cuba.

1960: Senator John F. Kennedy defeats incumbent Vice President Richard M. Nixon in one of the closest presidential elections of the twentieth century.

1961: The U.S.-supported Bay of Pigs invasion of Cuba fails.

The U.S. Supreme Court decides the case of *Mapp v. Ohio*, extending the exclusionary rule to apply to all state prosecutions.

1962: In response to the deployment of Soviet nuclear weapons in Cuba, the United States initiates a naval blockade, a series of events known as the Cuban Missile crisis.

1963: President John F. Kennedy is assassinated in Dallas, Texas. Vice President Lyndon B. Johnson succeeds Kennedy as president.

1964: The U.S. Supreme Court rules on the case of *New York Times v. Sullivan*, changing the rules regarding what constitutes libel in statements made by the media about public figures.

The Gulf of Tonkin incident leads to escalation of the Vietnam War.

The Food Stamp Act of 1964, part of President Lyndon B. Johnson's "Great Society" agenda, is approved by Congress.

The Warren Commission issues its final report on the John F. Kennedy assassination.

Incumbent Lyndon B. Johnson defeats Barry Goldwater in a landslide presidential election.

Rev. Martin Luther King Jr. receives the Nobel Peace Prize for his leadership in the American Civil Rights movement.

The U.S. Supreme Court decides the case of *Heart of Atlanta Motel v. United States*, the first major test of the Civil Rights Act of 1964.

1965: Black Muslim leader Malcolm X is assassinated in New York City.

The U.S. Supreme Court decides the case of *Griswold v. Connecticut*, affirming married couples' right to privacy in the bedroom.

Congress creates the Medicaid and Medicare health care programs, furthering President Lyndon Johnson's "Great Society" agenda.

Ralph Nader publishes *Unsafe at Any Speed: The Designed-In Dangers of the American Automobile*, bringing automotive safety to public attention.

1966: The U.S. Supreme Court case *Miranda v. Arizona* requires that criminal suspects be informed prior to questioning of their right to legal counsel and their right to remain silent.

1967: The Twenty-Fifth Amendment, establishing the procedure for replacing the president or vice president of the United States in the event that either office is unoccupied, is ratified.

The U.S. Department of Transportation is formed, consolidating authority over the national highway system, automotive and airline safety, and other transportation policy issues.

Thurgood Marshall becomes the first African-American justice of the U.S. Supreme Court.

Black Panther party leader Huey P. Newton is shot in a gun battle with police and charged with manslaughter in the death of a white police officer.

1968: Civil rights activist Martin Luther King Jr. is assassinated in Memphis, Tennessee, sparking riots in cities across the United States.

George C. Wallace receives substantial support for his independent run for the presidency but still falls a distant third to Democrat Hubert H. Humphrey and winner Richard M. Nixon.

1969: The U.S. Supreme Court upholds the "fairness doctrine" as constitutional in the case of *Red Lion Broadcasting Co. v. Federal Communications Commission*.

Warren Burger is appointed chief justice of the Supreme Court.

1970: The Racketeer Influenced and Corrupt Organizations Act (RICO) is signed into law as part of an effort to control organized crime in America.

The Occupational Safety and Health Act is signed into law.

The Clean Air Act of 1970 shifts primary responsibility for air quality control from the states to the federal government.

1971: The U.S. Supreme Court decides the case of *Lemon v. Kurtzman*, which finds that public funding of parochial schools violates the separation of church and state.

The U.S. Supreme Court rules that efforts to stop publication of the Pentagon Papers in the *New York Times* violated the First Amendment.

1972: The Equal Rights Amendment, establishing equal rights for women under law, passes through Congress. Over the next decade the amendment will fall three votes short of ratification.

J. Edgar Hoover dies, ending forty-seven years as head of the Federal Bureau of Investigation.

Title IX of the Education Amendments of 1972 prohibits gender discrimination by institutions of higher education that receive federal funds.

Five men, later revealed to be agents of the Richard M. Nixon administration, are caught attempting to break into the headquarters of the Democratic National Committee at the Watergate Hotel Complex.

The U.S. Supreme Court's ruling in *Furman v. Georgia* severely limits the death penalty's use based on the Eighth Amendment.

1973: The Drug Enforcement Administration is established to consolidate the government's narcotics control efforts.

The U.S. Supreme Court's decision in *Roe v. Wade* strikes down state laws that restrict women's access to abortions.

1974: The U.S. Supreme Court rules against President Richard M. Nixon's request for "executive priviledge," whereby Nixon claimed tape recordings of conversations he had with staffers in the Oval Office should be considered confidential.

Under threat of impeachment due to the Watergate scandal, Richard M. Nixon resigns as president of the United States and is succeeded by Vice President Gerald Ford.

Less than a month after taking office, President Gerald Ford issues a full pardon toward former President Richard M. Nixon, immunizing Nixon from any prosecution in the Watergate scandal.

The Internet is invented by scientists with the Advanced Research Projects Agency (ARPA).

1976: The U.S. Supreme Court upholds limits on donations to political campaigns in *Buckley v. Valeo*.

Georgia Governor Jimmy Carter defeats Republican incumbent Gerald Ford in the presidential election.

1977: The Department of Energy is established by Congress.

1978: The Federal Emergency Management Agency is created by executive order.

Congress passes the Ethics in Government Act, which allows for the appointment of an impartial, nonpartisan independent counsel to investigate and prosecute illegal acts by high-level government officials.

The U.S. Supreme Court decides the case of *City of Philadelphia v. New Jersey*, ruling that a state may not restrict importation of waste from other states.

The U.S. Supreme Court's decision in *Regents of the University of California v. Bakke* finds that affirmative action by the use of racial quotas is unconstitutional.

1979: A reactor malfunction at the Three Mile Island nuclear power plant results in the most serious mishap ever in the U.S. commercial nuclear power industry.

Islamic extremists take sixty-three Americans at the U.S. Embassy in Iran hostage.

1980: Former California Governor Ronald Reagan defeats incumbent Democrat Jimmy Carter in the presidential election.

1981: President Ronald Reagan is shot in an assassination attempt by a mentally disturbed man.

The first cases of acquired immune deficiency syndrome (AIDS) are identified in the United States.

Sandra Day O'Connor becomes the first female justice of the U.S. Supreme Court.

1982: The federal budget deficit exceeds $100 billion for the first time in history.

The U.S. Supreme Court decides the case of *Nixon v. Fitzgerald*, which upholds presidential immunity for official actions.

1983: The U.S. Supreme Court decides the case of *Bob Jones University v. United States*, which denies tax-exempt status to private colleges with racially discriminatory practices.

1984: Incumbent President Ronald Reagan wins a landslide electoral victory over former Vice President Walter Mondale.

1986: An independent counsel is appointed to investigate the Iran-Contra scandal.

1987: Alan Greenspan is named head of the Federal Reserve.

The District of Columbia Circuit Court decision in *Meredith Corporation v. FCC* finds that the government could discontinue enforcement of the Fairness Doctrine without legislative intervention.

The U.S. Supreme Court rules in *Cipollone v. Liggett Group, Inc.* that the federally mandated health warning on cigarette packages does not immunize cigarette manufacturers from being sued under state personal-injury laws.

1988: Incumbent Vice President George H. W. Bush wins the presidential election over Democratic candidate Michael Dukakis.

1989: The U.S. Supreme Court rules in *Texas v. Johnson* that burning the American flag is protected as free speech.

The federal government bails out the savings and loan industry at taxpayer expense exceeding $100 million.

1990: The U.S. Supreme Court decides the case of *Cruzan v. Director, Missouri Department of Health*, upholding the actions of the state of Missouri to maintain life support for a woman in a persistent vegetative state.

The Iraqi military invades and conquers Kuwait, initiating U.S. involvement in the Persian Gulf War.

1992: Businessman Ross Perot uses his own fortune to fund his presidential candidacy as an independent. Although Perot does not win a single electoral vote, he does capture nearly 19 percent of the popular vote.

Arkansas Governor Bill Clinton defeats incumbent George H. W. Bush in the presidential election.

1994: The North American Free Trade Agreement, which removes trade barriers among the United States, Canada, and Mexico, is implemented.

Independent counsel is appointed to investigate President Bill Clinton's involvement in the Whitewater real estate venture.

Before the midterm election Republicans propose a slate of reforms they call the "Contract with America"; the Republicans go on to take a majority in the House of Representatives for the first time in forty years.

1995: Ross Perot founds the Reform Party in anticipation of a second presidential bid.

A budgetary impasse in Congress causes the federal government to shut down many nonessential services for four weeks.

1996: Incumbent President Bill Clinton defeats Republican candidate Bob Dole in an electoral landslide.

1998: The impeachment trial of President Bill Clinton ends in acquittal.

2000: In one of the closest presidential elections in American history, Texas Governor George W. Bush defeats Vice President Al Gore after the U.S. Supreme Court stops the recounting of votes in Florida.

2001: On September 11th, terrorist hijackers fly commercial airliners into the twin towers of the World Trade Center in New York City and into the Pentagon, outside Washington, D.C.

The Department of Homeland Security is established in response to the terrorist attacks.

The United States invades Afghanistan after the Taliban government refuses to surrender the persons responsible for planning the attacks.

Congress passes the Patriot Act, granting the government broad powers to investigate and prosecute those suspected of terrorism.

2003: The United States invades Iraq, based on false reports that the Iraqi government is producing and stockpiling nuclear weapons.

2004: Incumbent George W. Bush defeats Massachusetts Senator John Kerry in the presidential election.

2005: The Kyoto Protocol on global warming goes into effect. The treaty, which the United States helped negotiate, is never submitted to the U.S. Congress for ratification.

Hurricane Katrina sweeps across the Gulf Coast, causing great damage in Mississippi and Louisiana, particularly in the city of New Orleans.

House Majority Leader Tom Delay is indicted in Texas of illegal campaign practices.

2006: The population of the United States exceeds three hundred million for the first time.

The Democratic Party takes control of both houses of Congress in the midterm elections. Representative Nancy Pelosi becomes the first female Speaker of the House.

Former Iraqi dictator Saddam Hussein is executed in Iraq for crimes against humanity.

2007: Massachusetts becomes first state to enact a universal health coverage plan.

Glossary

ANTEBELLUM: Before the Civil War.

BURGESS: A representative in a colonial legislature.

CLOTURE: Closing off debate over proposed legislation.

DEREGULATION: The removal of government restrictions on an industry.

DUE PROCESS: A legal doctrine by which the government is required to recognize and respect the legal rights of individuals.

ELECTORAL COLLEGE: The body of representatives that elects the president and vice president in the United States.

COMMON LAW: A legal tradition, brought to America from English law, in which judges, rather than legislatures, establish legal rules.

ENLIGHTENMENT: A philosophical movement of the seventeenth and eighteenth centuries that celebrated reason and the rights of the common people. Enlightenment ideals strongly influenced the framers of the U.S. Constitution.

FEDERALISM: A system of dual government sovereignty, where authority is divided between a central, federal government, and various local, state governments.

FREEMEN: Residents of the colonies having the full rights of a citizen.

GAG ORDER: A court order prohibiting discussion of information related to a case.

IMMUNITY: Freedom from legal requirements or liabilities. Diplomats, legislators, and some other government officials are granted immunity from prosecution in certain situations, most often related to their official actions in government service.

IMPERIALISM: Extension of power by a government that acquires territory or gains political and economic control over other countries.

IMPRESSMENT: Forcing sailors into military service. The British Royal Navy impressed American citizens into the nineteenth century.

INDENTURED SERVANT: A worker bound to his or her employer for a specified period of time as repayment for travel expenses.

ISOLATIONISM: A U.S. governmental policy of avoiding commitments to or alliances with other countries

JOINT STOCK COMPANY CHARTER: A charter granted by the British Crown to a group of investors who pooled their resources to fund the establishment of a North American colony and shared in the profits.

JUDICIAL REVIEW: The power of the Supreme Court to review government actions and legislation to determine whether or not they are permitted under the Constitution.

MERCANTILE: Commercial; relating to business or trade.

NATIONALISM: A strong sense of patriotism or a movement in favor of a nation's independence. Also, an extreme form of patriotism that leads to the exclusion of perceived outsiders.

NATIVISM: Advocacy of native inhabitants, coupled with opposition to immigration and immigrants.

POLL TAX: A flat tax paid by each individual. In some states, citizens were required to pay a poll tax to be eligible to vote. Because it discriminated against poor citizens, this practice was declared unconstitutional in 1966.

POPULISM: Advocacy of the common people.

PRIVATEER: A private ship licensed by a government to attack ships belonging to enemy nations. The word also applies to sailors serving on such ships.

PROGRESSIVE: Forward-looking. Progressives believe in government action to promote social improvement.

PROPRIETARY CHARTER: A charter granted by the British Crown to an individual to organize and operate an American colony.

SPOILS SYSTEM: The practice of rewarding political supporters by appointing them to government positions

SUFFRAGE: The right to vote.

SUNSET PROVISION: A clause stating that legislation will expire on a particular date.

SUPPLY SIDE ECONOMICS: Economic theories relating to the reduction of taxes as a means of expanding production and overall income.

SWING STATE: A state in which the race between presidential candidates is close. Because the electoral college system awards all of a state's electors to a single candidate, voters in these states are aggressively courted.

TARIFF: Taxes on imports or exports.

TEMPERANCE MOVEMENT: A social movement to encourage moderation in or complete abstinence from the consumption of alcoholic beverages.

TERM LIMITS: A limit on the number of terms a person may serve in a particular office.

TRADE GUILD: An association of artisans or merchants formed to pursue and protect their common interests.

TRANSCENDENTALISM: A nineteenth-century philosophical movement emphasizing the unity of nature and the precedence of intuition over experience.

TRUST: Corporations or firms that combine their resources in order to establish monopolies and reduce competition in an industry or business. Reduced competition allows trusts to control prices of the products they produce.

Introduction to the Progressive Era (1890–1930)

The Progressive era received its name from the forward-thinking, or "progressive," reformers who addressed a variety of social, economic, and political ills. They lived in all parts of the country, were often professionals from middle- or upper-class backgrounds, and belonged to both the Democratic and Republican parties. Many of the problems they sought to fix resulted from the rapid industrialization and urbanization and the huge surge of immigration at the turn of the twentieth century. They also sought to correct what they saw as the injustices of the Gilded Age (1870–1900), when corporations, along with corporate profits, grew, resulting in an ever-widening gap between the rich and the poor.

Progressives intended to make the United States more democratic, so they focused on political reforms that took power out of the hands of the few. One result was direct election of U.S. senators, which they achieved with ratification of the Seventeenth Amendment to the U.S. Constitution in 1913. Previously, state legislatures chose senators and controlled how they voted. Similarly, Progressives pushed for women's right to vote. The suffrage movement had started in the mid-nineteenth century; by the Progressive era it had become highly organized. In 1920, with ratification of the Nineteenth Amendment, twenty-six million women—half the population—suddenly became voters who could effect change.

Perhaps no one personified the progressive spirit more than President Theodore Roosevelt (1858–1919), who greatly expanded the powers of the government. He was the gleeful trust-buster, eager to break up huge business conglomerates that squelched competi-tion. He stepped into a miners' strike and got both business and labor to agree to arbitration to solve their disputes—an involvement in the economy that no president had risked before. He also came up with a plan to manage wilderness development and save many forests and unspoiled areas.

Reform did not come easy, nor did it touch all parts of society. Political and social opportunities for African-Americans, for example, were restricted by segregation. In 1896 the U.S. Supreme Court decided in *Plessy v. Ferguson* that "separate but equal" facilities for blacks and whites were constitutional. That would remain the law for fifty years.

Another failure came with Prohibition, which outlawed the manufacture, sale, import, and export of alcoholic beverages. Reformers saw it as a means of reducing domestic violence and crime, strengthening families, and increasing worker productivity. It became law with the Eighteenth Amendment, ratified in 1920. However, this "noble experiment" was repealed in 1933 because it unexpectedly led to the smuggling and sale of illicit liquor, an increase in organized crime, and widespread political corruption.

The reformers met repeated resistance from the more conservative members of society, who simply did not agree that it was government's responsibility to regulate industry and promote socially beneficial programs. Still, across the nation the Progressive era was an undisputed time of social, political, and economic transformation. The country was moving away from the agrarian economy of its early days toward a new and sometimes painful identity as an industrialized nation and participant in world affairs.

The Progressive Era (1890–1930)

✪ How They Were Governed

The Roosevelt Corollary

The Roosevelt Corollary, a statement of foreign policy proposed by President Theodore Roosevelt (1858–1919), declared that the United States would not tolerate European intervention in or colonization of independent nations in the Western Hemisphere. In addition, Roosevelt asserted that if any nation in the region—particularly in Central and South America—demonstrated instability or an inability to govern itself, the United States had the right to intervene and take over that nation's government to prevent it from falling into the hands of a European power. The corollary—a corollary is something that follows from or is added to another statement—was attached to the Monroe Doctrine of 1823, in which President James Monroe (1758–1831) called for an end to European intervention in the affairs of independent nations in the Americas. Roosevelt first proposed the corollary in May 1904, then repeated it in his annual message to Congress on December 6, 1904, and in a special message to Congress on February 15, 1905.

The European Presence Although Spain had lost its colony of New Spain, which included Mexico, to independence in 1821, Monroe and his secretary of state, John Quincy Adams (1767–1848), were growing increasingly concerned about the European presence in the Western Hemisphere. During the early 1820s France had briefly installed a king in Mexico—he was a member of the Hapsburg family, an Austrian-based dynasty that had ruled parts of Europe since the late Middle Ages—and England was attempting to exert its influence over Central America. In 1823 Monroe, in his annual address to Congress, declared that the United States would not tolerate any further European intervention in the hemisphere. His declaration became known as the Monroe Doctrine.

Even though the doctrine was a statement of U.S. isolationist, or noninterventionist, foreign policy, it contained no promise that the United States would refrain from intervention in Central and South America—the very action it was warning European powers against. In

fact, historians point to the Monroe Doctrine as an early example of U.S. expansionist plans in the hemisphere and the forerunner of manifest destiny, the belief that the United States was destined to expand its territories to include the entire North American continent.

A "Big Stick" Policy Roosevelt's assertive approach toward Latin America was sometimes referred to as the big stick policy because of his diplomatic motto: "Speak softly and carry a big stick." Although Roosevelt believed in diplomatic negotiations, he also believed in using military force when necessary to defend U.S. interests.

Roosevelt's corollary grew out of his fear of possible German naval intervention in the Caribbean and the use of force by Germany, Britain, and France to collect debts from Venezuela. Even though the United States opposed this possible use of force, the International Court of Justice in The Hague, the Netherlands, ruled that the three European nations had the right to exercise such power. The U.S. Department of State warned Roosevelt that this ruling would weaken the Monroe Doctrine. Another factor that led to the corollary was tension between the Dominican Republic and its German and French creditors. Roosevelt worried that the Europeans would invade the Caribbean island nation to protect their interests.

From Isolationism to Expansionism In his corollary, Roosevelt stated that the United States would intervene as a "last resort" to ensure that other nations in the Western Hemisphere fulfilled their international obligations and did not violate the rights of the United States or invite foreign aggression. Even though the Monroe Doctrine was essentially a passive request—it asked Europeans *not* to increase their influence or to recolonize any part of the Western Hemisphere—by the twentieth century a more confident United States was willing to take on the role of regional policeman. Therefore, the corollary was more than an addition to or emendation of the Monroe Doctrine; rather, it was a departure from the original doctrine. It opposed revolutions in Latin America, declared that the United States had the right to intervene in the region, facilitated U.S. economic control of those nations, and relied on force or the threat of force.

The Corollary's Impact Roosevelt's corollary declared that the United States had become an international police power that would uphold democracy and eliminate "flagrant cases" of wrongdoing wherever necessary. In practice, the United States increasingly used military force to restore what it referred to as "internal stability" to nations in the region.

Many historians note that, in the long run, the corollary had little to do with relations between the Western Hemisphere and Europe. Instead, it served as justification for U.S. intervention in the Caribbean and Central and South America for the next eighty years. They point to examples such as financial controls and interventions in Honduras, the Dominican Republic, Haiti, Cuba, and Nicaragua during the administrations of William Howard Taft (1857–1930) and Woodrow Wilson (1856–1924), which were defended on the basis of Roosevelt's corollary.

> *See also* **Isolationism**
> *See also* **Theodore Roosevelt**
> *See also* **Woodrow Wilson**

The Federal Trade Commission

The Federal Trade Commission (FTC) is an independent governmental agency that regulates foreign and interstate commerce to ensure that competition is not restricted by unfair and deceptive business practices. It also works to curb the growth of monopolies, which develop when people or groups gain control over the distribution or sale of a given product or service.

A Response to Excesses The creation of the FTC was a response to the excesses of nineteenth-century capitalism—a time when powerful industrialists who were thought to use unfair business tactics became known as robber barons—and political corruption. Social, economic, and political reform movements rose up, calling for an expansion of government to protect the public interest.

Some federal laws—for example, the Sherman Antitrust Act of 1890—were enacted, but no legislation had altered the shift toward the concentration of economic power. When President Theodore Roosevelt (1858–1919) took office in 1901, he asked Congress to create the Department of Commerce and Labor (DCL). Among its objectives were the promotion of domestic and foreign commerce and the encouragement of industrial growth in the United States. (In 1913 Congress divided the agency into the Department of Commerce and the Department of Labor.) As part of the DCL, Congress created the Bureau of Corporations, whose purpose was to investigate and publicize unethical and noncompetitive business practices. The bureau developed a series of informal agreements with large corporations; companies granted the government access to their records, and the bureau approved mergers that were deemed in the public interest.

"AN INTERNATIONAL POLICE POWER"

In his annual message to Congress on December 6, 1904, President Theodore Roosevelt (1858–1919) set forth a foreign-policy statement that later became known as the Roosevelt Corollary. The following is an excerpt:

> It is not true that the United States feels any land hunger or entertains any projects as regards the other nations of the Western Hemisphere save such as are for their welfare. All that this country desires is to see the neighboring countries stable, orderly, and prosperous. Any country whose people conduct themselves well can count upon our hearty friendship. If a nation shows that it knows how to act with reasonable efficiency and decency in social and political matters, if it keeps order and pays its obligations, it need fear no interference from the United States. Chronic wrongdoing, or an impotence which results in a general loosening of the ties of civilized society, may in America, as elsewhere, ultimately require intervention by some civilized nation, and in the Western Hemisphere the adherence of the United States to the Monroe Doctrine may force the United States, however reluctantly, in flagrant cases of such wrongdoing or impotence, to the exercise of an international police power. . . .
>
> Our interests and those of our southern neighbors are in reality identical. They have great natural riches, and if within their borders the reign of law and justice obtains, prosperity is sure to come to them. While they thus obey the primary laws of civilized society they may rest assured that they will be treated by us in a spirit of cordial and helpful sympathy. We would interfere with them only in the last resort, and then only if it became evident that their inability or unwillingness to do justice at home and abroad had violated the rights of the United States or had invited foreign aggression to the detriment of the entire body of American nations. It is a mere truism to say that every nation, whether in America or anywhere else, which desires to maintain its freedom, its independence, must ultimately realize that the right of such independence can not be separated from the responsibility of making good use of it.

SOURCE: *Transcript of Theodore Roosevelt's Corollary to the Monroe Doctrine, excerpted from his annual message to Congress, December 6, 1904. http://www.ourdocuments.gov/doc.php?doc=56&page= transcript (accessed April 11, 2007).*

Wilson and the Federal Trade Commission Act President Woodrow Wilson (1856–1924) and the Democrats won a sweeping victory in the 1912 election. A key component of their party platform was a program—

THE CLAYTON ANTITRUST ACT

The Clayton Antitrust Act, federal consumer-protection legislation enacted by Congress in 1914, clarified and strengthened the language of the Sherman Antitrust Act of 1890. It gave the government more power to prohibit companies from gaining exclusive control (a monopoly) of the market for goods or services.

The Sherman act had outlawed monopolies, trade restraints, and business combinations, called trusts, that were created for the sole purpose of limiting competition. (It exempted labor unions and agricultural cooperatives from antitrust action.) The purpose of the Sherman act—the first antitrust law in U.S. history—was to encourage a free-market system based on industry rivalries and competition. To encourage continuing competition, the law authorized the U.S. attorney general, as well as other companies or groups, to bring lawsuits against companies that were attempting to dominate the market. Because of its language, however, the law could be interpreted in various ways by attorneys representing large companies, such as Standard Oil and American Tobacco. Consequently, the companies continued to concentrate wealth, dominate their industries, and buy out smaller companies, thereby reducing competition.

The Clayton act, which was drafted by Henry De Lamar Clayton (1857–1929), a Democratic representative from Alabama, made clear what had been vague in the Sherman act. It contained extensive definitions and outlawed the following actions: the formation of a trust between two companies with a combined board of directors and access to more than $1 million in capital; price-fixing arrangements between companies that offered competing products; agreements that resulted in the power to control the supply of resources or products; and the use of an industry's power to gain or maintain a monopoly. The more precise language prevented companies from engaging in price-cutting strategies intended to eliminate competition and from merging with other companies to form monopolies.

The Clayton act was significantly amended in 1936 by the Robinson-Patman Act and in 1950 by the Celler-Kefauver Antimerger Act.

Wilson called it the New Freedom—to prevent and destroy industrial and financial monopolies. To accomplish this goal, he proposed a reduction in tariffs (or taxes) on foreign imports, reform of the banking and currency systems, and efforts to strengthen the Sherman Antitrust Act. In 1913 Congress passed a tariff-reduction bill and created the Federal Reserve System, a network of federal banks that regulate the U.S. money supply.

Originally, neither Wilson nor his primary economic adviser, Louis D. Brandeis (1856–1941), advocated the transformation of the Bureau of Corporations into a strong trade commission. Wilson envisioned an agency that would moderate but not excessively restrict business. In keeping with this philosophy, the administration supported a bill that would establish a commission to secure and publish information, conduct investigations as requested by Congress, and support methods of improving business practices and antitrust enforcement.

Congress encountered difficulty when it tried to specify all unlawful trade practices, however, so in consultation with Wilson, it decided on a strategy that would abandon a legislative solution for an administrative one. The result was an independent commission with broad regulatory powers.

The Commission's Duties The Federal Trade Commission Act, which was signed into law on September 26, 1914, created a commission with five members (no more than three could be from the same political party—an attempt to limit the control exercised by any president and his party) appointed by the president and confirmed by the U.S. Senate. The members served staggered, seven-year terms.

The FTC had two major tasks: to regulate trusts (combinations of businesses that functioned as monopolies or that engaged in other practices restricting free trade) and to prevent unfair competition or deceptive trade practices that affected interstate and foreign commerce. Its work usually started with investigations (of either a single company or an industry) based on consumer complaints, congressional inquiries, or even reports in the media. If the FTC discovered unlawful conduct, it could then seek voluntary compliance by the offending business through a consent order, file an administrative complaint, or initiate litigation in federal court. The FTC could also issue rules that addressed industrywide practices. Perhaps most important, the law did not require an actual deception to occur before the commission could take action; in fact, the FTC had only to find the likelihood that business practices could deceive consumers.

Reinforcing the FTC's Authority The last major item on the New Freedom agenda was legislation to strengthen the Sherman Antitrust Act, whose language was imprecise. The Clayton Antitrust Act, which was drafted by Henry De Lamar Clayton (1857–1929), a Democratic representative from Alabama, and signed into law on October 15, 1914, provided specific definitions as well as a list of business practices that were considered illegal.

The FTC's Impact Creating a bipartisan, independent commission with broad powers was viewed as a radical step in the government's relationship with business. The FTC was to become perhaps the most controversial of the independent regulatory commissions, largely because its broad authority allowed it to take action in some cases and not to take action in others. From the beginning advocates of the FTC demanded that the commission become more involved in foreign and interstate commerce to thwart unfair or corrupt business practices; however, many others have viewed any FTC action as tampering with the free-market system.

See also **Theodore Roosevelt**

See also **Woodrow Wilson**

Isolationism

Isolationism refers to a U.S. governmental policy of avoiding commitments to or alliances with other countries, particularly with nations in Europe. Although this policy had its roots in colonial America, the term was seldom used until the years between World Wars I (1914–1918) and II (1939–1945).

The Origins of the Policy American colonists, who crossed the ocean to escape war, religious persecution, and other hardships, believed that declaring independence from Britain in 1776 would be a definitive step in severing ties with Europe. Reflecting this desire, the country's founding fathers developed a foreign policy based on neutrality. To safeguard the independence of a new and struggling nation, they thought it best to avoid, if possible, involvement in military and political affairs of the major powers. As important, they wanted U.S. policies to remain free from foreign influence. Their position did not mean disengagement from world affairs, however; contacts with the outside world, especially through trade, were encouraged, and immigration was welcomed.

"A More Prominent Position in World Affairs" The traditional view began to break down early in the nineteenth century. In 1823 President James Monroe (1758–1831) signaled the nation's interest in events outside its borders when he issued the Monroe Doctrine, which called for an end to European intervention in the affairs of independent nations in the Western Hemisphere. In the years that followed, rapid industrialization and the opening of vast new lands to agriculture made the United States a serious player in the world economy: it became not only an importer but also an exporter of goods and services. Government officials saw a need for a strong navy to protect the country's trade and investments and expanded its military power. Advances in technology and communications also moved the country to a more prominent position in world affairs.

Then in 1898, after the U.S. battleship *Maine* exploded in the harbor of Havana, Cuba—at the time a Spanish colony—the United States declared war on Spain. U.S. victory ended Spanish colonial efforts in the Western Hemisphere and significantly changed the balance of power.

The United States responded to these sweeping economic and political changes with a more active foreign policy and greater international involvement, especially during the presidency of Theodore Roosevelt (1858–1919). In 1902 Roosevelt arbitrated agreements that protected longstanding U.S. interests in Latin America. In 1903 he recognized the new country of Panama and acquired territory there on which to build what would become the Panama Canal. A year later he offered the Roosevelt Corollary to the Monroe Doctrine, which said the United States had the right to exercise an international police power throughout the Western Hemisphere.

During the next twenty years, U.S. Marines landed in Cuba, the Dominican Republic, Nicaragua, Haiti, and Mexico. In 1905 Roosevelt used his world position to mediate a peace treaty between Russia and Japan. Despite this participation in international affairs, however, the U.S. policy of neutrality remained officially intact.

The United States Enters World War I Just three months before the outbreak of World War I, President Woodrow Wilson (1856–1924) declared that the United States remained neutral and reasserted a policy of friendship toward all nations and alliances with none. As the war progressed, the debate over possible U.S. entry into the fighting inspired a foreign policy of full-scale isolationism—as opposed to its traditional position of what might be called isolationist neutrality.

However, Wilson eventually supported U.S. involvement and helped create a national pro-war sentiment. He made the case that German actions, especially its submarine warfare, if left unchecked, would eventually threaten U.S. interests. In addition, the United States sent munitions, food, and goods to the Allied powers (including Britain, France, and Russia) at the war's outset, boosting trade relations as well as the U.S. economy, which gave the United States a tangible material stake in the outcome of the war. The nation formally entered World War I on April 6, 1917.

Wilson's League of Nations After the war Wilson advocated more active cooperation with other nations, largely because he was concerned that nations with political systems and economic goals that differed from those of the United States might dominate the world. So, despite his original devotion to neutrality, in a 1918 speech to Congress—referred to as the Fourteen Points speech—Wilson proposed the creation of an international organization to preserve peace and settle disputes by arbitration. His proposal called for full U.S. participation, including military support, in a system of collective security. The formation of that organization—the League of Nations—became one of the provisions of the Treaty of Versailles (1919), which ended World War I.

The U.S. Senate debate over the ratification of the treaty sharpened and clarified the U.S. isolationist position. In Wilson's view, changing world conditions required a departure from traditional policies. Americans, however, wanted to enjoy their prosperity—they thought getting entangled in the affairs of other nations was not worth the cost or the risk, particularly after the death toll of U.S. troops during World War I. Although many agreed that a traditional isolationist policy was no longer a realistic goal, they did not support Wilson's abrupt policy reversal. The Senate refused to ratify the Treaty of Versailles, and the United States did not join the League of Nations. Ironically, Wilson won the Nobel Peace Prize in 1919 for his role in creating the very organization that his country refused to join.

Isolationism's Peak and Decline The election in 1920 of President Warren G. Harding (1865–1923) signaled a new wave of political and economic conservatism.

Despite the continuing commercial expansion of the United States and its increasing influence on world affairs, the nation set an isolationist course that could best be described as cooperation without commitment. For the first time in its history, the United States sharply curtailed immigration, excluding Chinese, Japanese, and other Asians, as well as Europeans, particularly those from eastern and southern Europe. The United States did engage in negotiations that would make war less likely. The most celebrated achievement of the period was the Kellogg-Briand Pact (1928), an international treaty that renounced war as an instrument of national policy. Although most regarded the pact as a positive contribution to maintaining world peace and order, the agreement had no means of enforcement and did not formally commit the United States to action of any kind. Regardless, it was strongly supported by most of the major isolationists in Congress.

Isolationism was based on the assumption that the United States was safe from foreign attack and that U.S. trade and ideas would continue to find acceptance abroad. It reached its peak in the United States between 1934 and 1939, during the Great Depression, when national economic conditions took precedence over foreign policy and military spending. The rationale for isolationism began to crumble, however, as Nazi Germany, Italy, and Japan advanced their efforts toward world domination. The Japanese attack on Pearl Harbor, the U.S. naval station in Hawaii, in 1941 signaled that U.S. territory was vulnerable to foreign aggressors, and many Americans began to fear that a direct attack on the United States was possible. In 1941 isolationism ended forever when the United States moved into an alliance with Britain and entered World War II.

See also **Theodore Roosevelt**
See also **Woodrow Wilson**
See also **World War I**

✪ Important Figures of the Day

Jacob S. Coxey

Jacob S. Coxey (1854–1951), a social reformer and businessman, led a march of unemployed workers to Washington, D.C., in 1894. The first public protest of its kind, Coxey hoped that the march would motivate Congress to create jobs. The economic depression and widespread unemployment of the 1890s was caused by a stock market crash, often referred to as the Panic of 1893.

Early Life   Born in Pennsylvania, Coxey went to work in an iron mill at the age of sixteen. After several years in the scrap iron business, he bought a sandstone quarry in Massillon, Ohio, and formed the company Coxey Silica Sand Company, which provided silica sand to iron and steel mills. It was the mainstay of his business holdings for the next fifty years.

Supporting the Greenback   In 1877 Coxey joined the Greenback Party, which advocated switching to paper currency—the greenback—rather than a currency based

Jacob Coxey speaking from the Capitol steps, 1944.   *George Skadding/Time Life Pictures/Getty Images*

on gold or silver. Throughout his lifetime he remained devoted to the cause of paper currency.

After being forced to lay off forty workers, he sought ways to help the nation's unemployed. He got an idea from bicycling enthusiasts—it was a new sport at the time—who were calling attention to the poor condition of country roads. Coxey proposed a federal program, called the Good Roads Bill, to construct a national network of roads financed by $500 million in new greenbacks. Under the program the unemployed would be hired at $1.50 per day for an eight-hour day. A similar proposal, the Non-interest-Bearing Bond Bill, sought to aid the urban jobless through public works projects financed by federally subsidized bonds.

The March on Washington   Coxey, a mild-mannered man who lacked eloquence or charisma, had little success in publicizing his proposals until he met Carl Browne, a former rancher, carnival worker, labor editor, and Greenbacker who dressed like William "Buffalo Bill" Cody (1846–1917). Browne conceived the idea of a march of jobless men to Washington, D.C.

Coxey chose his hometown as the starting point for the march, which started with about one hundred workers and farmers; by the time it arrived in Washington, the group had grown to about five hundred. Coxey called the group the Commonweal of Christ, whereas observers called it Coxey's Army.

Coxey's Army of unemployed workers marching from Ohio to Washington in 1894.   © *CORBIS*

About forty other groups, inspired by Coxey's marchers but more militant in attitude, were also heading for Washington, particularly from the West. They made government officials apprehensive as Coxey and his followers marched toward the Capitol. When Coxey attempted to speak on the Capitol steps, he and two other men were arrested and sentenced to twenty days in jail for carrying banners (Coxey had a badge on his lapel) and fined for trespassing.

Although Coxey and other marchers remained in the Washington area from May until August, Congress made no attempt to assist the unemployed. Coxey's Good Roads Bill, which was introduced in Congress by William A. Peffer (1831–1912), a Populist Party senator from Kansas, got no further than a committee report.

Running for Office   For the rest of his life, Coxey combined business affairs with attempts to promote currency expansion. He repeatedly ran for office in Ohio, but was only successful in 1931 when he was elected mayor of Massillon as a Republican. He was not renominated in 1933. Although he later became a presidential candidate of the Farmer-Labor Party, he withdrew in favor of William Lemke (1878–1950), the Union Party candidate.

A campaign poster from 1900 for presidential candidate William McKinley and his running mate, Theodore Roosevelt. © *CORBIS*

Coxey's Legacy Although Coxey's march on Washington failed to achieve its goal, it was the first real protest march on the nation's capital. He publicized issues of relevance to ordinary citizens and pointed the way for others who felt they had a right to voice their demands. Many of the ideas he proposed were later adopted. For example, the public works programs he advocated influenced the efforts of President Franklin Roosevelt (1882–1945) during the Great Depression.

See also **Panic of 1893**

William McKinley

William McKinley (1843–1901), the twenty-fifth president, led the United States to victory during the Spanish-American War in 1898, resulting in the end of Spain's colonial rule in the Americas. He also pushed the Dingley Tariff Act, which created higher tariffs on foreign imports and helped get the nation out of an economic depression, which followed the stock market crash of 1893. McKinley was assassinated during his second term of office and was succeeded by Vice President Theodore Roosevelt (1858–1919).

Early Life McKinley, the seventh of nine children, was the son of an ironworker who instilled a strong work ethic in his children. After graduating from the Methodist seminary school in Poland, Ohio, McKinley entered Allegheny College in Pennsylvania, but dropped out after one term because of exhaustion and financial difficulties.

When the Civil War began in 1861, McKinley joined the Twenty-third Ohio Volunteer Army Infantry. He became known for taking risks on the battlefield, especially at the battle of Antietam, the single bloodiest day in U.S. military history (the death toll has been estimated at twenty thousand). Promoted to second lieutenant for bravery at Antietam, McKinley served under Colonel Rutherford B. Hayes (1822–1893), who would later become president. McKinley left the army a brevet major, a title that remained with him throughout his political career.

Following the Civil War, McKinley studied law and opened a practice in Canton, Ohio. After several years as a county prosecutor, he ran for the U.S. House of Representatives in 1876 and served nearly continuously until 1891.

As chairman of the House Ways and Means Committee in 1889, he drafted and steered to passage the McKinley

The assassination of President William McKinley, 1901. © *Library of Congress*

Tariff of 1890, the highest protective tariff in U.S. history to that point. The tariff, which was intended to protect U.S. business and manufacturing, raised consumer prices significantly; as a result, angry voters rejected McKinley and many other Republicans in the 1890 House elections. Stunned by his defeat, McKinley returned to Ohio and ran for governor in 1891, winning by a narrow margin.

As governor, McKinley worked to decrease the growing hostilities between management and labor, creating a system of arbitration to settle labor disputes. He persuaded Ohio Republicans, many of whom refused to acknowledge the rights of labor, to support it. Although sympathetic to workers, McKinley was unwilling to agree to all their demands. In 1894 he called out the National Guard to control violence that erupted during a strike by the United Mine Workers.

A Run for President One of the nation's most devastating economic collapses, referred to as the Panic of 1893, turned voters against the Democratic Party and gave McKinley a good chance at winning the presidential election in 1896. The Republican platform endorsed protective tariffs and the gold standard—using gold to back the value of money—while leaving open the door to an international agreement on bimetallism (using both gold and silver as standards for currency). McKinley argued that protective tariffs would solve the unemployment problem and stim-

ulate industrial growth. The Republican platform also supported the acquisition of Hawaii, construction of a canal across Central America, expansion of the U.S. Navy, immigration restrictions, equal pay for equal work for women, and a national board of arbitration to settle labor disputes.

McKinley defeated William Jennings Bryan (1860–1925), the Democratic candidate, in the largest Electoral College victory in twenty-five years. Four years later McKinley ran and defeated Bryan again. His victories launched a period of Republican power that lasted until 1913, when the Democrat Woodrow Wilson (1856–1924) was elected president, primarily because of a split in the Republican Party.

During his first year as president, he concentrated on the promises of the Republican platform. For most of 1897 the administration pursued an international agreement to include silver, along with gold, as an acceptable backing for the major currencies. McKinley said he would support bimetallism if England, France, Italy, and Russia would as well. When negotiations failed in late 1897, McKinley began advocating a gold-based currency. In 1900 he signed a law that formally placed U.S. currency on the gold standard, fully backed by gold at a fixed price of $20.67 per troy ounce. (The troy weight system is used primarily for precious metals and gemstones.)

He followed through on plans to increase tariff income as well, believing it would reduce internal taxes and encourage the expansion of domestic industry and employment. The Dingley Tariff Act of 1897, which was sponsored by Nelson R. Dingley (1832–1899), a Republican representative from Maine, raised tariffs on foreign goods to an average rate of 49 percent. McKinley, however, did not continue to support tariffs throughout his presidency. In 1901, only a day before his death, he announced his support for reciprocal trade agreements between nations, indicating a shift in his trade policy.

The Dingley tariff had a side benefit: it solidified McKinley's favorable standing with organized labor. Labor leaders also appreciated his endorsement of the Erdman Act of 1898, which made it illegal for railroads that participated in interstate commerce to hire only nonunion employees, and his support for the exclusion of Chinese workers. McKinley sent federal troops to keep order during a miners' strike in Coeur d'Alene, Idaho, but he still kept the support of organized labor.

A constituency he did not address was African-Americans. Unwilling to alienate southern white voters, McKinley did and said little about the disfranchisement and exclusion of blacks from political power. Even though he denounced lynching in his 1897 inaugural address, he did nothing formal to stop it. He refrained from taking action to curtail the general antiblack violence in the South, which had reached near epidemic proportions by the end of the nineteenth century. Instead, McKinley's initiatives in race relations were largely superficial: he appointed thirty African-Americans to positions in diplomatic and records offices.

The Spanish-American War

McKinley led the United States into its first international conflict with a European power since the War of 1812. The decision to go to the aid of Cubans, who were struggling to cast off Spanish colonial rule, was hastened by reports that Spain was responsible for the explosion of the U.S. battleship *Maine* in the Havana harbor. On April 25, 1898, Congress declared war on Spain and promised to secure independence for Cuba once the war ended.

After three months of fighting, the United States was victorious. Even though the peace treaty between the United States and Spain granted Cuba its independence, the island became a U.S. protectorate. The United States was also given control of the Philippines, Puerto Rico, and Guam, which had been Spanish colonies. Almost overnight the United States became a colonial power.

That status had its costs, however. Soon after the war with Spain had ended, a grassroots uprising against U.S. rule broke out in the Philippines. McKinley responded by sending thousands of troops to the islands, initiating a bloody conflict that left the United States open to atrocity charges similar to those lodged against Spain in Cuba. The war, which ended with U.S. victory in 1902, claimed the lives of more than five thousand Americans and two hundred thousand Filipinos.

The Open Door Policy in China

Britain, France, Germany, Japan, and Russia, among others, tried to establish their own spheres of influence in China during the 1890s. Concerned that they might close Chinese ports to U.S. commerce, McKinley had Secretary of State John Hay (1838–1905) issue an open door note on China. The statement expressed the U.S. desire to place all commercial nations on an equal footing in China, unrestricted by tariffs or other limitations, and declared U.S. support for Chinese independence from colonial rule.

Then in June 1900 a group of Chinese citizens revolted against foreign influence in their country, killing many Western missionaries and Chinese converts to Christianity. Popularly known as the Boxers (from the Chinese expression for "harmonious fists"), this group also threatened the lives of foreign diplomats in Peking (now Beijing).

Without congressional approval, McKinley sent twenty-five hundred U.S. troops and several gunboats to assist British, German, Japanese, and Russian forces to liberate the diplomats. Hay issued an open door note during the Boxer Rebellion, warning U.S. allies that the United States supported intervention only to rescue the diplomats and not to bring China under European and Japanese control. By August the allied force had successfully ended the rebellion. China was forced to pay compensation of $333 million—$25 million of which went to the United States—for damages, to modify commercial treaties to the advantage of foreign nations, and to allow the stationing of foreign troops in the Chinese capital.

Assassination

On the morning of September 6, 1901, McKinley gave a speech at the Pan-American Exposition in Buffalo, New York. That afternoon, at a public reception at the exposition's Temple of Music, Leon F. Czolgosz (1873–1901), an unemployed mill worker with anarchist tendencies, fired a revolver point blank at the president's chest. Although McKinley's doctors predicted recovery, gangrene set in, and he died on September 14, 1901, six months after he was inaugurated for his second term.

McKinley's Legacy

His contemporaries—and many historians—disagreed with his policies and doubted his leadership abilities. However, McKinley's difficult foreign policy decisions, especially his decision to go to war with Spain over Cuban independence and his policy toward China, helped the United States enter the twentieth century as a major world power.

See also **Gold Standard**
See also **Panic of 1893**
See also **Spanish-American War**

Theodore Roosevelt

Theodore Roosevelt (1858–1919), the twenty-sixth president of the United States, assumed office following the assassination of President William McKinley (1843–1901). Roosevelt was elected president in his own right in 1904 and served until 1909. He relished the role of trust-buster—his administration took many powerful business conglomerates to court—as well as protector of labor and the environment. Furthermore, he strengthened the U.S. Navy, because he accepted the country's new role as a world power, and secured the land for the Panama Canal. In 1906 he was awarded the Nobel Peace Prize for negotiating an end to a war between Japan and Russia.

Early Life Roosevelt was a frail and sickly child with poor eyesight and asthma, so as a teenager he undertook an exercise regimen to develop his physical stamina. He became an advocate of the "strenuous life."

When he was eighteen he entered Harvard College, where he excelled at both academics and sports, and developed interests in politics and history. He enrolled in Columbia University Law School, but soon discovered that he did not want to be a lawyer. So he left the university and entered politics, running for the New York State Assembly, where he served three terms. He quickly gained a reputation for attacking corruption and social problems. Among the many bills he steered through the assembly was a measure to regulate workplaces, a response to the sweatshop conditions that many workers faced.

In 1884, because of poor health and the death of his wife and his mother within hours of each other, Roosevelt abandoned his political career and moved to a cattle ranch in the Badlands of Dakota Territory (which became the states of North Dakota and South Dakota in 1889). An avid hunter, he developed a deep respect for the harsh landscape. In 1886 Roosevelt returned to New York, remarried, and reentered politics.

Over the next decade he was appointed to several posts, including assistant secretary of the navy in the first McKinley administration. After the U.S. battleship *Maine* exploded in the harbor of Havana, Cuba, and the United States declared war against Spain, Roosevelt resigned from the post and began recruiting the U.S. First Volunteer Cavalry. He went to Cuba as a lieutenant colonel of the regiment—its members became known as the Rough Riders—and gained national prominence for his exploits.

With his new fame, Roosevelt ran for governor of New York in 1898. During his two years in office, his forthright style led to clashes with state political bosses. Fed up with him, they helped him get nominated for vice president. McKinley and Roosevelt won the election in 1901.

Roosevelt had served as vice president for less than a year when McKinley was assassinated. Then forty-two years old, Roosevelt became the youngest president in U.S. history. In 1904 he was elected president on a platform known as the Square Deal.

Roosevelt did not share McKinley's conservative, pro-business views. Instead, he advanced an aggressive program of reforms, including the regulation of busi-

Poster for Theodore Roosevelt's presidential campaign, 1904. © *CORBIS*

ness. Invoking the Sherman Antitrust Act of 1890, his attorney general filed suit against the Northern Securities Company, a railroad trust, for illegally offering freight rebates—a practice in which railroads returned part of their fees to favored customers. In 1904 the U.S. Supreme Court ordered that the Northern Securities Company be dissolved. After that decision, the Roosevelt administration filed forty-two other trust-busting suits.

However, despite his fame as a trust-buster, Roosevelt wanted to regulate large corporations, not destroy them. In 1903 he pushed through Congress a bill to form a Bureau of Corporations, which was intended to investigate the business practices of interstate corporations. He also supported legislation that prohibited railroad rebates of the sort offered by the Northern Securities Company and asked Congress to create the Department of Commerce and Labor.

After winning the election in 1904, Roosevelt turned to more permanent business regulation. He successfully negotiated the passage of the Hepburn Act, which gave the Interstate Commerce Commission the

Theodore Roosevelt speaking on the campaign trail. © *Bettmann/ CORBIS*

authority to set maximum railroad rates and inspect railroad companies' financial records. Unlike his predecessors, he defended the right of labor to organize and join unions and objected to the use of federal troops to stop strikes. In 1902 he intervened in a United Mine Workers' strike and got management to agree to arbitration of the dispute. The arbitrators awarded the miners a wage increase and a shortened workday.

Consumer and Environmental Protection During his administration, journalists—often called muckrakers—reported on unsanitary conditions in food plants and harmful ingredients in certain foods and medications. In response, Roosevelt endorsed the Pure Food and Drug Act, which prohibited the sale of tainted or improperly labeled foods and medications, and the Meat Inspection Act, which established federal regulations for meatpackers and a system of inspection. Both passed in 1906.

It was also a time of growing public concern about the environment. Preservationists, as they were called, often clashed with businessmen who wanted to develop the country's natural resources and use wilderness land for commercial and residential development. Even though Roosevelt was a preservationist, he understood the need to compromise with business developers. He established a conservation program that regulated the use of wilderness areas and designated some two hundred million acres as national forests, mineral reserves, and potential waterpower sites. He also added five national parks and eighteen national monuments (including the Grand Canyon, Death Valley, and Crater Lake) to the list of protected lands. In 1908 he created the National Conservation Commission to inventory the nation's resources and better manage their use.

A "Big Stick" Diplomacy Roosevelt summed up his approach to foreign policy with the phrase "speak softly and carry a big stick"—he would engage in negotiations but was prepared to use military force if necessary. Having become president shortly after the U.S. victory in the Spanish-American War, he was confident of the country's status as a world power and sought to maintain that status through aggressive tactics.

Those tactics were especially evident when the United States decided to build a canal across Panama, which would link the Atlantic and Pacific oceans. Colombia, which controlled Panama at the time, rejected the terms that Roosevelt offered. His response: he supplied money to foment a revolution and established a naval blockade so Colombia could not land troops in Panama.

Roosevelt's intervention in Panama was representative of his general approach toward Latin America, where he asserted the Roosevelt Corollary to the Monroe Doctrine. The Monroe Doctrine was intended to discourage European nations from colonizing or asserting their influence in Central and South America; the Roosevelt Corollary went a step further, asserting the right of the U.S. government to intervene when European powers ventured into the region.

In 1904, with several European nations preparing to invade the Dominican Republic, Roosevelt declared that the United States, not Europe, should dominate Latin America. He claimed the United States had no expansionist intentions; however, he also asserted that any "chronic wrongdoing" by a Latin American nation would justify U.S. intervention as an international police power. During Roosevelt's presidency, the United States invoked the Roosevelt Corollary repeatedly to justify involvement in the affairs of the Dominican Republic, Haiti, Venezuela, Nicaragua, and Cuba.

The Russo-Japanese War Roosevelt used his clout in other world arenas as well. When war broke out between Russia and Japan in 1904—both countries wanted access to the rich natural resources of China—Roosevelt stepped in to maintain the balance of power between them. He invited delegates from Japan and Russia to the United States for a peace conference. The negotiations resulted in the Portsmouth Treaty in 1905, which effectively ended the war.

The Progressive Party Roosevelt lost the Republican presidential nomination to William Howard Taft in

1912, so he established the National Progressive Party (which was also known as the Bull Moose Party). During a campaign stop in Milwaukee, Wisconsin, Roosevelt was shot in the chest by an assassin, but the bullet was slowed by his steel eyeglass case and a copy of the speech he was carrying in his breast pocket. Despite being shot, he insisted on delivering his ninety-minute speech, declaring that it would take "more than a bullet to stop a bull moose."

His campaign platform, which he called the New Nationalism, was an ambitious program of economic and social reforms. The campaign focused on Roosevelt and Woodrow Wilson (1856–1924), the Democratic candidate, but Roosevelt divided the Republican vote with Taft, so Wilson was elected.

Roosevelt's final years were spent writing, exploring the Amazon jungles of South America, and raising money for the U.S. effort in World War I (1914–1918). He died in 1919 at the age of sixty.

Roosevelt's Legacy Even though some U.S. officials and citizens were disturbed by Roosevelt's push to increase the powers of the federal government, he thought it was the best way to represent and safeguard the interests of all Americans, not just the wealthy few. Roosevelt appreciated the energy that had been building in the United States in the decades following the Civil War (1861–1865), such as the explosion of industrial power and the desire to expand territorially, politically, socially, and economically. He used his presidency to channel this energy, leaving a legacy of sweeping reforms that anticipated the progressive movements of the 1930s and the 1960s.

> *See also* **Progressive Party, 1912**
> *See also* **Roosevelt Corollary**
> *See also* **Spanish-American War**
> *See also* **Square Deal**
> *See also* **William McKinley**

William Howard Taft

William Howard Taft (1857–1930), the twenty-seventh president of the United States and the tenth chief justice (1921–1930) of the U.S. Supreme Court, was the only person in U.S. history to hold both offices. Chosen by President Theodore Roosevelt (1858–1919) as his successor, Taft promised to carry out Roosevelt's progressive policies if elected.

After assuming office, however, Taft was unable to unite the warring factions within the Republican Party and vacillated from a progressive antitrust program, in which large, powerful companies that controlled markets were broken up, to reactionary conservatism, which opposed any kind of progress. More important, he often backed down from his positions when the criticism became too severe. Although Taft distinguished himself as an administrator, historians generally regard his presidency as a failure.

THE PANAMA CANAL

For many years U.S. naval leaders had envisioned building a passageway between the Atlantic and Pacific oceans through Central America. The need for this passageway became apparent during the Spanish-American War in 1898, which was precipitated by the sinking of the USS *Maine* in the Havana harbor. To join the U.S. fleet off the coast of Cuba, ships stationed in the Pacific had to sail around the southern tip of South America, a voyage that took two months.

In 1901 the United States negotiated with Britain for support of a U.S.-controlled canal that would be constructed either through Panama, which was under Colombian control, or Nicaragua. After a series of secret meetings, the U.S. Senate approved the Panama route, which was contingent on Colombian approval. Colombia resisted, so the Roosevelt administration backed a Panamanian revolution with money and a naval blockade that prevented Colombian troops from landing in Panama. In 1903 the United States signed the Hay-Bunau-Varilla Treaty with Panama, which gave the United States perpetual control of the canal at a cost of $10 million and an annual payment of $250,000.

The $400 million canal, which took nearly thirty thousand workers ten years to build, prompted advances in technology and engineering. It also made clear how much the balance of power had shifted: the Panama Canal Zone became a major U.S. military base, making the United States the dominant power in Central America.

On September 7, 1977, a new Panama Canal Treaty, signed by the Panamanian leader Omar Torrijos (1929–1981) and the U.S. president Jimmy Carter (1924–), transferred full control of the canal to Panama on December 31, 1999.

Early Life Taft was the son of Alfonso Taft, a lawyer who served as secretary of war and attorney general under President Ulysses S. Grant (1869–1977) and then as an ambassador. Raised in Cincinnati, he graduated with distinction from Yale University in 1878 and from Cincinnati Law School in 1880.

Taft worked as an assistant prosecuting attorney and a collector of internal revenue, but he wanted a judicial post. This goal was realized when he was appointed to fill a vacancy on an Ohio superior court in 1887. The following year he was elected to a term of his own—the only office other than the presidency that he won by election.

In 1890 President Benjamin Harrison (1889–1893) called Taft to Washington to serve as solicitor general, the attorney who represents the government before the U.S. Supreme Court. Two years later Harrison named him to the U.S. Circuit Court for the Sixth District. Taft's record as a state and federal judge showed that he was honest and competent and that he was receptive to the problems of labor.

The Philippines Taft gained national stature when President William McKinley (1843–1930) appointed him to two posts in the Philippine Islands, which became a U.S. possession following the Spanish-American War in 1898: he first headed the commission to end military rule in the islands and then became their first civil governor. Taft received high praise as a colonial administrator. He was sympathetic to the problems of the Filipinos and believed in giving them the widest possible degree of self-government. He recognized that the first steps toward Philippine independence were public education and the end of ownership of land by Roman Catholic friars.

The 1902 Philippine Organic Act removed Roman Catholicism as the state religion. Undertaking dollar diplomacy—the practice of using economic incentives rather than bullets to resolve disputes—Taft negotiated an agreement with the Vatican. In 1904 the United States bought most of the friars' land and then resold it, in small parcels, to Filipinos.

Secretary of War When Roosevelt succeeded McKinley, he and Taft became close personal friends and political allies—even though they were different in temperament: Roosevelt was dynamic and impulsive, and Taft was reserved and accommodating. Roosevelt came to regard Taft as his eventual successor and invited him to join his cabinet. Taft accepted the post of secretary of war with the understanding that he would continue to oversee Philippine affairs from Washington; he left the task of managing the army to the generals.

He had several other roles in the administration as well. Between 1904 and 1908 he was in charge of constructing the Panama Canal. In 1906, when revolution threatened in Cuba, he brought a degree of peace through negotiations. In Tokyo in 1907 he improved Japanese-American relations, which had been strained by the abuse of Japanese immigrants in California.

A Reluctant Candidate Initially, Taft had no desire to run for president, but on Roosevelt's insistence, and with the urging of his wife and brothers, he accepted the Republican nomination in 1908. Benefiting from the popularity of the Roosevelt administration, Taft defeated William Jennings Bryan (1860–1925), the Democratic candidate.

His term had few significant achievements. He inherited the widespread demand for a lower tariff and accepted the Payne-Aldrich Act of 1909, a compromise that was denounced by both big business and progressive Republicans. With a characteristic clumsiness that often marked his public statements, he referred to the Payne-Aldrich Act as the best tariff in history. He negotiated an agreement with Canada that promised relatively free trade between the two countries, but Canada ultimately rejected the proposal. Although Taft's attorney general initiated twice as many antitrust suits against

Plate commemorating President William Taft, Vice-President James Sherman, and all the Republican presidential candidates who preceded them, 1908. *© CORBIS*

big corporations as the previous administration, Roosevelt is remembered as the trust-buster.

When the Democrats captured control of the U.S. House of Representatives in 1910, progressive Republicans looked to Roosevelt to be their presidential candidate in 1912. Roosevelt, who had broken off his relationship with Taft in 1911 because he thought Taft was too conservative, ran as a Progressive Party candidate against the man whose candidacy he had backed four years earlier. Although Taft won the Republican nomination, he and Roosevelt split the Republican vote; the Democrat Woodrow Wilson (1856–1924) won the election.

Chief Justice When Chief Justice Edward D. White (1845–1921) died, President Warren G. Harding (1865–1923) appointed Taft to succeed him. Taft's greatest achievement as chief justice was to bring greater harmony and efficiency to a deeply divided court.

Taft's main interest was in speeding up the work of the courts. He never offered a dissenting opinion when the majority disagreed with his position, and he usually sided with property rights over labor interests and government power over civil rights. He retired from the court in 1930, because of heart disease, and died a month later.

Taft's Legacy According to many historians, Taft had little talent for leadership. He accepted the role of president with great reluctance, was indecisive, and took little initiative in legislative matters. His term had few significant accomplishments. Taft is often viewed as a conservative bridge between the activist reformers Roosevelt and Wilson.

See also **Dollar Diplomacy**

See also **Spanish-American War**

Robert M. La Follette

Robert M. La Follette (1855–1925) was a leader of the Progressive movement, which sought to address social problems that resulted from rapid industrial growth in the United States during the last quarter of the nineteenth century. He is remembered for battling political corruption and corporate greed during his long career in public service—as governor of Wisconsin and as a member of both the U.S. House of Representatives and the U.S. Senate. Known as "Fighting Bob" because of his commitment to reform, his fervent speeches, and his frequent clashes with party bosses, La Follette fought for higher wages and better working conditions for laborers, women's right to vote, and civil rights legislation.

Early Life La Follette worked on a farm until 1875, when he enrolled in the University of Wisconsin, where he excelled in social studies and oratory. He established a law practice in Madison and then ran successfully for district attorney—he won over a local political leader by going door to door and speaking to voters directly, an uncommon practice at the time. In 1884, at the age of twenty-nine, he became the youngest member of the House of Representatives. A Republican, he served three terms. Although he was defeated by the Democrat Allen Bushnell (1833–1909) in 1890 and returned to the office of district attorney, La Follette remained active in state politics.

The Political Turning Point The turning point in La Follette's career—and the beginning of his days as a political reformer—came in 1891, when Philetus Sawyer (1816–1900), a Republican senator and wealthy lumberman, offered him a bribe to fix a court case against several former state officials. La Follette was outraged; he denounced the attempt and for nearly ten years

Robert M. La Follette. © *CORBIS*

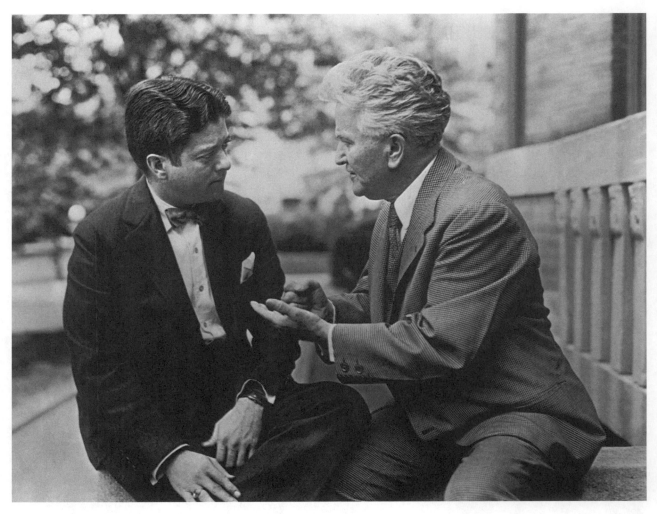

Robert M. La Follette with his son Robert M. La Follette, Jr., also a U.S. Senator. © *CORBIS*

traveled the state speaking out against the influence of dishonest politicians and the lumber barons and railroad interests that dominated his party.

The Republican Party machine twice stopped his nomination for governor, but he was finally elected to the office in 1900 and reelected in 1902 and 1904. Fighting Bob was popular among farmers, small businesses owners, professionals, and intellectuals who resented the control that wealthy eastern businessmen exercised over credit, railroad freight rates, and political power.

As governor, La Follette advocated what became known as the Wisconsin Idea, a broad agenda of social and political reform. To weaken the political influence of party machines and large corporations, he established primary elections that allowed voters, rather than party leaders, to nominate candidates for office—Wisconsin was the first state to adopt the primary system for state offices. He also instituted campaign-spending limits. To guide policy on railroad regulation, the environment, transportation, civil service, insurance, banking, and taxation, he created state commissions. His proposals for

taxing corporations, in particular, enraged big business but allowed the state to control tax rates. He also advocated increased funding for education. In an unprecedented move, La Follette employed political and social scientists and economists from the University of Wisconsin to draft bills and administer laws.

In 1905, having gained a national reputation, La Follette ran for the U.S. Senate, where he tried to apply the Wisconsin Idea on a national level. He worked to regulate the railroads and other industries, and he spoke about government corruption and the abuse of industrial workers. To check the power and "selfish interests" of large corporations, he supported the growth of trade unions. Among the most notable achievements of his three Senate terms was a 1915 bill protecting merchant seamen from exploitation.

In 1909 he and his wife, Belle La Follette, a suffragist and attorney, founded *La Follette's Weekly* (later called the *Progressive*). It promoted women's suffrage, racial equality, and other progressive causes.

President Woodrow Wilson married Edith Bolling Galt in December, 1915. After he was disabled by a stroke in 1919, Edith stepped in to handle many matters of state. © *CORBIS*

An Antiwar Senator La Follette was unsuccessful in seeking the Republican presidential nomination in 1908 and 1912. Although he supported the Democrat Woodrow Wilson (1856–1924) in the 1912 presidential election because of Wilson's commitment to social justice, La Follette opposed Wilson's determination to enter World War I (1914–1918). In April 1917 La Follette voted against declaring war, believing that war could be avoided and that U.S. involvement would most likely put a stop to domestic reforms. Military expansion, he argued, would only reward corporations and their investors. His leadership of the antiwar faction in the Senate made him an outsider: after he made an antiwar speech, members of the Senate tried to expel him for disloyalty. La Follette also opposed the terms of the Treaty of Versailles, the peace treaty that ended World War I and the Senate refused to ratify.

Wilson later adopted many of La Follette's reform programs, including public disclosure of campaign contributions and graduated taxation. Indirectly, La Follette worked with Wilson to limit the power of big business and was instrumental in the creation of the Department of Labor and the Federal Trade Commission.

Although his critics believed his opposition to the war would end his political career, La Follette was reelected to the Senate in 1922. In 1924 he ran for president on the Progressive Party ticket (a successful third party that advocated tax, judicial, and agricultural reform and government ownership of natural resources and public utilities) but lost to the Republican Calvin Coolidge (1872–1933). La Follette died in 1925.

La Follette's Legacy La Follette is remembered as one of the most important political and social reformers in U.S. history. In fact, in 1957 the Senate voted La Follette one of the five most outstanding senators of all time. His policies, which had appeal across party lines, set precedents for state and federal programs in the following decades and improved the lives of farmers, workers, women, and children.

> *See also* **Federal Trade Commission**
> *See also* **Progressive Party, 1924**
> *See also* **Woodrow Wilson**

Woodrow Wilson

Woodrow Wilson (1856–1924), the twenty-eighth president of the United States, advocated progressive reform, steered the United States through World War I (1914–1918), and persuaded members of the Paris Peace Conference of 1919—convened to negotiate the end of the war—to establish the League of Nations.

Early Years Thomas Woodrow Wilson, born in Staunton, Virginia, was the son of a Presbyterian minister and a minister's daughter. Like his father, he demanded total loyalty from friends and associates and had few friends he treated as equals. He had a strong sense of duty and justice—which is why, historians say, he treated those who disagreed with him in a condescending manner.

Wilson had difficulty learning to read when he was a boy. Even though he compensated with hard work, the difficulty remained with him throughout his life. He was physically frail and had to withdraw from Davidson College, where he was preparing for the ministry, and rest at home for a year. As an adult, he had several strokes, one of which left him partially paralyzed for the rest of his life.

Wilson studied history at the College of New Jersey, which later became Princeton University, and earned a law degree from the University of Virginia and a doctorate from Johns Hopkins University, the top graduate school in the country at the time. His first book, *Congressional Government*, was based on his doctoral dissertation.

He opened a law practice in Atlanta, Georgia, but the venture was not successful, so he turned to academia. In 1885 he taught briefly at Bryn Mawr College in Pennsylvania and then at Wesleyan University in Connecticut. In 1890 he was appointed professor of jurisprudence and economics at Princeton and became the school's most popular professor. When he was named president of the university in 1902, he introduced curriculum innovations and reforms.

Those reforms led to tiring battles with Princeton's wealthy, conservative trustees and alumni, however, so when he was offered the Democratic nomination for governor of New Jersey in 1910, he accepted. After an overwhelming victory, he worked with progressives—social, political, and economic reformers—and accomplished a great deal in a short time: he changed policies regarding schools and workmen's compensation; established direct primaries, which replaced a system in which parties nominated candidates; regulated public utilities; and passed antitrust legislation, which stopped large corporations from amassing too much economic power. Media attention to these sweeping reforms gave Wilson national prominence.

The Reform Candidate After a successful term as governor of New Jersey, Wilson ran for president in 1912 on a platform offering what the public demanded: reform. Wilson's opponents included the Republican president William Howard Taft (1857–1930), who favored progressive measures but did not implement them effectively; the former president Theodore Roosevelt (1858–1919), who ran on his Progressive Party platform, which was even more reformist than Wilson's; and the Socialist Party candidate Eugene V. Debs (1855–1926). The Republican vote was split between Taft and the formerly Republican Roosevelt, so Wilson was the unexpected winner.

Once elected, Wilson called a special session of Congress and appeared before it personally, which no president had done since John Adams (1735–1826) in 1800. Impressed by the speech, Congress quickly took up Wilson's proposal for a lower tariff on foreign imports. When lobbyists tried to persuade Congress not to cut tariff rates, the president called a news conference, another Wilson first. Newspaper reports generated public demand for tariff reform and a flood of mail to Congress, which, in response, passed the Underwood-Simmons Tariff Act of 1913. The law—which reduced tariffs to their lowest level since 1846—also reinstituted a federal income tax to compensate for the lost revenue.

Congress addressed other parts of Wilson's reform program as well, creating the Federal Reserve System, a centralized banking system for the nation, and the Federal Trade Commission, which investigates and curbs unfair business practices. It also passed the Clayton Antitrust Act of 1914, which clarified the language of the Sherman Antitrust Act of 1890, which had outlawed monopolies and other large business combinations that limited competition. Labor reforms included a forty-hour workweek for some employees and a law prohibiting child labor (an act later overturned by the U.S. Supreme Court). Congress granted funds for precollege agricultural and vocational education and also created the federal highway system.

A Novice at Foreign Policy Wilson tended to regard himself as an expert in domestic matters, but he had no experience in diplomacy. Regardless, world events would force him to make major foreign policy decisions, especially when World War I erupted in Europe in 1914. The assassination of the archduke Franz Ferdinand of Austria-Hungary by a Serb precipitated a war between Austria-Hungary and Serbia; many other European nations soon joined the conflict. Following traditional U.S. isolationist policies, Wilson vowed to keep the United States out of the war. Although he kept his promise for nearly three years, many U.S. citizens, who had strong ties to Europe, found neutrality difficult. Public sentiment favored the side of the Allies—the democracies of Britain, France, and Belgium—rather than the autocracies of Germany, Austria-Hungary, and, later, Ottoman Turkey and Bulgaria, where political power was held by individuals.

When Britain set up a naval blockade of Germany, Wilson did not seriously protest, even though the blockade cut the United States off from a huge trade market. He did warn Germany, however, that he would hold it accountable for any damage done to Americans or their property. The Germans were angered by Wilson's harsh words. Americans, in turn, became enraged when a German submarine sank the British ocean liner *Lusitania*, killing more than a thousand people, including 128 Americans. Wilson demanded that Germany end submarine attacks on civilian vessels. In 1916 the German government vowed not to attack unresisting merchant ships, but added that Wilson had to persuade the British to end the blockade. Wilson ignored the challenge.

THE LEAGUE OF NATIONS

Toward the end of World War I (1914–1918) President Woodrow Wilson (1856–1924) called for the creation of a League of Nations, an international body that would, he said, lead to an effective and lasting peace in Europe and the world. He made certain that the League of Nations was an essential part of the Treaty of Versailles, which ended the war.

Of the 440 articles in the treaty, the first twenty-six make up the Covenant of the League of Nations, a description of its operations. Article Ten, which caused the most debate in the U.S. Senate, reads as follows:

> Article 10. The Members of the League undertake to respect and preserve as against external aggression the territorial integrity and existing political independence of all Members of the League. In case of any such aggression or in case of any threat or danger of such aggression the Council shall advise upon the means by which this obligation shall be fulfilled.

Henry Cabot Lodge (1850–1985), a Republican senator from Massachusetts, led the opposition to the league. Although he and Wilson were bitter political adversaries, they had legitimate differences of opinion on the issue. Lodge maintained that, under Article Ten, the organization could require the United States to commit economic or military force to maintain the security of member nations. Wilson, the author of Article Ten, argued that because the United States would be a permanent member of the League Council—the body within the league that would arbitrate disputes—it could veto sanctions. Furthermore, he said, if the league voted unanimously for sanctions, that action amounted only to advice, and the United States would not be legally bound by the league's dictates. He did maintain, however, that the United States would be morally bound to adhere to the league's resolutions. From his perspective, a moral obligation was vastly superior to a legal one, and Article Ten was a serious obligation.

Although a compromise was possible—a sufficient number of pro-treaty Republicans would have joined the Democrats to achieve the necessary two-thirds majority—Wilson blocked any compromise after he suffered a massive stroke in October 1919. The vote to ratify the Treaty of Versailles failed.

The United States remained officially at war until August 1921, when President Warren G. Harding (1865–1923) approved a congressional resolution proclaiming that the war had ended. He later signed a separate peace treaty. The resolution and the treaty specified that, although the United States did not sign the Treaty of Versailles, the nation retained all rights and advantages accorded under its terms, with the exception of the League Covenant.

The League of Nations, which was established in 1920, remained in existence until it was superseded by the United Nations in 1945.

SOURCE: The Covenant of the League of Nations. *http://www.yale. edu/lawweb/avalon/leagcov.htm (accessed May 15, 2007).*

Even though Wilson had practical plans for war mobilization, he had increased army strength to only 223,000 by 1916—by contrast, Germany had an army of 11 million soldiers. In addition, the government was building mostly battleships; Wilson resisted building destroyers—small, fast ships that are efficient for sinking submarines—because doing so would be, in his words, "unneutral."

The United States Declares War Reelected president by a slim margin in 1916, Wilson continued his efforts to mediate a peace between Britain and Germany, but failed. In 1917 Germany began a new submarine campaign. After U.S. ships were sunk, Wilson broke diplomatic relations and threatened war. When the campaign continued, Wilson requested a declaration of war, which Congress granted on April 6, 1917.

Wilson mobilized not only an army of four million men but also all of U.S. industry to provide munitions and other supplies. He advocated a unified command on the western front in France and Belgium, which proved far superior to the four armies operating on their own.

Wilson's Peace Plan Wilson proclaimed that U.S. entry into the war made "the world safe for democracy." In an address to Congress in January 1918, he issued a plan for a lasting peace in Europe, which became known as his Fourteen Points speech. It offered details about the return of occupied lands to their previous owners and suggested that the war should have no victor, because peace could only exist between equals. The plan included the creation of an international organization to guarantee "political independence and territorial integrity to great and small state alike." That organization would later be called the League of Nations.

By the fall of 1918 Germany, which was near collapse from heavy casualties and the starvation of people and industry brought on by the British blockade, appealed to Wilson for peace on the basis of the Fourteen Points; he agreed. The European Allies, however, adopted only those points that fit their interests. The Treaty of Versailles, which ended the war, imposed harsh terms on Germany, forcing it to surrender its entire navy and air force and all artillery and to permit Allied forces to occupy western Germany. In addition, France recovered the regions of Alsace and Lorraine, and both France and Britain seized Arab regions from Turkey (arousing anger in what are now Syria, Lebanon, Iraq, Israel, and Jordan). France helped create a huge Poland that, because so many Germans, Russians, and Lithuanians lived within its borders, was not a cohesive country, and a large Yugoslavia, which contained many different ethnic and religious groups. In general, the armistice punished Germany so severely that Germans would soon desire revenge.

The Final Years When Wilson's pleas to the U.S. Senate to ratify the Treaty of Versailles failed, he took his appeals directly to the American people. On a trip of several thousand miles through the Midwest and West, he gave speeches to large crowds several times a day. Although he changed some voters' minds, most Americans rejected the League of Nations because they believed it would make the United States an international police power.

As he returned home to Washington, Wilson suffered a massive stroke that left him an invalid. Although extremely ill, he continued his efforts to get the Senate to accept the Treaty of Versailles and the League of Nations, but failed every time a vote was taken. He announced that the presidential election of 1920 would resolve the issue.

By then Americans were tired of reform crusades and war and were reluctant to be involved abroad. When the Republican Warren G. Harding (1865–1923) became the next president, the League of Nations was a dead issue in U.S. politics.

Wilson, who was awarded the Nobel Peace Prize in 1919 for the creation of the League of Nations, died at his home in Washington, D.C., on February 3, 1924.

Wilson's Legacy Historians sometimes refer to Wilson as the first modern president, noting that he understood the power of the president to deal directly with the people. He guided them from a policy of isolationism to one of global participation, and he believed they would eventually embrace his vision of the United States leading a world community of nations. Twenty-five years later, his dream, which was first expressed in the League of Nations, became a reality in the United Nations.

    See also **Isolationism**

    See also **World War I**

William Jennings Bryan

William Jennings Bryan (1860–1925) was a populist—he was called the Great Commoner because of his defense of the common man—lawyer, politician, and Democratic presidential nominee in 1896, 1900, and 1908. He is perhaps best known as the voice of religious fundamentalism in the 1925 "monkey trial," in which John T. Scopes (1900–1970), a high school teacher, was tried for teaching evolution. He was also a fiery orator who fought against the gold standard, a monetary system that sets the value of currency with gold. Yet, Bryan's legacy in U.S. politics is more far reaching: he is sometimes referred to as one of the founding fathers of the modern Democratic Party.

Early Life Born in Illinois, Bryan was the son of a circuit court judge and a high school teacher. Even though he excelled as a debater, he was not an outstanding student. After graduating with honors from Illinois College, he enrolled in the Union College of Law in Chicago. He then practiced law in Jacksonville, Illinois.

Bryan thought his chances for a career in Illinois politics were slim, so he and his wife, Mary Baird, moved to Lincoln, Nebraska, in 1887, where he opened a law office. In 1888 his wife passed the Nebraska bar.

Bryan gave up his law practice when he became a Democratic candidate for Congress. He won a seat in the U.S. House of Representatives—in a largely Republican district—by a large majority in 1890 and by a smaller margin in 1892. Two years later he announced his candidacy for the U.S. Senate and gave popular speeches but lost the election. To earn a living, he became the editor in chief of the *Omaha World-Herald*.

The Fight against the Gold Standard In his first term in the House, Bryan turned his attention to the growing debate over monetary policy in the wake of post–Civil War inflation, depression, and unemployment. The issue was the "free," or unlimited, coinage of silver versus an adherence to the gold standard.

Free-silver supporters—primarily farmers from the West and South—argued that the gold standard exploited them economically. Rather than enriching the bankers who loaned farmers money, the farmers advocated cheaper dollars to pay off their debts. Bryan supported the farmers and advocated free silver—at a ratio of sixteen ounces of silver to one ounce of gold. He voted against the repeal of the Sherman Silver Purchase Act of 1890, a law that increased the amount of silver that the U.S. Department of the Treasury was required to purchase each month.

Bryan gave several well-received speeches on the topic, including his famous Cross of Gold speech at the Democratic convention in 1896. It electrified the free-silver contingent, which took control of the convention, casting aside the New York leaders who had run the party for many years.

The day after his famous speech, Bryan was nominated as the Democratic Party's candidate for president. He also received nominations from the Populist Party, whose members were mostly farmers who opposed the gold standard, and the National Silver Party. His candidacy was even supported by Republicans who favored free silver.

William McKinley (1843–1901), the Republican candidate, was well financed and likeable. Although Bryan's speeches were clever and aroused patriotism, some found his solution to the nation's economic problems simplistic: they thought "free silver" and "sound money" were nothing more than empty campaign slogans. Eastern industrialists convinced their workers that Bryan was a revolutionary, so he failed to convert them to his cause. McKinley won the election.

William Jennings Bryan at the trial of John Scopes, who stood accused of teaching evolution in a public school, in violation of state law. Bryan, who represented the prosecution in that case, is seen here sitting with defense attorney Clarence Darrow (left) © *Bettmann/CORBIS*

Foreign Policy Initiatives Bryan ran unsuccessfully for president again in 1900 and 1908. He did, however, succeed in seeing many of his ideas enacted into law: the popular election of senators, the income tax, the creation of the Department of Labor, Prohibition (which banned the sale, manufacture, import, and export of alcohol), and suffrage for women.

After his 1908 loss, Bryan worked for the election of Woodrow Wilson (1856–1924) in 1912 and was rewarded with an appointment as secretary of state. Bryan used his political influence to push measures through Congress, particularly the creation of the Federal Reserve System, the network of banks that controls the money supply.

However, nothing in Bryan's training prepared him to direct U.S. foreign policy; he knew nothing about international law. A pacifist, Bryan was effective in promoting several treaties designed to delay World War I (1914–1918) in Europe, but his pleas for peace went unheeded. He resigned in protest when Wilson, who had been committed to neutrality, adopted a hard line

after a German submarine sank the British ocean liner *Lusitania* in 1915, killing over a thousand passengers, including 128 U.S. citizens. However, Bryan loyally supported the United States when it entered World War I.

The Scopes Trial Bryan, who had joined the Presbyterian church as a boy, believed in a literal interpretation of the Bible. As he grew older, he became increasingly hostile to the teachings of biological science. Theories of evolution, he thought, seemed to contradict the words of Genesis and devalue human life, so he undertook a great crusade against the Darwinian theory of evolution.

Bryan was one of the prosecutors at the 1925 trial of John T. Scopes, a Tennessee biology teacher who was accused of violating state law by teaching evolution in his classroom. The trial had a circus-like atmosphere, attracting worldwide attention as a battle between fundamentalism and the theory of the evolutionary origin of human beings. The press called it the "monkey trial." When Bryan offered to join the prosecution team—even

"CROSS OF GOLD"

At the 1896 Democratic convention in Chicago, William Jennings Bryan (1860–1925) made what would become one of the most memorable speeches in U.S. politics. The Cross of Gold speech recounted the effort to back currency with silver and challenged Democrats to make the decision that he believed most Americans had already made: to support the cause. The following is an excerpt:

> We have petitioned, and our petitions have been scorned; we have entreated, and our entreaties have been disregarded; we have begged, and they have mocked us when our calamity came. We beg no longer, we entreat no more; we petition no more. We defy the. . . .

> Having behind us the producing masses of this nation and the world, supported by the commercial interests, the laboring interests, and the toilers everywhere, we will answer their demand for a gold standard by saying to them: You shall not press down upon the brow of labor this crown of thorns, you shall not crucify mankind upon a cross of gold.

SOURCE: *The Cross of Gold Speech. http://douglassarchives.org/brya_a26.htm (accessed February 20, 2007).*

though he had not practiced law in more than thirty years—the renowned attorney Clarence Darrow, nearly seventy at the time, joined the defense team. It became a fierce battle between the two men. In a two-hour examination of Bryan, which was broadcast live on national radio, Darrow confused Bryan and revealed Bryan's ignorance of science. Scopes was eventually found guilty, but the trial took an enormous toll on Bryan. He died five days after the trial ended.

Bryan's Legacy Bryan's politics were staunchly anti-corporate and anti-imperialist. He was an early supporter of labor unions, women's rights, progressive taxation, and the federal government's central role in safeguarding the interests of the poor, the elderly, and the sick. He drove the conservatives out of the Democratic Party—they had dominated the party since the Civil War—by advocating high tariffs and low taxes. His efforts set the party on a course it would follow into the twenty-first century.

> *See also* **Gold Standard**
> *See also* **William McKinley**

Henry Cabot Lodge

Henry Cabot Lodge (1850–1924), a conservative Republican politician and adversary of the Democratic president Woodrow Wilson (1856–1924), favored a strong military and greater U.S. involvement in world affairs.

Lodge is best remembered for leading the U.S. Senate's successful effort to block U.S. entry into the League of Nations.

Early Life Lodge, who was born into a wealthy political family in Boston, earned a law degree from Harvard University as well as the school's first doctorate in political science. Rather than enter the legal profession, Lodge taught history at Harvard, wrote a series of books and magazine articles, and edited the journal *International Review* for four years. Lodge was first elected to the Massachusetts legislature and, after two unsuccessful bids, was elected to the U.S. House of Representatives in 1886. In 1892 he was elected to the Senate, where he served four terms.

As a senator, he was a strong supporter of the Spanish-American War (1898)—in which two of his three sons served—and supported U.S. involvement abroad during the presidency of Theodore Roosevelt (1858–1919). He sponsored a law against child labor, a law mandating an eight-hour workday, and worked on the Pure Food and Drug Act to help ensure food and drug safety.

The League of Nations From 1918 to 1924 Lodge chaired the Senate Foreign Relations Committee, a position he used to stop Wilson's efforts to establish the League of Nations. Lodge disliked both Wilson's policies and personality. Because the creation of the league was part of the Treaty of Versailles, which officially ended World War I (1914–1918), Lodge accused Wilson of jeopardizing the peace process for the sake of his project.

In 1919 Lodge addressed the Senate about the terms of the proposed league. He pointed out a direct conflict between the league and the Monroe Doctrine, which, he said, dictated that Americans settle their problems by themselves. He also questioned whether the United States could fulfill some of the promises outlined in Wilson's proposal and warned that it could lead to a loss of control over immigration.

Lodge and two other senators crafted a declaration of objections to the league, particularly those involving congressional rights, and gathered signatures of support from Republican senators. He also led a lengthy debate on the Senate floor, followed by hearings in which a variety of representatives from around the world were allowed to testify—all were tactics to wear down Wilson and his supporters and encourage a deadlock.

Ultimately, Congress did deadlock on the issue, and the U.S. public decided the fate of the league in the November 1920 presidential election. James M. Cox (1870–1957), the Democratic candidate, lost to Warren G. Harding (1865–1923), an opponent of the league.

Lodge died on November 9, 1924, at the age of seventy-four.

Lodge's Legacy Although Lodge's goal was to expand U.S. interests in the world, he was often regarded as an isolationist because of his successful effort to prevent the United States from entering the League of Nations. Ironically, Lodge's grandson, Henry Cabot Lodge Jr. (1902–1985), later served as the U.S. ambassador to the United Nations. The League of Nations was the forerunner of the United Nations.

See also **Woodrow Wilson**

Warren G. Harding

Warren G. Harding (1865–1923), the twenty-ninth president of the United States, was inarticulate and indecisive, avoided issues, and viewed the presidency largely as a ceremonial office. Although his ambition was to be the "best-loved president," historians often rank him as one of the worst, because his administration was rife with corruption and scandal.

Early Life Born in Ohio, Harding was the eldest of six children of two doctors. He studied at Ohio Central College and, after unsuccessful attempts to teach, study law, and sell insurance, became a newspaperman. In

1884 he and two friends purchased the near-bankrupt *Marion Star* for $300. Harding became the newspaper's publisher and editor, and he eventually bought out his partners. The growth of the city, his business skills—as well as those of his wife, Florence Mabel Kling DeWolfe—and his editorial abilities brought prosperity to the newspaper and some fame to Harding. Both Republicans and Democrats admired the paper because they considered its coverage of political news unbiased.

A Political Career An amicable conservative who let the party bosses set his agenda, Harding served two terms in the Ohio Senate and ran successfully for lieutenant governor in 1903. After returning to his newspaper for five years, in 1910 he ventured into politics again in a losing bid for governor. In 1914 he was elected to the U.S. Senate, where he never introduced bills of national importance, missed more sessions than he attended, and avoided taking a stand on issues so successfully that he made few enemies.

At their national convention in 1920, Republicans nominated Harding for president on the tenth ballot. During the campaign his word choice was often ridiculed and

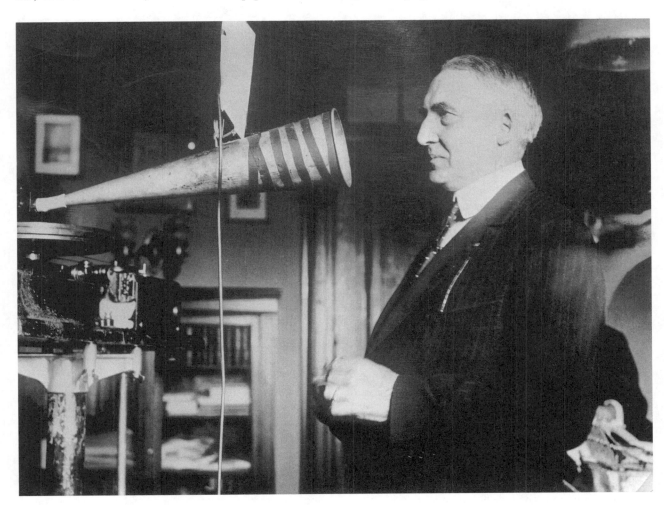

Senator Warren Harding making a phonograph record of a speech while campaigning in 1920. © *Bettmann/CORBIS*

President Warren Harding and his wife, Florence (far right), 1923.   © *CORBIS*

characterized as "pompous," "murky," and "unclear." In campaign speeches his inarticulate ramblings on, for example, the League of Nations—the international peace-keeping body advocated by President Woodrow Wilson (1856–1924)—stood in stark contrast to the impassioned crusades of the Democratic nominees: James M. Cox (1870–1957), the governor of Ohio, and Franklin D. Roosevelt (1882–1945), the governor of New York, who would later become president.

Harding told Americans what they wanted to hear: he promised to return the nation to "normalty"—he mispronounced "normalcy," which is how the media reported his statement. He won by a landslide. Harding's inaugural address became famous for its promotion of "normalcy."

Once in office he surrounded himself with both capable and dishonest men who were referred to as the Ohio gang. Many of them were later charged with crimes and sent to prison.

Conservative on trade and economic issues, Harding advocated a higher tariff on foreign products to protect manufacturers of U.S. goods and stricter immi-gration laws. The Johnson Immigrant Quota Act of 1921 was the first in a series of laws that limited immi-gration to the United States, especially from southern and eastern Europe.

Secretary of the Treasury Andrew W. Mellon (1855–1937) helped push through tax cuts for the rich; stopped antitrust actions, thereby allowing companies to form powerful conglomerates; and opposed organized labor. Harding left foreign policy to others, especially his secretary of state, Charles Evans Hughes (1862–1948), who convened the Washington Conference to regulate armaments among the major powers.

Teapot Dome and Other Scandals

The worst scandal of the Harding administration was referred to as the Tea-pot Dome scandal. Albert Fall (1861–1944), the secretary of the interior, secretly leased the Teapot Dome naval oil reserve in Wyoming and the Elk Hills oil reserve in Cal-ifornia to private companies in return for some $400,000 in bribes. Fall was eventually found guilty of bribery, fined, and sent to prison for a year. Another scandal involved Charles Forbes, the director of the Veterans Bureau, who diverted alcohol and drugs from veterans hospitals to bootleggers and narcotics dealers and took payoffs from contractors who were building the hospitals. He went to jail for two years. Several of Harding's closest advisers resigned and two committed suicide under the weight of other corruption charges.

Harding had personal scandals as well. He had a reputation for adultery and fathered a daughter out of wedlock when he was a presidential nominee. He also hosted poker parties at the White House, serving liquor—even though Prohibition, the law at the time, outlawed alcoholic beverages—and gambled away the White House china.

Shaken by talk of corruption among his key officials, including his attorney general, Harding and his wife traveled to Alaska to meet the people and explain his policies. He became suddenly ill—food poisoning was suspected—and was rushed to San Francisco, where, according to many accounts, he developed pneumonia, had a heart attack, and died quietly in his sleep on August 2, 1923. Other theories of his death include stroke, medical malpractice, and even poisoning by his wife because she wished to save him from the charges of corruption that were sweeping the administration. No

evidence ever confirmed the rumors about his wife's involvement in his death; regardless, she would not permit an autopsy. She died the following year.

Harding's Legacy Some historians see Harding as an important transitional figure between the idealism of Woodrow Wilson and the prosperity of the Calvin Coolidge (1872–1933) and Herbert Hoover (1874–1964) years. However, the majority of historians view Harding as an accommodating, but weak and ineffectual president because he lacked decisiveness and conviction.

See also **Temperance and Prohibition**
See also **Woodrow Wilson**
See also **World War I**

Calvin Coolidge

Calvin Coolidge (1872–1933), the thirtieth president of the United States, took office after the death of President Warren G. Harding (1865–1923). He restored confidence in an administration discredited by scandals and led the nation into a period of seeming prosperity. A strong supporter of business, Coolidge encouraged the financial investment that led to a stock market boom in

President Calvin Coolidge throwing out the first ball of the baseball season, 1924. *Henry Groskinsky/Time Life Pictures/Getty Images*

the 1920s. Eventually, however, stock speculation led to economic collapse and the Great Depression.

Early Life John Calvin Coolidge, who was born in Plymouth Notch, Vermont, earned a bachelor's degree at Amherst College in Massachusetts in 1895. He apprenticed in a law office in Northampton, Massachusetts, instead of attending law school—a common practice at the time—and was admitted to the bar in 1897. He opened his own law office in Northampton, where he practiced until 1919.

Coolidge won his first election in 1898, becoming a member of the Northampton city council. Although he lacked the skills of a professional politician, he had loyal supporters. Between 1900 and 1918 he held a variety of posts in Massachusetts. In 1919 he was elected governor.

Coolidge gained national prominence when the Boston police, seeking better wages and working conditions, attempted to join the American Federation of Labor. When the police commissioner suspended nineteen police officers for unionizing, the police voted to strike. At first, Coolidge refused to intervene, but he later sided with the commissioner, who announced that the striking police officers would not be allowed to return to their jobs. "There is no right to strike against the public safety by anybody, anywhere, any time," Coolidge said. His photograph and words appeared in newspapers across the country—he was heralded as the "law and order governor."

His supporters seized the opportunity to get him nominated for president at the 1920 Republican National Convention. However, party leaders chose Harding. Unhappy with that choice, a delegate from Oregon nominated Coolidge for vice president. In the balloting, Coolidge easily defeated Irvine Lenroot (1869–1949), a liberal senator from Wisconsin. Aided by disillusionment after World War I (1914–1918) and the policies of President Woodrow Wilson (1856–1924), the Republican ticket won by a huge margin.

Called "Silent Cal" because he sat quietly at cabinet meetings and while presiding over the Senate, Coolidge had little enthusiasm for his job and had no power as a national political figure. Then Harding died, and Coolidge was suddenly president. His honesty and simplicity appealed to the American people, as did his belief that government should interfere as little as possible in the lives of its citizens. He was elected president in 1924 and served until 1929.

Coolidge presided over an era of governmental frugality and pro-business policies. Through his appointees he transformed the Federal Trade Commission from an agency intended to regulate corporations into one dominated by big business. He vetoed measures to provide farm relief and bonuses to World War I veterans. With his blessing Congress maintained a high protective tariff on imported goods, instituted tax cuts that favored big

Calvin Coolidge delivering his inaugural address, 1925. *National Archive/Newsmakers/Getty Images*

business, and decreased government spending. Coolidge continued to oppose U.S. entry into the League of Nations, the international peacekeeping organization, although he did support U.S. participation in the World Court. Perhaps most important, through his public statements Coolidge encouraged the stock market speculation of the late 1920s.

Coolidge chose not to seek reelection in 1928. He retired to Northampton, Massachusetts, to write newspaper and magazine articles and his autobiography.

Coolidge's Legacy Coolidge is probably best known for his statement: "The business of America is business." As president, he adopted policies that favored business and discouraged government intervention in the economy. He influenced speculation in the stock market toward the end of the 1920s, which, most historians believe, precipitated the economic collapse of 1929. Although he was popular while in office, the Great Depression brought Coolidge's policies into disrepute, and most historians regard him as having been complacent, lacking in vision, and ill equipped to deal with the challenges of the period.

See also **Warren G. Harding**

Marcus Garvey Jr.

Marcus Garvey Jr. (1887–1940) founded a back-to-Africa movement that encouraged people of African descent everywhere to create their own sovereign nation on that continent. Sometimes referred to as the black Moses, he believed that global black unity was a necessary step toward improving the political, economic, and social conditions of the people of Africa and African descent.

Early Life The youngest of eleven children, Garvey left school in St. Ann's Bay, Jamaica, when he was fourteen to work as a printer's apprentice. He later worked at P. A. Benjamin Manufacturing Company, a printing company in Kingston, where he became a foreman. In 1907, when the printers union—the first trade union in Jamaica—went on strike to protest reduced wages following a company fire and an earthquake, the union elected Garvey their leader. Although the strike failed, most workers got their jobs back. Garvey, however, did not.

Garvey left for Costa Rica and found a job at the United Fruit Company, where he observed the working conditions and exploitation of the black fieldworkers. Although his protests on behalf of the workers were largely ignored and a political newspaper he founded was unsuccessful, his political commitment to the cause of black workers everywhere intensified.

From 1912 to 1914 Garvey lived in London, where he met with black laborers, businessmen, and intellectuals who inspired and educated him on the issues facing black workers in Europe and Africa. Following his return to Jamaica in 1914, he founded the Universal Negro Improvement Association (UNIA) and its governing body, the African Communities League (ACL). The organization's goals were to promote black unity through education, economic independence, and moral reform.

To raise funds for a Jamaican school, Garvey visited the United States in 1916. The school was to be modeled after the Tuskegee Institute, an industrial training school established by the African-American activist Booker T. Washington (1856–1915). Garvey embarked on a lecture tour of thirty-eight cities, encouraging black unity, pride, economic independence, and emigration to Africa.

In 1918 Garvey established the UNIA's first U.S. chapter in New York and transferred the organization's worldwide headquarters from Jamaica to Harlem. He also founded a weekly newspaper, the *Negro World*, which was the organization's official publication. It quickly developed a worldwide readership and became the most popular black publication in the United States. In the years that followed, Garvey became the most celebrated black leader in the West. The UNIA grew exponentially as well, with hundreds of chapters opening around the world.

The Black Star Line Fiasco

After starting several businesses—including the Negro Factories Corporation, a restaurant, a publishing house, and chain of grocery stores—Garvey founded an international steamship company, the Black Star Line, in 1919. (The company name was a play on the White Star Line, the British shipping company whose most famous vessel was the *Titanic*.) The steamship line was both a business venture and part of Garvey's back-to-Africa plan: the ships would transport raw materials, manufactured goods, and produce among black businesses in North America, the Caribbean, and Africa—thereby promoting the economic and political power of black communities—and transport

Black Nationalist leader Marcus Garvey, 1922. © *Bettmann/CORBIS*

those of African ancestry back to Africa. Shares of the steamship line were sold at UNIA meetings and conventions and through advertisements in the *Negro World*; many of Garvey's supporters invested their life savings in the venture. The company failed a few years later, however; Garvey was convicted of mail fraud stemming from the sale of stock in the Black Star Line and sentenced to five years in prison. The sentence was commuted in 1927, and Garvey was deported to Jamaica. Following his conviction, Garvey's reputation was destroyed, and his influence and popularity declined dramatically. He later moved to London, where he died in 1940.

Ku Klux Klan Connections

Although he claimed not to believe in black supremacy, Garvey said the UNIA and the Ku Klux Klan (KKK), the white supremacist organization in the United States, had common goals: racial autonomy and the separation of blacks and whites. In early 1922 Garvey met with Edward Young Clarke, the KKK's Imperial Wizard, a meeting that drew criticism from both black and white political, labor, and religious leaders. Among his harshest critics was W. E. B. Du Bois (1868–1963), the cofounder of the National Association for the Advancement of Colored People, who claimed that Garvey associated with the KKK only to maintain support for his failing back-to-Africa movement.

Garvey's Legacy Although his dream of organizing and unifying blacks everywhere met with limited success, the UNIA became the largest black secular organization in African-American history. Garvey remains a symbol of black freedom and pride and has inspired countless organizations, leaders, and movements worldwide, including the civil rights movement in the 1960s and the black power and black arts movements of the 1960s and early 1970s.

See also **W. E. B. Du Bois**

W. E. B. Du Bois

W. E. B. Du Bois (1868–1963) was one of the most influential scholars and civil rights activists of the twentieth century. A founding member of the National Association for the Advancement of Colored People (NAACP), he was committed to the struggle for economic, civil, and political equality for all Americans.

Early Life William Edward Burghardt Du Bois, the only child of Alfred Du Bois, a French Huguenot from Haiti, and Mary Silvina Burghardt, a descendant of slaves, was born in Great Barrington, Massachusetts. Du Bois's father left soon after his birth, and Du Bois lived with his mother until her death in 1884—shortly after his graduation from high school.

While studying at Fisk University in Nashville, Tennessee, Du Bois taught in rural areas, where he gained firsthand knowledge of Jim Crow laws, which mandated "separate but equal" status for African-Americans, as well as extreme poverty and ignorance. That experience ignited the flame of civil rights activism.

After receiving a bachelor's degree at Fisk, Du Bois earned a bachelor's degree at Harvard University. He then went to the University of Berlin, which offered an international perspective for his studies of race, history, economics, and politics. His funding was cut short, however, so Du Bois returned to the United States to complete his studies. In 1885 he became the first African-American to receive a doctorate from Harvard. His dissertation, *The Suppression of the African Slave Trade to the United States of America, 1638–1870*, remains the authoritative work in the field.

After teaching at Wilberforce University in Ohio, he accepted a fellowship at the University of Pennsylvania to conduct a sociological study of the black population of Philadelphia. The result of his research, *The Philadephia Negro*, was published in 1899. With this landmark work Du Bois became the first scholar to apply social science to the study of a racial group. His meticulous detail set the standard for future sociologists in their studies of ethnic groups.

In 1897 Du Bois accepted a teaching position at Atlanta University, where he continued his research and writing. One of his major works from that time was *The Souls of Black Folks*, a collection of essays published in 1903. It not only examined the damage inflicted by

African-American writer and activist W. E. B. Du Bois, 1918. © *Bettmann/Corbis*

racism but also celebrated the endurance of black people in the United States. More important, it took a strong stand against the political accommodation and passivity of the former slave and civil rights activist Booker T. Washington (1856–1915). Washington encouraged African-Americans to study vocational education and work for gradual change rather than to attempt higher education and engage in active protest against prejudice and injustice.

In 1905 Du Bois helped found the Niagara Movement, which renounced Washington's policies of accommodation. A group of African-American leaders met at Niagara Falls—they were denied accommodations on the U.S. side of the falls, so they met on the Canadian side—and drafted a plan for aggressive action, demanding full suffrage and civil rights, equal economic and educational opportunities for all, and an end to segregation. The group had limited success in achieving its goals, according to some historians, because of the militant personality of one member: Monroe Trotter (1872–1934). In addition, Washington's supporters charged the Niagara Movement with fraud and deceit, which hurt its credibility.

In 1909 the group—except for Trotter—formed the NAACP. Du Bois was named the association's director of publications and research and became the editor of *Crisis*, the organization's monthly magazine. The journal campaigned against lynching, Jim Crow laws, and sexual inequality. It also kept its readers informed about advances in civil rights. The magazine developed a huge following among both African-Americans and liberal whites.

A Rift with Marcus Garvey Although Du Bois initially supported the black nationalist cause, after World War I (1914–1918) he became highly critical of Marcus Garvey Jr. (1887–1940), a popular African-American leader who promoted a back-to-Africa movement and the Universal Negro Improvement Association, which Garvey founded. Du Bois considered Garvey a traitor and worked to expose corruption and mismanagement of Garvey's Black Star Line, which was set up for trade among black communities in Africa and the West and to take African-Americans back to Africa.

A Marxist Perspective Du Bois edited *Crisis* until 1934, when he returned to Atlanta University to chair the Department of Sociology. A former member of the Socialist Party—which advocates a nonracist, classless, feminist society controlled by the working class—Du Bois began to use Marxist theory in his historical investigations, applying ideas about economics to understand race relations. Among his most significant works of the period was *Black Reconstruction: An Essay toward a History of the Part Which Black Folk Played in the Attempt to Reconstruct Democracy in America, 1860–1880*. It detailed the role blacks played in the period following the Civil War (1861–1865), which had been largely ignored by white historians. Even though the book was often criticized for its use of Marxist concepts and for its claims that white historians overlooked black contributions because they were racist, it is still considered one of the most authoritative books on the era.

In 1945 Du Bois represented the NAACP at the conference that created the charter of the United Nations. In that same year he served as a delegate to the Pan-African Congress in Manchester, England, which demanded an end to racial discrimination, imperialism, and colonial rule in Africa and fought for human rights and equality of economic opportunity for all people of African descent.

In 1951 Du Bois, who had called on the United Nations to examine the crimes of the U.S. government against its own citizens, was indicted as an agent of the Soviet Union. Even though he was later acquitted of all charges, the U.S. Department of State denied him a passport until 1958.

Disillusioned by both U.S. capitalism and racism, he moved to Ghana in 1961 and joined the Communist Party at the age of ninety-three. In 1963 he became a Ghanaian citizen, after renouncing his U.S. citizenship, and died shortly thereafter. The Ghanaian president honored him with a state funeral.

Du Bois's Impact Du Bois, who is often referred to as the father of social science, was the first to take a scientific approach to the study of black history. His fight for freedom and justice—especially as cofounder of the NAACP—inspired millions of others to take up the cause. His written works include scholarly historical studies, essays, poetry, novels, and plays, many of which laid the groundwork for scholars and writers to follow.

See also **Marcus Garvey**

Alvin C. York

Alvin C. York (1887–1964) is often referred to as the greatest hero of World War I (1914–1918). He was awarded a Congressional Medal of Honor for his heroism.

Early Life The third of eleven children, Alvin Cullom York was born in the mountains of Tennessee, where his family lived in a two-room cabin. York attended school for only nine months and worked as a semiskilled laborer.

As a boy, he earned a reputation as an accurate shot with pistols and rifles. He spent much of his youth drinking, smoking, gambling, and fighting. However, in 1914, when his best friend was killed in a bar fight, York knew he needed to change his life, so he attended a church prayer meeting at which he experienced a

War hero Alvin York, c. 1918. © *AP/Wide World Photos*

"WHAT IS THE USE OF WORRYING?"

Alvin C. York (1887–1964), often referred to as the greatest hero of World War I (1914–1918), kept a diary during the war. The following is an excerpt:

July 1, 1918

Montsec Sector, France—A few words on Christian witness in war and why a Christian does worry. Yet there is no use worrying about anything except the worry of so many souls who have passed out into the Deep of an unknown world and have left no testimony as to the welfare of their souls. There is no use of worrying about shells, for you can't keep them from busting in your trench, nor you can't stop the rain or prevent a light from agoing up jest as you are half-way over the parapet.

So what is the use of worrying if you can't alter things? Just ask God to help you and accept them and make the best of them by the help of God. Yet some men do worry, and by doing so they effectually destroy their peace of mind without doing anyone any good. Yet it is often the religious man who worries. I have even heard those whose care was for the soldier's soul deplore the fact that he did not worry. I have heard it said that the soldier is so careless, he realizes his position so little.

SOURCE: Sgt. Alvin C. York's Diary. *http://www.alvincyork.org/Diary.htm* (accessed May 15, 2007).

religious conversion. The Church of Christ in Christian Union, a fundamentalist sect with a following limited to Ohio, Kentucky, and Tennessee, forbade drinking, dancing, movies, swimming, cursing, and popular literature. The church also held moral convictions against violence and war. Although he was raised a Methodist, York joined the church, changed his behavior, and became a Sunday school teacher.

When York received his draft notice in June 1917, he sought conscientious objector status, but local and state review boards denied his request because his church was not recognized as a legitimate Christian sect.

Nearly thirty years old, he set off for basic training at Camp Gordon, Georgia. As a member of Company G in the 328th Infantry, he gained a reputation as an excellent marksman—but one who would not shoot at cardboard targets shaped in human form. After weeks of counseling, York relented to the arguments of his company commander and agreed that there were times when war was moral and ordained by God. He and his unit sailed to France in the spring of 1918.

Heroism in Battle York's regiment was part of a company assigned to capture a heavily guarded hill near Château-Thierry, France. On October 8, 1918, York and sixteen other soldiers under the command of Sergeant Bernard Early were dispatched to disrupt German supply lines by taking control of the Decauville railroad. The men could not read their map, which was labeled in French, and mistakenly found themselves behind enemy lines. A firefight ensued. German machine gunners killed nine Americans, including York's best friend in the outfit. Early suffered seventeen bullet wounds and turned the command over to Corporals Harry Parsons and William Cutting. They ordered York to silence the German machine guns.

York maneuvered to a position where, as a sniper, he was able to shoot seventeen German soldiers with his rifle. He then killed eight more with his pistol. The demoralized Germans—4 officers and 128 soldiers—surrendered to the lone Corporal York. With his squad, York managed to get the prisoners to the headquarters of the 328th Regiment.

York was promoted to sergeant and awarded the Congressional Medal of Honor for his feat, even though he never claimed that he acted alone. He was also awarded the French Médaille Militaire and Croix de Guerre and the Italian Croce di Guerra. Early and Cutting were both awarded the Distinguished Service Cross in 1927.

York captured the American imagination because of what he symbolized: a humble, self-reliant, and religious patriot who moved to action only when sufficiently provoked and who refused to capitalize on his fame. Ironically, he also represented a rejection of mechanization and modernization because of his dependence on personal skill.

The Return Home In 1919 York was taken aback by the hero's welcome he received in New York, which included a ticker-tape parade down Fifth Avenue and a suite of rooms at the Waldorf Astoria Hotel. Once back in Tennessee, the Rotary Club of Nashville, in conjunction with other Tennessee clubs, planned to present York with a home and a farm. When donations fell short of the goal, the Rotarians gave York an unfinished house with a substantial mortgage but retained the property rights. York received lucrative offers from Hollywood, Broadway, and various advertisers, but he rejected them because he did not believe in profiting from the deaths of others.

As York tried to resume peacetime life, he established a goal: to provide practical education to the children of Fentress County, where he lived. During the 1920s he went on speaking tours to raise money for his school, the Alvin C. York Institute. He also used his fame to garner funds for road improvement and job creation.

In the 1930s, with the renewed threat of war in Europe, York initially spoke out against U.S. intervention. To achieve world peace, he said, Americans should first secure it at home. York changed his position, however, during the making of a film about his life. The Hollywood filmmaker Jesse L. Lasky believed that the United States had to be convinced that war was not only justifiable but sometimes necessary. York's story seemed to afford a perfect example.

York announced that Lasky's planned biographical movie, *Sergeant York*, would portray his life and wartime activities but would not be a war movie—a form his church condemned as sinful. York only agreed to the film because he decided that he could use the profits for his school. However, the film that opened in July 1941 promoted U.S. involvement in World War II (1939–1945). During the shooting of the film, York became convinced of the world threat and supported the call for the country's first peacetime draft. The Tennessee governor Prentice Cooper (1895–1969) put York in charge of the Fentress County draft board and appointed him to the Tennessee Preparedness Committee. York tried to reenlist in the infantry but was rejected because of age and weight. Through an affiliation with the U.S. Signal Corps, York traveled the country to encourage the sale of war bonds and to aid recruitment.

Later Life In 1951 the Internal Revenue Service (IRS) accused York of tax evasion related to his profits from the movie. Nearly destitute, York spent the next ten years wrangling with the agency. Eventually, Speaker of the House Sam Rayburn (1882–1961) and Joe L.

Evins (1910–1964), a Democratic representative from Tennessee, established the York Relief Fund to help cancel his debt. In 1961 President John F. Kennedy (1917–1963), who considered the actions of the IRS a national disgrace, ordered a resolution of the matter.

York's health deteriorated after World War II. In 1954 he suffered a stroke that left him bedridden for the remainder of his life. He died of a cerebral hemorrhage on September 2, 1964, in Nashville and was buried with full military honors.

York's Legacy An entire generation of Americans was inspired by the story of a humble man with simple values who served his country to the best of his ability and did not seek to profit from the deaths of others. Even though York was honored for his deeds on the battlefield, he wanted to use his fame for the common good. Through the school he founded, he gave the children of his home county educational opportunities that he never had.

See also **World War I**

Alice Paul

Alice Paul (1885–1977), an activist for women's rights, lawyer, and cofounder of the National Woman's Party, played a major role in the passage of the Nineteenth

Women's suffrage leader Alice Paul toasting the passage of the 19th Amendment, which gave women the right to vote, 1920. © *UPI/ Bettmann/CORBIS*

THE NINETEENTH AMENDMENT

The Nineteenth Amendment, which granted women the right to vote, required very few words:

Section 1. The right of the citizens of the United States to vote shall not be denied or abridged by the United States or by any State on account of sex.

Section 2. Congress shall have power to enforce this article by appropriate legislation.

SOURCE: *U.S. Constitution: Nineteenth Amendment. http://caselaw. lp.findlaw.com/data/constitution/amendment19/ (accessed May 15, 2007)*

Amendment to the U.S. Constitution, which granted women the right to vote. She was also the author and chief promoter of the Equal Rights Amendment.

Early Life Alice Stokes Paul, the eldest of four children, was born into a Quaker family in Moorestown, New Jersey. Her parents instilled in her and her siblings a belief in gender equality, education for women, and social activism—tenets that were central to their religion. Her mother, a member of the National American Woman Suffrage Association (NAWSA), often took her along to the organization's meetings.

Paul attended Swarthmore College in Pennsylvania, a Quaker college cofounded by her grandfather, and graduated with a bachelor's degree in biology in 1905. During her final year at Swarthmore, Paul developed what would become a lifelong interest in political science and economics.

In 1907 Paul received a scholarship to study social work at Woodbrooke Settlement, a Quaker training school, in Birmingham, England. There she became acquainted with the radical suffragette Emmeline Pankhurst (1858–1928) and her daughters. To raise public awareness of the suffrage issue, the Pankhursts resorted to violence, often throwing rocks and smashing windows. Paul's education as an activist grew with a series of arrests, imprisonments, hunger strikes, and force feedings. Paul and the Pankhursts made front-page news and gathered much public support for their cause in England. Paul maintained that the same militancy was necessary to generate publicity in the United States.

Paul returned to the United States in 1910, determined to renew her suffrage efforts. While a student at the University of Pennsylvania, where she was studying for a master's degree in sociology, Paul joined the NAWSA and worked for a federal suffrage amendment.

Paul gathered together a group of young women—many of whom had also worked with the Pankhursts in England—who were willing to depart from NAWSA's conservative tactics to get attention for their cause.

Picketing the White House In 1912 Paul and two of her friends, Lucy Burns (1879–1966) and Crystal Eastman (1881–1928), traveled to Washington, D.C., to organize rallies in support of suffrage. Paul and Burns organized a women's march on Pennsylvania Avenue on March 3, 1913, the day before the inauguration of President Woodrow Wilson (1856–1924). The women were verbally and physically attacked while police stood idly by. After newspapers ran stories about the march and the crowd's reaction, suffrage became a popular topic among the general population as well as the politicians.

Paul and Carrie Chapman Catt (1859–1947), the NAWSA president, disagreed on strategies for gaining the women's vote. Catt focused on state-by-state campaigns as well as the federal campaign; Paul wanted to work exclusively on the federal level for an amendment to the U.S. Constitution. In addition, Catt endorsed President Wilson, whereas Paul could not because she thought he neglected the issue of women's enfranchisement. Paul and her followers initially formed a semiautonomous group called the Congressional Union for Woman Suffrage; eventually, they severed all ties to the NAWSA and in 1916 formed the National Woman's Party (NWP), whose sole aim was to persuade Wilson to push federal legislation to guarantee women's suffrage.

When NWP members picketed the White House, Wilson ignored them. After the United States entered World War I in 1917, the picketers were attacked by crowds who thought the women were unpatriotic for focusing on the vote during a time of war. When the women were jailed in Virginia, Paul demanded that they be treated as political prisoners and staged hunger strikes. The women, some elderly and frail, were pushed around and beaten; the arrests and imprisonment continued, and Paul and a few other women were force fed. Prison officials even tried to get Paul declared insane and put in a sanitarium.

When news of the prison conditions and hunger strikes spread, however, the press, several politicians, and the public began demanding the women's release. Concern for the women led many to support their cause. When Paul was released, she had renewed hope for victory.

In 1917, responding to public outcry, Wilson reversed his position and announced his support for a suffrage amendment, which Congress passed two years later. Three-fourths of the state legislatures had to ratify the amendment; that number was reached in 1920 with the vote in Tennessee.

Her Fight Continues Paul continued her battle for equality after the Nineteenth Amendment was ratified. In 1923 she announced that she would work for a new constitutional amendment for full equality for women, at the time called the Lucretia Mott Amendment after the nineteenth-century abolitionist and suffragist. It was later called the Equal Rights Amendment (ERA).

Throughout her lifetime, Paul worked for passage of the ERA in the United States and for women's rights worldwide. In 1938 she created the World Woman's Party (WWP), with headquarters in Geneva, Switzerland. The WWP worked closely with the creators of the United Nations to ensure that gender equality was part of the organization's charter and that it would establish a United Nations Commission on the Status of Women.

Paul moved back to the United States in 1941 and once again became active in national women's issues. She led a coalition that was successful in adding a sexual discrimination clause to Title VII of the 1964 Civil Rights Act, which made it illegal to discriminate based on race, color, religion, national origin, or sex.

The reemergence of the women's movement in the late 1960s led to renewed interest in the ERA, and in 1972 Congress passed the amendment, which went to the states for ratification. However, only twenty-two of the necessary thirty-eight states ratified the amendment by the seven-year deadline Congress had set. The deadline was later extended and then eliminated, but as of 2007, the ERA had not become law.

Paul died on July 9, 1977, in Moorestown, New Jersey.

See also **National Woman's Party**
See also **Women's Suffrage Movement**

✪ Political Parties, Platforms, and Key Issues

The Populist Party

The Populist Party—originally called the People's Party—was established in 1881 through a merger of the Farmers' Alliance, a group of grassroots farmers organizations, and the Knights of Labor, the largest U.S. labor organization in the nineteenth century. The short-lived party advocated public ownership of railroads, steamship lines, and telephone and telegraph systems. It also supported the free and unlimited coinage of silver, graduated income tax, and direct election of U.S. senators (they were chosen by state legislatures at the time).

Origins of the Party In the late nineteenth century discontent rose among farmers, who were not sharing the nation's general prosperity. Even though their situation resulted mainly from fluctuations in international markets for agricultural products, they firmly believed that the democratic system was failing them. Starting in the 1870s they mounted political campaigns to rectify what they saw as corruption of the government and the economy by big business and the railroads.

The most successful of the agrarian political movements was the Populist Party. After the 1892 presidential campaign, in which the party's presidential candidate, James B. Weaver (1833–1912), won more than a million votes and carried four states—Colorado, Idaho, Kansas, and Nebraska—the party appeared to have gained enough support to become a powerful political force. Its major strength came from the nation's agricultural heartland—states in the South and Midwest—although its leaders reached out to eastern workers.

The party's 1896 platform had two major goals: to relieve the economic pressure on agriculture and to eliminate what the Populists viewed as the corrupt relationship between business and government. They did not merely object to big business; they also feared that the alliance between business and government would destroy U.S. democracy.

Before the 1896 election the leaders of the Populist Party entered into negotiations with the Democratic presidential nominee, William Jennings Bryan (1860–1925), who was one of the foremost promoters of populism in the country. Party leaders believed they had reached an agreement with Bryan that Tom Watson (1856–1922), a Populist senator from Georgia, would be Bryan's running mate. However, after receiving the party's support, Bryan announced that Arthur Sewall, a wealthy Democrat from Maine with a record of opposition to trade unions, would be his running mate. Bryan's decision and his subsequent defeat at the polls severely damaged the Populist Party's future. Although it continued to hold power in a few western states, the party largely disappeared from national politics after 1896.

The Party's Impact Many Populist Party proposals, such as the direct election of senators, the income tax, and tighter regulation of large corporations, were considered radical at the time. However, in following decades most of the party's issues were absorbed by the Democratic Party and transformed into law.

See also **Progressive Party, 1912**

The Socialist Party

The Socialist Party of America, formally organized in the United States in 1901, brought together people who were committed to replacing capitalism with a cooperative system in which property and the distribution of wealth were under public, rather than private, control. The party was made up of diverse, and often conflicting, ethnic, class, occupational, and regional constituencies that advocated a variety of methods for improving the daily life of workers.

The rise of socialism in the United States coincided with industrialization, which led to the exploitation of workers. It can be traced to the arrival of German immigrants in the 1850s, who formed such socialistic unions as the National Typographic Union, the United Hatters, and the Iron Molders Union of North America.

The Socialist Party was formed by a merger of two parties. The Social Democratic Party, which advocated a system of cooperative production and distribution of wealth, had been formed by members of the American Railway Union who had gone on strike against the Pullman Company. The other group was a branch of the Socialist Labor Party of America, the oldest socialist organization in the United States. It campaigned for reforms such as the eight-hour workday.

Unlike the Communist Party, the Socialist Party did not require adherence to an international party line. Socialists and other reformers campaigned at the local level for municipal ownership of waterworks and gas and electric plants; they often made progress in their endeavors.

The party related most popular issues to economics. For example, even though individual Socialists spoke out for racial equality—as the founders of the National Association for the Advancement of Colored People did in 1910—the party as a whole did not address specific issues pertaining to African-Americans. The party saw racial discrimination as part of a larger problem: capitalist exploitation.

The party achieved its greatest electoral success in the United States before World War I (1914–1918). In 1912 the party's five-time presidential candidate, Eugene V. Debs (1855–1926), the cofounder of the International Labor Union, received nine hundred thousand votes, or 6 percent of the popular vote. Debs took a strong stand against U.S. involvement in World War I and appealed not only to blue-collar workers who were seeking improved working conditions and higher wages but also to intellectuals, such as the novelist and social crusader Upton Sinclair (1878–1968).

Following the election of 1912, Socialist Party membership declined, largely because of internal conflicts. Some members envisioned revolution as the ultimate goal and joined the Communist Party; others advocated continuing reform and became Democrats—they believed they could best achieve their goals by working within a major political party dedicated to reform.

Two laws were factors in the party's decline as well. The Espionage Act of 1917, which was designed to punish those who "interfered with the draft or encouraged disloyalty" to the United States during World War I, sentenced offenders to jail terms of ten to twenty years. The Sedition Act of 1918 penalized those who obstructed the sale of war bonds, discouraged recruitment, or uttered "disloyal or abusive language" about the government, the Constitution, or the U.S. flag. Under those acts, the government arrested more than fifteen hundred people, many of whom—including Debs—were Socialists.

The party's membership revived briefly during the Great Depression of the 1930s, but was never a serious factor in national elections after 1936.

The Party's Impact   The Socialist Party adhered to the belief that social, economic, and political reform was both necessary and possible. The policies it advocated are reflected in a variety of government-owned, -funded, or -subsidized programs later created by both Democrats and Republicans. Social Security, for example, is seen by some as a socialistic system because it is run by the government. A part of the New Deal advanced by President Franklin D. Roosevelt (1882–1945), Social Security provides retirement benefits financed by mandatory contributions from workers.

The Square Deal

The name "Square Deal" was given by President Theodore Roosevelt (1858–1919) to his platform of economic and social reforms. He initially used the phrase, following the settlement of a miners' strike in 1902, to describe his ideal of peaceful coexistence of large corporations and organized labor. He also asserted that he would treat the rich and poor, labor and management, in a "fair and square" manner.

During his administration, Roosevelt was committed to addressing the problems between labor and management; he was also committed to trust-busting, in which huge business conglomerates that dominated markets and eliminated competition were broken up. Unlike his predecessors, Roosevelt defended the right of workers to organize and join unions and avoided calling in federal troops to ease the tensions between striking workers and management. In 1902 he intervened in a United Mine Workers' strike and got both sides to agree to arbitration of the dispute.

Based on his experiences during the strike, Roosevelt proposed the Square Deal, which advocated fairness for all citizens, whether they were businessmen or wage workers, whether they conducted their business as individuals or as members of organizations. He also thought the government should play an active role in achieving this goal.

He first used the phrase on Labor Day 1903 in a speech about the common interests of management and labor and the danger of allowing either side to pursue selfish goals. To ensure continued national prosperity, he maintained, both business and labor had to share in the wealth produced. To maintain this balance, business and labor had to remain equals and be subject to the same laws. Roosevelt also argued that people should not be judged on the basis of their social standing but on their character and behavior—their capacity for work, honesty, common sense, and devotion to the common good. These virtues were the hallmarks of good citizenship, he said, and their preservation was necessary for the future of the nation and the progress of civilization.

Over the next several years Roosevelt broadened the scope of the Square Deal to include economic, environmental, and international affairs. He also used the words in 1912 when he ran for president as a member of the Progressive Party, which was dedicated to social, economic, and political reform.

Roosevelt's Square Deal was politically significant in that it was the first attempt by a modern president to promote a unified domestic reform program. His program established several firsts that became important in future crises: for the first time labor and business came to the White House on equal terms (in the miners' strike), for the first time government used its influence to negotiate a settlement, and never before had a president appointed an arbitration board to settle such disputes. Although Roosevelt stepped beyond his legal authority to negotiate a settlement, his actions set powerful precedents. The Square Deal also served as inspiration for future reform-minded presidents, such as President Franklin D. Roosevelt (1882–1945), whose campaign called for a New Deal, and President Harry S. Truman (1884–1972), who offered a Fair Deal.

See also **Theodore Roosevelt**

See also **Progressive Party, 1912**

Dollar Diplomacy

The phrase "dollar diplomacy" was most commonly used to describe the foreign policy of President William Howard Taft (1857–1930). In his annual message to Congress in 1912, Taft summed up his goal as "substituting dollars for bullets." Taft advocated the use of diplomatic influence and economic pressure to expand and protect U.S. economic and business interests in foreign countries.

Dollar diplomacy had originated during the presidency of Theodore Roosevelt (1858–1919). In 1904 the Dominican Republic was $32 million in debt, primarily to European nations. Payments were infrequent or missed, so the Europeans threatened armed intervention. That same year Roosevelt introduced a sweeping new policy—it became known as the Roosevelt Corollary to the Monroe Doctrine—which asserted that the United States had the right to act as an international police power in the Western Hemisphere if "wrongdoing" threatened "civilized society." Concerned that Europeans would colonize the Dominican Republic, Roosevelt declared that they would not be allowed to use force to collect debts owed by Latin American nations.

Under diplomatic pressure from the United States, the Dominican Republic requested U.S. intervention to

---

"ALL FOR EACH AND EACH FOR ALL"

On Labor Day 1903 President Theodore Roosevelt (1858–1919) addressed the New York State Agricultural Association in Syracuse. The following is an excerpt:

> It is not enough to be well-meaning and kindly, but weak; neither is it enough to be strong, unless morality and decency go hand in hand with strength. We must possess the qualities which make us do our duty in our homes and among our neighbors, and in addition we must possess the qualities which are indispensable to the make-up of every great and masterful nation—the qualities of courage and hardihood, of individual initiative and yet of power to combine for a common end, and above all, the resolute determination to permit no man and no set of men to sunder us one from the other by lines of caste or creed or section.
>
> We must act upon the motto of all for each and each for all. There must be ever present in our minds the fundamental truth that in a republic such as ours the only safety is to stand neither for nor against any man because he is rich or because he is poor, because he is engaged in one occupation or another, because he works with his brains or because he works with his hands. We must treat each man on his worth and merits as a man. We must see that each is given a square deal, because he is entitled to no more and should receive no less.
>
> Finally, we must keep ever in mind that a republic such as ours can exist only by virtue of the orderly liberty which comes through the equal domination of the law over all men alike, and through its administration in such resolute and fearless fashion as shall teach all that no man is above it and no man below it.

SOURCE: *"The Square Deal" (September 7, 1903).* http://www.theodore-roosevelt.com/trsquaredealspeech.html *(accessed May 15, 2007).*

---

solve its financial problems. In 1907 the U.S. Senate approved a treaty that allowed the United States to take over the Dominican Republic's customs house and duty collection (its largest source of revenue) and use the revenues to pay off the country's foreign debt. This political domination by the United States caused disorder, which led to occupation of the country by U.S. Marines from 1916 to 1924. The United States continued to control the Dominican Republic's customs operations until 1941.

This implementation of the Roosevelt Corollary established a pattern of intervention in the region near what is now the Panama Canal. The policy was at first ignored by other Latin American nations, but it later generated much resentment when the United States intervened in Nicaragua and Haiti to protect U.S. investments.

Like Roosevelt, Taft had ambitious plans to expand U.S. influence abroad. With the assistance of Secretary of State Philander C. Knox (1853–1921), Taft developed a plan that encouraged U.S. bankers and industrialists to invest in foreign countries and used diplomatic pressure to force U.S. investment into regions where it was not welcomed.

One of the first regions Taft chose to exercise his new foreign policy was China. In 1910 he persuaded U.S. bankers to finance railroad construction in China and to help China purchase Japanese- and Russian-owned railroads in Manchuria, the northeastern part of China. When Japan and Russia protested, however, the plan was abandoned; the administration did not believe the United States had the military power to force Japan and Russia to agree to the plan.

To safeguard the Panama Canal, Taft intensified dollar diplomacy in the Caribbean. He promoted U.S. investment in the region, arranging it so that U.S. citizens were in charge of finances whenever possible. He sent in U.S. Marines when he could not achieve his objectives by persuasion.

The Policy's Impact Dollar diplomacy was severely criticized, both within and outside the United States. President Woodrow Wilson (1856–1924) repudiated it shortly after he was inaugurated. He said that encouraging bankers to invest in countries such as China implied the possibility of "forcible interference" if the loans were not repaid. In his view this possibility would betray the principles on which the United States was founded.

Most historians view dollar diplomacy as a failed policy, largely because it deepened the antagonism of Latin Americans and Asians toward the United States. As important, they note that the policy was established to avoid military action; in practice, the policy often led to military intervention to protect the interests of U.S. businesses and investors. Following the Taft administration dollar diplomacy took on a negative connotation, referring to the manipulation of foreign policy for economic gain.

See also **Roosevelt Corollary**
See also **Theodore Roosevelt**

The Progressive Party, 1912

The Progressive Party—also known as the Bull Moose Party—was an offshoot of the Republican Party. It was founded in 1912 by the former president Theodore Roosevelt (1858–1919) and his supporters, who had become dissatisfied with the conservative agenda of the Republican president William Howard Taft (1857–1930). When Roosevelt did not get the Republican nomination for president in 1912, he and his supporters

Progressive party election banner, 1912. © Bettmann/CORBIS

created the Progressive Party so he could run against Taft.

The Party's Beginnings Roosevelt became president following the assassination of William McKinley (1843–1901) and was elected in his own right in 1904. For his first two years as president, Roosevelt adhered to the conservative policies of his predecessor. However, Roosevelt was a progressive at heart. He attacked monopolies—he became known as a trust-buster for breaking up powerful groups of businesses that controlled markets and diminished competition. He staked his political future on the premise that individuals were the key to political power, so he became a very public president: he held daily press briefings and traveled on national speaking tours to raise support for his policies.

Roosevelt did not seek to run for president in 1908, holding to the two-term precedent set by George Washington (1732–1799). He chose Taft, who was a close friend, to succeed him. For many Republicans, however, Taft's policies as president were too conservative. Eventually, Roosevelt agreed and decided to run for another term in 1912.

In 1911 Robert M. La Follette (1855–1925), a Republican senator from Wisconsin, and some colleagues created the National Republican Progressive League, an offshoot of the Republican Party. It supported La Follette for the Republican presidential nomination until Roosevelt announced he would run. La Follette and the Progressive League then endorsed Roosevelt.

Republican Party leaders continued to support Taft, however. Roosevelt and his supporters refused to accept the party's decision and formed the Progressive Party. It nominated Roosevelt for president and Hiram W. Johnson (1866–1945) for vice president.

Certificate given to the charter members of Theodore Roosevelt's Progressive Party, 1912. © *Bettmann/CORBIS*

The party became known as the Bull Moose Party because of a campaign incident. Roosevelt, who had been frail and sickly as a child, had worked hard to build his stamina and took pride in his physical endurance as an adult. While he was in Milwaukee, Wisconsin, to deliver a speech, he was shot in the chest by an assassin. The script of the speech—which he had placed in his breast pocket—slowed the bullet. Even though he was bleeding, Roosevelt refused to go to the hospital. Instead, he went on with his ninety-minute speech, declaring that it would take "more than a bullet to stop a bull moose." The event—and his comment—made headlines.

The New Nationalism The party's platform, which was called the New Nationalism, sought a variety of social reforms, including direct election of U.S. senators (they were chosen by their state legislature at the time); the creation of three procedures by which citizens could affect legislation—the initiative, the referendum, and the recall; women's right to vote; a reduction in tariffs on foreign imports; laws against child labor; and pensions for the elderly. Roosevelt's agenda received broad support.

Roosevelt received 27 percent of the popular vote to Taft's 23 percent. However, Woodrow Wilson (1856–1924), the Democratic candidate, received 41 percent of the popular vote and most of the Electoral College votes, so he won the election.

In 1916 Roosevelt turned down the Progressive Party's nomination for president. Charles Evans Hughes (1862–1948) ran for president as a Republican and attracted most of the Bull Moose supporters, effectively ending the party.

The Party's Impact As a result of Roosevelt's rousing candidacy as a Progressive, the public accepted the idea of a more modern and activist president. In addition, most of Roosevelt's reforms later became law, such as the Seventeenth Amendment, which established the direct election of U.S. senators, and the Nineteenth Amendment, which granted women the right to vote.

See also **Theodore Roosevelt**
See also **Progressive Party, 1924**

The National Woman's Party

The National Woman's Party (NWP), founded in 1913, was an offshoot of the National American Woman Suffrage Association (NAWSA). The NWP organized protest marches and other public demonstrations to publicize its cause: passage of an amendment to the U.S. Constitution that guaranteed women's right to vote. When that amendment was ratified in 1920, the group began to advocate an Equal Rights Amendment.

The Party's Origins In 1890 the National American Woman Suffrage Association was formed from two rival suffrage groups: the National Woman Suffrage Association, led by Elizabeth Cady Stanton (1815–1902) and Susan B. Anthony (1820–1906), and the American Woman Suffrage Association, led by Lucy Stone (1818–1893), Henry Blackwell (1825–1909), and Julia Ward Howe (1819–1910).

Alice Paul (1885–1977) and Lucy Burns (1879–1966), who were both members of the NAWSA, believed the organization was not militant enough in its demands for women's suffrage. In addition, they preferred to work exclusively for passage of a federal amendment rather than on the state-by-state level, the strategy advocated by the NAWSA. So in 1913 Paul and Burns and their supporters founded the Congressional

Alice Paul, Vice-President of the National Woman's Party, broadcasting plans for the dedication of a new national headquarters in Washington, 1922. © *Bettmann/CORBIS*

Union for Woman Suffrage, which was renamed the National Woman's Party three years later.

Most NWP members were young, white, and educated middle- or upper-class women; men were not allowed to join the organization. It was not intended to be a political party—it did not, for example, nominate a candidate for U.S. president—although it did direct much of its protest against the Democratic president Woodrow Wilson (1856–1924), because it believed he ignored its cause.

Picketing the White House NWP members became the first women to picket for women's rights outside the White House; they also held a suffrage march on the day before Wilson's inauguration. Many were arrested for their protests and, once in jail, went on hunger strikes. Some, including Paul, were subjected to unsanitary conditions, force feedings, and beatings. The picketing continued, however.

Media coverage of the treatment of the women came at an inopportune time for Wilson: he was trying to build a reputation—for himself and the nation—as an international leader in human rights. The publicity may have contributed to Wilson's decision to request congressional support for a constitutional amendment that granted women's suffrage.

The Equal Rights Amendment Once the suffrage amendment was ratified in 1920, the NWP began lobbying for a measure that became known as the Equal Rights Amendment (ERA). It was intended to guarantee equal treatment of all U.S. citizens under the law. Most women's groups did not support the ERA, however, because they thought it would undo much of the legislation that protected women in the workplace. Because of its agenda, the NWP was supplanted by other women's groups as the 1920s progressed.

The NWP's Impact Along with other women's organizations, the NWP was instrumental in gaining women's suffrage in the United States. In the years that followed many former suffragists and their daughters became active in other reform initiatives, such as advocating regulation of workplaces and the workday, world peace, birth control, conservation of natural resources, consumer issues, and legislation against child labor and child abuse.

> *See also* **Alice Paul**
> *See also* **Nineteenth Amendment**
> *See also* **Women's Suffrage Movement**

The Progressive Party, 1924

Even though it was the heir of the Progressive Party founded in 1912 by the former president Theodore Roosevelt (1858–1919), the Progressive Party of 1924 was a separate and distinct entity with a far more radical agenda. For example, it called for public ownership of natural resources and railroads.

The Party's Origins Following World War I (1914–1918) left-wing political activity in the United States increased as farmers and laborers grew dissatisfied with their economic situation. Membership in the Workers' Party (the Communists), the Socialist Party, and the Farmer-Labor Party expanded in the early 1920s.

One liberal coalition, which called itself the Conference for Progressive Political Action (CPPA), successfully backed a number of liberal candidates in congressional races and envisioned even greater success in the presidential election of 1924. To that end the CPPA—which included members of the Socialist Party, the railroad unions, and the American Federation of Labor—formed the League of Progressive Political Action, popularly known as the Progressive Party.

To gain real political influence, the party sought a presidential candidate with a national reputation. Robert M. La Follette (1855–1925), a Republican senator from Wisconsin, suited their requirements. A reformer, he had failed to win the Republican presidential nomination in 1908 and 1912. At first, he was reluctant to become the standard bearer of the Progressive Party, largely because of possible communist influence on the organization. However, he grew increasingly dissatisfied with the Republican Party's conservative agenda, especially after the party nominated the incumbent Calvin Coolidge (1872–1933) for president. When La Follette was offered full control of the Progressive Party's platform and the choice of his running mate, he accepted the party's presidential nomination.

The platform La Follette created called for public control and conservation of natural resources, farm-relief measures, public ownership of railways, tax reduction for those with moderate incomes, the abolition of child labor, the right of labor to organize and bargain collectively, and the breakup of monopolies and other business conglomerates that stifled competition.

La Follette ran against Coolidge and John W. Davis (1873–1955), a Democratic representative from West Virginia. Although La Follette and his running mate, the Montana senator Burton K. Wheeler (1882–1975),

gained support from trade unions, the Socialist Party, and a major newspaper chain, the campaign ran short of funds and La Follette was smeared as unpatriotic and a communist. Coolidge won a landslide victory.

The Progressive Party unraveled quickly following the defeat in 1924. It staged a comeback in the 1930s on the state level when La Follette's sons, Robert Jr. and Philip, forged a successful movement in Wisconsin. That effort lasted until the end of World War II (1939–1945).

The Party's Impact La Follette ran for president on a reform platform, promising to do for the nation what he had done for Wisconsin. Although his bid was unsuccessful, many of La Follette's progressive ideas were transformed into law during the administration of the Democratic president Franklin Roosevelt (1882–1945).

> *See also* **Progressive Party, 1912**

✪ Current Events and Social Movements

The Panic of 1893

The Panic of 1893, a national financial crisis, began when the Philadelphia and Reading Railroad, one of the largest railroad companies and employers in the United States, went bankrupt. It was more than $125 million in debt. A short time later, the National Cordage Company, a group of rope manufacturers, also closed its doors. For the first time, gold reserves in the U.S. Department of the Treasury plunged below the accepted minimum level of $100 million, confidence in the U.S. dollar dropped around the world, and in May 1893 the New York Stock Exchange crashed. The financial crisis was followed by four years of depression during which millions of Americans lost their jobs and struggled to survive.

The Roots of the Crisis In November 1890 the collapse of Baring Brothers, a British banking company, triggered a widespread sell-off of securities in Britain, including a substantial amount of stock in U.S. companies. At the time, the United States was operating on the gold standard, which meant that actual gold backed the value of money. The sale of European-held securities resulted in a vast drain of gold from the United States. Gold reserves were also falling because of a sharp decline in revenue associated with the McKinley Tariff of 1890—the second-largest tariff on imported goods in U.S. history—and the massive pension grants made to veterans during the administration of President Benjamin Harrison (1833–1901). The flow of foreign capital into U.S. businesses slowed, and the export of gold increased.

Several other factors contributed to the crisis. At the beginning of the 1890s the U.S. economy was expanding quickly, particularly in the areas of agriculture and railroads. Prospective farmers and business owners were borrowing huge sums of money to finance their ventures, and many became overextended financially. Although the abundant wheat crop of 1891 caused a brief upturn, agricultural prices fell, as did exports and commerce in general.

Then in 1893 the collapse of the Philadelphia and Reading Railroad and the National Cordage Company—the most actively traded stock on the New York Stock Exchange—led to panic in the stock market. Banks and other investment firms began calling in loans, causing hundreds of businesses to go bankrupt. In particular, the failures of steel mills, banks, and railroads—including the Northern Pacific Railway, the Union Pacific Railroad, and the Atchison, Topeka & Santa Fe Railroad—took a huge toll on the U.S. economy. More than fifteen thousand businesses were forced to shut down, and about 25 percent of the nation's workforce was laid off. Homelessness soared as unemployed workers were unable to pay their rent or mortgages.

In response to the crisis, President Grover Cleveland (1837–1908) asked Congress to repeal the Sherman Silver Purchase Act of 1890. That law—sponsored by John Sherman (1823–1900), a Republican senator from Ohio—required the U.S. government to increase its purchases of silver by nearly 50 percent, substantially adding to the number of banknotes in circulation. Those notes could be redeemed in either silver or gold. As the government bought more and more silver, prices fell, so people holding the banknotes began to redeem them for gold rather than silver. By repealing the act, Congress reduced the pressure on the gold reserves.

The Economy Recovers Economic recovery finally started in 1896. The sale of a new series of treasury bonds brought in gold, allowing the country to sustain gold reserves above $100 million, and new gold was produced. The public and the financial markets became confident again. The depression did not lift substantially, however, until 1897, when poor European crops stimulated U.S. exports, leading to imports of gold. Only then did the stock market stabilize.

The Long-Term Impact The hard times the United States experienced during the Panic of 1893 forced the nation to alter the pattern and pace of its development. The depression also intensified the sensitivity—of both the government and the general public—to a wide range of economic, social, and political issues that accompanied the transition from an agrarian to an industrial economy.

The poorest elements of society believed they had once again been left at the mercy of large corporations because the reforms of the last quarter of the nineteenth century had not been sufficient. New leadership, they thought, was needed for the next century.

See also **Gold Standard**

The Spanish-American War

The Spanish-American War, a short military conflict between the United States and Spain, erupted after a U.S. battleship exploded in the harbor of Havana, Cuba, then a Spanish colony. The U.S. decision to declare war on April 25, 1898, was also prompted by anti-Spanish sentiment in the United States, the desire to protect U.S. economic interests in Cuba, and the Cubans' desire for independence from Spain.

On August 12, 1898, only four months after the war began, the United States was victorious. Spain's overseas empire came to an end, and the United States acquired status as a global military power.

The Spanish Empire Spain was the first European nation to explore and colonize the Western Hemisphere. It developed an empire in the Americas that extended from colonial Virginia to the southern tip of South America—with the exception of Brazil, which was controlled by Portugal—and westward to California and Alaska. In the Pacific the Spanish empire included the Philippines and other groups of islands. By 1825, however, much of Spain's empire had been conquered by other nations or granted independence. However, Spain still controlled Cuba and Puerto Rico in the Caribbean and the Philippine, Caroline, Marshall, and Mariana islands (including Guam) in the Pacific.

Anti-Spanish Sentiment The greatest challenge for President William McKinley (1843–1901) was managing the growing tension between the United States and Spain over Cuba. Spanish officials had suppressed an independence movement on the island, which was its most profitable Caribbean colony because of sugar exports. Spain forced Cuban men, women, and children into what were called re-concentration camps, ostensibly to protect the civilians by separating them from the rebels seeking independence. The Spanish general Valeriano Weyler y Nicolau (1883–1930), who was known as the Butcher, neglected the camps' three hundred thousand inhabitants. As a result, starvation and disease became rampant, and thousands died.

Cuban-Americans grew concerned about the treatment of their countrymen. Sensational newspaper articles printed—partly to increase newspaper circulation—by the publishers William Randolph Hearst (1863–1951) and Joseph Pulitzer (1847–1911) further inflamed anti-Spanish sentiment.

Even though McKinley was reluctant to go to war with Spain, he felt compelled to do so, especially after the mysterious explosion of the USS *Maine* in Havana harbor. In 1898 the United States sent the warship to Cuba on what was called a "courtesy visit"; in reality, the ship was sent to protect U.S. citizens and property in Cuba. On February 15, 1898, a mysterious underwater explosion destroyed the ship and killed 266 U.S. sailors. U.S. officials believed a Spanish mine caused the disaster (navy studies in the 1970s suggested that the explosion may have been caused by spontaneous combustion in the ship's coal bunkers). So McKinley ordered a naval

Battleship USS *Maine* in Havana Harbor, 1898. The sinking of the *Maine* launched the Spanish-American War.   © *Bettmann/CORBIS*

blockade of Cuba, and by April both the United States and Spain had declared war.

To assure the world that the United States was fighting only to protect Cuba and not for colonial gain, Congress passed legislation known as the Teller Amendment (1898), which promised that Cuba would become independent after the war. Once declared, the United States fought the war on a variety of fronts.

As soon as hostilities began, Theodore Roosevelt (1858–1919), then the assistant secretary of the navy, ordered Commodore George Dewey (1837–1913) to attack the Philippines. On May 1 Dewey destroyed the Spanish fleet in Manila harbor. Some historians see that action as a reflection of Roosevelt's desire to take over and dominate other territories; others maintain that his motivation was simply to attack enemy naval vessels wherever they existed. During the war the United States also invaded Guam and Puerto Rico.

The U.S. ground force in Cuba, under the leadership of General William R. Shafer, was disorganized. However, with the assistance of the First U.S. Volunteer

Cavalry and other units, the United States defeated the Spanish military relatively quickly. The cavalry, which became known as the Rough Riders, was led by Roosevelt, who resigned his navy post in May 1898 to join the group of volunteers.

The Peace Treaty The treaty ending the war, which was signed on December 10, 1898, established Cuban independence and ceded Puerto Rico and Guam to the United States. It also allowed the United States to purchase the Philippine Islands from Spain for $20 million.

After the war the United States made improvements in Cuban schools, courts, and other infrastructure and prepared to withdraw according to the terms of the Teller Amendment. However, in 1901, before its departure, the United States forced the Cubans to insert a clause into their constitution. Known as the Platt Amendment, the clause gave the United States the right to establish a permanent military base in Cuba at Guantánamo Bay.

In Puerto Rico the United States established a civilian government—based on the Foraker Act, which was

THE PLATT AMENDMENT

When the Spanish-American War ended, Cuba became independent. However, the U.S. government insisted that the Cubans add a clause, known as the Platt Amendment, to their constitution. The following is an excerpt from the amendment:

> The President is hereby authorized to "leave the government and control of the island of Cuba to its people" so soon as a government shall have been established in said island under a constitution which, either as a part thereof or in an ordinance appended thereto, shall define the future relations of the United States with Cuba, substantially as follows:
>
> I. That the government of Cuba shall never enter into any treaty or other compact with any foreign power or powers which will impair or tend to impair the independence of Cuba, nor in any manner authorize or permit any foreign power or powers to obtain by colonization or for military or naval purposes or otherwise, lodgement in or control over any portion of said island.
>
> II. That said government shall not assume or contract any public debt, to pay the interest upon which, and to make reasonable sinking fund provision for the ultimate discharge of which, the ordinary revenues of the island, after defraying the current expenses of government shall be inadequate.
>
> III. That the government of Cuba consents that the United States may exercise the right to intervene for the preservation of Cuban independence, the maintenance of a government adequate for the protection of life, property, and individual liberty, and for discharging the obligations with respect to Cuba imposed by the treaty of Paris on the United States, now to be assumed and undertaken by the government of Cuba.
>
> IV. That all Acts of the United States in Cuba during its military occupancy thereof are ratified and validated, and all lawful rights acquired thereunder shall be maintained and protected.
>
> V. That the government of Cuba will execute, and as far as necessary extend, the plans already devised or other plans to be mutually agreed upon, for the sanitation of the cities of the island, to the end that a recurrence of epidemic and infectious diseases may be prevented, thereby assuring protection to the people and commerce of Cuba, as well as to the commerce of the southern ports of the United States and the people residing therein.
>
> VI. That the Isle of Pines shall be omitted from the proposed constitutional boundaries of Cuba, the title thereto being left to future adjustment by treaty.
>
> VII. That to enable the United States to maintain the independence of Cuba, and to protect the people thereof, as well as for its own defense, the government of Cuba will sell or lease to the United States lands necessary for coaling or naval stations at certain specified points to be agreed upon with the President of the United States.
>
> VIII. That by way of further assurance the government of Cuba will embody the foregoing provisions in a permanent treaty with the United States.

SOURCE: *Platt Amendment (1903)*. http://www.ourdocuments.gov/doc.php?doc=55&page=transcript (accessed May 15, 2007).

passed in 1900—with a governor and executive council appointed by the U.S. president, a House of Representatives with thirty-five elected members, a judicial system with a Supreme Court, and a nonvoting resident commissioner in the U.S. Congress. In addition, all federal laws of the United States were to be in effect on the island.

When the United States assumed control of Puerto Rico, the Puerto Rican people expected the United States to liberate the island nation, as the United States had liberated Cuba; instead, the United States used Puerto Rico as a coaling station for U.S. ships. The people of Puerto Rico would not receive collective U.S. citizenship until 1917.

The United States annexed the Philippines in January 1899. The Filipinos immediately declared independence. Under Emilio Aguinaldo (1869–1964), who was proclaimed the first president of the Republic of the Philippines, they began a guerrilla war that lasted until March 1901, when the United States captured Aguinaldo.

The War's Impact The Spanish-American War signaled the emergence of the United States as a world power and a major player in international affairs. Ironically, the United States, a nation founded in opposition to imperialism, became an imperial power itself. Its response to the Cuban and Filipino struggles for independence inspired the kind of outrage and revolt that other colonial powers had encountered in previous centuries.

The war also revealed the growing power of the media to affect public opinion. Much evidence suggests that sensationalistic journalism, like that published by Hearst and Pulitzer, was intended to encourage anti-Spanish sentiment among Americans. The publishers wanted to encourage a war with Spain because a war would sell more newspapers. The Spanish-American War may have been the first media war in U.S. history.

See also **Theodore Roosevelt**
See also **William McKinley**

The 16th Infantry facing fire from San Juan Hill in the Spanish-American War, 1898. © *Bettmann/CORBIS*

The Women's Suffrage Movement

In the United States, the movement for women's suffrage—also called the franchise or the right to vote—began in the mid-nineteenth century. Through the efforts of many women and men, it ultimately led to ratification of the Nineteenth Amendment to the U.S. Constitution in 1920, which granted women the right to vote.

A History of Suffrage Several of the thirteen original colonies gave women of property limited voting privileges in local elections. With U.S. independence from Britain in 1776, however, even that limited right was withdrawn, except in New Jersey. Property-holding women took advantage of the vague wording of the New Jersey state constitution, which gave the vote to "all inhabitants" of the state. In 1807, when African-Americans as well as women voted in some elections, suffrage in the state was restricted to free white men.

The Seneca Falls Convention In 1848 some two hundred women and forty men, including the reformers Lucretia Mott (1793–1880), Elizabeth Cady Stanton (1815–1902), and Frederick Douglass (1818–1895), met in Seneca Falls, New York, for the first women's rights convention. The group laid claim to full citizenship for all U.S. women, rejecting Victorian domesticity and its separation of men's and women's spheres. The delegates believed that women were full citizens and not exclusively wives or mothers. Perhaps most significant, they began the suffrage movement.

The Reformers In the years following the convention, reformers failed to secure the vote for women in conjunction with the enfranchisement of blacks by the Fourteenth Amendment—which secured the rights of all citizens under the law—and the Fifteenth Amendment—which secured the rights of all citizens to vote, without regard to race, color, or previous servitude. The American Equal

Women's suffrage leader Alice Paul unfurling a banner from the balcony of the National Woman's Party headquarters, showing a star for each state that had ratified the 19th Amendment to give women the right to vote. The women celebrate ratification by Tennessee, which made the amendment law in August, 1920. © *Bettmann/CORBIS*

Rights Association was formed in 1866, but policy rifts developed over women's suffrage in 1869.

As a result, the American Woman Suffrage Association was formed by Lucy Stone (1818–1893), Henry Blackwell (1825–1909), and Julia Ward Howe (1819–1910) and the National Woman Suffrage Association was created by Elizabeth Cady Stanton and Susan B. Anthony (1820–1906). Although bitterly opposed by certain segments of society—including most conservatives, the liquor interests, and organized crime bosses—the suffragists widened their influence through the press and by circulating petitions, lobbying legislators, and speaking at congressional hearings.

Gradually, a few states granted women limited suffrage, usually in local elections. Then, in 1869, when Wyoming organized as a territory, it gave women the right to vote; when it became a state in 1890, the right

for women to vote was retained. In 1893 Colorado gave women the vote; in 1896 Utah and Idaho; in 1910 Washington state; in 1911 California; in 1912 Arizona, Kansas, and Oregon; and in 1913 Alaska Territory. In 1913 Illinois, by statute, gave women suffrage in presidential and municipal elections. In 1914 Nevada and Montana granted women full suffrage. In 1917, prompted by women's active participation in World War I, New York granted women the vote.

Women Challenge Their Roles More and more women entered public life in the years after the Seneca Falls convention, partly because of greater educational opportunities. Women's colleges sprang up around the country, enrolling mostly white, middle-class women. By 1870 there were eleven thousand female students in these institutions; a decade later, the number had grown to forty thousand.

THE SENECA FALLS DECLARATION

In July 1848 the first women's rights convention in the United States adopted a Declaration of Sentiments and Resolutions. The following is an excerpt:

> The history of mankind is a history of repeated injuries and usurpations on the part of man toward woman, having in direct object the establishment of an absolute tyranny over her. To prove this, let facts be submitted to a candid world.
>
> He has never permitted her to exercise her inalienable right to the elective franchise.
>
> He has compelled her to submit to laws, in the formation of which she had no voice.
>
> He has withheld from her rights which are given to the most ignorant and degraded men—both natives and foreigners.
>
> Having deprived her of this first right of a citizen, the elective franchise, thereby leaving her without representation in the halls of legislation, he has oppressed her on all sides.
>
> He has made her, if married, in the eye of the law, civilly dead.
>
> He has taken from her all right in property, even to the wages she earns.
>
> He has made her, morally, an irresponsible being, as she can commit many crimes with impunity, provided they be done in the presence of her husband. In the covenant of marriage, she is compelled to promise obedience to her husband, he becoming to all intents and purposes, her master—the law giving him power to deprive her of her liberty, and to administer chastisement.
>
> He has so framed the laws of divorce, as to what shall be the proper causes, and in case of separation, to whom the guardianship of the children shall be given, as to be wholly regardless of the happiness of women— the law, in all cases, going upon a false supposition of the supremacy of man, and giving all power into his hands.
>
> After depriving her of all rights as a married woman, if single, and the owner of property, he has taxed her to support a government which recognizes her only when her property can be made profitable to it.
>
> He has monopolized nearly all the profitable employments, and from those she is permitted to follow, she receives but a scanty remuneration. He closes against her all the avenues to wealth and distinction which he considers most honorable to himself. As a teacher of theology, medicine, or law, she is not known.
>
> He has denied her the facilities for obtaining a thorough education, all colleges being closed against her....
>
> He has created a false public sentiment by giving to the world a different code of morals for men and women, by which moral delinquencies which exclude women from society, are not only tolerated, but deemed of little account in man....
>
> He has endeavored, in every way that he could, to destroy her confidence in her own powers, to lessen her self-respect, and to make her willing to lead a dependent and abject life.

SOURCE: *Seneca Falls Declaration (1848). http://usinfo.state.gov/usa/infousa/ facts/democrac/17.htm (accessed May 15, 2007).*

Half of all college-educated women in the late nineteenth century never married. Instead, they allied themselves with married women and formed associations geared toward extending the maternal role into the public sphere: educating young children, instituting benefits for the poor, and improving health conditions for both women and children. The associations included settlement houses, which were community centers that served the needs of the urban poor, and reenergized suffrage organizations.

Yet, many segments of society challenged women's efforts to enter public life. Throughout the 1890s a variety of "scientific reports" were released that claimed too much education could seriously injure the female reproductive system. In 1905 the former president Grover Cleveland (1837–1908) wrote that allowing women to vote would upset the "natural equilibrium" between men and women and cause chaos.

In retaliation, women set out to demonstrate that rather than disrupt the social order, suffrage for women would improve it. The suffragists argued that bringing their roles as mothers into the public arena would impose a kind of civic housekeeping on government and encourage a more nurturing role of the state toward its people. Women such as the Reverend Anna Garlin Spencer (1851–1931), who represented the mainstream suffrage movement, argued for a conservative rather than a radical transformation of women's role in society.

New Leadership By 1890 the early suffrage leaders had died, and with a significant number of college-educated women and women's organizations behind it, the movement found new leadership, including Carrie Chapman Catt (1859–1947), who led the National American Woman Suffrage Association (NAWSA), which combined the earlier suffrage associations. The group's platform was moderate and argued that women, who were inherently different from men, would restore moral order and harmony if they were allowed the vote. However, the NAWSA excluded black women from membership and garnered significant support from southern women by asserting that the white man's vote would maintain white supremacy in the South. In response, black women, such as Mary Church Terrell (1863–1954), formed their own organization, the National Association of Colored Women, in 1896.

By 1910 women's suffrage had become a mass movement. A parallel and much more radical movement was under way in England. Led by the activist Emmeline Pankhurst (1858–1928), British suffragists resorted to violence: they burned buildings, blew up mailboxes, and staged hunger strikes—actions that garnered negative publicity for themselves and their cause. American activists such as Alice Paul (1885–1977) and Lucy Burns (1879–1966) trained under Pankhurst and participated in British suffrage demonstrations.

The Women's March on Washington When they returned to the United States, Paul and Burns were not satisfied with the slow gains made by working with state legislatures. Nor were they content with the conservative tactics of the NAWSA. They decided to focus on passage of an amendment to the U.S. Constitution. Paul and Burns broke from the NAWSA and formed the National Woman's Party (NWP) to continue their militant tactics.

On March 3, 1913, the day before President Woodrow Wilson (1856–1924) was inaugurated, about five thousand women united under the NWP's leadership to picket the White House and demand the right to vote. The women denounced Wilson and the Democratic Party for their failure to enfranchise women. The marchers were shouted and jeered at, and many were jailed. However, their tactics and arrests received publicity for their cause. In addition, Wilson eventually announced his support for the suffrage amendment.

A little girl shakes the hand of an American soldier as his troop marches through London, 1917. *A.R. Coster/Topical Press Agency/Getty Images*

The Nineteenth Amendment The efforts of both organizations were rewarded with the passage in 1919 of the Nineteenth Amendment. Ratification by three-fourths of the state legislatures did not come immediately, however; many southerners balked, believing that white (male) supremacy would be threatened if women gained the vote. So the NAWSA and the NWP continued to campaign until Tennessee's legislature voted in 1920 to ratify the amendment. The Nineteenth Amendment immediately granted twenty-six million women—half the nation's population—the right to vote.

The Movement's Impact Although suffrage did not produce the immediate results anticipated by its supporters or include minority women in its successes, it laid the groundwork for women to pursue a life of independence and public action. Women only gradually realized their power as citizens and as voters. The Nineteenth Amendment—like the Fourteenth Amendment before it—was one more step in the fight for equal rights for all U.S. citizens.

See also **Alice Paul**

World War I

World War I (1914–1918) erupted in Europe following the assassination of the archduke Franz Ferdinand (1863–1914), heir to the Austro-Hungarian throne, by the Serbian nationalist Gavrilo Princip (1894–1918). Within months, most of the nations of Europe were at war. The United States did not enter the conflict until 1917.

At the time of the assassination, Bosnia, which was a province governed by Austro-Hungary, was populated primarily by three groups: Croats, who were Roman Catholics; ethnic Serbs, who were Eastern Orthodox; and Muslims, who remained from the days of Turkish rule. Many Bosnian-Serbs resented Austrian rule and wanted their province joined with Serbia across the river, and many in Serbia shared this desire.

Austria declared war on Serbia (July 28, 1914). Then Germany declared war on Russia (August 1, 1914), on France (August 3), and invaded Belgium (August 4). Britain declared war on Germany (August 4). The Central Powers—the combined forces of Germany and Austro-Hungary—fought against the Allies—Britain, France, and Russia. In November 1914 Turkey allied itself with the Central Powers, and in 1915 Italy joined the Allies. The United States entered the war in support of the Allies in 1917.

U.S. Neutrality At the outset of the war President Woodrow Wilson (1856–1924), adhering to the nation's longstanding isolationist foreign policy, issued a declaration of neutrality. He advocated keeping the Atlantic Ocean open for U.S. trade with all the European nations at war. British naval supremacy, however, nearly eliminated U.S. trade with Germany, so U.S. shipments to the Allies increased dramatically. To curb this trend, German submarines, known as U-boats, torpedoed U.S. merchant vessels bound for Allied ports.

THE SINKING OF THE *LUSITANIA*

After the outbreak of World War I, ocean voyage became dangerous. To keep war matériel from getting through to Britain, German submarines, known as U-boats, constantly patrolled British waters in search of approaching vessels.

The *Lusitania*, a British ocean liner with 1,959 people on board—159 of whom were American—departed New York for Liverpool, England, on May 1, 1915. It sailed despite a warning from the German authorities, which had appeared in U.S. newspapers that morning.

By that point in the war, a number of British merchant ships had been sunk by German U-boats, but the ocean liner's speed was thought to be its best guarantee of safety. While the *Lusitania* was at sea, a German U-boat sank three British ships in the waters south of Ireland through which it was about to sail, and the ship's captain received repeated warnings that U-boats were active on his intended course. On May 7, as the *Lusitania* entered the most dangerous segment of its journey, Captain William Turner (1856–1915) slowed the ship, presumably because of fog. He also failed to use the standard zigzag maneuvers that were intended to evade enemy attacks.

Approximately fourteen miles off the coast of southern Ireland, unknown to either the captain or any of his crew, the German submarine U-20 spotted and targeted the ship. The U-boat launched a torpedo, which hit the *Lusitania*; almost immediately another explosion occurred.

At the time, the Allies thought the Germans had launched two or three torpedoes to sink the ship. The Germans later maintained that their U-boat fired only one torpedo. Many experts suggested the second explosion was caused by the ignition of ammunition hidden in the cargo hold; others said that coal dust, stirred up when the torpedo hit, exploded. Regardless of the exact cause, the damage from the second explosion caused the ship to sink in eighteen minutes.

Even though the ship had a sufficient number of lifeboats for all passengers, the severe shifting of the ship while it sunk prevented most of the boats from being launched properly. Of the 1,959 people on board, 1,198 died. The heavy death toll shocked the world.

Americans were especially outraged to learn that 128 U.S. civilians were killed in a war in which the United States was officially neutral. Attacking vessels not known to be carrying war matériel countered generally accepted international war protocols. The sinking of the *Lusitania* helped create a climate of indignation that later prompted the United States to enter the war.

In May 1915 a German submarine sank the British passenger ship *Lusitania*; more than a thousand passengers, including 128 Americans, died. A strong protest from Wilson subdued Germany's submarine campaign, but in January 1917 Germany announced its intention to destroy all ships heading to Britain. Although Wilson broke diplomatic ties with Germany, he still hoped to avert war and armed merchant vessels as a deterrent. Nevertheless, Germany began sinking U.S. ships.

The Zimmerman Telegram In February 1917 British intelligence gave the U.S. government a decoded telegram from Germany's foreign minister, Arthur Zimmerman (1864–1940). The telegram had been intercepted on its way to the German ambassador to Mexico. The telegram authorized the ambassador to offer Mexico the portions of the southwestern United States that it had lost in the 1840s if it joined the Central Powers. Because of a campaign promise to keep the United States out of the European war, Wilson did not publicize the telegram initially. He only released the message to the press in March, after weeks of German attacks on U.S. ships had turned public sentiment toward involvement in the war.

On April 2, 1917, Wilson asked Congress for a declaration of war. Four days later a war resolution was passed. The Selective Service System, which registered men between the ages of eighteen and twenty-five for possible military service, was created a month later. The draft, along with a large number of volunteers, built the army from less than 250,000 to 4 million during the course of the conflict.

Initially, the United States was not prepared to fight so large a war so far from U.S. soil: it took time to reorganize government and industry to coordinate a war and then recruit, train, equip, and ship out massive numbers of soldiers. General John Pershing (1860–1948), who commanded U.S. forces in Europe, led the first troops to France during the summer.

Building Support for a War Although many Americans supported the war and many volunteered for service, the scale of the undertaking and time pressures led the government to mount a massive propaganda campaign. The press received carefully selected information on the progress of the war, and more than 75,000 speakers were sent to 750,000 public events, rousing the patriotism of millions of spectators.

The government needed patriotic cooperation because it was completely unequipped to enforce many of the new regulations it adopted. A War Industries Board was charged with gearing up the economy to war production, but it lacked sufficient authority. The Overman Act of May 1918, which gave the president broad powers to commandeer industries if needed, failed to persuade industrialists to retool their manufacturing plants in support of the war effort.

The government took control of only one industry, the railroads, in December 1917, and then only temporarily. In all other industries federal investment, rather than coercion, achieved results. The Emergency Fleet Corporation invested more than $3 billion in the nation's inactive shipbuilding industry. U.S. production was just gaining strength as the war ended, but the threat that it represented helped persuade an exhausted Germany to surrender.

A soldier with a machine gun in a sandbagged enclosure, 1916. *Three Lions/Getty Images*

Repression and the War The war effort relied on a workforce of unprecedented diversity and on cooperation from increasingly powerful unions. To achieve its goals, the federal government sought to suppress elements that might harm the system. For the first time, it developed a significant intelligence-gathering apparatus whose primary targets were anticapitalist radicals and enemy aliens (e.g., German and Austro-Hungarian immigrants). Radicals were targeted by the Espionage Act of 1917, which outlawed the conveyance of information with intent to interfere with the operation or success of the U.S. armed forces or to promote the success of its enemies. After the Bolshevik Revolution in Russia, in which the czar was overthrown, the government sought even broader powers to control public speech. In 1918 Congress passed the Sedition Act, which prohibited "disloyal, profane, scurrilous, or abusive language" about the government, the flag, or the military and tightened restrictions on disclosure of government and industrial information pertaining to national defense.

The U.S. Department of Justice, through its U.S. attorneys and Bureau of Investigation, cooperated with local and state authorities to suppress radical organizers. Many government agencies developed some intelligence capacity and the private, but government-sanctioned, American Protective League recruited three hundred thousand citizen-spies to keep watch on their fellow Americans.

In this climate of suspicion, German-speaking aliens became fearful, especially when war propaganda dehumanized Germans and ridiculed their culture and language. Large numbers of aliens were screened by the Department of Justice; many who were considered disloyal had their movements restricted and were denied access to military and war-production sites.

U.S. Soldiers on the Front Lines The end of the war seemed a long way off when U.S. troops first engaged in significant fighting in the spring of 1918. The new Bolshevik government in Russia withdrew from the war in March, so Germany redirected its efforts to the western front. Under British and French pressure, Pershing allowed a limited number of his troops to join with those of the Allies. Now under foreign command, U.S. troops helped stop the renewed German offensive in May and June.

The First U.S. Army was given its own mission in August: to push back the German advance near Verdun, a town in northeastern France, and to seize the important railroad facilities at Sedan, a nearby village. The campaign, which began in September, was a success.

The Meuse-Argonne Offensive, which was launched in late September, proved to be much bloodier than the U.S. battle at Verdun. Even though the German position was heavily fortified, more than a million U.S. soldiers simply overwhelmed all resistance. This massive and relentless operation persuaded the German command that its opportunity to defeat the Allies before U.S. troops and industry were fully ready to enter combat had been lost. With U.S. troops ready for battle, the exhausted Central Powers surrendered on November 11, 1918. An armistice, a temporary peace agreement, was declared.

U.S. Casualties During the war, about two million U.S. soldiers engaged in combat in France. About fifty-three thousand died in battle, and more than two hundred thousand were wounded. An additional sixty thousand died from diseases—several contracted influenza during the epidemic that spread around the world in 1918 and 1919. Furthermore, many surviving combatants suffered psychological damage, known as shell shock, from the horrors of trench warfare.

The Treaty of Versailles After the war the Paris Peace Conference, which was convened by the Allies, hammered out the terms of peace treaties, including the Treaty of Versailles. Signed on June 28, 1919, it officially ended the war with Germany. Among its 440 articles were demands that Germany accept full responsibility for causing the war, pay heavy economic reparations to Allied countries, and lose territory and much of its right to develop militarily. Other treaties were created for other countries.

The Treaty of Versailles also included articles that established a League of Nations, an international peacekeeping organization like the one first advocated by Wilson in a speech to Congress in 1918. The treaty specified the rules and requirements of membership. However, joining the league ran counter to the traditional views of many members of Congress, who preferred a U.S. foreign policy of nonintervention. As important, many Americans, because of the heavy U.S. death toll during the war, wanted to detach politically from Europe. So the U.S. Senate failed to ratify the treaty, and the United States did not join the league. The United States negotiated a separate peace with Germany, which became official in August 1921.

Aftermath of the War World War I changed the political, social, and economic conditions of the entire world. Economies were drained, and boundaries shifted. The German and Austro-Hungarian empires ceased to exist. Much of eastern Europe was reconfigured along ethnolinguistic lines, and Hungary, Poland, Lithuania, Latvia, Estonia, and Finland became independent countries. Several other nations were haphazardly combined into the countries of Yugoslavia and Czechoslovakia. A major reorganization of the Middle East also took place, establishing the countries later known as Armenia, Turkey, Syria, Lebanon, Saudi Arabia, and Iraq.

Many historians believe that the Allies were excessive in their punishment of Germany after the war and that the harsh terms of the Treaty of Versailles, rather than fostering peace, encouraged the bitterness and resentment that led to World War II. Although Germany ultimately paid only a small percentage of the reparations, the country's economy was already stretched thin from the war, so the additional economic burden caused further resentment. Extremist groups, such as the Nazi Party, exploited this humiliation and took political control of the country during the next two decades.

See also **Influenza Epidemic**
See also **Isolationism**
See also **Woodrow Wilson**
See also **Alvin C. York**

The Influenza Epidemic

During 1918 and 1919 a particularly virulent strain of influenza swept the world, infecting approximately one billion people and killing an estimated fifty million—more than all the casualties of World War I. Within months, the pandemic, or worldwide epidemic, killed more people than any illness in recorded history.

Although the geographic origins of the deadly flu are still unknown, it was first believed that the pandemic originated in China from a rare genetic mutation of the swine virus. In 2005, however, researchers studying the genetic makeup of the virus suggested that it had jumped directly from birds to humans, bypassing swine, and that it probably did not originate in Asia (they were not able to identify the site of its origin). They also learned that the virus was not caused by a mutation of a previously existing virus but was a new strain of virus to which people had little, if any, immunity.

Before and after 1918 most influenza pandemics developed in Asia, then spread to the rest of the world. Unlike the others, the 1918 disease spread in three distinct waves over eighteen months in Europe, Asia, and North America.

Officials inspecting street cleaners in Chicago for Spanish influenza, 1918.   © *Bettmann/CORBIS*

The First Wave   The first outbreak of the flu in the United States was recorded on March 11, 1918, at Camp Funston, a military camp in Fort Riley, Kansas. In this early stage, the disease was mild in nature: it began with a cough, then headache and backache, fatigue, high fever, rapid heartbeat, loss of appetite, and difficulty breathing. Victims usually recovered in a few days, and no deaths were reported. In April and May a similar illness struck more than five hundred prisoners in San Quentin Prison in California. Then the disease spread to military camps throughout the United States. Within seven days every state was affected, and forty-eight people were dead. The disease spread particularly quickly where people lived in close quarters.

A Flu Moves with a War   As the armies of various nations, including U.S. soldiers from Camp Funston, moved across continents during the war, the flu spread with them. British and German soldiers were affected in April 1918. When the flu attacked France in May, the virus had mutated; the killer virus, referred to as *la grippe*, was contracted not only by French soldiers but also by African soldiers who had been recruited into the French army.

Next, the virus showed up in Spain in May and June 1918, and within a short time, eight million people were affected. Many countries involved in World War I censored news of the illness to keep their populations and

military personnel focused on the war effort. Spain, however, remained neutral during the war, so it had no need to censor news reports of the illness. Consequently, the Spanish press fully documented the illness and its effects on the human body, calling the disease the Spanish Flu.

Cases had appeared during the spring and summer of 1918 in other countries as well, from Norway to China to Costa Rica to India, where the mortality rate was extremely high. The disease was so deadly that some of the Allies (France, Italy, Russia, the United Kingdom, and the United States) thought the pandemic was a tool of biological warfare devised by the Central Powers.

The Second Wave   Then a second, more deadly, wave of influenza developed. By the end of August 1918 the mutated virus led to epidemics of unprecedented virulence—in the same week—in three port cities thousands of miles apart: Freetown, Sierra Leone; Brest, Belgium; and Boston, Massachusetts. Scientists still do not know if this outbreak was the result of three appearances of a single mutation or three different simultaneous mutations.

In August some of the sailors on a ship carrying supplies and machinery into the port of Boston were transferred to Michigan and Illinois, and the influenza spread to the Midwest. Thousands of soldiers fell ill at army bases across the country. By September the disease had spread to the civilian population and moved quickly along

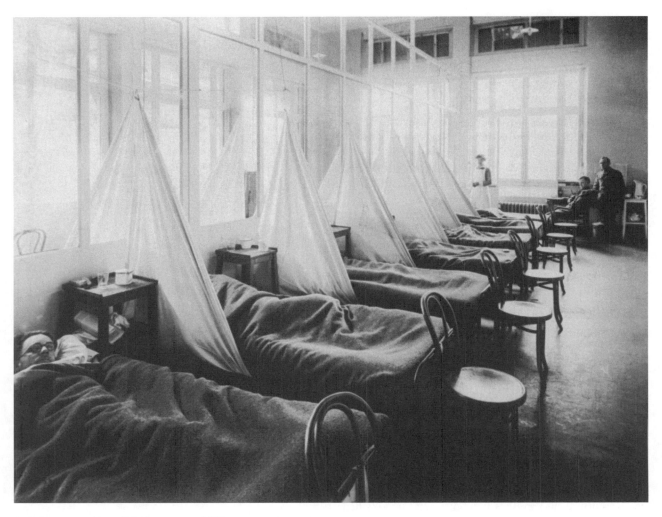

An influenza ward in a U.S. Army camp, 1918. © *CORBIS*

the eastern seaboard to New York, Philadelphia, and beyond. That month, twelve thousand Americans died of influenza.

Mysterious Symptoms Doctors across the nation were perplexed by the symptoms they saw among the flu victims: raging fever, delirium, and nosebleeds, followed by bloody pneumonia. The victims coughed up blood, their faces turned blue, and their autopsies revealed that their lungs had turned blue as well. Some victims died within hours of contracting the disease; others died more slowly. In many cases death was not caused by influenza but by pneumonia that accompanied the infection.

Medical researchers knew the disease was spread through the air (through coughing or sneezing) but were unable to see the organism under the unsophisticated microscopes of the time. They incorrectly identified the cause of the disease as bacterial. While vaccines had been developed for many bacterial diseases—smallpox, anthrax, rabies, diphtheria, and meningitis—doctors were helpless to stop the influenza of 1918. Viruses had not yet been

discovered in 1918, and, as was later determined, the epidemic was caused by a virus.

With medical science unable to help them, many people turned to folk remedies such as garlic, castor oil, quinine tablets, kerosene on sugar, morphine, enemas, aspirin, tobacco, hot and cold baths, and expectorants of pine tar.

Public Precautions When deaths from the disease grew more widespread, theaters, churches, and other public venues were closed. Public gatherings were often difficult to avoid, however. The war effort brought people into the streets for rallies and bond drives—and the influenza spread rapidly. Ordinances made it illegal to spit, cough, or sneeze in public, with the threat of $500 fines in New York City. When people left their homes, many wore gauze masks—often soaked in camphor or a medicine—over their nose and mouth.

In October 1918 the flu reached its peak, killing about 195,000 Americans. A casket shortage developed. In Philadelphia, the dead were left in gutters and stacked in caskets on front porches. Trucks drove through city streets, picking up the caskets and corpses. People stayed indoors and were afraid to associate with friends and neighbors.

On November 11, 1918, when the war ended, people gathered to celebrate Armistice Day with parades and parties for returning veterans. The occasion offered the virus another opportunity to spread.

The Disease Recedes   Just as suddenly as it struck, the disease began to disappear. By mid-November 1918 the numbers of those dying decreased dramatically. During the war about fifty-seven thousand U.S. soldiers died from influenza—more than the fifty-three thousand who had died in battle. An estimated six hundred thousand Americans died of influenza, and about 25 percent of the U.S. population was infected. Worldwide, about 20 percent of the population was affected. The flu killed people on every inhabited continent. The death toll was highest in Asia; the highest percentage of the population killed was in India.

The Third Wave   A third wave of the influenza, occurring at the beginning of 1919, was less severe. By then the world was better prepared, and the virus could be quarantined. Although the virus inflicted a rapid death toll, it also disappeared quickly.

New Research   Because viruses had not been discovered in 1918, no one had isolated or saved a specimen of the virus that caused the epidemic. In 2005, however, several teams of British government and university scientists reconstructed the 1918 virus using tiny pieces of lung tissue from people who died in the pandemic—two soldiers, whose tissue had been saved in an army pathology warehouse, and an Alaskan woman, whose body had been buried in permanently frozen ground. Although their results have been disputed, the scientists' research led them to conclude that the virus jumped directly from birds to humans—very unexpectedly—catching the human immune system off guard.

When they do exist, vaccines to fight viruses offer about 70 percent protection. In new or recently evolved viral strains, however, researchers find that vaccines may be relatively useless because the rate of evolution of the virus outpaces the rate at which new vaccines can be manufactured. For this reason, researchers often call pandemic influenza the largest immediate threat to global human health in the twenty-first century.

See also **World War I**

The Gold Standard

The gold standard is a monetary system in which a country's currency can be converted into a fixed weight of gold. The gold standard was shared by many countries—especially Britain, France, Germany, and the United States—between 1870 and 1914. The currencies of those nations were fixed at a set exchange rate to ounces of gold. The gold standard was virtually abandoned by all the major participating nations at the begin-

Political handbill for the 1900 presidential election, featuring William McKinley's support of the Gold Standard.   © *CORBIS*

ning of World War I, although the United States did not officially abandon the gold standard until 1971.

A Way to Stabilize the Global Economy   The gold standard was intended to stabilize the global economy and to require participating nations to limit their issued currency to the amount of gold they held in reserve. Britain officially adopted the standard in 1821; Germany and France followed in the 1870s.

During the days of the American frontier, news of the discovery of gold in a region attracted many new settlers who risked their lives to find gold. The most famous gold rush occurred in 1848 at Sutter's Mill in California. Gold rushes also occurred in Australia in 1851, South Africa in 1884, and Canada in 1897. Although the United States had technically been on a bimetallic monetary system—gold and silver both served as the basis for currency—the country was essentially on a gold standard during the 1800s because very little silver was traded.

Prompted by the increased supply of gold, the United States unofficially adopted the gold standard in the 1870s. Passage of the Gold Standard Act in 1900, which set the value of gold at $20.67 per troy ounce, made it official. (The troy weight system is used primarily for precious metals and gemstones.) The United States was one of the last developed nations to adopt the standard, largely because of powerful and vocal silver supporters.

From 1871 to 1914 the world was politically stable, and governments worked together to make the gold standard work. All trade imbalances between nations were settled with gold, so governments had a strong incentive to stockpile gold for economically difficult times. Dramatic increases in global trade and production in the nineteenth century—as well as large discoveries of gold—sustained the gold standard well into the twentieth century.

The Effects of World War The cooperation among countries using the gold standard disintegrated, however, with the outbreak of World War I in 1914. Political alliances altered, international indebtedness increased, prices of exports fluctuated, and government finances deteriorated. The instability stressed an economic system based on a fixed gold standard, creating a lack of confidence. It became increasingly apparent that the global economy needed a more stable monetary base.

As the gold supply continued to fall behind the growth of the global economy, the British pound sterling and the U.S. dollar became the global reserve currencies: smaller countries began holding supplies of these currencies instead of gold. The result was a growing consolidation of gold in the hands of a few large nations and a "gold-exchange standard": nations supplemented their gold reserves with currencies, such as U.S. dollars and British pounds, that were convertible into gold at a stable rate of exchange.

The Effects of the Great Depression The U.S. stock market crash of 1929, which began the Great Depression of the 1930s, was felt worldwide and marked the beginning of the end of the gold standard. In the United States the gold standard was revised, and the price of gold was devalued.

The exchange rates of the British pound and the French franc were poorly aligned with other currencies, war debts and repayments were still adversely affecting the German economy, commodity prices were collapsing, and banks were overextended. The high cost of the war, besides the economic depression, finally forced Britain to abandon the gold standard in 1931.

In the midst of the Great Depression, President Franklin D. Roosevelt (1882–1945) decided to make the U.S. government a large-scale borrower. Until then, the government's ability to borrow had been automatically controlled because currency was backed by physical reserves of gold: Americans had a constitutional right to demand gold in return for their U.S. banknotes.

In response to a drop in the nation's gold reserves, Roosevelt issued an executive order in 1933 that outlawed the personal ownership of gold (except for small amounts, such as jewelry and coins in collections). In 1934 the U.S. government revalued gold from $20.67

to $35 per troy ounce, raising the amount of paper money it took to buy one troy ounce. This higher gold price increased the conversion of gold into U.S. dollars. Gold production increased, and by 1939 there was enough gold in the world to replace all global currency in circulation.

A Standard Abandoned Following World War II (1939–1945) representatives of the major Western powers met in Bretton Woods, New Hampshire, to make financial arrangements for the postwar world. They put together the Bretton Woods Agreement (1946), which created a system of exchange rates that allowed governments to sell their gold to the U.S. Department of the Treasury at the price of $35 per troy ounce. They also created the International Monetary Fund, which became the official organization for securing monetary cooperation around the world.

The Bretton Woods system provided the framework for global currency markets until 1971, when President Richard M. Nixon (1913–1994) ended gold trading at the fixed price of $35 per troy ounce. At the time, gold reserves were dwindling, and the United States faced an unfavorable balance of payments with other countries. For the first time in history, formal links between the major world currencies and real commodities, such as gold, were severed.

See also **World War I**

✪ Legislation, Court Cases, and Trials

The Income Tax of 1894

The income tax of 1894 was a flat-rate federal tax on corporate and individual income. A year later the U.S. Supreme Court declared the tax unconstitutional. In its decision, the Court said the U.S. Constitution allowed Congress to impose direct taxes—taxes paid directly to the government, as opposed to an indirect tax, such as a sales tax, which is paid to an intermediary, such as a store—only if the taxes were levied in proportion to each state's population. The Court said the provisions of the income tax of 1894 did not meet that requirement. This decision eventually lead to the Sixteenth Amendment to the Constitution.

The First Income Tax An income tax was first proposed in the United States during the War of 1812—a war between the United States and Britain ostensibly over Britain's violations of U.S. maritime rights in European ports. After two years of war, the federal government had accumulated a huge debt and doubled the rates of its major source of revenue: customs duties on imports. The duties hindered trade, however, and generated less revenue than the earlier rates.

At the height of the war, the government imposed excise—nonincome—taxes on goods and commodities, housing, slaves, and land. In 1816 these taxes were repealed, and instead a high tariff on foreign imports was established to pay off the accumulated war debt. At the time an income tax was defeated by Congress.

Funding the Civil War The income tax reappeared as a means of funding the Union army in the Civil War (1861–1865), which was costly—about $2 million per day. To meet expenses, the Republican-controlled Congress borrowed heavily, doubled tariff rates, sold public lands, imposed various licensing fees, increased excise tax rates, and created new excise taxes. Revenues still did not meet the government's wartime needs.

The first income tax was moderately progressive—because it progressed, or increased, with the amount of income earned. The rate was set at 3 percent of annual income over $800. The tax exempted most wage earners, whose annual income fell below $800.

The Internal Revenue Act of 1862 The Internal Revenue Act of 1862 levied excise taxes on a wide variety of goods and services, including items considered luxuries, such as liquor, tobacco, playing cards, carriages, yachts, billiard tables, and jewelry. It also taxed patented medications and newspaper advertisements; imposed license taxes on virtually every profession or service except the clergy; instituted stamp taxes; set taxes for the value added to goods when they were manufactured or processed; established inheritance taxes; levied taxes on the gross receipts of corporations, banks, and insurance companies; and taxed dividends and interest paid to investors. To administer all these excise taxes, Congress created the Bureau of Internal Revenue. The bureau also administered the tariff system.

Most of these taxes and tariffs were consumption-oriented measures that affected lower-income Americans more than higher-income Americans. In an attempt to increase the fairness of the system, Congress implemented a supplementary system of taxation that more accurately reflected taxpayers' ability to pay. The income tax fulfilled this purpose.

Income Tax Reforms The 1862 law made important changes in the federal income tax. For example, a two-tiered rate structure was enacted, with taxable incomes up to $10,000 taxed at a rate of 3 percent and higher incomes taxed at 5 percent. A standard deduction of $600 was established, and deductions were permitted for rental housing, repairs, losses, and other taxes paid. In addition, to ensure timely collection, taxes were "withheld at the source" by employers. Taxes were also withheld from the salaries of government employees and from dividends paid to corporations.

In 1863 Congress passed a special 5 percent tax on incomes above $600 to pay for an army-recruitment program. In mid-1864 the income tax rates were raised again, and the tax on interest and dividends was also raised from 3 percent to 5 percent.

Penalties Imposed Initially, the income tax raised relatively little revenue. Presuming that many large-income earners were escaping the tax, Congress raised the rate on incomes of more than $5,000 to 10 percent and gave tax assessors the power to estimate income and increased the penalties for noncompliance. In addition, fines of 25 percent to 50 percent were assessed for filing fraudulent returns.

The Postwar Years After the Civil War ended, the government continued to collect an income tax to pay the war debt. However, resistance to the tax grew, so in 1867 a flat tax of 5 percent on annual incomes of more than $1,000 was introduced. The penalty for failure to pay was increased as well.

This income tax expired in 1870 and was replaced with a 2.5 percent tax on annual incomes of more than $2,000. When that law expired in 1872, the United States had no income tax. With a booming economy that produced tariff surpluses for decades, the need for tax revenue declined sharply. By 1868 the main sources of government revenue were the taxes on liquor and tobacco.

Passed and Repealed Amid the Panic of 1893—a financial crisis in the United States that led to a serious economic depression—Congress established a 2 percent tax on all annual incomes of more than $4,000. The 1894 law exempted the salaries of state and local officials, federal judges, and the president.

The income tax of 1894 was designed to shift the tax burden from the less wealthy to the wealthy. Even though it was not designed to redistribute wealth or restructure society, the tax was designed to redistribute the tax burden and restructure the revenue system. According to some historians, however, the 1894 tax was designed to prevent more drastic alternatives, including a more progressive income tax. They see it as a tool for protecting the status quo rather than an instrument of social and economic reform.

President Grover Cleveland (1837–1908) opposed the income tax of 1894 but allowed it to become law without his signature. In 1895 the Supreme Court ruled five to four against the measure, declaring that its provisions amounted to a direct tax, which was prohibited by the Constitution. Sections 8 and 9 of Article I state that direct taxes must be apportioned among the states according to the census.

Later Developments In 1909 Congress proposed an income tax that would not be based on the population of the states. To do so, it worked around the 1895 Supreme Court objection to the income tax of 1894. Ratification of the Sixteenth Amendment in 1913 made the income tax constitutional and allowed the federal government to tax the incomes of individuals directly, without regard to the population of each state. This amendment served as the basis for the federal income tax system—the largest source of federal receipts—into the twenty-first century.

See also **Panic of 1893**

Plessy v. Ferguson

Plessy v. Ferguson, a landmark case argued before the U.S. Supreme Court in 1896, concerned a Louisiana law that required separate railway cars for blacks and whites. To test the constitutionality of the law, Homer Plessy (1863–1925), who was seven-eighths Caucasian and one-eighth "African blood," as he later described himself, took a seat in a "whites only" car of a Louisiana train in 1892. He refused to move to the car reserved for blacks and was arrested.

Judge John H. Ferguson of the Criminal District Court of New Orleans found the law constitutional, as did the Louisiana Supreme Court. The U.S. Supreme Court upheld the lower courts' decisions. It ruled that "separate but equal" accommodations for white and nonwhite railroad passengers did not violate the Fourteenth Amendment, which provides equal protection under the law for all people. This decision provided the legal justification for segregating blacks and whites for decades.

Jim Crow Laws When slavery was abolished after the Civil War (1861–1865), southern and border states enacted a series of "separate but equal" laws that served to define blacks' "place" in the eyes of the dominant whites. They were called Jim Crow laws, after a fictional black-faced character in minstrel shows. The first Jim Crow law requiring railroads to transport blacks in separate cars or separated from whites by partitions was adopted by Florida in 1887. Mississippi followed in 1888; Texas in 1889; Louisiana in 1890; Alabama, Arkansas, Georgia, and Tennessee in 1891; and Kentucky in 1892. North and South Carolina and Virginia followed in the final three years of the nineteenth century.

Black Hopes Are Dashed The postwar commitment to equality, as demonstrated by the passage of a number of civil rights acts, was virtually repudiated by the Jim Crow laws. Mississippi and South Carolina already denied the vote to blacks, and many other states were preparing to follow suit.

On July 19, 1890, the Separate Car Act was passed by the Louisiana General Assembly. The law stated that all railroad companies transporting passengers within Louisiana state lines were required to provide "separate but equal" accommodations for white and nonwhite passengers. The penalty for sitting in the wrong compartment was a fine of $25 or twenty days in jail.

The black community of New Orleans, with its strong mix of French and other nationalities, was in a strategic position to lead resistance to segregation. The state legislature received an official protest from the American Citizens' Equal Rights Association of Louisi-

ana against Class Legislation, an advocacy group created by New Orleans black professionals in 1891. It denounced the Separate Car Act as unconstitutional, un-American, and unjust. It maintained that such a law would give free rein to anyone wishing to insult and humiliate people whose skin was dark. The advocacy group, along with the East Louisiana Railroad Company, which sought to abolish the law—largely because it cost the company money—sought a test case that would challenge the constitutionality of the law.

Plessy's Arrest The two parties chose Plessy, a twenty-nine-year-old shoemaker who was a Louisiana resident and U.S. citizen. On June 7, 1892, Plessy purchased a first-class train ticket from New Orleans to Covington, Louisiana, and sat in the railroad car designated For Whites Only. The railroad officials, following through on their arrangement with the American Citizens' Equal Rights Association of Louisiana Against Class Legislation, had Plessy arrested.

Louisiana Courts Hear the Case Two white lawyers, Albion Tourgée (1838–1905), a well-known advocate for black rights, and his assistant, James C. Walker, handled the case pro bono (without compensation). Tourgée entered a plea before Judge John H. Ferguson of the Criminal District Court for the Parish of New Orleans, arguing that the Separate Car Act was null and void because it violated the Thirteenth and Fourteenth amendments to the U.S. Constitution. The Thirteenth Amendment bans slavery, and the Fourteenth Amendment requires that the government treat all people equally under the law. In a previous court decision, Ferguson had stated that the Separate Car Act was unconstitutional if it applied to trains running outside of Louisiana. In this case, however, he argued that the act was constitutional because the train on which Plessy rode was running within the state of Louisiana. Therefore, he found Plessy guilty. The case was appealed to the Louisiana Supreme Court, which affirmed the decision.

The U.S. Supreme Court Hears the Case Plessy's attorneys argued the case before the U.S. Supreme Court in 1896. (The case bears Ferguson's name because he had been named in the petition to the Louisiana Supreme Court, not because he was a party to the initial lawsuit.) The majority (eight of the nine justices), in an opinion written by Justice Henry Billings Brown (1836–1913), upheld state-imposed racial segregation and ruled against Plessy. Separate facilities for blacks and whites satisfied the Fourteenth Amendment, the Court said, as long as those facilities were equal. Brown conceded that the Fourteenth Amendment intended to establish absolute equality for the races before the law, but noted that the amendment was not intended to abolish distinctions based on color or to enforce social

"OUR CONSTITUTION IS COLOR-BLIND"

In *Plessy v. Ferguson*, the U.S. Supreme Court ruled eight to one that the Fourteenth Amendment created "absolute equality" of blacks and whites, but those rights extended only to political and civil rights and not to social rights (e.g., the right to choose any seat on a train). The following is an excerpt from the dissenting opinion of Justice John Marshall Harlan (1833–1911):

> In view of the constitution ... there is in this country no superior, dominant, ruling class of citizens.... Our constitution is color-blind, and neither knows nor tolerates classes among citizens. In respect of civil rights, all citizens are equal before the law. The humblest is the peer of the most powerful. The law regards man as man, and takes no account of his surroundings or of his color when his civil rights as guarantied by the supreme law of the land are involved. It is therefore to be regretted that this high tribunal, the final expositor of the fundamental law of the land, has reached the conclusion that it is competent for a state to regulate the enjoyment by citizens of their civil rights solely upon the basis of race.
>
> In my opinion, the judgment this day rendered will, in time, prove to be quite as pernicious as the decision made by this tribunal in the Dred Scott Case. It was adjudged in that case that the descendants of Africans who were imported into this country and sold as slaves were not included nor intended to be included under the word "citizens" in the Constitution, and could not claim any of

the rights and privileges which that instrument provided for and secured to citizens of the United States; that at the time of the adoption of the Constitution they were "considered as a subordinate and inferior class of beings, who had been subjugated by the dominant race, and, whether emancipated or not, yet remained subject to their authority, and had no rights or privileges but such as those who held the power and the government might choose to grant them." The recent amendments of the Constitution ... had eradicated these principles from our institutions. But it seems that we have yet, in some of the States, a dominant race—a superior class of citizens, which assumes to regulate the enjoyment of civil rights, common to all citizens, upon the basis of race. The present decision ... will not only stimulate aggressions ... upon the admitted rights of colored citizens, but will encourage the belief that it is possible ... to defeat the beneficent purposes which the people of the United States had in view when they adopted the recent amendments of the Constitution, by one of which the blacks of this country were made citizens of the United States and of the States in which they respectively reside, and whose privileges and immunities, as citizens, the States are forbidden to abridge.

SOURCE: Plessy v. Ferguson *(163 U.S. 537 [1896]). http://caselaw.lp. findlaw.com/scripts/printer_friendly.pl?page=us/163/537.html (accessed May 15, 2007).*

---

equality; therefore, segregation did not in itself constitute unlawful discrimination.

A Dissenting Opinion Justice John Marshall Harlan (1833–1911) dissented from the majority opinion, asserting that justice should be color blind and that enforcing "separate but equal" measures interferes with the personal freedoms of individuals by legally forcing separation.

Impact of the Decision The majority decision in *Plessy v. Ferguson* served as the legal justification for racial segregation for the following fifty years. It was overturned by the Supreme Court in 1954 in *Brown v. Board of Education*, which declared that separate public schools for blacks and whites were unequal and, therefore, unconstitutional. This ruling signaled the fall of segregation in the United States.

The Seventeenth Amendment

The Seventeenth Amendment to the U.S. Constitution called for the election of two U.S. senators from every state by popular vote. Before the ratification of this amendment in 1913, state legislatures had elected or

appointed U.S. senators. The law was passed after decades of insistence that the public should have the power to elect members of both the U.S. House of Representatives and the U.S. Senate by popular vote.

A Change of Opinion The framers of the U.S. Constitution had reservations about the wisdom of majority rule and worried that uninformed voters would be determining public policy. Even though they allowed for direct election of members of the House of Representatives, who serve two-year terms, they decided that legislatures would select members of the Senate, who serve six-year terms. When the Constitution was being drawn up, only one proposal for senatorial election by popular vote was offered, and it was soundly defeated. The states did not protest when the Constitution was sent to them for ratification, and during the next several decades the system was generally supported.

By the late nineteenth century, however, the public wanted a more fully participatory democracy. Complaints rose that too much power was concentrated in the hands of state legislatures, which were dominated by party bosses who prevented citizen participation. Evidence of the practical disadvantages of the system, as well as the potential for abuse of power, mounted as well: deadlocks within legislatures resulted in Senate vacancies for long periods, legislative decisions were influenced by corrupt political organizations and special interest groups that "purchased" legislative seats, and the long electoral contests caused lawmakers to neglect their other government duties.

Before the passage of the Seventeenth Amendment, some states modified their laws to allow voters to choose senatorial candidates in primary elections. These unofficial nominations were then sent to the state legislatures, which elected senators from among the nominees—usually the candidate who received the majority of the votes. In several states candidates for the legislature had to promise to support the senatorial candidate receiving the most votes in the primary election, regardless of party affiliation. As a result of these legislative changes, by 1912—one year before the amendment was ratified—at least twenty-nine states were nominating senators on a popular basis.

Congress resisted the change, arguing that direct election of senators would rob states of their independence and sovereignty. By 1910, however, thirty-one state legislatures had requested that Congress hold a constitutional convention to propose an amendment. The next year Congress bowed to the pressure and passed the amendment. Within two years the Seventeenth Amendment had been ratified by the states.

The Effects of the Amendment Ratification of the Seventeenth Amendment changed some operations of the Senate. When states elected senators, they could direct their senators to vote a certain way on matters of great substance. The amendment formally ended that connection because senators were accountable only to voters. Historians disagree, however, on how much the change affected the actual practice of the Senate.

Historians and legal scholars also debate the amendment's effectiveness. Some view it as a serious surrender of state sovereignty; others see it as a harmless or even positive outgrowth of popular will. Direct election of senators may, in some places, have contributed to a decline in the power of party bosses, which would have suited progressive reformers.

Schenck v. United States

In *Schenck v. United States* (1919), the U.S. Supreme Court, for the first time, ruled directly on the extent to which the federal government could limit free speech. After reviewing the conviction of Charles T. Schenck, who circulated thousands of leaflets to men who had been drafted into military service, the Court found that, in certain contexts, speech could be curtailed under the U.S. Constitution. The speech had to create what the Court called a "clear and present danger" to bring about "substantial evils" to society.

"A CLEAR AND PRESENT DANGER"

In his opinion in *Schenck v. United States*, Justice Oliver Wendell Holmes Jr. (1841–1935) stressed that the context in which words are uttered determines whether those words violate the First Amendment. The following is an excerpt:

> We admit that in many places and in ordinary times the defendants in saying all that was said in the circular would have been within their constitutional rights. But the character of every act depends upon the circumstances in which it is done …

> The most stringent protection of free speech would not protect a man in falsely shouting fire in a theatre and causing a panic. It does not even protect a man from an injunction against uttering words that may have all the effect of force . . . .

> The question in every case is whether the words used are used in such circumstances and are of such a nature as to create a clear and present danger that they will bring about the substantive evils that Congress has a right to prevent. It is a question of proximity and degree. When a nation is at war many things that might be said in time of peace are such a hindrance to its effort that their utterance will not be endured so long as men fight and that no Court could regard them as protected by any constitutional right.

SOURCE: Schenck v. United States *(249 U.S. 47 [1919]). http://case-law.lp.findlaw.com/scripts/printer_friendly.pl?page=us/249/47.html (accessed May 15, 2007).*

Involuntary Servitude To acquire a sufficient number of troops to fight in World War I (1914–1918), Congress passed the Selective Service Act of 1917, which required men between the ages of twenty-one and thirty to register for military service. The age range was later changed to eighteen to forty-five.

Schenck, the general secretary of the U.S. Socialist Party, and his wife, Elizabeth Baer, who served on the party's executive board, opposed the war and believed that U.S. involvement was wrong. By forcing young men to fight and die for an unjust cause, in their view, the Selective Service Act violated the Thirteenth Amendment, which outlawed slavery and involuntary servitude except when a person had been convicted of a crime.

Schenck and Baer published their antidraft views in a leaflet, which they mailed to fifteen thousand recent draftees in Philadelphia. Asserting that the draft was morally wrong and perpetrated by the capitalist system, the leaflet informed draftees of their constitutional rights and urged them to resist. In addition, the leaflet advised the draftees to initiate peaceful forms of protest.

After a few recipients complained to postal inspectors about the leaflets, the Socialist Party headquarters was raided and documents were seized. Schenck and Baer were charged with conspiring to violate the Espionage Act of 1917, which made it illegal to interfere with the operation of the U.S. armed forces. According to the federal prosecutor in Philadelphia, Schenck and Baer's message promoted disloyalty toward the armed forces and made recruiting soldiers for the war more difficult. Schenck and Baer were found guilty and sentenced to fifteen years in federal prison.

The Appeal to the Supreme Court Schenck's attorneys argued, on appeal to the Supreme Court, that the contents of the leaflet were protected by the First Amendment's guarantee of freedom of speech. That freedom, they maintained, granted all citizens the right to speak or print their political opinions as long as those opinions do not incite immediate illegal action.

Attorneys for the U.S. government argued that the First Amendment's guarantee of free speech does not include the freedom to obstruct the draft by making disparaging remarks about it. As was argued in the lower court, the attorneys asserted that Schenck and Baer's message promoted disloyalty toward the armed forces and made it more difficult for the U.S. Army to recruit soldiers for the war.

The Court's Decision In a unanimous decision, the Court upheld Schenck's conviction. It said the circumstances in which words are spoken can determine their constitutionality and can allow them to be curtailed. According to the Court, in peacetime Schenck's pamphlets may have been protected by the Constitution; during wartime, however, no citizen has the right to speak or to publish with the intent of unlawfully obstructing—or inciting others to obstruct—the recruitment process. The Court also made a distinction between speech protected by the First Amendment (e.g., publicly criticizing the government) and unprotected speech (calling for an illegal action, such as resisting the draft).

Impact of the Decision Even though this ruling was later overturned, the Court's decision was significant in clarifying the standard—the clear and present danger test—by which certain political utterances were judged for the next fifty years. Justice Oliver Wendell Holmes Jr. (1841–1935) later maintained that the decision had been abused by the federal government in cases involving the prosecution of political dissidents. In 1919 in *Abrams v. United States* Holmes reversed himself and modified his test to include only those present dangers relating to immediate and illegal action rather than to ideas. He adhered to his interpretation of protected speech throughout the next decade, and by the 1930s, the test was generally accepted doctrine.

Decades later, the clear and present danger test was further, and most significantly, restricted in *Brandenberg v. Ohio*. The Court ruled in 1969 that inflammatory speech is only unprotected if it is a call to "imminent action." Despite the reformulation of the clear and present danger test in subsequent decisions, *Schenck v. United States* retained constitutional force in cases involving freedom of speech into the twenty-first century.

See also **Socialist Party**
See also **World War I**

The Nineteenth Amendment

The Nineteenth Amendment to the U.S. Constitution, which granted women the right to vote, was passed by Congress in 1919 and ratified by state legislatures in 1920. Achieving the vote took decades of agitation and protest.

A Variety of Strategies Beginning in the mid-nineteenth century, several generations of woman suffrage supporters lectured, wrote, marched, lobbied, and practiced civil disobedience to achieve what many Americans considered a radical change to the Constitution. Few early supporters lived to see final victory in 1920.

Between 1878, when the amendment was first introduced in Congress, and 1920, when it was ratified, advocates of voting rights for women tried a variety of strategies to achieve their goal. Some women pursued suffrage laws in each state; nine western states adopted woman suffrage legislation by 1912. Others challenged male-only voting laws in the federal courts. Militant suffragists, such as Alice Paul (1885–1977) and Lucy Burns (1879–1966), the founders of the National Woman's Party, organized parades, silent vigils, and hunger strikes. Often, supporters met fierce resistance and were heckled and jailed.

By 1916 almost all the major suffrage organizations were united behind the goal of a constitutional amendment. When New York adopted suffrage for women in 1917 and President Woodrow Wilson (1913–1921) changed his position to support an amendment in 1918, the political balance began to shift.

On May 21, 1919, the U.S. House of Representatives passed the amendment; two weeks later the U.S. Senate followed. Even though some states in the South rejected it, the amendment passed its final hurdle when Tennessee became the thirty-sixth state to ratify it on August 18, 1920.

The Amendment's Legacy When it became law, twenty-six million women—about half the population—suddenly became eligible to participate fully in U.S. politics. Traditional social and political systems were profoundly changed: issues of importance to women could no longer be ignored because they were supported by women's ability to vote for candidates for political office.

Some of the most significant changes in the following decades affected women's everyday lives, including regulation of workplaces and children's well-being (e.g., laws against child labor).

> *See also* **Alice Paul**
> *See also* **National Woman's Party**
> *See also* **Women's Suffrage Movement**

Gitlow v. New York

In *Gitlow v. New York*, the U.S. Supreme Court said for the first time that the First Amendment's free-speech clause applied to state governments as well as to the federal government. The 1925 ruling is considered a landmark case in First Amendment rights and in the relationship between the federal government and the states.

Details of the Case Benjamin Gitlow (1891–1965) was convicted in New York for publishing and circulating pamphlets and leaflets that advocated harm to the government. One of the pamphlets, the *Left Wing Manifesto*, called for the overthrow of the government by violent means so a socialist state could be established. Gitlow's attorney, Clarence Darrow (1857–1938), argued that the statute under which Gitlow was arrested—a New York law that punished those who advocated overthrowing the government by force—violated the First Amendment's guarantee of freedom of expression. The Supreme Court upheld the constitutionality of the state law and Gitlow's conviction.

The Gitlow case arose after the Russian Revolution of 1917, which overthrew the czar and began the advance toward communism, and in the midst of the Red Scare in the United States. During the Red Scare—a period of fear of communists, socialists, and other dissidents—Americans believed a revolution such as the one in Russia was possible in the United States.

Government officials fed this fear by spreading rumors of plots to overthrow the U.S. government. Attorney General A. Mitchell Palmer (1872–1936) staged raids against "subversive" groups, rounded up "radicals"—many of whom were immigrants and were deported—and set up an antiradicalism division at the U.S. Department of Justice. This new department, which was run by J. Edgar Hoover (1895–1972), later became the Federal Bureau of Investigation. Many states passed antirevolution laws that forbid public statements that called for violent revolution against the U.S. government.

During the Red Scare, New York officials actively sought to enforce a long-dormant law, the Criminal Anarchy Act. The law, which was passed shortly after the assassination of President William McKinley (1843–1901) in Buffalo, New York, by the anarchist Leon F. Czolgosz (1873–1901), imposed a criminal penalty on anyone who advocated violent overthrow of the government.

"A SUFFICIENT DANGER OF SUBSTANTIVE EVIL"

In *Gitlow v. New York*, the U.S. Supreme Court ruled that free speech is limited for anyone who advocates a doctrine of violent revolution. The following is an excerpt from the 1925 decision, written by Justice Edward Terry Sanford (1865–1930):

> That utterances inciting to the overthrow of organized government by unlawful means present a sufficient danger of substantive evil to bring their punishment within the range of legislative discretion is clear. Such utterances, by their very nature, involve danger to the public peace and to the security of the State. They threaten breaches of the peace, and ultimate revolution. And the immediate danger is none the less real and substantial because the effect of a given utterance cannot be accurately foreseen....

> In *People v. Lloyd*, it was aptly said: "Manifestly, the legislature has authority to forbid the advocacy of a doctrine designed and intended to overthrow the government without waiting until there is a present and imminent danger of the success of the plan advocated. If the State were compelled to wait until the apprehended danger became certain, then its right to protect itself would come into being simultaneously with the overthrow of the government, when there ... would be neither prosecuting officers nor courts for the enforcement of the law."

> We cannot hold that the present statute is an arbitrary or unreasonable exercise of the police power of the State unwarrantably infringing the freedom of speech or press, and we must and do sustain its constitutionality....

> The general statement in the Schenck Case [which involved the extent of the U.S. government's right to limit free speech] that "the question in every case is whether the words are used in such circumstances and are of such a nature as to create a clear and present danger that they will bring about the substantive evils"—upon which great reliance is placed in the defendant's argument—was manifestly intended, as shown by the context, to apply only in cases of this class, and has no application to those like the present, where the legislative body itself has previously determined the danger of substantive evil arising from utterances of a specified character.

SOURCE: Gitlow v. New York *(268 U.S. 652 [1925]). http://www.law.cornell.edu/supct/html/historics/USSC_CR_0268_0652_ZO.html (accessed April 7, 2007).*

In 1919 Gitlow, a member of the American Socialist Party, became dissatisfied with the party's moderate socialism. He and other members of the party's left-wing faction called for revolution and broke from the party at a convention in New York City. They began to advocate more aggressive tactics, including violence. The left-wing convention appointed a committee, under Gitlow's leadership, to create a manifesto modeled after the *Communist Manifesto* by Karl Marx (1818–1883) and Friedrich Engels (1820–1895). The committee's *Left Wing Manifesto* urged the overthrow of organized U.S. government by force, violence, and other "unlawful means" for the purpose of establishing a socialist state.

Under Gitlow's leadership, sixteen thousand copies of the manifesto were printed and distributed. The June 1919 issue of Gitlow's radical pamphlet, *The Revolutionary Age*, reprinted the document. Gitlow also supported the circulation of the manifesto among the American Socialist Party's left-wing members and traveled throughout New York publicly advocating the manifesto and its principles. He was arrested, charged with criminal anarchy, and convicted in 1923.

Constitutional Issues

Gitlow's case raised issues pertaining to the First and Fourteenth amendments to the U.S. Constitution. One issue was whether the New York law against criminal anarchy could deprive Gitlow of his liberty of expression under the due process clause of the Fourteenth Amendment, which prohibits any state from depriving "any person of life, liberty, or property, without due process of law." Another issue was whether the New York law was constitutional. For the first time, the Supreme Court was asked to consider whether the Fourteenth Amendment "incorporated" the freedoms of the Bill of Rights—the first ten amendments to the Constitution—into the constitutions of the states. In Gitlow's case the specific issue was whether the Fourteenth Amendment afforded Gitlow, in state court, the same protections provided by the First Amendment to a citizen in federal court. The Fourteenth Amendment requires states to provide equal protection under the law to all people within their jurisdictions The question became which portions of the Bill of Rights were guaranteed by the Fourteenth Amendment.

Gitlow's attorneys argued that New York could not show that any harm resulted from their client's exercise of freedom of speech and press. They also maintained that the Constitution protected Gitlow's speech unless that speech presented a "clear and present danger" to society. There was no evidence, they said, that anyone had been influenced to any action by Gitlow's manifesto. In addition, they claimed that the New York law was an unconstitutional limit imposed by a state on a First Amendment right. The Fourteenth Amendment's guarantee that states could not make or enforce a law that would curtail the "privileges or immunities" of citizens of the United States was, they argued, violated in this case.

Attorneys for New York argued that any state had the authority to prevent violence and disorder and that the New York legislature had acted properly and constitutionally in creating laws to ensure the public safety.

They said Gitlow had violated those laws by engaging in actions that threatened great harm to the people of New York. Furthermore, they argued that the Supreme Court should not interfere in the internal affairs of a state because that action would violate the principles of federalism. Lastly, they maintained that Gitlow's First Amendment rights to freedom of speech were protected in the New York state constitution.

Decision and Rationale

In a seven to two decision, the Court upheld the conviction and ruled the New York law constitutional. Justice Edward Terry Sanford (1865–1930), who wrote the majority opinion, emphasized that freedom of speech and of the press, which is guaranteed by the Constitution, does not mean that a person is allowed to say anything at any time or that a person is allowed to speak without responsibility.

The Court, Sanford wrote, could not hold that the state infringed on Gitlow's freedom of speech or press without warrant. Gitlow's manifesto was not merely "the expression of philosophical abstraction" but was phrased in such a way as to call for direct incitement against the U.S. government. New York had determined that certain utterances involve "danger of substantial evil" and that Gitlow's utterances involved such evil and deserve to be punished.

Justices Oliver Wendell Holmes Jr. (1841–1935) and Louis Brandeis (1856–1941), in their dissenting opinion, argued that "every idea is an incitement" and that "eloquence can set fire to reason." They wrote, however, that regardless of what others thought about Gitlow's manifesto, there was no chance that the pamphlet could cause a "present conflagration." Therefore, it presented no "clear and present danger," and Gitlow's conviction should be overturned.

Significance of the Case

Even though the Supreme Court upheld the state law and Gitlow's conviction, the importance of the case lies in the arguments that Gitlow's attorneys brought before the Court. For the first time, the Court considered the implications of what has become known as "incorporation doctrine"—how provisions of the First Amendment were incorporated or added into state constitutions by the Fourteenth Amendment. The argument over incorporation opened the door to landmark decisions in future years.

See also **Schenck v. United States**

See also **Socialist Party**

Temperance and Prohibition

The temperance movement (1830s–1918) was an organized effort to encourage moderation in or complete abstinence from the consumption of alcoholic beverages. Political pressure from the movement resulted in the ratification in 1919 of the Eighteenth Amendment to the U.S. Constitution, which banned the "manufacture, sale, or transportation of intoxicating liquors" in the

Raiding a still in Mt. Vernon, New York, 1925.   © *Bettmann/CORBIS*

United States. It created a period known as Prohibition, which came to an end in 1933 with the ratification of the Twenty-first Amendment, which repealed the Eighteenth Amendment and restored control of alcohol to the states.

Origins of the Movement

In the colonial era informal social controls in the home and community were effective in maintaining general moderation in the use of alcohol. As the colonies expanded and cities grew, economic change and urbanization led to increasing poverty, unemployment, and crime—which were often blamed on alcoholism. Following the Revolutionary War (1775–1783) the new nation experienced major social, political, and economic changes that affected every segment of society. Social control over alcohol use decreased, antidrunkenness ordinances were relaxed, and alcohol-related problems increased dramatically.

The Rise of Temperance Associations

Given the environment, people sought explanations and solutions for drinking problems. One suggestion came from the physician Benjamin Rush (1713–1813), who signed the Declaration of Independence. In 1784 he noted that excessive use of alcohol was harmful to physical and psychological health. His solution was temperance, or moderation; he did not, however, propose banning the consumption of alcohol. Apparently influenced by Rush's ideas, which were widely disseminated and discussed, some two hundred farmers in Connecticut formed a temperance association in 1789. Similar associations were formed in Virginia in 1800 and New York in 1808. Within the next decade, temperance organizations formed in eight other states.

The early movement advocated temperance rather than abstinence. Many of the leaders expanded their activities and took positions on gambling, profanity, and other moral issues as well. Political disagreements turned into bickering, so by the early 1820s the movement's efforts stalled.

Some leaders persevered, however. The American Temperance Society was formed in 1826, aided by a renewed interest in religion and morality in the nation. Within ten years the society had more than 1.5 million members. By 1839 fifteen temperance journals were being published, and many Protestant churches began to promote temperance.

Temperance Leads to Prohibition

Although the temperance movement began with a belief in moderation, between 1830 and 1840 most temperance organizations maintained that the only way to prevent alcoholism was to ban the consumption of alcohol entirely. The Temperance Society was transformed into the Abstinence Society. The Independent Order of Good Templars, the Sons of Temperance, the Templars of Honor and Temperance, the Anti-Saloon League, the National Prohibition Party, and other groups were formed and expanded rapidly. The temperance societies also grew increasingly extreme in their actions, proclaiming their cause with an almost religious zeal.

For temperance advocates the legal prohibition of alcohol became a major issue in every political election from the national to the local level. Prohibitionists turned to pressure politics—not only on candidates running for office but also on voters. Women in the movement sometimes took their children to marches, where they sang temperance songs—one more way to exert pressure on voters.

The Anti-Saloon League stressed its religious character and presented itself as an agent of the churches. Therefore, anything it did was seen as moral and justified because the organization was working to bring about God's will. The league grew so powerful that national politicians feared its strength.

Woman's Christian Temperance Union

The Woman's Christian Temperance Union (WCTU) was founded after the Civil War (1861–1865). Its name was misleading, for it did not promote moderation or temperance; rather, it insisted on Prohibition. To achieve its goals, it focused on education. Its founders believed that if the organization could gain access to students, it could create an anti-alcohol, or "dry," reaction that would eventually help the Prohibition cause.

In 1880 the WCTU established a Department of Scientific Temperance Instruction in Schools and Colleges, with Mary Hunt (1830–1906) as the national superintendent. She believed that to make alcohol illegal voters would need to be educated about its dangers. Because students would be the next generation of voters,

Federal agents emptying liquor bottles into a sewer, c. 1933. *© Bettmann/CORBIS*

she encouraged legislation to coerce students toward her point of view. Her ideas led to the compulsory Scientific Temperance Instruction Movement, an anti-alcohol education program in schools.

By 1900 Hunt's efforts had proved successful. Nearly every state had strong legislation mandating that all students receive anti-alcohol education. The implementation of this legislation was closely monitored—at the classroom level—by vigilant WCTU members. Many historians view the WCTU's program of compulsory temperance education as a major factor in the establishment of national Prohibition.

Temperance Movement Expands Because it saw a correlation between drinking and domestic violence, the temperance movement existed alongside various women's rights groups, including the suffrage movement, which fought to establish the vote for women. Former abolitionists, who had worked to end slavery, joined the temperance movement as well.

The movement was also strongly supported by what is considered the second Ku Klux Klan (KKK). The first KKK, formed by former Confederate (southern) soldiers

from the Civil War, worked to stop the integration of freed slaves into the U.S. political, social, and economic systems. The first KKK was disbanded under the Civil Rights Act of 1871. A second KKK, however, was revived in Georgia in 1915, largely to defend that state's Prohibition laws but also to promote racism, anti-Semitism, and anti-Catholicism. Promoting and even enforcing temperance became a major focus of the KKK's agenda

Prohibition Laws Passed After the Eighteenth Amendment was ratified in 1919, Congress passed the Volstead Act to enforce national Prohibition. It established definitions for "intoxicating alcohol" and criminal penalties for violation of the law. It also superseded all state laws regarding Prohibition.

For decades many Americans had embraced Prohibition as a remedy for all of society's ills, including poverty, crime, and violence. Many communities were so certain it would solve their criminal problems that they sold their jails. The actual consequences of Prohibition were unanticipated—and ranged from undesirable to disastrous and deadly.

The law was immediately countered by illegal activity. Bootlegging, which became the common name for the buying and selling of illegal alcohol, was widespread. Bootleggers sold alcohol brought into the United States from Canada and other countries by organized smuggling operations. Among the most common smuggling operations were the rum rows—lines of ships that anchored just beyond the three-mile limit off the coasts of large cities—that off-loaded their cargo onto speedboats, which smuggled the liquor ashore. Murder and hijacking were common in this dangerous and lucrative business. Prohibition led to massive corruption of politicians and law enforcement officers and helped finance powerful crime syndicates, such as the operation run by Al Capone (1899–1947) in Chicago.

Perhaps the most unexpected side effects of Prohibition were the death and disability caused by bootleg liquor: blindness and paralysis often resulted from contaminants such as lead, embalming fluid, industrial alcohol, and creosote in bootleg liquor.

The Fight for Repeal Enthusiastic support from industrialists and business leaders had helped enact Prohibition. As time passed, however, an increasing number of those same business leaders, such as John D. Rockefeller (1839–1937), became disillusioned because of the consequences of the law.

As surprising, women, who had been pivotal in bringing about national Prohibition because of moral interests—protecting the family, women, and children from the effects of alcohol abuse—proved to be equally pivotal in repealing Prohibition. Their interest, once again, was moral: Prohibition was undermining the family and corrupting the morals of women, children, and all of society.

When the president of the WCTU declared to Congress that she represented the views of all U.S. women, Pauline Sabin (1887–1955) decided to organize women for repeal. In 1929 she founded the Women's Legion for True Temperance, which was later renamed the Women's Organization for National Prohibition Reform. Even though she had been a proponent of Prohibition, Sabin became disturbed by what she saw as hypocrisy once the law was passed: politicians would vote for stricter enforcement of the Eighteenth Amendment and then illegally drink alcohol themselves. She also became convinced that Prohibition was counterproductive. Once the law was passed, moderate drinking declined and binge drinking increased, resulting in more public intoxication and disrespect for law and law enforcement. Furthermore, Sabin saw an erosion of personal liberty at the hands of an increasingly intrusive centralized government.

Sabin and millions of other women came to oppose Prohibition for the very reasons they originally supported it: they wanted the world to be a safer place for

their children. Furthermore, politically women were much more powerful than before Prohibition; since 1920 they were able to vote.

The number of repeal organizations grew, and the demand for repeal intensified. The country had entered the Great Depression, when millions were unemployed, agricultural prices fell, tax revenues dropped, and the future appeared desolate. Many came to believe that legalizing alcohol would increase prices for grain and other farm commodities; increase the demand for labor to produce, transport, and sell alcohol; and increase revenues from taxes on alcohol.

Prohibition Repealed In the 1932 presidential election the Democratic Party platform included an anti-Prohibition plank, and Franklin D. Roosevelt (1882–1945), the Democratic governor of New York, ran for president promising to repeal Prohibition. Congress passed a constitutional amendment to repeal Prohibition in February 1933; it had achieved ratification by December. The Twenty-first Amendment, which officially

---

"THE TEMPERANCE ARMY"

"The Temperance Army" was sung by Christian women during the latter part of the nineteenth century. Written by J. M. Kieffer and published by S. Brainard's Sons of Cleveland, it is part of the collection *Music for the Nation, 1870–1885* at the Library of Congress.

1. Now the temp'rance army's marching,
   With the Christian's armor on;
   Love our motto, Christian Captain,
   Prohibition is our song!

2. Now the temp'rance army's marching,
   Firm and steady in our tread;
   See! the mothers they are leading,
   Marching boldly at the head.

3. Now the temp'rance army's marching,
   Wives and Sisters in the throng;
   Shouting: "Total Prohibition!"
   As we bravely march along.

Chorus:

Yes, the temp'rance army's marching,
And will march forevermore,
And our triumph shall be sounded,
Round the world from shore to shore,
Marching on, Marching on forevermore,
And our triumph shall be sounded,
Round the world from shore to shore.

SOURCE: *"The Temperance Army."* http://memory.loc.gov/learn/features/timeline/progress/prohib/song.html (accessed May 15, 2007).

---

brought the Prohibition era in the United States to an end, repealed the Eighteenth Amendment; made it again legal to import, produce, and sell alcoholic beverages; and delegated to the individual states authority for regulating alcohol.

Some states continued to enforce Prohibition at the state level; Mississippi was the last to repeal it in 1966. Almost two-thirds of all states adopted some form of local option, which enabled residents to vote for or against local Prohibition.

Impact of the Movement Constitutionally mandated Prohibition was generally regarded as an abysmal failure. Its most adverse effects on society included the growth of a large and powerful underworld of bootlegging, smuggling, organized crime, and brutal violence. However, the failure of Prohibition to cure society's ills eventually made people take a more realistic look at the factors that caused disruptions in families and the workplace. In the decades that followed reformers would call for an end to child labor, advocate better working conditions and the eight-hour workday, and initiate programs that reduced economic uncertainty.

BIBLIOGRAPHY

Books

Cashman, Sean Dennis. *America in the Gilded Age: From the Death of Lincoln to the Rise of Theodore Roosevelt.* 3rd ed. New York: New York University Press, 1993.

Chambers, John Whiteclay, II. *The Tyranny of Change: America in the Progressive Era, 1890–1920.* 2nd ed. New Brunswick, N.J.: Rutgers University Press, 2000.

Crunden, Robert M. *Ministers of Reform: The Progressives' Achievement in American Civilization, 1889–1920.* New York: Basic Books, 1982.

Daniels, Roger. *Coming to America: A History of Immigration and Ethnicity in American Life.* New York: HarperCollins, 1990.

Dawley, Alan. *Struggles for Justice: Social Responsibility and the Liberal State.* Cambridge, Mass.: Belknap Press of Harvard University, 1991.

Gould, Lewis L. *Reform and Regulation: American Politics from Roosevelt to Wilson.* 3rd ed. Prospect Heights, Ill.: Waveland Press, 1996.

Harris, Thomas E. *Analysis of the Clash over the Issues between Booker T. Washington and W. E. B. Du Bois.* New York: Garland Publishers, 1993.

Hine, Robert V., and John Mack Faragher. *The American West: A New Interpretive History.* New Haven, Conn.: Yale University Press, 2000.

Hofstadter, Richard. *The Age of Reform: From Bryan to F.D.R.* New York: Vintage, 1955.

———. *The Progressive Movement: 1900–1915.* Englewood Cliffs, N.J.: Prentice-Hall, 1963.

Holli, Melvin. *The Progressive Era*, edited by Louis Gould. Syracuse, N.Y.: Syracuse University Press, 1986.

Keller, Morton, and R. Shep Melnick, eds. *Taking Stock: American Government in the Twentieth Century.* Cambridge, U.K.: Cambridge University Press, 1999.

Kennedy, David M. *Over Here: The First World War and American Society.* New York: Oxford University Press, 1980.

Link, Arthur S., and Richard L. McCormick. *Progressivism.* Wheeling, Ill.: Harlan Davidson, 1983.

McMath, Robert C., Jr. *American Populism: A Social History, 1877–1898.* New York: Hill and Wang, 1990.

Milkis, Sidney M., and Jerome M. Mileur. *Progressivism and the New Democracy.* Amherst: University of Massachusetts Press, 1999.

Mowry, George E. *Theodore Roosevelt and the Progressive Movement.* New York: Hill and Wang, 1960.

Rodgers, Daniel T. *Atlantic Crossings: Social Politics in a Progressive Age.* Cambridge, Mass.: Belknap Press of Harvard University Press, 1998.

Skocpol, Theda. *Protecting Soldiers and Mothers: The Political Origins of Social Policy in the United States.* Reprint, Cambridge, Mass.: Belknap Press of Harvard University Press, 1995.

Wood, Stephen B. *Constitutional Politics in the Progressive Era: Child Labor and the Law.* Chicago: University of Chicago Press, 1968.

Periodicals

Buenker, John D. "The Progressive Era: A Search for a Synthesis." *Mid-America* 51 (1969): 175–193.

Diggins, John P. "Republicanism and Progressivism." *American Quarterly* 37 (Autumn 1985): 572–598.

Filene, Peter G. "An Obituary for the Progressive Movement." *American Quarterly* 22 (Spring 1970): 20–34.

Fox, Richard W. "The Culture of Liberal Protestant Progressivism." *Journal of Interdisciplinary History* 23 (Winter 1993): 639–660.

McCormick, Richard L. "The Discovery That Business Corrupts Politics: A Reappraisal of the Origins of Progressivism." *American Historical Review* 86 (April 1981): 247–274.

Ross, Dorothy. "Woodrow Wilson and the Case for Psychohistory." *Journal of American History* 69 (1982): 659–668.

Testi, Arnoldo. "The Gender of Politics Reform: Theodore Roosevelt and the Culture of Masculinity." *Journal of American History* 81 (March 1995): 1509–1533.

Thelen, David P. "Social Tensions and the Origins of Progressivism." *Journal of American History* 56 (September 1969): 323–341.

Web Sites

Humanities and Social Services Online. "Gilded Age and Progressive Era Resources." http://www.h-net.msu.edu/~shgape/internet/index.html (accessed May 15, 2007).

Ohio State University History Department. "Temperance and Prohibition History." http://prohibition.osu.edu/ (accessed May 15, 2007).

Library of Congress. "Progressive Era, 1890–1910." *America's Story from America's Library.* http://www.americaslibrary.gov/cgi-bin/page.cgi/jb/progress (accessed May 15, 2007)

Public Broadcasting Service. "The Great War and the Shaping of the Twentieth Century." http://www.pbs.org/greatwar/ (accessed May 15, 2007).

Susan B. Anthony Center for Women's Leadership. "Suffrage History." http://www.rochester.edu/SBA/suffragehistory.html (accessed May 15, 2007).

Theodore Roosevelt Association. http://www.theodoreroosevelt.org/ (accessed May 15, 2007).

Introduction to the Great Depression and World War II (1929–1945)

The era of the Great Depression and World War II was a roller-coaster ride for the United States. When the stock market crashed, ending the plenty of the 1920s, the country slid into an economic crisis that brought unemployment, hunger, and hardship to millions of people. A severe drought deepened the misery, as winds scraped dried-out soil into dust storms and turned a huge part of the Great Plains into a desolate dust bowl. America's entry into World War II rejuvenated the economy but also thrust the nation into years of hard-fought battle with high casualty rates. In the end massive U.S. military might and a new weapon—the atomic bomb—made the difference. Victory by the United States and its allies brought euphoria and a hope that the new United Nations could avert future warfare.

The United States came out of World War II extremely strong, both economically and politically: it had become one of the world's true superpowers. This amazing transformation—from destitution to power and wealth—occurred in little more than a decade.

Two presidents served during most of those years—Herbert Hoover (1874–1964) and Franklin Roosevelt (1882–1945). Hoover was elected in 1928 during a time of prosperity for most Americans. He left office in 1933 as the scapegoat for the nation's deep economic troubles. In 1932 Roosevelt was elected in a landslide with promises of a "new deal" for Americans. The population, enchanted by his charismatic, folksy style, returned him to office three more times. Only death could stop the political juggernaut that he became.

The Depression era was a time of great law-making. Dozens of new programs and agencies were created, largely because Roosevelt enjoyed a highly cooperative Congress that agreed with most of his agenda. The U.S. Supreme Court was not as cooperative, at least during his early years in office. It declared several of the New Deal laws unconstitutional, which so angered the president that he tried to reorganize and expand the Court—critics called it his "court-packing plan." A major misstep, his proposal did not find political support. Ultimately the New Deal was an economic and social experiment with mixed results. While many of its efforts were temporary, some of its programs and agencies have survived to the present day.

Within his own party Roosevelt walked a tightrope between northern and southern Democrats. Much of the South was still dominated by "Jim Crow laws," under which African-Americans were supposed to have access to "separate but equal" facilities. While separation was strictly enforced, equality was nowhere close to a reality. The burgeoning civil rights movement found enthusiastic supporters in some quarters, including the president's wife, Eleanor Roosevelt (1884–1962). Her more cautious husband chose to tread carefully on matters of race, lest he offend his southern supporters. The result was an era with mixed messages for minorities. Some progress was made, and some opportunities were lost.

The overriding political story of the era was federalism—the division of power between the federal government and state and local governments. Before this time the federal government had little impact on the everyday lives of Americans. They were much more affected by the actions of their state and local authorities. The Great Depression and World War II were such overwhelming events—truly national emergencies—that Americans accepted a much more powerful role for their federal government, particularly the executive branch. Millions were desperate; they put their faith in Roosevelt. This political shift had a long-term effect on the national psyche, considerably raising people's expectations of the federal government.

The Great Depression and World War II (1929–1945)

✪ How They Were Governed

The Tennessee Valley Authority

The Tennessee Valley Authority (TVA) was established in 1933 to bring flood and navigation control, electricity production, and agricultural and industrial development to parts of southern Appalachia. It played a vital role in national defense during World War II by providing electricity to industries important to the war effort and to a top-secret government complex that helped develop the atomic bomb.

The Tennessee Valley The Tennessee River flows southward from the Great Smoky Mountains in eastern Tennessee, across northern Alabama, and then northward across western Tennessee into Kentucky. The river basin, as well as the nearby Ohio and Mississippi rivers, was prone to floods that brought malaria-bearing mosquitoes and hardship to local residents. Decades of flooding and soil erosion, combined with local farming practices, had depleted the agricultural productivity of the area. Navigation of the Tennessee River was complicated by steep drops in elevation along its course and a series of massive sandbars in the Alabama stretch.

During World War I the federal government built a dam on the river and operated nitrate plants for munitions production near the town of Muscle Shoals, Alabama. Oklahoma Senator George Norris (1861–1944), a progressive Republican who championed the causes of small farmers, persuaded President Franklin Roosevelt (1882–1945) to use the government-owned complex at Muscle Shoals as the headquarters for a new agency devoted to improving the environmental, economic, and social conditions of farmers in the valley. Roosevelt created an independent agency that operated almost like a private corporation.

In May 1933 Congress passed the Tennessee Valley Authority Act to "improve the navigability and to provide for the flood control of the Tennessee River; to provide for reforestation and the proper use of marginal lands in the Tennessee Valley; to provide for the agricultural and industrial development of said valley; to provide for the national defense by the creation of a corporation for the operation of Government properties at and near Muscle Shoals in the State of Alabama, and for other purposes." The new agency developed fertilizers, planted trees, controlled forest fires, and improved habitats for fish and wildlife. It also began an ambitious dam-building program along the Tennessee River to rein in its unpredictable waters.

The Dam Controversy The first dam was completed in 1936 and named for Norris; more than a dozen more were constructed by 1944, an unprecedented feat of U.S. engineering. Besides much-needed jobs, the projects provided electrical power that was distributed through a network of

Workers with the Tennessee Valley Authority. © *Arthur Rothstein/ CORBIS*

Water pouring from the spillways of the Pickwick Landing Dam, a project of the Tennessee Valley Authority. © *CORBIS*

municipal power boards and rural electric cooperatives—the TVA law had specifically called for the extension of electrical service to rural areas. By the end of World War II the agency was the largest electrical supplier in the country.

Because the dams were built to generate electricity, private utility companies viewed them as unfair competition from the government and took TVA to court. The U.S. Supreme Court considered the issue in *Ashwander v. TVA* (1935) and *Tennessee Electric Power Company v. TVA* (1939). In both cases, the constitutionality of the TVA was upheld.

The War Effort During World War II TVA played a vital role by providing nitrate for munitions and electrical power to key industries in the region, particularly the Alcoa Company near Knoxville, Tennessee, which operated the largest aluminum plant in the world. Nearby was a small community, Oak Ridge, that was chosen for a top-secret government complex devoted to development of the first atomic bomb.

The Postwar Decades Following the war TVA continued to operate and expand its growing electrical network.

During the 1950s the agency began building coal-fired power plants in the Tennessee Valley. Eventually those plants provided more electricity than the hydroelectric plants at TVA's dams. In 1959 Congress passed amendments to the TVA law, allowing the agency to sell bonds to finance its operations, instead of depending on government appropriations. By that time the Tennessee Valley had evolved into a thriving region with a huge appetite for electrical power. During the 1960s and 1970s TVA constructed three nuclear power plants in the area. The agency's expansion slowed over the following decades because of increasing energy costs and deregulation within the utility industry. Nevertheless, TVA remains the largest public power supplier in the United States.

The Federal Communications Commission

The Federal Communications Commission (FCC) was created in 1934 to regulate interstate communications via the airwaves. The telecommunications industry, at the time in its infancy, included only telegraph, telephone, and radio transmissions. Technological advances since then have greatly expanded the types of transmitting services subject to FCC jurisdiction and raised questions about the relevancy of the agency.

Formation of the FCC In January 1934 President Franklin Roosevelt (1882–1945) suggested that the regulation of interstate communications be centralized in one agency. Regulatory authority had been fragmented between the Interstate Commerce Commission, the Postmaster General, and the Federal Radio Commission. Congress passed the Communications Act of 1934 with little debate because it made only modest changes to the existing regulatory framework. Title I of the law established the Federal Communications Commission to oversee telephone-service providers and radio broadcasting. The Federal Radio Commission was abolished.

The FCC had a seven-person board appointed by Roosevelt. Eugene Sykes (1876–1941), a Democrat from Mississippi, was its first chairman.

The Telephone Giant When the FCC was created the nation's telephone service was dominated by one company, American Telephone and Telegraph (AT&T), which included a number of companies that handled local telephone services (the Bell Operating Companies) and Western Electric, which manufactured telephone equipment. In 1935 AT&T companies serviced nearly 96 percent of the nation's 14 million telephone subscribers. The federal government chose to tighten regulation of the corporate giant, rather than dismantle it.

After focusing intense scrutiny on the policies of AT&T, the FCC in 1938 released a report (known as the Walker report, after Commissioner Paul Walker) that harshly criticized the company's business practices. The backlash from AT&T and the press caused the FCC to issue a milder version of the report a year later. World War II precluded any government action for a decade. In 1949 the U.S. Department of Justice filed an antitrust lawsuit against the company, using many of the same arguments that had been raised in the Walker report. After a seven-year court battle AT&T agreed to change some of its operations.

Regulating Radio As successor to the Federal Radio Commission, the FCC assumed jurisdiction over commercial AM and FM radio and amateur (ham) radio transmissions. In the Radio Act of 1927 Congress had declared that the electromagnetic frequencies over which radio waves are propagated are a national resource because they are limited—radio signals can be transmitted over a finite number of frequencies. That decision created fierce competition for licenses from the FCC.

The authority of the FCC to regulate and license radio stations was upheld by the U.S. Supreme Court in two major cases, *Columbia Broadcasting System v. United States* (1942) and *National Broadcasting System v. FCC* (1943). In the majority opinion in the first case Justice Felix Frankfurter wrote: "The Act itself establishes that the Commission's powers are not limited to the engineering and technical aspects of regulation of radio communica-

tion. Yet we are asked to regard the Commission as a kind of traffic officer, policing the wave lengths to prevent stations from interfering with each other. But the Act does not restrict the Commission merely to supervision of the traffic. It puts upon the Commission the burden of determining the composition of that traffic. The facilities of radio are not large enough to accommodate all who wish to use them. Methods must be devised for choosing from among the many who apply. And since Congress itself could not do this, it committed the task to the Commission." The opinion in the second case, also written by Frankfurter, used similar language: "Regulation of radio was therefore as vital to its development as traffic control was to the development of the automobile."

Universal Access The Communications Act of 1934 required the FCC to "make available, so far as possible, to all the people of the United States a rapid, efficient, nationwide, and worldwide wire and radio communication service with adequate facilities at reasonable charges." This clause has been interpreted to mean that universal access to telephone service should be provided. During the 1930s few rural areas were serviced by AT&T because the costs to the company of installing telephone lines and associated facilities were prohibitive. A similar problem with electric power was addressed by the Rural Electrification Administration (REA), an agency created by President Roosevelt in 1935, which brought electricity to rural areas not served by private utilities. In 1949, when just over a third of all farms had telephones, Congress added the provision of rural telephone service to the REA's mandate. By 1979 REA loan programs had helped provide phone service to more than 90 percent of the nation's farms.

The Telecommunications Explosion The decades that followed the creation of the FCC witnessed an explosion in new telecommunications services. Television became popular following World War II and fell under the jurisdiction of the agency. Initially television signals were transmitted through the airwaves. The development of cable television raised questions about the FCC's regulatory authority. In 1968 the Supreme Court upheld the agency's jurisdiction in *United States v. Southwestern Cable Company*. Fifty years after its passage the Communications Act was amended by the Cable Communications Policy Act of 1984, which established policies relating to cable ownership, channel usage, subscriber rates, and other issues. Congress also clarified the jurisdictional boundaries between federal, state, and local governments regarding the regulation of cable television.

The space age presented new challenges to the FCC as well. Satellite transmissions, fiber optics, cell phones, and digital and broadband technologies have greatly changed telecommunications. Deregulation and competition in the telephone industry have eliminated the job of the FCC as a monopoly regulator. Some critics question whether the agency is still relevant and blame it for slowing industry innovations. The FCC has defended its actions, claiming that regulatory barriers on the

A WPA road construction project in New York City. © *Bettmann/CORBIS*

telecommunications industry have been put in place by Congress and the courts.

The Works Progress Administration

The Works Progress Administration (WPA) was a massive federal jobs program implemented by President Franklin Roosevelt (1882–1945) during the Great Depression to relieve high unemployment. The WPA employed millions of people, primarily as construction workers or laborers on public works projects, such as dams and bridges. Smaller programs created work for unemployed people in the arts—writers, artists, musicians, and actors. The WPA paid just enough for people to afford the bare necessities of life.

The WPA was a part of the New Deal, Roosevelt's program to revitalize America. The Emergency Relief Appropriations Act of 1935 authorized the president to fund programs providing aid and work to Americans. Executive Order 7034 created the WPA, which was placed under the leadership of Harry Hopkins (1890–1946)—a close adviser to Roosevelt with a history of social work. Because of the size and budget of the programs under Hopkins's control, he was often referred to as the second most powerful man in America.

The WPA was widely criticized. Labor leaders complained that it depressed wages for workers in private industry. Roosevelt's Republican critics accused him of using the WPA to buy votes from the nation's unemployed. Some people viewed it as a government boondoggle that created "busy work." Said Roosevelt in response: "If we can boondoggle ourselves out of this depression, that word is going to be enshrined in the hearts of the people for many years to come."

Blue-Collar Jobs   The bulk of employment provided by the WPA was menial labor. Workers constructed more than six hundred thousand miles of roads; built or repaired thousands of schools, hospitals, sports stadiums, police stations, city halls, courthouses, museums, and bridges; enlarged and improved hundred of airports; planted millions of trees in parks and other public areas; and laid thousands of miles of storm drains and sewer lines around the country. The vast majority of WPA workers were men. Women were employed primarily in lower-paying positions as seamstresses or in educational and recreational fields, such as nursery schools or school lunch programs.

The Arts Program   The WPA's Arts Program was known as Federal Project Number One—Federal One, for short. It originally included four components—the Federal Writers' Project, the Federal Theatre Project, the Federal Music Project, and the Federal Art Project. In 1936 the Historical Records Survey, a part of the Federal Writers' Project, was designated a separate program under Federal One.

The Federal Writers' Project employed approximately 6,500 people at its peak and produced nearly a thousand publications, including some very popular tourism guidebooks. Some writers interviewed thousands of people around the country to create anthologies about Americans

Demonstrators in San Francisco protesting the layoff of WPA workers in 1936.   © *Horace Bristol/CORBIS*

from different walks of life. The material was never published, but is maintained by the Library of Congress for researchers interested in the life stories of people who lived during the Great Depression. The Historical Records Survey made an inventory of all county government records; incomplete when Federal One ended, it was taken over in some cases by county and state officials.

The Federal Theatre Project funded plays, musical revues, and circuses, which were performed around the country, either for free or for a small fee. The project was led by Hallie Flanagan (1890–1969), a longtime friend of Hopkins. Government funding of plays proved to be especially controversial and attracted the scrutiny of the Dies Committee, a House committee that investigated "un-American activities." The WPA's theater program was accused of employing many Communist sympathizers and was shut down in 1939. The Federal Music Project financed traveling orchestras and paid for the writing of new musical compositions. Those employed by the Federal Art Project created thousands of sculptures and murals for public buildings, primarily post offices.

The Legacy By December 1942 the nation was deeply involved in World War II and facing a labor shortage. Roosevelt ended the WPA, noting that it had wielded "a creative hand" and "strengthened the country." The creative mis-

sion of the WPA's Arts Program was resurrected in 1965 in the National Foundation on the Arts and the Humanities, an independent government agency created to promote the humanities, arts, and cultural heritage of the United States. Its programs have grown to include the National Endowment for the Arts, the National Endowment for the Humanities, the Federal Council on the Arts and the Humanities, and the Institute of Museum and Library Services.

The Federal Bureau of Investigation

The Federal Bureau of Investigation (FBI), the first agency to fight crime on a national level, built a strong reputation during the Great Depression for capturing gangsters and during World War II for thwarting wartime espionage. The agency, which was created from an existing agency in 1935, gained prominence under the leadership of J. Edgar Hoover (1895–1972), who was its director for more than three decades. Hoover realized his vision of establishing a force of well-trained professionals equipped with high-technology tools for fighting crime. His leadership, however, also raised serious questions about the agency's infringements of citizens' civil rights and abuse of its power. He left a mixed legacy for an agency motivated by the motto "Fidelity. Bravery. Integrity."

The Roots of the FBI In 1908 U.S. Attorney General Charles Bonaparte (1851–1921) formed a squadron of special agents within the U.S. Department of Justice to investigate federal crimes—crimes that crossed state lines or occurred on federal lands, such as Native American reservations. A year later the squadron was named the Bureau of Investigation (BOI). Although it was headquartered in Washington, D.C., it established a network of field offices around the country to handle the few offenses that were federal crimes—at the time state and local authorities had jurisdiction over most crimes. Nevertheless, the agency's work increased as Congress passed such laws as the Mann Act (1910), which outlawed interstate transport of women for "immoral purposes," and the National Motor Vehicle Theft Act (1919), which outlawed interstate transport of stolen vehicles.

During World War I the BOI investigated people suspected of spying for foreign governments or conducting espionage, sabotage, or sedition (speech or conduct intended to incite insurrection against the government). Following the war the BOI concentrated on rooting Communists and their sympathizers out of the United States. In 1919 a bombing by radicals of the home of U.S. Attorney General A. Mitchell Palmer (1872–1936) sparked a series of raids, conducted without search warrants, during which hundreds of people were rounded up on suspicion of engaging in radical activities. Many were later deported. The raids were spearheaded by Hoover, then a young investigator. He so impressed his superiors that in 1924 they appointed him director of the BOI.

Prohibition and the Depression With the passage in 1919 of a constitutional amendment that prohibited the manufacture, transport, and sale of alcoholic beverages—Prohibition—a national crime wave was brought on after the amendment became law the following year. Liquor laws were widely violated, and bootleggers flourished. Automobiles made them and other criminals more mobile—they could simply move from one law-enforcement jurisdiction to the next and avoid capture. Eventually criminal syndicates gained power and exploited corrupt law-enforcement officials to further their organizations. A spirit of lawlessness took hold.

The stock market crash of 1929 and the ensuing Great Depression made the public cynical about government authority. Magazines, novels, and movies specialized in hard-core crime fiction that featured tough-guy gangsters. The exploits of real criminals were widely covered in the media and made celebrities of such outlaws as Bonnie Parker (1910–1934), Clyde Barrow (1909–1934), Al Capone (1899–1947), John Dillinger (1903–1934), Charles "Pretty Boy" Floyd (1901–1934), and Kate "Ma" Barker (1871–1935) and her gang.

Hoover launched a media campaign to turn public opinion against these romanticized criminals. His effort was helped by two tragic events. The first was the 1932 kidnapping of Charles Lindbergh, Jr., the infant son of the first aviator to fly solo across the Atlantic Ocean nonstop. The BOI joined the investigation at the invitation of President Franklin Roosevelt (1882–1945) and, through painstaking detective work, tracked down Bruno

WARNING
from the
FBI

The war against spies and saboteurs demands the aid of every American.

When you see evidence of sabotage, notify the Federal Bureau of Investigation at once.

When you suspect the presence of enemy agents, tell it to the FBI.

Beware of those who spread enemy propaganda! <u>Don't repeat vicious rumors or vicious whispers.</u>

Tell it to the FBI!

  J. Edgar Hoover, *Director*
Federal Bureau of Investigation

The nearest Federal Bureau of Investigation office is listed on page one of your telephone directory.

An FBI poster signed by J. Edgar Hoover warning against espionage. © *CORBIS*

Hauptmann (1899–1936), who was executed for murdering the baby. That case led to the Federal Kidnapping (or Lindbergh) Act, which made kidnapping a federal crime. In 1933, in the "Kansas City Massacre," four law-enforcement officers were killed when Pretty Boy Floyd tried to free a friend being transported to prison. The shootings mobilized the public and Congress to action. A series of new federal laws greatly expanded the role and scope of the BOI. For the first time its agents were authorized to carry guns and make arrests.

Under Hoover's direction the agency conducted research in criminology and forensics, which led to new methods for investigating crimes and to sophisticated laboratory equipment for identifying suspects. In 1935 the BOI was renamed the Federal Bureau of Investigation, and the FBI National Academy was established to train law-enforcement officials from around the country (and later from around the world). Hoover's public-relations efforts succeeded as well: government agents (eventually referred to as "G-men") became the heroes in the movies and the media, feeding the public's desire for some order in a chaotic time of economic depression.

Subversion and World War II By 1936 all of the notorious gangsters were dead or captured, so Roosevelt authorized the FBI to focus on national security concerns. Growing political unrest in Europe and the Far East had Roosevelt worried about Fascist and Communist threats in the United States. When the nation entered World War II in 1941 the FBI was already deeply involved in investigating subversive activity. The Smith Act (or Alien Registration Act) of 1940 made it illegal for anyone to conduct any activity or make any statement advocating the violent overthrow of the U.S. government. With the help of a double agent, the FBI broke up a spy ring, headed by Frederick Duquesne (1887–1956), that was working on behalf of Nazi Germany. Thirty-three people were convicted. After Congress created the first peacetime military draft, the FBI became responsible for tracking down draft dodgers and military deserters.

Immediately after the Japanese attack on Pearl Harbor, the U.S. naval station in Hawaii, on December 7, 1941, the FBI began rounding up Japanese citizens who were considered security threats and turned them over to military or immigrations officials. Because Hoover considered this action sufficient to protect national security, he viewed as unnecessary the relocation of many Japanese American and Japanese-born citizens to internment camps. Other government officials—especially the military—thought otherwise. In 1942 the FBI captured a group of German agents that had come ashore on the East Coast intent on conducting sabotage. One of the men turned himself in and helped the agency capture the others. That incident, in particular, helped bolster confidence in the FBI. By the end of 1943 the agency employed more than thirteen thousand people, including some four thousand specially trained agents.

In 1940 Roosevelt established an elite corps of FBI agents called the Special Intelligence Service (SIS). Working undercover, SIS agents were dispatched throughout Central and South America where they rooted out hundreds of Nazi spies, smugglers, and saboteurs and discovered dozens of secret radio stations that passed information to Germany. U.S. agents destroyed many of the stations, but used others to feed misleading information to the German military. Although the SIS was abolished after World War II, its work was continued by the Central Intelligence Agency, which was created in 1947.

Civil Rights In 1939 U.S. Attorney General Frank Murphy (1890–1949) created the Civil Rights Section (CRS) of the Department of Justice. Relying on the investigatory skills of the FBI, it prosecuted cases in which the civil rights of citizens had been infringed. Because segregation was legal throughout the South, the CRS concentrated on more easily prosecuted issues, such as peonage—involuntary work to pay off a debt or obligation. For example, because laborers were scarce during the war, young African-American men were often lured to farms with promises of well-paying jobs—only to learn that their transportation or room and board had to be paid off through labor. In 1942 the U.S. Sugar Cor-

poration was indicted on charges of holding laborers in peonage in Florida, but the charges were dropped.

At the same time that the FBI was investigating alleged civil rights abuses, it was also collecting information and spying upon U.S. citizens who were believed to pose threats to national security. In 1949 the FBI learned that Soviet spies had infiltrated the top-secret Manhattan Project, which was established to develop an atomic bomb, and had obtained key data. Information about the spy network came from the Venona Project, a secret undertaking by U.S. and British intelligence agencies to decode Soviet diplomatic messages they had intercepted. The decryption revealed activities by Soviet spies within the United States and led to the convictions of several people, most famously Julius (1918–1953) and Ethel (1915–1953) Rosenberg, who were executed. Hoover believed the "red menace," as communism was called, extended deeply into U.S. society, so he authorized intelligence gathering on many prominent Americans. Labor leaders and vocal advocates of civil rights, including Eleanor Roosevelt (1884–1962), the president's wife, were his primary targets during the 1930s and 1940s.

An Expanded Role for the FBI The FBI played a much larger role in the civil rights struggles of the 1950s and 1960s as the government acquired greater legal leeway to prosecute violations at the federal level. FBI agents investigated cases involving voter rights, murders of civil rights workers, and the Ku Klux Klan, the fraternal organization that advocated white supremacy. Organized crime became the focus in 1957 after Congress created or broadened federal jurisdiction over crimes involving racketeering and gambling. In addition new laws expanded the FBI's authority to use electronic surveillance techniques.

An FBI poster for James Earl Ray, the assassin of Martin Luther King, Jr., 1968. © *Bettmann/CORBIS*

A TRAIL OF GOLD TO THE LINDBERGH BABY

The kidnapping and murder of the Lindbergh baby was considered the "crime of the century" in 1932. The twenty-month-old toddler was the son of aviator Charles Lindbergh (1902–1974), who had thrilled Americans with his nonstop solo flight across the Atlantic Ocean in 1927, and writer Anne Morrow Lindbergh (1906–2001). The baby disappeared from his second-story bedroom on the evening of March 1, 1932. The local police found a broken, homemade wooden ladder outside the house, which suggested that the kidnapper had fallen as he escaped. A crudely written note left on the windowsill demanded a $50,000 ransom. News of the crime spread quickly, and the Lindberghs announced publicly that they intended to pay.

The day after the kidnapping President Franklin Roosevelt (1882–1945) asked the FBI—then called the Bureau of Investigation—to assist local and state authorities, even though kidnapping was not then a federal crime. The case took many bizarre twists. The baby's nurse committed suicide after being questioned repeatedly by authorities. A retired school principal in New York, John Condon, placed an ad in a newspaper, offering to pass messages between the kidnapper and the Lindberghs. Surprisingly, the kidnapper contacted Condon and passed along additional ransom notes and the baby's pajamas. After the ransom was paid, the kidnapper gave

Condon a note with the supposed location of the baby, but it proved to be false. On May 12, 1932, the baby's body was found by accident only a few miles from the Lindbergh home. He had died of skull fractures. Authorities believed the baby died instantly when he and his kidnapper tumbled from the ladder on the night of the crime.

The Lindberghs had paid the ransom in gold notes—a form of paper currency that could be exchanged immediately for gold. The FBI had recorded the serial numbers of the gold notes and began to look for them at banks and businesses. Their mission was made easier by the president's decision to require Americans to turn over nearly all of their gold to the government. Gold coins and gold notes streamed into federal banks. More than two years after the kidnapping the notes used in the ransom were found and traced back to the businesses that had deposited them. At one of those businesses, a gas station, an employee had scribbled down the license-plate number of a car driven by the man who had given him the gold note. Investigators captured that man, Bruno Hauptmann (1899–1936), at his home in New York. Hauptmann was convicted of murder and executed by electrocution. The FBI earned high praise for its role. The case spurred Congress to make kidnapping a federal crime.

Until 1971 the FBI operated the Counterintelligence Program, or COINTELPRO, in which it spied on people and organizations it deemed to be threats to national security, including civil rights leaders and antiwar protesters. After the public learned about COINTELPRO, new limits were placed on the FBI's abilities to conduct such investigations.

Hoover remained as director of the FBI until his death in 1972. During his long tenure he collected a wealth of personal and often embarrassing information about many public figures for his "private files." Although he is credited with building a highly professional and effective crime-fighting force, the revelations about his personal files and COINTELPRO seriously damaged the FBI's reputation. During the subsequent decades the agency has increasingly dealt with nontraditional threats to law and order, such as white-collar crime, gangs, the international drug trade, Internet-related crime, and terrorism.

Japanese American Internment

During World War II the U.S. government forcibly relocated 120,000 Japanese immigrants and their descendants from their homes on the West Coast because it feared they could aid the Japanese war effort. More than 60 percent of those affected were U.S. citizens. Approximately ten thousand people were relocated to cities in the interior of the United States, while the remainder were resettled in internment camps. Although the United

States was also at war with Germany and Italy and there were far greater numbers of German-born and Italian-born immigrants in the country, no blanket action was taken to avoid possible treason by members of those groups. The U.S. government officially apologized for this policy nearly forty years later.

Fear after Pearl Harbor The Japanese attack on Pearl Harbor, the U.S. naval station in Hawaii, on December 7, 1941, plunged the nation into war with Japan and its European allies, Germany and Italy. The attack also temporarily crippled the Pacific Fleet, which had been headquartered and docked at Pearl Harbor. Fear rose that Japan, taking advantage of that weakness, would attack or even invade the U.S. mainland. At the same time apprehension grew that Japanese agents inside the country could aid an attack through espionage or sabotage.

Political Support for Internment Soon after the attack politicians and citizens' groups in California began accusing Japanese Americans on the West Coast of collaboration with Japan and called for Japanese immigrants and Japanese Americans to be "secured" by the federal government. Among the prominent politicians supporting these measures were California Representative Leland Ford (1893–1965) and California Attorney General Earl Warren (1891–1974), who would later be chief justice of the U.S. Supreme Court. In the military, support for evacuation of these groups from the Pacific Coast was led by Major

Japanese Americans at an internment camp lining up for a meal, 1942. © *Seattle Post-Intelligencer Collection; Museum of History and Industry/ CORBIS*

General Allen W. Gullion, the U.S. Army's chief law enforcement officer, and Lieutenant General John L. De-Witt, the commander of the army's Western Defense Command.

Many of those calling for action had actually supported laws to restrict Japanese immigration long before hostilities broke out. In the early twentieth century labor groups and farming concerns on the West Coast formed anti-Asian associations to fight the economic effects of inexpensive Asian labor. In 1907 agitation by such groups led to a gentlemen's agreement, under which Japan agreed to stop issuing passports to Japanese citizens for travel to the United States, in effect curtailing new immigration. In return the United States agreed to allow the immigration of current residents' spouses, children, and parents and pledged that Japanese schoolchildren would not be forced to attend racially segregated schools.

The Government Takes Action On February 19, 1942, President Franklin Roosevelt (1882–1945) signed

Executive Order 9066, which authorized the creation of "military areas … from which any or all persons may be excluded, and with respect to which, the right of any person to enter, remain in, or leave shall be subject to whatever restrictions" the military decided to impose. Roosevelt's order did not name the Japanese specifically, but rather delegated blanket authority to exclude "any and all persons" to the secretary of war or to any military commanders designated by the secretary. That meant DeWitt—who was famously quoted as saying, "A Jap's a Jap…. It makes no difference whether he is an American citizen or not"—would eventually have the authority to evacuate Japanese Americans from the western states.

On March 2, 1942, DeWitt issued a proclamation declaring the Pacific Coast Military Area No. 1 and informing all persons of Japanese ancestry that they would eventually be evacuated from the area. On March 24 he declared a curfew from 8 p.m. to 6 a.m. for Japanese Americans in Military Area No. 1. Three days later, seeing that Japanese were leaving the Pacific Coast of their own

KOREMATSU V. UNITED STATES (1944)

In the U.S. Supreme Court case *Korematsu v. United States*, the Japanese internment was challenged on behalf of Fred Korematsu (1919–2005), a U.S.-born citizen of Japanese descent who disobeyed orders to relocate to an internment camp. The following excerpt is from the Court's majority opinion, written by Justice Hugo Black (1886–1971):

It should be noted, to begin with, that all legal restrictions which curtail the civil rights of a single racial group are immediately suspect. That is not to say that all such restrictions are unconstitutional. It is to say that courts must subject them to the most rigid scrutiny. Pressing public necessity may sometimes justify the existence of such restrictions; racial antagonism never can....

Like curfew, exclusion of those of Japanese origin was deemed necessary because of the presence of an unascertained number of disloyal members of the group, most of whom we have no doubt were loyal to this country. It was because we could not reject the finding of the military authorities that it was impossible to bring about an immediate segregation of the disloyal from the loyal that we sustained the validity of the curfew order as applying to the whole group.... That there were members of the group who retained loyalties to Japan has been confirmed by investigations made subsequent to the exclusion. Approximately five thousand American citizens of Japanese ancestry refused to swear unqualified allegiance to the United States and to renounce allegiance to the Japanese Emperor, and several thousand evacuees requested repatriation to Japan.

This excerpt is from the dissenting opinion written by Justice Robert H. Jackson (1892–1954):

Korematsu was born on our soil, of parents born in Japan. The Constitution makes him a citizen of the United States by nativity and a citizen of California by residence. No claim is made that he is not loyal to this country.... Korematsu, however, has been convicted of an act not commonly a crime. It consists merely of being present in the state whereof he is a citizen, near the place where he was born, and where all his life he has lived. Even more unusual is the series of military orders which made this conduct a crime. They forbid such a one to remain, and they also forbid him to leave. They were so drawn that the only way Korematsu could avoid violation was to give himself up to the military authority. This meant submission to custody, examination, and transportation out of the territory, to be followed by indeterminate confinement in detention camps....

Now, if any fundamental assumption underlies our system, it is that guilt is personal and not inheritable. Even if all of one's antecedents had been convicted of treason, the Constitution forbids its penalties to be visited upon him, for it provides that "no attainder of treason shall work corruption of blood, or forfeiture except during the life of the person attainted." But here is an attempt to make an otherwise innocent act a crime merely because this prisoner is the son of parents as to whom he had no choice, and belongs to a race from which there is no way to resign.

SOURCE: Korematsu v. United States, *323 U.S. 214 (1944), U.S. Government Printing Office, http://www.fedworld.gov/cgi-bin/waisgate?waisdocid= 2479331490+1+0+0&waisaction=retrieve (accessed February 7, 2007).*

accord, DeWitt issued a proclamation prohibiting any person of Japanese ancestry from leaving Military Area No. 1 without military authorization.

Through Executive Orders 9095 and 9102, the president created the Office of the Alien Property Custodian, which had the authority to freeze or confiscate the property of non-U.S. nationals, and the War Relocation Authority (WRA), which would be responsible for the relocation and internment of Japanese Americans. To head the WRA the president chose Milton S. Eisenhower (1899–1985), brother of General Dwight Eisenhower (1890–1969), who commanded U.S. troops in Europe during the war and became president in 1953.

On May 3, 1942, DeWitt issued a Civilian Exclusion Order requiring all persons of Japanese ancestry in the Military Areas to report to assembly areas, bringing with them only as much luggage as they could carry. From the assembly areas, they were taken to the WRA's internment camps.

Life in the Camps WRA operated ten internment camps in California, Arizona, Colorado, Utah, Arkansas, Wyoming, and Idaho. The most famous of them was the Manzanar War Relocation Center in inland California, which at its peak held more than ten thousand internees. Accommodations at most camps consisted of crudely built wooden houses with tar-paper roofs and shared latrines. Families lived together in a single room, and single individuals shared rooms with people to whom they were not related. The camps had schools for the many interned children.

The internees were required to sign loyalty oaths, in which they proclaimed sole loyalty to the U.S. government. Signing such an oath did not ensure release from the camps, but refusing to sign targeted people for transfer to tougher camps or for deportation to Japan. Within the camps, tension ran high between those who opposed internment and those internees suspected of cooperating with the WRA.

Some internees joined the armed forces to prove their loyalty to the United States, serving in Europe during the war. Others were able to leave the camps by securing employment away from the West Coast or by having churches or other organizations in the interior of the country sponsor them. Most remained interned until the war was nearly over.

Legal Challenges to the Internment With the assistance of the American Civil Liberties Union, internees mounted legal challenges. Four of those cases reached the U.S. Supreme Court. *Hirabayashi v. United States* and *Yasui v. United States* were both brought in 1943 on behalf of Japanese Americans who violated curfew, but the Court found that the curfew imposed by De-Witt's orders was constitutional. A third challenge was brought on behalf of Fred Korematsu (1919–2005), a U.S. citizen who disobeyed the relocation order. In a 1944 ruling the Court upheld the constitutionality of the order, citing the judgment of military commanders that the evacuation of Japanese Americans from the West Coast was a "military imperative." At the same time the *Korematsu v. United States* decision set forth the principle that any law that singled out a racial group for disparate treatment would be subject to "strict scrutiny"—that is, the highest standard of judicial review regarding an action's constitutionality. That concept would later be used in such segregation cases as *Brown v. Topeka Board of Education.*

In the fourth case, *Ex parte Endo*, the Court ordered the WRA to release Mitsuye Endo, a Japanese American who had continued to be held in an internment camp despite having been granted leave, but the case was considered a limited victory because the decision turned on technical rather than constitutional issues. The December 1944 ruling came too late to inspire additional challenges to the internment. In January 1945 President Roosevelt decided that the camps had served their purpose and ordered the WRA to release the internees.

Aftermath and Reparations Many of the interned Japanese Americans returned from confinement to find that nothing tangible remained of the lives they had left behind. Many had sold their farms, homes, and businesses at steeply discounted prices prior to being sent to the camps. Those who had not sold their property frequently found that they had been foreclosed upon in absentia or that their property had been vandalized while it lay vacant. The vehicles of many internees had been appropriated by the military "to aid in the war effort." Some internees who had left their personal property in the charge of churches or in storage for safety found that those places had been looted.

Many could not return to the West Coast. They had been released to work or into the custody of charitable groups in the interior of the country. Japanese Americans who returned to California faced the threat of violence from those who saw their release as "a second Pearl Harbor."

In 1948 Congress passed the Evacuee Claims Act, which was meant to provide restitution for monetary losses suffered by those who had been evacuated or interned. Payments under the law, however, generally fell far below the losses that the evacuees and internees had suffered, and activists continued to press for equitable reparations and an apology from the government. In 1976 President Gerald Ford (1913–2006) officially rescinded Executive Order 9066, and twelve years later Congress passed the Civil Liberties Act of 1988, which authorized an official apology from the government and a payment of $20,000 to each surviving internee, at a total cost of $1.2 billion.

✪ Important Figures of the Day

Herbert Hoover

Herbert Hoover (1874–1964), the thirty-first president of the United States, started his administration with optimism: "I have no fears for the future of our country," he said in his inaugural address in March 1929. "It is bright with hope." That hope was crushed the following October when the stock market collapsed and the nation plunged into the Great Depression. Despite Hoover's efforts to ameliorate its effects, he became the scapegoat for the economic woes that befell the nation.

Early Public Service Born in Iowa to a poor Quaker family, Hoover was raised by relatives after his parents died. He earned an engineering degree from Stanford University and developed a successful mining company, which made him a millionaire. Hoover was also a dedicated public servant. During World War I he headed the U.S. Food Administration, which ensured that farmers produced enough food for the nation and its allies. Following the war he headed the American Relief Administration, which transported food to millions of people in Europe. Hoover served as secretary of commerce in the administrations of two presidents—Warren Harding (1921–1923) and Calvin Coolidge (1923–1929).

Hoover's Presidency In 1928 the Republican Party, which had held the presidency and dominated Congress throughout the prosperous 1920s, nominated Hoover for president. He won easily, garnering 444 of the 531 electoral votes, even though he had never been elected to public office before. He was rather shy and tended to speak in a dull monotone, but he was viewed as a compassionate humanitarian and a practical problem-solver—his nickname was the Great Engineer.

Hoover initiated a number of programs and reforms: he cut taxes for low-income Americans; established a Federal Farm Board to aid struggling farmers and the Veterans Administration to assist war veterans; and reorganized the Bureau of Indian Affairs and the federal criminal justice system—reform of the prison system shifted the focus from punishment to rehabilitation.

Presidential candidate Herbert Hoover campaigning with his running mate, Charles Curtis, 1928. © AP/Wide World Photos

The legacy of Hoover's presidency, however, was to be the Great Depression.

Onset of the Great Depression In previous years the federal government had taken a hands-off, or laissez-faire, approach to the economy. So when it began to falter, Hoover's secretary of the treasury, Andrew Mellon (1855–1937), and other economists advised him to limit government intervention. They held the traditional view that factors of supply and demand would eventually allow the economy to recover on its own. Hoover was not convinced.

During his service as secretary of commerce Hoover had forged strong ties with the business community, so as president he held several conferences at which he asked industry leaders to raise production, to keep employment rates high, and to avoid cutting wages. At first the business community was agreeable—industrialist Henry Ford even raised wages as a sign of confidence; eventually, however, the measures could not be sustained as prices and profits fell.

Past economic turndowns had been temporary dips in prosperity, so the nation remained optimistic through early 1930. Food prices began to recover, indicating improving conditions for farmers, and Hoover received the credit. The recovery was short-lived. The summer of 1930 brought a devastating drought to the South and Midwest, with repercussions across the country. During

the 1930 midterm elections Democratic candidates capitalized on the nation's dissatisfaction with Hoover and took control of Congress. Throughout the remainder of his term Hoover accused his opponents of sabotaging his efforts for their own political gain.

The Depression Deepens In 1931 the Depression swept across Europe, which was still struggling to recover from World War I. Part of the blame went to the Smoot-Hawley Tariff Act of 1930, which Hoover originally championed as a way to get better prices for U.S. agricultural products. The act had grown in scope, however, creating high tariffs on many imported goods. The nation's trading partners retaliated by imposing their own tariffs. As a result international trade dropped sharply, spreading the economic downturn worldwide.

Although Hoover agonized in private over the Depression's effects, in public he refused to acknowledge that it was as serious as it was. In fact, he often assured the public that it would soon end. His radio addresses were filled with economic statistics and did not speak to the suffering endured by millions of people. Hoover's critics persuaded the public that he was a cold and callous man. Shantytowns that sprang up around the country were called "Hoovervilles."

A staunch believer in personal responsibility, Hoover was at first opposed to federal aid programs for individuals. His Reconstruction Finance Corporation borrowed

Advertisement for a Hoover campaign film, c. 1928. © *CORBIS*

money from the U.S. Treasury and lent it to ailing banks and railroad corporations, public works projects, and state agencies engaged in relief efforts. As conditions got worse, however, he changed his mind and began providing some direct financial aid to individuals. The money arrived too late to mitigate the damage already done to his image.

As the Depression lingered it severely curtailed the amount of money received by the federal government. Spending outpaced revenues, creating a federal deficit. The Revenue Act of 1932, which instituted broad tax increases, primarily on the consumption of goods, hit Americans already burdened by high unemployment and low wages. Hoover began his campaign for reelection as a very unpopular president.

Hoover Leaves Office The presidential election of November 1932 pitted a demonized Hoover against the charismatic Democratic governor of New York, Franklin Roosevelt (1882–1945). Roosevelt, exuding confidence,

promised a "new deal" for Americans, which captured the hearts of the voters. He won the election in a landslide.

Hoover's final months in office were filled with turmoil. In February 1933 a banking crisis led to the failure of many banks. Hoover blamed the crisis on investor nervousness caused by Roosevelt's continuing silence about his plans for the economy—he had revealed few details about the New Deal. Hoover asked Roosevelt to make public assurances that the federal budget would be balanced and that paper money would be backed by gold, but Roosevelt refused to do so. By the time Hoover left office on March 4, 1933, nearly every bank in the country had ceased operating for lack of currency.

Hoover's Postpresidential Life Hoover's memoirs and personal papers reveal that he left the White House a bitter man. He insisted that his programs were working and would have succeeded had they not been thwarted by a Democratic-controlled Congress and an uncooperative Roosevelt. Throughout the remainder of the Depression he toured the country, denouncing Roosevelt's New Deal programs as excessive meddling by government in economic affairs.

Following World War II Hoover advised President Harry Truman (1884–1972) about food relief for war-torn Europe and, later, streamlining the executive departments of the government. The Hoover Commission Reports, as they came to be called, included a variety of suggestions for making the government "do more with less." Many of the recommendations were adopted. In 1953 Hoover headed a similar committee for President Dwight Eisenhower (1890–1969). Hoover continued to advise presidents, write books, and give speeches until his death in 1964 at age ninety.

Hoover's Legacy Hoover's actions to stem the Great Depression get mixed reviews. Some criticize his reluctance to render direct government aid to millions of lower- and middle-class Americans, while others believe he interfered far too much in the economy and laid the groundwork for the radical social programs of Roosevelt's New Deal. All agree that Hoover failed to connect with the people in a way that made them confident about his leadership and vision.

Huey Long

Huey Long (1893–1935) was a colorful, controversial figure in Louisiana politics who advocated national wealth redistribution by taxing the rich and giving the money to the poor. The Kingfish, as he called himself, dominated government in Louisiana because of the political machine he created while serving nearly simultaneously as the state's governor (1928–1932) and senator (1930–1935, but he did not take office until 1932). A charismatic speaker, Long used national radio addresses to garner support for his views. He was considered a strong contender for president in 1936 against Franklin Roosevelt (1882–1945), but was killed by an assassin in 1935. The fiercely dedicated "Longites" who held government positions continued to wield power in Louisiana for decades after his death.

Early Life Long was born into a middle-class farming family in northern Louisiana in 1893, one of ten children. After only a year in law school he passed the bar and began practicing law in 1915. Long quickly made a name for himself in local and regional politics and in 1924 ran an unsuccessful campaign to win the state's Democratic nomination for governor. Four years later he ran again and won using the campaign slogan "every man a king"—a phrase borrowed from William Jennings Bryan (1860–1925), the Populist politician. Like Bryan, Long championed himself as a defender of the rural poor and an enemy of big business and the wealthy.

Building an Empire Long was elected governor in 1928 and immediately began fulfilling the promises he had made during the campaign: his administration built

Senator Huey Long speaking at a campaign event for Senator Hattie Caraway, 1932. © *Bettmann/CORBIS*

nearly thirteen thousand miles of roads in Louisiana; provided free textbooks to public schoolchildren; and secured funding to expand the state's hospital and university systems and to enlarge the port of New Orleans. Despite these accomplishments Long's administration was tainted by corruption and cronyism. In 1929 the Louisiana House voted to impeach Governor Long for a variety of misdeeds, including abuse of power and misuse of state funds. The charges were dropped by the Louisiana Senate.

While Long was popular among the poor, he was lambasted by the major newspapers in the state. In 1934 the state government adopted a newspaper tax, which Long called "a tax on lying, at two-cents a lie." The newspapers took the state to court, claiming that the tax violated the First Amendment right to freedom of the press. In 1936 the U.S. Supreme Court, in *American Press Co. v. Grosjean*, ruled the tax unconstitutional.

Senator Huey Long In 1930 Long was elected to the U.S. Senate; he did not, however, assume his duties until January 1932, after state elections had been held. He chose one of his most dedicated cronies—Oscar Kelly Allen (1882–1936)—to succeed him as governor and used his political power to ensure that Allen and other Longites were elected before he moved to Washington, D.C. Critics scornfully called the new governor O.K. Allen for his role as a puppet controlled by Long.

In the U.S. Senate Long carried his radical platform to a national audience. He supported Roosevelt in his presidential bid of 1932, but became disillusioned when he realized the president's programs, which were called the New Deal, would not achieve wealth redistribution. He made his presidential aspirations clear in two books, *Every Man a King* (1933) and *My First Days in the White House* (1935), in which he described how he would run the nation, humiliate his political rivals, and see his "Share-the-Wealth" plan successfully upheld by the U.S. Supreme Court. Roosevelt called him "one of the two most dangerous men in America." (The other, according to Roosevelt, was General Douglas McArthur.)

The Assassination In August 1935 Long announced his intention to run against Roosevelt. A month later Long was shot and killed while walking through the state capitol with armed bodyguards. His suspected assassin, Carl Weiss (1906–1935), was the son-in-law of a judge who, Long had stated publicly, had African-American ancestors—a statement that could destroy the career and social status of a white Louisianan at the time. Because Long had so many enemies, his assassination spurred conspiracy theories that persisted for decades. Speculation arose as well that the senator had been accidentally shot by one of his bodyguards because of the barrage of gunfire they unleashed during the incident.

Following his death Long's wife, Rose (1892–1970), was appointed to complete his Senate term. A "Longite" named Richard Leche (1898–1965) was elected governor in 1936, but was forced to resign after being indicted for fraud. Lieutenant Governor Earl Long (1895–1960), Huey Long's younger brother, then became Louisiana's governor.

Franklin Delano Roosevelt

Franklin Delano Roosevelt (1882–1945), the thirty-second president of the United States, led the nation during most of the Great Depression and World War II. Through a variety of programs, which he called the New Deal, he changed the government's role in the economy and the people's expectations of what the government could—and should—do for them. His stewardship of the war effort brought the United States to new prominence as a leader among nations.

Early Life and Career Born into a wealthy family in Hyde Park, New York, Roosevelt attended Harvard University and Columbia Law School. In 1905 he married a distant cousin, Eleanor Roosevelt (1884–1962). They had six children, one of whom died in infancy. In 1910 he was elected to the New York Senate as a Democrat, where he caught the attention of President Woodrow Wilson (1856–1924), who appointed him assistant secretary of the navy. In 1920 Roosevelt was a candidate for vice president with James Cox (1870–1957). Although

President Franklin Roosevelt delivering his first "fireside chat," 1933. © *CORBIS*

they lost the election, Roosevelt gained valuable political experience during the campaign.

In 1921, when he was thirty-nine years old, Roosevelt was diagnosed with poliomyelitis—a viral disease that attacks the spinal cord. The disease left him paralyzed from the waist down. He refused to believe the paralysis was permanent, however, and moved to Warm Springs, Georgia, because its natural spring waters were considered therapeutic. After an intense course of swimming therapy he was able to walk with braces. Roosevelt was so enamored with the Warm Springs facility that he bought it. Meanwhile, his wife had immersed herself in New York politics and, in 1928, helped persuade him to run for governor. He was elected by a narrow margin.

In his two terms as governor, Roosevelt made a name for himself in state and national politics. In 1932 he began campaigning for president, promising the public "a new deal." Roosevelt's charismatic style captivated voters. He defeated President Herbert Hoover (1874–1964) in a landslide, capturing 472 of the 531 electoral votes.

The New Deal When Roosevelt was inaugurated in March 1933 the country was in the throes of the Great Depression. Millions of Americans—approximately 25 percent of the nation's labor force—were unemployed. Those who had jobs found their wages and benefits

THE TROJAN HORSE AT OUR GATE

CONSTITUTION OF THE UNITED STATES

NEW DEAL TYRANNY

VOICE OF THE PEOPLE

Cartoon equating the New Deal with a Trojan Horse threatening the Constitution and American people, 1935. © *CORBIS*

slashed, as company profits declined. People stood in long lines at soup kitchens. Almost all the banks had closed.

The newly elected president benefited from a heavily Democratic Congress. During his first one hundred days in office his congressional allies passed more than a dozen pieces of New Deal legislation, creating such programs and agencies as the Civilian Conservation Corps, which put young men to work on public works projects, and the Agricultural Adjustment Administration, which tried to raise farm prices by limiting agricultural production. Other New Deal innovations tightened banking regulations, provided aid to the unemployed, and subsidized mortgage payments.

Some of the legislation from the first one hundred days was later declared unconstitutional by the U.S. Supreme Court and had to be modified or discarded. The most notable example was the National Industrial Recovery Act of 1933, which encouraged companies within industries to form alliances and set prices and wages. In 1935 the Supreme Court unanimously ruled the law unconstitutional on the grounds that it improperly delegated legislative powers to the executive branch. It was one of several judicial setbacks that greatly aggravated Roosevelt. In 1937 he proposed a reorganization plan for the Supreme Court that would have allowed

him to expand the number of sitting justices. Quickly dubbed the "court-packing plan," the legislation was quietly dropped.

One revolutionary program, Social Security, which was introduced in 1935, provided federal benefits to the elderly and assisted the states in providing for "aged persons, blind persons, dependent and crippled children, maternal and child welfare, public health, and the administration of unemployment compensation laws." Social Security was decried by Roosevelt's critics as "socialist," but was viewed by people in crisis as a much needed safety net.

A Popular President   From the beginning of his presidency Roosevelt used his oratorical skill and personal charm to persuade the people that he understood their problems and would do his utmost to alleviate them. In his 1933 inaugural address he assured the nation "the only thing we have to fear is fear itself." In the following years he gave more than two dozen radio addresses, called "fireside chats," in which he laid out in simple, folksy language his ambitious plans for the nation.

While it was largely World War II and not the New Deal that pulled the country out of the Great Depression, Roosevelt's programs did bring relief and comfort to millions. For his efforts, he enjoyed enormous popularity and was easily reelected in 1936, 1940, and 1944.

Throughout his presidential years Roosevelt hid his disability from the public as much as possible. While campaigning he rode in the back of open-air cars equipped with steel bars that he could use to support himself while standing and addressing crowds. In other public appearances he leaned on specially designed podiums or discreetly held the arms of aides to maintain his balance. He also established a gentlemen's agreement with the press to ensure that he was not photographed in his wheelchair. All of these maneuvers were designed to further his public image as a strong and able leader.

Roosevelt Prepares for War   Following World War I, the United States took an isolationist stance, determined to stay out of foreign conflicts. The 1930s, however, saw the rise of powerful dictators in Germany, Italy, and Japan, and Roosevelt became concerned as they launched military campaigns against their neighbors. In 1939 Britain, France, Australia, New Zealand, and Canada declared war on Germany after it invaded Poland. By mid-1941 German forces occupied France, Denmark, Norway, the Netherlands, Belgium, and large parts of Eastern Europe. German troops had also invaded the Soviet Union and North Africa. The very survival of Britain was threatened. Meanwhile Italy had invaded Ethiopia, Greece, and other areas along the Mediterranean, and the Japanese military had attacked China and islands in the South Pacific.

Publicly Roosevelt assured the people that the United States would stay out of the war; as early as 1939, however, he began quietly expanding the nation's military capabilities and increasing the defense budget. He got Congress to pass the Selective Training and Service Act of 1940, which created the nation's first peacetime draft. He sent his advisers on secret missions to Britain and offered all possible U.S. aid short of direct military action. In August 1941 he met secretly with British Prime Minister Winston Churchill (1874–1965), with whom he had been corresponding for months about possible American involvement in the war.

Officially the United States had to remain neutral, as dictated by the Neutrality Act of 1935. In early 1939 Roosevelt urged Congress to repeal the law, but it refused. It did, however, amend the act to allow the sale of certain military assets to warring nations in exchange for cash. Roosevelt knew that this measure was not enough because Great Britain was on the brink of bankruptcy. In 1940 he used his presidential powers to bypass the Neutrality Act and trade fifty aged destroyers for British naval bases in Newfoundland and the Caribbean. In October 1941 he achieved passage of the Lend-Lease Act, which granted him permission to "lend" U.S. goods to "any country whose defense the President deems vital to the defense of the United States." Roosevelt authorized the first shipments to Britain even before the act was passed.

World War II On December 7, 1941, Japanese forces waged a surprise attack on Pearl Harbor, the U.S. naval station in Hawaii. Roosevelt called it "a date which will live in infamy" and asked Congress to declare war on Japan. Within days, Germany and Italy had declared war on the United States, and the country had entered World War II. The nation's industrial strength became a huge asset, as the country began to churn out war goods worth billions of dollars. Roosevelt abandoned his longtime commitment to a balanced federal budget, believing the war had to be won at any cost.

The federal government established a host of agencies to oversee wartime production, labor relations, and prices. Some goods were rationed to prevent dramatic price increases. Businesses rushed to increase production and hire workers to produce the goods needed for the war effort. Unemployment dropped dramatically and even unskilled laborers found themselves in high demand. This employment effectively ended the Great Depression.

Throughout the war Roosevelt took a hands-on approach, carefully selecting and sometimes overruling his military commanders. U.S. strategy and manpower, plus the flood of American-made materiel, helped defeat Germany and Italy by early 1945. In August of that year Japan surrendered after the United States dropped atomic bombs on Hiroshima and Nagasaki. The bombs had been developed in a top-secret program initiated by Roosevelt in 1939.

Roosevelt did not live to see the end of World War II. He died in April 1945 after suffering a massive stroke at age sixty-three.

A New World Order Part of Roosevelt's political legacy was the postwar alignment of nations. When he met secretly with Churchill in August 1941, Britain was already at war and the United States would soon join the effort. The two leaders developed a document, the Atlantic Charter, which spelled out their commitment to a postwar world in which differences between nations would be settled diplomatically. Roosevelt wanted an international body ruled by democratic principles, a successor to the failed League of Nations, and suggested it be called the United Nations. He believed the organization would need the active support of the United States to be successful and obtained congressional approval for U.S. membership. He persuaded the nation's allies to pledge their participation as well.

In February 1945 he met in Yalta, a resort town in what is now Ukraine, with Churchill and Soviet leader Joseph Stalin (1879–1953). The war in Europe was nearly won by that time, and the three leaders gathered not to discuss battle strategy, but to map out the future of the world. They negotiated territorial boundaries and the fate of governments. A new world order was established that recognized the economic and military prowess of the world's new superpowers, the United States and the Soviet Union. Under Roosevelt's leadership the United States had evolved from an isolationist nation to one of prominence in world affairs.

Roosevelt's domestic legacy exists in many government programs, for he greatly expanded the influence of the executive branch and the federal government in social and economic matters. Conventional wisdom prior to the Great Depression had been that supply and demand would eventually fix an ailing economy. Roosevelt dismissed that notion and manipulated the economy with program after program. While those efforts can be seen as only marginally successful—it was largely World War II that pulled the nation out of the economic abyss—Roosevelt's attempts at reform did have far-reaching effects on the nation's psyche: they accustomed many Americans to the idea that the government has a responsibility to provide for their social and financial welfare.

Eleanor Roosevelt

(Anna) Eleanor Roosevelt (1884–1962), the wife of President Franklin Roosevelt (1882–1945), was more visible and vocal than previous first ladies—she was the first to hold a press conference—and developed her own agenda on social issues. She elicited both praise and criticism for her outspokenness, particularly her support for minority rights.

Early Life and Career Roosevelt, born into a well-to-do family in New York, was the niece of Theodore Roosevelt (1858–1919), who would become president while she was a teenager. By the time she was ten her parents had died, so she was raised by her maternal grandmother. She attended a prestigious school in England. After returning to the United States she became

Eleanor Roosevelt delivering a radio broadcast, 1942. © *Hulton-Deutsch Collection/CORBIS*

interacting with the public as much as possible. As one reporter noted, "Eleanor uses No. 1600 Pennsylvania Ave. less as a home than as a base of operations."

Her speeches and writing conveyed her passion for social reform and the government's responsibility to care for people in need: she was an enthusiastic advocate for her husband's programs, which he called the New Deal. Because she understood the ability of the press to spread her message, she developed a reputation as a publicity seeker. Her friendly, unassuming style charmed many Americans, but some were put off by her vocal social activism.

Civil Rights   In a 1933 magazine article she urged Americans to write to her. Over the next twelve years she received more than half a million letters. Many writers sought help with problems brought on by the Great Depression and World War II, but racial discrimination was an equally frequent subject. After a young African-American man wrote to complain about racist treatment in a drugstore, she urged him to keep working on behalf of his race for better treatment and noted "you are gradually gathering behind you a larger and larger group of white people who are conscious of the wrongs and who are helping to correct them."

She often met and corresponded with leaders of the early civil rights movement, including Mary McLeod Bethune (1875–1955), A. Philip Randolph (1889–1979), and Walter White (1893–1955). When African-American singer Marian Anderson (1897–1993) was barred from performing at Constitution Hall in Washington, D.C., in 1939, Roosevelt protested by resigning from the Daughters of the American Revolution, which owned the building. Along with White, she encouraged the secretary of the interior to arrange a free concert by Anderson on the steps of the Lincoln Memorial. More than seventy-five thousand people attended.

World War II   Like many Americans in the 1930s, she was opposed to U.S. intervention in the escalating conflicts in Europe. In 1935 she declared that war was "obsolete." International problems, she said, could be dealt with much better through diplomacy. Her optimism faded as Nazi Germany's plans for conquest in Europe became clear. By 1939 she was hinting in public that U.S. neutrality might not be possible—or right. Two years later the United States entered World War II.

During the war she visited U.S. troops and toured veterans hospitals to bolster morale. She lobbied Congress unsuccessfully for changes in immigration law that would have allowed fleeing European refugees, particularly Jews, to enter the United States. As women and African-Americans entered the workforce in large numbers, she spoke out in favor of "equal pay for equal work" and urged her husband to sign Executive Order 8802, which prohibited government contractors from engaging in employment discrimination based on race, color, or national origin.

engaged to Franklin Roosevelt, who was a distant cousin. They married in 1905 and had six children, one of whom died in infancy.

During the 1920s she worked as a teacher and for a variety of social and humanitarian causes, including the Red Cross. A trip to Europe, which had been devastated by World War I, touched her deeply and ignited a fierce antiwar sentiment. She was devoted to her politically ambitious husband and watched as his career progressed from state senator to assistant secretary of the navy. In 1921 he was stricken with poliomyelitis, which left him paralyzed from the waist down. He moved to Warm Springs, Georgia, where he spent seven years in water therapy trying to regain the use of his legs. During that time she became active in the Democratic Party, developing political savvy and confidence, maturing from a shy young woman into an accomplished public speaker. She persuaded her husband to run for governor of New York in 1928; his victory was a surprise. Four years later he was elected president of the United States.

First Lady   Like her predecessors, she graciously entertained guests at the White House; nevertheless, she also had her own agenda for her public life. She held press conferences; gave lectures and radio talks; and wrote books, magazine articles, and a daily syndicated newspaper column, "My Day." She also traveled extensively,

MRS. ROOSEVELT AND LYNCHING LEGISLATION

Eleanor Roosevelt (1884–1962) was an avid supporter of civil rights for minorities. One of the most contentious debates of her era centered around making lynching a federal crime. Lynching incidents involving African-Americans increased dramatically during the early years of the Great Depression. Achieving federal anti-lynching legislation was a top priority in the 1930s for the National Association for the Advancement of Colored People (NAACP). NAACP president Walter White (1893–1955) was of mixed race and had a very light skin color. As a young man during World War I he had interviewed members of lynch mobs in the South by passing as a white person. Shortly after the war ended ten African-American veterans were lynched by white mobs—two of the men were burned alive.

In 1918 Missouri Congressman Leonidas Dyer introduced a federal anti-lynching bill, which passed the House in 1922. However, it was derailed by a filibuster in the Senate led by Southern legislators. The same technique doomed a 1935 bill championed by New York Senator Robert Wagner and Colorado Senator Edward Costigan. Nearly three hundred African-Americans were lynched by white mobs in the years between the two failed bills. In 1937 a white mob in Mississippi used blowtorches to torture two African-Americans seized from a local jail. The men were killed after their forced confessions. A third African-American man, their supposed accomplice, was burned alive. Horror at this act sparked the House to pass the Gavagan bill, introduced by New York Congressman Joseph Gavagan. Once again, a southern filibuster blocked passage of the act. The following year Wagner and Indiana Senator Frederick Van Nuys tried again, but were thwarted in a similar fashion.

Civil rights leaders like White had the ear of Mrs. Roosevelt and desperately hoped that her reform-minded husband would use his influence to push through federal anti-lynching legislation, but they were disappointed. In a 1936 letter the first lady told White that she was "deeply troubled" about the issue, but the president believed lynching to be a state matter and outside the constitutional jurisdiction of the federal government. Historians agree that the president was actually afraid of angering his large bloc of southern supporters in Congress, whom he needed to pass his New Deal agenda. Mrs. Roosevelt's letter to White was marked "personal and confidential." The political constraints of the time prevented her from speaking openly and publicly on this polarizing subject.

In 2005 the U.S. Senate issued a formal apology for failing to pass any of the nearly 200 federal anti-lynching bills presented to it for consideration between 1882 and 1968. During that time period, more than 4,700 people—primarily African-Americans—were killed by lynch mobs.

After the White House When her husband died in April 1945, just months before the war's end, she moved back to New York, expecting to fade from public view. In December 1945, however, her husband's successor, Harry Truman (1884–1972), asked her to join the U.S. delegation to the newly created United Nations (UN). It was a task for which she was well suited. In 1948 she helped draft and oversaw passage by the UN of the Universal Declaration of Human Rights, a document that affirms the fundamental rights of all human beings.

She considered Truman woefully inadequate for the job he had inherited, however, and wrote him hundreds of letters containing both advice and scathing criticism during his presidency. Although he complained about her privately, he knew that she was a political asset and called her "first lady of the world." She resigned from her UN post following the election of President Dwight Eisenhower (1890–1969) in 1952. President John F. Kennedy (1917–1963) reappointed her to the post in 1961. She died in 1962 at age seventy-eight.

Eleanor Roosevelt's Legacy By most standards Eleanor Roosevelt was a distinctive first lady. She stepped out of the shadow of her charismatic and popular husband and expressed her own political views. As one magazine of her time put it, "She is a one-woman show in herself." In 1998 *Time* declared her among the one hundred most influential people of the twentieth century. She is most remembered for her social activism and outspoken support for minority causes.

Charles Evans Hughes

Charles Evans Hughes (1862–1948), chief justice of the U.S. Supreme Court from 1930 through 1941, worked effectively behind the scenes to defeat an attempt in 1937 by President Franklin Roosevelt (1882–1945) to reorganize the Supreme Court. Hughes and other critics claimed Roosevelt was trying to "pack the court" with justices friendly to his programs, which he called the New Deal.

Early Career Hughes was born in New York, the son of immigrant parents from Wales. After graduating first in his class from Columbia Law School he went into private practice. In 1906 he was elected governor of New York as a Republican, defeating publishing magnate William Randolph Hearst (1863–1951). After two terms Hughes was nominated and confirmed as a justice of the Supreme Court, a position he held from 1910 to 1916. Hughes ran for president in 1916 but lost by a narrow margin to his Democratic challenger, Woodrow Wilson (1856–1924).

From 1921 through 1925 Hughes served as secretary of state under two presidents—Warren Harding (1865–1923) and Calvin Coolidge (1872–1933). In

New York Governor Charles Evans Hughes, c. 1900. © *CORBIS*

1930 Hughes became chief justice after being nominated by President Herbert Hoover (1874–1964).

Hughes as Chief Justice At the time of Hughes's appointment, four of the eight justices were considered conservative and three liberal. The eighth justice and Hughes were more centrist in their views. In 1935 and 1936 they heard several challenges to New Deal legislation. In *Panama Refining Co. v. Ryan* and *Schechter Poultry Corp v. United States* the justices declared unconstitutional portions of the National Industrial Recovery Act, a law that gave the federal government broad powers over private businesses. In writing for the majority, Hughes argued that the law granted power to the executive branch that rightly belonged to the legislative branch.

Roosevelt, reelected in a landslide in 1936, became frustrated by Supreme Court rulings against his programs, so he pushed Congress for legislation that would allow him to reorganize the Supreme Court and increase the number of justices. Hughes quietly joined forces with Democratic Senator Burton Wheeler (1882–1975) of Montana to fight the Judiciary Reorganization Bill, which was ultimately dropped.

Hughes served as chief justice until 1941, when he retired at age seventy-nine. By that time Roosevelt had appointed eight justices who tilted the court in favor of New Deal reforms.

The Legacy of Charles Evans Hughes Hughes earned a reputation as a socially progressive, but practical, reformer. While he supported Prohibition, which prohibited the manufacture, transportation, and sale of alcoholic beverages, and regulation of business, both of which strengthened the power of the government, he also fiercely protected civil rights, property rights, and free speech under the Constitution. During the late 1930s he began supporting New Deal legislation; he was opposed, however, to the more extreme goals of the Progressive movement, such as wealth redistribution.

Frances Perkins

Frances Perkins (1882–1965), secretary of labor from 1933 to 1945, was the first woman to be appointed to a cabinet-level post. She advocated reform of wage and employment laws and spearheaded the passage of the Social Security Act of 1935.

Early Life and Career While still in college Perkins—who was born into a well-to-do Boston family—visited factories to learn firsthand about working conditions. What she witnessed began her lifelong quest for social reform. In 1910 she joined the National

U.S. Secretary of Labor Frances Perkins, the first female Cabinet member, shown here with President Franklin Roosevelt in 1943. © *Bettmann/CORBIS*

Consumers' League, an organization devoted to improving industrial safety and health conditions. The following year she witnessed a fire at the Triangle Shirtwaist Company in New York that killed 146 workers, mostly immigrant girls and women. Survivors claimed that one of the exit doors had been locked by management. The deaths not only intensified Perkins's efforts, but also elicited public support for many of the reforms she had been advocating.

Secretary Perkins In the 1920s she held a number of labor-related posts in New York state government. When President Franklin Roosevelt (1882–1945) asked her to join his cabinet, she agreed only after gaining his assurance that he supported her goals—reform of state and local labor laws, limits on work hours and child labor, minimum wage laws, and programs of government assistance for unemployed and retired workers. Perkins was instrumental in gaining passage of such legislation as the Wagner-Peyser Act of 1933, which established a national

system of public employment offices; the National Labor Relations Act of 1935, which granted workers the right to form unions and bargain collectively with their employers and created the National Labor Relations Board; and the Fair Labor Standards Act of 1938, which set minimum wage standards and prohibited child labor. All were parts of Roosevelt's program, which he called the New Deal.

In 1934 Perkins chaired the Committee on Economic Security, which was established by the president to make recommendations regarding unemployment and "old-age" insurance. Its suggestions led to a new government program, Social Security. Perkins worked diligently for passage of the Social Security Act of 1935, speaking on the radio to a national audience on many occasions. In one of those addresses she said, "We have come to learn that the large majority of our citizens must have protection against the loss of income due to unemployment, old age, death of the breadwinners, and disabling accident and illness, not only on humanitarian grounds, but in the interest of our national welfare."

Later Life Perkins resigned her post in 1945 following Roosevelt's death. The next year President Harry Truman asked her to serve on the federal Civil Service Commission, a position she held until her retirement from government service in 1952. She spent the remainder of her life teaching and lecturing at universities. Perkins died in 1965 at age eighty-three.

Transforming Government's Role Perkins once described her motivation to become secretary of labor as follows: "I came to work for God, FDR, and the millions of forgotten, plain, common workingmen." Her view of the government as a protector of working people was typical of New Deal liberalism. She helped to achieve workplace reforms and strengthened the government's authority to intervene in business-labor relations.

Dorothea Lange

Dorothea Lange (1895–1965) was a photographer best known for her poignant photographs of impoverished Americans during the Great Depression and of Japanese Americans interned in camps during World War II. Her photographs are valued for their frank depiction of the gritty conditions endured by her subjects.

Early Life and Career Lange got polio at age seven, which left her with a disfigured leg and a limp. After taking photography lessons in New York, she set up a photography studio in San Francisco and specialized in portraits for well-to-do clients. The onset of the Great Depression awakened within Lange a passion to evoke through film the misery endured by many Americans. Exhibitions of her early photographs captured the attention of state and national authorities.

Lange was employed first by the California State Emergency Relief Administration and later the federal Resettlement Administration, whose goal was to garner public support and government funds for the construction of livable work camps for the thousands of people migrating into California each month. In 1937 Lange reported to her supervisor that "the region is swamped with homeless moving families. The relief association offices are open day and night twenty-four hours. The people continue to pour in and there is no way to stop them and no work when they get there."

While some of Lange's photographs were exhibited or published, most were not embraced by mainstream publications. Some were even published out of context with captions fabricated to put a more optimistic spin on the nation's condition.

Lange's Photographic Style Lange's black-and-white photographs are noted for capturing the mood and circumstances of her subjects. Her shy, low-key manner allowed her to circulate unobtrusively among the migrant workers, so her photographs were not posed for effect,

Migrant Mother, by Dorothea Lange, 1936. This iconic portrait of Florence Owens Thompson, a poverty-stricken mother of young children, came to symbolize the Great Depression for many Americans. © *Library of Congress. Photograph by Dorothea Lange*

but starkly realistic. One of her most famous photographs, which she titled "Migrant Mother," shows a weary dark-haired woman staring woefully into the distance. She has two small children huddled against her. Lange snapped the photograph in 1936 in a field in California where the woman, a widow at age thirty-two, lived in a shabby tent with her seven children. According to Lange's account, they survived by eating leftover vegetables from the fields and birds the children caught.

During World War II Lange was one of several photographers hired by the War Relocation Authority, a federal agency that moved thousands of Japanese Americans to internment camps in the West. Lange documented the story of the internees as they left their homes, registered with the government, traveled to the camps, and were resettled. Unlike many of her contemporaries Lange was appalled by the camps. The government and most photographers of the time presented the camps to the public as pleasant places with cheerful inhabitants, but Lange saw them as prisons: she purposely included barbed wire and guard towers in many of her photographs. As a result the government censored her work; many of her photographs were not seen by the public for decades.

A. Philip Randolph (left) leading picketers for African-American rights outside the Democratic National Convention in Philadelphia, 1948. © *Bettmann/CORBIS*

A "Social-Documentary" Photographer Lange continued to take photographs until her death in 1965 at age seventy. A year later her husband donated her portfolio, which included more than twenty-five thousand images, to the Oakland Museum of California. Lange is now referred to as a "social-documentary" photographer because she captured her subjects in their natural conditions and publicized their plight in the hope of social reform.

A. Philip Randolph

A. (Asa) Philip Randolph (1889–1979) was an African-American labor leader and civil rights activist. He successfully fought for the rights of railroad porters to form a union during the Great Depression and pressured the government to eliminate job-related discrimination against African-Americans as the United States geared up for World War II.

Early Life and Career Randolph was born in 1889 in Florida, but moved as a young man to the Harlem neighborhood of New York City. He joined the Socialist Party and campaigned vigorously for Socialist causes.

In 1917 Randolph and his friend, Chandler Owen, started a newsletter, the *Messenger*, which addressed issues of importance to African-Americans, particularly discrimination in the workplace. They called it "the first voice of radical, revolutionary, economic and political action among Negroes in America." During the late 1920s the title changed to the *Black Worker*. It continued to address the ongoing struggle of thousands of African-American men.

During the 1920s trains were the primary means of long-distance travel, so the Pullman Company built luxuriously equipped train cars, called sleeping cars, in which passengers could relax on long journeys. About twelve thousand porters, almost all African-American men, attended to the needs of passengers. Frustrated by their working conditions, which included long hours at low pay, a group of porters asked Randolph to help them organize a labor union. Negotiations with the

President Lyndon Johnson presenting A. Philip Randolph with the Presidential Medal of Freedom, 1964.   © *Bettmann/CORBIS*

company dragged on for more than a decade. In 1937 the Brotherhood of Sleeping Car Porters was recognized and won the right to negotiate wages, hours, and working conditions for its members.

Pressuring Presidents for Change   When war broke out in Europe in 1939 the United States began ramping up its military forces and defense industries, which provided much-needed jobs in a depressed economy. African-Americans were thwarted, however, by racist recruiting and hiring procedures. Randolph and other civil rights leaders organized African-Americans for a protest march through the nation's capital on July 1, 1941. President Franklin Roosevelt (1882–1945) feared the march would arouse racial strife. At the urging of his wife, Eleanor (1884–1962), he signed Executive Order 8802 in June 1941, which prohibited discrimination in employment by government contractors. Randolph canceled the march planned for Washington; smaller protest marches, however, were held throughout the early 1940s in other major cities. Although Executive Order 8802 was poorly implemented and enforced during Roosevelt's administration, it demonstrated the growing political influence of the civil rights movement.

In 1948 Randolph and his allies used the threat of civil disobedience to pressure President Harry Truman (1884–1972) into issuing Executive Order 9981, which banned discrimination in the nation's armed forces. It led to an arduous transformation of the military into a desegregated institution.

A Civil Rights Pioneer   Randolph is considered one of the most influential pioneers of the civil rights movement. His effective use of nonviolent protest and civil disobedience to achieve political change inspired social activists of the 1950s and 1960s, including Bayard Rustin (1912–1987) and Martin Luther King Jr. (1929–1968). In 1963 Randolph organized the March on Washington for Jobs and Freedom at which King made his now famous "I have a dream" speech. Randolph continued to speak out against discrimination until his death in 1979 at age ninety.

George C. Marshall

George C. Marshall (1880–1959) was a brilliant military strategist during World II and architect of the Marshall Plan, a postwar relief and reconstruction program for Europe. The Marshall Plan provided billions of U.S. dollars in aid to war-devastated Western Europe both for humanitarian reasons and to ward off the encroachment of communism.

Early Life and Career Marshall was born into a prosperous Pennsylvania family with a long and distinguished history of government service. After graduating from the Virginia Military Institute he served as an army officer at posts in the Philippines and in the United States. During World War I Marshall was appointed to the military's General Staff and planned decisive battles in France. He was a favorite of General John Pershing (1860–1948), serving as his assistant through 1924. During the following fourteen years Marshall held a variety of roles in the peacetime army, primarily as an instructor of infantrymen. By 1939 he had been promoted to general and named army chief of staff by President Franklin Roosevelt (1882–1945).

World War II Following the horrors of World War I the United States assumed an isolationist stance in international affairs. When World War II broke out in Europe in 1939 the United States had only a poorly trained army of fewer than two hundred thousand soldiers; Marshall expanded it into a fighting force of more than eight million. When the United States decided to enter the European war, Marshall planned Operation Overlord, the massive invasion of Normandy, France, by Allied troops on June 6, 1944, which became known as D-day. Roosevelt put General Dwight D. Eisenhower (1890–1969) in command of the invasion, telling Marshall, "I feel I could not sleep at night with you out of the country." Throughout the remainder of the war Marshall guided U.S. military policy in Europe. He also served on the committee that oversaw the development of the atomic bomb.

The Marshall Plan World War II left most of Europe in ruins. Infrastructure, industries, and agriculture were devastated. Millions of people were displaced from their homes and faced severe food, fuel, and job shortages. U.S. and British leaders feared that communism, which had been forced upon Eastern European nations by the victorious Soviet Union, would attract the disenfranchised masses of Western Europe. To counteract that possibility and to save Europe from starvation, Marshall devised the European Recovery Program. Marshall, who had been appointed secretary of state by President Harry Truman (1884–1972) in 1947, outlined the plan in a commencement speech at Harvard University. "Our policy is not directed against any country or doctrine," Marshall said, "but against hunger, poverty, desperation, and chaos." Despite its worthwhile goals the plan—which quickly became known as the Marshall Plan in honor of its chief protagonist—was not initially well received in the United States: war-weary Americans were not anxious to assume new foreign responsibilities, and Congress was not keen on spending billions of dollars in foreign lands. That attitude changed in February 1948

General George C. Marshall, c. 1943. *© Bettmann/CORBIS*

when Soviet-backed Communists seized control of the Czechoslovakian government. Two months later Congress passed the Foreign Assistance Act, which implemented the Marshall Plan.

Between 1948 and 1952 the program funneled approximately $13 billion in U.S. aid to Western Europe. In addition to food, it financed the reconstruction of key industries and the redevelopment of agriculture, allowing nations to become self-sufficient and politically stable. The plan also benefited the United States by fostering goodwill and creating robust markets for U.S.-made goods and services. For his role in the European Recovery Program, Marshall received the Nobel Peace Prize in 1953.

Marshall served as secretary of state from 1947 to 1949. He went on to head the American Red Cross and was secretary of defense for one year during the Korean War. He resigned in 1951 because of poor health. He died in 1959 at age seventy-eight.

Marshall's Legacy Marshall was a true public servant, during both war and peace. First he rebuilt the army as World War II was erupting and then, when the United States decided to enter the conflict, created the military strategy for U.S. participation. In peacetime the Marshall Plan, which he championed, not only gave immediate help to war-torn Europe but later gave impetus to the formation of the North Atlantic Treaty Organization and the European Common Market as well.

Hugo Black

Hugo Black (1886–1971) was a justice of the U.S. Supreme Court from 1937 through 1971. As the first Supreme Court nominee of Franklin Roosevelt (1882–1945), Black was a fervent supporter of the president's programs, which were called the New Deal. During his long tenure on the Court he was best known for rulings that protected civil rights, particularly those of minorities, and the First Amendment guarantees of free speech and the press.

Early Life and Career Born in Alabama, Black never finished high school, but graduated from the University of Alabama Law School in 1906. He spent the next two decades in private practice, as a county prosecutor, and in the U.S. Army. In 1926 Black, a Democrat, was elected to the U.S. Senate, where he backed issues associated with the Progressive movement and southern Populism, which advocated government aid for farmers and working-class people, stronger labor unions, and a crackdown on corporate corruption.

During Black's second term, he was an ardent supporter of Roosevelt and his New Deal agenda, including the Fair Labor Standards Act of 1938, which set minimum wages and maximum working hours. Black also supported Roosevelt's effort in 1937 to reorganize the Supreme Court—which quickly became known as the "court-packing plan." Roosevelt was unhappy with rulings against New Deal legislation by justices he believed to be overly conservative. The plan was quietly dropped. Later that year, when conservative Justice Willis Van Devanter (1859–1941) resigned, Roosevelt nominated Black for the vacated position.

The Ku Klux Klan Controversy During his confirmation hearings questions arose about Black's membership during the 1920s in the Ku Klux Klan, the fraternal organization that advocated white supremacy. In a series of articles in the *Pittsburgh Post-Gazette*, reporter Ray Sprigle revealed that Black had joined the Klan in 1923 and relied heavily on Klan support to win his Senate seat. Although Black resigned from the Klan before taking office, Sprigle claimed that the Klan never recognized the resignation and had given Black a card conferring lifelong membership in the organization. After calls for his resignation, Black addressed the controversy in a national radio address, a rare action by a Supreme Court justice. He admitted that he had joined the Klan, but insisted that he later resigned and never rejoined. He acknowledged that the Klan had presented him with a card but called it "unsolicited" and said he had not kept it or used it and did not consider it "as a membership of any kind in the Ku Klux Klan." While his address helped to calm concerns that he was a racist, his decisions on the Court would vanquish any doubts about him.

The Record of Justice Black Black served on the Supreme Court for more than four decades. His record

Supreme Court Justice Hugo Black, 1965. © *Bettmann/CORBIS*

is largely one of ardent support for civil rights under the First Amendment (particularly freedom of speech and the press), due process of law under the Fourteenth Amendment (for instance, the right to a fair trial), and strict separation of church and state.

During the 1930s and 1940s segregation and discrimination against African-Americans was institutionalized throughout the South. Black greatly angered his former southern supporters by siding with the majority in decisions that overturned convictions of African-American defendants in cases that involved forced confessions, poor legal representation, and all-white juries. Black publicly described the courts as "havens of refuge" for the weak, the helpless, and "victims of prejudice and public excitement." This protection, however, did not extend to Japanese American civilians interned by the U.S. government during World War II. In a departure from his historical support for civil rights, Black wrote for the majority in *Korematsu v. United States* (1944) that the detention was justified for reasons of national security.

During the anticommunism fervor following World War II, Black criticized Senate hearings delving into activities deemed un-American and defended the rights of people to criticize the U.S. government. In 1962 he wrote the Court's decision in *Engel v. Vitale*, which banned state-sanctioned prayer in public schools. He died in 1971 at age eighty-five, just two days after retiring from the Court.

See also **Japanese American Internment**

A sticker for the New Deal National Recovery Administration, c. 1934. © *Bettmann/CORBIS*

✪ Political Parties, Platforms, and Key Issues

The New Deal

The New Deal was the name given to a massive campaign of economic and social reform waged by the administration of President Franklin Roosevelt (1882–1945) during the Great Depression. The reforms greatly expanded the size of the federal government and increased its influence over banking, investment, farming, utilities, and business-labor relations. The New Deal also provided relief to impoverished Americans and set up temporary job programs for the unemployed. Although it lessened the hunger and hardship of millions of people, it did not pull the country out of the Great Depression. That occurred only when the nation entered World War II.

Roosevelt Connects with the People Herbert Hoover (1874–1964) was president when the stock market crashed in 1929. He quickly became the nation's favorite scapegoat for the severe economic crisis that followed. During the presidential campaign of 1932 Americans became enraptured with Roosevelt, then the Democratic governor of New York, who was a charismatic politician. People believed that he cared about their desperate condition and would do everything he could to alleviate their plight. When he accepted his party's nomination in July 1932, he said, "I pledge you, I pledge myself, to a new deal for the American people."

Although Roosevelt gave few details about his plan, he indicated that he would focus on relieving the suffering of Americans, recovery of farms and businesses, and reform of the stock market and banking industry. To do so he relied on a trusted circle of political, academic, and economic advisers, known as his "brain trust." Roosevelt's win was so decisive and so many Democratic candidates were swept into Congress that legislation he and his brain trust championed was nearly guaranteed passage, particularly during the early years of his administration. Dozens of new agencies were created to oversee the administration and funding of New Deal programs—they were often called "alphabet soup" agencies because their names were quickly turned into acronyms and initialisms.

During his first two years in office Roosevelt focused primarily on building government-business-labor relations and providing financial aid to the states for distribution to the needy and unemployed. In 1935 the priority shifted to large-scale public works programs; the responsibility to provide direct financial aid to people reverted to state and local governments, as it had been under the Hoover administration. The programs created after this policy shift are often called the "second New Deal."

Banking and Investment One of Roosevelt's first acts under the New Deal was to increase confidence in the nation's banks. Banks had begun to collapse after the stock market crashed. Because deposits were not insured at that time, people lost their savings when the banks failed. In addition "bank runs"—when large numbers of nervous depositors rush to remove their money all at once—forced many banks out of business because they had insufficient assets to meet demand. Between 1929 and 1933 depositors lost in excess of $1 billion when banks failed.

Immediately after his inauguration in March 1933 Roosevelt declared a nationwide bank holiday, freezing all deposits until U.S. Treasury inspectors could verify the soundness of the banks. The Emergency Banking

Relief Act—quickly passed by Congress to legalize what Roosevelt had done—required closed banks to meet certain criteria before they could reopen. Later in the year the Banking Act of 1933 (also called the second Glass-Steagall Act) extended federal oversight to all commercial banks and created a temporary agency, the Federal Deposit Insurance Corporation (FDIC), with authority to regulate and supervise banks and to provide them with deposit insurance. The FDIC was made permanent by the Banking Act of 1935. Other new laws regulated savings and loan companies and authorized the formation of federally chartered credit unions.

Several New Deal laws addressed problems that were believed to have contributed to the crash of the stock market. The federal Securities Act (1933) regulated the selling of investment instruments, such as stocks, to ensure that buyers were better educated about their purchases and to prevent fraudulent practices. The Securities Exchange Act (1934) regulated the stock exchanges and created the U.S. Securities and Exchange Commission to enforce the regulations.

Agriculture The Agricultural Adjustment Act (AAA) of 1933 paid farmers to reduce production of specific crops and set target prices. Decreasing supply was intended to increase prices, which would improve the living standards of farmers. The money to pay the farming subsidies was raised by levying a tax on the companies that bought agricultural goods and processed them. In 1936 the U.S. Supreme Court in *United States v. Butler* invalidated parts of the AAA. The law was revamped and passed again in 1938.

Other New Deal legislation provided farm mortgage holders with easier credit terms; lent money to farmers so they could recover foreclosed property; and allowed farmers to reduce their debts to avoid bankruptcy. A 1933 executive order created the Farm Credit Administration to provide credit to farmers and ranchers. The Taylor Grazing Act (1934) set up a system for orderly grazing by private ranchers on public lands—an effort to prevent the type of overgrazing that helped turn parts of the Great Plains into a dust bowl. The Drought Relief Service (DRS), created in 1935, purchased cattle from farmers and ranchers who could not afford to feed their livestock. The beef was turned over to the Federal Surplus Relief Corporation, which was created to distribute surpluses to people without food. The Resettlement Administration, established in 1935 by Executive Order 7027, was responsible for a variety of programs, including resettling poor families and providing loans and grants to small farmers.

Labor and Business The National Industrial Recovery Act (NIRA) of 1933 was groundbreaking legislation because it gave the federal government a major role in the financial and labor affairs of private businesses. The NIRA encouraged companies within industries to form alliances, set production quotas, and fix prices and wages.

ROOSEVELT GOES FOR THE GOLD

In April 1933, in one of the most controversial actions of his administration, President Franklin Roosevelt (1882–1945) nationalized private gold supplies. Executive Order 6102 required all private citizens and businesses to turn their gold over to the federal government by May 1 in exchange for cash. Exceptions were allowed for gold used for industrial, professional, or artistic purposes and for rare gold coins that were in collections. In addition each citizen was allowed to keep up to $100 worth of gold. Violation of the order was punishable by a fine of up to $10,000 and imprisonment for up to ten years.

Roosevelt claimed authority to nationalize private gold under existing law. The Trading with the Enemy Act of 1917, a relic of World War I, granted the president power to prevent the hoarding of gold during wartime. Only days after Roosevelt took office Congress passed the Emergency Banking Relief Act (1933), which amended the 1917 law to apply during "any period of national emergency declared by the President." Roosevelt and Congress deemed the Great Depression to be a national emergency.

The gold grab had a variety of objectives. The administration wanted people to spend cash to spur the economy, which they could not do if their assets were hoarded in gold. It also wanted to induce inflation, which occurs when demand outpaces supply, making prices go up. Higher prices, the New Deal officials believed, would encourage more production and raise employment. They also knew that, under the gold standard, each U.S. dollar was backed by a specified amount of gold. One way to encourage inflation is to devalue money by not backing it with gold. That was essentially what the government did, because it refused to exchange paper money for gold. While that action did cause a spike in inflation, it did not bring about the desired drop in unemployment.

The federal ban on private ownership of gold remained in effect for more than four decades. It was finally reversed in 1974 when President Gerald Ford (1913–2006) issued Executive Order 11825.

The companies that participated were exempted from antitrust laws, which ordinarily would have forbidden such collusion. The National Recovery Administration was established to develop "codes of fair competition" to which businesses were required to adhere. The codes were highly controversial and unpopular, particularly with the owners of smaller companies, who believed the codes favored big businesses.

When the U.S. Supreme Court ruled, in *Schechter Poultry Corp. v. United States*, that the codes section of the NIRA was unconstitutional, the administration abandoned that approach to business regulation. The NIRA had also, however, guaranteed the right of employees to organize and bargain collectively with their employers.

Furthermore, it barred employers from requiring or prohibiting union membership as a condition of employment. Those labor stipulations were resurrected in the National Labor Relations (or Wagner) Act of 1935, which was administered by the National Labor Relations Board (NLRB). That law was declared constitutional by the Supreme Court in *NLRB v. Jones & Laughlin Steel Corp* in 1937.

The Fair Labor Standards Act of 1938 established a national minimum wage of twenty-five cents per hour and a maximum workweek of forty-four hours in some industries. It also prohibited child labor. Unlike legislation of the early days of the Roosevelt administration, this bill languished in Congress for more than a year as various factions bickered over its provisions. Although controversial for its time, the legislation was upheld as constitutional by the Supreme Court in *United States v. Darby Lumber Company* in 1941. The Fair Labor Standards Act was the last major piece of legislation of the New Deal era.

Public Works Programs In 1933 Congress passed the Reforestation Relief Act, which created the Civilian Conservation Corps (CCC). It put hundreds of thousands of young men to work building roads and developing national parks for tourism. NIRA, also passed in 1933, created the Public Works Administration, a program of temporary jobs constructing roads and public buildings. Later that year Roosevelt issued an executive order establishing the Civil Works Administration (CWA), which provided millions of other temporary jobs.

The Emergency Relief Appropriation Act of 1935 provided funding for a variety of programs, including the National Youth Administration (NYA) and the Works Progress Administration (WPA). NYA provided grants to students so they could stay in school and economic aid and job training for unemployed youths. WPA became one of the most popular New Deal programs, providing jobs for as many as three million people at a cost of more than $1 billion per year. WPA workers built or repaired thousands of schools, hospitals, sports stadiums, and bridges; planted millions of trees; and laid thousands of miles of storm drains and sewer lines. Other WPA programs provided work for actors, authors, artists, and musicians.

Public Utilities During the 1920s private utility companies experienced a business boom, thanks to strong demand for electricity. By the end of the decade a handful of electric corporations held a near monopoly. Many of them had unstable financial structures, however: they were made up of layers of companies, some of which were "holding companies" that sold securities (stocks and bonds) for "operating companies" beneath them. In addition, because large holding companies often had assets in several states, they were able to skirt state regulations that were supposed to control them. These vast pyramids of businesses suffered huge losses when the stock market crashed in 1929. One of the goals of the New Deal was to tighten government control of utility holding companies. To do so Congress passed the Public Utility Holding Company Act in 1935. The Federal Power Act, enacted the same year, gave the federal government the authority to regulate electricity rates.

Roosevelt also wanted to make electricity available to rural areas that were not served by the private utilities. In 1935 he issued Executive Order 7037, which created the Rural Electrification Administration (REA). The Norris-Rayburn Act (1936) provided hundreds of millions of dollars in funding for the REA, which became a permanent federal agency with passage of the Rural Electrification Act (1936). By the end of the decade 25 percent of the nation's rural households and farms had electricity, up from around 10 percent at the beginning of the 1930s.

Tennessee Valley Authority The Tennessee Valley Authority (TVA) Act of 1933 created a corporation to oversee agricultural and industrial development of government-owned lands near the Tennessee River. As part of its mission TVA built dams to improve the navigability of the river and to implement flood-control measures for the benefit of people living in the river basin. The corporation became controversial because many of the dams it built to control flooding also generated electricity. Private utility companies fought the program in court because they viewed it as unfair government competition. The constitutionality of selling government-generated electric power was upheld by the Supreme Court in *Ashwander v. TVA* (1935) and *Tennessee Electric Power Company v. TVA* (1939). More than a dozen TVA dams were constructed during the Roosevelt administration to provide jobs and electricity to the region.

Social Security One of the most sweeping New Deal programs was Social Security. In a June 1934 speech to Congress Roosevelt introduced his concept of "social insurance" to prevent "social unrest and economic demoralization." The following year Congress passed the Social Security Act to provide federal benefits to retired workers and to assist the states in providing for "aged persons, blind persons, dependent and crippled children, maternal and child welfare, public health, and the administration of unemployment compensation laws."

Social Security, which required millions of Americans to apply for Social Security numbers, was funded by taxes paid by employers and employees. In 1939 the program was expanded to include benefits for the spouses and children of retirees and of covered workers who died before they retired. In January 1940 the first monthly Social Security benefit checks were mailed. Although repeatedly challenged in court, the Social Security system withstood constitutional scrutiny and became one of the enduring legacies of the New Deal era.

New Deal Taxes Roosevelt's New Deal programs were expensive undertakings during a time of economic depression, so a variety of tax measures were implemented to help cover the costs. The Revenue Act of 1935 significantly raised taxes for the wealthiest corporations and individuals in society: the so-called Wealth Tax Act required payment of up to 75 percent of income by some Americans. Estate and gift taxes were also increased—critics called it the "soak the rich" plan. In 1939 taxes were raised on corporations and, for the first time, levied on the compensation of state employees. In addition the repeal of Prohibition, which had prohibited the manufacture, transportation, and sale of alcoholic beverages since 1920, allowed the government to collect taxes on the sale of alcohol.

The Supreme Court Roosevelt's early New Deal programs may have sailed through Congress but they often encountered opposition in the courts. During the mid-1930s the U.S. Supreme Court declared some of the new laws unconstitutional, particularly the Agricultural Adjustment Act and the National Industrial Relations Act. Roosevelt was incensed by the rulings and believed the Supreme Court was dominated by overly conservative justices. In 1937 he proposed a "reorganization" plan under which he would be allowed to expand the size of the Court. Quickly dubbed the "court-packing plan," it was seen by many as a brazen attempt to load the Court with justices sympathetic to the New Deal. The plan received little public or political support and was soon abandoned. The issue became moot as the more conservative justices began to retire and Roosevelt nominated more liberal replacements.

Legacy of the New Deal Most New Deal programs were considered temporary, emergency measures for dealing with an unusual circumstance, the Great Depression. Roosevelt himself referred to some of them as "experiments." Although many of the programs disappeared as the Depression abated, some have become fixtures in society—most notably Social Security and the TVA. The farm subsidies begun during the New Deal became permanent components of U.S. agricultural policy. Perhaps the greatest effect of the New Deal was the planting of the idea in the national psyche that the federal government can be—or should be—a manipulator of economic forces and a provider of benefits to individual citizens.

✪ Current Events and Social Movements

Black Tuesday

Black Tuesday refers to Tuesday, October 29, 1929, the day on which the stock market "crashed," reducing the value of stocks in corporations and utilities by billions of dollars. The day is generally considered the starting point for the Great Depression. The crash severely damaged the U.S. economy and caused the public to lose faith in the soundness of big business, the banking system, and the government.

The Plenty of the 1920s The 1920s had seen robust economic growth in the United States. Mass-production techniques and the growing availability of electricity allowed industries to increase their output—and profits—dramatically. Employment levels surged, and many workers saw improvements in their standards of living. Consumer demand for new products also drove creation of new loan programs: for the first time middle-class Americans were able to purchase such goods as refrigerators, washing machines, and automobiles by making payments, rather than by paying cash up front. Many people, optimistic that prosperity would continue, borrowed heavily, certain that they would be able to pay back the loans.

By the end of the decade the stock market had become a major influence on the economy. Investors were being richly rewarded as stock prices increased, which caused some observers, including President Herbert Hoover (1874–1964), to worry about "speculation"—when overly optimistic investors buy stocks rashly, driving their prices higher than their actual value.

One reason for the concern was the common practice, by both individuals and companies, of buying stocks with money borrowed from banks. Investors also bought stock "on margin," an arrangement that allowed them to make a small down payment (often as little as 10 percent) on a stock purchase. The remainder of the balance would conceivably be paid by the future increase in the value of the stock. Margin purchases allowed many people to invest heavily in the stock market without using much of their own money.

A Selling Frenzy Erupts During the autumn of 1929 the stock market became erratic, with stock values dropping unexpectedly and then recovering. Suddenly on October 24, 1929, a frenzy erupted as people tried to sell stocks they thought might be overvalued. The day became known as Black Thursday. The following day the market rebounded somewhat; nevertheless, the recovery was short-lived.

On Tuesday, October 29, frantic sellers sold their stocks for prices far below what they had paid for them, which started a downward spiral that hurt all investors, but particularly those who had bought stocks on margin. As stock values dropped, lenders demanded that margin buyers pay cash to keep their stocks. If margin buyers could not pay, the lenders sold the stocks to recoup the money. Throughout the day desperate margin buyers turned over their cash in hopes of saving their stocks for an expected recovery, but no recovery came. As stock values kept falling, lenders demanded more money. By the end of the day many margin buyers had lost both

Panicked stock traders outside the New York Stock Exchange after the Black Tuesday market crash, 1929. © *Bettmann/CORBIS*

their life savings and their stocks. Those who managed to keep their stocks found they were worth only a fraction of their former value.

Causes of the Crash Economists disagree about the causes of the crash. Some point to excessive speculation, which created a stock market "bubble"—a state in which stock prices are much higher than their actual worth—that was followed by a "market correction" that went too far. Other economists insist that stocks were not overvalued; instead, they assert, skeptics spooked investors into setting off a selling frenzy. Additional forces cited include the federal government's decision to increase interest rates; investor nervousness over the impending Smoot-Hawley Tariff Act; widely publicized scandals in the British financial markets; and warnings from U.S. regulators about the economic soundness of some public utilities.

The consequences of Black Tuesday were not immediately apparent. The next day the headline in the *New York Times* read "Stocks Collapse in 16,410,030-Share Day, but Rally at Close Cheers Brokers; Bankers Optimistic, to Continue Aid." The stock market did in fact

recover dramatically several times during the following months, but it always fell again, finally bottoming out in 1932. By that time many businesses had failed, banks had closed, workers were out of jobs, and homes and farms had been lost to foreclosure.

Black Tuesday did not immediately affect a large number of people, for only about 5 percent of Americans owned stocks at the time. The ripple effects of the crash were far-reaching, however. So much of the money had been borrowed for investments that banks were ruined when loans could not be repaid. That made less money available for everyday purposes, such as building homes and businesses. Companies that had invested their profits in the stock market suddenly found themselves in financial difficulty and had to lay off employees and cut wages. Unemployed people and underpaid workers could not pay back loans and were reluctant to spend any money, further crippling the nation's banks and businesses.

The crash had psychological repercussions as well, for the public lost faith in the stock market and, by association, the banking system, big business, and the government. Heady optimism about the nation's future was replaced

The "Bonus Army" arriving at the Capitol after their march up Pennsylvania Avenue to demand passage of the Bonus Bill, which would provide for immediate payment of the Soldiers' Bonus, 1932. © *Bettmann/CORBIS*

with disillusionment, and the country sank into an economic depression that would last for more than a decade.

The Government Response After holding hearings, Congress passed the Securities Act of 1933, which required companies that sold stocks and other securities to communicate important information to consumers and set up systems to prevent fraud. The law was strengthened in 1934 when Congress created the Securities and Exchange Commission, a federal agency charged with overseeing the securities markets. Additional laws were enacted during the 1930s and early 1940s to strengthen government control over the nation's banks, public utilities, and investment companies and advisers.

See also **Great Depression**

The Bonus March

The Bonus March brought thousands of World War I veterans to Washington, D.C., in 1932. They sought early payment of a cash bonus the government was scheduled to pay them in 1945. When the early payment was denied, many of the protesters refused to leave the city and were forcibly ejected by the U.S. Army. The event was a public-relations disaster for President Herbert Hoover (1874–1964) and a major impetus for passage of the GI Bill of Rights during World War II.

Origins of the Bonus In 1924 the nation was enjoying financial prosperity. Congress decided to reward World War I veterans with a bonus called the Veteran's Compensation Certificate to be payable in 1945. Each bonus was based on the number of days a veteran had served during the war; the average bonus was $1,000. When the Great Depression began in 1929 veterans started pressuring the government for early payment of the bonus. In 1932 Representative Wright Patman (1893–1976), a Democrat from Texas, introduced legislation to authorize payment of the bonuses immediately.

Walter Waters, a veteran living in Oregon, heard about the Patman bill and recruited veterans to travel to Washington, D.C., as a show of solidarity for its passage. Waters called the group the Bonus Expeditionary Force (BEF). Small groups of veterans in the Northwest began making their way toward the nation's capital, often hitching illegal rides on freight trains because cross-country travel by car or passenger train was too expensive. Word of the march spread; by the time Waters's group reached Washington, the city was packed with thousands of veterans. Some had brought their entire families with them.

Waters, determined to keep the Bonus March peaceful, worked closely with Washington, D.C., police superintendent Pelham Glassford (1883–1959), who was a veteran and sympathetic to the cause. Glassford arranged for the protestors to get food and supplies and allowed them to set up camps around the city. Waters and other march organizers formed a military-type hierarchy for maintaining order. They forbade drinking alcohol, panhandling for money, or engaging in "radical" activities. Suspected anarchists and Communist agitators, were forced to leave the camps.

Violence Erupts By June 1932 an estimated twenty thousand protesters were in Washington. During that month the Patman bill was narrowly passed by the House, but defeated in the Senate. Some of the protesters left town quietly; many did not. Tension intensified when Waters announced that they would stay until the bonus was paid. City leaders feared violence and decided to evict the BEF from camps near the White House and Capitol. Violent confrontations erupted and at least two protesters were killed by police. In July the city asked the federal government to send in troops.

Army Chief of Staff Douglas MacArthur (1880–1964) was convinced that the BEF was a Communist plot to spread anarchy. On July 28, 1932, his troops fixed their bayonets, drew their swords, and swept through the camps in the heart of the city. They used tear gas to force protesters to leave. MacArthur disobeyed orders from Hoover and cleared out the main BEF camp across the Anacostia River from downtown Washington. Shacks in the camp burned to the ground; how the fire started was never determined. The next morning the *New York Times* reported "a pitiful stream of refugee veterans of the World War walked out of their home of the past two months, going they knew not where."

The Fallout The government's handling of the incident sparked outrage, much of it directed at Hoover. The Bonus March was one of many factors that led to his defeat by Franklin Roosevelt (1882–1945) in the 1932 presidential election. During World War II memories of the Bonus March debacle spurred veterans groups to push Congress for passage of a bill granting financial incentives to future war veterans. The Servicemen's Readjustment Act, which became known as the GI Bill of Rights, passed in 1944.

The Dust Bowl

Dust Bowl was the name given to parts of the Great Plains in the 1930s after severe drought and high winds degraded farmland. Huge dust storms literally buried farmhouses and equipment, forcing people to flee. The disaster was not entirely due to natural causes: years of overproduction and poor farming techniques had stripped the land of protective topsoil and left it vulnerable to the winds. The Dust Bowl spurred a massive migration of people, desperate for work, from the plains into California. The struggling migrants became symbols of the misery endured by so many Americans during the Great Depression.

Overproduction and Drought The Great Plains, a swath of land east of the Rocky Mountains, extend from North Dakota and eastern Montana in the north to western Texas in the south. During the early 1800s explorer Zebulon Pike (1779–1813) reported that the prairies were "incapable of cultivation." Hordes of pioneers moved into the area and began farming and ranching anyway. Cattle overgrazed the land, stripping it of the shrubby grasses that had held the soil in place for centuries. Farmers unfamiliar with the semi-arid climate of the region used growing methods common to the more humid eastern United States. Although droughts occurred occasionally, the land provided abundant crops, particularly of grains, such as wheat.

During World War I demand for agricultural goods skyrocketed, particularly in Europe. Optimistic U.S. farmers took out loans to buy more land and newly developed mechanized equipment. Plains farmers ramped up production, using tractors and plows that churned the ground more deeply than before. In the 1920s, however, many farmers suffered economic hardship when agricultural supply outpaced demand and pushed prices downward. The agricultural sector was already in crisis when the stock market crashed in October 1929.

The drought began in the summer of 1930 in the southeastern United States and spread across the plains. The Southeast suffered until late 1931, when rain fell regularly again. The central plains, however, experienced nearly continuous drought for almost a decade. As the dust storms turned the sky black and scoured the landscape, people lost their farms and homes to foreclosure and farmworkers and tenant farmers—those who live on and farmland that is owned by others—lost their livelihoods.

Western Migration Thousands of farmers uprooted from the Dust Bowl traveled west, hoping to find jobs in the fertile agricultural fields of California. Some found temporary work picking crops—usually for very low pay and usually competing for work and wages with each other and the Mexican and Filipino farmworkers already in the state. Migrants wandered from place to place, living in tents and makeshift shacks or in their cars. Although not all were from Oklahoma, they were commonly called "Okies."

Two Dust Bowl refugees walking along the highway toward Los Angeles, 1937. *© Bettmann/CORBIS*

In the mid-1930s the federal government erected more than a dozen camps in California to provide clean living quarters for the migrant workers. For the residents and government of the state of California, however, the camps were small comfort. They considered the dilapidated shantytowns and temporary camps to be menaces to the public health. Sheriffs set up roadblocks at the state's border and refused entry to bedraggled migrants. For a few months in 1936 the Los Angeles Police Department deployed more than a hundred officers to border towns to stop vehicles and freight trains as part of a "bum blockade." California began enforcing a decades-old law that prohibited anyone from transporting into the state "any indigent person who is not a resident of the state." In 1941 the U.S. Supreme Court ruled in *Edwards v. People of State of California* that the law was unconstitutional because it violated the freedom of interstate commerce. The Court acknowledged that migrants produced "staggering" problems for the state in terms of "health, morals, and especially finance," but insisted that it could not be allowed simply to "shut its gates" as a remedy.

Labor Unrest Tension between California residents and migrants was aggravated by ongoing labor strife: dozens of farm strikes erupted in 1933, some led by Communist organizers or their sympathizers. In response a group of wealthy farmers and businessmen formed an antiunion group, Associated Farmers (AF), which recruited local sheriffs and citizens to harass migrant workers who were considered troublemakers. Major strikes in 1936 by lettuce pickers in Salinas and in 1937 by cannery workers in Stockton ended in violence when the AF sent hundreds of armed vigilantes to break up the strikes with tear gas. In 1939 Senator Robert La Follette, Jr. (1895–1953), a Republican from Wisconsin, formed a committee to investigate the AF and its union-busting activities. The La Follette Civil Liberties Committee found many activities that violated labor laws; its findings, however, were overshadowed by the nation's entry into World War II in 1941.

Public Attention The plight of the migrant workers was publicized widely. Some newspapers and magazines printed the photographs of Dorothea Lange (1895–1965), who became famous for her frank portrayals of down-and-out people and their living conditions. More common were articles such as "The Harvest Gypsies," a series written by John Steinbeck (1902–1968) in 1936 for the *San Francisco News*. "They arrive in California," wrote Steinbeck, "usually having used up every resource to get here, even to the selling of their poor blankets and utensils and tools on the way to buy gasoline. They arrive bewildered and beaten and usually in a state of semistarvation, with only one necessity to face immediately, and that is to find work at any wage in order that the family may eat."

In 1939 Steinbeck used his research to write a novel about a fictionalized migrant family, the Joads, who were tenant farmers from Oklahoma. Driven west from the Dust Bowl, they roamed the migrant camps, encountering discrimination against Okies and mistreatment by local authorities and farmers. The novel, *The Grapes of Wrath*, which became the definitive work about the Great Depression, created a storm of controversy. Californians were outraged by the negative depiction of their state. Some critics complained that Steinbeck exaggerated the poor condition of the migrants and that he had Communist leanings. First Lady Eleanor Roosevelt (1884–1962) came to his defense, praising the book in her daily syndicated newspaper column, "My Day."

The Rain Returns   Not all farmers left the Dust Bowl. Those who remained behind scraped out a living as best they could or depended on government aid. Twenty-one percent of rural residents in the plains states received federal emergency aid in 1936—as many as 90 percent of the residents in the hardest-hit counties. The government supplied cash payments, farming supplies, and feed for livestock and set up medical-care facilities to meet the everyday needs of poor farmers and ranchers. It also conducted research to determine and implement better land-management techniques for the region. During the spring of 1938 the rains finally returned. By 1941 the drought was over, and the prairies of the Dust Bowl had been rejuvenated.

The Legacy of the Dust Bowl   The drought of the 1930s would have been ruinous on its own, but its arrival at the same time as the Great Depression greatly magnified its effects. Local relief agencies—the traditional source of aid to rural America—were overwhelmed, so the federal government became involved in the lives and financial affairs of the nation's farmers in an unprecedented way. Besides financial aid, it created programs to inspire new farming methods. The Soil Erosion Service (1933) fostered such techniques as contouring, terracing, and crop rotation to preserve valuable topsoil. The Soil Conservation and Domestic Allotment Act of 1935 established the Soil Conservation Service (now the National Resource Conservation Service), which made land use and conservation a high priority in agriculture.

The Great Depression

The Great Depression was a deep economic crisis that began in 1929 and lasted until the nation's entry into World War II in 1941. Depressions had occurred several times before, but had always been short-lived. The Great Depression, by contrast, lasted for more than a decade and brought long-term unemployment, hunger, and hardship to millions of people. It completely dominated the social and political landscape of American life and dramatically altered the relationship between the nation's government and the people.

The Roaring Twenties   The roots of the Great Depression lay in the prosperous 1920s, when U.S. industries embraced techniques of mass production that allowed them to increase their output and their profits. High employment levels meant that standards of living improved. Consumer demand increased dramatically, especially for such newly available products as electrical appliances and automobiles. Many people were so optimistic about the future they borrowed money to finance their purchases or bought items through installment plans. The stock market was on a bullish—or upward—trend, providing handsome profits to investors. In fact, the stock market had become a popular investment vehicle, despite its inherent risks.

Prosperity was not shared by all sectors of the economy in the 1920s. Farmers, in particular, had financial difficulties because of overproduction. During World War I demand for agricultural goods had soared, particularly in Europe. Optimistic farmers had borrowed money to invest in new equipment, only to see food prices plummet during the 1920s when supply outpaced demand. Lower profits made it difficult for farmers to pay back their loans, which stressed banks in rural areas. At the same time there were downturns in the coal mining and railroad industries.

The Depression Begins   By early 1929 demand had slackened for some goods, even automobiles. Wages in the industrial sector were not keeping pace with huge gains in production and profits. Business and government leaders, however, were still confident about the economy. During the autumn of 1929 the stock market began behaving erratically. Several sharp dips were quickly alleviated by rallies. On October 29, 1929, the stock market dropped so severely that the event became known as "the great crash." Stocks lost billions of dollars of value in a single day. Fortunes were wiped out. Investors who had borrowed money to buy stocks were particularly hard hit, as were the banks that had lent the money.

During the following months the stock market occasionally rebounded, only to fall again. Investor and consumer confidence faded, and people began holding onto their money instead of spending or investing it. The

A Hooverville, or makeshift village, in Seattle, Washington, 1934. These impoverished communities were named after President Herbert Hoover, whose administration was blamed for the widespread unemployment and homelessness of the Great Depression. © *Bettmann/ CORBIS*

economy underwent deflation—a condition in which depressed demand pushes prices downward. Lower prices for agricultural and industrial goods hurt farmers and businesses, particularly those with high debt. Businesses laid off employees to cut costs and did not hire new employees. As more people became unemployed or fearful about their jobs, they spent even less, which led to more business cutbacks and closures.

To make matters worse a decade-long drought began in 1930; dried-out and degraded soil, loosened by high winds, turned parts of the Great Plains into a "dust bowl" and scattered homeless migrants across the West. By 1933 the nation's unemployment rate stood at nearly 25 percent, up from only 3 percent in 1929.

The Banking Crisis

The stock market crash spurred a crisis in the banking industry. The prosperity of the early 1920s had encouraged the development of many new banks and the granting of many loans. At the time the

banking system was only loosely regulated by the government, and deposits were not guaranteed and could be lost when banks failed. Many banks did fail after the stock market crash because they had invested their depositors' money in the stock market or lent large amounts of money to stock market investors. Fear of additional failures caused "bank runs" in which large numbers of depositors rushed to withdraw their money at the same time. By the beginning of 1933 nearly every bank in the country had been forced to close for lack of funds.

Hoover Responds

President Herbert Hoover (1874–1964) had been in office only a few months when the stock market crashed in October 1929. Secretary of the Treasury Andrew Mellon (1855–1937) advised the president not to interfere, believing that the forces of supply and demand would allow the economy to correct itself. Hoover was not convinced, so he tried a variety of measures: he adjusted taxes, asked industry not to cut

NATIVISM DURING THE GREAT DEPRESSION— MEXICANS AND FILIPINOS

Nativism is the policy of giving preference to natives over aliens. During the Great Depression American nativists argued, often successfully, that aliens from Mexico and the Philippines took American jobs, placed an undue burden on the government, and should be repatriated (returned to their country of origin).

During the prosperous 1920s Mexican workers crossed the border illegally to work in the United States. Many found employment in the agricultural industry in the southwest, particularly California. The Great Depression brought unemployment and wage cuts to these people, as it did to most Americans. However, nonnatives were often denied relief from state and local agencies. Expulsion of these people became a priority on many political agendas. Beginning in 1931 the Los Angeles County Department of Charities paid for repatriation trains to transport thousands of Mexicans back to their homeland. Officials argued that the aliens were a drain on relief funds and posed a health risk because they were not clean.

The Philippines became a U.S. territory after Spain's defeat in the Spanish-American War in 1898. As such, Filipinos were considered "nationals" and entered the United States in large numbers during the early decades of the twentieth century. Many settled in southern California. Racial tensions reached a climax between Filipinos and white Americans during the late 1920s and early 1930s. The Tydings McDuffie Act of 1934 established the Philippines as a U.S. Commonwealth, but changed the legal status of Filipinos from "nationals" to aliens. A year later Congress passed the Repatriation Act, which provided funds to repatriate Filipinos as long as they agreed not to return to the United States. Before the act expired in December 1938 only approximately 2,000 Filipinos were repatriated.

Mexican and Filipino workers who remained in the United States during the Great Depression played a major role in organizing dozens of agricultural labor unions in the West. Strikes by these unions resulted in most cases in better wages and working conditions for the employees.

wages, and pushed for public works projects. None of these measures was effective. As the Great Depression deepened, Hoover got the blame. Homeless people built shantytowns that were called "Hoovervilles."

In the summer of 1932 thousands of World War I veterans traveled to Washington, D.C., demanding early payment of a war bonus that was scheduled to be paid them in 1945. Federal troops armed with bayonets used tear gas to forcibly expel the "bonus marchers" from the city. The negative publicity damaged Hoover's already poor image.

Roosevelt's New Deal In late 1932 Americans overwhelmingly chose a new president—New York State Governor Franklin Roosevelt (1882–1945), who promised "a new deal" for the nation. Roosevelt initiated a variety of programs to revive the economy, with various levels of success. Unemployment was reduced, but still averaged above 10 percent throughout the 1930s. Many people, particularly young men, were employed through public works projects, building roads, dams, bridges, airfields, and post offices and developing national parks for tourism. The government began paying farm subsidies to stabilize agricultural markets.

Some of Roosevelt's New Deal programs did not survive U.S. Supreme Court challenges and had to be discarded or revamped. They did, however, bring reform to the banking and investment industries. A series of new laws regulated the stock market, ensuring that investors were educated about their purchases and preventing fraudulent investment practices. The Federal Deposit Insurance Corporation, which safeguarded bank deposits, helped greatly to restore confidence in the nation's banking system.

In 1935 Congress passed two pieces of New Deal legislation that would have long-term repercussions. The National Labor Relations Act guaranteed the right of employees in most private industries to organize, form labor unions, and bargain collectively with their employers. It also established the National Labor Relations Board to investigate unfair labor practices. The Social Security Act established a program to provide federal benefits to the elderly and assist the states in providing for "aged persons, blind persons, dependent and crippled children, maternal and child welfare, public health, and the administration of unemployment compensation laws."

Roosevelt's New Deal greatly expanded the size and scope of the government, with more than a dozen new federal agencies influencing the nation's social and economic systems. To offset some of the costs, Roosevelt implemented a number of tax increases. In 1933 Congress repealed Prohibition—a constitutional amendment passed in 1919 to prohibit the manufacture, transportation, and sale of alcoholic beverages—and the government began collecting liquor taxes.

Breadlines and Soup Kitchens During the Great Depression hunger and unemployment became a way of life for millions of people. Breadlines and soup kitchens became symbols for the era: churches and charities in major cities served free meals to hundreds of thousands of people each day. Those who lost their homes and jobs traveled the country looking for work—some illegally hopped aboard freight trains. Shantytowns called "jungles" sprang up near rail lines.

Much of the population lacked the most basic necessities—food, shelter, and clothing. While people with farms or gardens grew food to sustain themselves, malnutrition became a serious problem among children, particularly in the big cities. The drought and winds that turned parts of the Great Plains into the Dust Bowl

Unemployed men waiting in line for bread and handouts in New York City, c. 1930. © *Bettmann/CORBIS*

drove hundreds of thousands of migrant workers into California looking for a better life, only to find little work and poor living conditions. African-Americans migrated in large numbers from the rural South to northern cities in search of factory jobs, but found work scarce and encountered racist employment policies that made it difficult for them to compete in the workplace.

The early years of the Depression were the toughest, particularly for young people. Some that could not find work left their homes so their parents would have fewer mouths to feed. The government estimated that as many as 250,000 people younger than age twenty-one wandered the country aimlessly, getting food and shelter where they could. Several New Deal programs were created specifically for young people, including the Civilian Conservation Corps, which put young men to work on conservation projects; the National Youth Administration, which provided training and jobs for youths; and a college aid program under the Federal Emergency Relief Administration.

Labor Unrest Labor unions played a minor role in the booming economy of the 1920s. Once the Great Depression set in they took on greater importance, particularly after the election of pro-union Roosevelt. In 1933 union membership stood at about three million. In June of that year Congress passed the National Industrial Recovery Act (NIRA), which was the first federal law to give employees the right to organize and bargain collectively with their employers. The law forbade employers from requiring or forbidding union membership as a condition of employment.

Passage of the NIRA gave unions the impetus to strike for better pay and working conditions. During 1933 and 1934 major strikes were organized in California by agricultural workers and longshoremen and in the Midwest by autoworkers and teamsters. Although sometimes violent, the strikes ultimately achieved their goals, which served to make unionization more appealing.

During the mid-1930s the economy began to show signs of improvement. Unemployment dropped to around 15 percent. Then in 1937 and 1938 the stock market took a steep dive, and unemployment spiked to 20 percent. This "depression within a depression" coincided with labor troubles in the nation's largest industries.

The National Labor Relations Act of 1935—passed because parts of the 1933 law had been declared unconstitutional by the Supreme Court—required businesses to negotiate with any union supported by a majority of employees. At that time the dominant organization of labor unions in the United States was the American Federation of Labor (AFL), which concentrated on organizing trade unions of skilled craftspeople, such as electricians and typesetters. In 1935 a faction of AFL organizers split off and formed a committee—later called the Congress of Industrial Organizations (CIO)—with the goal of unionizing unskilled workers in mass-production jobs, mostly in the steel, rubber, automobile, and meatpacking industries.

CIO unions, including the United Auto Workers (UAW), embraced a militant organizing strategy that encouraged confrontations between workers and management. In late 1936 the UAW began a series of sit-down strikes at General Motors (GM) plants around the country. After several tense months violence broke out between strikers and police in Flint, Michigan. Dozens of people were injured. Under pressure from Roosevelt, GM officials met with UAW leaders and ultimately agreed to bargain with the union. Similar campaigns began at other major industrial plants. By 1940 more than 20 million workers had joined unions.

Roosevelt easily won reelection in 1936 and 1940, even though his New Deal programs had had only mixed results. While they had reduced the hardship experienced by many Americans, they had not pulled the nation out of the Great Depression. In 1941 the unemployment rate stood at 10 percent, still high historically.

Later that year, after Japan attacked Pearl Harbor, the U.S. naval station in Hawaii, the United States entered World War II. The government poured billions of dollars into wartime industries, which put millions of people back to work. By 1942 the unemployment rate had fallen below 5 percent and continued to drop. The economy recovered from the depths of the Great Depression and maintained its healthy state even after wartime spending ended.

A Lasting Imprint The Great Depression left its imprint on an entire generation of Americans. The length and breadth of the hardship changed people's expectations about the quality of their lives and made them receptive to a more active role for the federal government in the day-to-day business of the population. They had seen where the "hands-off" approach to the economy had taken them and began to appreciate government as a caretaker with responsibilities for the economic and social well-being of businesses and individual citizens. Many New Deal programs, which created

safeguards and regulations that became fixtures of the U.S. economy, often had their most important effect on the national psyche: they offered reassurance and optimism, which had been missing for more than a decade.

World War II

World War II, a nearly worldwide conflict during the late 1930s and early 1940s, pitted the armed forces of Germany, Italy, and Japan (known as the Axis powers) against the Allies—primarily the United States, the Soviet Union, and Britain and its dominions (Australia, Canada, and New Zealand). The war profoundly affected the course of U.S. history. It permanently brought the nation out of its isolationist stance toward foreign conflicts and established America as one of the world's economic and military superpowers.

Unrest Stirs the World The 1920s and 1930s saw the rise of several powerful militaristic governments. In 1931 Japan invaded the Chinese region of Manchuria and set up a puppet government. During the following years Japan greatly increased its military might until, in 1937, it began a full-scale war against China that spread throughout Southeast Asia and the islands of the South Pacific. Meanwhile in Europe the armies of Nazi Germany and Fascist Italy were launching their own wars of conquest. In 1935 Italy invaded Ethiopia. Three years later Germany seized control of Austria and the German-speaking region of Czechoslovakia. In May 1939 Germany and Italy signed an agreement to support each other militarily—they called it "the pact of steel." When German forces invaded Poland on September 1, 1939, France and Britain declared war on Germany. The Soviet Union did not react, because it had recently signed a nonaggression pact with Germany. The United States officially remained neutral.

In 1940 Italy declared war against Germany's foes. Japan, Germany, and Italy then signed a pact, sealing their alignment as the Axis powers. By that time Germany's relationship with the Soviet Union had soured. In June 1941 German forces surged across the Soviet border, opening a second front in what was rapidly becoming a worldwide war. German forces had already seized France and parts of North Africa and were planning an invasion of Britain.

America Clings to Isolationism The United States was preoccupied with the Great Depression during the 1930s, but watched uneasily as war spread in Europe, Asia, and Africa. Many Americans had developed an isolationist attitude following the horrors of World War I. In 1935 the first of several neutrality acts was passed by Congress to ensure that the United States would not be dragged into international conflicts. The next year a Senate committee, led by Gerald Nye (1892–1971), a Republican from North Dakota, investigated U.S. involvement in World War I. The committee's report suggested that the nation's

The *USS Arizona* sinking into Pearl Harbor after the Japanese attack on December 7, 1941. © *AP/Wide World Photos*

munitions industry had wielded considerable influence over the political decision to enter the war and had profited handsomely from it. A peace movement swept across college campuses and was embraced by many other parts of society. As he campaigned for reelection in the fall of 1940 President Franklin Roosevelt (1882–1945) repeatedly promised that the United States would not enter the war. He won the election easily and began his third term in office.

Despite his assurances to the contrary, Roosevelt had already begun preparing the nation's military and industries for war and was using every political tool at his disposal to render aid to Britain. In 1939 he asked Congress to repeal the Neutrality Act; while it refused, it did amend the law to allow the United States to sell military assets to Britain. Knowing that Britain was nearly bankrupt, in 1940 Roosevelt worked around the Neutrality Act to trade fifty older American destroyers to Britain in exchange for some of its naval bases. He also got Congress to enact the Selective Training and Service Act, creating the nation's first peacetime draft.

In December 1940, Roosevelt gave a radio address in which he reiterated his goal to keep the United States

out of the war; nevertheless, he also warned the public that the very survival of the United States would be jeopardized if Britain were defeated. He pledged to provide the country's allies with war implements, saying "we must be the great arsenal of democracy." In July 1941, after months of private correspondence, Roosevelt and British Prime Minister Winston Churchill (1874–1965) met for the first time on a ship off the coast of eastern Canada. They created a document, the Atlantic Charter, in which they pledged "the final destruction of the Nazi tyranny" and laid out plans for a postwar world based on diplomacy, rather than aggression. A few months later Roosevelt attained passage of the Lend-Lease Act, which granted him permission to "lend" goods to other countries in the interests of U.S. defense. He authorized the first shipments to Britain even before the act was passed.

America Enters the War On December 7, 1941, Japanese forces attacked Pearl Harbor, the U.S. naval station in Hawaii. Within days the United States was at war with Japan, Germany, and Italy. In an address to the nation Roosevelt said, "We don't like it—we didn't want to get in it—but we are in it and we're going to fight it with everything we've got." The nation's military, relatively small and ill-equipped for war at the time, was expanded quickly through recruitment and the draft. Eventually a fighting force of some eight million soldiers would be trained and equipped.

Civilian industries quickly converted to produce military goods, with new federal agencies to oversee wartime production, labor relations, and prices. Businesses hired workers, so unemployment dropped dramatically, effectively ending the Great Depression. The growth in employment spurred workers to join labor unions in record numbers, consolidating their power to seek better working conditions.

Although Roosevelt gave the war in Europe first priority and wanted to liberate France as soon as possible, the British suggested—and he eventually agreed—that U.S. forces should fight the Germans in the air over Europe and launch their first ground attacks in North Africa. Soon thereafter the German war effort began to falter: the influx of U.S. troops and equipment and the military supremacy of the Soviet army took their toll. By late 1943 the Axis powers had been driven from North Africa and parts of Italy. On June 6, 1944—which became known as D-day—U.S. and British forces began an offensive to take back France. By the end of the summer they had liberated Paris. At the end of the year they fought back a fierce German offensive, the Battle of the Bulge, in which the United States suffered more than nineteen thousand casualities. By the spring of 1945 the Allies occupied Germany—Soviet troops had swept in from the east and U.S. and British forces from the west. On May 7, 1945, Germany surrendered.

The War in the Pacific

The first months of the war in the Pacific did not go well for U.S. forces. During early 1942 Japanese troops captured a number of islands in the South Pacific, forcing thousands of American soldiers to surrender. The turning point came in May 1942 when the United States achieved a decisive victory on Midway Island. From then on U.S. forces, suffering heavy casualties, fought their way island by island, wresting Guadalcanal, the Solomon Islands, Wake Island, Guam, Iwo Jima, the Philippines, and Okinawa from Japanese control. Meanwhile British forces liberated Burma.

In the spring of 1945 the U.S. military began preparing for Operation Downfall, an invasion of Japan. Nevertheless, the possibility of a huge American death toll from an invasion, as well as other political considerations, led to another tactic: on August 6, 1945, a U.S.-made atomic bomb was dropped on Hiroshima, Japan, killing thousands of people immediately. When the Japanese did not surrender, a similar bomb was dropped on Nagasaki three days later. On August 14, 1945, Japan surrendered. World War II had ended.

The human toll of the war was staggering. An estimated 40 million to 60 million people were killed worldwide. U.S. military casualties included more than 400,000 dead and more than 670,000 wounded.

Mushroom cloud rising over Nagasaki, Japan, on August 9, 1945, after a U.S. nuclear attack. Japan surrendered five days later. *© Bettmann/CORBIS*

Changes in the Economy

On the home front life changed dramatically during World War II. The federal government imposed widespread controls over the economy to ensure that the military received the goods it needed. Sales of many products, such as gasoline and sugar, to the civilian population were rationed. The wartime production boom put many unemployed Americans to work and put more money into their pockets. Shortages and rationing, however, dampened consumer spending. Americans were encouraged to buy war bonds to help the government raise money.

Roosevelt abandoned his Depression-era attempts to balance the federal budget: he believed the war had to be won at any cost. Wartime government spending far outpaced federal revenues. By 1945 the government was spending around $90 billion per year and taking in about half of that amount. The national debt skyrocketed from about $40 billion in 1940 to $258 billion in 1945.

Labor Issues

In 1942 Roosevelt obtained commitments from the large labor unions that they would not organize strikes during the war and that labor disputes would be settled peacefully. He also issued Executive Order 9017, creating the National War Labor Board (NWLB), which was to mediate any labor disputes that could not be settled by unions and employers themselves. Despite these measures, a number of strikes erupted during the war, most notably in 1943 by the mine-workers union. The government responded by taking control of the coal mines.

The War Labor Disputes Act (1943) gave the government the power to seize businesses in which labor disputes were believed detrimental to the war effort. In 1944 Roosevelt used that power to take control of Montgomery Ward—a large company that manufactured consumer goods. The company's chairman, Sewell Avery (1873–1960), was carried out of his office and into the street by two soldiers after he refused to cooperate with labor directives from the NWLB.

The NWLB was notable in that it insisted on equal pay for equal work by minorities. Women and African-Americans entered the workforce in large numbers during the war, particularly in factory jobs that had previously been closed to them. The NWLB abolished the separate classifications of "colored laborer" and "white laborer," which were commonly used by industries at the time. The agency pointed out that "discrimination on account of race or creed is in line with the Nazi program." Such measures met with various success in practice. Many of the strikes during the war were "hate strikes" waged by white workers protesting the employment or promotion of African-Americans.

At the urging of his wife, Eleanor Roosevelt (1884–1962), and civil rights leaders, Roosevelt issued several executive orders during the war intended to eliminate employment discrimination by government contractors and in the war industries. In 1943 he created the Fair Employment Practices Committee, which had limited success at integrating the nation's workplaces.

Civil Rights Issues The prospect of good-paying factory jobs during the war lured many African-Americans from the South to northern industrial cities. Many white factory workers resented this influx and staged slowdowns and protests. Away from the factories a severe housing shortage increased racial tensions until street violence erupted. In the summer of 1943 race riots in Detroit killed dozens of people. Cars were overturned and set afire and people beaten at random based on the color of their skin. The police arrested more than eighteen hundred people, most of them African-Americans. Leaders of the National Association for the Advancement of Colored People, including Thurgood Marshall (1908–1993), who would later become a U.S. Supreme Court justice, complained bitterly about the police response. The president sent federal troops to the city to maintain order; he avoided, however, making the riots a political issue for fear of alienating his southern supporters. Racial problems continued to simmer around the country during the war and intensified as returning African-American veterans ran into segregation and discriminatory labor practices.

Elsewhere another civil rights issue festered: the forced internment, or relocation to camps, of thousands of Japanese Americans during the war. In February 1942 Roosevelt issued Executive Order 9066 granting authority to the military to exclude people for national security

THE DECISION TO USE ATOMIC BOMBS

The government's decision to use atomic bombs in World War II started with a 1939 letter from physicist Albert Einstein (1879–1955) to President Franklin Roosevelt (1882–1945). Einstein told the president about ongoing work in nuclear physics that could possibly lead to the construction of "extremely powerful bombs of a new type" and suggested the U.S. government become involved in the research. Just as important, he warned that Nazi Germany was likely engaged in a similar program. The result in the United States was the Manhattan Project, a top-secret partnership that combined the efforts of academics, military strategists, and industrial planners.

The goal at first was to develop an atomic bomb before the Germans did. By early 1945 it was obvious that Germany was not going to win the war and had made little progress in atomic-bomb research. The U.S. government turned its focus toward Japan. An invasion of Japan was expected to lead to many U.S. casualties, so government officials hoped to use the atomic bomb to persuade the Japanese to surrender unconditionally and quickly; U.S. leaders wanted the surrender before the Soviet Union entered the war in the Pacific and gained any control over the future of the region.

Shortly after Roosevelt died in April 1945, some of the scientists involved in the Manhattan Project petitioned his successor, Harry Truman (1884–1972), hoping to persuade him to demonstrate the atomic bomb on uninhabited territory before dropping it on Japan. They had begun to realize the terrible destruction their invention could cause, and they thought a demonstration would be enough to bring about Japan's surrender. The president's advisers did not believe such a demonstration would deter a fanatical enemy. Truman, reminded of the many casualties the United States suffered throughout the South Pacific and fearing an even larger death toll if the United States invaded Japan, decided to go ahead with the bombing.

On August 6, 1945, an atomic bomb was dropped on Hiroshima, Japan. Approximately seventy thousand people died in the blast or soon afterward. America warned the Japanese that more bombs of that type would be used against them if they did not surrender. Stubborn elements within the Japanese military refused to agree. On August 9, 1945, an atomic bomb was dropped on Nagasaki, Japan. Approximately forty thousand people were killed immediately. Japan's emperor intervened and forced the Japanese government to surrender, ending World War II.

reasons from designated "military areas." The Pacific Coast region was declared a military area, and all people of Japanese descent were ordered to relocate to internment camps away from the coast. The order applied even to U.S. citizens. The government's actions were challenged in the courts, but in *Korematsu v. United States* (1944) the Supreme Court ruled the internment constitutional. In January 1945 Roosevelt disbanded the camps and freed their inhabitants. Decades later the surviving internees received an official apology and reparations from the government.

A New Role for the United States World War II catapulted the United States into a position of world leadership. U.S. agriculture and industry were not damaged during the war, as they were in every other major country, so the nation's economy flourished. It decided to extend economic aid to rebuild Japan and Western Europe, creating valuable allies and trading partners in the process. It also abandoned its prewar isolationist stance and took a leading role in the new United Nations, a body designed to use diplomacy to settle international differences. The United States also, however, began to build and maintain its military might and nuclear arsenal: it had become a superpower and saw a need to provide a deterrent against future aggressors.

U.S. Ratification of the United Nations Charter

On July 28, 1945, the U.S. Senate ratified the United Nations (UN) charter, making the nation one of the founding members of an international organization

The United Nations building in New York. © *Paul Almasy/CORBIS*

formed to achieve peace in the world through diplomacy. The organization grew out of a 1941 meeting between President Franklin Roosevelt (1882–1945) and British Prime Minister Winston Churchill (1874–1965), at which they developed the Atlantic Charter: the document laid out their hopes for a world in which differences between nations could be settled by diplomats, rather than armies. Roosevelt suggested an international organization called the United Nations to ensure that peace and security were maintained. The UN was to have much more authority than the League of Nations, which had resulted from the peace treaties that ended World War I but which had failed to prevent the outbreak of World War II.

Representatives of fifty countries met in San Francisco, California, in April 1945 to finalize the UN charter, which was based on an outline drawn up the previous year at Dumbarton Oaks, a mansion in Washington, D.C. The charter contained 111 articles describing the goals, structure, and activities of an organization whose stated purpose was "to save succeeding generations from the scourge of war." Among the most important elements of the organization's framework was the Security Council, which was made up of eleven (later fifteen) member states. Five nations—Great Britain, the Republic of China, France, the Soviet Union, and the United States—were designated permanent members of the Security Council. The remaining positions were to rotate among the other member countries. Most important, each permanent member of the Security Council got veto power over resolutions dealing with substantive issues, even if those resolutions had been approved by all other members of the Security Council.

Fifty countries signed the charter; nevertheless, for the United Nations to become an official organization, the charter had to be ratified by the governments of the five permanent members of the Security Council and a majority of the other signatories.

The Senate Ratification The U.S. Senate spent just six days considering ratification of the UN charter. In the end only two senators voted against it—Henrik Shipstead (1881–1960), a Republican from Minnesota, and William "Wild Bill" Langer (1886–1959), a Republican from North Dakota. Senator Burton Wheeler (1882–1975), a Democrat from Montana, gave an impassioned three-hour speech against the charter, but reluctantly voted to ratify.

The most serious objections were aimed at Article 43, Section 1, of the charter, which read: "All Members of the United Nations, in order to contribute to the maintenance of international peace and security, undertake to make available to the Security Council, on its call and in accordance with a special agreement or agreements, armed forces, assistance, and facilities, including rights of passage, necessary for the purpose of maintaining international peace and security." Opponents argued that the provision took war power away from Congress, violating the U.S. Constitution.

On October 24, 1945, the last required ratification was obtained, and the UN became an official organization. World War II had ended only two months before. The major victors in the war were the permanent members of the Security Council. It was hoped that they could ensure international peace and security. The United States had been allied with the Soviet Union and China during the war, but their relationships soured over the following decades as the cold war came to dominate world politics.

✪ Legislation, Court Cases, and Trials

Near v. Minnesota

In *Near v. Minnesota* (1931), the U.S. Supreme Court ruled that the government could not prevent publication of materials by the press, except in "exceptional" circumstances. The case involved a tabloid, the *Saturday Press*, published in Minneapolis by Jay Near. In 1927 Near published several articles that accused local officials and citizens of wrongdoing. County officials ordered him to cease publishing because of a state law that barred publication of "malicious, scandalous, and defamatory" information. Near complained that the order violated his right of freedom of the press under the Constitution. The Supreme Court agreed and invalidated the Minnesota law.

Background of the Case In his newspaper Near claimed that Jewish gangsters were blatantly conducting criminal acts in Minneapolis and that police and local government officials knew about the crimes, but did nothing to stop them. The stories accused the chief of police of being in cahoots with the gangsters and alleged that the city's mayor and major newspapers were also involved in the conspiracy.

Near was ordered by the county attorney not to publish "any future editions" of the newspaper, which in legal terms is known as abatement or prior restraint. It is equivalent to issuing a gag order to prevent someone from making information public.

The Court Decision Chief Justice Charles Evans Hughes (1862–1948), writing for the Court, noted that freedom of the press had historically been interpreted to mean that the government could not censor or prevent publication of materials except in certain "exceptional" circumstances. As an example, he wrote, "No one would question but that a government might prevent actual obstruction to its recruiting service or the publication of the sailing dates of transports or the number and location of troops."

Hughes warned that the Minnesota law could lead to situations in which government officials forced newspaper publishers to disclose what they intended to publish in the future. This, he reasoned, would be "a step to a complete system of censorship." The Minnesota statute under which Near had been charged was ruled to be an infringement of freedom of the press guaranteed by the Fourteenth Amendment of the U.S. Constitution. The Court noted that freedom of the press does not protect publishers against prosecution for publishing material that is libelous or slanderous. That determination, however, has to be made after the material is published, not before.

The Ramifications

Four decades later the issue of prior restraint was raised when the *New York Times* began publishing excerpts from the so-called Pentagon Papers, a massive U.S. Department of Defense document that examined how and why the United States had become involved in the Vietnam War. Copies of the document had been leaked to the press by a government employee. The Nixon administration took the newspaper to court to stop it from publishing additional excerpts. The U.S. Department of Justice used the "exceptional" example cited by Hughes in 1931 as grounds for its attempted abatement. The Supreme Court ultimately heard the case and ruled in *New York Times v. United States* (1971) that the government did not have sufficient reason to exercise prior restraint.

Powell v. Alabama

In *Powell v. Alabama* (1932) the U.S. Supreme Court ruled that the right to due process had not been afforded to nine young African-American men convicted of raping two white women in Alabama. The "Scottsboro boys," as they became known, had received hasty trials without being given a chance to hire lawyers. All nine were convicted, and eight of them were sentenced to death. Their cases were appealed to the Supreme Court, which invalidated their convictions in concurrent rulings in *Powell v. Alabama*, *Patterson v. Alabama*, and *Weems v. Alabama*.

The Criminal Trials

On March 25, 1931, groups of white and African-American male youths got into a fight while riding a freight train in northern Alabama. The train was stopped by a local sheriff, and nine African-Americans were arrested and charged with assault. Two young white women who had been aboard the train claimed the youths in custody had raped them. Six days later a grand jury indicted the Scottsboro boys, and a week after that the trials began. Huge crowds of angry whites congregated around the courthouse during the trials, so the military was called in to guard and transport the defendants.

The Scottsboro boys were tried in groups, with each trial lasting only a day or two. By April 9 eight of the defendants had been found guilty and sentenced to death. The trial of the ninth defendant—the youngest of the group at fourteen years of age—ended in a hung jury when one jury member held out for life in prison instead of a death sentence.

The verdicts received national attention and were soundly condemned by socially progressive groups, such as the National Association for the Advancement of Colored People and the International Labor Defense. The executions were delayed while the convictions were appealed to higher courts.

The Supreme Court Rulings

In May 1932 the Supreme Court considered appeals based on three issues: the lack of a fair and impartial trial, the denial of the right to counsel, and the lack of African-Americans on the juries. In *Powell v. Alabama*, the Court considered only the issues related to the denial of right to counsel.

The judge who had presided at the criminal trials had vaguely appointed "all members of the bar" to represent the defendants. At the outset of the first trial, he asked if all parties were ready to proceed. No one answered for the defense. An attorney from out of state told the court that he was present at the request of the defendants' families to observe the proceedings and would lend his assistance to whatever local attorney took the case. He pointed out, however, that he had not prepared a defense and was not familiar with Alabama law. He was promptly appointed to represent the defendants and reluctantly did so. Justice George Sutherland (1862–1942), writing for the Supreme Court, noted that "until the very morning of the trial no lawyer had been named or definitely designated to represent the defendants." He added: "[Given] the ignorance and illiteracy of the defendants, their youth, the circumstances of public hostility, the imprisonment and the close surveillance of the defendants by the military forces, the fact that their friends and families were all in other states and communication with them necessarily difficult, and above all that they stood in deadly peril of their lives—we think the failure of the trial court to give them reasonable time and opportunity to secure counsel was a clear denial of due process." The convictions were overturned.

The Trials Continue

The saga of the Scottsboro boys continued to unfold for decades after the Supreme Court decision, as most of the youths were retried in Alabama courts, convicted, and sentenced to death again. The executions, however, were delayed as legal maneuvers continued. The International Labor Defense persuaded well-known attorney Samuel Leibowitz (1893–1978) to take one of the cases, and in 1935 he argued before the Supreme Court that the criminal convictions were invalid because African-Americans had been intentionally left out of the jury pools. The Court agreed in *Norris v. Alabama* (1935). Another round of criminal trials resulted in convictions and lengthy prison sentences. Continued public scrutiny helped most of Scottsboro boys achieve parole by the end of the 1940s.

The Legacy of the Cases To many Americans the trials of the Scottsboro boys have come to epitomize the racial injustices common to the era. The Supreme Court decisions gave the burgeoning civil rights movement new vigor to fight racism, particularly the Jim Crow—or separate-but-equal—laws that were common throughout the South. During the 1950s and 1960s this battle achieved such results as *Brown v. Board of Education*, which abolished segregation in the public schools, and the Civil Rights Act of 1964.

The Emergency Relief Appropriation Act of 1935

The Emergency Relief Appropriation Act of 1935 granted President Franklin Roosevelt (1882–1945) the authority to establish programs to provide aid and work during the Great Depression. Ultimately nearly $5 billion in funding was devoted to these programs, which were part of the New Deal, the president's socioeconomic agenda. The programs included the Works Progress Administration, the National Youth Administration, the Resettlement Administration, and the Rural Electrification Administration.

The Second New Deal When Roosevelt took office in 1933 his programs focused primarily on direct aid. Relief funds were provided to the states to distribute to the unemployed and needy. Three work programs did exist: the Civilian Conservation Corps employed young men in forestry and conservation projects; the Public Works Administration provided jobs in the construction of roads, dams, and public buildings; and the Civil Works Administration created short-term employment during the winter of 1933–1934.

In January 1935 the president decided to change New Deal policies to put more able-bodied Americans into work programs and return the responsibility for providing direct financial aid to state and local governments. In most cases direct aid was reserved for people unable to work, usually because of age or disability. The programs that resulted from this policy change were dubbed the "second New Deal."

Executive Order 7027 established the Resettlement Administration (RA), whose mission included resettling "destitute or low-income families" from rural and urban areas to new communities; setting up programs devoted to forestation, soil and beach erosion, water pollution, flood control, and drought relief; and providing financing to farmers and farmworkers for the purchase of land and equipment. The RA also supervised the migrant-worker camps that were built in California to handle the huge influx of refugees from the Great Plains, where drought and winds had created the Dust Bowl.

The Works Progress Administration (WPA), created by Executive Order 7034, employed millions of people who built and repaired schools, hospitals, sports stadiums, and bridges; planted trees in parks; and installed public storm drains and sewer lines. Other WPA programs provided work for actors, authors, artists, and musicians. Executive Order 7086 created the National Youth Administration, which gave grants to students so they could stay in school and supplied economic aid and job training for unemployed youths.

Executive Order 7037 established the Rural Electrification Administration (REA), which brought electricity to rural areas not served by private utilities. The REA received hundreds of millions of dollars in funding after passage of the Norris-Rayburn Act in 1936. With REA help 25 percent of the nation's rural households and farms had electricity by 1939, up from around 10 percent at the beginning of the decade.

Paying for Relief Roosevelt hoped his emergency relief programs would jump-start American business, but that did not happen. His critics complained that the programs created "busy work" for the unemployed at the expense of the nation's more affluent citizens. Four months after passage of the Emergency Relief Appropriation Act, a massive tax bill made its way through Congress. It included sharp tax increases for the wealthiest individuals and corporations, which some observers now believe may have stymied investment in new businesses at a time when it was most needed.

Schechter Poultry Corp. v. United States

In *Schechter Poultry Corp. v. United States* (1935) the U.S. Supreme Court invalidated portions of the National Industrial Recovery Act (NIRA), which created a government-business-labor partnership during the Great Depression. The Court ruled that the NIRA was unconstitutional because it allowed the president to set "codes of fair practice" for industries and because it attempted to enforce the codes on businesses engaged in in-state commerce that did not directly affect interstate commerce. (Interstate commerce may be regulated by Congress under the Commerce Clause of the U.S. Constitution.)

The NIRA (1933) gave the federal government a major role in the economic and labor affairs of private businesses, for it encouraged companies within industries to form alliances, set production quotas, and fix prices and wages. The law exempted these arrangements from federal antitrust laws, which would have forbidden such collusion. The law created the National Recovery Administration to develop the fair-competition codes and, in Section 3, specifically authorized the president to approve them. The codes, which regulated work hours, wages, and other business practices, became extremely unpopular, particularly with smaller companies whose owners believed that the codes favored big businesses. Violations of the codes were criminal misdemeanor offenses punishable by fines.

Within a year the law was challenged in court. The case involved chicken slaughterhouses and markets operated by the Schechter family in New York City, which were subject to the Live Poultry Code. Authorized by Executive Order 6675-A, the code specified a forty-hour workweek for most employees and a minimum wage of fifty cents per hour. The business operators were tried and convicted in New York for eighteen violations related to trade practices, minimum wages, and maximum work hours. They appealed the conviction, arguing that the NIRA represented an unconstitutional delegation by Congress of legislative power to the president and that the law attempted to regulate in-state transactions that were outside the authority of Congress.

In 1935 the U.S. Supreme Court ruled unanimously in *Schechter* that the codes section of the NIRA was unconstitutional. Chief Justice Charles Evans Hughes (1862–1948), writing for the Court, acknowledged that the NIRA was crafted by Congress in the midst of a grave national crisis, the Great Depression. He cautioned, however, that "extraordinary conditions do not create or enlarge constitutional power," adding that "Congress cannot delegate legislative power to the President to exercise an unfettered discretion to make whatever laws he thinks may be needed or advisable for the rehabilitation and expansion of trade or industry." In addition the Court ruled that the code's attempted regulation of in-state transactions was invalid because the transactions did not directly affect interstate commerce.

President Franklin Roosevelt (1882–1945) was said to be infuriated by the Court's decision in *Schechter*. It played a major role in his attempt in 1937 to "reorganize" the Supreme Court: he pushed legislation that would have allowed him to appoint one additional justice for each sitting justice aged seventy or older. His proposal, which failed to pass, was criticized widely as an overextension of presidential power, just as the NIRA had been denounced by the Supreme Court.

The National Labor Relations Act of 1935

The National Labor Relations Act (NLRA) of 1935 was designed to improve labor relations during the Great Depression by encouraging workers to form labor unions and bargain collectively with their employers. It granted authority to enforce the law to a National Labor Relations Board. Because the stated purpose of the law was to limit the effects of labor disputes on interstate commerce, the law passed U.S. Supreme Court scrutiny in 1937.

Background of the Law Although the NLRA is often heralded as a revolutionary step in labor history, its provisions actually evolved from a series of older acts. The government's national labor policy had its roots in the War Labor Board, a temporary agency established in 1918 that recognized the right of workers to organize unions and bargain collectively. In 1926 Congress passed the Railway Labor Act, which guaranteed that right to workers in the railway industry. The law was amended in 1934 to create the National Mediation Board, an independent agency that helped settle railroad labor disputes.

Prior to the Great Depression the federal courts usually considered labor organizing activities and strikes to be impediments to interstate commerce, so court injunctions or restraining orders were commonly issued. The Norris-LaGuardia Act of 1932 greatly limited this court authority and clarified federal labor policy, recognizing the freedom of employees to unionize and bargain collectively. The policy was reinforced in 1933 by passage of the National Industrial Recovery Act (NIRA), which contained a number of provisions affecting the government-business-labor relationship. Section 7(a) of the law specified that employees had the right to organize and bargain collectively and that employers could not interfere in those activities or force employees to join or refrain from joining a union.

When the Supreme Court invalidated other sections of the NIRA in *Schechter Poultry Corp. v. United States* (1935), the provisions of NIRA's section 7(a) were incorporated into the NLRA. Section 1 includes the following statement: "It is declared to be the policy of the United States to eliminate the causes of certain substantial obstructions to the free flow of commerce and to mitigate and eliminate these obstructions when they have occurred by encouraging the practice and procedure of collective bargaining and by protecting the exercise by workers of full freedom of association, self-organization, and designation of representatives of their own choosing, for the purpose of negotiating the terms and conditions of their employment or other mutual aid or protection." The NLRA, also known as the Wagner Act—one of its chief proponents was Robert Wagner Sr. (1877–1953), a Democratic senator from New York—was administered by the National Labor Relations Board (NLRB), an independent agency that had been created earlier. The NLRA greatly strengthened the scope and power of the board.

The Supreme Court Ruling The NLRA was widely condemned by business and employer groups; in 1937, however, the U.S. Supreme Court ruled five to four, in *National Labor Relations Board v. Jones & Laughlin Steel Corp.*, that the law was constitutional. Chief Justice Charles Evans Hughes (1862–1948) wrote that the NLRA served "to safeguard the right of employees" to organize and bargain collectively with their employers. He called it a "fundamental right" and noted that "employees have as clear a right to organize and select their representatives for lawful purposes as the respondent has to organize its business and select its own officers and agents."

The Smith Committee The controversy festered, however, as business leaders complained bitterly that the NLRB was biased against them. In 1939 Howard

First meeting of the National Labor Relations Board, 1934. © *Bettmann/CORBIS*

Worth Smith (1883–1976), a conservative Democratic representative from Virginia, formed a committee to investigate their claims. Smith, who believed that the NLRB espoused a Communist agenda and wanted to limit its power, complained that more strikes had taken place between 1935 and 1939 than in any period since the early 1920s. The NLRB defended its actions and pointed out that fewer workers had been involved in the strikes in question than in previous strikes. Smith introduced legislation in 1940 that would have curtailed the NLRB's power, but the bill died in the Senate. His hearings, however, did tarnish the image of the NLRB and led to internal changes in the board's administration.

The Decades Since The NLRA was substantially amended in 1947 by the Taft-Hartley Act, which incorporated some of the changes that Smith had sought. Strikes were common at the time, which was also the beginning of the cold war between the Soviet Union and the West. Many Americans had suspicions about ties between labor unions and communism. The Taft-Hartley Act granted greater power to government and business to prevent union activities and strikes. In particular the president was given the authority to obtain court injunctions to end strikes considered damaging to the national economy. That authority has been exercised on several occasions.

The Social Security Act of 1935

The Social Security Act of 1935 established a federal program of pensions for retirees and financial aid for the disabled and needy. A groundbreaking law, it was designed to help the most vulnerable victims of the Great Depression. During the following decades the scope of the program was greatly expanded to provide coverage for more segments of the population. Social Security is one New Deal program that survives to the

Female labor protesters at a General Motors plant, 1937.   © *Bettmann/CORBIS*

present day; its survival, however, has been repeatedly threatened by funding shortages.

Building a Safety Net   The early twentieth century witnessed the establishment of a number of state programs to provide benefits or pensions for the unemployed, elderly, blind, disabled, or needy. The payouts were small, however, and tight restrictions limited the number of people who could participate. These drawbacks did not become a major issue until the Great Depression, when the idea of a national benefit system gained popularity.

Several pension schemes were proposed, including the "Share-the-Wealth" plan of Louisiana Governor Huey Long (1893–1935), which called for heavy taxes on the wealthiest Americans to provide monthly benefits for everyone else. By the mid-1930s Share-the-Wealth clubs claimed to have more than 7 million members around the country. Another program, the Townsend Old-Age Revolving Pension Plan, was championed by

Francis Townsend (1867–1960), a California doctor. It called for a national sales tax to fund pensions for every American aged sixty or older.

In 1934 Congress passed the Railroad Retirement Act, a centerpiece of the New Deal agenda of President Franklin Roosevelt (1882–1945). It established benefits for retired and disabled workers in the industry and lump-sum payments to their survivors. Although it was later ruled unconstitutional by the U.S. Supreme Court, the law provided a blueprint for a larger and more sweeping program. The Committee on Economic Security, established by Roosevelt's Executive Order 6757, developed recommendations that became part of the Economic Security Bill of 1935. While it was being deliberated in Congress, the bill's name was changed to the Social Security Act. After the House of Representatives and the Senate both passed it by wide margins, Roosevelt signed it into law on August 14, 1935.

The president referred to Social Security as "social insurance." It was a contributory program that required

President Franklin Roosevelt signing the Social Security Bill, 1935. © *Bettmann/CORBIS*

wage earners and their employers to pay taxes into the system; when they retired those workers could collect monthly payments to sustain them in their old age. In addition Social Security assisted the states in providing for "aged persons, blind persons, dependent and crippled children, maternal and child welfare, public health, and the administration of unemployment compensation laws."

Social Security Evolves The new law was not universally embraced, particularly by those who had supported other alternatives. A filibuster led by Long prevented passage of a budget bill in 1935, which included funding to set up the new program. Congress finally provided the funding the following year.

The law was challenged repeatedly in the courts—conservatives believed it was an improper expansion of government power and an intrusion into the private lives of citizens, and businesses opposed the new taxes created by the law. In 1937, however, a series of Supreme Court decisions upheld the constitutionality of the Social Security Act. The rulings came in *Helvering v. Davis*,

Steward Machine Company v. Davis, and *Carmichael v. Southern Coal & Coke and Gulf States Paper*.

In 1939 the law was amended to provide benefits for the dependents (spouses and children) of retired workers and for the survivors of covered workers who died before retiring. Additional amendments in the 1950s and 1960s dramatically increased benefit levels, included coverage for the disabled, and lowered the age at which retirees became eligible for benefits. In 1965 Congress created Medicare, a program that provided medical health insurance to covered retirees in exchange for deductions from their Social Security checks.

By the early 1970s the Social Security program was in financial difficulty. Expansion of benefits and coverage, combined with longer life spans for beneficiaries, put the future of the program in jeopardy. In 1940 the program included slightly more than two hundred thousand beneficiaries. By 1970 that number had jumped to 26 million and was growing rapidly. Congress responded by amending the Social Security Act to increase the taxes collected, raise the retirement age, and reduce benefits. When the post–World War II baby boom ended, the drop in the birthrate resulted in fewer workers to pay into the system even as more retirees reached retirement age. Most observers believe that, unless a politically acceptable solution to the funding problem is found, a serious shortfall will occur, resulting in sharp cuts in benefits.

The Judiciary Reorganization Bill of 1937

The Judiciary Reorganization Bill of 1937 was an attempt by President Franklin Roosevelt (1882–1945) to increase the number of U.S. Supreme Court justices. The "court-packing plan," as it was quickly called, was assailed by critics as an effort to create a court more favorable to the New Deal, Roosevelt's socioeconomic agenda. He was known to be frustrated by the Court's repeated invalidation of early New Deal legislation. The plan did not gain political popularity—in fact, the opposite happened. It is considered one of Roosevelt's greatest missteps as president.

The Early New Deal in Court Roosevelt, who had won the presidency by a landslide in 1932, was reelected easily in 1936, which he took as a sign that the voters were overwhelmingly in favor of his New Deal programs. During its first few years in office his administration pushed dozens of bills through Congress. New Deal–type legislation was also adopted in some states. Many of the new laws were challenged in court, with a few of the cases reaching the Supreme Court. The Court declared unconstitutional portions of the Railroad Retirement Act (*Railroad Retirement Board v. Alton*, 1935), the National Industrial Recovery Act (*Schechter Poultry v. United States*, 1935), the Agricultural Adjustment Act (*United States v. Butler*, 1936), and New York state's minimum-wage law (*Morehead v. New York*, 1936).

The plan Roosevelt presented to Congress in February 1937 specified that, in the future, a president could make a new appointment for any federal judge or justice who did not retire at age seventy. In 1937 six of the nine Supreme Court justices were older than seventy. His proposal capped the total number of justices at fifteen—an increase from nine, the figure most common throughout the nation's history. He presented this plan to the people in a March 9, 1937, radio address—one of his "fireside chats"—arguing that "the Court has been acting not as a judicial body, but as a policy-making body." He noted that the Supreme Court was acting to "thwart the will of the people" and "reading into the Constitution words and implications which are not there." Roosevelt complained of "hardening of the judicial arteries" and urged his listeners to "save the Constitution from the Court and the Court from itself."

Roosevelt's critics considered the plan a brazen attempt to appoint liberal-minded justices who would look favorably upon New Deal legislation. Even some Democratic members of Congress were aghast at the proposal. It was debated on the Senate floor in July 1937 but was not enacted.

The Switch In the spring of 1937 the Supreme Court made several rulings that seemed to indicate a change in attitude. They upheld as constitutional the state of Washington's minimum-wage law (*West Coast Hotel Co. v. Parrish*), the National Labor Relations Act (*National Labor Relations Board v. Jones & Laughlin Steel Corp.*), and the Social Security Act (*Helvering v. Davis, Steward Machine Company v. Davis*, and *Carmichael v. Southern Coal & Coke and Gulf States Paper*). The media jokingly called it "the switch in time that saved nine," a twist on the common proverb. Historians still debate whether the "switch" occurred because the justices were intimidated by Roosevelt's reorganization plan or because later New Deal legislation was more carefully written to be within constitutional bounds.

West Virginia Board of Education v. Barnette

In *West Virginia Board of Education v. Barnette* (1943) the U.S. Supreme Court held that the government could not require children in public schools to salute the American flag. The family that brought the case to court believed saluting the flag constituted worship of an icon, which violated their religious beliefs. *Barnette* reversed the Court's decision of three years earlier in which it said that civic responsibility to salute the flag outweighed religious sensibilities.

The Salute During the early decades of the twentieth century it was common practice to salute the flag during the Pledge of Allegiance by holding the right arm stretched upward toward the flag. The so-called Bellamy salute was named after Francis Bellamy (1855–1931), who first suggested it in 1892 when he printed the pledge in his youth magazine. During World War II the Bellamy salute lost favor in the United States because it was similar to the salute used by the Nazi Party in Germany. The salute was replaced by a hand-over-heart gesture, which Congress officially made part of the Flag Code in 1942.

In 1940 the Supreme Court debated the case of *Minersville School District v. Gobitis*. Two children of the Gobitis family, who were Jehovah's Witnesses, had been expelled from a public school in Pennsylvania for refusing to salute the flag. The Jehovah's Witnesses are a religious group who believe they are forbidden by biblical text from worshipping anyone or anything other than God. They found the flag salute objectionable on these grounds. The Supreme Court ruled in an 8–1 decision that the government's interest in maintaining "national cohesion" justified the mandatory flag salute in public schools.

A Change in Perspective In 1943 the Barnette family of West Virginia, who also were Jehovah's Witnesses, protested the local school district's policy requiring that all children salute the flag during the recital of the Pledge of Allegiance. The school district's policy specified a Bellamy salute with the palm of the hand turned upward. Children who refused to salute the flag could be expelled, and their parents were subject to criminal

Children and teachers saluting the American flag. The Supreme Court held that compulsory flag salutes are unconstitutional.   © *Underwood &*
Underwood/CORBIS

prosecution under West Virginia law for contributing to the delinquency of minors.

The Supreme Court ruled 6–3 that West Virginia authorities had exceeded constitutional limits on their power by requiring mandatory flag salutes. Justice Robert Jackson (1892–1954), writing for the Court, stated that the "validity of the asserted power to force an American citizen publicly to profess any statement of belief or to engage in any ceremony of assent to one, presents questions of power that must be considered independently of any idea we may have as to the utility of the ceremony in question."

In 1919 Justice Oliver Wendell Holmes Jr. (1841–1935) had established the "clear and present danger" test as a measure of whether utterances in public were covered by the First Amendment right to freedom of expression. Jackson noted in the West Virginia case that the government was not even alleging that failure to salute the flag constituted a "clear and present danger" to the nation. Furthermore, he wrote, "to sustain the

compulsory flag salute we are required to say that a Bill of Rights which guards the individual's right to speak his own mind, left it open to public authorities to compel him to utter what is not in his mind." He concluded that the mandatory flag salute "invades the sphere of intellect and spirit which it is the purpose of the First Amendment to our Constitution to reserve from all official control."

By either odd coincidence or purposeful action, the Supreme Court's decision in this case was handed down on June 14—Flag Day. Debates over the government's authority to regulate the behavior of Americans regarding the flag have not abated since that day. In 1989 the Supreme Court ruled in *Texas v. Johnson* that a Texas law forbidding desecration of the flag—in this case the burning of an American flag during a political protest—was unconstitutional. On several occasions since then politicians have tried unsuccessfully to pass an amendment to the Constitution that would make flag desecration illegal.

BIBLIOGRAPHY

Books

Galenson, Walter. *The CIO Challenge to the AFL: A History of the American Labor Movement, 1935–1941*. Cambridge, MA: Harvard University Press, 1960.

Law, Gordon T., Jr., ed. *A Guide to Sources of Information on the National Labor Relations Board*. Abingdon, UK: Routledge, 2002.

Neal, Steve, ed. *Eleanor and Harry: The Correspondence of Eleanor Roosevelt and Harry S. Truman*. New York: A Lisa Drew Book/Scribner, 2002.

Periodicals

Berg, Gordon. "Frances Perkins and the Flowering of Economic and Social Policies." *Monthly Labor Review* 112 (June 1989): 28–32.

Collins, William J. "Race, Roosevelt, and Wartime Production: Fair Employment in World War II Labor Markets." *American Economic Review* 91 (March 2001): 272–286.

Kilborn, Peter T. "From Binge to Bust: The Legacy of the Crash." *New York Times*, September 23, 1979. http://select.nytimes.com/mem/archive/pdf?res=F70A1EF93A5D11728DDDAA0A94D1405B898BF1D3 (accessed March 13, 2007).

Kort, Michael. "Racing the Enemy: A Critical Look." *Historically Speaking* 7, no. 3 (January/February 2006). http://www.bu.edu/historic/hs/kort.html (accessed March 23, 2007).

Los Angeles Times, "LAPD Blocked Dust Bowl Migrants at State Borders," March 9, 2003. http://pqasb.pqarchiver.com/latimes/access/303634661.html?dids=303634661:303634661&FMT=FT&FMTS=ABS:FT&type=current&date=Mar+9%2C+2003&author=Cecilia+Rasmussen&pub=Los+Angeles+Times&edition=&startpage=B.4&desc=Los+Angeles (accessed March 20, 2007).

Morrow, Lance. "George C. Marshall: The Last Great American?" *Smithsonian* 28 (August 1997): 104–115.

Neuberger, Richard L. "Who Are the Associated Farmers?" *Survey Graphic* 28, no. 9 (September 1939): 517. http://newdeal.feri.org/survey/39b12.htm (accessed March 19, 2007).

New York Times, "Anacostia Camp No More." July 29, 1932. http://select.nytimes.com/mem/archive/pdf?res=F00C17F73E5513738DDDA00A94DF405B828FF1D3 (accessed March 10, 2007).

Rural Migration News, "Farm Labor in the 1930s," October 2003. http://migration.ucdavis.edu/rmn/comments.php?id=788_0_6_0 (accessed March 19, 2007).

Seeber, Frances M. "'I Want You to Write to Me': The Papers of Anna Eleanor Roosevelt." *Prologue* 19 (Summer 1987): 95–100.

Smith, Richard Norton, and Timothy Walch. "The Ordeal of Herbert Hoover, Part 2." *Prologue* 36, no. 2 (Summer 2004). http://www.archives.gov/publications/prologue/2004/summer/hoover-2.html (accessed February 5, 2007).

Time, "The Boondoggle Recalled," March 6, 1972. http://www.time.com/time/magazine/article/0,9171,910233,00.html (accessed March 20, 2007).

Time, "Headlines v. Breadlines," March 31, 1930. http://www.time.com/time/magazine/article/0,9171,738940,00.html (accessed March 17, 2007).

Uelmen, Gerald F. "The Vindication of Hugo Black." *Champion*, January–February 2003:18.

Web sites

Bierman, Harold, Jr. "The 1929 Stock Market Crash." Robert Whaples, ed. EH.Net Encyclopedia. http://eh.net/encyclopedia/article/Bierman.Crash (accessed March 13, 2007).

Couch, Jim. "The Works Progress Administration." EH.Net Encyclopedia. http://eh.net/encyclopedia/article/couch.works.progress.administration (accessed February 20, 2007).

Federal Bureau of Investigation. "FBI History." http://www.fbi.gov/fbihistory.htm (accessed April 3, 2007).

Federal Communications Commission. "Communications Act of 1934." Collected Engineering Documents from the Audio Division, Media Bureau. http://search.fcc.gov/query.html?qt=Communications+Act+of+1934&col=fccall&ht=0&qp=&qs=&qc=&pw=100%25&ws=0&la=en&qm=0&st=1&nh=300&lk=1&rf=0&oq=&rq=0&si=0&Submit+search+request.x=10&Submit+search+request.y=9 (accessed April 21, 2007).

Franklin and Eleanor Roosevelt Institute. "Eleanor Roosevelt Biography." Archives and Resources. http://www.feri.org/archives/erbio/ (accessed March 7, 2007).

Library of Congress. "Dorothea Lange." http://www.americaslibrary.gov/cgi-bin/page.cgi/aa/writers/lange (accessed February 27, 2007).

National Labor Relations Board. "The First Sixty Years: The Story of the National Labor Relations Board, 1935–1995." http://www.nlrb.gov/About_Us/History/thhe_first_60_years.aspx (accessed March 27, 2007).

National Museum of American History, the Smithsonian Institution. "America on the Move: Lives on the Railroad; Pullman Porter." http://americanhistory.si.edu/onthemove/exhibition/exhibition_9_6.html (accessed March 5, 2007).

Our Documents (an initiative of National History Day; the National Archives and Records Administration; and U.S. Freedom Corp). "National Labor

Relations Act (1935)." http://www.our documents.gov/doc.php?doc=67 (accessed March 27, 2007).

Public Broadcasting Service. "American Experience: Scottsboro, an American Tragedy." http://www.pbs.org/wgbh/amex/scottsboro/ (accessed March 29, 2007).

Public Broadcasting Service: "The Court and Democracy: Biographies of the Robes; Charles Evans Hughes." http://www.pbs.org/wnet/supremecourt/democracy/robes_hughes.html (accessed February 9, 2007).

Samuelson, Robert J. "Great Depression." *The Concise Encyclopedia of Economics.* http://www.econlib.org/LIBRARY/Enc/GreatDepression.html (accessed February 6, 2007).

Social Security Online. "Historical Background and Development of Social Security." http://www.ssa.gov/history/briefhistory3.html (accessed March 30, 2007).

Supreme Court Historical Society. "Historical Documentary Feature: FDR & the Court-Packing Controversy." http://www.supremecourthistory.org/02_history/02.html (accessed March 27, 2007).

Tennessee Valley Authority. "From the New Deal to a New Century: A Short History of TVA." http://www.tva.gov/abouttva/history.htm (accessed March 31, 2007).

Triebwasser, Marc A. "Radio and Television." Internet and Multimedia Studies, Central Connecticut State University. http://www.ims.ccsu.edu/Radio.htm (accessed April 2, 2007).

U.S. Department of Energy, Office of History and Heritage Resources. "The Manhattan Project: An Interactive History." http://www.mbe.doe.gov/me70/manhattan/ (accessed April 2, 2007).

U.S. Department of State. "Basic Readings in U.S. Democracy: Backgrounder on the Court Opinion on the *Near v. Minnesota* Case." http://usinfo.state.gov/usa/infousa/facts/democrac/45.htm (accessed February 20, 2007).

U.S. Department of State. "Basic Readings in U.S. Democracy: Introduction to the Court Opinion on the *West Virginia Board of Education v. Barnette* Case." http://usinfo.state.gov/usa/infousa/facts/democrac/46.htm (accessed March 27, 2007).

U.S. Department of State. "The United States and the Founding of the United Nations, August 1941–October 1945." http://www.state.gov/r/pa/ho/pubs/fs/55407.htm (accessed March 8, 2007).

U.S. Supreme Court Center. "*A. L. A. Schechter Poultry Corporation et al. v. United States*, 295 U.S. 495 (1935)." http://supreme.justia.com/us/295/495/case.html (accessed March 28, 2007).

U.S. Supreme Court Center. "*Powell et al. v. State of Alabama*, 287 U.S. 45 (1932)." http://supreme.justia.com/us/287/45/case.html (accessed March 29, 2007).

Zechowski, Sharon. "Public Interest, Convenience, and Necessity." Archives, the Museum of Broadcast Communications. http://www.museum.tv/archives/etv/P/htmlP/publicintere/publicintere.htm (accessed April 2, 2007).

Introduction to the Postwar Era (1945–1970)

Three important political events define the period between the end of World War II in 1945 and 1970: the Cold War, the civil rights movement, and the Vietnam War. These three events provide the overarching framework for a rich array of social and political changes that took place in America during that time.

The United States emerged from World War II in a strong position in world politics. Because the war was not fought on American soil, the nation's infrastructure was largely untouched. In contrast, the cities and economies of Western Europe suffered such a degree of destruction that it would require years and billions of dollars to repair. The biggest postwar concern of U.S. foreign policy was the perceived threat posed by the Soviet Union, the world's only other "superpower." Curbing the spread of communism became the chief principle behind every foreign policy decision. The United States poured vast sums of money into the war-torn economies of Europe and sent financial and military assistance to many Third World countries in hopes of keeping them from turning to communism.

The first major Cold War flare-up was the Korean War (1950–1953). During the early 1960s Cuba was a flashpoint for Cold War conflict, with the Cuban missile crisis bringing the United States and Soviet Union to the brink of nuclear war in 1962. Meanwhile, fear of communism was a major domestic issue during much of the 1950s as well. Unsubstantiated accusations by Republican Senator Joseph McCarthy (1908–1957) and hearings conducted by the House Committee on Un-American Activities ruined the careers of many innocent citizens based on warped notions of the magnitude of the communist threat within U.S. borders.

By the middle of the 1950s the civil rights movement emerged as a powerful force for social change in the United States. The U.S. Supreme Court's 1954 decision in *Brown v. Board of Education of Topeka*, which declared school segregation unconstitutional, helped to jump-start the movement. In addition to landmark civil rights legislation, laws were enacted to protect the environment and consumer safety. Important Supreme Court rulings expanded personal privacy rights, freedom of the press, and freedom of expression.

The nation suffered tragedy when President John F. Kennedy (1917–1963) was assassinated in November 1963. For many this event signified the end of innocence in American national consciousness. Kennedy's successor, Lyndon B. Johnson (1908–1973), launched a number of important social programs, collectively called the Great Society. Aimed at addressing poverty and racial injustice, the programs included Medicare, Medicaid, food stamps, and Head Start. These domestic accomplishments were overshadowed, however, by Johnson's escalation of U.S. involvement in Vietnam. By the final months of Johnson's term, opposition to the Vietnam War had grown fierce enough to play a central role in his decision not to seek reelection.

By the late 1960s the United States was a nation in conflict with itself. The civil rights movement had largely disintegrated, as the rise of more radical groups, which rejected Martin Luther King Jr.'s (1929–1968) pacifist approach, alienated many former supporters. Rioting erupted in several major cities. Vietnam had become an enormously unpopular quagmire. Nevertheless, the United States rose above the upheaval of the era and emerged from it with a greater understanding of its own identity.

The Postwar Era (1945–1970)

⭐ How They Were Governed

The Central Intelligence Agency (CIA)

Created by the National Security Act of 1947, the Central Intelligence Agency (CIA) is an independent government agency that collects and analyzes information, often covertly, about adversaries of, and potential threats to, the United States.

The United States has spied on its enemies ever since it came into existence. Over time, American intelligence capabilities evolved into an uncoordinated effort scattered over many different offices of the federal government. For example, the Army and Navy each had their own code-breaking operations, and those units did not share information with each other. This situation persisted until World War II.

Office of Strategic Services (OSS)   After U.S. intelligence services failed to warn of the impending Japanese attack on Pearl Harbor in December 1941, President Franklin D. Roosevelt (1882–1945) asked New York lawyer and decorated World War I hero William J. Donovan to craft a plan for a consolidated national intelligence service. Out of that plan, the Office of Strategic Services (OSS) was created in June 1942, with Donovan as its first leader. The OSS was charged with the tasks of gathering and analyzing strategic information to be used by the Joint Chiefs of Staff and leaders of all branches of the military, and to conduct additional covert operations not assigned to other agencies. Throughout the rest of World War II, the OSS provided the military with important intelligence pertaining to enemy troop strength and weapons capabilities.

When the war was over, questions arose as to who should carry out intelligence activities during peacetime and who should be in charge of coordinating those efforts. These questions became more important as concerns began to arise about the potential threat posed by the Soviet Union at the dawn of the Cold War. In October 1945, President Harry S. Truman (1884–

1972) disbanded the OSS and divided its former responsibilities between the Department of War and the Department of State. About the same time, Donovan suggested that an independent, civilian agency be created to coordinate all of the nation's intelligence gathering operations. He proposed that the new agency be responsible for overseas espionage operations, but have no role in domestic law enforcement. Initially, both the military and the Federal Bureau of Investigation (FBI), which was responsible for domestic spying, opposed Donovan's idea, fearing that it would reduce their own influence with the federal government.

Truman opted for an approach halfway between Donovan's proposal and the position of its critics. In January 1946 he created the Central Intelligence Group (CIG), which had the authority to coordinate the intelligence efforts of the departments and agencies already involved in spying. The CIG was led by a newly created position, Director of Central Intelligence. The CIG was short-lived. In 1947 Congress passed the National Security Act, which created an entirely new intelligence structure. It established the National Security Council (NSC), which oversaw the activity of the newly created Central Intelligence Agency (CIA). The position of Director of Central Intelligence was retained as head of the CIA. A law passed two years later, the Central Intelligence Agency Act, established means for the CIA's budget to remain secret and allowed the agency to skirt some of the limitations of federal budget appropriations. It also exempted the CIA from having to disclose information about its employees.

Cold War Role   The CIA's role expanded dramatically during the Korean War. Truman appointed a new director, Lt. General Walter Bedell Smith, who succeeded in putting many more efficient systems in place at the agency. During this period the CIA absorbed the Office of Policy Coordination, which the NSC had created in 1948 to engage in secret anticommunist operations abroad. Allen Dulles served as DCI from 1953 to 1961 during the presidency of Dwight D. Eisenhower (1890–1969). Under Dulles's leadership, the CIA grew into a formidable force on the world scene, mounting massive propaganda campaigns, influencing the outcomes of foreign elections, and in some cases directly sponsoring political coups when it would benefit U.S. interests. The CIA was largely responsible for restoring the pro-Western Mohammad Reza Pahlavi, Shah of Iran, to power in that country in 1953, and it orchestrated the 1954 overthrow of Guatemalan president Jacobo Arbenz.

In 1961 the CIA was the driving force behind the disastrous Bay of Pigs Invasion, a failed attempt to topple Cuban leader Fidel Castro from power. The following year, CIA surveillance was instrumental in detecting the buildup of Soviet missiles in Cuba, which led to the Cuban Missile Crisis of 1962. During the rest of the 1960s, the Far East occupied much of the CIA's attention. As part of its effort during the Vietnam War, the CIA undertook a secret arm of the war in neighboring Laos under director Richard Helms. As opposition to the war increased, the CIA became a target of criticism for its role not only in Vietnam, but also in supporting brutal dictatorships in other parts of the Third World.

Controversies In the 1970s the CIA came under increased scrutiny by Congress. When Helms refused the request of President Richard M. Nixon (1913–1994) to use the CIA to help him cover up the Watergate scandal, Nixon replaced him with James Schlesinger in early 1973. By 1975 the press had uncovered information about past CIA involvement in an assortment of assassination attempts and incidents of domestic spying, leading to investigations by a special presidential commission and select committees in each house of Congress. Permanent intelligence oversight committees were created over the next two years.

Cold War tensions were renewed during the first half of the 1980s, and President Ronald Reagan (1911–2004) expanded the CIA's role accordingly with additional funding and personnel. The agency was embroiled in controversy in the mid-1980s for its role in the Iran-Contra Affair, in which members of the Reagan administration and their operatives orchestrated the illegal sale of weapons to Iran and funneled the proceeds, also illegally, to the right-wing Contra rebels in Nicaragua.

With the demise of the Soviet Union in 1991, the CIA's involvement in fighting communism gave way to a new emphasis on fighting terrorism. Since the terrorist attack of September 11, 2001, the CIA has once again received massive financial and logistical support in the federal budget for its clandestine activities.

The Department of Defense

The Department of Defense (DoD) is a department of the executive branch of the U.S. government with responsibility for all defense and military activities. Under the direction of the president and the secretary of defense, the DoD is responsible for fifteen military departments including the three major military branches: the U.S. Army, U.S. Navy, and U.S. Air Force. The DoD determines troop deployment, obtains and distributes defense revenues, invests in the development of military technology, and functions as a crucial link between military leaders and the executive branch. The DoD is headquartered in the Pentagon office complex, located in Arlington, Virginia.

Establishment of the Department of Defense Before the establishment of the DoD, the responsibility for national defense was divided between the Department of War and the Department of Navy. During World War II, persistent interdepartmental conflicts interfered with military operations as the departmental leaders disagreed about engagement strategies and troop deployment. In 1945 President Harry S. Truman (1884–1972) spearheaded a proposal to unify the defense departments under a single executive office. The primary issue in the debate was whether or not the military would be more functional under centralized control.

In September 1947 Truman's proposal was accepted and the departments were combined into the National Military Establishment (NME). Truman appointed former Secretary of Navy James Forrestal (1892–1949) as the nation's first secretary of defense. Under the original framework, the heads of the three military divisions—army, navy, and air force—were designated members of the executive cabinet.

Over the next two years, as tensions grew over a possible military conflict in the Korean Peninsula, the structure of the NME was refined and amended. In 1949 the NME was renamed the Department of Defense, and the secretaries of the army, navy, and air force were joined into the Joint Chiefs of Staff, under the supervision of the secretary of state, who was thereafter the only department member to serve in the cabinet.

The Korean War The first major task for the Department of Defense was to mobilize the united military for the Korean War (1950–1953). During the first months of the conflict, the DoD was disorganized and unable to meet the president's guidelines for progress. In 1950 Truman called for the resignation of secretary Louis Johnson (1891–1966) and asked former Secretary of State George C. Marshall (1880–1959) to come out of retirement to take control of the DoD.

Known for his skill as a diplomat, in 1947 Marshall had developed a comprehensive foreign aid initiative, known as the "Marshall Plan," to stimulate the recovery of Europe after the devastation of World War II. For his innovative strategies and focus on humanitarian aid, Marshall received the 1953 Nobel Peace Prize. Marshall's tenure as secretary of defense lasted for only one year, and his main contributions were in helping to establish an administrative structure that allowed for command decisions to be quickly implemented in the field. Marshall and his deputy secretary, Robert A. Lovett (1895–1986), were also responsible for defining the relationship between the DoD and the Central Intelligence Agency.

Throughout the Korean conflict, public opinion of the war effort remained low, and Marshall was subject to extensive criticism for his role. In 1951 Senator Joseph McCarthy (1908–1957) attacked Marshall as the individual most directly responsible for military failures in Korea. In the wake of McCarthy's character assaults, Marshall resigned and left the post to Lovett. Though operations in Korea were largely unsuccessful, Lovett's administration succeeded in creating a more efficient system for mobilization, securing funding needed to encourage military growth, and creating an ongoing military preparedness that served as a model for peacetime operation of the DoD.

The Vietnam War   The Vietnam War (1959–1975) began during the administration of President Dwight D. Eisenhower (1890–1969), when the DoD was under the leadership of Thomas S. Gates Jr. (1906–1983). In 1961, when President John F. Kennedy (1917–1963) defeated Eisenhower to win the presidency, he replaced Gates with Robert S. McNamara (1916–), a business executive who had been recommended by former secretary Robert Lovett.

Kennedy and McNamara fundamentally altered the focus of the military by reducing the concentration on preparing for major engagements in favor of training in flexible strategies for use in localized conflicts. The primary objective was to contain enemy forces without allowing a major escalation that might lead to nuclear conflict. McNamara further centralized the DoD administration and encouraged greater civilian involvement and leadership. Under McNamara, civilian strategists and analysts took part in military planning in an effort to foster innovation and to make the DoD more adaptable in responding to the unique challenges of the Vietnam War.

McNamara and Kennedy were responsible for approving the Bay of Pigs operation, in which the United States armed and supported a group of exiled Cuban nationalists in attempting to overthrow Cuban dictator Fidel Castro (1927?–). The insurgency failed, and the United States narrowly avoided military conflict with Cuba. In the wake of the incident, both the United States and the Soviet Union (the world power that was Cuba's patron) began stockpiling weapons in preparation for conflict. The ensuing Cuban Missile Crisis is often regarded as the closest the world has come to nuclear war. After his retirement, McNamara cited the Bay of Pigs as his primary failure.

After the assassination of Kennedy in 1963, McNamara remained secretary under President Lyndon B. Johnson (1908–1973). By 1966, after U.S. public opinion had turned against the American involvement in Vietnam, McNamara began to depart from state policy and disagreed with Johnson's recommendations for deploying additional troops. McNamara recommended decreasing troops and abandoning bombing operations in North Vietnam. When McNamara announced his decision to resign in 1968, many opponents of the war saw the resignation as an admission that U.S. policy in Vietnam had failed.

In 1971 an employee of the State Department leaked crucial DoD policy documents, which became known as the Pentagon Papers, to the *New York Times.* The documents were part of a comprehensive analysis of the Vietnam conflict commissioned in 1967 by McNamara. Among other things, the Pentagon Papers revealed covert military activities including secret aerial attacks authorized by the president and executive efforts to mislead Congress regarding the status of the war effort. The lasting effect of the Pentagon Papers was an increase in popular dissent against the administration of President Richard M. Nixon (1913–1994), who continued the war effort after Johnson.

Ongoing until 1975, the Vietnam War resulted in more than 58,000 American combat deaths and the loss of more than one million Vietnamese lives (many of them civilians), and saw the development of the largest antiwar movement in American history. When the war ended, the DoD shifted its focus toward domestic defense and, more specifically, toward developing contingencies for nuclear war.

The End of the Cold War   In 1975 newly elected president Gerald R. Ford (1913–2006) appointed Donald Rumsfeld (1932–) secretary of defense. During Rumsfeld's administration the military was dealing with the aftereffects of the Vietnam crisis, including transitioning to an all-volunteer system after the abandonment of the draft in 1973. Rumsfeld's administration helped increase emphasis on research and development.

During the period from 1985 to 1990, the annual DoD budget exceeded $400 billion, largely focused on research, development, and anti-nuclear defense strategies in response to the Cold War—a period of tension between the United States and the Soviet Union that had been ongoing since the 1940s. The DoD budget continued to increase until the collapse of the Soviet Union in the early 1990s, when the Cold War drew to a close.

Dick Cheney (1941–), who served as chief of staff under the Ford administration, was named secretary of defense under President George H. W. Bush (1924–). Cheney supervised the DoD during the 1991 Operation Desert Storm, in which the United States sent a military force to rebuff an Iraqi invasion of Kuwait. After Bill Clinton (1946–) became president in 1993, military spending and the influence of the DoD gradually diminished. During Clinton's two terms as president, the military budget reached its lowest levels since before the Vietnam War.

The War on Terror   The next president, George W. Bush (1946–), asked Donald Rumsfeld to serve a second term as secretary of defense, beginning a new period of prominence for the U.S. military. The terrorist attacks of September 2001 initiated a rapid military escalation that Bush referred to as the "Global War on Terror," which included the 2003 American invasion of Iraq despite no evidence that Iraq had ties to terrorist organizations. By 2007 the annual military budget, at more than $600 billion, had reached its highest levels since World War II, even when adjusted for inflation. Nearly 75 percent of the budget was allocated to the ongoing American occupation of Iraq, while the remainder funded development projects and peacekeeping efforts in other parts of the world. The DoD faced intense criticism at home and abroad for both the invasion of Iraq and the implementation of the war effort, which was widely viewed as bungled. Under extreme pressure from his Republican constituency, Bush accepted Rumsfeld's resignation, replacing him with Robert M. Gates (1943–) in December 2006.

The Department of Transportation

The U.S. Department of Transportation (DOT) is a cabinet-level department of the federal government that coordinates national transportation policy. Created in 1967 with the passage of the National Traffic and Motor Vehicle Safety Act of 1966, DOT consolidated transportation-related functions previously scattered among at least fifty different federal agencies. This allowed for the first time the development of a cohesive nationwide approach to highway system development, aviation and automobile safety, and many other kinds of transportation planning. Today, DOT contains eleven individual agencies, including the Federal Aviation Administration, the Federal Highway Administration, and the Federal Transit Administration.

Unsafe at Any Speed   For years prior to passage of the National Traffic and Motor Vehicle Safety Act, proposals had been put forward for the creation of a single agency that would oversee all federal transportation functions. However, the coordination of transportation functions was not an issue that was considered a high priority by legislative leaders, and independent agencies continued to operate with limited oversight and authority. By the mid-1960s developments in transportation technology and growing public concern about an escalating number of traffic deaths brought the issue to the forefront of national politics. This public awareness of the need for a national approach to automobile safety was reinforced by the publication in 1965 of consumer advocate Ralph Nader's (1934–) influential book *Unsafe at Any Speed*, which was highly critical of auto manufacturers for prioritizing power and styling over vehicle safety.

On March 2, 1966, President Lyndon B. Johnson (1908–1973) proposed in a message to the U.S. Congress the formation of a new department that would bring together a host of federal functions involved in transportation planning and regulation. After some negotiation over exactly what duties would be included in the new department, the National Traffic and Motor Vehicle Safety Act

BIRTH OF THE FEDERAL AVIATION ADMINISTRATION

The federal government has been regulating civil aviation since 1926, when the Air Commerce Act was passed. That law put the secretary of commerce in charge of issuing and enforcing air traffic rules, pilot licensing, aircraft certification, and other key aviation functions. In 1938 responsibility for regulating civil aviation was moved from the U.S. Department of Commerce to the newly created Civil Aeronautics Authority, which was given the power to regulate airline fares and determine commercial airline routes. Two years later, the agency was split into the Civil Aeronautics Administration (CAA), which was in charge of certification, safety enforcement, and airway development; and the Civil Aeronautics Board (CAB), which took care of making safety rules, investigating accidents, and regulating the airlines' economics.

As commercial flight grew—along with the number of midair collisions and near misses—and with jet airliners getting ready to make their appearance, Congress passed the Federal Aviation Act of 1958. The act created the independent Federal Aviation Agency, and transferred all of CAA's functions to the new entity. The Federal Aviation Agency also took over CAB's role as maker of safety rules, and gave the new agency sole responsibility for developing and maintaining an air traffic control system to be used for both civil and military flight. When the DOT went into operation in 1967, the Federal Aviation Agency—renamed the Federal Aviation Administration (FAA)—became one of its core components. The FAA continued to gain new powers over the years that followed. In 1968 Congress gave it the authority to implement aircraft noise standards, and the Airport and Airway Development Act of 1970 put the FAA in charge of safety certification of airports served by commercial carriers.

was signed into law on October 15, 1966. The DOT was officially activated on April 1 of the following year. Incorporated into the department were the Federal Aviation Administration, Bureau of Public Roads, Coast Guard, Alaska Railway, St. Lawrence Seaway Development Corporation, Great Lakes Pilotage Administration, high-speed surface transportation program, and various new regulatory and safety functions mandated by the act.

Upon its birth, DOT instantly became the fourth-largest cabinet-level department. Johnson appointed Alan S. Boyd, a former chairman of the Civil Aeronautics Board and undersecretary of commerce for transportation, as DOT's first secretary, charged with organizing it according to instructions from Congress and bringing the act to life.

New Responsibilities   The department expanded its authority soon after it was established when oversight of urban mass transit systems was brought under DOT administration in 1968. Initially, urban transit was under the control of the U.S. Department of Housing and Urban Development (HUD), with the idea that it would be easier for one agency to coordinate cities' transportation needs with housing patterns. However, President Johnson believed these functions could more efficiently be managed by the DOT.

Several important developments took place at DOT during the first term of President Richard Nixon (1913–1994), which began in 1969. With the nation's passenger rail system in crisis in the late 1960s, a new consolidated system was proposed, leading to the creation in 1971 of the quasi-public National Railroad Passenger Corporation, better known as Amtrak. By law, the secretary of transportation sits on Amtrak's board of directors. In 1970 the Highway Safety Act separated highway safety from administration of the nation's highway design, construction, and maintenance programs, creating the National Highway Traffic Safety Administration to assume safety administration duties.

Several structural changes have taken place at DOT since its early days. In the early 1980s, President Ronald Reagan (1911–2004) shifted the Maritime Administration from the U.S. Department of Commerce to DOT. In 1984 the Office of Commercial Space Transportation was created within the department. The 1991 passage of the Intermodal Surface Transportation Efficiency Act created two new entities: the Bureau of Transportation Statistics and the Office of Intermodalism, both aimed at promoting a more coordinated, data-driven approach to the nation's intermodal (using more than one type of transportation in a single trip) transportation system. And finally, in 2002 the Transportation Security Administration was transferred out of DOT and into the newly created U.S. Department of Homeland Security.

See also **Ralph Nader**

✪ Important Figures of the Day

Harry S. Truman

As the thirty-third president of the United States, Harry S. Truman (1884–1972) led the country through the critical

President Harry S. Truman at the signing of the Medicare Bill, 1965. *Francis Miller/Time Life Pictures/Getty Images*

DEWEY DEFEATS TRUMAN ... OR DOES HE?

The *Chicago Daily Tribune*'s erroneous "DEWEY DEFEATS TRUMAN" headline in 1948 is remembered as one of the biggest gaffes in the history of American journalism. It is hard to imagine such a mistake taking place today, but in retrospect it is not hard to see how the *Daily Tribune*'s blunder came about.

Perhaps the biggest factor was that most pollsters had Harry Truman (1884–1972) trailing Thomas Dewey (1902–1971) by a substantial margin, and few thought Truman could pull off a victory. After all, the Democratic Party had splintered, and offered three different candidates for president. Many analysts believed that some Southern states, long considered safely Democratic, would instead go for the Dixiecrat candidate Strom Thurmond (1902–2003). Some also thought that Progressive candidate Henry Wallace (1888–1965) could steal enough votes from Truman to tip some of the tighter state races toward Dewey. All of these thoughts influenced the decision of *Daily Tribune* editors to jump the gun in the face of slow election returns and looming print deadlines. The early election returns seemed to indicate a Dewey victory was in progress, and, based on pre-election polling, newspaper staff had no reason to suspect those early returns were misleading. In addition, a portion of the *Daily Tribune*'s regular staff was on strike, meaning the type was being set by novices. These inexperienced workers even set five lines of type upside down in this historic edition.

As more election returns came in across the nation, it became apparent that the race was very close. But it was too late, the newspaper had already hit the stands. Soon it was clear that Truman had won the election. Panic set in at the *Daily Tribune*. Trucks were dispatched to pick up newspapers that had already been delivered, and thousands of copies were retrieved. Truman went to bed on election night behind in the race. When he woke the next morning, he had won. Traveling to Washington, D.C., that day by train, he was handed a copy of the erroneously headlined newspaper. This moment was captured in a photograph that quickly became famous. Asked to comment on the fiasco, a grinning Truman simply replied, "This is one for the books."

Perhaps even more than the *Daily Tribune*, the nation's prominent pollsters came out of the 1948 presidential election with egg on their collective faces. They wondered how they could have been so wrong. One problem was their sampling methods. Much of Truman's support was from working-class people, minorities, and the poor. These groups were grossly underrepresented in most polls compared to the affluent, who were more likely to support Dewey. Moreover, even as the latest polls showed the gap between Truman and Dewey narrowing, the media stubbornly refused to revise their earlier predictions. They still believed Truman had no chance to win. In the aftermath of the debacle, major pollsters, such as Gallup and Roper, reexamined their methods.

---

transition from global conflict to peacetime prosperity during the late 1940s. He also ushered in the Cold War era in America, positioning the United States as the chief impediment to the worldwide spread of communism. Truman was the last of a breed of "ordinary citizens" to rise to the highest levels in politics, reinforcing the traditional American notion that anybody could become president of the United States through hard work and common sense.

Harry Truman was born on May 8, 1884, in Lamar, Missouri, the eldest of John and Martha Truman's three children. His middle name was "S.," as a tribute to both his maternal grandfather, Shipp Truman, and his paternal grandfather, Solomon Young. Truman grew up in and around Independence, Missouri, where his father operated a successful family farm. A somewhat sickly child, he did not participate in sports and needed thick eyeglasses from the time he was six years old. Truman graduated from high school in Independence in 1901 at age seventeen. He hoped to attend the U.S. Military Academy at West Point, New York, but after failing the vision exam, he instead enrolled at the local business college. A family financial downturn prevented him from completing his studies, however, so Truman went to work at a series of jobs in the Kansas City, Missouri, area, including bank clerk and timekeeper for a railroad builder. In 1906 he left the city and moved back home to work on the family farm. He stayed there for twelve years.

From Humble Haberdasher to Powerful Politician
In 1917, soon after the United States entered World War I, Truman enlisted in the U.S. Army. He was shipped to France, where he was put in charge of an artillery unit and rose to the rank of captain. In 1919 he returned to Kansas City, where he married Bess Wallace and opened a haberdashery with a friend. The business went bankrupt within a few years.

About this time Truman became interested in politics. One of his army friends had family connections to Thomas J. Pendergast, a powerful boss of Missouri's Democratic "machine." At the suggestion of his friend, Truman decided to run for an administrative position in the Jackson County court. He won the 1922 election, but was defeated in his 1924 reelection bid. With Pendergast's support, however, Truman was elected to the top administrative post in the county in 1926. He served in this position until 1934. Despite his ties to Pendergast, whose corruption was common knowledge, Truman was able to forge a reputation as an honest and committed public servant.

As a dedicated soldier in Missouri's Democratic ranks, Truman was recruited to run for the U.S. Senate in 1934. With Pendergast's help again, Truman secured narrow victories in both the Democratic primary and the general election. In the Senate, Truman was a staunch supporter of President Franklin Roosevelt's (1882–1945) New Deal policies aimed at correcting the nation's foundering Great Depression–era economy. While Truman was serving his first term in the Senate, Pendergast's political machine collapsed, with some two hundred functionaries convicted of election fraud and other charges. Pendergast himself was sentenced to prison.

Because of his longstanding ties to Pendergast, Republicans saw Truman as an easy target when he came up for reelection in 1940. By then, however, Truman was associated much more closely with the popular Roosevelt than with Pendergast in the minds of voters, and he easily won another election victory. Early in his second term, Truman was named to head a special Senate committee formed to investigate possible corruption in the National Defense Program's contracting process.

Rewarded for Loyalty

Throughout his tenure in the Senate, Truman remained fiercely loyal to Roosevelt—not terribly difficult, since he was a firm believer in Roosevelt's New Deal philosophy. Truman was rewarded for this loyalty when he was nominated as Roosevelt's running mate at the 1944 Democratic national convention. That November, he was elected vice president of the United States.

Truman was vice president for only eighty-three days. Roosevelt, whose health was already failing as he ran for an unprecedented fourth term as president, died on April 12, 1945, and Truman became president. Truman's first challenge was to win the confidence of Roosevelt's advisers, many of whom viewed him as an unsophisticated "hick." Truman quickly made it clear that he intended to carry on with Roosevelt's policies, both domestic and foreign.

As Truman took office, World War II was nearing its end. The war in Europe was already under control, and indeed victory there was declared just weeks into Truman's presidency. Japan was another matter. Made aware of the availability of a powerful new weapon capable of ending the war quickly, Truman in July 1945 authorized the military to drop atomic bombs on the Japanese cities of Hiroshima and Nagasaki. The bombs were dropped in early August, and the war effectively came to an end soon afterward; on September 2 the Japanese formally surrendered.

Guided Nation's Postwar Transition

With the war over, Truman immediately turned his attention to shifting the American economy back into peacetime mode. The years immediately following World War II were marked by high inflation, shortages of consumer goods, and labor unrest. Truman responded by seizing government control of a handful of key industries and transportation systems, and intervening aggressively in labor strikes. Some of his tactics were not well received—especially by the newly Republican-controlled Congress—and his political popularity suffered. His move to desegregate the military and his support of civil rights legislation further cost him support among Southerners.

America's victory celebration was soon cut short by the realities of the Cold War. Truman responded to the threat of Soviet aggression by involving the United States much more in world affairs. Known as the Truman Doctrine, the aim of U.S. foreign policy during the postwar period was to oppose Soviet expansion wherever it occurred around the globe. Challenging Soviet expansion remained at the core of American foreign policy for decades to come. When Soviet-backed rebels threatened to take control in Greece and Turkey in 1947, Truman provided substantial financial support to the existing governments. He orchestrated an airlift of food and supplies into West Berlin when the Soviets blockaded the city in 1948. Over the years that followed, Truman and his administration implemented the European Recovery Program, known as the Marshall Plan. Named for Secretary of State George C. Marshall (1880–1959), the program was based on the premise that aiding the war-shattered nations of Europe would promote regional economic stability and usher in a period of international peace and prosperity. Under the Marshall Plan the United States provided more than $13 billion in aid to Western Europe over four years.

Truman entered the 1948 presidential campaign in a weakened political position. In addition to Republican candidate Thomas Dewey (1902–1971), the governor of New York, Truman found himself in a race against two other candidates representing parties that had splintered off of the Democrats: Henry Wallace (1888–1965), who had been the vice president before Truman, and whom Truman had fired from his job as secretary of commerce after he criticized Truman's anti-Soviet policies, representing the new Progressive Party; and South Carolina governor Strom Thurmond (1902–2003) of the States' Rights Democratic Party, better known as the Dixiecrats. National polls had Truman trailing Dewey, and most major newspapers gave Truman little chance of winning. Truman went on the offensive with a whistle-stop campaign tour, covering more than 22,000 miles by train and making over two hundred speeches. Rallying under the campaign slogan "Give 'em hell, Harry," he focused his campaign on industrial workers and agricultural centers. He was also the first major presidential candidate to actively court voters in the predominantly African-American Harlem section of New York City. On election night the *Chicago Daily Tribune* famously prepared an extra edition to be distributed the next morning featuring the banner headline "DEWEY DEFEATS TRUMAN." The *Tribune*'s projection was inaccurate; Truman won the popular election by more than two million votes. His party also regained control of Congress.

Korean War

The Cold War intensified during the first year of Truman's second term in office when the

Soviet Union exploded its first atomic bomb in 1949. In June 1950 communist North Korean forces, backed initially by the Soviets and later by the People's Republic of China, invaded South Korea. Truman quickly sent American troops to repel the attack, sanctioned by the United Nations. The following year Truman fired General Douglas MacArthur (1880–1964) from his post as head of the Far East Command of the U.S. Army, citing repeated acts of insubordination. The firing of MacArthur, a hero of World War II, brought down new waves of criticism on Truman. Burdened by difficulties both at home and abroad, Truman announced in 1952 that he would not run for reelection to a second full term.

When his presidency was over, Truman eased into a quiet retirement back home in Independence, Missouri. He published two volumes of memoirs, in 1955 and 1956. While his reputation had suffered considerably during the final years of his presidency, Truman enjoyed a surge in public esteem once out of office. He came to be admired as a "straight shooter" in an era when Americans were growing increasingly skeptical of the intentions and honesty of politicians. Truman died on December 26, 1972, and was buried on the grounds of the Truman Library in Independence. His reputation improved after his death, as the public reacted with disgust to the political scandals of the Nixon era. Truman's stature seemed to grow throughout the ensuing decades. He was the subject of an award-winning biographical movie on HBO in 1995 and was quoted by presidential candidates of both major parties during the 1996 campaign season. In 2003 an unmarked notebook discovered at the Truman Library turned out to be Truman's handwritten diary from 1947, sparking yet another wave of interest in his presidency. By 2007 Truman was a frequent topic of biographical studies, volumes of correspondence, and military and political analyses concerning his presidency, in particular his straightforward leadership style, his decision to use nuclear weapons to end World War II, and his attempt to contain the spread of communism.

> *See also* **The Cold War**
> *See also* **The Korean War**
> *See also* **The Marshall Plan**

J. Edgar Hoover

J. Edgar Hoover (1895–1972) directed the Federal Bureau of Investigation (FBI) for nearly forty-eight years, from 1924 until his death in 1972. He transformed the agency from a small, poorly trained outfit into a modern, highly effective, and professional crime-fighting organization. Hoover gained almost cult-like status among the American public for upholding law and order and espousing conservative, wholesome virtues. However, his dedication to protecting the country evolved into an obsession in which his agency trampled civil liberties in the name of national security. The FBI investigated and hounded people who had not committed crimes, but were deemed by Hoover to threaten U.S. interests. In the process he collected personal and embarrassing information about many prominent personalities. His power and ruthless reputation for seeking revenge kept his critics at bay until after his death, when his excesses became widely known. The FBI achieved many admirable feats during his long tenure as its director, but fairly or unfairly, Hoover is remembered more for his faults than his successes.

Early Life and Career John Edgar Hoover was born on January 1, 1895, in Washington, D.C., to a middle-class family. His father was in civil service with the U.S. Coast Guard. His mother was a disciplinarian who strongly impressed her Victorian-era moral values on young Hoover. His father died in 1921, and Hoover continued to live with his mother until her death in 1938. He never married.

In high school, Hoover excelled at debating and hoped to go into politics. He earned a law degree at George Washington University and accepted a legal position at the Department of Justice (DOJ). He impressed his superiors with his organizational skills and clean-cut, patriotic image. Hoover made a name for himself in 1919 by playing an integral role in the Palmer Raids—a series of raids initiated by Attorney General Mitchell Palmer against suspected communists in the United States. The country was in the midst of a "red scare," an intense and fiercely paranoid fear about communism, that Hoover took to heart and embraced for the rest of his life.

In 1924 a new Attorney General, Harlan Fiske Stone, asked Hoover to take over the Department of Justice's Bureau of Investigation (BOI), a small law enforcement agency that had been in operation for more than a decade. The BOI had a poor reputation. There were few federal crimes at the time, and the agency was full of appointees who were considered cronies of their political benefactors. Stone wanted Hoover to transform the BOI into an agency resembling Scotland Yard, the metropolitan police service in London, England, that is known for its success in crime detection. Hoover, who was only twenty-nine years old at the time, agreed to take the position, but only if he was given broad authority to make personnel decisions at the agency. Stone granted his request.

Building a New Image Hoover took the reins of the BOI in the midst of Prohibition. A national crime wave was driven by public antipathy toward the liquor laws and the availability of two innovations—the automobile and the machine gun. Local and state law enforcement authorities proved ineffective against heavily armed gangsters and bank robbers who easily crossed state lines. The stock market crash of 1929 and the ensuing Great Depression produced public cynicism about the

J. Edgar Hoover pointing to a map of the United States, 1940s.   © *Bettmann/CORBIS*

government's authority and made outlaws like John Dillinger and Bonnie and Clyde into cultural celebrities.

Hoover launched a massive and highly successful media campaign to turn public opinion against these romanticized criminals. He pushed his media contacts to cast the outlaws as heartless villains and his government agents, or G-men, as brave heroes. His efforts were aided by a tragic shootout in June 1933 that left four law enforcement officers dead from an ambush by gangster Pretty Boy Floyd. Congress passed new laws greatly expanding the power of the BOI in fighting federal crimes. In a few short years almost all of the notorious gangsters had been killed or captured. The agency also earned high praise for its role in catching the kidnapper and murderer of the baby of famous aviator Charles Lindbergh. A new law making kidnapping a federal crime solidified the BOI's involvement in future similar cases.

Hoover worked diligently to modernize the agency, which was renamed the Federal Bureau of Investigation in 1935. Under his direction the FBI obtained sophisticated laboratory equipment, established a centralized fingerprint file, conducted research in criminology and forensics, and developed high-tech methods for investigating crimes and identifying suspects. He established a national academy to train law enforcement officials from around the country (and later from around the world) in professional crime-fighting techniques.

Spies and Subversives During the 1930s President Franklin D. Roosevelt (1882–1945) was worried about threats to national security from fascists and communists. He ordered Hoover to investigate potential agitators. The FBI director seized on this authority and dramatically increased surveillance of Americans he believed embraced left-leaning politics. Years later it would be learned that the president's own wife, Eleanor Roosevelt (1884–1962), was among Hoover's targets, because of her liberal political views. With America's entry into World War II in 1941 the FBI garnered sweeping new powers in its investigations of espionage, sabotage, and suspected subversion (support for the overthrow of the government). The Smith Act (or Alien Registration Act) of 1940 had outlawed activities and even statements deemed to be subversive.

In 1942 the FBI scored a public relations victory when it captured dozens of German spies. The FBI obtained convictions of nearly three-dozen people for violations of the Smith Act and/or for espionage. Later that year the agency arrested eight German spies who had snuck onto U.S. shores from a submarine. The men were sent to conduct sabotage operations against American targets. Before they could carry out their missions, one of the spies had a change of heart and turned himself into the FBI, which quickly captured the others.

By the end of 1943 Hoover oversaw more than 13,000 employees at the FBI, including approximately 4,000 specially trained agents. By this time he had been the FBI director for nearly two decades and had earned the nation's respect as a protector of U.S. security and values.

A New Red Scare Following the war Hoover's anti-communist zeal found momentum in a new "red scare." His acquisition of power was helped by several events that occurred during the administration of President Harry Truman (1884–1972). In 1947 Truman's Executive Order 9835 created the Federal Employee Loyalty Program. The FBI began running background checks on millions of federal employees looking for a variety of misdeeds, including connections to subversive organizations. The next year the DOJ used the Smith Act to obtain the first of numerous indictments against American members of the Communist Party. Meanwhile, Republican Senator Joseph McCarthy (1908–1957) and other politicians fanatically hounded Americans on the slightest suspicion that they were communists or had communist leanings. At first, Hoover heartily supported these efforts and even supplied information from FBI files; however, he gradually saw McCarthy as a political threat to his power and ended his support.

By the mid-1950s anticommunist hysteria had somewhat diminished. McCarthy was censured by the U.S. Senate and ended his political service in disgrace. The U.S. Supreme Court weakened the government's power under the Smith Act to prosecute communists. Hoover was determined to take on the battle himself. By that time the FBI was learning much from a top-secret U.S. and U.K. intelligence program called Venona in which Soviet diplomatic messages were slowly being decoded. Venona information indicated that a number of Soviet spies had been working in the United States for some time. These revelations led to the convictions of several people, most famously Julius (1918–1953) and Ethel (1915–1953) Rosenberg, who were executed for spying.

Hoover believed the "red menace" posed a grave threat to American society. In 1956 he initiated a secret FBI program called COINTELPRO that would go on for nearly two decades and ultimately tarnish his hard-fought image as America's guardian of law and order.

COINTELPRO COINTELPRO was short for Counterintelligence Program. It combined surveillance techniques with trickery designed to harass suspected subversives. Hoover had long advocated the use of electronic bugs and secret tape recorders with or without legal permission from his superiors. These techniques were used liberally by the FBI during COINTELPRO. Originally limited to communists and their supporters, the program was soon expanded to cover other groups Hoover considered threatening to American security. These included civil rights leaders, like Martin Luther King Jr. (1929–1968), protesters against the Vietnam War, anti-government radicals, and members of the Ku Klux Klan. A typical COINTELPRO scheme was to send anonymous letters to the wives, families, or employers of suspects. These letters would include damaging or embarrassing information designed to ruin marriages, careers, and reputations. Tape recordings of sexual encounters were obtained by the FBI and used in a similar manner.

Hoover's Last Years In 1966 a *Time* article noted "An unwritten rule of American politics is: Never tangle with J. Edgar Hoover." For decades Hoover had been rumored to be compiling his own secret files containing personal information about prominent Americans, including politicians, Hollywood celebrities, journalists, and others. His biographers would later say that these files helped cement his grip on power for so many decades. Politicians, in particular, feared what Hoover might know about them and what he might do with the information. It was all part of the immense legend that grew around the man and insulated him and his agency from presidential and congressional criticism. One administration after another kept Hoover as FBI director, long after he had reached retirement age.

In 1971 Hoover's public façade began to crack when allegations flew around Washington, D.C., that the FBI had planted secret listening devices in congressional offices. House Democratic Leader Hale Boggs of Louisiana accused Hoover of using "the tactics of the Soviet Union and Hitler's Gestapo" and called for the FBI director to be replaced. The accusations followed a break-in at an FBI office in Pennsylvania in which numerous documents were stolen and turned over to the press. They provided the first tantalizing clues about the existence of the COINTELPRO program, which Hoover terminated soon afterward. The full story would come out after his death.

Hoover died of a heart attack at his home on May 2, 1972. He was seventy-seven years old and had served as FBI director under eight U.S. presidents.

The Fallout Hoover's death was quickly followed by the fall from grace of President Richard Nixon (1913–1994) in the Watergate scandal. Congressional hearings into those matters uncovered unsavory activities by the FBI, including bugging the offices of White House aides, National Security Council members, and prominent reporters. Nixon resigned in 1974, before he could be impeached. By the end of the next year Hoover's COINTELPRO program had become public knowledge and was widely criticized as a gross violation of American civil liberties. Many of the FBI's operations had targeted law-abiding Americans engaged in peaceful activities, such as protesting the Vietnam War or speaking out against the government. The reputations of Hoover and the FBI were severely damaged by the revelations. New limits were placed on the FBI's authority to conduct counter-intelligence and domestic security investigations.

The existence of Hoover's long-suspected secret files was confirmed by his private secretary who testified before Congress that she had destroyed many of the files after he died. Those that remained became a source of frequent Freedom of Information requests by curious journalists and provided much insight into the workings of the FBI during the long Hoover era.

In death, Hoover elicited a flood of negative publicity about COINTELPRO and other matters. He became the focus of numerous books, some of which claimed that he had engaged in scandalous sexual behavior. Critics have also faulted Hoover for the FBI's slow response in the 1950s and 1960s to organized crime and civil rights abuses perpetuated against minorities. As a result, Hoover's legacy is decidedly mixed. He is reviled for the abuses of power that characterized his dictatorial reign at the FBI, but he is also praised for building a premier law enforcement agency renowned for its technological and investigatory skills.

See also **The Federal Bureau of Investigation**

Alger Hiss

Alger Hiss (1904–1996), a high-ranking official in the U.S. Department of State, was an early victim of McCarthyism, an anticommunist political climate that ruined the careers of many innocent Americans. Hiss was convicted in 1950 of perjury after having allegedly provided classified documents to *Time* magazine editor Whittaker Chambers (1901–1961), an admitted member of a communist organization.

A Stellar Government Career Hiss was born on November 11, 1904, in Baltimore, Maryland. He and his four siblings were raised in a genteel environment by their mother and an aunt following the suicide of his father, an executive with a dry goods firm. Hiss excelled in school. He received a scholarship to Johns Hopkins University, where he performed well enough to earn entrance into Harvard Law School. He continued to stand out academically at Harvard. After graduating from law school in 1929, he served as a clerk for legendary U.S. Supreme Court Justice Oliver Wendell

Holmes (1841–1935), serving in that capacity for about a year.

After short stints at two prestigious East Coast law firms, Hiss accepted a position in 1933 with the federal government, working on a variety of New Deal projects within President Franklin Roosevelt's (1882–1945) administration. In 1936 Hiss transferred to the State Department. He moved quickly up the State Department's organizational ladder over the next decade. By the end of World War II he was high enough in the departmental bureaucracy to serve as an aid to Roosevelt at the Yalta Conference of 1945. Hiss attended conferences that led to the development of the United Nations (UN) charter, and was an adviser to U.S. delegation at the very first meeting of the UN General Assembly. He left his government post in 1946 to become president of the Carnegie Endowment for International Peace.

Chambers's Damaging Testimony Hiss's promising career came to a screeching halt in 1948. On August 3, Chambers, a senior editor at *Time* who had acknowledged his own past association with the Communist Party, named Hiss as a communist sympathizer in his testimony before the House Committee on Un-American Activities. Chambers also claimed that in the late 1930s Hiss had stolen classified documents from the State Department and given them to Chambers for delivery to the Soviets. Hiss sued Chambers for slander, whereupon Chambers produced a substantial paper trail implicating Hiss.

Because the statute of limitations had run out on his alleged actions, Hiss could not be charged with espionage. He was instead tried for perjury, based on his testimony before Congress that he had never met Chambers before. A 1949 trial ended in a hung jury, but Hiss was retried the following year and found guilty of perjury. He was sentenced to five years in prison, of which he ended up serving forty-four months. He was also disbarred. He was released from prison in 1954, but his life was in shambles and his political career was over.

The conviction of Hiss fueled the anticommunist hysteria gripping the country, as it supported the notion that communists had successfully infiltrated the highest levels of American government. Throughout his incarceration and afterward, Hiss and his supporters strenuously argued that he was innocent and had been framed; and indeed over the years credible evidence emerged that the evidence against him had been mishandled, or perhaps even fabricated. Nevertheless, accusations about Hiss continued in the post-Soviet era as previously unavailable documents were declassified and translated. Several historians have identified Hiss as the Soviet spy who is code-named "Ales" in intercepted Soviet communications. However, the question of his guilt or innocence has never been definitively resolved. Hiss died in 1996 at the age of ninety-two.

See also **McCarthyism**

Former State Department official Alger Hiss on his way to jail for espionage, 1951. © *Bettmann/CORBIS*

Julius and Ethel Rosenberg

During the height of anticommunist hysteria in the United States in the early 1950s, Julius (1918–1953) and Ethel (1915–1953) Rosenberg, an otherwise nondescript married couple, were convicted of espionage and executed for their alleged role in passing nuclear secrets to the Soviets. While information that has surfaced in the years since their trial tends to confirm that their guilty verdict was correct, the trial itself ignited outrage among liberals worldwide, as did their death sentence, which seemed to many wildly out of proportion to the severity of their offense.

Background Julius Rosenberg was born into a Jewish family in New York on May 12, 1918. While still in his teens, he became active in the Young Communist League, where he met his future wife, Ethel Greenglass,

a Jewish woman three years his senior. Julius received a degree in electrical engineering from the City College of New York in 1939, and the following year he began working for the U.S. Army Signal Corps. Ethel was a frustrated singer and actress who was active in labor organizing. The couple married in 1939 and had two sons, Michael, born in 1943, and Robert, born in 1947. Active members of the Communist Party until Michael was born, the couple then dropped out of the party and lived an apparently quiet domestic life in Brooklyn.

In June 1950, Ethel Rosenberg's brother David Greenglass, a machinist at the Los Alamos, New Mexico, nuclear research facility, confessed to the Federal Bureau of Investigation (FBI) that he had passed sensitive information about the Manhattan Project—the project that led to the development of the first atomic weapons—indirectly to the Soviets. He also said that he had given

Ethel and Julius Rosenberg seated in a police van shortly before their execution for espionage, 1953. © *Getty Images*

secret documents to his sister Ethel and her husband. FBI agents visited the Rosenberg household the next day. The Rosenbergs firmly denied that they were involved in spying, but others involved in the ring implicated them. Julius Rosenberg was arrested in July 1950, and Ethel was taken into custody the following month. A grand jury indicted both of them on August 17, 1950, for conspiracy to commit espionage, though the evidence against them was not very strong.

The Rosenberg Trial At trial, a handful of witnesses testified that the Rosenbergs had indeed been part of the spy ring at various times during the 1940s, though no other concrete evidence against them materialized. The most damaging information seemed to be that Julius Rosenberg had begun making preparations to leave the country upon learning that Dr. Karl Fuchs, a Manhattan Project scientist, had confessed to passing atomic secrets to the Soviet Union. The other major strike against them was their indisputable involvement with the Communist Party, despite membership in the party being fairly common during the period in which they were active, and that the Soviet Union was an ally of the United States at the time. When asked on the witness stand about their affiliation with the Communist Party, both Rosenbergs invoked their Fifth Amendment right to avoid incriminating themselves. Meanwhile, their defense attorney Emmanuel Bloch was of little help,

failing miserably in his attempts to play down the importance of the information the Rosenbergs were accused of helping deliver to the Soviets.

The Rosenbergs maintained throughout the trial that they were innocent, but the jury believed the prosecution. They were both convicted of espionage, and on April 5, 1951, they were sentenced to die in the electric chair.

Around the world, a wave of protest rang out regarding the unfairness of the government's treatment of the Rosenbergs and the severity of their punishment. The Rosenbergs attempted for two years to appeal their convictions, taking the case all the way to the U.S. Supreme Court, but they were unsuccessful. They were both executed on June 19, 1953, at the Sing Sing prison in New York. The case of the Rosenbergs continues to stir debate. While more recent examinations of the evidence against them suggest they had in fact engaged in spying for the Soviet Union, the idea of executing a married couple for passing relatively unimportant information to a nation that was not even an enemy at the time is difficult to comprehend more than half a century later. However, the sentencing judge at their trial asserted that by helping the Soviets acquire nuclear weapons sooner than they otherwise would have, the Rosenbergs contributed to causing thousands of deaths in the Korean War and to the "constant state of tension" that characterized the nuclear stalemate of the Cold War era.

See also **McCarthyism**

Dwight D. Eisenhower

Dwight D. Eisenhower (1890–1969) parlayed his fame as a leader of Allied forces during World War II into a successful political career that culminated in his election as the thirty-fourth president of the United States. Eisenhower led the nation during a period of unprecedented worldwide power and great postwar prosperity, but did so under the cloud of the Cold War.

Dwight David Eisenhower was born on October 14, 1890, in Denison, Texas, and raised in the small farming community of Abilene, Kansas. The third of seven sons of David Eisenhower and Ida Stover Eisenhower, he was originally named David Dwight Eisenhower, but his first and middle names were flipped at an early age to avoid the confusion of having two Davids in the house. A standout both in the classroom and on the athletic field, Eisenhower earned an appointment to the U.S. Military Academy at West Point, New York, after graduating from high school and working with his father at the local creamery for two years.

Average Student, Competent Officer Eisenhower was only an average student at West Point, graduating sixty-first in a class of 164 in 1915. After graduation, he was commissioned as a second lieutenant and stationed at Fort Sam Houston in Texas. There he met Mamie Doud, and the two were married in 1916. When the United States entered World War I in 1917, Eisenhower hoped he would be assigned a combat command in Europe. Instead, he remained stateside, where he instructed troops at various training camps. When he finally received a European command, it was just a month before the war came to an end; by then his services overseas were no longer needed.

Eisenhower proved to be a competent officer over the next several years of his military career, but his superiors perceived his chief skills to be organization and administration rather than in the more glamorous realm of battle. So rather than being assigned to a field position in some distant part of the world, Eisenhower became a senior aide to General Douglas MacArthur (1880–1964) in 1932. A few years later, MacArthur made him his assistant military adviser for the Philippine Commonwealth, a position in which he remained until 1939.

Though he was successful in his job and well respected by army commanders, Eisenhower was frustrated with the pace of his career advancement in the military, having reached only the rank of lieutenant colonel by 1940. The entrance of the United States into World War II finally gave him the opportunity to demonstrate his leadership abilities. Just days after the Japanese attack on Pearl Harbor in December 1941, Eisenhower was called to Washington, D.C., and put in charge of the War Plans Division (later renamed the Operations Division) of the War Department. Because of his experience in the Philippines, he was initially con-

President Dwight D. Eisenhower in the Oval Office, 1956.
© *Bettmann/CORBIS*

sulted on matters relating to the war in the Pacific. Soon, however, Eisenhower was advocating a "Europe first" policy, which called for the United States to take the offensive in Europe and Africa while holding the line in the Pacific theater. Eisenhower was quickly promoted to one-star general, and his influence in the conduct of the war in Europe expanded. By 1942 he was in charge of U.S. forces based in Great Britain.

Normandy Invasion A short time later, Eisenhower was promoted again, and was named to lead joint U.S.-British efforts in North Africa. Under Eisenhower's leadership, Allied forces succeeded in defeating the Axis powers in North Africa, forcing the surrender of enemy forces in Tunisia in May 1943. From there, Eisenhower, now a four-star general, led the amphibious assaults on Sicily and, in September of that year, Italy. Based on his efforts in these successful campaigns, Eisenhower was named supreme commander of Operation Overlord, the code name for the huge Allied incursion into Nazi-occupied France. The invasion at Normandy, launched in June 1944, was the biggest amphibious attack in the history of the world. It proved to be a key turning point in the war in Europe, and made Eisenhower a celebrity in the United States. Allied forces moved on into Germany, ultimately forcing the Nazi surrender and ending

NATIONAL AERONAUTICS AND SPACE ADMINISTRATION

Many Americans reacted with dismay in 1957 to the news that the Soviet Union had successfully launched *Sputnik*, the first manmade satellite, into orbit. The news was especially disturbing coming in the wake of the Soviet news agency's announcement the previous summer that Russia had successfully tested an intercontinental ballistic missile (ICBM) capable of delivering a nuclear warhead to targets within the United States. To observers already disappointed by the perceived "missile gap" between the United States and the Soviet Union was now added a perceived "space lag." It did not help matters that the United States' initial attempt at putting a small satellite into orbit ended disastrously when the rocket carrying it exploded a few seconds after liftoff.

By early 1958 the United States had managed to send two satellites—*Explorer* and *Vanguard*—into orbit, and the United States' ICBM supply grew over the next few years. President Dwight D. Eisenhower (1890–1969) was convinced that the American nuclear arsenal was adequate, but he also believed that an overall national space program was in order. While the military implications of space superiority over the Soviets were obvious, he was more interested in a space program that was primarily nonmilitary and believed that such a program should be run by civilians. He decided to form a national space program using as its foundation an existing agency called the National Advisory Committee for Aeronautics, which had been established in 1915 but had never been awarded much of a budget.

The new, improved version of the agency, to be known as the National Aeronautics and Space Administration (NASA), was created with the signing of the National Aeronautics and Space Act on July 29, 1958. Eisenhower named T. Keith Glennan, president of the Case Institute of Technology and a former member of the Atomic Energy Commission, as NASA's first administrator. NASA formally went into action on October 1, 1958. Within a year, NASA had realized its first successful satellite launch. NASA's attentions soon shifted from satellites to manned spaceflight, starting with Project Mercury, established in November 1958. Between 1961 and 1963, NASA carried out half a dozen successful manned missions.

In spite of these successes, the assertion by President John F. Kennedy (1917–1963) in May 1961 that the United States could land on the moon "before the decade is out" seemed unduly optimistic to many at the time. However, when two American astronauts set foot on the lunar surface in July 1969, Kennedy's optimism proved justified.

and the eventual erection of the Berlin Wall, the Cold War's most visible symbol.

In 1945 Eisenhower returned to the United States a hero. He was named army chief of staff, replacing General George C. Marshall (1880–1959). Eisenhower held that position for two years, but he did not particularly enjoy it, and retired from the military altogether in 1948. Because of his overwhelming popularity, there was much talk at that time of a presidential run. Instead, Eisenhower wrote a book about his wartime experiences, *Crusade in Europe* (1948), and accepted a position as president of Columbia University. After only a few years at that job, Eisenhower was summoned out of retirement from the military by President Harry Truman (1884–1972) to serve as supreme commander of Allied forces in Europe during the formation of a new alliance designed to counter potential communist aggression. This new entity would evolve into the North Atlantic Treaty Organization.

From War Hero to President By 1952 Republican leaders had managed to persuade Eisenhower to run for president. Still immensely popular from his wartime exploits, Eisenhower easily defeated Democratic nominee Adlai Stevenson (1900–1965) in the 1952 election. Eisenhower took office at a time when war was raging in Korea and the Cold War was simmering everywhere else. At home, the communist "witch hunt" spearheaded by Senator Joseph McCarthy (1908–1957) was in high gear. During the first year of his presidency, Eisenhower managed to extricate the United States from Korea, negotiating a cease-fire that was signed in July 1953. Eisenhower moved to reduce military spending by beefing up the U.S. nuclear arsenal—which he considered the most effective deterrent to Soviet aggression—while reducing the size of the nation's expensive conventional forces and weaponry.

After the death of Soviet leader Joseph Stalin (1879–1953), Eisenhower made attempts to improve relations between the United States and the Soviet Union. These efforts met with little success, though he did meet with Soviet leaders in 1955. While Eisenhower kept the United States out of full-scale wars for the remainder of his presidency, he was aggressive in battling communism around the globe. In 1953 the Central Intelligence Agency (CIA) directed the overthrow of the democratically elected government of Iran based on the notion that they were pro-communist. A similar overthrow was orchestrated in Guatemala the following year. In 1954 Eisenhower oversaw the creation of the Southeast Asia Treaty Organization, a military alliance formed to combat the spread of communism in that region.

Eisenhower suffered a heart attack in 1955, but his recovery progressed quickly enough to allow him to run for reelection in 1956. Once again, he defeated Democratic challenger Stevenson by a comfortable margin.

the European portion of the war. During the war's closing stages, Eisenhower made a critical decision that would have a lasting impact on the Cold War that followed: he left the capture of Berlin to the Soviet army, while he focused the attentions of Western forces elsewhere, thus setting the stage for the partition of the city

Second Term In 1957 Eisenhower faced his next Cold War crisis when the Soviet Union successfully launched the first manmade satellite into orbit. This development represented a major blow to the American psyche; to many it meant that the Soviets had surpassed the United States in technological sophistication. In response, Eisenhower urged Congress to commit more funding for scientific and military research, and in July 1958 the National Aeronautics and Space Administration was formed. The space race had begun.

Cuba represented Eisenhower's next Cold War challenge. In the late 1950s, the Eisenhower administration became disenchanted with the brutality and corruption of the government of Cuban president Fulgencio Batista y Zaldívar (1901–1973), and in 1958 the United States withdrew its military support of the Batista regime. The Cuban government quickly collapsed, and in the power struggle that ensued, leftist guerrilla leader Fidel Castro (1926–) emerged as the new Cuban head of state. Castro immediately developed a close alliance with the Soviet Union, guaranteeing that relations between Cuba and the United States would remain distant. Eisenhower assigned the CIA to develop a plan to support an invasion of Cuba by Cuban exiles living in the United States. The plan was still in development when Eisenhower's term as president came to an end. Launched in the spring of 1961, the Bay of Pigs invasion failed miserably and was a great embarrassment to the new president, John F. Kennedy (1917–1963).

While Eisenhower's main area of interest was always on foreign policy, a number of important domestic developments took place during his presidency as well. The civil rights movement gained considerable momentum during the 1950s. In 1954 the U.S. Supreme Court, under Eisenhower-appointed Chief Justice Earl Warren (1891–1974), unanimously declared school segregation unconstitutional in the landmark case *Brown v. Board of Education of Topeka*. When Arkansas governor Orval Faubus tried to block implementation of the law, Eisenhower intervened, sending federal troops to Little Rock in 1957 to address the situation. Eisenhower was also the first president to hire African-Americans to positions of consequence within his administration, most notably Assistant Secretary of Labor J. Ernest Wilkins. Eisenhower's other domestic achievements included signing the legislation that created the national highway system and creating the new cabinet-level U.S. Department of Health, Education, and Welfare.

Eisenhower was the first president subject to the Twenty-second Amendment to the U.S. Constitution, which states that no one may serve as president of the United States for more than two four-year terms. He left office in 1961, and he and his wife, Mamie, retired to their homes in Gettysburg, Pennsylvania, and Palm Desert, California. Over the next few years, he wrote three more books of memoirs: *Mandate for Change* (1963),

The White House Years (1963–1965), and *At Ease: Stories I Tell to Friends* (1967). While he was occasionally called on to play the role of elder statesman for the Republican Party, he mostly played golf and painted with watercolors. Eisenhower had several heart attacks in 1968 and died in 1969.

See also **The Cold War**
See also **The Korean War**
See also **McCarthyism**

Rosa Parks

Rosa Parks (1913–2005) was responsible for one of the defining moments of the civil rights movement when she refused to give up her seat to a white man on a crowded Montgomery, Alabama, bus on December 1, 1955. Her act of defiance galvanized African-Americans across the country and made her an instant civil rights heroine. Her subsequent arrest and fine led to a successful boycott of the Montgomery bus system by African-American riders, sparking a sequence of events that changed race relations in the South forever.

Youth in Segregated Alabama Parks was born Rosa McCauley on February 4, 1913, in Tuskegee, Alabama, the daughter of James McCauley, a carpenter, and Leona (Edwards) McCauley, a schoolteacher. Shortly after her younger brother Sylvester was born, her parents separated. Leona McCauley took the children to live with their grandparents in Pine Level, Alabama. James McCauley migrated north and had little contact with his children after the move.

When she was a child, Parks was a good student, but not the kind who would have led teachers to predict that she was destined to become a historical figure. She attended the Montgomery Industrial School for Girls, then graduated from the all-black Booker T. Washington High School in 1928. For a short time she attended Alabama State Teachers College in Montgomery.

In 1932 Rosa married Raymond Parks, a barber with little formal education. With both Rosa and Raymond holding steady jobs, the young family enjoyed a degree of financial stability. They were, nevertheless, held back by the harsh reality of segregation and second-rate service for African-Americans at many establishments in Alabama. As they became increasingly incensed with sitting in the back of the bus and using "colored" facilities inferior to those reserved for "whites only," both Rosa and Raymond became increasingly involved in civil rights endeavors. They worked on voter registration drives, and Rosa became active in the National Association for the Advancement of Colored People (NAACP). She was named secretary of the NAACP's Montgomery branch in 1943.

Fateful Bus Ride The segregation laws in Montgomery in 1955 reserved the first four rows of seats on city buses for whites. The middle section was a sort of "no

Rosa Parks (center) riding on a newly integrated bus in 1956. Parks sparked a 381-day boycott of segregated buses when she was arrested for refusing to give up her seat to a white person.   *Don Cravens/Time Life Pictures/Getty Images*

man's land," where blacks could sit if there were no white riders occupying the seats. The rear section of the bus was African-American only. Often, African-American riders had to stand even if there were empty seats available in the front of the bus. If an African-American passenger was seated in the middle section, she was expected to give up her seat if a white rider boarded and the first four rows were full. To add to the humiliation, African-Americans were often made to exit out the front door after paying their fare, then reenter through the back door so that they would not pass by the white riders up front. Parks was certainly not the first African-American to stand up to this policy. Riders were frequently kicked off of buses or even arrested for refusing to abide by these racist laws.

Parks worked at a number of different occupations over the years, including insurance sales, housecleaning, and sewing. In 1955 she was working as a seamstress at the Montgomery Fair department store. On December 1, she was exhausted after a grueling day at work. When she boarded the bus to go home, she found an available seat in the middle section. A few stops later, a white rider entered the bus, and the driver ordered Parks and three other African-American passengers to move. The other

three riders obeyed, but Parks had had enough, and she continued to resist even after the driver threatened to call the police.

Parks was taken to jail. She used her one phone call to contact a prominent member of the local NAACP chapter, and word of her arrest quickly spread in the African-American community. Community leaders recognized Parks's case as an opportunity to challenge Montgomery's backward segregation laws. Parks agreed to take part in the challenge, refusing to pay her fine and appealing her guilty verdict to the Montgomery Circuit Court. Under the leadership of the NAACP and Montgomery's black churches, a boycott of the city's buses was organized. One of the key organizers was Martin Luther King Jr. (1929–1968), the young pastor of a Baptist church in Montgomery. African-Americans, who accounted for nearly three-quarters of the bus company's business, were urged to stop riding on buses until the company agreed to abolish its racist rules and to begin hiring African-American drivers.

Bus Boycott Spurs Change   The boycott was highly successful, as nearly every African-American in Montgomery used other means to get around. Meanwhile, the newly formed Montgomery Improvement Association filed suit to have Alabama's segregation laws declared unconstitutional. The case made its way to the U.S. Supreme Court, and on December 20, 1956, Montgomery officials were ordered to end discriminatory practices on their buses. Thus the boycott came to an end after 381 days.

Though victorious in her battle against the humiliation of Montgomery's racist bus policies, the struggle took a toll on Parks and her family. There was a great deal of backlash from the white community, and she and Raymond were unable to find stable employment afterward. In 1957 Parks, her husband, and her mother all moved to Detroit, where her brother Sylvester already lived. She continued her civil rights activism in Detroit, working with the Southern Christian Leadership Conference and the NAACP. Parks was now a civil rights icon and was in great demand as a public speaker. A boulevard in Detroit was named after her, and she received dozens of other awards and honors over the years, including the Presidential Medal of Freedom and the Congressional Gold Medal. In 1965 Parks was hired to work in the Detroit office of Congressman John Conyers, where she remained employed until her retirement in 1988. After she died at her Detroit home on October 24, 2005, she became the first woman to lie in honor in the U.S. Capitol Rotunda.

See also **The Civil Rights Movement**

Thurgood Marshall

A leading civil rights crusader for much of the twentieth century, Thurgood Marshall (1908–1993) was the first African-American to serve on the U.S. Supreme Court. He was influential in bringing about the desegregation of public schools and universities in the United States and fought for equal treatment for people of color in the military. As a private lawyer, as the legal director of the National Association for the Advancement of Colored People (NAACP), and as a judge, Marshall represented the interests not only of African-Americans, but of all the nation's disadvantaged populations. He brought a progressive viewpoint to U.S. policymaking on behalf of those who lacked the money or clout to otherwise be heard.

Early Life Marshall was born into a middle-class family on July 2, 1908, in Baltimore, Maryland. His mother was a teacher in a segregated public elementary school. His father worked at a posh all-white yacht club. Marshall grew up in a comfortable home in a racially diverse neighborhood, where black children and white children played together unselfconsciously. He was popular in school, though somewhat of a class clown, which prevented him from achieving stellar grades. After graduation from high school, Marshall entered Lincoln University, an all-black college near Philadelphia, Pennsylvania. He graduated with honors in 1930 and

enrolled in law school at Howard University, the historically all-black institution in Washington, D.C. Marshall graduated from law school at the top of his class in 1933, and later that year was admitted to the Maryland bar. He set up a private legal practice in Baltimore, specializing in civil rights and criminal cases. Many of his clients could not afford to pay him, but he believed it was important that all people have access to legal representation regardless of their economic status.

Marshall also began serving as counsel to the Baltimore chapter of the NAACP, and it was in that capacity that he handled his first important case, representing an aspiring African-American law student who was trying to get into the all-white University of Maryland law school. Marshall's team won the case, and he was soon invited to work at the NAACP's national headquarters in New York. In 1938 the organization named Marshall head special counsel, and two years later he was named director of the newly created NAACP Legal Defense and Education Fund.

Marshall spent the next twenty years litigating civil rights cases across America—often under threat of physical violence—challenging the nation's racist status quo. He was indisputably one of the key legal forces against racial discrimination in America, arguing thirty-two cases before the U.S. Supreme Court during the 1940s and 1950s and winning twenty-nine of them. Among his victories were cases dealing with white-only primary elections, discrimination in jury selection, and racist housing policies.

Brown v. Board of Education The case that put Marshall in the national spotlight was *Brown v. Board of Education of Topeka* (1954), the landmark school desegregation case. In *Brown*, Marshall successfully argued before the Supreme Court that the "separate but equal" doctrine that had been established in the 1896 *Plessy v. Ferguson* case was unconstitutional, based on the obvious conclusion that separate educational systems were by their very nature unequal. The Court's decision in *Brown v. Board of Education* began the slow, controversial, sometimes violent process of desegregating the nation's schools. Another slow, painful battle, that of cancer, took the life of Marshall's first wife, the former Vivian Burey (better known as "Buster"). About a year later, he married Cecilia Suyat, a secretary at the New York office of the NAACP.

Marshall continued to battle against discrimination over the next several years, attempting to integrate Little Rock Central High School in Arkansas and the University of Alabama in the late 1950s. When the Democrats gained the White House in the 1960 presidential election, Marshall made clear to party leaders that he was interested in a judicial appointment. He did not have to wait long to realize this desire. In 1961 President John F. Kennedy (1917–1963) nominated Marshall for a spot as federal judge on the U.S. Court of Appeals for the

Supreme Court Justice Thurgood Marshall, 1967.   © *Bettmann/CORBIS*

Second Circuit, which covers New York, Vermont, and Connecticut. The confirmation process stretched for nearly a year because of resistance from Southern segregationists, but he eventually prevailed. In his four years on the circuit court, Marshall wrote more than one hundred opinions, with none reversed by the Supreme Court. Four years later, President Lyndon Johnson (1908–1973) appointed Marshall solicitor general, meaning he would argue the federal government's position in Supreme Court cases. In 1967 Johnson nominated Marshall to become the first African-American justice on the nation's highest court. In spite of reluctance from Southern conservatives in the Senate—most notably Strom Thurmond (1902–2003) of South Carolina—Marshall was confirmed after two months, thus breaking the Supreme Court racial barrier.

U.S. Supreme Court In his earliest years on the Supreme Court, Marshall fit right in among the liberals he joined, including Chief Justice Earl Warren (1891–1974). Over time, however, the Court grew more conservative as long-serving liberals retired and were replaced by justices appointed by Republican presidents Richard M. Nixon (1913–1994), Gerald R. Ford (1913–2006), Ronald Reagan (1911–2004), and George H. W.

Bush (1924–). Marshall often found himself an isolated liberal voice on a court moving gradually but steadily to the right. In case after case he was the Court's most consistent defender of society's underdogs. For example, in *Powell v. Texas* (1968), Marshall wrote that habitual drunkenness was a medical condition rather than a criminal act. He was also a fierce guardian of the rights to free speech and privacy. In 1969 Marshall wrote the Court's opinion in *Stanley v. Georgia*, in which he and his colleagues overturned a man's conviction for possessing obscene material in his own home. Marshall was also a strong opponent of capital punishment. One of his most important pieces of work was his sixty-page concurring opinion in *Furman v. Georgia* (1972), the case that ended the death penalty in a number of states as it was applied at the time, resulting in many death sentences being overturned.

By the 1970s Marshall had become quite reclusive. He gave very few interviews and did his best to avoid big public events. He spent his workdays in his chambers and spent the majority of his off time with his family, consisting of his wife, Cecilia, and their two sons, Thurgood Jr. and John. As the Court drifted to the right under Chief Justice Warren Burger (1907–1995) and his successor

William Rehnquist (1924–2005), Marshall clung to his liberal principles, but more and more often found himself on the losing side of key decisions, along with his friend and fellow liberal Justice William J. Brennan Jr. (1906–1997). Supreme Court justices have traditionally restrained themselves in expressing their political views, but in the 1980s, Marshall was unable to contain his contempt for Republican Presidents Reagan and Bush. Dismayed by the Court's reversals of important decisions related to affirmative action and minority set-aside programs, Marshall criticized these presidents sharply for their support of policies that he believed turned back the clock on civil rights, undoing much of the movement's hard-won progress. So deep was his disapproval of Reagan that he was once quoted in *Ebony* as saying, "I wouldn't do the job of dogcatcher for Ronald Reagan," a burst of public disrespect rare for a justice.

Brennan's retirement in 1990 left Marshall even more isolated as the lone remaining genuine liberal on the Supreme Court. Marshall, whose health had been deteriorating for several years, announced his own retirement a year later. His retirement may have had as much to do with his frustration level as with his medical problems. Less than two years later, on January 24, 1993, Marshall died of heart failure.

Earl Warren

Earl Warren's (1891–1974) sixteen-year tenure as chief justice of the U.S. Supreme Court was marked by an unprecedented series of landmark decisions related to civil rights, freedom of speech, and other individual civil liberties. As detested by conservatives for his "judicial activism" as he was adored by liberals for championing progressive ideals, Warren led a Court that helped change American society during the 1950s and 1960s.

Warren was born on March 19, 1891, in Los Angeles, California. His father, a Norwegian immigrant, was a railroad worker. The family moved to Bakersfield, California, when Warren was a child. During his college years, Warren supported himself by working summers on a railroad crew. After receiving a bachelor's degree from the University of California (UC) at Berkeley, Warren went straight into UC's law school, earning a law degree in 1914. He enlisted in the U.S. Army in 1917, then returned to Northern California to practice law when his World War I tour of duty was over.

Early Career In 1920 Warren took a job with the Alameda County, California, district attorney's office, initially intending to stay just long enough to gain some legal experience. In 1925, however, he was elected to the first of his three terms as district attorney.

As district attorney, Warren, a liberal Republican, gained a reputation as a tough-but-fair prosecutor. In 1938 he was elected attorney general for the state of California. A few years later, Warren earned one of the few black marks on his career. Following the Japanese

Supreme Court Chief Justice Earl Warren. © *United States Supreme Court*

attack on Pearl Harbor in December 1941, Warren was one of the most prominent state officials calling for the internment of Japanese-Americans living on the West Coast, which history has judged to be a gross violation of the rights of those individuals, the majority of whom were American citizens.

Governor of California In 1942 Warren was elected governor of California, winning by a considerable margin. He proved to be a popular governor, and was reelected in 1946 and 1950 with broad, bipartisan support. In 1948 he suffered the only electoral defeat of his career, as the vice-presidential candidate on Thomas Dewey's (1902–1971) 1948 Republican ticket that lost to Harry Truman (1884–1972).

Warren was instrumental in garnering support for Dwight D. Eisenhower's (1890–1969) nomination as the 1952 Republican presidential candidate. Eisenhower rewarded Warren by appointing him to replace U.S. Supreme Court Chief Justice Fred Vinson (1890–1953) when Vinson died unexpectedly in 1953.

Supreme Court Warren was quickly faced with a case of historical importance in *Brown v. Board of Education of Topeka*. In that case, the Warren Court ruled unanimously that the "separate but equal" doctrine that had allowed states to maintain segregated schools was

Secret Service agent climbing onto the back of President Kennedy's car in an attempt to save the mortally wounded president, November 22, 1963. © Bettmann/CORBIS

unconstitutional. The decision helped kick the civil rights movement into high gear, but it also infuriated segregationists in the South, many of whom called for Warren's impeachment.

In addition to civil rights and segregation, the Warren Court also made its mark in the area of criminal justice with a series of key decisions. In *Griffin v. Illinois* (1956), Warren with the majority ruled that states had to furnish an indigent defendant with a copy of the evidence against him. *Mapp v. Ohio* (1961) extended the constitutional protection against unreasonable search and seizure to apply to state courts and officers. Similarly, *Gideon v. Wainright* (1963) extended the right to legal counsel to state as well as federal criminal proceedings. *Miranda v. Arizona* (1966) required that suspects be informed of their right to counsel before interrogation. Another key area in which the Warren Court made important rulings was the geography of representation in government. In *Baker v. Carr* (1962) and *Reynolds v. Sims* (1964), Warren and his colleagues held that state legislatures must be apportioned based on population rather than geography, a doctrine known as "one person, one vote."

Warren Commission In 1963 President Lyndon B. Johnson (1908–1973) appointed Warren to head a commission created to investigate the circumstances surrounding the assassination of John F. Kennedy (1917–1963). The Warren Commission, as it was popularly known, issued a massive report in 1964 in which the members concluded that Lee Harvey Oswald had acted alone in assassinating Kennedy, and that there was no convincing evidence of a broader conspiracy. The *Warren Report* has remained somewhat controversial since the day it was issued; a number of vexing questions about the assassination have never been answered to the satisfaction of many Americans.

Warren retired from the Supreme Court in July 1969 and was succeeded as chief justice by Warren Burger (1907–1995). Earl Warren died in 1974.

See also **The Warren Commission**

Fidel Castro

Fidel Castro (1926–) has been president of Cuba since 1959, when he led the revolution that ousted dictator Fulgencio Batista y Zaldívar (1901–1973) and formed the Western Hemisphere's first communist government. One of the world's most recognizable leaders on the basis of his trademark bushy beard and military fatigues, Castro is revered by some as a man of the people who dramatically improved most Cubans' standard of living, and loathed by others as a ruthless despot who brutally represses all opposition. Under Castro's leadership, Cuba remains steadfastly communist even after the disintegration of its longtime ally the Soviet Union.

Fidel Castro Ruz was born on August 13, 1926 (or, according to some sources, 1927), in Cuba's Oriente Province, and grew up on his family's thriving sugar plantation. As a child, Castro had an unquenchable thirst for knowledge. He pestered his parents to provide him with a formal education, and though they had not planned on sending him to school, his persistence eventually paid off when they relented. Castro attended Jesuit schools in Santiago for several years before entering Belén College, an exclusive college preparatory high school in Havana, in 1941. He excelled in nearly every subject, and was a standout athlete as well.

Revolutionary Climate   In 1945 Castro began studying law at the University of Havana. Revolution was in the air at the university, and Castro quickly became interested in politics. He acquired a reputation as a fiery speaker and committed activist. In 1947 he left school temporarily to take part in an attempt to overthrow dictator Rafael Trujillo Molina of the Dominican Republic. The revolt was aborted en route on the sea, and Castro was forced to swim ashore through shark-infested waters while holding his gun above his head. The following year, while attending a conference in Bogotá, Colombia, Castro took part in the *Bogotazo*, a series of riots there that took place in the wake of the assassination of Liberal Party leader Jorge Eliécer Gaitán.

Later that year, Castro married Mirta Díaz-Balart, and in 1949 the couple had a son, Fidelito. Fidel Castro completed his legal studies in 1950 and helped establish the law firm of Azpiazu, Castro y Rosendo. Much of his work involved representing poor and working-class individuals, often for free. Castro continued his political activity, joining the liberal Ortodoxo Party, which emphasized social justice and economic independence. In 1952 Castro began campaigning for a seat in the Cuban parliament. His run for office was cut short, however, when Batista, a general in the army, staged a coup that overthrew democratically elected president Carlos Prio Socarras.

Outraged, Castro officially challenged Batista's actions by filing a petition with the Court of Constitutional Guarantees. The petition was rejected. Castro, however, was not ready to give up quite so easily. He formed a small band of about 165 rebels, and on July 26, 1953, launched an attack on the Moncada barracks in Santiago de Cuba, in hopes that the assault would spark a broader uprising in Oriente Province. The attack failed miserably; half the participants

THE MARIEL BOATLIFT

During the first decade of Fidel Castro's (1926–) rule in Cuba, very few people were allowed to leave the country permanently. It was not until 1980 that a window of opportunity opened for those seeking to emigrate from Cuba. Over several months during that year, about 125,000 Cubans fled their homeland and crossed the Straits of Florida on boats of all shapes, sizes, and levels of safety to resettle in the United States. Known as the Mariel boatlift, the mass exodus carried these migrants from the port of Mariel on the northern coast of Cuba between April and October 1980.

With Cuba suffering myriad social problems in 1980, including housing shortages and job shortages and an overall stagnant economy, thousands of Cubans gathered at the Peruvian Embassy in Havana in hopes of gaining permission to leave the country. As the number of would-be emigrants swelled to over ten thousand, most of them lacking food and water, Castro came up with a novel way to deflect the embarrassment the situation was causing: he announced that anybody who wanted to leave Cuba was free to go, a major departure from the nation's longstanding, rigid emigration policies. Beginning on April 15, a flotilla of watercraft, many of them arriving from the Miami area, where a large number Cuban exiles were already living, began transporting Cubans across the narrow channel between Cuba and South Florida.

The sudden influx of so many Cuban immigrants placed a huge burden on the U.S. immigration system. Many of the newcomers were detained in American prisons, some because they had criminal backgrounds, others simply because they did not have an American sponsor. Having grown up in Cuba's socialist climate, the "marielitos," as they came to be called, generally expected the state to take care of many of their needs, such as housing and health care. Nevertheless, while U.S. President Jimmy Carter (1924–) released several million dollars in emergency aid for the refugees, most of them found that they were on their own. Even the established Cuban population in South Florida was less than enthusiastic about receiving this sudden wave of immigrants, in part because the majority were young, poor, dark-skinned, and ill-equipped to successfully plunge directly into the American economy. The media tended to exaggerate the criminal histories of the marielitos; in fact only a small percentage had records that warranted incarceration in the United States. And contrary to the fears of Miamians, the big influx of unskilled workers did not have a negative impact on the local economy in the long run.

were captured, tortured, and/or killed. Castro and his brother Raúl were taken into custody, and Fidel Castro was sentenced to fifteen years in prison.

Movement Regroups in Mexico   Castro was released under a general amnesty order in May 1955, having served only a year-and-a-half of his sentence. A few months later, Castro and a small number of followers

Cuban leader Fidel Castro in 1962 denouncing the United States for firing on Havana's shoreline from gunboats. Anti-Castro Cuban exiles later claimed responsibility for the cannon fire, which damaged several homes and a hotel.   *Alan Oxley/Getty Images*

left Cuba and regrouped in Mexico, where they formed the "26th of July" movement, named after the date of the failed Moncada barracks attack. There he met a young Argentine doctor and revolutionary named Ernesto "Che" Guevara (1928–1967). Together, they trained their small army in military tactics and skills.

Led by the Castro brothers and Guevara, a tiny army of about eighty-two men returned to Cuba on an old yacht in December 1956. The ragtag force was met by Batista's army almost the moment they landed on the north shore of Oriente, and more than half of the rebels were killed. The survivors, including the Castros and Guevara, retreated to the Sierra Maestra mountains. Over the next two years, Castro and his followers worked to build support among the local peasants, winning them over with promises of land reform. The revolutionaries spent most of their time avoiding Batista's forces and engaging in occasional ambushes and small attacks. Meanwhile, word of Castro and his band of revolutionaries spread across Cuba, and revolutionary fervor began to arise among the nation's poor.

Castro's rebel movement began to gain the upper hand in early 1958. It helped that the United States,

aggravated by the corruption and brutal tactics of the Batista government, suspended its military support of his regime. In December of that year, Guevara led an attack on a government train column and dealt Batista's army a devastating blow. Sensing imminent defeat, Batista fled the country on New Year's Day 1959. Castro marched into Havana the next day and assumed control of Cuba.

Socialist Reforms To his supporters, Castro was a charismatic hero. To his enemies, Castro was a criminal. Some members of the Batista regime were arrested and executed. Castro began confiscating the property of Batista supporters, as well as the inherited wealth of Cuba's elite families. In all, 1,500 new laws were passed the first day of the revolution. One law passed early in Castro's reign, the Agrarian Reform Act, confiscated land from anyone with an estate of more than 1,000 acres. While wealthy Cubans were horrified by Castro's moves to redistribute the nation's wealth, the impoverished masses were elated. They were equally delighted by Castro's campaigns to promote literacy and improve access to health care. These campaigns were highly successful. Average life expectancy in Cuba rose dramatically, and Cuba now boasts one of the highest literacy rates in the

Fidel Castro with Jesse Jackson, 1984.   © *Jacques M. Chenet/CORBIS*

Western Hemisphere. Schools and universities were built, and postgraduate education was made free.

Castro's early socialistic policies and nationalistic rhetoric did not please the administration of U.S. President Dwight D. Eisenhower (1890–1969). U.S.-Cuban relations were strained further when Castro signed an agreement with the Soviet Union to trade sugar for oil. In response, the United States reduced its imports from Cuba, and in January 1961 Eisenhower cut off relations with Cuba completely. Cuba's ties with the Soviets quickly intensified.

Eisenhower was naturally distressed by the presence of a Soviet ally so close to the U.S. mainland. This unease carried over into the Kennedy presidency. In April 1961 the United States supported a mission to invade Cuba and overthrow Castro that was conducted by a small army of Cuban exiles trained by the Central Intelligence Agency. Landing at the Bay of Pigs on Cuba's southern coast, the exile army was quickly overwhelmed by Castro's military, and the invasion ended in a colossal failure. The event was a major embarrassment to the United States, and solidified support for Castro within Cuba. Following the Bay of Pigs debacle, Castro officially proclaimed Cuba to be a communist state with a Marxist-Leninist orientation akin to that of the Soviets.

October 1962: Cuban Missile Crisis Relations between Castro and the Americans continued to deteriorate. In October 1962 U.S. intelligence detected the presence of powerful Soviet missiles in Cuba. The resulting showdown, known as the Cuban missile crisis, brought the United States and the Soviet Union to the brink of nuclear war, as the United States imposed a blockade on the island, and both superpowers issued ultimatums to each other. The Soviets eventually agreed to remove their Cuban-based missiles, after the United States agreed to various concessions negotiated in secret meetings. The crisis brought Cuba even closer to the Soviet Union, and isolated it from most of its neighbors. This isolation grew when, in the aftermath of the crisis, the Organization of American States (OAS) suspended Cuba's membership, and, two years later, cut off all diplomatic and trade relations. Among OAS nations, only Mexico opted not to participate in the boycott.

While he was reforming Cuba's economy—nationalizing its industries, centralizing economic planning, and seizing government control of the media—Castro also resorted to repressive tactics to maintain social order. Tens of thousands of political prisoners were locked up during the 1960s, as were thousands more simply for being homosexuals or for being artists or intellectuals whose work was deemed subversive.

Castro also sought to export his revolution to other countries. In 1966 he helped found the Organization of Solidarity of the People of Asia, Africa and Latin America, which supported anti-imperialist struggles in Third World countries all over the world. In the years that followed, he sent Cuban personnel to fight in Angola's civil war, to assist Ethiopia's efforts to repel attacks from Somalia, and to support guerrilla movements in several Latin American countries, including the Sandinistas in Nicaragua.

Castro's hold on the reins of power in Cuba has not been seriously threatened since the 1959 revolution. As the Soviet Union reformed its economic system and dismantled itself in the late 1980s and early 1990s, Castro clung to his socialist policies in Cuba. In 2006 serious illness forced him to transfer leadership duties to his brother Raúl. With Castro entering his eighties, it was unclear whether he would ever again be healthy enough to fully resume his role as president.

See also **The Cuban Missile Crisis**

John F. Kennedy

John F. Kennedy (1917–1963), the thirty-fifth president of the United States, became the most recent U.S. head of state to die in office when he was assassinated on November 22, 1963. Kennedy was the youngest American president ever elected, as well as the youngest to die. He was also the first Roman Catholic to occupy the White House.

Privileged Childhood John Fitzgerald Kennedy was born on May 29, 1917, in Brookline, Massachusetts, just outside of Boston. He was raised at the Kennedy family's homes in New York and Hyannis Port, Massachusetts, on Cape Cod. He was second-oldest among Joseph and Rose Kennedy's nine children. The Kennedy clan was immensely wealthy and immensely powerful politically. His paternal grandfather, Patrick Joseph Kennedy, rose from poverty to become a successful liquor importer, and translated his business achievements into political clout, as he became an important backroom power broker in the Boston area and eventually a member of the Massachusetts legislature. His maternal grandfather, John Francis Fitzgerald, was also a political figure, serving three terms in Congress and two terms as mayor of Boston.

President John F. Kennedy speaking at a labor convention, 1961. © *Bettmann/CORBIS*

President John F. Kennedy making a dramatic television broadcast to announce the blockade of Cuba during the Cuban Missile Crisis, 1962. *Keystone/Getty Images*

Patrick Kennedy's son Joseph—John F. Kennedy's father—built on his father's success through well-timed investments in a range of industries, including banking, shipbuilding, motion pictures, and the family's main line, liquor. These investments made him one of the wealthiest men in America. Joseph Kennedy used his vast wealth to support the presidential candidacy of Franklin Roosevelt (1882–1945) in 1932, and was rewarded with a series of appointments to coveted government posts, including chair of the U.S. Securities and Exchange Commission in 1934, chair of the U.S. Maritime Commission in 1937, and finally the one he sought most, the ambassadorship to Great Britain in December 1937.

John F. Kennedy, who went by "Jack," grew up in the shadow of his older brother, Joe Jr. It was Joe Kennedy who was the apple of his father's eye, destined to carry on the family legacy of power and prominence. Jack followed Joe, two years his senior, through the prestigious prep school Choate and into Harvard University. Jack struggled with various medical problems, in contrast to his strong, healthy brother. Jack Kennedy graduated cum laude from Harvard in 1940. With the onset of World War II, he enlisted in the U.S. Navy, initially serving as an intelligence officer in Washington, D.C. After the Japanese attack on Pearl Harbor in December 1941, Kennedy was reassigned to sea duty on a PT boat—a small, fast vessel used to torpedo larger surface ships—in the Pacific. He was given his own PT boat to command in March 1943. A few months later, his boat, PT109, was rammed and sunk by a Japanese destroyer. Kennedy swam three miles to safety, towing an injured crewmate along with him. Though Kennedy tended to play down his act of heroism, he was honored for his courageous act, and it became part of the Kennedy aura that would serve him well during his political career.

Early Political Career The following year, his brother Joe was killed while flying a dangerous mission over Europe. The entire family was devastated. Joseph Sr., who had long groomed Joe Jr. to go into politics, tapped Jack to take his brother's place. Supported by his father's financial fortune and political connections, Kennedy ran for a seat in the U.S. House of Representatives in 1946. He was a political novice, but won the election handily, taking the congressional seat held by his grandfather John "Honey Fitz" Fitzgerald a half-century earlier.

In the House of Representatives, Kennedy did nothing that stood out among his peers. In spite of the Kennedy family's privileged economic status, he tended to support policies that favored workers and ordinary people. In 1947 Kennedy was diagnosed with Addison's disease, a degenerative condition that affects the adrenal glands. The condition improved in 1950, when he began receiving cortisone treatments. Meanwhile, he was reelected to the House twice. In 1952 Kennedy ran for U.S. Senate, taking on the incumbent Republican Henry Cabot Lodge (1902–1985). The Republicans rode a wave of anticommunist hysteria to victory in most congressional races that year; but on the strength of his personal charisma and the growing Kennedy mystique, Kennedy was able to score a rare victory for the Democrats in that race.

During his first year as a U.S. senator, Kennedy married Jacqueline Bouvier. In the Senate, Kennedy was assigned to several key committees: the Labor and Public Welfare Committee, the Government Operations Committee, the Select Committee on Labor-Management Relations, the Foreign Relations Committee, and the Joint Economic Committee. From there, he was able to guide several bills designed to help the Massachusetts fishing and textile industries through the legislative process.

Profiles in Courage During the mid-1950s, Kennedy began to suffer intense pain from an old back injury, for which he underwent dangerous surgeries in 1954 and 1955. The surgeries were not entirely successful; Kennedy lived with chronic back pain for the rest of his life. As he recuperated from surgery, he spent several months writing a book about U.S. senators who had taken courageous stands and demonstrated remarkable integrity. The book, *Profiles in Courage*, was published in 1956 and awarded a Pulitzer Prize the following year.

THE KENNEDY CURSE

Fabulous wealth and power have not spared the Kennedy family from tragedy. In fact, the Kennedy clan has suffered through an extraordinary number of tragic events over the years, leading some observers inclined toward superstition to believe the Kennedys are "cursed."

The so-called curse goes back to the 1940s. Rosemary Kennedy, the sister of President John F. Kennedy (1917–1963), suffered from violent mood swings. She was given an experimental treatment called a lobotomy, which involved blindly poking an instrument into a patient's brain. The results in her case were terrible, and she remained institutionalized for the rest of her life. She died in 2005.

In 1944 Joe Kennedy Jr., President Kennedy's older brother, was killed over the English Channel while flying a mission during World War II. Four years later another sister, Kathleen Kennedy Cavendish, died in a plane crash in France. In the mid-1950s, as John F. Kennedy was making his name as a U.S. senator and struggling with severe back ailments, his wife Jacqueline had a miscarriage one year and gave birth to a stillborn daughter the next. In August 1963 John and Jacqueline had a son, Patrick Bouvier Kennedy. He was born nearly six weeks premature, and died two days after his birth. John Kennedy was assassinated that November.

In 1964 one of Kennedy's younger brothers, Edward "Ted" Kennedy (1932–), was severely injured in a plane crash that killed one of his aides and the pilot. He spent weeks in the hospital recovering from injuries that included a punctured lung, broken ribs, and internal bleeding. Another brother, Robert F. Kennedy (1925–1968)—the former attorney general of the United States, whom many thought to be the leading contender for the 1968 presidential election—was assassinated while leaving an event celebrating his victory in the California Democratic presidential primary in June 1968.

The following year, Ted Kennedy drove a car off a bridge after a party on Chappaquiddick Island near Martha's Vineyard in Massachusetts, killing his passenger Mary Jo Kopechne, a former aide to Robert Kennedy. Ted Kennedy escaped serious injury, but questions surrounding the event may have thwarted his own future presidential aspirations. In 1999 John F. Kennedy Jr., his wife, Caroline Bessette-Kennedy, and her sister were killed when the plane Kennedy was piloting crashed into the Atlantic Ocean.

Amazingly, even this list is incomplete. Similar tragedies have befallen distantly related members of the clan, and the family has experienced a variety of additional, less dramatic misfortunes over the years.

Despite his physical struggles, Kennedy was considered a rising star in the Senate by this time. He was nearly nominated to be the Democratic Party vice-presidential candidate in 1956, but narrowly lost the nomination battle to Senator Estes Kefauver of Tennessee. By 1960 Kennedy was in a position to vie for the top spot on the Democratic ticket. Running on a campaign theme of achieving "national greatness" through sacrifice, and arriving at a "New Frontier," Kennedy coasted through the Democratic convention and was named the party's presidential candidate.

Kennedy's opponent in the 1960 presidential election was Richard M. Nixon (1913–1994), who was running on his reputation as a fierce Cold Warrior, tough on communism and hostile to the proliferation of costly domestic programs. This was the first election in which television played an important role, and Kennedy benefited mightily from four televised debates at which he appeared to be the more poised, sophisticated, and charismatic of the two candidates. Kennedy prevailed in what was one of the closest presidential elections in the nation's history. He won in part by carrying 68 percent of the African-American vote, more than three-quarters of the Catholic vote, and, largely thanks to his savvy selection of Texan Lyndon B. Johnson (1908–1973) as his running mate, by winning a handful of Southern states.

Kennedy Presidency As president, Kennedy was immediately faced with a number of challenges associated with the Cold War. In 1959 Fidel Castro (1926–) had become leader of Cuba after successfully toppling President Fulgencio Batista y Zaldívar (1901–1973). As Castro began forging close ties with the Soviet Union, American leaders grew increasingly nervous about the presence of a communist client state so close to American soil. Kennedy inherited a plan first conceived by the Central Intelligence Agency (CIA) under the Eisenhower administration to support with money, weapons, and training an invasion of Cuba by Cuban exiles living in the Unites States, in hopes of ousting Castro from power. In April 1961 Kennedy authorized the execution of the plan. The invasion, focused at a site called the Bay of Pigs, failed miserably and was a major embarrassment for the young Kennedy administration.

Another crisis involving Cuba emerged the following year, when American intelligence detected signs that the Soviets were deploying powerful missiles in Cuba that were capable of carrying atomic warheads to targets across the United States. A high-stakes showdown between the United States and the Soviet Union ensued, as threats and ultimatums were exchanged, bringing the world to the brink of nuclear war. This time, Kennedy was able to avert a catastrophe. A flurry of secret, high-level negotiations resulted in a deal under which the Soviets agreed to remove their Cuban-based missiles in return for a U.S. promise not to invade Cuba. Undisclosed at the time was another part of the agreement: the United States would remove its missiles based in Turkey.

No sooner was the Cuban missile crisis defused, however, than Vietnam began to emerge as the nation's next Cold War crisis. Determined to resist efforts by North Vietnam to unify Vietnam under communist rule,

Kennedy increased the number of military advisers there, creating the conditions that would explode into full-blown U.S. participation in the Vietnam War under Kennedy's successor Lyndon Johnson.

Despite these crises, the Kennedy years are generally remembered as a time of great prosperity and hope in America. Among Kennedy's historic accomplishments were the creation of the Peace Corps and the Agency for International Development. He was also supportive, if not aggressively so, of the civil rights movement. On a handful of occasions Kennedy intervened when Southern officials and establishments sought to prevent racial desegregation from taking place as mandated by U.S. Supreme Court rulings.

Kennedy Assassination Kennedy was assassinated on November 22, 1963, while touring Dallas, Texas, in a motorcade. The presumed assassin, Lee Harvey Oswald, was himself gunned down two days later, while in police custody, by Dallas nightclub owner Jack Ruby. A number of questions lingered in the wake of the murders, the most important being whether Oswald had acted alone or been part of a broader conspiracy. Incoming president Johnson convened a special panel to investigate the strange circumstances surrounding the Kennedy assassination. The panel, led by U.S. Supreme Court Chief Justice Earl Warren (1891–1974) and generally referred to as the Warren Commission, released an 888-page report in September 1964, in which it concluded that there was no persuasive evidence of a conspiracy and Oswald had in fact acted alone.

The conclusions of the Warren Commission remain controversial today, and many Americans remain convinced that a conspiracy was at work. Regardless of how the assassination was orchestrated, Kennedy's death is widely perceived as a transforming moment in American history. Over the next several years, a general mood of optimism gave way to one of conflict and upheaval, with the escalation of U.S. involvement in Vietnam, the rise of racial strife in many cities, and other divisive social phenomena taking hold.

See also **The Cuban Missile Crisis**
See also **The Warren Commission**

William Brennan

During his thirty-four years on the U.S. Supreme Court, Justice William J. Brennan Jr. (1906–1997) was one of the nation's most consistent and passionate champions of individual liberties. A staunch advocate for racial and gender equity, Brennan was undoubtedly one of the most influential justices in the nation's history. As a mainstay of the Court's liberal wing over a period that spanned eight presidencies and saw sweeping social and political changes, Brennan wrote landmark opinions on such critical issues as freedom of speech, civil rights, and separation of church and state. Brennan wrote more than 1,200 opinions while serving on the Supreme Court, more than

any other justice except William O. Douglas (1898–1980).

Son of a Working-Class Politician Brennan was born on April 25, 1906, in Newark, New Jersey. He was the second of eight children born to William J. Brennan Sr. and Agnes McDermott, both Irish immigrants. William Sr. was a coal shoveler in a brewery before becoming active in politics, first as a labor union official and later as a member of the Newark City Commission. He eventually became police commissioner and, finally, director of public safety, one of the most powerful posts in Newark's municipal bureaucracy.

After graduating with honors from the University of Pennsylvania, William Jr. moved on to Harvard Law School, where he served as president of the student Legal Aid Society. He graduated from law school near the top of his class in 1931. Returning home to Newark, Brennan took a job with the corporate law firm of Pitney, Hardin and Skinner, becoming a partner in 1937. In this position, Brennan often found himself arguing on behalf of corporate management, which contradicted his natural inclination, inherited from his labor activist father, to champion the interests of underdogs and regular working folks.

Brennan served in the U.S. Army during World War II, working on labor and procurement matters, and was discharged with the rank of colonel. After the war, he returned to the law firm, where two senior partners had passed away, leaving Brennan as top manager. Brennan soon became involved in efforts to reform the New Jersey judicial system. In 1959 he was appointed to the appellate division of the New Jersey Superior Court, and two years later he was named to the state's Supreme Court.

U.S. Supreme Court When Justice Sherman Minton (1890–1965) announced his retirement from the U.S. Supreme Court in 1956, President Dwight D. Eisenhower (1890–1969) sought to replace him for political reasons with a fairly young, sitting judge who was Catholic and a Democrat. Brennan, who had already impressed Attorney General Herbert Brownell, fit the profile precisely. Brennan was appointed to the Supreme Court on October 16, 1956, and confirmed by the Senate the following March, with only Republican Senator Joseph McCarthy (1908–1957) of Wisconsin voting against his confirmation.

During his first thirteen years on the Court under Chief Justice Earl Warren (1891–1974), with whom he had a very close working relationship, Brennan was a key member of the Court's liberal majority. Brennan wrote his first landmark opinion in 1962 in the case *Baker v. Carr*. In this ruling, the Court held that cases challenging unequal legislative apportionment could be heard in federal court, leading to the series of "one person, one vote" reapportionment cases that essentially revolutionized electoral districting and redistricting in the United States. The following year, Brennan—one of the most religious justices on the Court—made a strong

Supreme Court Justice William Brennan, 1972. © *Library of Congress*

statement for the strict separation of church and state in his seventy-page concurring opinion in *Abington School District v. Schempp* and *Murray v. Curlett*, which held that state-mandated Bible reading and recitation of the Lord's Prayer were unconstitutional. In 1964 Brennan wrote the Court's unanimous opinion in the landmark First Amendment case *New York Times v. Sullivan*. This case established that the press was free to criticize public officials as long as the statements were not deliberately false or made with malicious intent.

Endured Court's Rightward Swing Brennan's role on the Court was diminished slightly when Warren was replaced as chief justice by Warren Burger (1907–1995), with whom Brennan did not enjoy such a close friendship. Nevertheless, he remained the Court's most consistent liberal voice and vote, usually in alliance with Thurgood Marshall (1908–1993). In 1970 Brennan wrote the majority opinion in *Goldberg v. Kelly*, a case in which the Court ruled that states cannot cut off welfare benefits without first giving the recipient a hearing.

During the second half of Brennan's tenure on the bench, the Supreme Court became much more conservative. President Ronald Reagan (1911–2004) and his allies on the right criticized Brennan for using the Court

to effect social changes they believed were more appropriately handled through legislation, if at all. He saw many of the progressive changes he had been part of undone by the conservative courts of the 1980s. One of Brennan's last major cases was *Texas v. Johnson* (1989), in which he and others in the majority ruled that laws banning flag burning as a political statement were unconstitutional.

Brennan retired in 1990, leaving a judicial legacy matched by only a few other Supreme Court justices in the history of the nation. He died in 1997 in Arlington, Virginia.

Martin Luther King Jr.

Martin Luther King Jr. (1929–1968) was one of the most important leaders of the civil rights movement in the United States during the 1950s and 1960s. King advocated a nonviolent approach to protest, a philosophy influenced by the Indian leader Mahatma Gandhi (1869–1948). King's passion and determination inspired countless Americans to action as the nation struggled with issues of social justice and racial equality.

King was born Michael King Jr. on January 15, 1929, in Atlanta, Georgia, the second child of Michael King Sr. and Alberta Williams King. Both King and his father later changed their names to honor Martin Luther, the religious leader who spearheaded the Protestant Reformation in the sixteenth century.

Early Life King attended public schools in Atlanta. Upon graduation from high school, he enrolled at Morehouse College, a historically all-black liberal arts school in Atlanta. While still a student at Morehouse, King was ordained into the ministry of the National Baptist Church. He was also exposed for the first time to the philosophy of Mahatma Gandhi, the pacifist Indian leader. King graduated from Morehouse in 1948 and entered Crozer Theological Seminary in Pennsylvania. King graduated from Crozer in 1951, and then moved on to Boston University to begin working toward a Ph.D. in theology. During his time in Boston, King met Coretta Scott, a voice student at the New England Conservatory of Music. King and Scott were married on June 18, 1953.

In 1954, while he was still working on his doctoral dissertation, King was named pastor of the Dexter Avenue Baptist Church in Montgomery, Alabama. He was awarded his Ph.D. in June of the following year. It did not take long after King's arrival in Montgomery for him to become a central figure in the civil rights movement. In December 1955 an African-American woman named Rosa Parks (1913–2005) was arrested for refusing to give up her seat on a Montgomery bus to a white man, as was required by local law. The African-American community was outraged by Parks's treatment. King and other religious leaders and activists, including Alabama state NAACP chairman Ralph Abernathy (1926–1990), quickly organized a boycott of the segregated Montgomery bus system. As the leader of the boycott, King

Civil rights leader Martin Luther King, Jr., during the 1963 March on Washington.   *CNP/Getty Images*

came under harsh criticism from proponents of segregation. At one point his home was firebombed, and he received a steady stream of threats. The boycott lasted for more than a year, and in the end, after the U.S. Supreme Court ruled that segregation on the city's buses was unconstitutional, the bus company relented. Segregation on Montgomery's buses was ended, and the success of the bus boycott brought national attention to King.

In January 1957 several dozen African-American religious leaders met in Atlanta to organize a permanent group that would work on civil rights issues. The group became the Southern Christian Leadership Conference (SCLC), and King was chosen as its first president. The following year, the SCLC launched the "Crusade for Citizenship," an initiative to register thousands of new black voters across the South. In support of the project King traveled to cities all over the region to speak on the importance of voting in the overall campaign for social justice.

King moved to Atlanta in 1960 to become associate pastor at the Ebenezer Baptist Church. That year, he helped coordinate the "sit-in" movement, in which groups of African-Americans occupied "whites-only" lunch counters and other segregated venues. As the movement gained momentum, King encouraged the students at the core of the movement to remain independent of the SCLC, leading to the formation of the Student Nonviolent Coordinating Committee (SNCC, pronounced "snick").

Freedom Riders   The sit-ins were highly successful in raising public awareness of segregation in public places. Their success led to the idea of bringing sit-ins to the interstate transportation system. The SCLC, SNCC, and the Congress of Racial Equality (CORE) formed a coalition, chaired by King, to organize a series of actions in which pairs of African-American and white volunteers would board interstate buses scheduled to travel through Southern states. These volunteers, called Freedom Riders, were brutally assaulted upon their arrival in some Southern cities. Nevertheless, the project was effective; as a result the Interstate Commerce

BLOODY SUNDAY

One of the most dramatic moments in the civil rights movement took place in Selma, Alabama, in March 1965. The Civil Rights Act had passed the previous year, but it did nothing to explicitly ensure the voting rights of minorities. Throughout 1963 and 1964, Selma was a focal point for voter registration efforts by the Student Nonviolent Coordinating Committee (SNCC) and other groups. The segregationists who held power in Selma resisted these efforts forcefully. By early 1965, civil rights activists were pouring into Selma to help the cause. A protest march from Selma to Montgomery, the state capital, was planned to raise awareness of what was going on in Selma.

The first attempt at the march took place on Sunday, March 7, 1965. Over five hundred participants headed out of Selma on U.S. Highway 80. The march, led by Hosea Williams of the Southern Christian Leadership Conference and John Lewis of SNCC, made it only as far as the Edmund Pettus Bridge six blocks away before they were set upon by Alabama state troopers and officers from the Dallas County Sheriff's Department wielding clubs, whips, and tear gas. The attack was brutal; seventeen marchers were hospitalized, and about sixty more were treated at the hospital and released. The event became known as Bloody Sunday.

Footage of the violence was broadcast nationwide, resulting in an outpouring of support for the movement. A second march was planned for March 9, led by King, but it was merely a prenegotiated symbolic crossing of the Pettus Bridge, and many participants were left confused and dissatisfied. Even the scaled-down second march was not without bloodshed; after the march a Unitarian minister named James Reeb was brutally assaulted by a group of racists, and died later at the hospital.

After much political maneuvering, a third march was organized. This time the march was authorized by a judge, and state and local authorities were ordered not to interfere. About eight thousand people began the third march on Sunday, March 24 and over thirty thousand participated in it overall, including a number of celebrities, such as Harry Belafonte, Tony Bennett, and Leonard Bernstein. Even the successful third march was marred by deadly violence: a white Michigan housewife and mother named Viola Liuzza was shot and killed in her car as she drove some African-Americans home from the historic march.

The same day the march began, President Lyndon B. Johnson (1908–1973) sent his voting rights bill to Congress. The following year, it became the Voting Rights Act of 1965.

descended on Washington, D.C., for a gigantic rally, where King delivered his famous "I have a dream" speech. King's efforts paid off a year later when President Lyndon B. Johnson (1908–1973) signed the Civil Rights Act of 1964 into law. In December of that year, King was given the Nobel Peace Prize in recognition of his inspiring leadership of the civil rights movement.

In spite of the passage of the Civil Rights Act, King found that much work remained to be done. African-American citizens were being denied their voting rights through a variety of underhanded mechanisms in many parts of the South. King and the SCLC decided to focus their efforts first on Selma, Alabama. To raise awareness of the issue, in 1965 King helped organize a march from Selma to Montgomery, Alabama. Alabama Governor George C. Wallace (1919–1998) ordered state troopers to stop the march, and many participants were beaten viciously. The march continued, however, with more than ten thousand people taking part. It helped promote the passage of the Voting Rights Act, which President Johnson signed in 1965.

Decline of Nonviolent Protest In spite of this progress, the civil rights movement had begun to splinter by the mid-1960s. Some factions of the movement had lost patience with King's nonviolent approach. SNCC, for example, no longer believed in nonviolence, and the Nation of Islam preached a distrust of all white people, even those who had been supportive of civil rights. Militant groups such as the Black Panthers emerged, and as racial violence ignited in major cities, many white liberals who had been active in the movement became disengaged.

Another significant factor was the emergence of the Vietnam War as the main target of political dissatisfaction among American liberals. In 1967 King became a vocal critic of American involvement in Vietnam, to the chagrin of some longtime civil rights crusaders who saw involvement in antiwar protest as a distraction from their main objective.

In March 1968 King traveled to Memphis, Tennessee, to support striking city sanitation workers. The protests erupted in violence and chaos, and the police responded with violence of their own. On April 3 King addressed a rally, calling on followers to remain committed to nonviolent protest. He also spoke of threats on his life, and the need for the movement to continue on the nonviolent path regardless of what happened to him. The following evening, King was shot to death as he stood on the balcony of his room at the Lorraine Motel. News of his death sparked rioting in more than one hundred cities around the United States. Tens of thousands of people were injured and forty-six killed before order was restored more than a week later. In 1986 Martin Luther King Jr. Day was made a national holiday, celebrated on the third Monday of January each year.

See also **The Civil Rights Movement**

Commission began enforcing existing laws prohibiting racial segregation on interstate buses.

Support for the civil rights movement continued to grow, as did the militancy of the resistance against it. Violence erupted repeatedly when schools began the process of court-ordered desegregation. In June 1963 King and 125,000 supporters marched in a Freedom Walk in the streets of Detroit, Michigan, and in August of that year twice that many activists of many races

George Wallace, the American Independent Party presidential candidate, with his running mate Curtis LeMay at a campaign rally in New York, 1968. *Bernard Gotfryd/Getty Images*

George C. Wallace

Before entering the 1968 presidential race as an independent candidate, George C. Wallace (1919–1998) was best known for his efforts as governor of Alabama to preserve racial segregation in his state. Wallace repeatedly attempted to defy the federal government's attempts to integrate public schools and other institutions across Alabama. During his time as governor, Alabama was the epicenter of the civil rights movement, as activists repeatedly clashed, sometimes with violent results, with Wallace and his segregationist allies. Ironically, on most other issues Wallace was considered a moderate, even tilting toward the liberal side at times.

Early Years George Corley Wallace was born on August 25, 1919, in Clio, Alabama, located in the rural southeastern corner of the state. His father was a cotton farmer, his mother a school music teacher. As a youth, Wallace was a skilled boxer, winning two state Golden Gloves titles while in high school. After graduating from high school, Wallace attended the University of Alabama, where he received a law degree in 1942. He

married Lurleen Burns, a sixteen-year-old store clerk, the following year.

Wallace served in the U.S. Air Force from 1942 to 1945, serving first as an airplane mechanic and later flying several missions over Japan during World War II. Returning from the war, Wallace immediately went into politics. In 1946 he landed a job as assistant state attorney general, and later that year he won election to the Alabama House of Representatives. In the state legislature, Wallace forged a reputation as being a somewhat liberal Democrat, even on issues related to race. As a delegate at the 1948 Democratic National Convention, Wallace refused to join in the walkout orchestrated by fellow Southerners who splintered from the party and formed the Dixiecrats.

Wallace continued to represent Barbour County in the Alabama House until 1953, when he was elected as a state district court judge in Alabama's Third Judicial District. He held that position until 1958. That year, Wallace launched his first campaign for governor, running as a racially tolerant moderate. His opponent was state attorney general John Patterson, who campaigned as a solid segregationist. Wallace was clearly the more progressive candidate; he even had the endorsement of the National Association for the Advancement of Colored People (NAACP). Wallace lost the election in a runoff vote. This defeat marked a turning point in Wallace's political career. In its aftermath, he resolved to never again lose an election by being "out-segged," or appearing to be less supportive of segregation than his opponent.

Governor of Alabama   After spending four years in private law practice with his brother Gerald, Wallace ran for governor again in 1962, this time as a strict segregationist. His opponent was former governor—and Wallace's former political mentor—James Folsom. This time Wallace had the backing not of the NAACP, but of the Ku Klux Klan. In his inaugural speech, he made clear his intentions with regard to race: "Segregation now! Segregation tomorrow! Segregation forever!"

Wallace's first year as governor was marked by all-out war between segregationists and civil rights proponents. On June 11, 1963, Wallace personally blocked an entrance at the University of Alabama to prevent two African-American students from enrolling. He backed down only after being confronted by federal marshals and the Alabama National Guard. That September, Wallace sent Alabama state troopers to various parts of the state to prevent African-American students from entering all-white public schools in several different cities. When Martin Luther King Jr. (1929–1968) led a major protest march from Selma to Montgomery, Alabama, in 1965, Wallace ordered state troopers to block their way. The encounter erupted in violence, and emerged as a watershed moment in the civil rights movement.

Alabama's state constitution prevented Wallace from serving two consecutive terms as governor, so in 1966 his wife Lurleen ran instead, winning easily. Wallace, officially her special assistant, essentially continued to call the shots. Lurleen died in office of cancer two years later. In 1968 Wallace made a serious run as an independent candidate for president of the United States. Appealing to voters fed up with paying taxes and other forms of federal interference in their lives, he managed to gain the support of many conservatives, both wealthy and blue collar, almost all white. Wallace managed to capture more than 13 percent of the popular vote, and won outright in five Southern states.

Reversal on Racism   Wallace ran for governor again in 1970, and won handily. In 1972 he mounted another presidential campaign, this time running as a Democrat. Wallace was running well, with strong showings in early primaries, when he was shot by Arthur Bremer while campaigning in Maryland. Wallace suffered a severe spinal injury in the shooting and used a wheelchair for the rest of his life.

Wallace successfully ran for governor in 1974 and again, after a three-year break, in 1982. By then he had renounced his former racist positions and apologized publicly for his earlier segregationist policies. He appointed African-Americans to a number of high-ranking posts in his administration, and developed relationships with civil rights leaders. Wallace declined to run for governor again in 1986—the state law preventing consecutive terms having been erased—because of health problems. Wallace died in 1998, at the age of 79.

See also **The Civil Rights Movement**

Malcolm X

Malcolm X (1925–1965) was a prominent Black Muslim minister and a leader of the black nationalist movement in the United States. A central figure in the fight for racial justice in America in the 1950s and the first half of the 1960s, Malcolm X preached an aggressive brand of black self-reliance and rebellion against white authority, in contrast to the more peaceful civil rights message Martin Luther King Jr. (1929–1968) was advocating at the same time.

Malcolm X was born Malcolm Little on May 19, 1925, in Omaha, Nebraska. His childhood was marked by ongoing trauma and violence. His father, Earl Little, was a Baptist minister and an organizer for Marcus Garvey's (1887–1940) Universal Negro Improvement Association. As an outspoken advocate of black nationalism, Earl Little was a regular target for harassment by various white groups. The family lived under a constant threat of Ku Klux Klan violence, and eventually their home was burned down.

A Traumatic Childhood   The family moved to Lansing, Michigan, in 1929, where Earl Little continued to deliver rousing sermons that infuriated the white community. In 1931 Earl was found dead on the streetcar tracks, his body nearly severed in half and his skull caved in. The death was ruled a suicide, but there was widespread speculation in the community that he had actually died at the hands of the Klan or another racist group. Malcolm's mother, Louise Little, was devastated by the death of her husband. Unable to tolerate the strain of raising seven children on her own, she suffered a mental breakdown shortly afterward and was committed to an institution. She remained institutionalized until 1963.

With their father dead and their mother incapacitated, Malcolm and his siblings were placed in different foster homes and state facilities. Even while bouncing between foster families over the next several years, Malcolm proved to be an excellent student. When he confided to a teacher his dream of becoming a lawyer, however, he was told to come up with a different goal that was "more realistic" for an African-American.

Disillusioned, Malcolm dropped out of school after eighth grade and moved to Boston, where he lived with his half-sister. In Boston, he worked at a series of menial jobs, including shoe shining and restaurant work. Gradually, he drifted into a life of petty crime. In about 1942 Malcolm moved to the Harlem neighborhood of New York City, where his criminal activities escalated. He began selling drugs and organized a gambling ring,

Malcolm X addressing a rally in New York, 1963. © *Bettmann/ Corbis*

operating under the nickname Detroit Red. In 1946 Malcolm was sentenced to ten years in prison for burglary. In prison, Malcolm began filling in the gaps in his education, absorbing books on religion, history, and philosophy. He became especially interested in the religion of Islam, and began studying the teachings of Nation of Islam leader Elijah Muhammad (1897–1975).

Nation of Islam Upon his release from prison in 1952, Malcolm went to Chicago to meet Muhammad. He was quickly welcomed into the Nation of Islam, and given a new name, Malcolm X. The X symbolized a rejection of the "slave name" his family had been given upon arrival from Africa. Malcolm was appointed assistant minister of the Detroit mosque. A year later he went back to Chicago to study directly with Muhammad. He was then sent to Philadelphia to open a mosque there. In 1954 Malcolm X became leader of the movement's flagship mosque in Harlem, where he became the most visible public face and voice of the Nation of Islam.

Malcolm's charisma helped the Nation of Islam grow from a small fringe group of about four hundred to a movement more than one hundred thousand people strong in 1960. Malcolm preached a philosophy almost diametrically opposite that of mainstream civil rights leaders such as King. He endorsed black separatism, urging African-Americans to defend themselves, with violence if necessary, against their white oppressors. This

approach terrified not only most white Americans, but also many blacks, who feared he was stirring up a brutal race war that would result only in more bloodshed.

When President John F. Kennedy (1917–1963) was assassinated in November 1963, Malcolm described it as an instance of "the chickens coming home to roost," meaning such events were deserved by a society that tolerated violence by the white majority against blacks. Muhammad quickly suspended Malcolm, ordering him not to speak publicly on behalf of the Nation of Islam for ninety days. In March 1964 Malcolm announced that he was breaking with the Nation of Islam completely and forming his own group, the Organization of Afro-American Unity.

No More "White Devils" That spring, Malcolm embarked on a series of trips to Africa and the Middle East, including a pilgrimage to Mecca, Saudi Arabia, the holiest place in the world for Muslims. During the course of his travels, Malcolm was struck by the sight of Muslims of all skin colors worshipping together. He came to the realization that the Nation of Islam's characterization of all whites as evil was wrong-headed. He sought to practice a more "pure" version of Islam, and changed his name to el-Hajj Malik el-Shabazz.

Upon his return, Malcolm became increasingly critical of Muhammad and the Nation of Islam. He disavowed his old rhetoric, which he now considered racist. He now believed that the enemy was racism itself, and pledged to work with progressively minded white leaders to improve race relations worldwide. His new philosophy still emphasized black pride and anticolonialism, but he now believed separatism was counterproductive. He was more interested in forging bonds of shared culture and heritage among black people worldwide than in encouraging them to shun their white neighbors. He also made a number of public accusations against Muhammad, claiming his former boss had engaged in numerous affairs with his young secretaries, as well as financial irregularities. These accusations made Malcolm a marked man. He began receiving a steady stream of death threats.

Hostilities between Malcolm and Muhammad continued to escalate through the rest of 1964 and into 1965. The threats on Malcolm's life evolved into actual attempts. His home was firebombed on February 14, 1965. Exactly one week later, on February 21, Malcolm was shot more than a dozen times by three men who rushed the stage of the Audubon Ballroom in Harlem, where he was about to begin a speech to an audience of several hundred followers. Malcolm died at the hospital a short time later.

In the years that followed, responses to Malcolm's life and death were mixed. His message of black pride and unity resonated strongly with a generation of young African-Americans who came of age during the 1960s. The more radical aspects of his teachings were taken up by members of the militant elements of the Black Power movement of the late 1960s and early 1970s, while the more moderate message Malcolm delivered in his later speeches influenced such mainstream figures as U.S.

THE NATION OF ISLAM

The Nation of Islam was founded as the Allah Temple of Islam in 1930 in Detroit, Michigan. Its founder, Wallace D. Fard (1877?–1934?), showed up in a poor, black Detroit neighborhood as a peddler with a murky background. He began dispensing spiritual advice to his customers, informing them of their "true religion," which was not Christianity but the Islamic faith practiced by dark-skinned people in Asia and Africa. As he gained followers, he set up a temple in a rented space. Fard taught his adherents that white people were "blue-eyed devils" who had come to power through violence and trickery. He established several special purpose branches: the University of Islam, to spread his teachings; the Muslim Girls Training, which instructed girls in their role as homemakers; and the Fruit of Islam, the sect's paramilitary arm.

One of Fard's early aides was Robert (or Elijah) Poole. Poole, who quickly became Fard's most trusted assistant, took on the Muslim name Elijah Muhammad (1897–1975). Poole's family had migrated to Detroit from the South in 1923. In 1934 Fard mysteriously disappeared, leading to a power struggle within the fledgling organization. Muhammad emerged from the tussle as leader of the Nation of Islam. He moved his family to Chicago in 1936, where he set up Temple of Islam No. 2. This eventually became the organization's national headquarters. Muhammad led the Nation of Islam until his death in 1975. Under Muhammad's leadership, the Nation of Islam developed a philosophy of self-reliance for black people. In addition to temples, they set up grocery stores, restaurants, and other small businesses in black neighborhoods, in part for their own economic gain and in part so that members would not have to patronize white-owned establishments.

After Muhammad's death, one of his six sons, Wallace Muhammad (who later changed his name to Warith Deen Muhammad), was named the head of the Nation of Islam. Warith Deen Muhammad soon disavowed the organization's position on the evil of white people, and moved the Nation of Islam toward a more mainstream form of Sunni Islam. He also changed the name of the organization several times. Warith's reforms caused resentment among some Nation of Islam leaders, leading to a schism within the organization. In 1978 a group led by Louis Farrakhan (1933–) that sought to retain the organization's separatist values reconstituted the Nation of Islam under its old name. Farrakhan's Nation of Islam continues to thrive in many urban areas of the United States.

Supreme Court Justice Clarence Thomas (1948–), a political conservative by any measure.

See also **The Civil Rights Movement**

Robert McNamara

As secretary of defense under Presidents John F. Kennedy (1917–1963) and Lyndon B. Johnson (1908–1973), Robert McNamara (1916–) was one of the key advisers behind the escalation of the Vietnam War. He later became disillusioned with the war, and left that post in 1967. Soon after that, McNamara was named head of the World Bank, where he focused on promoting economic development in Third World countries. After leaving the World Bank in 1981, McNamara became a vocal critic of nuclear weapons proliferation, writing several books and articles on the subject.

Early Life Robert Strange McNamara was born on June 9, 1916, in San Francisco, California, the son of a manager at a shoe wholesale company. He was a standout student in the public schools of Piedmont, California, and went on to attend the nearby University of California (UC) at Berkeley, majoring in philosophy and economics. He graduated from UC in 1937 and enrolled at Harvard University's Graduate School of Business Administration, earning a master's degree in business administration two years later.

After a year with the accounting firm Price Waterhouse & Company, McNamara returned to Harvard as an assistant professor of business administration. When the United States entered World War II, he taught a course for U.S. Air Force officers under a special arrangement between Harvard and the U.S. Army. He also worked as a consultant to the army on statistical systems for handling military logistical problems. In 1943 McNamara took a leave of absence from Harvard and saw active duty with the Air Force overseas—though poor eyesight prevented him from flying—until his release from service in 1946.

After the war, McNamara joined an elite team of statistical specialists that was hired by Ford Motor Company. He rose quickly up the ranks of Ford's corporate bureaucracy, becoming company president in 1960, the first non-Ford family member ever to hold that position. After only about a month on the job, however, the call came from president-elect Kennedy offering him the top post at the U.S. Department of Defense.

Secretary of Defense In January 1961 McNamara was sworn in as secretary of defense. Selected mainly for his business wizardry, he brought with him to the department many of the "whiz kids" with whom he had climbed the ladder at Ford. At the time, he knew very little about nuclear strategy and other key military issues. What he did know about was management and organizational efficiency, and he applied his expertise to what had become a bloated, dysfunctional bureaucracy.

McNamara's relative inexperience in the politics of nuclear arms did not last long. Under President Dwight D. Eisenhower (1890–1969), the United States had become reliant on a policy of nuclear deterrence, the idea that a powerful nuclear arsenal would prevent aggression on the part of hostile countries. McNamara focused on changing the direction of the military, reinvigorating the nation's conventional forces and placing

Defense Secretary Robert S. McNamara (in short sleeves) visiting a U.S. infantry division in Vietnam, 1965. © *Bettmann/CORBIS*

less emphasis on nuclear deterrence. At the same time, however, political realities demanded that McNamara and the new president who had appointed him respond to the perceived "missile gap" between the U.S. arsenal and that of the Soviet Union. While McNamara promoted a doctrine of "flexible response," meaning being prepared to respond to threats in a variety of ways beyond using nuclear weapons, he simultaneously presided over a massive buildup of nuclear arms.

Containing communism was the driving force behind most U.S. foreign policy decisions at the time, and McNamara became one of Kennedy's key advisers on the military aspects of that objective. In 1961 McNamara was one of the voices arguing in favor of supporting the efforts of Cuban exiles to overthrow Cuban leader Fidel Castro (1926–). This support culminated in the failed Bay of Pigs invasion, a project McNamara later regretted as being doomed from the start. The following year, McNamara was part of the small committee of presidential advisers gathered to contend with the sequence of events that became known as the Cuban missile crisis. McNamara was an advocate of Kennedy's policy to quarantine Cuba in order to stop the flow of additional weapons from the Soviet Union into the island nation.

Meanwhile, U.S. involvement in Vietnam increased under President Kennedy and, after Kennedy's assassination in 1963, President Johnson. Under Johnson, McNamara was the chief engineer of U.S. endeavors in Vietnam. Journalists took to calling the conflict "McNamara's War." The expansion of the U.S. role in that conflict became the central issue of McNamara's career. McNamara fully supported Johnson's decision to increase the number of U.S. troops in Vietnam and to launch a massive bombing campaign there in 1965. By 1966 McNamara had become convinced that the United States could prevail in Vietnam by using its technological superiority to create an "electronic battlefield," an idea that became known as the "McNamara line."

World Bank While McNamara continued to support the Vietnam War in his public statements, he gradually became disillusioned, and was expressing doubts about the war in private. By late 1967 McNamara had changed his mind about many of the policies he had previously supported, including the heavy bombing of North Vietnam. In November of that year he resigned from his post as secretary of defense. In April 1968 Johnson appointed McNamara president of the International Bank for Reconstruction and Development, better known as the World Bank. McNamara remained at the head of the

World Bank until 1981. During his last year there, McNamara oversaw some 1,600 economic projects in more than 100 developing countries, with a total value of about $100 billion, though some critics of the World Bank argue that the conditions attached to the loans for these projects pinch domestic social spending in recipient nations and ultimately harm the poorest people who live there.

After he retired from the World Bank in 1981, McNamara continued to speak and write on a number of different issues, most notably economic development and poverty in developing countries, and nuclear policy. He became a vocal critic of nuclear proliferation, advocating for a dramatic reduction in the number of nuclear missiles in the arsenals of both the United States and the Soviet Union. In 1995 McNamara published a book, *In Retrospect: The Tragedy and Lessons of Vietnam*, in which he admitted that he had lied to Congress and the American people about the rationale for U.S. involvement in the Vietnam War. While he takes responsibility in the book for some of the war's negative impact, the book came across as self-serving and shallow to some critics. A 2003 documentary by Errol Morris, *The Fog of War: Eleven Lessons from the Life of Robert S. McNamara*, shed additional light on McNamara's ideas and activities during one of the most divisive periods in the nation's history.

See also **The Cuban Missile Crisis**
See also **The Vietnam War**

Lyndon B. Johnson

Lyndon Baines Johnson (1908–1973), the thirty-sixth president of the United States, served in the White House from late 1963, when he took office after the assassination of John F. Kennedy (1917–1963), to January 1969 after he declined to run for a second full term. Johnson presided over a nation struggling with an assortment of divisive issues, from civil rights to the conflict in Vietnam (1964–1975). Along the way, he launched a number of ambitious domestic initiatives aimed at defeating poverty in America in hopes of transforming the nation into a "Great Society."

Early Years Johnson was born on August 27, 1908, near Stonewall, Texas, the oldest of five children. His father, Sam Johnson, was a rancher who had served in the Texas legislature. The family moved to Johnson City, about fifteen miles from Stonewall, in 1913. Johnson graduated from high school there in 1924, before enrolling at Southwest State Teachers College in San Marcos, Texas. While working toward his degree, Johnson earned money teaching at an all-Hispanic junior high school in Cotulla, Texas. He also became involved in student government activities at Southwest State, and gained a reputation as a personable leader with a gift for motivating people to do what he wanted, a good formula for success in politics.

Upon graduating from college, Johnson accepted a teaching job at Sam Houston High School in Houston, where he taught an assortment of courses in such varied subjects as public speaking, geography, and math. Johnson proved to be an excellent teacher, but his interest in politics was stronger. In 1931 he accepted a position on the staff of newly elected congressman Richard Kleberg. Johnson essentially ran Kleberg's Washington office, taking care of correspondence with constituents and dealing with lobbyists and other insiders. Johnson also became active in the "Little Congress," an informal organization of congressional staffers. He was elected speaker of that body, and was able to use that position to leverage a certain amount of political power of his own. Over his four years in Kleberg's office, Johnson learned the ins and outs of federal politics quite thoroughly. He also found time to court Claudia Alta Taylor, known to all as Lady Bird. The couple was married in 1934.

In 1935, through the connections he had developed in government, Johnson was appointed Texas director of the National Youth Administration, a project of the Works Progress Administration that provided relief funds and work opportunities for children and young adults. Two years later, the congressman representing Texas's 10th District died unexpectedly. Johnson quickly added his name to the already crowded list of candidates vying in the special election to replace him. Johnson won the race, and at the tender age of twenty-eight became a member of the U.S. House of Representatives. He was reelected to serve a full term a year later. Another death, that of Texas senator Morris Sheppard, prompted Johnson to run for the U.S. Senate in 1941. Johnson lost a close race to Texas governor W. Lee O'Daniel, the only election he would ever lose; for years afterward, Johnson claimed the election had been stolen from him through underhanded tactics. Johnson, defeated but not demoralized, returned to Washington to serve out the remainder of his term in the House.

When the Japanese attacked Pearl Harbor in 1941, Johnson fulfilled a campaign promise by requesting active duty in the U.S. Navy. He served as a lieutenant commander in the Pacific, participating in a bombing mission over New Guinea before President Franklin Roosevelt (1882–1945) called all members of Congress in the military back to Washington in 1942.

Senate Leadership Johnson's second bid for a Senate seat was successful, albeit controversial. Learning from the dirty tricks of his opponent in his previous Senate attempt, Johnson reportedly employed several underhanded tactics during his 1948 Senate campaign, including vote fraud, voter intimidation, bribery, and mudslinging. Johnson prevailed by just eighty-seven votes over popular Texas governor Coke Stevenson, earning the ironic nickname "Landslide Lyndon" in reference to his slim margin of victory. After Johnson's

President Lyndon Johnson in the Oval Office, c. 1967.   © *Wally McNamee/CORBIS*

death it was established fairly conclusively that this election was fixed.

It quickly became clear that Johnson was not a typical Senate rookie. He arrived with a deep understanding of both the key issues of the day and the unwritten rules of Senate politics. He used his political connections and savvy to land prime jobs and contracts for businessmen who had supported his campaigns for office. In 1951 he was named Democratic Party whip, a rare honor for a newcomer to the Senate. Two years later he was selected minority leader, and when the Democrats seized control of both houses of Congress in 1954, Johnson became the youngest Senate majority leader in the nation's history. As the most powerful Democrat in the country, Johnson worked closely with Republican president Dwight D. Eisenhower (1890–1969), and was instrumental in the passage of many of the most important pieces of legislation of the 1950s, including the extension of Social Security benefits, the 1956 highway bill, the Civil Rights Act of 1957, and the omnibus housing bill also passed in 1957.

By 1960 it was clear that Johnson could be a serious contender for the presidency. Johnson briefly mounted a campaign, but it quickly became apparent that Kennedy had more support. Since Kennedy was a New Englander, it made sense for him to seek a running mate from the South to help attract votes from that region, and Johnson's Texas roots seemed to make him the ideal candidate to add to the ticket as vice president. With Johnson's help, Kennedy defeated Republican candidate Richard Nixon (1913–1994) in one of the closest presidential elections in history.

Vice Presidency As vice president of the United States, Johnson took on a much bigger role than was traditionally associated with that post. As a Senate leader a few years earlier, he had helped shepherd through Congress the legislation that created the National Aeronautics and Space Administration, and space exploration remained a keen interest. Kennedy rewarded that enthusiasm by appointing Johnson chairman of the Space Council, a position from which he could closely monitor the progress of the budding space program. Johnson also took an active role in the civil rights efforts of the Kennedy administration. Early in his career, Johnson had supported segregation, a more or less necessary position for a politician from Texas to take in the 1930s and 1940s. By the 1950s, however, he had shifted

President Lyndon Johnson signing the Civil Rights Act of 1964. © *Bettmann/CORBIS*

his position, and was now a supporter of civil rights initiatives, making him a reasonable choice to head the newly formed President's Committee on Equal Employment, a federal program aimed at expanding job opportunities for African-Americans.

Johnson made substantial progress in these roles—especially civil rights, where he helped lay the groundwork for the landmark legislation to come a few years later—but as vice president serving under a young, enormously popular president, it seemed unlikely that Johnson would ever rise any higher than his current job. That changed suddenly and horribly on November 22, 1963, when Kennedy was assassinated. Johnson was instantly thrust into the spotlight as leader of the world's most powerful country.

The Johnson presidency was marked by important achievements at home—exemplified by the Civil Rights Act of 1964 and the creation of a variety of programs designed to combat poverty in the United States—which in the end were all overshadowed to some degree by the escalation of U.S. involvement in Vietnam. In his first State of the Union address, Johnson declared a "War on Poverty," and made that the cornerstone of his domestic agenda. He successfully pushed the Economic Opportunity Act of 1964 through Congress. The act created the Office of Economic Opportunity, home to such new antipoverty programs as Job Corps, Head Start, Community Action, and Volunteers in Service to America. Through these programs and others, Johnson sought to attack the root causes of the nation's domestic problems, including illiteracy, joblessness, urban decay, and inadequate public services. Taken together, these initiatives were designed to move America closer to Johnson's vision of the "Great Society," a concept he outlined in a May 1964 speech in Ann Arbor, Michigan. In that address, he said,

> We are going to assemble the best thought and the broadest knowledge from all over the world to find those answers for America. I intend to establish working groups to prepare a series of White House conferences and meetings—on the cities, on natural beauty, on the quality of education, and on other emerging challenges. And from these studies we will begin to set our course toward the Great Society.

The breadth of legislation enacted to help the poor during Johnson's first term rivaled that of Franklin Roosevelt's New Deal initiatives a few decades earlier.

Vietnam War Drags On On the strength of these achievements, Johnson cruised to an easy victory in his

1964 presidential bid against conservative Republican Barry Goldwater (1909–1998), one of the most lopsided races in the nation's history. Johnson leveraged this popularity by pushing vast amounts of legislation through Congress. Federal spending on education and health care increased dramatically during the Johnson presidency. The Civil Rights Act of 1964 was followed by the Voting Rights Act of 1965, which prohibited discrimination in the electoral process. Blue-collar wages increased during these years, and the United States enjoyed several consecutive years of economic growth.

Johnson was unable to savor his domestic accomplishments, however. In August 1964 it was reported that two U.S. destroyers in the Gulf of Tonkin off the coast of North Vietnam had been the recipients of unprovoked attacks. Johnson took this news—which later turned out to be distorted and overblown—as justification for a strong military response. He quickly authorized retaliatory air raids on selected North Vietnamese targets. He then persuaded Congress to pass the Gulf of Tonkin Resolution, which essentially gave Johnson a blank check to escalate American involvement in Vietnam as he saw fit in order to repel North Vietnamese aggression "by all necessary measures."

The Vietnam War—technically a "police action" rather than a war, since war was never formally declared—quickly became an all-consuming issue for Johnson and the nation. As the conflict dragged on, Johnson sent increasing numbers of young Americans overseas to fight a war that began to seem unwinnable. Opposition to the war grew with every television newscast showing dead and injured Americans. By 1968 a large percentage of the American public, including many returning Vietnam veterans, was fed up with the quagmire Vietnam had become. In the face of massive protest, Johnson announced in March 1968 that he would not seek reelection that November. He served out the rest of his term quietly, then retired to his ranch near San Antonio, Texas, where he tended to cattle and worked on his memoirs. He died of a heart attack in 1973.

See also **The Model Cities Program**
See also **The Vietnam War**

Betty Friedan

With the publication of her 1963 book *The Feminine Mystique*, Betty Friedan (1921–2006) effectively launched the modern feminist movement. A few years after the book came out, Friedan helped found the National Organization for Women (NOW), the most visible and effective political arm of the feminist movement.

Background The United States of the late 1940s and 1950s was a place where women were expected to assume the traditional roles of wife, mother, and homemaker. During World War II, when a large percentage of the nation's men were fighting overseas, women took

THE GREAT SOCIETY

As the nation mourned the death of President John F. Kennedy (1917–1963), his successor, Lyndon B. Johnson (1908–1973), committed himself to following through with many of Kennedy's domestic proposals. The time was ripe for such a push. The economy was relatively stable, and Americans' emotions were running high in the aftermath of the assassination of the popular president. Seizing the initiative, Johnson proposed a sweeping array of laws covering poverty, employment, civil rights, education, and health care. Together, these proposals represented steps toward establishing what Johnson dubbed the "Great Society," a term he coined in a May 1964 speech in Ann Arbor, Michigan.

In many ways the Great Society mirrored the New Deal enacted by Franklin Roosevelt (1882–1945), one of Johnson's political heroes. The main difference was that the New Deal was a response to the Great Depression, a time when a large portion of the American public was suffering from the effects of a collapsed economy; the Great Society initiative, in contrast, came at a time when the American economy was strong. It was instead an attempt to spread the nation's wealth more equitably, reaching corners of the population whom the prosperity of the time had somehow bypassed.

The list of programs and agencies that were created during the War on Poverty waged by Johnson includes many that now form the heart of the nation's social safety net. Medicaid and Medicare were founded to ensure access to health care for the poor, the elderly, and the disabled. The U.S. Department of Housing and Urban Development was established to improve the condition and supply of the nation's housing stock, especially in major cities. Head Start was created to improve school readiness among disadvantaged children. On the cultural front, the National Endowment for the Humanities and the Corporation for Public Broadcasting emerged as contributors to the development of a Great Society. As the federal government became more conservative during the 1980s and 1990s, funding for many of these programs dwindled, with many politicians turning to private sector solutions to social problems and championing the notion of "small government."

their places in many crucial jobs that had previously been filled almost exclusively by men. After the war, women were encouraged and expected to leave the workforce and return to their former domestic roles. Higher education was an afterthought for most women, and political activity was considered unseemly. By the 1960s, increasing numbers of women had grown disenchanted with the role that was being forced on them by society. They wanted to enjoy the same opportunities as their male counterparts—the right to pursue a top-notch education, a rewarding career, and political power. During that decade, the feminist movement emerged, giving voice to the collective frustration of American women

Betty Friedan speaking at a political rally in New York, 1971.   *© JP Laffont/Sygma/CORBIS*

who wanted more out of life than to be defined only as a wife or mother. Friedan was one of the early leaders of the movement.

Friedan was born Betty Naomi Goldstein on February 4, 1921, in Peoria, Illinois. Her parents, Harry and Miriam Goldstein, were the children of Jewish immigrants from Eastern Europe. In high school, Friedan founded a literary magazine, and she graduated at the top of her class. After high school, she attended Smith College, graduating summa cum laude in 1942. Friedan was offered a fellowship to pursue a doctorate in psychology, but seeing no future for herself in academia, she instead moved to New York to be a journalist. In 1947 she married Carl Friedan. The couple settled in Queens, New York, and soon had three children. After being fired from her writing job for taking maternity leave, she continued to work as a freelance writer.

The Feminine Mystique Over time, Friedan found herself increasingly dissatisfied with her life as a typical suburban American housewife. In 1957 she decided to find out if other women felt the same way. She sent an extensive questionnaire to two hundred of her former Smith classmates. She learned that she was not alone in her feelings of frustration, and that a great many women felt trapped and resentful in their culturally mandated roles as housewives and mothers. Friedan wrote an article about her findings, but none of the women's magazines she sent it to was interested in publishing it. Rather than give up, she expanded her ideas into a book. The resulting work, *The Feminine Mystique*, struck a nerve with women across the United States. It was a best seller and sparked a revolution of consciousness among American women.

Friedan instantly became one of the women's movement's preeminent spokespersons, both nationally and internationally. Three years after the publication of *The Feminine Mystique*, Friedan was instrumental in creating NOW, and she became the organization's first president. Under her leadership, NOW fought hard for equality in the workplace, including enforcement of Title VII of the 1964 Civil Rights Act, which prohibited employment discrimination on the basis of gender. NOW also advocated for passage of the Equal Rights Amendment, which had been failing to achieve Congressional approval for more than forty years. In 1969 Friedan helped launch another organization, the National Association for the Repeal of Abortion Laws (NARAL; the name changed in 1973 to National Abortion and Reproductive Rights Action League), which was instrumental in the movement that led to the legalization of abortion in 1973 by virtue of the U.S. Supreme Court's decision in *Roe v. Wade*.

Friedan stepped down from the presidency of NOW in 1970. For the next few years, she wrote a regular column for *McCall's* magazine called "Betty Friedan's Notebook." As the feminist movement went through inevitable changes over time, Friedan became less visible as a spokesperson. She nevertheless continued to write prolifically on a range of topics. In her 1981 book *The Second Stage*, she called for a new focus in the movement that would emphasize the needs of families, allowing both men and women to gain freedom from the shackles of gender-based stereotypes. In 1993 she published *The Fountain of Age*, in which she explored the rights and challenges of elderly and aging people. Friedan died in 2006.

Ralph Nader

Ralph Nader (1934–) essentially invented the consumer protection movement and is without question the most important advocate for consumer safety and corporate accountability in recent history. While his status as a crusader for consumer rights is unassailable, he enraged many Democrats by running for president on the Green Party ticket in 2000, siphoning crucial votes away from Democratic candidate Al Gore and, in the view of his detractors, helping hand the election to Republican George W. Bush (1946–). Nader ran for president again in 2004, but he attained limited support and was not a factor in the outcome.

Nader was born on February 27, 1934, in Winsted, Connecticut, the youngest child of Lebanese immigrants Nadra and Rose (Bouziane) Nader. His parents, who owned a restaurant and bakery, were interested in politics; current affairs were a standard topic of discussion around the family dinner table. His father's ideas about social justice impressed Nader at an early age, and he was still young when he decided that he wanted to study law. A brilliant student, Nader graduated in 1955 with highest honors from Princeton University's Woodrow Wilson School of Public and International Affairs. He then moved on to Harvard Law School, earning a law degree in 1958. Nader's first experience as an activist came while he was at Princeton, where he attempted—unsuccessfully—to persuade the university to stop spraying campus trees with the harmful pesticide dichlorodiphenyltrichloroethane, or DDT.

Vehicle Safety While at Harvard, Nader became interested in vehicle safety, an issue with which he would later make his mark professionally. Nader was convinced that poor vehicle design, not just driver error, was responsible for many traffic fatalities. In 1958 he published his first article on the topic, "American Cars: Designed for Death," in the *Harvard Law Review*. That article foreshadowed the major work of his career.

After law school, Nader served briefly in the U.S. Army, then traveled extensively overseas. Returning to Connecticut, he went into legal practice and lectured on history and government at the University of Hartford from 1961 to 1963. In 1964 Nader moved to Washington, D.C., where he hoped to continue his work on automobile safety. He landed a job as a consultant at the U.S. Department of Labor, and there he wrote a report

Consumer rights advocate Ralph Nader on the television program *Face the Nation*, 1970.   *CBS Photo Archive/Getty Images*

calling for expanded federal regulation of vehicle safely. Nader left the Labor Department in May 1965 in order to devote himself full time into the task of writing a book on the subject that had become his passion. The book, *Unsafe at Any Speed: The Designed-In Dangers of the American Automobile*, was published later that year. It caused an immediate stir, and quickly became a best seller. Federal hearings were held, at which Nader provided key testimony.

The major car manufacturers, particularly General Motors—whose Chevrolet Corvair was singled out as being especially unsafe—were antagonized by Nader's crusade, and they embarked on a campaign of harassment and intimidation. Nader withstood the pressure and pressed on with his effort. The eventual result was the passage in 1966 of the National Traffic and Motor Vehicle Safety Act, which created the National Traffic Safety Agency to enforce the new safety regulations established by the act. Ralph Nader became a household name.

Nader's Raiders   After his success with automobiles, Nader moved on to address safety issues in other industries. He took on the meatpacking industry, resulting in the 1967 passage of the Wholesome Meat Act. He also scrutinized coal mining and natural gas pipelines. Living a frugal lifestyle, Nader used the money he earned from book sales and lectures to assemble a small army of young people to help him with research and data collection. The group, composed mainly of students at law schools and other colleges, became known as "Nader's Raiders." In 1969 Nader formed the Center for the Study of Responsive Law, a think tank devoted to consumer safety issues. Two years later, he founded Public Citizen, an advocacy group that lobbies for public policy related to consumer protection. Nader founded various other groups over the next several years including the Public Interest Research Groups that sprang up on college campuses in many states during the 1970s.

Nader continued to write prolifically during the 1970s. His influence in Washington began to wane in the 1980s as the atmosphere in the nation's capital grew more conservative, though he continued to score occasional successes, such as the rollback of California auto insurance rates in 1988. Nader made token runs for president in 1992 and 1996 before mounting a serious campaign with the Green Party in 2000, which generated nearly three million votes.

See also **The U.S. Department of Transportation**

Cesar Chavez

The son of Mexican immigrants, Cesar Chavez (1927–1993) rose from humble beginnings as a migrant worker in California to become one of the most important labor leaders in U.S. history as founder and leader of the United Farm Workers. Chavez spent his entire career battling for the rights of agricultural workers in the face of exploitation by companies looking for a cheap and vulnerable workforce, often composed largely of immigrant families.

Cesar Estrada Chavez was born on March 31, 1927, near Yuma, Arizona, one of five children in a poor family that ran a grocery store and a small farm. During the Great Depression, the Chavez family lost their farm, and they joined the burgeoning host of families in the rural Southwest that headed for California to become temporary agricultural workers. The family moved from farm to farm in search of work, living in tents in small encampments wherever there was work to be done. The wages for these migrant workers were extremely low, and the living conditions were primitive.

When Chavez was about twelve years old, the Congress of Industrial Organizations (CIO), a conglomeration of labor unions, began trying to organize workers in the dried fruit industry. His father and uncle supported these efforts, and Chavez observed some of their early labor actions. Organizing migrant workers, however, is difficult, mostly because they make up an inherently mobile workforce, so the CIO made little progress initially.

Community Service Organization Chavez attended school from time to time, but he was never in one place long enough to graduate. He joined the U.S. Navy in 1944 and served for two years during World War II. After the war, he returned to the California fields and was reunited with his family. In 1948 he married Helen Fabela, a fellow migrant worker. The couple settled in Delano, California, a town near San Jose, and began raising a family that eventually included eight children. Chavez began his career as a labor activist in 1952, while working as a migrant grape and cotton farmer. That year he joined the Community Service Organization (CSO), a group working to register and mobilize Mexican-Americans. Chavez proved to be a highly skilled organizer, and he quickly moved into a leadership role within the CSO. Over the next several years, he led voter registration drives and worked on a variety of issues affecting Mexican-Americans, including immigration practices,

THE CHEVY CORVAIR: UNSAFE AT ANY SPEED?

The Chevrolet Corvair was one of a handful of American cars produced in response to the popularity of the sporty, fuel-efficient European imports showing up on U.S. streets during the middle part of the twentieth century. General Motors (GM) manufactured the Corvair from 1960 to 1969. The Corvair had a number of unique design features, such as an air-cooled aluminum engine in the rear of the car. It also had an unusual suspension design that required the owner to inflate the tires to a pressure exceeding the tire manufacturers' recommendations, and with a striking imbalance between the front and rear tire inflation pressures.

Ralph Nader (1934–) deemed the Corvair inherently unsafe in his breakthrough book *Unsafe at Any Speed* (1965), and while seven of the book's eight chapters have nothing to do with the Corvair, it is the model with which the book has always been most closely associated. Nader wrote that the car's unusual features made the Corvair more prone to roll over. He also criticized the car's steering column, remarking that because of its rigidity it was likely to impale the driver in a head-on collision.

Sales of the Corvair plummeted following the publication of *Unsafe at Any Speed*, in spite of GM's attempts to discredit Nader. Some of the company's personal attacks on Nader were highly unethical and resulted in a successful lawsuit by Nader. Nader's claim that the Corvair was inherently unsafe, however, was not universally accepted, and critics point out that his assessment was not based on the kind of sophisticated testing available today. Tests run by the National Highway Traffic Safety Administration in 1971 found that the Corvair actually handled better than several comparable models. Nevertheless, Nader's book made the powerful point—based on many more examples beyond the Corvair—that automakers were thinking a lot more about looks than about safety, and that it was the consumer who ultimately paid the price for those misguided priorities.

welfare policy, and police abuse. He also successfully launched several new CSO chapters. Chavez was named national general director of the CSO in 1958.

Chavez was able to accomplish a great deal with CSO, but the organization was not involved in the issue that was most important to him: labor conditions for migrant farm workers. He proposed that the CSO start working to organize migrant laborers, but the board of directors declined to take up the cause. In response, Chavez resigned from his job, and with $1,200 of his own savings he founded a new organization, the National Farm Workers Association (NFWA), in 1962.

La Causa In spite of the difficulties inherent in trying to organize a migrant workforce, Chavez managed to build a membership of about 1,700 workers by 1965. In

Labor leader Cesar Chavez leading a strike outside the San Diego headquarters of the Safeway supermarket chain, 1973.   © *Bettmann/CORBIS*

September of that year, Filipino grape pickers in the Delano area went on strike demanding higher wages. The NFWA voted to join the strike. They also pledged to keep their actions nonviolent. One of Chavez's chief role models was the Indian leader Mahatma Gandhi (1869–1948), and like Gandhi, Chavez championed the strategy of passive resistance. He brought attention to his cause through such tactics as inviting arrests and undertaking well-publicized fasts. Over time, the strike began to blossom into a full-blown movement called La Causa, which is Spanish for "the cause."

The grape growers resisted the workers' challenge, but gradually the strike began to gain the support of consumers around the country. A nationwide boycott of California grapes was in place by 1968, and the financial impact was great enough that the growers were forced to begin negotiating a settlement with the workers. The strike lasted a total of five years. Following the success of the grape boycott, Chavez next decided to take on iceberg lettuce growers in Arizona and California. Working against the combined forces of the growers, large agricultural corporations, and a rival union (the Teamsters), Chavez and his organization managed to initiate a successful nationwide boycott of California lettuce, forcing the growers to come to the bargaining table. His efforts also resulted in the passage of California laws to protect agricultural workers, including California's Agri-

cultural Labor Relations Act in 1975, which led to the formation of the Agricultural Labor Relations Board.

Along the way, the NFWA became part of the gigantic labor umbrella organization the American Federation of Labor and Congress of Industrial Organizations (AFL-CIO) and changed its name to the United Farm Workers Organizing Committee, which was shortened to United Farm Workers (UFW) in 1972.

Union Power Declines   By the early 1980s the UFW's membership and political clout were both in decline. Later in that decade Chavez set his sights on a new issue: growers' use of pesticides that were harmful to the health of farm workers. In 1987 he called for another grape boycott aimed at forcing the growers to change their pesticide practices. To publicize the boycott, Chavez undertook his longest fast yet, lasting thirty-six days.

Chavez died unexpectedly in his sleep on April 23, 1993. By the time of his death, UFW membership was a small fraction of what it had been at its peak, and agricultural workers had been forced to give back many of the gains they had made in wages and working conditions. Nevertheless, Chavez's contribution to the well-being of agricultural workers is unparalleled in history, a fact recognized by President Bill Clinton (1946–) when he posthumously awarded Chavez the Presidential Medal of Freedom, the nation's highest civilian honor, in 1994.

Henry Kissinger

Henry Kissinger (1923–) was the most influential foreign policy adviser to Presidents Richard Nixon (1913–1994) and Gerald R. Ford (1913–2006) during the late 1960s and early 1970s. As national security adviser and then secretary of state, Kissinger made popular the term *shuttle diplomacy*, a strategy in which he acted as a go-between to defuse tensions between hostile nations. Kissinger was awarded the Nobel Peace Prize in 1973 for his efforts to bring the Vietnam War to a conclusion.

Kissinger was born Heinz Alfred Kissinger on May 27, 1923, in Furth, Germany. As a Jewish family, the Kissingers suffered anti-Semitic discrimination as the Nazis rose to power in the 1930s. His father, Louis, lost his job as a schoolteacher, and the young Kissinger was forced to switch to an all-Jewish school. The Kissingers fled Germany in 1938, just in time to escape the horrors of the Holocaust. They initially went to London, then moved on to the United States several months later.

The Kissinger family settled in New York, where Heinz changed his name to Henry. He attended high school at night while working in a factory during the day to help support his family. After graduating from high school in 1941, Kissinger entered the City College of New York and began studying accounting. He became a naturalized American citizen in 1943, and the same year he was drafted into the armed forces to serve in World War II. In the U.S. Army, Kissinger was assigned to military intelligence service in Germany, where he served as an interpreter for a general.

Academic Career After the war, Kissinger returned to the United States and resumed his college education, enrolling at Harvard University in 1947. He graduated with honors in 1950, then received a master's degree two years later and a Ph.D. in 1954. After completing his studies, Kissinger stayed at Harvard as an instructor. He also joined the Council on Foreign Relations, an independent foreign policy think tank based in New York. While there, Kissinger wrote a book called *Nuclear Weapons and Foreign Policy* (1957), which earned him a reputation as a rising star in the field of international relations. Kissinger was hired as a lecturer at Harvard in 1957. He was promoted to associate professor in 1959 and to full professor in 1962.

As his standing among foreign affairs specialists increased, presidents began seeking Kissinger's counsel on matters of state. He served as a consultant to the National Security Council in the early 1960s. In 1965 the U.S. Department of State hired Kissinger as a consultant, focusing specifically on the situation in Vietnam. During the

Henry Kissinger at a press conference in 1971. © *Bettmann/CORBIS*

1968 presidential campaign, he worked as a speechwriter and policy adviser to Republican candidate Nelson Rockefeller (1908–1979). Although Rockefeller failed to win the Republican nomination, Kissinger impressed eventual winner Nixon enough to prompt Nixon to hire him as head of the National Security Council upon taking office in 1969.

Key Presidential Adviser   Kissinger quickly became Nixon's most trusted adviser on foreign policy matters, wielding more influence than members of Nixon's own cabinet. Kissinger traveled the globe conducting secret talks with the Soviet Union, China, and North Vietnam, engaging in a practice that was tagged shuttle diplomacy. Kissinger believed that the Kennedy and Johnson administrations had taken the wrong line in their relations with the Soviet Union. While he was as troubled as they were by the prospect of communist expansion, he recognized that the Soviet Union was a legitimate world power, and that the most sensible policy was therefore to maintain a workable balance of power between the United States and the Soviets. He sought to ease tensions between the two superpowers, advocating an approach that became known as detente, a French word roughly meaning "relaxation." The right wing of the Republican Party was not particularly happy with the approach, coming from the more moderate Kissinger. They believed that this sort of appeasement was wrongheaded, a sign of weakness, and that the correct strategy was to take a hard line against communism.

Kissinger also played a key role in the later stages of the Vietnam War. He advocated secret bombings and a ground invasion of Cambodia in 1970, a controversial strategy at a time when most Americans were calling for a de-escalation of American involvement in the Far East. Kissinger also, however, conducted a series of secret meetings in Paris with North Vietnamese diplomat Le Duc Tho (1911–1990), leading directly to the end of the conflict. As a result of those talks, Kissinger and Tho shared the Nobel Peace Prize in 1973 (although it was declined by Tho).

Kissinger scored a number of other diplomatic breakthroughs during the early 1970s. He initiated the Strategic Arms Limitation Talks (SALT) with the Soviet Union, which resulted in the 1972 signing of the historic SALT I treaty between the two superpowers. He was also deeply involved in efforts to settle the explosive situation in the Middle East, working with Egypt, Syria, Israel, and other nations in the region.

Nixon named Kissinger secretary of state at the beginning of his second presidential term in 1973, and Kissinger remained in the post under Ford after Nixon was forced to resign in disgrace in the wake of the Watergate scandal. Since 1977 Kissinger has mostly remained out of the public eye, though he has continued to write prolifically on foreign policy and has been consulted by government leaders from time to time on diplomatic issues, including meetings with President George W. Bush (1946–) and Vice President Dick Cheney (1941–) about the war in Iraq.

See also **The Vietnam War**

Jesse Jackson

Jesse Jackson (1941–) emerged in the 1960s as a leading crusader for civil rights and social justice in the United States. A follower of Martin Luther King Jr. (1929–1968), Jackson was in King's entourage when King was assassinated in 1968. In the 1970s Jackson left the Southern Christian Leadership Conference (SCLC) to start his own organization, People United to Save Humanity, better known as Operation PUSH, based in Chicago. In the 1980s Jackson formed the National Rainbow Coalition, a group dedicated to mobilizing the nation's dispossessed of all races. Operation PUSH and the National Rainbow Coalition were merged into a single organization in the 1990s.

Jackson was born Jesse Louis Burns on October 18, 1941, in Greenville, South Carolina, the son of Helen Burns and her married next-door neighbor Noah Robinson. In 1943 his mother married Charles Henry Jackson, who later adopted Jesse. A star athlete at Greenville's Sterling High School, Jackson was awarded a football

Jesse Jackson, c. 1974.   *© Jeff Albertson/CORBIS*

scholarship to attend the University of Illinois. When he learned that an African-American would not be allowed to play quarterback, Jackson left Illinois and enrolled at North Carolina Agricultural and Technical College in Greensboro, a traditionally African-American institution. There he was elected president of the student body. He also became active in the civil rights movement during his senior year, and worked for a short time with the Congress of Racial Equality (CORE). After graduating in 1964 with a degree in sociology, Jackson entered the Chicago Theological Seminary to prepare to become a minister. He was ordained in 1968.

Operation Breadbasket In 1966 Jackson joined the Atlanta-based Southern Christian Leadership Conference (SCLC), the renowned civil rights group led by King. With King, he participated in the SCLC-orchestrated protest activities in Selma, Alabama, around that time. Later that year, King assigned Jackson to head the Chicago branch of Operation Breadbasket, an SCLC project that promoted economic development and employment opportunities in African-American communities. Jackson was also a leading figure in protests against alleged racial discrimination on the part of Chicago mayor Richard J. Daley (1902–1976).

Within a year, King appointed Jackson national director of Operation Breadbasket. In that capacity, Jackson worked to put pressure on businesses and industries with large African-American customer bases, such as bakeries and soft-drink bottlers. When businesses refused to comply with the SCLC's demands regarding fair employment practices and contracts with minority-owned companies, Jackson organized boycotts, often resulting in a negotiated compromise.

In April 1968 Jackson was with a group of SCLC leaders accompanying King in Memphis, Tennessee, when King was assassinated while standing on the balcony of his hotel room. Jackson appeared on national television the next day wearing a shirt covered with what he claimed to be King's blood, saying he had held King in his arms after the shooting and was the last person to speak to the fallen hero. Others present at the scene disputed Jackson's account. Regardless of the accuracy of Jackson's statements, his emotional television appearance made him the new face of the civil rights movement in the minds of many Americans and, perhaps more important, the media.

Operation PUSH After King's death, tensions grew between Jackson and new SCLC leader Ralph Abernathy (1926–1990). Abernathy considered Jackson a self-promoter, using Operation Breadbasket to advance his own agenda without regard to SCLC direction. He disliked Jackson's attention-seeking antics and aggressive personality. In 1971 the SCLC suspended Jackson for what organization leaders termed "administrative improprieties and repeated acts of violation of organizational policy."

After his suspension, Jackson broke with the SCLC entirely and founded his own organization, Operation

"WAVING THE BLOODY SHIRT"

When Jesse Jackson (1941–) appeared on television wearing a shirt allegedly covered with the blood of Martin Luther King Jr. (1929–1968), it was not the first time a bloody shirt has been used to inspire political sympathy. In fact the phrase "waving the bloody shirt" has long referred to the practice of politicians pointing to the blood of a martyr in order to gain support or deflect criticism. During times of war, politicians routinely "wave the bloody shirts" of fallen soldiers—in the metaphorical sense, of course—as they seek to defend the foreign policy decisions that ultimately led to battlefield casualties. The phrase originated after the American Civil War, when Republicans used it as part of their anti-Southern rhetoric to associate Democrats with the bloodshed of the war and the assassination of Abraham Lincoln (1809–1865). Benjamin Franklin Butler (1818–1893), during a speech before his fellow congressmen, held up what he claimed was the shirt of a federal tax collector who had been whipped by the Ku Klux Klan. The "bloody shirt" ploy was used similarly even earlier than that. One of the first known uses occurred in AD 656, when a bloody shirt and some hair allegedly from the murdered Uthman, the third caliph (worldwide Muslim leader), were used to build support for seeking revenge against his opponents. There is also a scene in William Shakespeare's *Julius Caesar* in which Mark Antony waves Julius Caesar's bloody toga in order to whip up the emotions of the Roman populace (though the phrase "waving the bloody toga" apparently never quite caught on).

PUSH. Operation PUSH carried on many of the strategies of Operation Breadbasket, and expanded them into the social and political realms. Over the next two decades, Jackson evolved into the nation's leading civil rights activist. He ran for president in 1984 and 1988, making an impressively strong showing on the second try, when he garnered nearly seven million votes in Democratic primaries.

Since 1990 Jackson has kept a substantially lower profile, though he has not hesitated to employ his abundant oration skills when moved to comment publicly about an important issue. In 2000 President Bill Clinton (1946–) awarded Jackson the Presidential Medal of Freedom, the highest honor the federal government can give to a civilian.

See also **The Civil Rights Movement**

✪ Political Parties, Platforms, and Key Issues

The Dixiecrats (States' Rights Democratic Party)

As President Harry S. Truman (1884–1972) and the Democratic Party began to embrace civil rights legislation and racial integration policies in the months leading up to the 1948 elections, a number of Southern Democrats

A Dixiecrat meeting, 1948. *Thomas D. Mcavoy/Time Life Pictures/Getty Images*

created an offshoot political entity called the States' Rights Democratic Party, better known as the Dixiecrats, as an alternative for Southerners who opposed Truman's platform. Subscribing to a philosophy of "states' rights"—that is, that states have the right to govern themselves without interference from the federal government—the Dixiecrats argued that states had the right to maintain segregationist policies and that the federal government could not, therefore, impose integration measures.

An Anti–Civil Rights Campaign   As his first term in office—the term he inherited upon the death of President Franklin Roosevelt (1882–1945)—drew to a close, President Truman proposed civil rights legislation to Congress. Many Democratic politicians from the South were adamantly opposed to Truman's civil rights gestures, and they were frustrated in their attempts to obstruct the proposals. On May 10, 1948, Mississippi Governor Fielding Wright (1895–1956) convened a regional meeting of fifteen hundred delegates in Jackson, Mississippi, to discuss their response. They decided that if Truman received the party's nomination at the upcoming Democratic National Convention, they would break from the Democratic Party. Leaders of the movement articulated the

group's position clearly. In his keynote address at the meeting, South Carolina Governor (and later U.S. Senator) Strom Thurmond (1902–2003) declared that "all the laws of Washington and all the bayonets of the army cannot force the Negro into our homes, our schools, our churches, and our places of recreation."

Truman received the Democratic Party's nomination at the convention on July 15, 1948, defeating Richard Russell of Georgia. Delegates at the convention also endorsed by a narrow margin an ambitious civil rights agenda, to the chagrin of states' rights proponents. Immediately after the vote, the Mississippi delegation and half of the delegates from Alabama walked out of the hall. A mere two days later, the States' Rights Democratic Party was created at a meeting of six thousand states' rights advocates in Birmingham, Alabama. The party was soon given the nickname "Dixiecrats" by Bill Weisner, a North Carolina journalist. The Dixiecrat platform centered on preserving segregation in the South, but the party also embraced a handful of other conservative policies, including opposition to labor unions and rolling back the federal welfare system, which had grown dramatically during the Roosevelt era.

The Dixiecrats nominated their own ticket. Their presidential candidate was Thurmond, and Wright was his running mate. The hope was that the Dixiecrat ticket would draw enough votes away from both Truman and Republican candidate Thomas Dewey (1902–1971) to prevent either from gaining the required majority of votes in the electoral college. If that happened, the presidential contest would then move to the House of Representatives, where Southern members could bargain for concessions on civil rights legislation.

Thurmond and Wright campaigned aggressively across the South, and gained substantial support in several states. Their views were not universally accepted by Southern Democrats, however. Their position on matters of race was considered too extreme by even some fairly conservative voters.

Victorious in Four States Thurmond and Wright received about 1.2 million votes in the 1948 presidential election, and carried South Carolina, Mississippi, Louisiana, and Alabama, totaling 39 electoral votes. However Truman prevailed in the rest of the South, and won the election—carrying 28 states and receiving 303 electoral votes—despite nearly universal predictions by pollsters and the media that Dewey (who received not quite 22 million votes and 189 electoral votes) would be the next president.

The States' Rights Democratic Party disbanded shortly after the election, and most members returned to the regular Democratic Party, but politics in the South were never the same. The region would never again be considered "safely" Democratic. Thurmond was elected to the U.S. Senate as a Democrat in 1954, where he joined with other conservative Democrats in attempting to impede the civil rights movement. In 1964, with the civil rights struggle raging, Thurmond led a mass defection of conservative Southern elected officials from the Democratic Party over to the Republicans.

✪ Current Events and Social Movements

The Marshall Plan

The European Recovery Program, better known as the Marshall Plan, was an investment by the United States of nearly $15 billion in economic assistance to rebuild the devastated agricultural and industrial infrastructures of Western European countries in the aftermath of World War II. It was named after Secretary of State George C. Marshall (1880–1959), who first proposed this infusion of money in a 1947 speech.

Bolstering War-Torn Economies In 1946 Europe was in shambles. Six years of war had left every nation involved in the war in a state of physical and economic chaos. Industrial centers and transportation hubs had been reduced to rubble by years of relentless bombing. Even the countries that had been on the winning side faced years of rebuilding before their economies would be capable of performing at their prewar levels. So thorough was the destruction that there was not nearly enough capital or raw materials available to complete the job.

The United States, in contrast, emerged from World War II in better shape economically than it had entered it. Not only had the war not taken place on American soil—with the notable exception of the attack at Pearl Harbor—but wartime production had kept money flowing into the coffers of the nation's big industrial companies, the heart of the U.S. economy.

Former General Hatches a Plan Marshall had first made his mark as a military man. He was a key tactical officer in France during World War I, and in 1939 he was named chief of staff of the U.S. Army, effectively placing him at the very top of the U.S. fighting machine that fought World War II. Marshall retired from the army in November 1945, and was named secretary of state by President Harry S. Truman (1884–1972) in 1947.

One of Marshall's first assignments as secretary of state was to attend a conference in Moscow, along with representatives of Britain, France, and the Soviet Union, to discuss the future of vanquished Germany and Austria. Over the course of the meetings, it became clear that the Soviet Union saw the collapsed economies of Europe as an opportunity to spread communism across the continent. Marshall came away from the conference determined to forge an American response that would help restore those economies to viability and keep them operating according to free-market principles.

A team of Truman administration policy experts, which included William L. Clayton (1880–1966), George F. Kennan (1904–2005), and Dean Acheson (1893–1971), quickly put together a plan for a gigantic aid package that they hoped would stabilize the war-ravaged economies of Europe, with the idea that economic stability was the key ingredient in the recipe for political stability. Marshall officially unveiled the plan during his June 5, 1947, commencement address at Harvard University. In the address, Marshall played down the role of perceived Soviet aggression in the eagerness of the United States to lend a helping hand, stating that the program was "directed not against any country or doctrine but against hunger, poverty, desperation, and chaos." Marshall invited the nations of Europe to inventory their own needs and suggest a plan for the most effective use of American economic assistance.

Sixteen Countries Form Core Group A month later, representatives of eighteen Western European countries met in Paris to discuss such plans. Together, these countries—Austria, Belgium, Denmark, France, Great Britain, Greece, Iceland, Ireland, Italy, Luxembourg, the Netherlands, Norway, Portugal, Spain, Sweden, Switzerland, Turkey, and West Germany—and the United States formed the Organization for European Economic Cooperation. The Soviet Union was invited, but American policy makers doubted that Soviet leaders would join the coalition, and doubted even more that Congress would agree to any plan that gave a large amount of aid to the

Demonstration in Germany against the Marshall Plan, c. 1952. © *CORBIS*

Soviets. Planners ensured that outcome by attaching conditions they knew would be unacceptable to the Soviet Union, including movement toward a unified European economy. As expected, the Soviet Union refused to join the organization, and representative Vyacheslav Molotov (1890–1986) abruptly left the Paris gathering. The Western European counties put together a proposal for $16 billion to $22 billion in aid to boost their economies until 1951.

While the plan met with some resistance in Congress, U.S. lawmakers eventually agreed to President Truman's request for $17 billion in economic assistance for Europe. The Economic Cooperation Administration (ECA) was created in 1948 to administer the program. The Soviets refused to let their client nations Poland and Czechoslovakia participate in the program, and launched their own version, the Molotov Plan, to promote Soviet-style economic development in Eastern Europe. The Molotov Plan integrated Eastern European countries into the Soviet Union's socialist economy and led to the creation of the Council for Mutual Economic Assistance (COMECON). The creation of the ECA and COMECON set the stage for the economic aspects of the East-West rivalry that would dominate world affairs for the next four decades.

The Marshall Plan was completed in 1951, having added about $15 billion to the economies of Western Europe. Marshall himself was awarded a Nobel Peace Prize in 1953 for his role in revitalizing industrial and agricultural productivity in Europe after World War II. The Marshall Plan was instrumental in shifting U.S. foreign policy from isolationism to internationalism. It resulted in the creating of the European Economic Community, or "Common Market," the predecessor to today's European Union.

See also **The Cold War**

The Cold War

From the end of World War II until 1991, Western capitalist democracies led by the United States engaged in an ongoing ideological conflict against the Communist Soviet Union. Known as the Cold War, this forty-five-year period of hostilities between the two superpowers never exploded into direct warfare; the war was instead fought on the political, economic, and philosophical levels. Only indirectly did the two sides square off militarily, as they battled for supremacy and influence throughout the developing world by supporting and arming forces and factions in regions that were politically unstable.

Emblem stamped on relief packages for the European Recovery Program, also known as the Marshall Plan. © *Bettmann/CORBIS*

The "Iron Curtain" The United States and the Soviet Union were allies during World War II, working together to defeat Nazi Germany. After the war, however, relations between the two countries quickly deteriorated. There is no consensus as to the precise beginning of the Cold War, but many historians point to a 1946 speech given in Fulton, Missouri, by British statesman Winston Churchill (1874–1965). In the speech, Churchill decried the Soviet Union's moves to achieve regional domination over all the countries of Eastern Europe, stating that "an iron curtain has descended across the Continent. Behind that line lie all the capitals of the ancient states of Central and Eastern Europe. Warsaw, Berlin, Prague, Vienna, Budapest, Belgrade, Bucharest, and Sofia, all these famous cities and the populations around them lie in what I must call the Soviet sphere, and all are subject in one form or another, not only to Soviet influence but to a very high and, in many cases, increasing measure of control from Moscow."

Regardless of whether Churchill's use of the term *iron curtain* actually marked a significant turning point in history, there is no doubt that the Cold War had begun by the time President Harry Truman (1884–1972) implemented the Truman Doctrine—the proclamation that the United States would take proactive measures to prevent the spread of communism in Europe—in 1947. The following year, Truman put into effect the Marshall Plan, a

program of economic assistance to the war-ravaged countries of Western Europe, aimed at stabilizing the economies of those nations in hopes of keeping them from turning to communism as they sought to rebuild their infrastructures. As U.S. concerns about Soviet aggression in Europe continued to escalate, the United States worked with several Western European nations to form the North Atlantic Treaty Organization (NATO), a military coalition designed to reinforce its members' ability to resist any attempt by the Soviet Union to make inroads in the region. A few years later, the Soviet Union countered by forming its own military alliance, called the Warsaw Treaty Organization, or Warsaw Pact.

The geographic focal point of the early stages of the Cold War was Germany. After World War II, the country was split into two separate states: East Germany, controlled by the Soviets; and West Germany, controlled by the United States and its Western allies. The city of Berlin, located within the boundaries of East Germany, was itself split into Eastern and Western halves under the control of the two sides. When the Soviet Union blockaded West Berlin in 1948 to stop the inflow of American supplies, the United States responded by flying over the blockade and delivering via airlift the supplies necessary to keep the city alive. Soviet leader Joseph Stalin (1879–1953) finally disassembled the failed blockade in May

Testing a bomb shelter in Bronxville, New York, 1952. © *Bettmann/CORBIS*

1949. More than a decade later, in 1961, the East German government erected a wall between the two halves of Berlin—the Berlin Wall—to prevent East Germans from emigrating to the West.

The Cold War Expands   In the early 1950s the Cold War spread to Asia. In 1950 the Soviet Union forged an alliance with the Communist government of China, and that year China supported an invasion of South Korea by forces from Communist North Korea. Fearing that communism would expand throughout the region, the United States rushed to South Korea's assistance, helping form the Southeast Asia Treaty Organization, the region's version of NATO. The Korean War lasted until 1953, and thirty-seven thousand Americans lost their lives in it.

Meanwhile, the Soviet Union had leveled the nuclear playing field. At the beginning of the Cold War, the United States was the only country to possess nuclear weapons, giving it a huge strategic edge as it sought to counterbalance the might of the Soviets' huge and powerful conventional forces. In 1949, however, the Soviet Union tested its first atomic bomb, prompting the United States to intensify its own nuclear weapons development efforts. Thus the arms race was on.

At home in the United States, fear of communism bordered on hysteria. Convinced that communism threatened the very fabric of American society, anybody with a history of ties to communist organizations— which had been fairly common in the United States before World War II, especially during the Great Depression—was viewed as an enemy of the state, and was at risk of having his or her career ruined. This "witch hunt" mentality peaked in Congress with the work of the House Committee on Un-American Activities, whose highly publicized hearings targeted a number of celebrated entertainers and artists, and Senator Joseph McCarthy (1908–1957) of Wisconsin, who was eventually discredited for being overzealous in his search for communist operatives hiding in every corner of American society. Much of the American public lived under a cloud of terror, convinced that the Soviets intended to launch a nuclear attack on their hometown at any moment. Bomb shelters were dug in backyards across the nation, and schoolchildren were instructed to "duck and cover"—to get under a desk or table and cover their heads with their hands—in the event of such an attack.

The death of Stalin in 1953 brought hope that relations between the Soviet Union and the West might thaw, and the proliferation of nuclear weapons come to a halt. This hope was short-lived, however, as tensions mounted once again after just a couple of years, with Prime Minister Nikita Khrushchev (1894–1971) taking over as Soviet leader. Khrushchev is perhaps best remembered for shouting "We will bury you" during a meeting with Western ambassadors in 1956. His statement was interpreted at the time as being overtly hostile. There is some doubt, however, about that translation of his

American schoolchildren being taught to "duck and cover" under their desks in case of nuclear attack, 1951.   © *Bettmann/CORBIS*

Russian words; they are probably more accurately translated as "We will outlive you," or "We will attend your funeral." Nevertheless, when the Soviet Union launched the *Sputnik* satellite in 1957, it ushered in a new era of heightened competition between the Americans and Soviets. This round of conflict centered on technology for space exploration and bigger, better missiles.

Meanwhile, in nearly every part of the world, including not only Southeast Asia but also Africa, the Middle East, and Latin America, the United States and Soviet Union continually jockeyed for position by supporting leaders they thought would best help their cause in the region, often willingly turning a blind eye to a regime's brutality or corruption if they believed that regime was most likely to keep the other side at bay. Wherever a civil war broke out, the two superpowers were likely to be pulling the strings behind the opposing sides in the skirmish.

Crises in Cuba   In the early 1960s, the island nation of Cuba became the Cold War's most dangerous flash point. In 1959 Communist leader Fidel Castro (1926–) took power in Cuba after helping lead the overthrow of President Fulgencio Batista y Zaldívar (1901–1973). Castro developed close ties to the Soviet Union, which naturally was delighted to have a good friend located so close to the United States. Disturbed by the presence of a Soviet-sponsored communist country just ninety miles off the

HOLLYWOOD'S COLD WAR

The culture of the Cold War was captured, and to some extent created, by the Hollywood film industry. In the 1950s movie studios churned out anticommunist pictures by the score, partly in response to consumer demand, but also to deflect the scrutiny many top filmmakers had come under from "commie-hunters" in the nation's capital. Studios, with the blessing of Washington, had made numerous pro-Soviet movies during World War II—after all, they were U.S. allies at the time. These movies included *Mission to Moscow* (1943) and *Song of Russia* (1944). By the time the House Un-American Activities Committee (HUAC) was in full swing in the 1950s, however, those films had come back to haunt their makers. The HUAC-led backlash against Hollywood resulted in the production of such anticommunist propaganda films as *I Married a Communist* (1950), *I Was a Communist for the FBI* (1951), and *Invasion U.S.A.* (1952).

One of the best Cold War dramas was *The Manchurian Candidate* (1962), which addressed the prospect of U.S. soldiers captured during the Korean War being brainwashed by the Chinese to become political assassins upon receipt of a signal from their handlers. The movie, based on a 1959 novel by Richard Condon, starred Laurence Harvey as a war-hero-turned-assassin.

Hollywood turned its attention to a different aspect of the Cold War in the 1960s: the specter of nuclear annihilation. Two 1964 films exemplified this theme. *Fail-Safe*, based on a popular novel of the same title, was about a technical foul-up that accidentally sends American nuclear bombers on their preassigned mission toward Moscow. The other movie, Stanley Kubrick's *Dr. Strangelove, or: How I Learned to Stop Worrying and Love the Bomb*, was a satire in which actor Peter Sellers played several roles, including the president of the United States and the wheelchair-bound, ex-Nazi, nuclear weapons expert Dr. Strangelove.

Simultaneously, a separate line of movies focusing on espionage was hitting the nation's cinemas, including the wildly popular James Bond movies based on books by British writer and former intelligence officer Ian Fleming (1908–1964). These movies, which included *Dr. No* (1962), *From Russia with Love* (1963), and *Goldfinger* (1964), spawned a huge wave of Bond-influenced spy thrillers for both the cinema and television.

After the thaw of the 1970s, Hollywood joined with President Ronald Reagan (1911–2004) in renewing tensions with the Soviet Union with a new wave of anticommunist movies. *Red Dawn* (1984) showed a band of brave American teenagers rebelling guerrilla-style in a United States suffering under Soviet occupation. The 1985 movie *Invasion U.S.A.*—unrelated to the 1952 film of the same name—pitted martial arts expert Chuck Norris against a small army of Soviet infiltrators sent to destroy American society. Sylvester Stallone's *Rambo III* (1988) had the title character battling Russian villains in Afghanistan.

By the end of the 1980s, the Cold War was winding down. A popular, if sometimes hackneyed, Hollywood genre died along with it.

Florida coast, President John F. Kennedy (1917–1963) in 1961 armed a group of Cuban exiles and helped them launch an invasion at the Bay of Pigs in southwest Cuba, aimed at removing Castro from power. The invasion was poorly executed and failed miserably. It succeeded in only further damaging the relationship between the United States and Cuba, and by extension, the relationship between the United States and the Soviet Union.

There were a number of "near misses" over the course of the Cold War, but the event that probably brought the United States and the Soviet Union closest to a nuclear exchange was the Cuban missile crisis of October 1962. That fall, U.S. intelligence detected the presence of Russian nuclear missiles in Cuba. President Kennedy issued an ultimatum to the Soviet Union to remove the missiles, and the world waited anxiously to see which superpower would back down first. The crisis was essentially a game of "chicken," with nuclear annihilation the penalty for guessing wrong. After much diplomatic negotiation, the Soviet Union announced that it would dismantle and remove the missiles.

Communism Seen as Threat in Vietnam The Cold War, and the overriding foreign policy imperative that communism be contained in every region of the globe, provided the backdrop for the Vietnam War, which dominated political debate in the United States through the remainder of the 1960s and into the 1970s. In the mid-1950s, an uprising led by Ho Chi Minh (1890–1969) resulted in the ouster of the French colonialists who had dominated the region for about a century. The agreement that ended the fighting "temporarily" divided Vietnam into two separate nations in the north and south, with North Vietnam coming under communist control.

Naturally, the United States rushed to support South Vietnam in hopes of preventing it from being overrun by its neighbors to the north, which was supported by Communist China. Whereas China did not possess the "superpower" status of the Soviet Union, it was nevertheless perceived as the major communist threat in the region, setting up a classic East-West Cold War face-off by proxy.

Detente Relations between the United States and the Soviet Union thawed a bit during the early 1970s. This period was dubbed *detente*, a French word meaning "easing" or "relaxing." Between 1969 and 1972, the two superpowers engaged in negotiations aimed at slowing down the arms race. The dialogue, known as the Strategic Arms Limitation Talks (SALT I), led to the creation of two treaties designed to put a halt to the proliferation of nuclear arms for five years. The treaties were signed in May 1972 by U.S. President Richard M. Nixon (1913–1994) and Soviet General Secretary Leonid Brezhnev (1906–1982). The success of the SALT I negotiations led to a follow-up series, SALT II, which resulted in the signing of several more arms limitation treaties. This round of treaties was not ratified by Congress, however, as tensions between the two nations began to rise once more later in the decade. New conflicts in the Middle East, Angola, and Chile brought hostilities into the open once again.

By early in the presidency of Ronald Reagan (1911–2004), the Cold War was back in full swing. Reagan increased military spending, intensified the arms race, and engaged in a war of rhetoric, referring to the Soviet Union as the "evil empire." Reagan sent assistance, sometimes illegally, to anticommunist guerillas in Central America. He also sent covert aid to the mujahideen (Islamic guerrilla fighters) who were battling against the Soviet occupation of Afghanistan. Some of these mujahideen evolved into the Taliban.

The beginning of the end of the Cold War came in the mid-1980s, when Mikhail Gorbachev (1931–) took power in the Soviet Union. With the Soviet economy crumbling, in part due to the expense of its disastrous invasion of Afghanistan, Gorbachev introduced major reforms that completely overhauled the political and economic systems of Communist bloc countries. These reforms were known collectively as *perestroika* (economic and government restructuring) and *glasnost* (openness). By 1990 the Soviet economy had collapsed, the Communist governments of several Eastern European countries had been ousted, and, in the most important symbolic act of all, the Berlin Wall was dismantled, effectively bringing the Cold War to a decisive conclusion.

> *See also* **The Cuban Missile Crisis**
> *See also* **The Marshall Plan**
> *See also* **McCarthyism**

The Korean War

The Korean War (1950–1953) was the first conflict in which U.S. military forces were fully engaged in the years following World War II. The United States fought

U.S. soldiers in Seoul, 1950. © *CORBIS*

A squadron of American fighter planes returning from a mission over North Korea to the aircraft carrier *USS Boxer*, 1951. © *CORBIS*

on behalf of South Korea in hopes of preventing its occupation by Communist North Korea, backed first by the Soviet Union and later China. The war lasted just over three years, and resulted in about 140,000 American casualties, including approximately 37,000 deaths.

The Korean peninsula was under Japanese control from nearly the beginning of the twentieth century through World War II. After the Allies defeated the Japanese, Korea was partitioned into two separate countries for occupation purposes. The Soviets controlled the area north of the 38th parallel, where they set up a socialist regime. In 1948 that regime officially became the Democratic People's Republic (DPR) of Korea, with longtime Communist leader Kim Il Sung (1912–1994) as the new nation's first premier. In the South, many different factions struggled for power before a United Nations–sponsored election resulted in the selection of Syngman Rhee (1875–1965), widely called the father of Korean nationalism, as president of the newly formed Republic of Korea (ROK).

The division of Korea was supposed to be temporary, but both sides had their own ideas about how reunifica-

tion should be structured. Military incursions across the border took place constantly, though the ROK army was ill equipped and poorly trained, while the DPR's armed forces had access to the best Soviet weapons and training. Rhee's government was riddled with corruption, and engaged in repressive tactics against political dissenters. From the U.S. perspective, one objective was paramount: Korea could not be allowed to reunify under Communist rule. In spite of the potential for conflict, the United States withdrew most of its troops in June 1949, leaving only a small group of about five hundred technical advisers in place to help train the South Korean military.

Surprise Attack by DPR   On June 25, 1950, North Korean troops stormed across the border without warning. They met with little resistance from the shocked and outgunned South Koreans, and within a couple days they had advanced to the outskirts of the South Korean capital, Seoul. The United Nations (UN) Security Council immediately convened a special meeting, and passed a resolution calling on the North Koreans to withdraw instantly. The resolution was ignored. Two days later, the Security Council met again and passed another resolution authorizing

THE RETURN OF MACARTHUR

Few World War II military commanders achieved greater fame than General Douglas MacArthur (1880–1964). A hero of the war in the Pacific, MacArthur went on to lead the United Nations troops battling against North Korea a few years later. His trademark sunglasses and pipe made his likeness one of the most recognizable images of the era.

MacArthur was born on January 26, 1880, in Little Rock, Arkansas. He seemed destined for a military career; many in his family had been career soldiers, and his father, Arthur MacArthur, was himself a prominent general. As a child, Douglas MacArthur was a mediocre student. It was not until he entered the military academy at West Point in 1899 that he began to stand out in the classroom. He graduated from West Point in 1903 at the very top of his class.

MacArthur's first military assignment took him to the Philippines, and his climb through the army's ranks was rapid. In 1906 he was appointed aide-de-camp to President Theodore Roosevelt (1858–1919). During World War I, he earned a reputation as a skilled and daring leader and a variety of honors and decorations. After the war, he was promoted to brigadier general and was made superintendent of West Point, a position he held until 1922.

From 1930 to 1935, MacArthur served as chief of staff of the U.S. Army. During this period, an incident took place that most of his admirers would prefer not to remember. In 1932, during the heart of the Great Depression, MacArthur led a brutal assault on a gathering of thousands of ragged World War I veterans who were in Washington, D.C., to request that Congress dispense their war service bonuses earlier than scheduled. MacArthur set upon the shantytown, where the men were encamped with their families, with tanks and columns of bayonet-wielding soldiers. He rationalized the attack by insisting that he had just quelled an impending communist uprising.

MacArthur was sent back to the Philippines in 1935, and he continued to live there after retiring from the army. In July 1941 he was recalled to active duty as commander of U.S. forces in the Far East. MacArthur's forces were driven from the Philippines when the Japanese attacked the islands, prompting the general to utter his most famous line, "I shall return," in 1942. He made good on that prediction two years later, after battling his way back through the South Pacific from Australia, giving him an opportunity to deliver another, less famous, line, "I have returned. . . . Rally to me." For his exploits, MacArthur was rewarded with the privilege of accepting Japan's surrender on September 2, 1945.

When the war was over, President Harry Truman (1884–1972) named MacArthur supreme commander of Allied occupation forces in Japan, from where he launched the brilliant attack at Inchon that drove the North Koreans out of the South in the early stages of the Korean War. As the war dragged on, however, the headstrong MacArthur's defiance eventually crossed the line with Truman, and MacArthur was relieved of his command in April 1951.

UN members to intervene as necessary to turn back the assault. President Harry S. Truman (1884–1972) quickly accepted the mandate, committing U.S. air and naval forces to the conflict—technically a "police action," since war had not been officially declared. Fifteen other countries offered assistance, some of it substantial, some of it largely symbolic.

Initially, U.S. military involvement was limited to U.S. Air Force sorties from Japan and carrier strikes by the U.S. Navy, leaving the overmatched South Korean army to hold its own on the ground. They were not up to the task, and on June 28 North Korean forces took Seoul. By early August, enough UN forces had arrived to bolster the sagging ROK army and create a stable line of defense around the important port of Pusan. In mid-September 1950, General Douglas MacArthur (1880–1964), commander of U.S. forces in the Far East and supreme commander of the UN forces, launched a brilliantly conceived amphibious attack at Inchon, a port city on the western coast just a few miles from Seoul. American forces recaptured Seoul two days later. MacArthur's successful tactics threatened to encircle the overextended North Korean army, forcing them to retreat back above the 38th parallel.

With the momentum having swung in favor of the UN and American forces, a crucial decision had to made at this point: should they continue to pursue the enemy and advance across the 38th parallel into North Korean territory? Yielding to public pressure, and given the go-ahead by most UN members, Truman—sensitive to criticism throughout his presidency of being "soft" on communism—authorized MacArthur to continue moving northward into North Korea, crossing the 38th parallel on October 1. They took the DPR capital of P'yŏngyang on October 19. By late November, UN and ROK forces had driven the North Korean army nearly to the Yalu River, the boundary between North Korea and the People's Republic of China.

Chinese Entry Then the momentum of the war reversed once again. China, which had said all along that an invasion of North Korea would not be tolerated, began to send vast numbers of conscripts to assist the North Korean army. Thousands of Chinese soldiers crossed the Yalu and attacked the vulnerable flank of MacArthur's forces, and now it was the UN's turn to retreat. P'yŏngyang was abandoned on December 5 and on January 4, 1951, Communist forces once again captured Seoul.

A new line of scrimmage was established south of the 38th parallel, and over the next few months the line moved back and forth moderately without decisive progress made by either side. By July 1951 the conflict had become more or less a stalemate. MacArthur wanted to break the deadlock by attacking China, possibly with atomic weapons, but Truman was firmly against that approach. When MacArthur continued to press the matter, Truman eventually became fed up and relieved MacArthur of his command on April 11, 1951. In July of that year, the two sides began negotiating an end to hostilities. The talks, however, broke down repeatedly amid accusations of germ warfare and disagreements about plans to exchange prisoners.

It ultimately took two years to arrive at an agreement acceptable to all parties. By then the United States had a new president, Dwight D. Eisenhower (1890–1969), and thousands more soldiers had been killed and wounded. A final armistice was signed at P'anmunjŏm on July 27, 1953, calling for a cease-fire and the withdrawal of both

armies from a battle line that stretched the entire width of the peninsula, not far from the original border at the 38th parallel. Both sides claimed victory, but the mutual goal of a reunified Korea was not achieved.

McCarthyism

During the late 1940s and early 1950s, U.S. Senator Joseph McCarthy (1908–1957), a Wisconsin Republican, led a tidal wave of anticommunist political repression in the United States. McCarthy and his allies claimed that communists had infiltrated the federal government and other institutions, and were threatening the American way of life. The attacks were often baseless, but they nevertheless destroyed the careers of thousands of individuals, some of whom had done nothing more than attend a left-wing political meeting ten or fifteen years earlier. Originally associated with generic Cold War

Senator Joseph McCarthy in 1952, waving a document while delivering a report claiming that Democratic presidential candidate Adlai Stevenson had a record of associations with subversive groups. McCarthy maintained that Stevenson endorsed "the suicidal Kremlin-shaped policies of this nation." © *Bettmann/CORBIS*

THE HOLLYWOOD TEN

Artists and intellectuals, with their enduring interest in maintaining freedom of expression, have long been attracted to left-wing politics. The Hollywood film industry is no exception, from Jane Fonda's activism against the Vietnam War to the outspoken progressive views of Tim Robbins in the Iraq War era. In the fall of 1947, ten prominent movie writers and directors were subpoenaed to appear before the House Committee on Un-American Activities (HUAC) as part of a broad investigation into "the extent of Communist infiltration in the Hollywood motion picture industry." Dubbed the "Hollywood Ten," these artists were Alvah Bessie, Herbert Biberman, Lester Cole, Edward Dmytryk, Ring Lardner Jr., John Howard Lawson, Albert Maltz, Samuel Ornitz, Robert Adrian Scott, and Dalton Trumbo.

All ten members of the group refused to answer the committee's questions, on the grounds that their right to hold and communicate whatever personal and political beliefs they wanted was protected by the First Amendment to the Constitution. HUAC saw things differently, and as a result of their refusal to cooperate, the Hollywood Ten were tried in federal court and found guilty of contempt. They were each sentenced to one year in jail and fined $1,000. In addition, they were blacklisted from the movie business. For years most of them were able to eke out a living by working in the film industries of other countries, or else by using a pseudonym to continue working in Hollywood. The most famous pseudonym used by a member of the Hollywood Ten was Robert Rich, who won an Oscar in 1956 for writing *The Brave One*. Rich was actually the blacklisted Trumbo.

The example of the Hollywood Ten ushered in a dark period for Hollywood. Called to appear before HUAC, some three hundred witnesses from Hollywood clung to their own careers by admitting their previous communist affiliation and naming others whom they knew to have similar connections in their past. Many of the film industry's brightest stars took the high road by refusing to name names, and paid for the noble gesture with their careers, at least temporarily.

Of the original Hollywood Ten, only Dmytryk backed down and later cooperated with HUAC. He appeared a second time before the committee and named twenty-six members of left-wing groups.

Hollywood blacklisting finally subsided in the late 1950s along with the anticommunist hysteria that had gripped the entire nation. Many formerly blacklisted writers and directors were able to rebuild their careers. Trumbo was the first of the Hollywood Ten to successfully resume work in Hollywood, appearing in the credits of the classic *Spartacus* (1960), which he adapted from the novel of the same name by fellow blacklistee Howard Fast. The climactic scene in *Spartacus* reflects Trumbo's own traumatic McCarthyist experience, as captured rebel slaves refuse to betray Spartacus to the ruthless Crassus. As a result, Crassus has the slaves crucified one by one.

anticommunism, the term *McCarthyism* eventually came to refer to a particularly mean-spirited and groundless accusation based on paranoia and characterized by political grandstanding.

Seeds of Anticommunism Communism was under attack by conservatives in the United States long before the onset of the Cold War. The industrialization that took place in the late nineteenth and early twentieth centuries gave rise to a fairly large and active socialist movement in response to horrible working conditions and poor wages. Large segments of the labor movement embraced socialist philosophies, and the movement gained momentum with the arrival of waves of European immigrants who brought with them traditions of militant labor activism. The dawn of the Great Depression in 1929 sparked a period of dramatic growth for communism in the United States, as Americans searched for a response to the economic upheaval the nation was experiencing. Communist rhetoric became common among displaced workers as well as artists and intellectuals.

As the 1930s progressed, many people who had embraced communism began to sour on the ideology as news spread of such world events as the brutal purges carried out by Soviet leader Joseph Stalin (1879–1953) and the Soviets' signing of a nonaggression pact with Nazi Germany. There was also a backlash among some conservatives against President Franklin Roosevelt's (1882–1945) New Deal policies, which were too socialistic for their tastes.

By the time the United States entered World War II in late 1941, communism had largely fallen out of favor in the United States. In 1938 the House of Representatives formed the Committee on Un-American Activities (HUAC). Two years later the Smith Act was passed, making it illegal to advocate the violent overthrow of government. Various loyalty programs designed to weed out communists from jobs in the federal government were put into place over the next few years.

Growing Paranoia After the end of World War II in 1945, halting the spread of communism became a central theme of American policy both at home and abroad. In 1947 President Harry Truman (1884–1972) signed an executive order barring all communists and fascists from government work, and the following year, Communist Party leaders in the United States were prosecuted under the Smith Act. Communist paranoia continued to escalate as the Soviet Union expanded its global reach. The 1949 victory of Communist forces under Mao Zedong (1893–1976) in China's civil war further unsettled American nerves. Another law, the McCarran Internal Security Act, was passed by Congress in 1950, virtually outlawing communism altogether.

The act actually went even further than that, turning into outlaws even those who were shown simply to have a "sympathetic association" with undesirable organizations and individuals. In spite of these actions, conservative critics continued to assault the Truman administration as being too soft on communism. Such was the national mood when Senator McCarthy made his appearance in the national spotlight.

McCarthy was elected to the U.S. Senate in 1947 after a brief and undistinguished career as a lawyer and circuit court judge in his home state of Wisconsin. McCarthy's first few years in the Senate were fairly uneventful. That changed abruptly in February 1950, when McCarthy announced in a speech to the Republican Women's Club of Wheeling, West Virginia, that he was in possession of a list—presumably written on the piece of paper he was waving around—of the names of 205 known members of the Communist Party who were currently working for the U.S. State Department. The number tended to shift in subsequent versions of the claim over the weeks that followed.

McCarthy's claim created a nationwide stir, coming close on the heels of the conviction of State Department official Alger Hiss (1904–1996) for perjury related to his testimony about involvement with Soviet espionage agents. McCarthy moved quickly to exploit his new-found fame. He was extremely skillful at manipulating the media. At no point did he manage to produce concrete evidence to back up his claims, but it did not seem to matter, even after a Senate subcommittee investigated his allegations in the spring of 1950 and found them to be baseless. Bolstered by the onset of the Korean War and the arrests of Julius (1918–1953) and Ethel (1915–1953) Rosenberg for allegedly spying for the Soviets, Americans were primed to believe in the authenticity of McCarthy's "Red scare" assertions. The Republicans happily played on these fears, laying the blame for the spread of communism in the United States squarely on the shoulders of the Democrats, who had controlled the federal government for twenty years. McCarthy went so far in 1951 as to call this period of Democratic domination and in particular the leadership of Truman's secretary of state, George C. Marshall (1880–1959), part of "a conspiracy so immense and an infamy so black as to dwarf any previous such venture in the history of man." In this sense, McCarthy's tactics were an unqualified success; in 1952 the Republicans seized control of Congress and, with the election of Dwight D. Eisenhower (1890–1969), the White House.

The Role of the FBI Throughout the McCarthyism period, Senator McCarthy himself never actually documented the existence of a single communist in a government job, but his power to deflate his political enemies with false accusations was enormous. He also had a powerful ally in Federal Bureau of Investigation (FBI) director J. Edgar Hoover (1895–1972), perhaps the most virulent anticommunist in the federal government. The FBI provided much of the information, sketchy though it often was, that fueled the investigations and prosecutions of suspected communists and communist sympathizers. So eager was Hoover to expose the "Red menace" that he regularly resorted to such underhanded methods as unauthorized and often illegal wiretaps, break-ins, and media leaks.

Once identified as a communist or sympathizer, many individuals were forced to testify before one of several investigating bodies, most notably the House Un-American Activities Committee. HUAC members would browbeat their prey—some of whom were there on the basis of the flimsiest of evidence gathered through questionable means—into not only admitting their own past ties to the Communist Party, but also informing on others who had participated with them. Those who refused to cooperate could claim their Fifth Amendment right to avoid self-incrimination, but they usually lost their jobs just the same, and saw their lives thrown into chaos.

People who defied HUAC often learned the hard way that their name had been placed on an unofficial "blacklist." Many industries had blacklists containing the names of people who were no longer employable because they had been identified as communists or communist sympathizers. The most famous blacklist was the one for the Hollywood movie industry. It included the names of the so-called Hollywood Ten, a group of screenwriters and directors who had stood up to HUAC in 1947.

Discredit and Censure The threat of losing one's job turned out to be a powerful deterrent, leading people to avoid association with any organization that could be remotely considered leftist. Thousands of people were fired during the peak years of McCarthyism. Academia was a favorite target; about 20 percent of those called to testify before a state or federal investigative body were college faculty or graduate students.

Ironically, the Republican takeover of Congress turned out to be the beginning of the end of McCarthyism. With Republicans in control in Washington, McCarthy could no longer weave tales of communist conspiracies within the federal government. He turned his attention instead to the military, which turned out to be a major strategic blunder. With World War II still fairly fresh in the minds of most Americans, the military was generally revered by the public. McCarthy's new round of attacks was met with hostility, and, perhaps more important, he lost the support of the Eisenhower administration, whose leader was himself a military hero.

It soon became clear that McCarthy had invented many of his accusations out of thin air, and while Americans still feared the spread of communism as much as ever, they lost their taste for the witch-hunt. In 1954 McCarthy was censured by the Senate for his misconduct. He died three years later a bitter and disgraced has-been. By the late 1950s the repression and hysteria that characterized the McCarthyism era had pretty much evaporated, and Americans understood that many of their neighbors had been unjustly ruined.

> *See also* **The Cold War**
> *See also* **Alger Hiss**
> *See also* **Julius and Ethel Rosenberg**

The Civil Rights Movement

While the struggle for racial equality in the United States has been ongoing since the arrival of the first Africans in North America, the civil rights movement of the 1950s and 1960s was an especially critical period, marked by intensive activity, protest, and substantial progress in reducing discrimination in employment, education, politics, and housing.

Roots of the Movement The roots of the civil rights movement were planted nearly a century earlier, during the post–Civil War period known as the Reconstruction. After the war, the victorious North tried to impose economic and social changes on the vanquished South. The Thirteenth through Fifteenth Amendments to the Constitution—known collectively as the Civil War Amendments—granted fundamental citizenship rights to blacks, but the reality in the South was quite different. Even as eighteen states in the North and West were putting antidiscrimination laws in place by the end of the century, Southern states were moving in the opposite direction, creating a system of laws designed to prevent African-Americans from attaining equal status with whites. These laws became known as Jim Crow laws. They essentially institutionalized racial segregation and discrimination, ensuring that blacks would remain second-class citizens in the South, where 90 percent of the nation's African-Americans lived at the time. Jim Crow laws were accompanied by a wave of violence by white supremacist groups against African-Americans who dared challenge this systematic discrimination. By the dawn of the twentieth century, most black males in the South were disenfranchised, victims of such discriminatory policies as poll taxes and literacy tests required in order to vote. (Women of any race could not vote either.)

Institutionalized racism was not confined to the South. The federal government tacitly approved of Jim Crow policies when the U.S. Supreme Court ruled in *Plessy v. Ferguson* (1896) that the policy of "separate but equal" facilities for African-Americans did not violate the Constitution.

African-Americans began to battle back against Jim Crow in the early 1900s, though much of the protest took place in the North, where it was less dangerous to speak out. Massachusetts-native W. E. B. Du Bois (1868–1963) was one of the most visible and vocal crusaders for racial justice during this period. In 1905 he launched an equality initiative in Niagara Falls, New York, called the Niagara Movement, but it lasted only a few years and accomplished little. In 1909 Du Bois and a handful of other individuals of diverse ethnicities founded the National Association for the Advancement of Colored People (NAACP). The NAACP worked for racial equality through a combination of litigation and public education, including publication of their own magazine, *Crisis*, edited by Du Bois.

Progress after World War II The NAACP scored some notable legal victories beginning in the 1930s and early 1940s. Several law schools and graduate schools were desegregated because of the group's efforts, and through litigation culminating in the U.S. Supreme Court case *Smith v. Allwright* (1944) they were able to halt the formal exclusion of blacks from party primary elections in the South. Other efforts were less successful, however. Prodded by the NAACP, the U.S. House of Representatives passed strong antilynching legislation in 1937 and 1940, only to see the bills thwarted in the Senate by filibusters orchestrated by members from Southern states.

The civil rights movement gained much momentum after World War II, as Americans began to understand the hypocrisy of segregation and discrimination after years of witnessing the Nazi version of race policy. During this period, a vast migration of blacks from the rural South into Northern cities took place. As these individuals began registering to vote, a new and potentially powerful political force was created. In the North, a growing number of religious and labor leaders, intellectuals, and others were dissatisfied with the racist status quo, and began organizing to bring about change. In 1948 President Harry S. Truman (1884–1972) included a broad civil rights plank in his campaign agenda. It cost him the support of many white Southerners, a voting bloc that had long been reliably Democratic. A number of these people splintered from the Democrats to create a new party, the Dixiecrats, who fielded their own presidential candidate, Strom Thurmond (1902–2003). Truman prevailed in spite of this defection, with the help of 70 percent of the votes of blacks in the North.

A watershed moment in the civil rights movement occurred in the late 1940s, when the NAACP, driven by its chief legal counsel (and later Supreme Court Justice) Thurgood Marshall (1908–1993), began confronting segregation head-on through a series of landmark legal cases. Marshall's chief argument was that "separate but equal" was basically nonsense, since separate facilities, whether in education, housing, or other contexts, almost always meant inferior facilities for blacks. This drive culminated in the U.S. Supreme Court's 1954 decision in *Brown v. Board of Education of Topeka*, which brought the doctrine of "separate but equal" to an end with regard to public schools.

Brown v. Board of Education provided a surge of momentum to the civil rights movement, as African-American activists and their allies sought to extend the victory to other corners of society beyond education.

African-American students in Greensboro, North Carolina, staging a sit-in at a "whites only" lunch counter in 1960. © *Jack Moe/CORBIS*

Meanwhile, Southern whites saw the case as an omen that their comfortably segregated way of life was under attack. They responded by digging in stubbornly against the progress of the civil rights movement.

Rosa Parks In December 1955 Rosa Parks (1913–2005), the secretary of the Alabama NAACP chapter, was arrested after refusing to give up her seat to a white man on a Montgomery city bus, as was required by a city ordinance. Following her arrest, the NAACP, local churches, and other individuals and organizations launched a boycott by African-American riders of the Montgomery bus system. One of the boycott's chief organizers was Martin Luther King Jr. (1929–1968), at the time a young local preacher who advocated non-violent resistance and civil disobedience as the best route to social change. The Montgomery boycott lasted for more than a year. In the end, in spite of periodic violence that included the firebombing of King's house, the boycott was successful. In late 1956, the Supreme Court ruled that Montgomery's discriminatory bus law was unconstitutional.

Momentum for civil rights activism continued to grow with each victory. In 1957 King founded the Southern Christian Leadership Conference (SCLC) in order to help develop the generation of leaders who would drive the movement in the coming years. Still, the movement met with fierce resistance from racist groups, primarily in the South. In 1957 President Dwight D. Eisenhower (1890–1969) sent federal troops to Little Rock, Arkansas, when local authorities refused to allow nine African-American students to enroll in the previously all-white Central High School. A few years later, President John F. Kennedy (1917–1963) deployed U.S. marshals to ensure that James Meredith (1933–) could enroll as the first black student at the University of Mississippi in 1962.

Meanwhile, a steady series of smaller protest actions took place regularly across the South. Many of these actions were carried out by the Student Nonviolent

Civil rights activists in Memphis, Tennessee, in 1968, being blocked by National Guard troops with bayonets on one side and tanks on the other. © *Bettmann/CORBIS*

Coordinating Committee (SNCC, pronounced "Snick"), a youth-oriented organization that had branched off of the SCLS. On February 1, 1960, a group of four students sat down at a whites-only Woolworth's lunch counter in Greensboro, North Carolina, and refused to leave until physically evicted. A series of similar sit-ins followed, targeting not only lunch counters but also segregated theaters, swimming pools, and other facilities. Segregated interstate buses and bus stations were another target. In 1961 a group of these "Freedom Riders" organized by James Farmer (1920–1999), cofounder nearly twenty years earlier of the Congress of Racial Equality (CORE), boarded segregated buses traveling from Washington, D.C., into the South, where they were beaten viciously by Southern racists in some cities, receiving no help from local police. Segregation in interstate transportation was finally ended in September of that year when the Interstate Commerce Commission implemented the Supreme Court's 1960 decision in the case of *Boynton v. Virginia,* which deemed such segregationist transportation policies unconstitutional.

Civil Rights Act of 1964 By 1963 racial polarization in the South had escalated to dangerous levels. Violence was widespread. For several days in May, police in Bir-

mingham, Alabama, beat and set attack dogs on followers of King engaged in nonviolent protests. These brutal assaults were captured by television news cameras. Their broadcast outraged much of the American public, and led President Kennedy to address the nation on June 11 calling on Congress to enact strong civil rights legislation. One of the civil rights movement's defining moments took place on August 28, 1963, when a coalition of African-American groups and their allies organized a huge march on Washington to promote passage of the civil rights bill that had been introduced in Congress. This was the event at which King delivered his famous "I have a dream" speech before hundreds of thousands of supporters of many races.

After the assassination of Kennedy in November 1963, incoming President Lyndon B. Johnson (1908–1973) made passage of the civil rights bill a priority of his administration. Behind fierce lobbying by religious groups of many different denominations, the bill was signed into law by Johnson on July 2, becoming the Civil Rights Act of 1964. The act dealt a tremendous blow to the legal structures that had allowed segregation and racial discrimination to survive up to that time. It prohibited discrimination in places of public accommodation, such as restaurants, motels, and theaters; it denied federal funding to programs with discriminatory policies; it established the Equal Employment Opportunity Commission; and it outlawed discrimination in private businesses with twenty-five or more employees and in labor unions.

Meanwhile, the violence raged on. In 1963 Medgar Evers, field secretary of the NAACP in Mississippi, was gunned down while organizing a boycott to protest voter discrimination. In June 1964, two white civil rights activists, Andrew Goodman and Michael Schwerner, and an African-American associate, James Chaney, were murdered while promoting voter registration among blacks in Mississippi. In spite of the Civil Rights Act, discrimination in election policies was rampant. In 1965 King led a march from Selma, Alabama, to Montgomery to protest voting restrictions that unfairly disenfranchised African-Americans. More than twenty-five thousand people participated in the march, making it one of the largest civil rights protests of the 1960s. The march had a powerful impact; Congress soon responded by passing the Voting Rights Act of 1965, which prohibited the use of literacy tests and other discriminatory policies to filter out minority voters.

Fragmentation of the Movement In spite of this progress, the movement began to disintegrate in the mid-1960s. SNCC began to lose patience with the nonviolent approach advocated by King, who had been awarded the Nobel Peace Prize in 1964 for his inspiring leadership. SNCC leader Stokely Carmichael (who later changed his name to Kwame Ture; 1941–1998), later influential in the rise of the militant group the Black Panthers, was vocal in his criticism of King's pacifist philosophy. He began promoting distrust of whites who supported the movement, urging African-Americans to become more aggressive and self-sufficient. This approach was threatening to many white liberals, and it alienated many less-militant African-Americans as well. Bursts of violence broke out in large cities, the first major flare-up being the six-day Watts riot in South Central Los Angeles, California, in August 1965.

As these new, more militant factions of the civil rights movement grew angrier, the appeal for black separatism became louder. The Black Muslims were among those calling for a reorganization of African-American culture that would eliminate dependence on the white establishment. Large race riots took place in Detroit, Michigan, and Newark, New Jersey, during the summer of 1967. As African-American protest grew increasingly violent, many white liberals shifted their energies to protesting against the Vietnam War.

King was assassinated on April 4, 1968, in Memphis, Tennessee. The murder of King touched off riots in 125 cities over the next week. Parts of Washington, D.C., were in flames for three days. Congress reacted by passing the Civil Rights Act of 1968, the most important part of which was Title VIII, known as the Fair

MISSISSIPPI BURNING

One of the most shocking events associated with the civil rights movement was the 1964 murder in Philadelphia, Mississippi, of three young activists who were helping to organize a voter registration drive. The three men were James Chaney, a twenty-one-year-old African-American from Mississippi; Andrew Goodman, a white, twenty-year-old anthropology student from New York; and Michael Schwerner, a white, twenty-four-year-old social worker also from New York.

The trio arrived in Philadelphia on June 20, 1964, soon after finishing a weeklong training session in Ohio on minority voter registration strategies. At about 5:00 p.m. their car was stopped by Neshoba County Deputy Cecil Price. Chaney was arrested for allegedly speeding, and his passengers were detained "for investigation."

During their time in jail, the three were not allowed to make phone calls, and when their fellow civil rights workers called the jail, the secretary was ordered to lie and say the men were not there. They were finally released at 10:30 p.m. and ordered to leave the county. Police soon found the charred remains of their car. Local authorities and Mississippi Governor Paul Johnson played down the incident, suggesting that Schwerner, Goodman, and Chaney were probably fine and had just gone somewhere else to make trouble. However, after offering a $25,000 reward for information about the men's whereabouts, the Federal Bureau of Investigation received a tip that led them to a farm six miles southwest of Philadelphia, where they found the bodies of the three men on August 4, 1964. Autopsies showed that all three had been shot and Chaney had been severely beaten as well.

Eighteen suspects went to trial in 1967, and seven of them were found guilty, but only of civil rights violations. The event was recapped in several films over the next few decades, most notably the 1988 motion picture *Mississippi Burning*, starring Willem Dafoe and Gene Hackman, but no further legal action took place. Finally, after years of intensive scrutiny by award-winning investigative reporter Jerry Mitchell of the *Jackson Clarion-Ledger*, however, the case was reopened. In 2005 Edgar Ray Killen, a local minister who had been a prime suspect in the case from the start but been set free in 1967 by a deadlocked jury, was convicted of three counts of manslaughter.

Housing Act. The act outlawed discrimination in the sale and rental of most housing.

By this time, however, the civil rights movement was fragmented beyond recognition. Emphasis during the 1970s was on programs aimed at compensating for the impact of past discrimination by giving special consideration to minority applicants for jobs, university admissions, government contracts, and the like. This approach to reducing racial inequality is called "affirmative action." Critics of affirmative action tend to characterize it as "reverse discrimination" because it uses race rather than other qualifications to award opportunities.

During the 1980s national politics took a dramatic conservative swing, and there was considerable backlash against some of the civil rights movement's gains of the 1960s. The administration of President Ronald Reagan (1911–2004) reduced the number of lawyers in the Civil Rights Division of the U.S. Department of Justice from 210 to 57. Reagan went so far as to attempt—unsuccessfully—to disband the U.S. Commission on Civil Rights entirely. The Supreme Court under conservative Chief Justice William Rehnquist (1924–2005) chipped away further at government protections against racial discrimination. In a batch of 1989 rulings, the Court said, among other things, that (1) the Civil Rights Act of 1866 did not protect blacks from racial harassment by employers; (2) the burden of proof in employment discrimination cases was with the employee, not the employer; and (3) programs setting aside a portion of city contracts for minority businesses were unconstitutional unless there was evidence of flagrant discrimination. The Court has continued to struggle with the parameters of affirmative action into the twenty-first century.

See also **Brown v. Board of Education of Topeka**
See also **Martin Luther King Jr.**
See also **Rosa Parks**
See also **Affirmative Action**

The National Association for the Advancement of Colored People

The National Association for the Advancement of Colored People (NAACP) was founded in 1909 by a multiracial group of activists based in New York City. Its mission is to ensure the political, educational, social, and economic equality of all Americans by eliminating racial hatred and discrimination.

As the nation's oldest and largest civil rights organization, the NAACP played a key role in the civil rights movement in the United States, particularly during the 1950s and 1960s. The NAACP's strategy stressed using the federal courts to attack segregation laws and practices and secure the rights of all Americans, as guaranteed by the U.S. Constitution.

A note about language: At the time of the NAACP's founding, the words *colored* and *Negro* were the accepted terminology for describing nonwhite people of African descent. In the late 1960s, the word *black* started to be preferred. In the 1980s, the term *African-American* emerged as the descriptor of choice.

The NAACP and the Civil Rights Movement
The NAACP's strategy for promoting racial equality, and guaranteeing it in the law, was to present the legal arguments for its necessity by fighting in state and federal courts to strike down segregationist laws. An impetus for the NAACP's strategy to fight racism via the judicial system stemmed from its belief that the U.S. Supreme

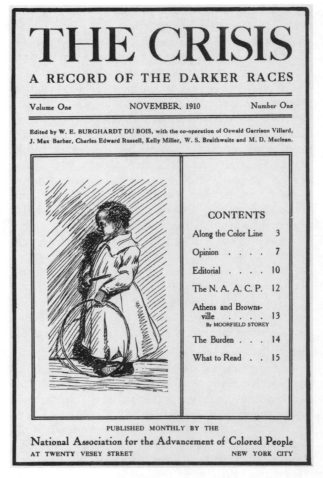

Cover of the first issue of the NAACP's monthly magazine *The Crisis*, 1910. *Public domain*

Court made an invalid decision in *Plessy v. Ferguson* (1896), which legalized segregation by establishing the "separate but equal" principle.

The NAACP's attorneys, among them future Supreme Court Justice Thurgood Marshall (1908–1993), argued that under segregation, the conditions in which blacks lived were *separate* but never *equal* to the higher standards afforded whites. The NAACP's legal challenges and victories revolved around that idea, which ultimately resulted in the Supreme Court decision in *Brown v. Board of Education of Topeka* (1954), which rejected *Plessy* by dissolving and deeming unconstitutional the concept of "separate but equal." The *Brown* decision inspired the marches and demonstrations of the civil rights movement by motivating a previously intimidated black populace with the possibility of change. The resulting protests and activism helped secure the enactment of the Civil Rights Act of 1964, the Voting Rights Act of 1965, and the Fair Housing Act of 1968.

The NAACP and Other Civil Rights Organizations
While courtroom victories could slay state-sponsored

discrimination, changing a predominantly white nation's long-held attitudes toward blacks could not be resolved with the simple strike of a gavel. To civil rights leaders such as the Reverend Martin Luther King Jr. (1929–1968) and his Southern Christian Leadership Conference (SCLC), and groups such as the Congress of Racial Equality (CORE) and Student Nonviolent Coordinating Committee (SNCC, pronounced "snick"), the battle for equal rights needed to also be waged through emotional entreaties. That is, to enlist the energies of sympathetic whites and the masses of black Americans, the civil rights movement needed to emphasize the moral reasons for equality, and by doing so motivate regular people to act in force by expressing their heartfelt desire for equal rights and protection under the law.

At times, the NAACP viewed King's theatrical speeches and dramatic but nonviolent demonstrations, marches, and acts of defiance as showboating, in part to enhance his own celebrity. King and his similarly passionate followers thought that while the NAACP's efforts at working through the judicial system were important, the results were too slow in coming. For instance, a single legal victory was typically preceded by a decade of work. Public adherence to—and the legal enforcement of the rights secured by—such victories often became battles unto themselves. As is often the case with activist causes, the ultimate goals of the various civil rights groups were the same, only the means for getting there differed.

As King himself observed about the civil rights movement's various approaches, on more than one occasion: "The law cannot make a man love me, but it can keep him from lynching me." The fight for equality, he said, was "a three-lane road with some emphasizing the way of litigation and mobilizing forces for meaningful legislation, and others emphasizing the way of nonviolent direct action, and still others moving through research and education and building up forces to prepare the Negro for the challenges of a highly industrialized society."

Reactions to Brown The *Brown* decision in 1954 raised the ire of segregationists, which led to an escalation of violence against blacks. However, by showing black Americans that their lot in life could change for the better, "the Negro has seen the exit sign to freedom," said King. "The whole nation put itself on record then as saying that segregation is wrong." Speaking about the decision in 1960, NAACP leader Roy Wilkins (1901–1981) noted the irony of his organization's work being considered controversial: "We ask nothing that is not guaranteed by the American Constitution, that has not been affirmed and reaffirmed in the nation's noblest expressions of democratic faith from the Declaration of Independence to the United Nations Charter, that is not rooted in our accepted Judeo-Christian ethic."

After *Brown*, the NAACP's profile was raised so high that the group and its members were targeted by extremists and politicians bent on disrupting racial progress. In Alabama, legislation outlawed the NAACP, a policy that held for a decade. NAACP activists including Henry Moore and Medgar Evers were assassinated at their homes. (In 1995 the latter's wife, Myrlie Evers-Williams, would become executive director of the NAACP.) Because NAACP activities were often less visible—engaging in legal proceedings, for example—some historians credit King and SNCC with making the civil rights movement the powerful cultural force that it was. At the same time violence against civil rights activists was building in the South, the NAACP was working behind the scenes in Washington. It successfully lobbied the administration of President John F. Kennedy (1917–1963) for assistance in securing the rights of black Americans. After Kennedy's assassination in November 1963, President Lyndon B. Johnson (1908–1973) continued his predecessor's efforts and signed the Civil Rights Bill of 1964, which outlawed segregation in public places. The following year, Johnson signed into law the Voting Rights Act of 1965.

The Post–Civil Rights Era Within days of President Johnson signing the Voting Rights Act, racial riots exploded in the Watts section of Los Angeles, California; in the following years other riots occurred in Cleveland, Ohio; Detroit, Michigan; Newark, New Jersey; Washington, D.C.; and other cities. In April 1968 Martin Luther King Jr. was assassinated in Memphis, Tennessee, by a white man named James Earl Ray. Two months later, Democratic presidential candidate and civil rights advocate Senator Robert F. Kennedy (1925–1968) was shot and killed by a deranged Palestinian immigrant, Sirhan Sirhan. That November, Republican Richard M. Nixon (1913–1994) won the presidency, replacing the Democrat Johnson who, bogged down by the Vietnam War, chose not to pursue a second full term in office.

Having gained legal victories in such areas as voting, housing, and education, NAACP leaders and other civil rights activists had to work to ensure that the new laws were being implemented and enforced. Frustrated at seeing integration efforts stalled by ingrained racism, young black people started to advocate for "Black Power" (a catchphrase of the Black Panther Party) in a movement that dismissed integration, espoused black self-determination, and promoted pride in being black; the movement was often viewed as antiwhite. Clashes between blacks and segregationists, and the police forces sympathetic to the segregationists, continued. When the Supreme Court ruled in *Swann v. Charlotte-Mecklenburg Board of Education* (1971) that busing children from black neighborhoods to white ones (and vice versa) could be federally mandated in order to achieve integration in public schools, white Americans launched violent protests. The issue of busing became a hot-button topic among whites and

A banner outside the headquarters of the NAACP in New York City calling attention to lynching, c. 1937. © *Library of Congress*

conservatives who were resistant to some or all of the changes brought on by the civil rights movement.

The influence and purpose of the NAACP during the Nixon years and after is not as easily defined as it was in the 1950s and 1960s. Because of the various civil rights acts, black Americans were beginning to have representatives in or near positions of power. Reliance on the NAACP was no longer as necessary. By the late 1970s the NAACP had serious financial and institutional problems. At the start of the Reagan era in 1981, the civil rights movement had lost both momentum and governmental support.

A century after its founding, however, the NAACP is still a primary player in challenging racial discrimination.

The organization's recent focus has been on equality cases of broad significance involving such issues as employment, education, housing, criminal law, and voting rights.

Affirmative Action

Affirmative action policies seek to redress the past discrimination and disadvantages inflicted upon minorities and women. Such policies often call for giving certain groups of people special consideration in employment and education in order to encourage diversity and promote equal opportunity.

Reasons for Affirmative Action Prior to the civil rights movement of the 1950s, discrimination on the

MILESTONES IN THE HISTORY OF AFFIRMATIVE ACTION

1961: In Executive Order 10925, President John F. Kennedy (1917–1963) declares that federal contractors may not discriminate in their hiring practices against "any employee or applicant for employment because of race, creed, color, or national origin." He then says that federal contractors need to use "affirmative action" to ensure that all employees and applicants are treated fairly. Kennedy also creates the Committee on Equal Employment Opportunity.

1964: The Civil Rights Act of 1964 is signed into law, prohibiting racial discrimination. The act also establishes the Equal Employment Opportunity Commission.

1965: In Executive Order 11246, President Lyndon B. Johnson (1908–1973) requires that all government contractors and subcontractors take "affirmative action" to expand job opportunities for minorities, and ensure that minority employees have the same chances for promotions and pay raises as white employees.

1967: Johnson amends his 1965 executive order to include affirmative action for women.

1970: In a regulation called Order No. 4, the U.S. Department of Labor under President Richard M. Nixon (1913–1994) authorizes the use of goals and timetables to correct the "underutilization" of minorities by federal contractors. (In 1971, Order No. 4 is revised to include women.) The rationale of Order No. 4 is that simply advertising job openings is not enough. Employers need to show that they are actually hiring minorities.

1973: To discourage the use of simple "quotas" for minority hiring, the Nixon administration issues goals and timetables for affirmative action hiring by state and local governments.

1978: In *Regents of the University of California v. Bakke*, the U.S. Supreme Court upholds the use of race as one factor in choosing among qualified applicants for admission, but rules unlawful the practice of reserving a set number of seats in each entering class for disadvantaged minority students.

1985: The Reagan administration is unsuccessful in its efforts to repeal the 1965 Executive Order 11246.

1995: President Bill Clinton (1946–) declares his support for affirmative action programs by announcing his administration's policy of "Mend it, don't end it."

1996: With the ballot measure Proposition 209, California abolishes all public sector affirmative action programs.

1997: The University of California ends affirmative action programs at its graduate schools, disallowing the use of race, gender, ethnicity, or national origin as a factor in admissions decisions.

1998: Voters in Washington State pass "Initiative 200" banning affirmative action in higher education, public contracting, and hiring.

2003: In two cases involving the University of Michigan, the U.S. Supreme Court holds, in *Grutter v. Bollinger*, that the use of race among other factors in the law school's admissions is constitutional because the program obtains "an educational benefit that flows from student body diversity." Nevertheless, in *Gratz v. Bollinger*, the justices reject an undergraduate admissions program that grants points based on race and ethnicity.

---

basis of race, ethnicity, gender, and religion was legal and rampant. Women and blacks were routinely prohibited from educational opportunities in both public and private institutions of higher education. Both were prohibited from entire fields of work opportunities. Newspaper job listings were gender specific and women rarely worked outside the home once they married or became pregnant. Black people were routinely relegated to menial jobs, regardless of their education or talents. At the time the United States was founded, all women and all nonwhite men were forbidden from owning property or having any significant measure of self-determination.

Policy makers and social activists in the 1960s realized that although judicial and legal victories had been achieved on behalf of equal rights, changing statutes was not enough. Beliefs and attitudes change gradually, regardless of the rules of law.

The 1954 landmark U.S. Supreme Court case of *Brown v. Board of Education of Topeka* declared as unconstitutional the segregationist practice of educating black and white children in separate schools. However, changing the instilled attitudes and behaviors of an entire society was not as straightforward, especially in a nation that

since its founding two centuries earlier had accepted the subjugation of women and blacks. Ingrained prejudice continued despite the *Brown* decision and the equality guarantees of the Civil Rights Act of 1964 and the Voting Rights Act of 1965. During the 1960s and 1970s predominantly white-male colleges and workplaces continued to be the norm.

How Affirmative Action Was Instituted The term *affirmative action* first appeared in 1961, in an executive order issued by President John F. Kennedy (1917–1963). In Executive Order 10925, Kennedy declared that "affirmative action" should be taken to ensure that federal employees are treated equality, regardless of "race, creed, color, or national origin."

Following Kennedy's lead, in 1965 President Lyndon B. Johnson (1908–1973) issued Executive Order 11246, which reiterated the points made by Kennedy but with a stronger, enforced directive. Three years later, Johnson added protections against gender discrimination. Articulating his support for equality and affirmative action in a speech to students at Washington, D.C.'s all-black Howard University in 1965, Johnson said:

EXECUTIVE ORDER 11246

On September 24, 1965, President Lyndon B. Johnson (1908–1973) issued an executive order prohibiting employment discrimination based on race, color, religion, and national origin by organizations receiving federal contracts or subcontracts. In 1967 the order was amended to also prohibit discrimination based on gender. Future affirmative action efforts were based on Johnson's combined orders.

> The contractor will not discriminate against any employee or applicant for employment because of race, color, religion, sex, or national origin. The contractor will take affirmative action to ensure that applicants are employed, and that employees are treated during employment, without regard to their race, color, religion, sex, or national origin. Such action shall include, but not be limited to the following: employment, upgrading, demotion, or transfer; recruitment or recruitment advertising; layoff or termination; rates of pay or other forms of compensation; and selection for training, including apprenticeship.

SOURCE: *U.S. Department of Labor, Employment Standards Administration, Office of Federal Contract Compliance Programs, "Executive Order 11246," Part II, Subpart B, Sec. 202(1), http://www.dol.gov/esa/regs/statutes/ofccp/eo11246.htm (accessed April 17, 2007).*

You do not wipe away the scars of centuries by saying: Now you are free to go where you want, and do as you desire, and choose the leaders you please.

You do not take a person who, for years, has been hobbled by chains and liberate him, bring him up to the starting line of a race and then say, "you are free to compete with all the others," and still justly believe that you have been completely fair.

Thus it is not enough just to open the gates of opportunity. All our citizens must have the ability to walk through those gates.

This is the next and the more profound stage of the battle for civil rights. We seek not just freedom but opportunity. We seek not just legal equity but human ability, not just equality as a right and a theory but equality as a fact and equality as a result.

In 1969 President Richard M. Nixon (1913–1994) expanded affirmative action in the federal government by establishing goals and issuing a timetable for construction-related federal contractors to meet certain diversity benchmarks, which became required a year later. In his autobiography that was published in 1978, Nixon wrote that his support of such policies came from his belief that, "A good job is as basic and important a civil right as a good education."

For an even wider reach, antidiscrimination language pertaining to private sector hiring was written into the Civil Rights Act of 1964. Enforcement was assigned to the newly created Equal Employment Opportunity Commission.

How Affirmative Action Works Affirmative action policies encouraged employers and educational institutions to set goals and timetables for increasing diversity within their workforce or school, by use of recruitment efforts and preferential hiring. In theory, affirmative action was not supposed to set aside quotas (that is, mandating the number of minority or female individuals to be hired or enrolled), nor was it to be used for the benefit of unqualified candidates. In its purest form, affirmative action would, in the case of two identically qualified candidates, encourage preference to the one from the previously routinely disregarded minority.

So-called weak affirmative action efforts are those that encouraged equal opportunities for all by, for example, banning segregation or discrimination. The more controversial affirmative action efforts were the "hard" policies that required a certain number of set-asides (or quotas) be included specifically for minorities or women.

The Arguments For and Against Affirmative Action The opponents of such hard affirmative action programs generally believed that past injustices are past. What is important is to provide equal opportunity going forward, without preferences for any race or gender. Otherwise, a quota system is being established in which education and work privileges and opportunities are being given to people based on their gender or race, and not on their academic or career skills. The program to "right past wrongs," a phrase often used in affirmative action debates, instead created "reverse discrimination," in which white men were on the losing side.

Supporters of affirmative action argued that minority-friendly policies were necessary in order to level the playing field between whites and people of color and between men and women. Years of oppression cannot be erased and equal opportunity cannot be created if for generations some people—because of their race, ethnicity, gender, or religion—have been denied the educational and vocational experiences available to the more privileged class (specifically white Anglo-Saxon Protestant males). Another argument raised by supporters of affirmative action is that institutionalized racism and violence (such as lynching and other Ku Klux Klan activities) are not in the distant past and, in some cases, are still ongoing. Many of the establishments that practiced and supported racist and sexist policies in the 1960s are still in existence.

The main court case to challenge affirmative action policies is *Regents of the University of California v. Bakke* (1978). Allan Bakke, a white man, sued the university because he was twice refused admission to the medical school in favor of less-qualified black applicants because, he claimed, of the school's quota for minority students

The Postwar Era (1945–1970)

and the preferential treatment they received during the admissions process. In a 5 to 4 decision, the U.S. Supreme Court ruled that while it was indeed illegal for the university to set aside for certain classes of people a specific number of places (quotas) in the absence of proof of past discrimination, it allowed that in order to achieve a diverse student body, minority status could be used as a factor in admissions.

When the United States fell into a recession in the 1970s, white men (pejoratively dubbed "angry white men") asserted that they were losing their jobs to minority hires, despite having seniority and better skills. Some accused black Americans of playing the "race card"— blaming racial discrimination—whenever a black person was denied an opportunity or felt victimized. Using such minority groups as Jews and newly immigrated Asians as examples, others asserted that minorities could achieve success on their own, without mandated special treatment. While women and minorities benefited from the way affirmative action made educational and career opportunities available to them, many bristled at any assumption that they were hired for their race or gender as opposed to their skills. Another argument in the debate held that if schools at the elementary and high school levels were providing the same quality of education to all, regardless of race or gender, by the time young people reached college and the workforce, all would be arriving from a level playing field, hence the need for affirmative action would be moot.

The White House and Affirmative Action Starting with the presidency of Ronald Reagan (1911–2004) in 1981, Republican leaders have challenged affirmative action policies. In the 1990s President Bill Clinton (1946–), a Democrat, asserted that the job of ending discrimination remained unfinished, "Mend it, but don't end it," he said of affirmative action in a 1995 speech at the National Archives.

From its outset, affirmative action was envisioned as a temporary policy, needed just until Americans of all races and genders could operate on a so-called level playing field. In 1996 voters in California decided that four decades of affirmative action had evened that field enough. They approved a ballot measure that declared: "The State shall not discriminate against, or grant preferential treatment to, any individual or group on the basis of race, sex, color, ethnicity, or national origin in the operation of public employment, public education, or public contracting."

Since 2001 a Republican White House again challenged affirmative action policies, specifically any types of quotas or preference standards. In 2003 the administration of President George W. Bush (1946–) joined arguments before the U.S. Supreme Court against affirmative action policies used by the University of Michigan. The Bush administration objected to the school's race-influenced admission policy, comparing it to a "quota system." An irony of the Bush White House's opposition to affirmative action was that two of its top cabinet appointees, successive secretaries of the Department of State, Colin Powell (1937–) and Condoleezza Rice (1954–), both of whom are African-American, had acknowledged that affirmative action policies gave them access and opportunities they would have been denied a generation earlier. It was also noted that Bush himself owed his Yale University admission to a quota system giving preferential treatment to the children of Yale graduates. As the son and grandson of two Yale alums, Bush was granted admission to the Ivy League school despite his less than stellar academic record because of the institution's "legacy" system, which sets aside spots in each year's class for the children of alumni.

The Cuban Missile Crisis

The placement of Soviet nuclear missiles in Cuba brought the United States and the Soviet Union to the brink of war in the fall of 1962. This showdown, which became known as the Cuban missile crisis, marked one of the most dangerous moments of the Cold War, as the world waited nervously to see if either superpower would back down in order to avoid a full-blown military confrontation.

Imperialist Threat versus Communist Aggression In the wake of the botched 1961 U.S.-backed Bay of Pigs invasion aimed at toppling the Castro regime, tensions had risen between the United States and Cuba. In spring of 1962 the Soviet Union, under the leadership of Premier Nikita Khrushchev (1894–1971), initiated plans to secretly deploy nuclear missiles in Cuba. A few months later, Khrushchev began to make public the Russians' commitment to protecting Cuba against what they perceived as the "imperialist threat" from the United States. That meant supplying additional arms and personnel, as well as indicating that any American attack on Cuba or on Soviet ships going there could result in war.

During August and September of that year, U.S. intelligence detected an increase in the amount of Soviet military aid arriving on the island, as well as other unusual activity. This included the arrival of sophisticated surface-to-air missile installations, bombers capable of carrying nuclear weapons, and thousands of Soviet technical experts. Politics played a key role in the American response. With Congressional elections approaching, the Republicans sensed an opportunity to pick up seats by attacking Democratic President John F. Kennedy's (1917–1963) response to the Soviet posturing. Kennedy understood that politically, he could not afford to be perceived by the American public as being weak against communism. He therefore responded in September by warning the Soviets that "the gravest consequences would arise" if offensive Soviet weapons were definitively found in Cuba.

U.S. aerial reconnaissance photo of Cuban missile launch pads, fueling vehicles, and missile-ready buildings, October 23, 1962. *Time Life Pictures/Department of Defense (DOD)/Getty Images*

Mounting Evidence On October 14, a U-2 reconnaissance plane returned from a flight over Cuba with pictures of long, canvas-covered objects. Over the next twenty-four hours, American analysts scrutinized the photographs, and finally determined that the Soviets were installing medium-range ballistic missiles and launch pads in Cuba. Located within 100 miles of Florida, these weapons were easily capable of striking a large portion of the United States. President Kennedy was informed of the discovery on October 16, and he quickly called a meeting of his top security advisers. This group later took on the name Executive Committee of the National Security Council, or ExComm.

ExComm conducted a series of meetings at which they considered several different courses of action. These options included a direct military attack on the Cuban missile sites; an all-out invasion of Cuba; a trade-off with the Soviets in which the United States would remove its own missiles positioned in Turkey; and a blockade of Cuba. Kennedy decided to implement a blockade. He also gave the Soviets an ultimatum, delivered in a nationally televised speech, demanding that they remove the

missiles and warning that any missile attack on the United States would be met with a U.S. attack on the Soviet Union.

The blockade was scheduled to go into place on October 24. That day, U.S. strategic nuclear forces were placed on their highest status of alert below actual nuclear war, DEFCON 2, as Americans waited anxiously to see how the Soviet Union would respond to this strategy. On the 25th, U.S. Ambassador to the United Nations (UN) Adlai Stevenson (1900–1965) confronted Soviet representative Valerian Zorin with photographic evidence of the buildup at a televised meeting of the UN Security Council. The Soviets denied everything and accused the United States of pushing the world to the edge of a nuclear exchange.

War Narrowly Averted Tensions ran high over the next several days, as the two sides engaged in secret dialogues. The crisis peaked on October 27, when an American U-2 surveillance plane was shot down over Cuba by a surface-to-air missile. Meanwhile, U.S. intelligence personnel reported that Soviet embassy officials

The U.S. Navy destroyer *Sullivan* in Guantanamo Bay at the time of the Cuban Missile Crisis, 1962. *Robert W. Kelley/Time Life Pictures/Getty Images*

at UN headquarters in New York City were destroying sensitive documents, which is often a sign that war is about to break out.

Behind the scenes, furious negotiations were taking place in an effort to avert a war. A Soviet intelligence agent contacted the Kennedy administration through an ABC news correspondent indicating that the Soviet government would consider removing its missiles from Cuba only if the United States removed its own missiles from Turkey and promised not to invade Cuba. By the end of the next day, Khrushchev had formally agreed to dismantle the missiles and ship them back to the Soviet Union. Kennedy's public part of the deal was a pledge not to invade Cuba, and an agreement to lift the blockade as soon as removal of the missiles could be verified. Out of the public eye, Kennedy also agreed to remove the American Jupiter missiles from Turkey.

In the aftermath of the crisis, the Democrats ended up gaining seats in the U.S. Senate and losing only two in the House, a much better result than anticipated, largely on the strength of Kennedy's handling of the situation. The Republicans, who had initially taken

the president to task for his inaction on the budding crisis in Cuba, now accused him of manipulating the crisis in order to build support for Democratic Congressional candidates.

While the Cuban missile crisis ultimately ended peacefully, it served as a startling illustration of how quickly Cold War mistrust could escalate into a nuclear confrontation capable of producing unprecedented destruction. The realization of how close the two superpowers had come to nuclear war led to the installation of a "hotline," a direct communication link between Washington and Moscow that would enable the leaders of the two nations to communicate directly in the event of another crisis, rather than relying on go-betweens to adequately deliver critical messages in volatile situations. The first hotline was ready for action in August 1963. U.S.-Soviet relations improved in a variety of other ways in the months that followed the Cuban missile crisis. In July 1963 the United States, the Soviet Union, and Great Britain signed a treaty prohibiting aboveground testing of nuclear weapons. The United States also began selling wheat to the Soviet Union around that time. Nevertheless, the arms race between the United States and Soviet Union went on unabated for many more years.

See also **Fidel Castro**
See also **The Cold War**
See also **John F. Kennedy**

The Warren Commission

A week after the assassination of President John F. Kennedy (1917–1963) in November 1963, incoming president Lyndon B. Johnson (1908–1973) issued an executive order creating the U.S. Commission to Report upon the Assassination of President John F. Kennedy, a seven-person panel charged with evaluating "all the facts and circumstances surrounding [the] assassination, including the subsequent violent death of the man charged with the assassination." Johnson named U.S. Supreme Court Chief Justice Earl Warren (1891–1974) to head the panel, and thus it quickly became best known as the Warren Commission.

The Assassination of JFK The assassination of Kennedy on November 22, 1963, shocked the nation at a time when the United States was enjoying a period of relative peace and prosperity. There were many questions swirling about the circumstances of the assassination. On November 24 the speculation intensified when the suspected assassin, Lee Harvey Oswald, while in the custody of the Dallas police, was gunned down by a local nightclub owner, Jack Ruby. Seeking to calm the nation's collective jangled nerves, Johnson, freshly sworn in as the thirty-sixth president of the United States, quickly moved to investigate the suspicious events surrounding the murder of his predecessor. On November 29, he issued Executive Order 11130, establishing the Warren Commission. Membership on the commission reflected careful planning in maintaining an acceptable political balance. In addition to Chief Justice Warren, the group included U.S. Senators John Sherman Cooper (a Republican from Kentucky) and Richard Russell (a Democrat from Georgia); Representatives Gerald Ford (a Republican from Michigan) and Hale Boggs (a Democrat from Louisiana); former Central Intelligence Agency (CIA) director Allen Dulles; and John J. McCloy, chair of the Council on Foreign Relations and formerly president of the World Bank and assistant secretary of war.

Proceedings of the Warren Commission began on December 3, 1963. Over the next ten months, the commission scrutinized immense amounts of evidence, including the testimony of 552 witnesses and reports from ten different federal agencies, such as the Federal Bureau of Investigation (FBI), CIA, the State Department, and the Secret Service. The hearings were closed to the public unless the individual testifying specifically requested that the public be invited to attend. Only two witnesses made such a request.

Warren Report On September 24, 1964, the Warren Commission presented President Johnson with an 888-page final report, officially titled *Report of the President's Commission on the Assassination of President John F. Kennedy* but almost universally referred to as the *Warren Report*. The report was made public three days later. Twenty-six additional volumes of testimony and exhibits were later published as well. The commission concluded unanimously that Oswald had acted alone in assassinating Kennedy, and that Ruby had likewise been a lone vigilante when he in turn killed Oswald two days later. While the conclusion of the commission was unanimous, the report did not, contrary to popular belief, completely dismiss the possibility of a conspiracy. It merely stated that given the information available to the commission, no substantial evidence had been uncovered to suggest that Oswald was acting in concert with others.

In its report, the commission subscribed to the "single bullet theory," concluding that only one bullet had caused the nonfatal injuries to both Kennedy and Texas Governor John Connally (1917–1993), who was sitting directly in front of Kennedy in the car. According to this view, a second bullet killed the president, and a third shot missed the motorcade entirely. The commission found no connection between the assassination and Oswald's association with communism and the Soviet Union. They also found no connection between Oswald and Ruby.

Conspiracy Theories Abound It did not take long for skepticism to bloom in some circles. Critics found numerous flaws in the commission's reasoning, citing photographs and X-rays from the autopsy and film footage shot by eyewitness Abraham Zapruder as evidence contradicting the official conclusions. Conspiracy theories abounded, and have continued to proliferate ever since. Two books published in 1966—*Inquest* by Edward Jay Epstein and *Rush to Judgment* by Mark Lane—charged that the commission had failed to dig deeply enough to uncover the truth with any certainty. The same year, a New Orleans district attorney named Jim Garrison unearthed what he believed to be persuasive evidence of a conspiracy, leading to charges against prominent businessman Clay Shaw. A trial ensued, and Shaw was acquitted in 1969. Film director Oliver Stone later replayed the Garrison-Shaw episode in his 1991 hit movie *JFK*.

Conspiracy theories and doubts about the accuracy of the Warren Commission's conclusions have continued to circulate and multiply over the years, though no conclusive evidence has ever emerged that Oswald acted in league with anybody else. One popular theory has it that the assassination was masterminded by Cuban leaders, in retaliation for an alleged plot on Fidel Castro's (1926–) life orchestrated by the Kennedy administration. Another points the finger at organized crime figures, acting in response to the Kennedy administration's crackdown on Mafia activities.

See also **John F. Kennedy**

See also **Earl Warren**

The Vietnam War

The eleven-year conflict in Vietnam (1964–1975) was the United States' longest and costliest war of the twentieth century, and unquestionably one of the most divisive events in modern American history. The war was responsible for the deaths of about 58,000 Americans and more than 3 million Vietnamese. The United States, operating under the "domino theory"—the fear that each small country allowed to fall into communist hands would inevitably lead to a chain reaction of similar events in other neighboring nations—entered the fray with the goal of preventing the reunification under Communist rule of Communist North Vietnam and the U.S.-backed South Vietnam. The United States ultimately failed to achieve its objective, as the North Vietnamese managed to subdue the South and unify the country soon after the withdrawal of U.S. forces in 1973. Along the way, the war bred massive, often violent, dissent inside the United States, creating social scars that took a generation to heal.

War's Colonial Roots The roots of the Vietnam conflict can be found in the European colonialism of the previous century. Vietnam, which stretches along the eastern edge of the Indochina peninsula just south of China, became a French colony in the mid-nineteenth century. Resistance to French domination began to grow in the early twentieth century, and a budding independence movement began to emerge in the years following World War I, under the leadership of Ho Chi Minh (1890–1969). During World War II, the Japanese occupied Vietnam, and the French were forced to abandon the colony.

With the defeat of Japan, France assumed that it would resume control of Vietnam and the rest of the territory they called French Indochina, which also included the neighboring countries of Cambodia and Laos. Ho Chi Minh and his nationalist organization, called the Viet Minh, opposed French rule, however, and beginning in 1946 they engaged the French in the First Indochina War. The United States, seeking to squelch the spread of communism in the region, channeled millions of dollars into France's efforts in Vietnam. That war finally ended when Viet Minh military forces trapped several thousand French troops in a fifty-six-day siege of the French fort at Dien Bien Phu in 1954. France's surrender at Dien Bien Phu led to peace talks in Geneva, Switzerland, at which the French agreed to withdraw all of their troops from Vietnam. The Geneva agreement also divided Vietnam "temporarily" into separate states in the north and south, with Ho Chi Minh and the Communists in control in the north. National

THE MAGIC BULLET

One of the most controversial conclusions of the Warren Commission is the contention that a single bullet—separate from the one that actually killed the president—entered John F. Kennedy's (1917–1963) back, exiting through his neck; hit Texas Governor John Connally (1917–1993) in the back, exiting through his chest; passed through Connally's wrist, and finally lodged in his leg. According to the theory, the bullet later fell out of Connally's leg and landed on a stretcher at Parkland Hospital, where it was eventually found. To do this, the bullet had to have passed through 15 layers of clothing, 7 layers of skin, about 15 inches of body tissue, and hit the knot of a necktie, taking out 4 inches of rib and shattering a radius bone along the way. The bullet itself was a 1-inch long, copper-jacketed, lead-core, 6.5-millimeter rifle bullet. It was entered as Warren Commission Exhibit 399, more commonly referred to as CE399.

This "single bullet theory"—derisively dubbed the "magic bullet theory" by skeptics—was central to the theory that Lee Harvey Oswald was the lone gunman. The theory is generally credited to Warren Commission Junior Counsel Arlen Specter, who is now a Republican U.S. senator from Pennsylvania. Only three spent shells were found at the site from which Oswald is believed to have shot Kennedy, meaning that only three shots could have been fired in order for the Commission's theory to be correct. According to the *Warren Report*, the first shot missed the president's limousine entirely, the second was the "magic" bullet, and the third struck Kennedy in the head and killed him. While the single bullet theory was plausible enough to sway members of the commission, it contains quite a few unlikely enough elements that doubts have been raised in the minds of those inclined to suspect a conspiracy.

For one thing, Connally himself and his wife Nellie were certain that he was struck by a second bullet, separate from the one that hit Kennedy in the back. There are also questions about the trajectory of the bullet. A bullet shot from the sixth floor of a building would have had to negotiate some bizarre turns and angles in order to cause all the damage credited to it. There are also problems with the time line: the amount of time it takes to fire three shots from a bolt-action Mannlicher-Carcano rifle—the type of weapon found at the shooter's location—does not correspond with the timing of the bullets' arrival at the limousine.

In spite of the myriad questions raised by the single bullet theory, it has never been decisively debunked.

elections to unify Vietnam as a single, independent nation were to be held in 1956.

Instability in South Vietnam President Dwight D. Eisenhower's (1890–1969) administration was rightfully worried that Ho Chi Minh would prevail in the election over Ngo Dinh Diem (1901–1963), the U.S.-backed leader of the South Vietnamese government. The U.S. government proceeded to undermine the Vietnamese elections. Diem, with Eisenhower in agreement, argued

Helicopters of the 1st Division of Airborne Infantry in Vietnam, 1966. © *Christian Simonpietri/Sygma/CORBIS*

that free elections in the North were impossible. Elections were held in South Vietnam, and Diem was elected by an overwhelming majority in a vote that was certainly rigged. He quickly declared South Vietnam an independent nation. The United States pledged millions of dollars in financial support to prop up Diem's fledgling government, and established a military presence in South Vietnam to ensure the stability of the border between North and South Vietnam.

By 1957 Communist guerrillas, known as the Vietcong, had begun an underground campaign to gain control of South Vietnam. In 1959 two U.S. soldiers were killed during a Vietcong attack north of Saigon, the South Vietnamese capital, marking the first American deaths of the Vietnamese conflict. The following year, North Vietnam openly acknowledged that they were sponsoring efforts to overthrow Diem's government and force the United States out of Vietnam altogether. Ho Chi Minh and his allies established a political wing of the Vietcong, calling it the National Front for the Liberation of South Vietnam.

In response, the United States ratcheted up its presence in Vietnam. President John F. Kennedy (1917–1963) increased the number of U.S. "advisers" there from eight hundred when he took office to more

than sixteen thousand by 1963. The insurgency in the South continued to intensify, fueled not only by North-sponsored propaganda and violence, but also by Diem's own heavy-handed, repressive methods, which did more to alienate large swaths of the South Vietnamese population than they did to contain the insurgency. In 1963 Diem was assassinated and his government overthrown by elements of the South Vietnamese military. A series of no less than ten unstable governments were put in place in South Vietnam over the next eighteen months.

The Gulf of Tonkin Meanwhile, American casualties began to reach levels too high to ignore. Forty-five Americans were killed in 1963; the total more than doubled the next year to 118. The year 1964 was a turning point for U.S. involvement in Vietnam. In August of that year, it was reported that two U.S. ships in the Gulf of Tonkin off the coast of North Vietnam were fired upon without provocation by North Vietnamese vessels. In fact, as it was later revealed, one of the American ships had not been fired on at all and the other had been engaged in supporting a South Vietnamese military operation on North Vietnamese turf. Nevertheless, the event gave President Lyndon B. Johnson (1908–1973) a rationale for dramatically escalating U.S. operations in Vietnam.

Anti-Vietnam War protesters, 1968. © *Harvey L. Silver/Corbis*

In response to the events in the Gulf of Tonkin, at least as they were portrayed at the time, President Johnson ordered a large air attack on North Vietnam's oil facilities and ship bases, and he sought Congressional approval for the power to run a broad military operation in Southeast Asia. Congress quickly gave him that power in the form of the Gulf of Tonkin Resolution, which authorized the president to take whatever measures were necessary to repel Vietcong aggression. Initially, Johnson used this "blank check" to authorize small covert operations by South Vietnamese troops in North Vietnam, and he ordered bombing along the Ho Chi Minh Trail, the name commonly used for North Vietnamese supply routes that snaked through Laos. Undeterred, the Vietcong accelerated their attacks on American outposts, prompting Johnson to commit thirty-five hundred U.S. combat troops to Vietnam on March 8, 1965. That commitment grew to eighty thousand by the end of 1965, as General William Westmoreland convinced Johnson that there were already large numbers of North Vietnamese soldiers operating in the South, and it would therefore take a major commitment of U.S. troops to save South Vietnam.

Over the next year, U.S. involvement in Vietnam blossomed into a full-blown military venture, involving every branch of the American armed services. Vietnam presented a new kind of challenge for U.S. forces. The conflict was fought mostly in rural areas covered with dense foliage, making it difficult to identify enemy soldiers, much less kill or capture them. One strategy employed by the American military was the use of defoliants, such as Agent Orange, to remove the natural vegetation that provided cover for enemy troops. Agent Orange was later found to cause cancer and other problems, and has been blamed for damaging the health of thousands of U.S. fighters and an unknown, massive number of Vietnamese villagers.

Growing Dissent As the war dragged on, the American public began to tire of the news they were receiving daily about dead and injured young people from their communities. By the late 1960s the war had become quite unpopular at home and the antiwar movement had broadened its support. Historians generally point to the 1968 Tet offensive—a coordinated assault by the North Vietnamese on nearly every South Vietnamese city or town with a substantial population—as the turning point in the war. The Tet offensive was named after the holiday celebrating the lunar new year. It was an all-out plunge designed to end the war in one devastating swoop, with the idea that many South Vietnamese city dwellers already sympathized with the Vietcong, and would help rather than hinder their efforts when they arrived. In all, eighty-four thousand troops attacked

VIETNAM VETERANS AGAINST THE WAR

In April 1967 a handful of disenchanted American service personnel who had returned to the United States after completing their tours of duty in Vietnam formed an antiwar organization called Vietnam Veterans Against the War (VVAW). After marching together in the Spring Mobilization to End the War demonstration along with over four hundred thousand other protesters, the group decided to assemble like-minded Vietnam veterans into a formal organization. As people who had seen the horrors of the war firsthand, VVAW added a degree of credibility to the antiwar movement.

In its earliest stages, VVAW's posture was composed and dignified, as they sought to contrast themselves from some of the movement's more radical elements. Wearing suits and ties, they lobbied legislators on military spending issues. VVAW chapters quickly began to spring up around the country, particularly in the Midwest and on the West Coast. Membership grew slowly but steadily as President Richard M. Nixon (1913–1994) maintained the United States' involvement in the war during the late 1960s. Events beginning in 1970, such as the deployment of U.S. combat troops in Cambodia and the shooting of students at Kent State University in Ohio by National Guardsmen during an antiwar rally, helped accelerate the organization's growth. Gradually, VVAW became more aggressive in its tactics, as organization leaders began associating with more radical groups, such as the Black Panthers. Members disrupted meetings and staged guerrilla theater events. Revelations about the My Lai massacre and other atrocities committed by U.S. forces sparked additional interest in VVAW on the part of returning soldiers disturbed by what they had witnessed in Vietnam. At one major VVAW protest in April 1971, hundreds of members marched to Arlington National Cemetery, while others gathered on the steps of the Capitol Building in Washington, D.C., to dramatically throw down the medals and ribbons they had been awarded. Congress convened hearings on the war. One of the speakers at the televised hearings was U.S. Navy veteran and Silver Star recipient John Kerry, a VVAW member who would later became a U.S. senator and the 2004 Democratic presidential nominee.

In addition to their activities aimed at ending the war, VVAW also served as a support group for veterans returning from overseas. The organization formed "rap groups," which gave veterans the opportunity to talk about their experiences in Vietnam and the problems they were facing readjusting to civilian life. By the end of 1971, membership in VVAW had begun to decline, in spite of a handful of high-profile events orchestrated by the group. More than thirty years later, VVAW was in the news once again. The organization leaped to Kerry's defense during the 2004 presidential campaign when he was attacked by a group called Swift Boat Veterans for Truth, whose members challenged Kerry's account of the events that led to his wartime honors.

---

seventy-four towns and cities, catching the American and South Vietnamese armies more or less by surprise.

From a military standpoint, the Tet offensive was a colossal failure. The Vietcong army was decimated, and they made no significant strategic gains. In the war of public opinion, however, it was a gigantic success. The attack took a heavy toll on the morale of U.S. forces, and an even heavier toll on the will of the American public to carry on with the seemingly endless effort to keep South Vietnam out of Communist hands, which a lot fewer people seemed to think was important compared to a few years earlier. The strength of the Tet offensive cast doubt on the Johnson administration's constant assertions that victory was just around the corner.

Nixon's Exit Strategy Dragged down by an unpopular war, the financial cost of which had stymied all of his ambitious domestic plans, Johnson announced that he would not seek reelection. By 1969 there were more than half a million U.S. troops fighting in Southeast Asia. Johnson's presidential successor, Richard M. Nixon (1913–1994), took a different approach, initiating a policy he called "Vietnamization," which meant gradually turning over more and more of the day-to-day fighting to the South Vietnamese army. Nixon began to slowly and systematically withdraw U.S. troops from the ground war, while simultaneously expanding the use of air attacks. He launched the most intensive bombing campaign in U.S. military history. Meanwhile, he sought to negotiate a settlement that would end the war in a way that would save face for America.

Meanwhile, opposition to the war continued to grow, fueled in part by new reports of atrocities committed by U.S. troops. The most highly publicized was the massacre of hundreds of unarmed civilians, mostly women and children, by U.S. soldiers at the tiny South Vietnamese village of My Lai in March 1968 (though the first reports of this massacre did not reach the media for more than a year). When Nixon sent troops into Cambodia in 1970 to root out Vietcong guerillas, the opposition at home reached new heights. In January 1973, Nixon and his key adviser Henry Kissinger (1923–) finally managed to negotiate a settlement that allowed the United States to complete their withdrawal from Vietnam without conceding defeat. The government of South Vietnam strongly opposed the American pullout, arguing that they were doomed without the support of U.S. troops. Their predictions were correct. In 1975—after Nixon had already been brought down by the Watergate scandal—North Vietnamese forces plowed through the South, capturing the capital city of Saigon in April of that year.

The domino theory that had been the basis for America's involvement in Vietnam to begin with turned out to be false. Rather than steamrolling across the region, communism ultimately petered out in many countries. The unified Vietnam nationalized some businesses and instituted a number of socialist reforms, but within a decade elements of capitalism began to creep into the nation's economy. By the mid-1990s, the Vietnamese economy was decidedly mixed, with private ownership of businesses on the rise, and in 1995 full diplomatic relations between the United States and Vietnam were established.

✪ Legislation, Court Cases, and Trials

The GI Bill

The GI Bill of Rights, usually referred to simply as the GI Bill, refers to two pieces of legislation for two different eras—the Servicemen's Readjustment Act of 1944, which offered World War II veterans a comprehensive package

of benefits, most notably financial assistance for college and mortgage subsidies; and the Montgomery GI Bill, passed in the 1980s to attract more volunteers into the military in the post-Vietnam era.

As the end of World War II approached, many lawmakers remembered what had happened at the end of World War I. When millions of veterans returned from service overseas in 1918, the United States entered a severe recession that cast many of these servicemen into unemployment or homelessness or both. With about twice as many veterans expected to return after World War II, there was great concern that the impact of their reintegration into the American economy would be even more disruptive than before.

Servicemen's Readjustment Act When World War II was still in progress, a number of groups began meeting to consider how to avert the economic problems

William Oskay, Jr., a student attending Pennsylvania State College under the G.I. Bill, and his family, 1946. © *Bettmann/CORBIS*

QUONSET HUTS

The GI Bill had a democratizing effect on U.S. college campuses. With the influx of millions of veterans into the higher education system after World War II, colleges and universities were suddenly no longer seen as gathering places for children of the nation's elite. While concerns about colleges being swamped with veterans were not borne out in any damaging way, there was the issue of where to house and instruct this new, oversized generation of budding scholars. The answer on many campuses was the use of prefabricated structures such as Quonset huts.

A Quonset hut is a lightweight, prefabricated building made of corrugated steel with an arched top. The structures got their name from the place where they were manufactured, the Davisville Naval Construction Battalion Center at Quonset Point in Rhode Island. Quonset huts were first used by the U.S. Navy in 1941. The navy needed a type of all-purpose structure that could be shipped easily over long distances and assembled on-site by unskilled workers. The navy awarded the contract to make the first Quonset huts to the George A. Fuller construction company; it took only two months from the day the contract was signed for the company to make their first hut.

The inside of a Quonset hut was open, so it could be configured for any of a variety of uses, from barracks to medical facilities to bakeries. During World War II, between 150,000 and 170,000 Quonset huts were manufactured. When the war was over, the government made surplus huts available to the general public for the very reasonable price of $1,000 per hut. Quonsets proved to be an ideal solution to many building challenges. They saw use as grocery stores, restaurants, churches, and, most important, as cheap shelter during the postwar housing crunch. Quonset huts put in place during the post–World War II years to house GI Bill students can still be found on many college campuses across the United States.

associated with masses of returning veterans. President Franklin Roosevelt (1882–1945) organized the National Resources Planning Board Conference on Postwar Readjustment of Civilian and Military Personnel, which held its first meeting in July 1942. The following year, the conference issued a report calling for the government to provide veterans with at least a year of education at any level. Meanwhile, another group, the Osborn Committee of the Armed Forces Committee on Postwar Educational Opportunities for Service Personnel, headed by General Frederick Osborn, was focusing on similar approaches. In the fall of 1943 the American Legion, an organization of U.S. wartime veterans, got involved in the discussion, and began crafting a comprehensive proposal that covered a wide range of needs, including health care, unemployment compensation, education and job training, and home and farm loans.

The American Legion's proposal became the Servicemen's Readjustment Act, though their public rela-

tions department quickly gave it a catchy nickname, the GI Bill of Rights. One of the bill's most vocal advocates was newspaper magnate William Randolph Hearst (1863–1951). With sponsorship from Hearst's nationwide media empire, public support for the bill mounted quickly. Both houses of Congress passed the bill unanimously in the spring of 1944, and on June 22 of that year, just days after the decisive D-day invasion at Normandy, Roosevelt signed the GI Bill into law.

The GI Bill offered veterans an impressive array of benefits. Two of the benefits that had a major impact on postwar American society were educational assistance and mortgage subsidies. Veterans were eligible to receive $500 per year for college tuition and other costs, more than adequate for a university education at the time. During 1947, at the peak of GI Bill usage, nearly half of all students on American college campuses were veterans. From the time the Servicemen's Readjustment Act was enacted in 1944 to its sunset in 1956, about 7.8 million out of the 15 million eligible veterans received education and job training with GI Bill assistance. The education and training component of the program cost the federal government a total of $14.5 billion over the twelve years it lasted. In spite of early concerns that college campuses would quickly be overrun with veterans, the program was highly successful. It brought a financial windfall for colleges and universities. It also enabled many people to attend college who otherwise would not have had the opportunity, and led to an increase in the nation's median income, and in turn increased tax revenue.

A New Middle Class The Serviceman's Readjustment Act's mortgage subsidy provision likewise had a transforming effect on American society. About 20 percent of the single-family homes built in the United States in the two decades after World War II were financed with GI Bill assistance. This supercharged demand for new housing stimulated the economy, built wealth among the nation's multiplying middle-class families, and led directly to the development of the country's suburban areas.

The Montgomery GI Bill, in contrast to the Servicemen's Readjustment Act, was enacted during a time of peace as a way to make military service more attractive to potential recruits. Unlike World War II veterans, military personnel who served in Vietnam were not generally greeted as heroes upon their return from war. Because the war had became so unpopular, the number of young adults willing to volunteer for the armed forces began to decline once the draft ended in 1973. In response to the sagging number of volunteers, Congressman G. V. (Sonny) Montgomery, a Mississippi Democrat who chaired the House Veterans Affairs Committee, proposed in 1984 a new version of the GI Bill designed to promote military service, even when the United States was not at war. President Ronald Reagan (1911–2004) signed the Montgomery GI Bill into law later that year.

Under this plan, participants could choose to have $100 deducted from their pay every month during their first year of service. In return, the government would provide up to $400 per month toward educational expenses for up to three years.

The Employment Act of 1946

The Employment Act of 1946 represented the federal government's attempt to head off a post–World War II depression by taking an active role in promoting full employment during the nation's transition back to a peacetime economy. The new law created the Council of Economic Advisers to help the president accomplish his administration's employment goals, and established the Joint Economic Committee in Congress to analyze relevant public policy strategies and proposals.

As World War II wound down, the American public and policy makers began to consider the economic challenges that lay ahead. Eleven million men were about to return from military service, and would have to be reintegrated somehow into the nation's civilian economy. Meanwhile, the American people had become accustomed to an economy stimulated by wartime production. A slowdown would remind them too much of the Great Depression that had ended just a few years earlier. Some economists were predicting massive unemployment, skeptical about the economy's ability to absorb so many returning servicemen.

Keynesian Theory Both major political parties made full employment a cornerstone of their platforms going into the 1944 election season. President Franklin Roosevelt (1882–1945), in his annual message to Congress in January 1944, talked about a new Economic Bill of Rights, which would include the "right to a useful and remunerative job." Roosevelt's thinking was strongly influenced by the work of the British economist John Maynard Keynes (1883–1946), whose groundbreaking 1936 book *The General Theory of Employment, Interest and Money* argued forcefully that governments could pull their nations out of economic depression by actively stimulating the economy through public works spending and other investment, even if it meant running a deficit budget. He rejected the traditional view that capitalism worked best when the government refrained from interfering and let the system make its own adjustments. The full mobilization of U.S. production capacity during World War II had been one of the first real-world applications of what became known as Keynesian theory.

On January 22, 1945, Senator James E. Murray (1876–1961) of Montana, chairman of the influential War Contracts Subcommittee of the Military Affairs Committee, introduced a bill calling for full employment. Murray's bill promoted the principle that everyone who was "able to work and seeking work" had the

GUNS, BUTTER, AND THE COUNCIL OF ECONOMIC ADVISERS

The Employment Act of 1946 created the Council of Economic Advisers, a three-member panel that advises the president on economic policy matters. The first chairman of the Council was Edwin G. Nourse, vice president of the Brookings Institution, a prominent Washington, D.C.–based think tank. A few years after its creation, the Council of Economic Advisers had its first quarrel over the classic "guns versus butter" debate. Nourse believed that the government had to make a choice between guns and butter, meaning that the government could invest public resources either in a strong defense or in generous domestic programs, but not both. Another member, Leon Keyserling, disagreed, arguing that in an expanding economy, the country could afford both a strong military and a high standard of living. Their disagreement came to a head in 1949. Keyserling gained the upper hand in the debate by garnering the support of two influential Truman advisers, Clark Clifford (1906–1998) and Dean Acheson (1893–1971). Nourse resigned as chairman of the council, departing with warnings about the hazards of deficit spending. He was succeeded as chairman by none other than Keyserling.

Keyserling's notion that one could have one's guns and eat one's butter too held sway in both parties for the next two decades, before the advent of stagflation in the 1970s cast doubt on the infallibility of the Keynesian approach to economic policy. By the 1980s a ballooning federal budget deficit became a hot-button political issue. Both Democrats and Republicans began to champion balanced budgets and proclaim the evil of deficit spending, though neither party had much success at crafting budgets whose combined spending on guns and butter did not exceed revenue.

right to a job, and it was the federal government's responsibility to see that this right was upheld.

No Guarantees The bill passed the Senate easily in nearly its original form, which directed the president to provide full employment when necessary through a program of public investment and expenditures on works programs. In the House of Representatives, however, the bill met with resistance from conservatives, who saw in it the seeds of socialism. They negotiated away some of what they regarded as the more offensive provisions, making sure the bill did not "guarantee" anybody a job or mandate full employment. Congress also got rid of any specific references to public works or other spending on government-created jobs, instead substituting vague language about using "all practicable means . . . to promote maximum employment, production, and purchasing power." The version of the law that eventually passed both houses did not mandate any particular action on the part of the federal government to stave off an economic slump. It did direct Congress to set up a Council of Economic Advisers, to consist of three qualified economists, which would help the president produce an annual report on the state of the economy. It also created a joint congressional committee whose assignment was to review that report and make its own recommendations. Most important, the bill articulated the federal government's commitment to playing a role in maintaining economic stability. It passed both houses of Congress easily, and was signed into law by President Harry Truman (1884–1972) on February 20, 1946.

As it happened, the postwar depression many economists had predicted did not materialize. In fact, in some ways the opposite of what was predicted took place. Instead of surplus production, there were shortages of many goods. Instead of an economic slowdown there was inflation. There was no gigantic wave of unemployment; instead, the U.S. economy entered one of its longest booms in history. Nevertheless, the logic of Keynesian theory became mainstream, and in the many brief recessions that have occurred since passage of the Employment Act of 1946, the federal government has generally reacted with some combination of increasing public works expen-

ditures, lowering interest rates, and cutting taxes, as advocated by Keynes. The Keynesian model did, however, lose some of its luster in the 1970s when the country experienced an unexpected bout of "stagflation," a previously rare combination of inflation and economic stagnation. This resulted in many conservatives, including President Ronald Reagan (1911–2004), embracing a competing theory known as "supply-side" economics.

Brown v. Board of Education

In its 1954 decision in *Brown v. Board of Education of Topeka, Kansas,* the U.S. Supreme Court held that school segregation was unconstitutional, effectively ending the "separate but equal" doctrine that had been established in the 1896 case *Plessy v. Ferguson.*

Background *Brown v. Board of Education* did not come about suddenly. It was the result of a long-term effort spearheaded by the National Association for the Advancement of Colored People (NAACP) beginning as early as the 1930s to attack school segregation across the South. Leading the charge was NAACP lawyer and future U.S. Supreme Court Justice Thurgood Marshall (1908–1993). The NAACP coordinated separate lawsuits in five states:

Arkansas National Guard troops outside Little Rock High School to halt enforcement of court-ordered racial desegregation, 1957.
© *CORBIS*

Elizabeth Eckford, one of the nine African-American students whose admission to Little Rock's Central High was ordered by a federal court, 1957. © AP/Wide World Photos

Maryland, Kansas, Virginia, South Carolina, and Delaware. The suits charged that forcing children to attend segregated schools violated their right to equal protection under the law as guaranteed by the Fourteenth Amendment to the Constitution.

Oliver Brown was a railroad employee who lived with his family in Topeka, Kansas. The Browns lived near a major railroad switchyard, which the Brown children had to cross every day in order to attend an all-black school. Brown was unhappy that because of their race his children were not allowed to attend another school that was much closer to home.

When his daughter Linda was entering third grade in the fall of 1950, Brown took her to the nearby whites-only school to attempt to enroll her. Not surprisingly, the principal refused to allow her to attend. Brown, who had no history of civil rights activism up to that time, decided to take action, and approached the head of the local branch of the NAACP for help. NAACP lawyers representing Brown filed a suit in the U.S. District Court on March 22, 1951. The District Court decided against Brown, and he filed an appeal.

Meanwhile, parallel suits were being filed in other states. The U.S. Supreme Court decided in 1952 to consolidate the suits into a single case. After hearing initial arguments in June of that year, the Supreme Court put the case on hold, requesting that both sides reargue their cases the following year with specific regard to the original intent and history of the Fourteenth Amendment as it pertained to educational institutions. The NAACP's Marshall argued before the Court that racially segregated schools were not and could never be made "equal," suggesting that segregation could be upheld only if the Court were "to find that for some reason Negroes are inferior to all other human beings."

Unanimous Decision Marshall's argument struck a chord with the justices. They decided unanimously against segregation, erasing the half-century-old "separate but equal" doctrine that had been established in *Plessy v. Ferguson.* Writing for the Court, Earl Warren (1891–1974), who had just replaced Fred Vinson (1890–1953) as chief justice, opined that "in the field of public education the doctrine of 'separate but equal' has no place." While the Court's ruling meant schools could no longer legally keep the races separate, the decision did not offer a remedy to the situation. In 1955 the Supreme Court issued a supplemental opinion, known as *Brown II*, which considered the challenges of desegregating the nation's thousands of segregated school districts. Instead of ordering all schools to instantly desegregate, the Court called on local districts to implement their own desegregation plans in good faith "with all deliberate speed."

The impact of *Brown v. Board of Education* was explosive. The Supreme Court had ruled segregation unconstitutional, but attitudes about race do not change overnight. Many school districts across the nation—not just in the South—initially refused to abide by the new reality brought about by *Brown*. This resistance led to numerous delays in implementing *Brown;* in fact, even a decade after the decision was handed down, fewer than 1 percent of public schools in the South had been desegregated. In many cities, riots erupted when African-American students tried to enroll in previously all-white schools as the Court had ordered. The standoff reached a boiling point in 1957 in Little Rock, Arkansas, when President Dwight D. Eisenhower (1890–1969) was forced to call in the military to overcome Arkansas governor Orval Faubus's blockade of the entrance to Central High School. It took at least another decade for school desegregation to truly penetrate a substantial portion of the Deep South.

Brown v. Board of Education marked a monumental turning point for the civil rights movement. Never again would racial segregation in any institution, be it a school district, a business, or other public facilities, be taken for granted. One by one, segregation in other kinds of institutions—from libraries to public restrooms—was shot down by a series of landmark Supreme Court decisions over the years that followed. Demographic shifts in the nation's major cities made school desegregation increasingly difficult to accomplish in the decades that followed, as white families fled to the suburbs and urban areas themselves grew more segregated. Nevertheless, the principle that the Constitution supports intentional efforts to eradicate segregation has remained a powerful force in social policy.

See also **The Civil Rights Movement**
See also **Thurgood Marshall**

The Exclusionary Rule

The exclusionary rule dictates that any evidence obtained by police or other government agents through an illegal search in violation of the Fourth Amendment to the Constitution is inadmissible in court during a criminal trial. The U.S. Supreme Court affirmed the exclusionary rule with regard to federal courts in 1914—though the central issues were raised as early as 1886—but not until 1961 did the Court extend the rule to apply to courts and law enforcement officials at all levels, from federal down to local.

The main purpose of the exclusionary rule is to deter police misconduct. Before the exclusionary rule came into practice, police had little reason to pay atten-

tion to the Fourth Amendment, which protects people against the unreasonable search for and seizure of evidence. Even if the evidence was gathered illegally, it could still be used in criminal trials. The method through which the evidence was obtained did not matter, as long as the evidence itself was relevant to the case. The defendant had no way of stopping the government from using this evidence; he or she could seek a remedy only through other channels, such as a lawsuit against the officers or agents for damages caused by their misconduct.

Weeks v. United States   The Supreme Court addressed this situation in 1914 with its ruling in the case of *Weeks v. United States*. In that case, a federal agent had conducted a warrantless search of the home of Fremont Weeks, who was suspected of violating gambling laws. The evidence found in the search helped convict Weeks, who then appealed the verdict on the grounds that the Fourth Amendment prohibited the use of evidence obtained via a warrantless search. The Supreme Court agreed with Weeks. His conviction was overturned, and the exclusionary rule was born.

Because the Supreme Court's decision in *Weeks* applied only to federal courts, however, state courts were free to continue considering evidence that had been obtained illegally. Moreover, there remained a loophole for federal courts as well. Through what was called the "silver platter doctrine," a federal court could still legally use illegally secured evidence if the evidence had been obtained by a state or local agent and then subsequently handed over to federal officials on a "silver platter." So as long as it was not a federal officer who violated the Fourth Amendment, the evidence was still admissible in court.

The Supreme Court revisited the issue in the early 1950s. In *Rochin v. California* (1952), the Court held that evidence was inadmissible if the manner in which it was obtained was an egregious violation of the Fourth Amendment. In this case, the defendant's stomach had been pumped in order to retrieve evidence that he had used illegal drugs. This ruling made clear that if officials' actions were offensive enough, they would be punished by having the evidence thrown out. Even after this ruling, however, states could still use evidence obtained illegally in all but the most wanton instances, and the silver platter doctrine still allowed federal courts to use evidence obtained illegally by state agents regardless of whether the search had violated Fourth Amendment protections. The Supreme Court finally did away with the silver platter doctrine in 1960 with its ruling in the case *Elkins v. United States,* though a vestige of the doctrine pertaining to evidence seized by foreign officials remained intact.

Mapp v. Ohio   It was not until its 1961 decision in *Mapp v. Ohio* that the Supreme Court effectively extended the exclusionary rule to apply to all state criminal prosecutions. In that case, Cleveland police suspected that Dollree Mapp was harboring the perpetrator of a firebombing. They arrived at her home and demanded entry, which she refused. The police forced their way in, handcuffed her, and proceeded to search the home without a warrant. They did not find the firebombing suspect, but they did find a pornography collection that allegedly violated obscenity laws. Mapp was arrested, convicted, and sentenced to seven years in prison. After the Ohio Supreme Court upheld the case, she appealed to the U.S. Supreme Court. In overturning the conviction, the Supreme Court established that the exclusionary rule applied to criminal proceedings at the state level.

In most cases, the exclusionary rule is invoked by defendants in a hearing before the presiding judge, at which they request to have evidence suppressed on the grounds that it was obtained through an illegal search. Within the exclusionary rule resides what is called the "fruit of the poisonous tree" doctrine, which requires that any evidence obtained on the basis of information or other evidence that was obtained through an illegal search is also inadmissible. In other words, violating the Fourth Amendment in a search "poisons" any evidence that follows from anything discovered in the original breach.

More recently, the exclusionary rule has been diluted and its applications narrowed. In 1984 the Supreme Court established a "good faith" exception to the rule, meaning that if the police's violation was inadvertent, then the evidence may be admissible. Subsequent decisions have carved out a variety of other exceptions, as the balance between individuals' right to privacy and the investigative needs of law enforcement continues to evolve.

The Clean Air Acts

As public awareness of environmental issues rose sharply in the 1960s, a series of laws was passed that promoted air pollution research, regulated vehicle and factory emissions, and created standards for air quality. Current U.S. policy regarding efforts to control air pollution is grounded in the Clean Air Act of 1970, as updated through major amendments in 1977 and 1990. Nevertheless, Congress has been passing laws aimed at protecting air quality since the 1950s, and local efforts at tackling air pollution go back as far as the late nineteenth century.

Some of the nation's earliest efforts to control air pollution include laws passed in 1881 in Chicago, Illinois, and Cincinnati, Ohio, to curb industrial smoke and soot. Other cities soon followed suit, and such laws were soon common in major industrial hubs. The first statewide air pollution control program was launched in Oregon in 1952. The federal government became involved in nationwide air quality control for the first time three years later, when Congress passed the Air

Pollution Control Act of 1955, which did not do much to actually improve air quality, but granted $5 million a year for five years to the U.S. Public Health Service to conduct research on the problem. Congress extended the program for another four years in 1960.

Clean Air Act of 1963 The first version of the Clean Air Act was enacted in 1963. This act provided a permanent stream of federal funding—initially $95 million over three years—for pollution research and support for states to set up their own pollution control agencies. The Clean Air Act of 1963 also included language recognizing the hazards of exhaust fumes from automobiles, and called for the development of auto emissions standards for the first time. In addition, the act encouraged research on new technologies to remove sulfur from fuels with high sulfur content, whose use was degrading air quality, with the federal government taking responsibility for these sorts of interstate pollution issues.

While passage of the Clean Air Act was an important step, guidelines developed by the U.S. Department of Health, Education, and Welfare (HEW) pertaining to motor vehicle emissions were still merely advisory; state and local agencies were not obligated to enforce them. In 1964 HEW published a report called *Steps toward Clean Air*, which made a strong case for mandatory emissions standards. A new Senate Subcommittee on Air and Water Pollution was created, with Democratic Senator Edmund Muskie (1914–1996) of Maine as its chair. With public awareness of the problem growing quickly, the first amendments to the Clean Air Act were passed in 1965, in the form of the Motor Vehicle Air Pollution Control Act. This act established nationwide motor vehicle emissions standards, to be administered by HEW; the Environmental Protection Agency (EPA) would not come into existence for another five years. Reactions to the Motor Vehicle Air Pollution Control Act were mixed. On the one hand, auto companies were predictably horrified, because they would for the first time be required to adapt their technology to meet environmental mandates. Consumer advocate Ralph Nader (1934–), on the other hand, criticized the new law as being too lenient.

Another batch of amendments to the Clean Air Act was passed in 1967. This legislation, called the Air Quality Act, divided the nation into Air Quality Control Regions for monitoring purposes. It also set a timetable for states to develop "state implementation plans" for meeting new standards for emissions from stationary sources, such as factories and fuel-processing facilities.

Clean Air Act of 1970 The Clean Air Act of 1970 represented a complete rewriting of the air pollution control laws that had been passed during the previous decade. It dramatically changed the nation's approach to addressing the problem of air pollution, and established the backbone of the air pollution control systems that have remained in place ever since. Championed by Senator Muskie and President Richard M. Nixon (1913–1994), the Clean Air Act of 1970 shifted primary responsibility for air quality control from the states to the federal government, though states were charged with monitoring and enforcing compliance.

There were four key components to the regulatory structure established by the 1970 act. First, it created National Ambient Air Quality Standards for six major categories of pollutants. Second, the newly created EPA was to set New Source Performance Standards for determining how much pollution new plants would be allowed to produce. Third, it instituted new motor vehicle emissions standards. Finally, it required states to produce implementation plans, to be approved by the EPA, outlining how they would go about meeting all these new federal guidelines.

The next round of substantial amendments to the Clean Air Act took place in 1977. One main purpose of the 1977 amendments was to address the widespread failure of industries, including automobile manufacturers, to meet the deadlines set out in the 1970 act. These deadlines were extended, but other, more stringent standards were put into place as well. One new feature was the addition of a program for prevention of significant deterioration of air that was already clean, such as in some national parks.

No substantial changes in the Clean Air Act were made during the 1980s, as the administration of President Ronald Reagan (1911–2004) opposed any strengthening of environmental regulations that might negatively impact the growth of American industry. In 1990, however, a new version of the Clean Air Act was passed. The Clean Air Act of 1990 addressed some new topics that had come to the fore in the years since the last round of amendments, including acid rain and ozone layer depletion. In 2003 Republicans in the House and Senate introduced the Clear Skies Act, which would weaken some of the Clean Air Act's standards. The Clear Skies Act failed to garner enough support to pass through Congress; even without new legislation, however, some of its features were implemented administratively through the EPA.

Sex Discrimination in Employment: Title VII

While the Civil Rights Act of 1964 is best known for its impact on racial discrimination, Title VII of the act also included language prohibiting employment discrimination on the basis of gender. This legislation marked a critical step forward in the movement toward equal opportunity for women in the United States.

For generations, men had traditionally been the primary breadwinners in American families, while women were in charge of the home and children. World War II changed the employment landscape for women, however, as they moved into the workplace to perform jobs formerly held by the men who were now overseas fighting the war. During the war, the National War Labor Board recommended that women be paid the same wages as men. However, equal compensation was a completely voluntary policy, and most employers did not comply.

Equal Pay Act   During the early 1960s President John F. Kennedy (1917–1963) and his associates had worked hard to produce a sweeping bill that would outlaw once and for all various forms of employment discrimination. One result was the Equal Pay Act of 1963, which amended the Fair Labor Standards Act of 1938. The Equal Pay Act essentially made it illegal to pay women less than men for doing the same work.

The Civil Rights Act of 1964 added a number of protections against gender-based employment discrimination, and the presence of sex as a protected class in Title VII of the act played an interesting role in the law's passage. As originally drafted, Title VII prohibited employment discrimination on the basis of race, color, religion, and national origin. It did not cover gender discrimination.

In February 1964 Congressman Howard Smith, the powerful Virginia Democrat who chaired the House Rules Committee, offered an amendment to the bill that added sex as a prohibited basis for employment discrimination. Many observers were baffled, as Smith had been a longtime opponent of civil rights legislation. Some supporters of the bill believed he was trying to sabotage it by adding language about sex discrimination in order to smash apart the bipartisan consensus required to pass the bill. The bill's sponsors opposed Smith's amendment, thinking the bill should focus exclusively on matters of race. Labor unions, many of which had a history of discrimination against women, were not happy about the amendment either.

Possible Poison Pill   Smith may not have had an ulterior motive. While he was no friend to the civil rights movement historically, he had a longstanding alliance with feminist leader Alice Paul (1884–1977), and had always been a supporter of the Equal Rights Amendment. He recognized the Civil Rights Act as a potential vehicle for advancing some of the women's rights he believed in. Regardless of Smith's motives, it is clear that many other Southern Democrats viewed Smith's amendment as an opportunity to scuttle the bill; most of them supported adoption of the amendment. The amendment was adopted on a vote of 164 to 133.

Most of the Democrats from the South who had supported Smith's amendment ended up voting against the full bill, which would seem to confirm that they had hoped the sex discrimination provision would be a "poison pill." The bill passed anyway, and the Civil Rights Act, with Title VII expanded to included gender discrimination, was enacted on July 2, 1964. Title VII empowered the Equal Employment Opportunity Commission to enforce the act's prohibitions against employment discrimination.

In the years since passage of the Civil Rights Act, Title VII has been expanded a few times. In 1986 the U.S. Supreme Court ruled in the case *Meritor Savings Bank v. Vinson* that women had the right to protection from a "hostile work environment." Later expansions protected women from discrimination based on pregnancy and broadened the definition of sexual harassment in the workplace.

Griswold v. Connecticut

The 1965 U.S. Supreme Court case *Griswold v. Connecticut* affirmed married couples' right to privacy in the bedroom. Specifically, this case determined that a Connecticut law preventing married couples from using birth control was unconstitutional. This outcome resulted in all state laws on the books prohibiting the use of contraceptives by married couples being struck down. It also set the stage for other landmark sexual privacy rulings that followed over the next decade, including *Eisenstadt v. Baird* (1972), which upheld the right of unmarried people to use birth control, and *Roe v. Wade* (1973), which made abortion legal.

Background Connecticut passed a law in 1879 making it illegal to use any kind of birth control drug or device, regardless of whether the use was by a married couple. In addition it became illegal to provide medical advice or information having to do with birth control. A number of other states passed similar laws around that time. By the middle of the twentieth century, the law was hopelessly out of date and rarely enforced. It nevertheless remained on the books in spite of its unpopularity. In 1942 the Planned Parenthood League of Connecticut, a group involved in public education about birth control, attempted to challenge the law in the U.S. Supreme Court. In that case, the appellant was a doctor, and the Court ruled that he did not have standing to sue, as he himself was not harmed by his inability to dispense, or advise patients about, birth control.

Another attempt to bring down the law was made in 1961, when a group of women brought suit. This time, the Court refused to decide the case (*Poe v. Ullman*) on the grounds that it was never enforced, calling it "dead words" and "harmless empty shadows." Not all members of the Court felt this way, however. In his dissenting opinion, Justice John Marshall Harlan (1899–1971) wrote that the law represented an "unjustifiable invasion of privacy," and should therefore be struck down.

In November 1961, four months after the Supreme Court's nondecision in the *Poe* case, Estelle Griswold, executive director of the Planned Parenthood League of Connecticut, and Dr. Charles Lee Buxton, chairman of Yale University's obstetrics department, opened a birth control clinic in New Haven, Connecticut. They contended that by declaring the law dead, the Supreme Court's language in the *Poe* case made it legal for doctors in Connecticut to prescribe birth control. However, nine days later, their clinic was closed and the two were arrested.

Conviction Leads to Test Case Both Griswold and Buxton were convicted at trial in the Sixth Connecticut Circuit Court, in spite of defense attorney Catherine Roraback's argument that the Connecticut birth control law violated her clients' constitutionally protected right to freedom of speech. They were each fined $100. The convictions were upheld in both the Appellate Division of the Sixth Connecticut Circuit Court and the State Supreme Court of Errors. In both cases, the courts held that it was the legislature's job, not theirs, to change a bad law. This set the stage for the case's arrival on the U.S. Supreme Court docket.

Oral arguments before the Supreme Court began on March 29, 1964. Attorney Thomas Emerson, a Yale law professor, argued on behalf of Griswold and Buxton that Connecticut's birth control law deprived his clients of their First Amendment right to free speech, as well as their Fourteenth Amendment right to liberty, which could not be abridged without "due process of law," and their right to privacy as guaranteed by the Ninth Amendment. Emerson also asserted that the Connecticut law was based on a moral judgment—the notion that the use of contraceptives is immoral even within a marital relationship—that did not "conform to current community standards."

Thomas Clark, the attorney for the State of Connecticut, was repeatedly called on to explain the purpose of the law. He maintained that the law was put into place in order to deter sex outside of marriage. He found it difficult, however, to explain (1) why then the law should apply to married couples; and (2) why the law was necessary when there were already laws on the books prohibiting fornication and adultery.

Supreme Court Reversal The Supreme Court voted 7–2 to reverse the convictions of Griswold and Buxton, vaporizing the 1879 Connecticut law in the process. In his majority opinion, Justice William O. Douglas (1898–1980) wrote that enforcing laws such as the Connecticut birth control ban represented a gross violation of the right to privacy, presumably guaranteed by the Ninth Amendment, which reads: "The enumeration in the Constitution, of certain rights, shall not be construed to deny or disparage others retained by the people." In other words, just because the Constitution does not specifically mention the right to use birth control in the privacy of one's own home does not mean that the government can search your bedroom for evidence of contraceptives if it sees fit to do so.

The *Griswold* case marked a significant change in the way the Ninth Amendment had historically been

PLANNED PARENTHOOD OF CONNECTICUT

Planned Parenthood of Connecticut was founded in 1923 by Mrs. Thomas N. Hepburn—mother of the actress Katharine Hepburn—and a few of her friends. After attending a speaking engagement in Hartford, Connecticut, that year by birth control advocate and Planned Parenthood pioneer Margaret Sanger (1879–1966), the group decided to launch the Connecticut Birth Control League. One of their main objectives was to get their state's law banning the use of and dissemination of information about birth control overturned. Connecticut's law was one of several state laws collectively known as Comstock Laws, named after Anthony Comstock (1844–1915), who had gotten similar laws passed in several states in the 1870s.

In spite of the group's efforts and the growth of their organization, their nine attempts to get the state legislature to change the law between 1923 and 1931 all failed. Nevertheless, the Birth Control League opened the state's first birth control center in Hartford in 1935, and by the end of that decade had opened clinics in nine other cities as well. The clinic in Waterbury, Connecticut, was raided by police six months after it opened, and two doctors and a nurse were arrested. Their defense attorneys argued that the state's Comstock Law was unconstitutional, but the Connecticut Supreme Court upheld the law in its 1940 ruling. The league continued to attack the law through litigation, but was unsuccessful until *Griswold v. Connecticut* presented an ideal test case with which to directly challenge the law.

By the time the *Griswold* case was decided, Planned Parenthood of Connecticut was serving about 300 women a year. In 2004 the organization provided medical services to more than 58,000 individuals, and provided information to over 16,000 people through its public education and outreach programs.

interpreted. Prior to 1964 it had usually been interpreted to mean that any right not specifically granted to the federal government by the Constitution fell by default into the domain of state government. The interpretation articulated by Douglas was more literal, reserving such rights "to the people" as per the actual language of the amendment.

This expanded interpretation of the right to privacy laid the groundwork for two important challenges over the next several years to state laws restricting people's reproductive behavior. In 1972 the Supreme Court ruled in the case *Eisenstadt v. Baird* that single people had the right to buy and use contraceptives. Writing for the majority, Justice William Brennan (1906–1997) pointed to the line of reasoning first outlined in *Griswold* as the basis for the decision. If the Ninth Amendment protected the privacy of married people, he noted, then it should also apply to nonmarried people, because it is actually the *individuals* making up the marriage with whom the right resides. Brennan opined that being married is not a prerequisite to freedom from "unwarranted governmental intrusion into matters so fundamentally affecting a person as the decision whether to bear or beget a child."

The following year, similar reasoning was used to extend this right of privacy to include a woman's right to choose to terminate a pregnancy in the controversial case *Roe v. Wade*.

New York Times v. Sullivan

In its ruling on the landmark case *New York Times v. Sullivan*, the U.S. Supreme Court changed the rules regarding what constituted libel in statements made by the media about public figures. Prior to *Sullivan*, standards for libel cases were determined at the state level. False statements about public figures were not generally considered to be free speech protected by the First Amendment to the Constitution, but each state was free to interpret libel laws as its leaders saw fit. This case limited states' authority to award libel damages, putting in place a national standard requiring the presence of "actual malice" for determining libel cases that involved public figures. In granting new protections to the press, *Sullivan* fundamentally changed the way the U.S. media dealt with controversial issues. Because they no longer had to fear a costly libel suit for inadvertently getting a fact wrong about a public figure, newspapers and other media outlets were able to go after perceived wrongdoers more aggressively than in the past.

Background   The events leading to *Sullivan* took place in the context of the civil rights movement. In 1960 Martin Luther King Jr. (1929–1968) and other civil rights leaders were engaged in a series of antisegregation protests in Montgomery, Alabama. Officials in Montgomery reacted strongly to the protests, and acted aggressively to thwart them. In March of that year, a group calling itself the Committee to Defend Martin Luther King and the Struggle for Freedom in the South took out a full-page advertisement in the *New York Times* that asked readers to contribute money to support their civil rights efforts. The ad, running under the headline "Heed Their Rising Voices" and signed by sixty-four prominent political, religious, and artistic leaders, was published in the March 29 edition of the *Times*, of which six hundred thousand copies were printed.

The ad claimed that state and local officials in Alabama had responded with a "wave of terror" to peaceful demonstrations by thousands of African-American students in the South. Events supporting this charge were described, but the ad did not mention any particular public official by name.

When Montgomery city commissioner L. B. Sullivan, who supervised the city's police department, heard about the ad, he was outraged. On April 19 he filed a libel suit against the *Times*, claiming that the ad's reference to

Police Commissioner L.B. Sullivan (second from left) with his attorneys after winning a $500,000 libel judgment against the *New York Times* in 1960. That judgment would be reversed by the U.S. Supreme Court four years later. © *Bettmann/CORBIS*

"Southern violators of the Constitution" in Montgomery had unjustly defamed him. His suit asked for $500,000 in damages. During the trial, Sullivan was able to establish that the ad contained a number of inaccurate statements about the events that had taken place. The judge instructed the jury that under Alabama law, it did not matter whether Sullivan had suffered any financial loss, and that if the statements were found to be libelous, then malice was presumed to be present. Therefore, the jury really had to decide only whether the ad actually concerned Sullivan, which was not clear because he was not specifically mentioned in it.

Circuit Court Ruling On November 3, the circuit court in Montgomery ruled in favor of Sullivan, and awarded him the full $500,000. The Alabama Supreme Court upheld this decision in 1962, applying an extremely broad definition of libel. The court wrote: "Where the words published tend to injure a person libeled by them in his reputation, profession, trade or business, or charge him with an indictable offense, or tends to bring the individual into public contempt [they] are libelous per se.... We hold that the matter complained of is, under the above doctrine, libelous per se."

The *Times* appealed the Alabama Supreme Court's ruling, and the case moved up to the U.S. Supreme Court. In unanimously overturning the Alabama court's decision, the Supreme Court on March 9, 1964, established a totally new standard for libel in cases concerning public officials. In his opinion, Justice William J. Brennan (1906–1997) wrote: "We hold that the rule of law applied by the Alabama courts is constitutionally deficient for failure to provide the safeguards for freedom of speech and of the press that are required by the First [Amendment] in a libel action brought by a public official against critics of his official conduct." Brennan went on to write that in order to succeed in such a libel case, the public official must prove that the statement was made with "actual malice," defining actual malice as "knowledge that it was false or with reckless disregard of whether it was false or not." Clearly, Sullivan had not proven that the *Times* acted with actual malice as so defined.

This new libel standard, applicable to every state, placed a much heavier burden on public officials seeking to sue for libel. The Supreme Court's position was that the press must be free to criticize the actions of officials related to controversial matters—such as civil rights—of great importance to the public, without fear of facing a suit just for getting a few minor facts wrong.

A Victory for Freedom of Press The Supreme Court's decision in *New York Times v. Sullivan* marked a major shift in the law's attitude toward the press. For the first time, the law was willing to look the other way on certain types of falsehoods published in the press, on the grounds that the importance of the free exchange of ideas far outweighed the damage caused by inevitable, inadvertent errors. In the "absence of malice," public officials cannot recover damages from those who publish false statements about them.

While the Court's decision was unanimous, not all of the justices agreed entirely with Brennan's thoughts on the case. Justices Hugo Black (1886–1971) and William O. Douglas (1898–1980), in separate concurring opinions, questioned whether the press should *ever* be held liable for defaming public officials. Their interpretation of the freedom of the press provisions in the First Amendment led to the conclusion that the press must be absolutely immune from liability for criticizing how public officials perform their duties.

In the years following the *Sullivan* decision, a sequence of decisions in other cases helped hash out such lingering questions as who is a public official, what constitutes official conduct as opposed to private conduct, and where the line should be drawn regarding the right of public figures to keep personal information private. Throughout this thread of cases, the Court made sure the new libel rules were applied effectively, and issued rulings that gave the press even more latitude. In *Rosenblatt v. Baer* (1966), the Court extended the *Sullivan* rule to public officials of lesser stature, and the following year, in *Associated Press v. Walker*, the rule was further stretched to cover not just public officials, but public figures outside the realm of government service. Over the years, the position on libel staked out by *Sullivan* has come under criticism from both directions. Public officials derided the policy for making it too difficult to recover damages from libel, while the news media have argued that because the ruling did not go far enough they are still subject to long, costly litigation, even though they usually win.

See also **William Brennan**

The Food Stamp Act of 1964

The Food Stamp Act of 1964 created a permanent food stamp program in the United States that assists poor families with food purchases, while also supporting the nation's farmers by boosting consumption of agricultural products. The Food Stamp Act was a central piece of President Lyndon B. Johnson's (1908–1973) social agenda known as the "Great Society." The stated goals of the act were to "strengthen the agricultural economy; to help achieve a fuller and more effective use of food abundances; [and] to provide for improved levels of nutrition among low-income households through a cooperative Federal-State program of food assistance to be operated through normal channels of trade."

Food Stamp Origins The origins of the food stamp program were in the Great Depression, as the federal government sought to counter overproduction by raising the amount of agricultural goods Americans consumed. The U.S. Department of Agriculture (USDA) saw the program as a way to address two crucial problems—low demand for farm products and increasing hunger among the poor and

Food stamps, 1991. © *Charles O'Rear/CORBIS*

unemployed—with a single government initiative. The first food stamp program was launched in Rochester, New York, in 1939. It spread to about fifteen hundred other counties before the economic upswing triggered by World War II made the program less necessary.

Over the next twenty years, various advocates proposed reviving the food stamp program, but the federal government made no move to do so. The idea finally took hold in 1960. While campaigning in parts of the poverty-stricken Appalachian Mountains that year, John F. Kennedy (1917–1963) witnessed firsthand the prevalence of severe hunger in the region. After he was elected president, Kennedy instructed the USDA to establish food stamp pilot programs. The first of these test programs was set up in McCowell County, West Virginia, in May 1961.

The idea behind food stamps is to create a mechanism—namely the stamps—for transferring surplus food grown by farmers to the people who need the food but cannot afford it. Rather than subsidizing farmers directly, food stamps provide a way to increase demand for food at stores, which in turn translates into increased

FOOD STAMP FRAUD

Since the food stamp program was first implemented, policy makers have always been concerned about fraud and abuse. In the decades since the Food Stamp Act was passed, Congress has tweaked the rules on a number of occasions to make it harder for people to cheat the program. In reality, only a tiny percentage of food stamp recipients have engaged in fraud or abuse. However, when it comes to entitlement programs, lawmakers and the media have always tended to play up such activities when they are uncovered.

There are two basic kinds of fraud that people engage in with regard to the food stamp program: providing false information when applying for the program in order to cheat on the eligibility restrictions; and trafficking in food stamp coupons for financial gain. The first type of cheating is relatively straightforward to address by requiring people to document their information more thoroughly when applying for the program. However, some advocates who work on behalf of the poor are against making it more burdensome to apply for food stamps. They argue that many people who need financial assistance have limited education and poor literacy skills, and that making the application process more complicated will prevent some eligible families from receiving assistance that they desperately need. According to this view, because the incidence of fraud is fairly low, it is better to allow a few cases of fraud to go undetected than to create unnecessary barriers to enrollment for those who legitimately qualify.

The other type of abuse is more difficult to address. Some stores illegally allow people to use food stamps for nonfood purchases, in violation of program rules. These stores usually give the customer only partial value for their food stamps. For example, they might allow somebody to use $5 in food stamps to cover $3 toward the purchase of laundry detergent or magazines. According to the federal government's Food and Nutrition Service (FNS), this sort of practice is much more common in small stores than in large ones. While only about 15 percent of food stamps are redeemed in small grocery stores, those stores accounted for about $190 million in food stamp fraud in 2005.

One recent development that is helping to eliminate this type of abuse is the replacement of paper food stamp coupons with an electronic benefits transfer (EBT) system, which works a lot like bank-issued debit cards. EBT has a lot of advantages. Besides helping to cut back on fraud, EBT also reduces the problem of food stamp theft, because a personal identification number is needed to use an EBT card. According to the FNS, about $241 million in food stamp benefits were stolen in 2005.

purchases of crops from farmers. The food stamp pilot programs were very successful in achieving this objective.

When Johnson inherited the presidency after the assassination of Kennedy, he prepared an ambitious agenda of social programs he referred to collectively as the Great Society. Johnson's Great Society initiative encompassed a range of programs designed to solve the problem of poverty. He aimed to improve access to health care, job training, education, and a variety of other services crucial to disadvantaged families. Johnson made food stamps one of his Great Society programs. The Food Stamp Act, which would make food stamps a permanent, nationwide program, was introduced into Congress with strong bipartisan support, as well as the backing of the USDA, the National Farmers Union, and a host of poverty groups. It was enacted on August 31, 1964.

Federal-State Partnership Like the Depression-era version of the program, the new food stamp program had two constituencies: poor people and farmers. The program was a collaborative effort between federal and state governments. The USDA distributed the stamps through state welfare offices, and recipients could then spend them almost like cash at their local grocery stores (certain items, such as alcohol, were excluded). The federal government was responsible for reimbursing stores for the value of the stamps, while state agencies handled eligibility determination and distribution. The cost of administering the program was shared between the two levels of government.

In the years following passage of the Food Stamp Act, the program evolved. For one thing, poverty was becoming more of an urban problem. The USDA adapted to the changing demographics of hunger by transforming food stamps from a way of disposing of the nation's agricultural surplus while feeding the hungry to more of a straightforward welfare program. Eligibility requirements were loosened, and benefits increased. The Food Stamp Reform Bill of 1970 solidified and standardized these changes in eligibility rules and nutritional standards. Additional legislation in 1973 made food stamps an entitlement program, meaning states must offer it to anybody who is eligible. As the 1970s continued, however, the food stamp program, and many other assistance programs, came under increased criticism for being lax in their detection of fraud and abuse. The Food Stamp Act of 1977 tightened eligibility standards and established more rigid guidelines for administering the program.

Criticism of assistance programs grew more insistent during the 1980s, as the administration of President Ronald Reagan (1911–2004) sought to reduce federal spending on assistance for the poor. Concerns were raised that easy access to benefits was functioning as a disincentive to work and was attracting illegal immigrants. This growing hostility culminated in the 1996 passage of the Personal Responsibility and Work Opportunity Reconciliation Act (PRWORA), sometimes referred to as the Welfare Reform Act. While food stamps remained an entitlement program, PRWORA ushered in an assortment of policies designed to shrink enrollment in public assistance programs, shifting the burden of aiding families in crisis from government agencies to private charities and food banks.

See also **Lyndon B. Johnson**

Heart of Atlanta Motel v. United States

The U.S. Supreme Court's decision in *Heart of Atlanta Motel v. United States*—the first major test of the Civil Rights Act of 1964—advanced the cause of the civil rights movement by affirming that the federal government's power to regulate interstate commerce could be used to combat racial discrimination. This landmark case upheld the constitutionality of Title II of the act, which guaranteed minorities full access to places of public accommodation.

Civil Rights Act Challenged The Heart of Atlanta Motel was a 216-room facility in downtown Atlanta, Georgia. Prior to passage of the Civil Rights Act of 1964, the Heart of Atlanta consistently refused to rent rooms to African-Americans. The ownership of the motel hoped to continue their whites-only policy, so they filed a lawsuit in the U.S. District Court for the Northern District of Georgia, in which they contended that Title II of the act violated their constitutional rights. Heart of Atlanta also filed for an injunction to prevent the government from enforcing the provision dealing with public accommodations.

In the suit, lawyers for the Heart of Atlanta made several arguments. They claimed above all that Congress had overstepped its power under the Commerce Clause—which gives Congress the ability to regulate interstate commerce—by seeking to regulate local private businesses such as their motel. They also argued that the act violated the Fifth Amendment, which prohibits the taking of liberty and property without due process of law, by depriving the motel's operators of their right to choose customers as they saw fit.

The federal government counter sued, asking that the act be enforced and the motel be forced to stop discriminating against African-Americans. Lawyers for the government contended that refusing to provide accommodations to African-Americans interfered with interstate commerce by making it harder for them to travel on business. Noting that some three-quarters of the motel's clients were from out of state, the government argued that this situation was clearly covered by the Commerce Clause.

Commerce Clause The District Court ruled against the Heart of Atlanta, and ordered the operators to stop denying service to African-Americans solely on the basis of their race. The motel appealed the decision, and the U.S. Supreme Court agreed to hear the case. In December 1964 the Supreme Court ruled unanimously against the Heart of Atlanta, upholding the constitutionality of Title II of the Civil Rights Act. In his opinion, Justice Tom C. Clark (1899–1977) wrote, based on transcripts of Congressional debate over the Civil Rights Act, that the discrimination African-Americans faced when they tried to find accommodations clearly "had the effect of discouraging travel on the part of a substantial portion of the Negro community." The evidence, he continued, was "overwhelming ... that discrimination by hotels and motels impedes interstate travel," which in turn impedes interstate commerce. He noted that the authority of Congress under the Commerce Clause of the Constitution to intervene in order to keep interstate commerce flowing freely had been long established.

Clark further argued that the Commerce Clause allowed Congress to regulate not only interstate commerce, but also to regulate commerce within a state if that commercial activity had a harmful effect on interstate commerce. So however "local" the Heart of Atlanta's discriminatory policies seemed, they were fair game for regulation by the federal government if they stopped African-Americans from traveling for purposes of interstate commerce.

In the aftermath of the Supreme Court's decision in *Heart of Atlanta Motel v. United States*, the Commerce Clause became an important weapon for the federal government to wield in its efforts to eliminate racial discrimination nationwide. In another case decided the same day, *Katzenbach v. McClung*, the Court gave a similar rationale in deciding against a small restaurant that did not serve African-Americans. According to the Court, because the restaurant purchased some of its food and supplies from out of state, it was engaging in interstate commerce, and was therefore subject to the Commerce Clause. That most of its customers were local was deemed irrelevant.

See also **The Civil Rights Movement**

Medicare and Medicaid

As part of his Great Society package of domestic programs, President Lyndon B. Johnson (1908–1973) signed into law two important government health-care programs in 1965: Medicare, which provides health insurance coverage for the elderly and people with disabilities; and Medicaid, which provides coverage for the poor.

Origins The seeds of government-sponsored health insurance in America were planted during the Great Depression. Historically in the United States, people have obtained health insurance through their employers. During the Depression, when a large percentage of Americans were unemployed, President Franklin Roosevelt's (1882–1945) administration developed New Deal

Demonstrators rallying in New York to oppose cuts to the Medicare program. © *Viviane Moos/CORBIS*

programs to help people cover their medical costs. The nonprofit Blue Cross and Blue Shield programs were created in the 1930s as the health insurers of last resort. During World War II, many employers improved their employee insurance plans as a worker retention strategy, because fringe benefits were exempt from wartime wage freezes. Nevertheless, those without insurance through an employer or labor union, such as retirees, were often out of luck.

The problems of the uninsured became more acute after World War II, as medical breakthroughs and advanced technology drove up the cost of health care. Health-care costs more than doubled during the 1950s. By 1960 it was estimated that the average senior citizen in the United States was spending 15 percent of his or her income on health care. That year, Congress passed the Kerr-Mills Act, named for Senator Robert Kerr (D-AR) and Congressman Wilbur Mills (D-OK), which provided federal grants for state-run programs that subsidized health-care expenditures for elderly persons who could not afford it on their own. Few states ended up participating in the Kerr-Mills program because of its unfavorable cost-sharing system, but it did spark the dialogue that would lead to more comprehensive reform a few years later.

In 1961 Congressmen Cecil R. King (D-CA) and Clinton Anderson (D-NM) introduced a proposal for a program, which they called Medicare, that would provide hospitalization coverage for Social Security recipients. The program would be funded through an additional Social Security tax, and included an annual deductible participants would have to pay before benefits kicked in. Doctors, represented by the American Medical Association (AMA), lobbied fiercely against the proposal, arguing against any government interference in patient care. Medical groups mounted a public relations campaign designed to spread anxiety over "socialized medicine" among ordinary Americans.

Social Security Act Amendments of 1965   The King-Anderson proposal stalled in Congress, as civil rights legislation dominated debate in 1963 and 1964. Johnson's landslide victory in the 1964 presidential election—coupled with Democratic control of both houses of Congress—removed many obstacles from his ambitious agenda of social reforms, collectively known as the Great Society. As he began his first full term in office, Johnson called for quick action on the issue of health care for the poor and the elderly. The AMA saw the writing on the wall, and rather than oppose the creation of government programs, they worked with lawmakers to craft a compromise. Medicare and Medicaid were both passed by Congress in 1965 as amendments to the Social Security Act, and Johnson signed the legislation into law on July 30, 1965. Former president Harry Truman (1884–1972) and his wife, Bess, were given the first Medicare cards.

The newly created Medicare program, created by Title XVIII of the Social Security Act, was divided into two separate components. Medicare Part A automatically covered hospitalization for people who were age sixty-five or older and eligible for Social Security. It also covered those eligible for railroad retirement benefits. People with disabilities under age sixty-five who received Social Security were also eligible for the program. Medicare Part B was a voluntary program in which eligible individuals could have a monthly premium deducted from their Social Security payment to receive coverage for 80 percent of their doctors' fees and medical supplies, after paying a $50 deductible.

Title XIX, a separate amendment to the Social Security Act, created the Medicaid program. Medicaid was built on the model first established with the Kerr-Mills program. Costs and administrative responsibilities would be shared by state and federal governments. In general, people receiving welfare or other public assistance were eligible for Medicaid, but each state was free to set up its own program with its own specific eligibility criteria within certain parameters. California was the first state to develop a program, launching Medi-Cal in 1966. Nearly every state had a Medicaid program within a couple of years.

As health-care costs continued to increase nationwide, Medicare and Medicaid were altered several times over the years that followed. Funding limits were put in place, and were adjusted on a number of different occasions. Gaps in coverage and loopholes that increase costs to either patients or the government have been an ongoing issue. One strategy implemented in recent years to hold down costs has been to require or encourage Medicaid participants to enroll in health maintenance organization plans. Health-care spending currently makes up a large and growing percentage of every state's budget, prompting louder and more frequent calls for an overhaul of the nation's health-care finance system.

See also **Lyndon B. Johnson**

The Immigration and Nationality Act of 1965

The Immigration and Nationality Act of 1965 made significant changes to the immigration policies of the United States by repealing the national origins quota system, which had restricted the number of people who could legally move to the United States from any one country. Under the new first-come, first-served system, immigrant applications were given preference if the immigrants had family in the United States or skills needed within the American workforce.

What Is an Immigrant? Foreign-born people who come to the United States with the intent to live and work are required to have immigration visas, which allow them to become "legal resident aliens" or, if they so choose, naturalized citizens (generally after five years). Such immigration visas are typically referred to as "green cards," due to the color of the card once used. Tourists, students, and other categories of foreigners seeking entry to the United States for short-term visits are considered "nonimmigrants" and, if they are from a nation for which the United States requires a visa, receive a visa with restrictions as to their activities (e.g., many cannot legally work) and length-of-stay. Such persons are expected to at some point leave the United States. Those who do not are considered "illegal aliens" and are subject to deportation.

Background: The National Origins Quota System
Since the 1920s, U.S. immigration policy for people seeking to stay in the United States held that foreigners were admitted based on the nation they were from. At the time, the bias favored immigrants from the Western Hemisphere, limited immigrants from the Eastern Hemisphere, and prohibited all immigration from Asian nations. A temporary version of a national origins quota system was enacted in 1921. A permanent policy was announced in 1924.

For the countries upon which the United States placed restrictions, the national origins quota system limited immigration to 2 percent of each foreign-born group living in the United States in 1890. For instance, if 100,000 people born in the United Kingdom were living in the United States in 1890, 2,000 Brits would be allowed permanent residency visas into the United States. The use of the 1890 census is significant because it purposely excluded the large wave of immigrants who arrived from southern and eastern Europe between 1890 and 1920. Under the new law, all of the nations under the quota system would be allowed a combined total of no more than 154,000 immigrants each year. Italy's quota, for example, reduced the migration from that country from roughly 42,000 immigrants annually to just 3,845 people per year. (Another barrier: applicants who were disabled, ill, poor, illiterate, or in some way considered unsavory could and would be denied visas.)

There were no quota limitations on refugees, religious ministers, spouses of U.S. citizens, temporary visitors, and immigrants from the North and South American continents. Not only did the United States not want to alienate its neighbors, it needed workers from Mexico and other points south who were employed as farm laborers.

Because of the quota system and a worldwide economic depression in the 1930s, many nations never even met their quotas. At the same time, however, Jews and other persecuted people trying to escape Nazi Germany and other totalitarian regimes were denied refuge in the United States.

EXCERPTS FROM PRESIDENT LYNDON B. JOHNSON'S REMARKS UPON SIGNING THE IMMIGRATION AND NATIONALITY ACT OF 1965

With Ellis Island in the background and the Statue of Liberty looming above, on October 3, 1965, President Lyndon B. Johnson (1908–1973) addressed a group of several hundred guests who had crossed to the island by boat for the ceremony.

This bill that we will sign today is not a revolutionary bill. It does not affect the lives of millions. It will not reshape the structure of our daily lives, or really add importantly to either our wealth or our power.

Yet it is still one of the most important acts of this Congress and of this administration.

For it does repair a very deep and painful flaw in the fabric of American justice. It corrects a cruel and enduring wrong in the conduct of the American Nation....

This bill says simply that from this day forth those wishing to immigrate to America shall be admitted on the basis of their skills and their close relationship to those already here.

This is a simple test, and it is a fair test. Those who can contribute most to this country—to its growth, to its strength, to its spirit—will be the first that are admitted to this land.

The fairness of this standard is so self-evident that we may well wonder that it has not always been applied. Yet the fact is that for over four decades the immigration policy of the United States has been twisted and has been distorted by the harsh injustice of the national origins quota system.

Under that system the ability of new immigrants to come to America depended upon the country of their birth. Only 3 countries were allowed to supply 70 percent of all the immigrants.

Families were kept apart because a husband or a wife or a child had been born in the wrong place.

Men of needed skill and talent were denied entrance because they came from southern or eastern Europe or from one of the developing continents.

This system violated the basic principle of American democracy—the principle that values and rewards each man on the basis of his merit as a man.

It has been un-American in the highest sense, because it has been untrue to the faith that brought thousands to these shores even before we were a country.

Today, with my signature, this system is abolished.

We can now believe that it will never again shadow the gate to the American Nation with the twin barriers of prejudice and privilege....

SOURCE: Public Papers of the Presidents of the United States: Lyndon B. Johnson, 1965. *Volume II, Entry 546, 1037–1040. Lyndon Baines Johnson Library and Museum. http://www.lbjlib.utexas.edu/Johnson/archives.hom/ speeches.hom/651003.asp (accessed April 14, 2007).*

1950s Legislation: The McCarran-Walter Bill The Immigration and Nationality Act of 1952, originally known as the McCarran-Walter Bill, repealed the long-held anti-Asian immigration policies but reaffirmed the national origins quota system. Under the act, the U.S. immigration system continued to set aside the vast majority of permanent residency visas for people from just three Western European nations: Ireland, the United Kingdom, and Germany. People wishing to immigrate to the United States from such Eastern and southern European nations as Poland, Italy, and Greece often waited years for their numbers to be called. According to a February 1965 session of the Senate Subcommittee on Immigration and Naturalization, Italy at that time had an annual allowed quota of 5,666 immigrants, yet the waiting list for admission into the United States tallied just short of 250,000 people.

Believing the 1952 act was simply perpetuating past wrongs, President Harry Truman (1884–1972) vetoed the bill when it landed on his desk. In his veto, he wrote "These are only a few examples of the absurdity, the cruelty of carrying over into this year of 1952 the isolationist limitations of our 1924 law. In no other realm of our national life are we so hampered and stultified by the dead hand of the past, as we are in this field of immigration." Congress, however, overrode Truman's veto.

Passage of the 1965 Immigration and Nationality Act The Immigration and Nationality Act of 1965 was signed by President Lyndon B. Johnson (1908–1973) on October 3; it had as its backdrop the civil rights movement, which aspired to expand rights and freedoms to all people. The new statute discarded considerations of nationality, race, and ethnicity that had dictated the quota system of U.S. immigration policy for forty years. The 1965 policy granted permission to immigrate based on, in the following order of preference, the reunification of families, the acquisition by the United States of needed workforce skills, and, in the fewest instances, the moral obligation to provide assistance to refugees. This new plan, much of which remains in effect in the twenty-first century, is described as a "preference system."

The 1965 act—also called the Hart-Celler Immigration Bill—capped the previously unrestricted immigration from Western Hemisphere nations to an annual maximum of 120,000, and placed a limit on immigration from Eastern Hemisphere nations at 170,000, but with no more than 20,000 persons per country. Overall, the ceiling on annual worldwide immigration increased from 150,000 to 290,000.

With national origin no longer a consideration, the United States would now fill each hemisphere's quota by choosing on a first-come, first-served basis from pools of prospective immigrants, based on a seven-category preference system for relatives of U.S. citizens and permanent resident aliens (President Johnson was particularly eager to help families separated by Fidel Castro's [1926–] revolutionary takeover of Cuba) and for people with work skills needed in the United States. According to one report, more than three-quarters of each hemisphere's quota went to people with family ties to American citizens. Roughly 10 percent was reserved for people who possessed knowledge, experience, or skills that would be useful to the U.S. economy. The remaining admissions went to refugees, such as those escaping racial, religious, or political persecution.

The Impact of the 1965 Legislation

By opening immigration possibilities to the entire world, the 1965 act, viewed by many as a symbolic effort in line with other civil rights objectives of the time, unintentionally led to a huge wave of new immigration. Upon signing the legislation, President Johnson stated, "This bill we sign today is not a revolutionary bill. It does not affect the lives of millions. It will not restructure the shape of our daily lives."

Dean Rusk (1909–1994), Johnson's secretary of state, estimated that a total of eight thousand people would immigrate to the United States from India within the first five years of the new policy. In a February 1965 Senate subcommittee hearing he stated: "I don't think we have a particular picture of a world situation where everybody is just straining to move to the United States," he said. In fact, more than twenty-seven thousand people came from India during that time frame. From 1965 to 1993, the total number was just short of six hundred thousand.

Later Changes

In the mid-1970s amendments were enacted and the policy was revised again. The hemisphere distinctions were removed and replaced by an overall annual limit of 290,000 for the number of immigrants from throughout the globe allowed into the United States per year. By this time, the majority of immigrants into the United States were coming from Asia and Latin America, not Europe. (Between 1970 and 1992 more than one million Indochinese immigrants came to the United States, most of them refugees from Vietnam, Cambodia, and Laos.)

In the 1974 *Lau v. Nichols* case, brought on behalf of immigrant Chinese children, the U.S. Supreme Court ruled that public schools have an obligation to provide bilingual educational services to students whose learning is impeded by their difficulty in understanding or speaking English. The Court agreed with the plaintiff's argument that such services were required by the clause in the Civil Rights Act of 1964, which stated, "No person in the United States shall, on the ground of race, color, or national origin, be excluded from participation in, be denied the benefits of, or be subjected to discrimination under any program or activity receiving Federal financial assistance."

An immigration-related statute, the Refugee Act of 1980, broadened the definition of what the U.S. government would consider to be a refugee. Whereas a refugee was once considered mainly someone who was fleeing persecution (typically from a Communist or Middle Eastern country), the new act opened the definition to be in line with the more generous criteria used by the United Nations. This act set an annual refugee admissions number at 50,000 and, separately, reduced the annual worldwide ceiling for immigrants to 270,000.

With the Immigration Reform and Control Act of 1986, Congress attempted to cope with the growing problem of illegal immigration. The act provided amnesty to certain individuals who were in the country illegally and at the same time increased the penalties for employers who hired undocumented aliens.

A revision in 1990 raised the overall annual global immigration limits to nearly seven hundred thousand, maintained family reconciliation as an important criterion, increased employment-based immigration (including allowances for temporary workers), and recognized as a category *diversity immigrants*, the term used to describe people from underrepresented countries.

Over the course of nearly a century, the immigration policies of the United States have evolved from a system based on national quotas—determined by ethnic and racial preferences—to one where entry for permanent residency is reserved for immigrants with desired job skills (employer sponsored) or immigrants with immediate legal family in the United States (family sponsored). Other changes in immigration policy have aimed at detecting and deporting criminals, terrorists, and undocumented aliens.

Immigration at the Start of the Twenty-First Century

In 2004 the largest legal immigrant groups to the United States were from Mexico, India, and the Philippines. (Complicated formulas exist to prevent one nation from monopolizing all of the open slots.) Since few people in the United States can trace their lineage through the centuries to Native American tribes that flourished on what is now U.S. soil, America is a nation built by immigrants. Some immigration opponents, however, argue that times have changed. They feel that with the nation's population exceeding the three hundred million mark in 2006, the United

States no longer needs or has the space or financing to accommodate vast migrations of foreigners. Immigration proponents argue that the United States has a moral obligation to keep its borders open and promote diversity. It is a problem that will not go away. From 2000 to 2005, nearly one million immigrants were granted legal permanent residence in the United States each year (though the majority were already living in the United States). By the middle of the first decade of the 2000s, an additional 8.7 million people were believed to be in the country illegally.

Miranda v. Arizona

Miranda v. Arizona is the U.S. Supreme Court case that affirmed the requirement that criminal suspects be informed of their constitutional rights to refrain from making statements to the police until they have had the advice of counsel and to have legal representation during questioning. Thus *Miranda* established the need for police officers everywhere to utter the phrase immortalized in countless television cop shows: "You have the right to remain silent...." Prior to *Miranda*, the law pertaining to the treatment of suspects in custody varied from state to state. *Miranda* clarified on a national level exactly what information regarding their constitutional rights—primarily those stemming from the Fifth Amendment right not to incriminate oneself—suspects must be informed about in order for any evidence produced by their questioning to be valid in court.

Arrest of Ernesto Miranda

On March 3, 1963, an eighteen-year-old Phoenix, Arizona, woman was grabbed on the way home from her movie theater job, forced into a car, driven into the desert, and raped. Her attacker then drove her back into the city and dropped her off not far from her home. When she reported the attack to police, the woman's account of the event was somewhat jumbled and contradictory. She described the assailant as a Mexican in his late twenties with glasses, driving either a Ford or Chevrolet from the early 1950s.

A week later, the woman and her brother-in-law spotted a 1953 Packard that she believed to be the car driven by the rapist. They reported that the vehicle's license plate number was DFL-312. That license turned out to be registered to a late model Oldsmobile, but a similar number, DFL-317 belonged to a Packard registered to a woman, Twila N. Hoffman, whose boyfriend, Ernesto Miranda, fit the woman's description of her attacker.

Miranda had a substantial criminal history, and had served a year in jail for attempted rape. Police placed Miranda in a lineup with three other Mexicans of similar physical type—though none of them wore glasses. The victim indicated that of the men in the lineup, Miranda looked the most like her attacker, but she was unable to provide a positive identification.

Two detectives, Carroll Cooley and Wilfred Young, took Miranda into another room and began interrogating him. As is common during questioning, the detectives misled their suspect, telling him he had been positively identified, and they asked him to make a statement. Miranda signed a written confession two hours later. There was no evidence that he had been coerced or abused in any significant way.

Questionable Police Practices

Because he was unable to afford private counsel, Miranda was given a court-appointed lawyer, Alvin Moore. While the case against Miranda was strong given the signed confession, Moore was disturbed by how the confession had been obtained. At trial in the Arizona state court, the prosecution presented only four witnesses: the victim, her sister, and the two detectives who had obtained Miranda's confession. Moore presented a spirited defense on behalf of Miranda, pointing out a number of inconsistencies in the victim's version of the event. Moore made his most important argument, however, during cross-examination of Detective Cooley. During this questioning, Cooley acknowledged that Miranda had never been informed of his right to the advice of an attorney before making a statement, and that informing suspects of this right was not part of the police department's standard procedure when questioning suspects.

Based on this information, Moore asked Judge Yale McFate to throw out Miranda's confession as tainted evidence. McFate rejected Moore's request, and the jury was allowed to hear the confession. On June 27, 1963, Miranda was convicted of the rape and kidnapping and sentenced to two concurrent terms of twenty to thirty years in prison.

Moore's arguments, however, had set off a chain of events that would dramatically change the way law enforcement officials go about their work. Miranda appealed to the Supreme Court of Arizona on the basis of Moore's argument that he had not been informed of his right to have a lawyer present, but his conviction was upheld. After that defeat, he appealed to the U.S. Supreme Court, which agreed to hear the case in 1965. The *Miranda* case, along with three other cases involving similar issues, was argued before the Supreme Court between February 28 and March 2, 1966. In each of the four cases that made up the *Miranda* review, the suspect had not been notified of his rights, leading to a confession that resulted in a conviction.

Warren Court Ruling

On June 13, 1966, the Supreme Court voted 5 to 4 in Miranda's favor. Writing for the majority, Chief Justice Earl Warren (1891–1974) established clear-cut guidelines for police behavior during an interrogation. He wrote:

> Prior to any questioning, the person must be warned that he has a right to remain silent, that any statement he does make may be used as evidence against him, and that he has a right to the presence of an attorney, either retained or appointed.

"You have the right to remain silent . . ." Los Angeles police officer reads Miranda warning to handcuffed suspect during a training exercise. © *Kim Kulish/CORBIS*

Warren and the other justices in the majority—Hugo Black (1886–1971), William Brennan (1906–1997), William O. Douglas (1898–1980), and Abe Fortas (1910–1982)—believed that the inherently intimidating atmosphere of a police interrogation must be counterbalanced by strong safeguards that the suspect's rights were upheld. To arguments that the new *Miranda* rules would hamper law enforcement efforts, Warren answered that similar rules were already in place at the Federal Bureau of Investigation, and that they did not seem to interfere with that agency's ability to fight crime.

The *Miranda* ruling instantly changed the way suspects were treated in the United States. With the implementation of the "Miranda rules," police officers all over the country began carrying "Miranda cards," from which they would read verbatim the rights of detainees before questioning them. Conservatives hated the decision, fearing that large numbers of criminals would be cut loose on technicalities after the failure of police to properly "Mirandize" them, as the procedure came to be known.

The fears of those who have opposed the *Miranda* decision do not seem to have been borne out. The change did not appear to have an impact on the willingness of those arrested to give statements to police, and while individual cases have been thrown out when confessions have been found to be inadmissible because of failure to Mirandize, the law has generally not hindered prosecutors. In practice, the *Miranda* case actually appears to have had a dramatic positive impact on police behavior, as incidences of abusive interrogation practices have decreased. While coercion continues to take place, *Miranda* led to greater standardization and professionalization of police practices, and an increased awareness on the part of police of the rights of the accused. Attempts have been made over the years to chip away at the rights established by *Miranda v. Arizona*, but to date those efforts have not succeeded in any substantial way.

Ernesto Miranda received a new trial after his conviction was overturned by the Supreme Court, but he was convicted a second time on the strength of new evidence and sentenced to twenty to thirty years in jail. He was released on parole in 1972. Four years later, Miranda was stabbed to death in a bar fight. However, his name lives on in the words associated with it, invoked nearly every time somebody in America is arrested.

The Freedom of Information Act

The Freedom of Information Act (FOIA), first passed in 1966, provides citizen access to information held by agencies that are part of the executive branch of the federal government of the United States. The act requires that unreleased documents in the custody of the executive branch be made available to any individual on request. The law does, however, carve out nine exceptions to this mandate, under which the requested information may be withheld.

Before passage of FOIA, people seeking government documents had to state the purpose of their request, and government officials had a great deal of latitude as to whether the benefits of disclosing the requested material outweighed the value of keeping it secret. Such requests were frequently denied, with little justification given.

Roots of the Act The movement to require the federal government to be more forthcoming with government documents was driven by journalists. At the dawn of the Cold War, an atmosphere of secrecy had descended upon Washington, D.C., as scare stories of communists hiding in every dark corner of every government office spread throughout federal agencies. Meanwhile, the federal government had grown dramatically since the 1930s, with the creation of many new agencies resulting in a sprawling, difficult-to-navigate bureaucracy.

In 1955 John Moss, a Democratic congressman from Sacramento, California, as chair of the Special Subcommittee on Government Information, led the first of a series of hearings on the issue of excessive government secrecy. His efforts were backed by an intensive lobbying campaign by newspaper editors who were fed up with the government's frequent refusal to release information crucial to the thorough coverage of key issues and events of the day. With a Republican president, Dwight D. Eisenhower (1890–1969), in the White House, however, there was little chance that Moss's proposed legislation to open government records to the public could move forward.

When the Democrats seized control of the White House at the beginning of the 1960s, Republicans became more receptive to the idea of opening access to government information. With Congressman Donald Rumsfeld (1932–), a Republican member of Moss's subcommittee, signed on as a cosponsor—quite ironic in light of Rumsfeld's role in promoting secrecy less than a decade later as President Gerald R. Ford's (1913–2006) chief of staff and secretary of defense, and even more so as President George W. Bush's (1946–) defense secretary during the War on Terror—Moss's freedom of information bill was finally ready to make headway in Congress.

Passage of FOIA President Lyndon B. Johnson (1908–1973) was adamantly opposed to the bill at first, and spent considerable energy stalling its progress in 1965. In another interesting twist, one of the leading voices against passage of the bill was Johnson's press secretary Bill Moyers, who later went on to become a leading muckraking journalist dependent on the availability of government documents. By the spring of 1966 the Senate had passed a version of Moss's bill, and

HOW TO FILE AN FOIA REQUEST

By law, anybody can request information for any reason from the federal government under the Freedom of Information Act (FOIA). For relatively small requests made for noncommercial purposes, there is usually no fee associated with filing a FOIA request. There are three general categories of requesters defined by the law. The first category includes members of the news media, educational institutions, and noncommercial scientific institutions. Usually this type of requester has to pay a standard document copying charge, but the fee is often waived for individual journalists and scholars if their goal is to disseminate information to the public. The second category consists of nonprofits, public interest groups, and individuals seeking information for personal use. This category must usually pay a fee for both document reproduction and the time it takes to perform the search. The last category is those requesting information for commercial use in order to make a profit. This group is usually assessed additional fees.

The first thing to do when seeking information is to figure out which department the information resides in. While there is no central office in the federal government that coordinates FOIA requests, the U.S. Department of Justice serves as the source of information about FOIA and the different government departments and agencies.

The next step is to make sure that the information you are looking for is not already available on the department's Web site. The department Web site will usually have information posted about where to send a FOIA request. It is usually a good idea to send the request to both the department's FOIA office and to the specific office within the department that has the information you hope to obtain.

The last step is to simply write a letter to the agency indicating in as much detail as possible the information you are looking for, making sure to mention in the letter that it is a formal FOIA request. Most departments' FOIA Web pages contain sample letters that you can use as a model when making your own FOIA request. Once the right agency has received the request, and if the request is complete and correct, the agency has twenty working days to respond with a determination as to whether they will grant the request. If the request is denied, the agency must give the reason within those twenty days. If the request is approved, the agency is then supposed to provide the information promptly, though there is no specific time frame within which they must act.

Moyers and other White House staff began to sense that passage in the House might be inevitable. Even Moyers began speaking in favor of the legislation.

The House of Representatives passed the bill unanimously on June 20, 1960, and sent it to Johnson for his signature. By that time, only one federal agency, the Department of Health, Education, and Welfare, was still recommending a veto. Johnson signed FOIA into law on July 4, 1966, albeit reluctantly. He was not happy about the prospect of open public access to his government's documents.

FOIA mandated that federal government documents be made available to any person who requests them; nevertheless, the act included nine exemptions to that requirement. Those exceptions are: (1) material that is classified in the interest of national defense; (2) internal guides that discuss enforcement strategies; (3) material whose disclosure is prohibited by other laws; (4) confidential or privileged commercial or financial information; (5) information protected by privileges such as attorney-client or work product; (6) information whose release would constitute an unwarranted invasion of personal privacy; (7) information compiled for law enforcement purposes that might cause harm if released; (8) information related to oversight of financial institutions; and (9) geophysical and geological information about oil wells.

FOIA has been amended a number of times since 1966. The most significant amendments took place in 1974 and 1996. The 1974 amendments, coming in the aftermath of the Watergate scandal, sought to tighten the requirements of the law, force greater agency compliance, and narrow the exceptions. President Ford vetoed this legislation, but Congress overrode his veto. The Electronic Freedom of Information Act of 1996 essentially updated the act to reflect changes that have taken place in information technology since the act was first established.

The Demonstration Cities and Metropolitan Development Act

The Model Cities program—originally called Demonstration Cities—was an ambitious attempt from the mid-1960s to the mid-1970s to revitalize selected urban neighborhoods through a comprehensive system of social programs and planning efforts. The program coordinated public and private resources and promoted participation by residents in efforts to rehabilitate their own communities. The Model Cities program was a cornerstone of President Lyndon B. Johnson's (1908–1973) Great Society initiative, a set of programs and policies aimed at eliminating poverty and racial injustice.

Early Roots During the late 1950s and early 1960s, the civil rights movement raised awareness among Americans of racial discrimination in the South and a litany of social problems plaguing poor African-Americans in northern cities. During this period a number of foundation-funded programs were instituted in various cities to address the social ills associated with poverty and discrimination. One of the first was Mobilization for Youth, an antidelinquency program launched in the late 1950s on New York's Lower East Side. Within a few years, the Ford Foundation had established an initiative known as the Gray Areas program. This program, which

absorbed Mobilization for Youth as well as similar programs that had developed elsewhere, provided grants to neighborhood improvement agencies in Boston, Massachusetts; New Haven, Connecticut; Philadelphia, Pennsylvania; and Washington, D.C. As these privately financed programs took hold, the federal government decided to take action as well. In 1964 the Economic Opportunity Act created the Community Action Program, which combined community participation with antipoverty programs.

By the mid-1960s a number of high-profile individuals representing the private and public sectors as well as academia began advocating for the creation of a national-scale approach to urban problems. National Institutes of Health psychiatrist Leonard Duhl, Tufts University dean Antonia Chayes, and Detroit mayor Jerome Cavanagh, among others, began pushing an idea for an overarching program that would address cities' problems on the social, economic, political, and physical levels simultaneously. Johnson convened a series of presidential task forces, which he asked to come up with solutions to the pressing urban problems of the day. One of the first recommendations to come out of the task forces was for the creation of a cabinet-level Department of Housing and Urban Development (HUD), which was established in 1965. Next the task forces took up the idea of Demonstration Cities. As initially conceived, the program would cover only a handful of cities, but it quickly grew into something much broader. The final report of the task forces quickly transformed into a bill requesting $2.3 billion to provide select cities with comprehensive assistance in several areas, including education, housing, and social services. Johnson directed leaders of the newly formed HUD to make passage of the Demonstration Cities project one of their top priorities in 1966.

The Demonstration Cities and Metropolitan Development Act was signed into law on November 3, 1966. When riots began to erupt in cities across the United States the next summer, the program's name was quickly changed to Model Cities, because the word *demonstration* was too closely associated with rioting. The first Model Cities grants were awarded in November 1967. Totaling over $300 million, they went to sixty-three cities and towns across the country. Another $200 million was handed out in a second round of grants in September 1968, following another summer of violence in America's cities.

Decline under Nixon In 1968 the Democrats lost control of the White House and lost ground in Congress. With that change in the political climate in Washington, along with waning support from suburban and rural Americans growing weary of scenes of urban violence on television, the Model Cities approach fell out of favor. Initially, HUD secretary George Romney persuaded President Richard Nixon (1913–1994) to leave Model Cities and a handful of other urban programs intact. With his reelection in 1972, however, Nixon began to reexamine the urban aid programs he had inherited from Johnson. Funding for the Model Cities program was suspended in 1973, and soon afterward the remnants of the program were folded into the Community Development Block Grant program, which was created by the Housing and Community Development Act of 1974.

It is difficult to assess the overall impact of the Model Cities program. In some senses, it was a success; supporters point to the development of a generation of involved citizens who became engaged in the political process through the program's resident participation requirement. Critics tend to point out that there was little improvement in most social problems; urban poverty certainly did not go away. While the Community Development Block Grant program that survives lacks the kind of comprehensive approach of Model Cities, it has resulted in the development of many highly successful community organizations that have had a positive and lasting effect in many cities.

See also **Lyndon B. Johnson**

The Presidential Succession Amendment

The Twenty-fifth Amendment to the Constitution, ratified on February 10, 1967, established the procedure for replacing the president or vice president of the United States in the event that either office is unoccupied. First proposed following the assassination of John F. Kennedy (1917–1963), the amendment has been used several times since its passage.

The term *presidential succession* refers to procedures for transferring presidential authority to another individual through means other than the normal electoral process that takes place every four years. That includes situations in which a sitting president dies while in office as well as when the president resigns, is removed through impeachment, or is unable to perform the duties of the office because of health or other reasons. The procedures for presidential succession are defined in three different parts of the U.S. Constitution—Article II, Section 1, Clause 6, and the Twentieth and Twenty-fifth Amendments—and in the presidential succession law passed by Congress in 1947.

Need for Clear Procedures During the twentieth century, the importance of a well-defined presidential succession system became obvious, as five vice presidents ascended to the presidency during the first three-quarters of the century, four of them because of presidential deaths and one as a result of a resignation. More than one-third of the presidents between 1841 and 1975 either died in office, became disabled, or, in the case of one, Richard M. Nixon (1913–1994), resigned.

The basic principles of presidential succession were laid out in Article II of the Constitution, which states

Vice President Spiro T. Agnew announcing his resignation on October 10, 1973, outside a federal courthouse in Baltimore, Maryland. The resignation triggered the first use of the 25th Amendment, invoked by President Richard Nixon to nominate Gerald Ford as the next vice president. © *Bettmann/CORBIS*

that the vice president shall assume the duties of the president if the president dies or is removed from office, or, if the president becomes disabled, until the disability is no longer present. Article II also directs Congress to figure out a plan for situations in which neither the president nor vice president is able to serve.

The Twentieth Amendment, ratified in January 1933, added to the formula that if the president-elect dies or is unable to take office, then the vice president–elect will be sworn in as president. Coincidentally, just twenty-three days after the amendment was ratified, an attempt was made to assassinate President-Elect Franklin Roosevelt (1882–1945). Had it succeeded, Vice President–Elect John Nance Garner (1868–1967) would have been sworn in as president in March. After World War II, Congress passed the Presidential Succession Act of 1947, which put in place the current order of succession after the vice president. If neither the president nor the vice president is able to serve, next in line are the

Speaker of the House of Representatives, the president pro tempore of the Senate, and then the cabinet officers, starting with the secretary of state, followed by the secretary of the treasury, secretary of defense, and attorney general.

Kennedy Assassination In spite of these laws, however, some procedural issues still remained unclear at the time Kennedy was assassinated. The Twenty-fifth Amendment was proposed to resolve some of these questions. Section 1 of the amendment simply reaffirmed the long-standing precedent of the vice president taking over as president upon the death or resignation of the president. Section 2 established a new procedure for selecting a new vice president if that office becomes vacant. This is precisely the situation Lyndon B. Johnson (1908–1973) faced when he assumed the presidency after Kennedy's death.

Sections 3 and 4 of the amendment address presidential disability. Prior to the passage of the Twenty-fifth Amendment, the Constitution did not cover situations in which a president becomes temporarily disabled. Section 3 establishes procedures for situations in which the president communicates that he "is unable to discharge the powers and duties of the office," in which case the vice president temporarily assumes those powers and duties until the president is once again able to serve. Section 4 addresses situations in which the vice president and a majority of cabinet members determine that the president is incapable of performing. In such a case, the vice president becomes acting president until four days after the time the president declares himself able to resume his duties. The vice president and cabinet members may dispute the president's assertion of capability, in which case the matter is resolved by Congress.

Twenty-fifth Amendment Invoked The Presidential Succession Amendment saw plenty of action in the 1970s. President Richard M. Nixon (1913–1994) used the procedure outlined in Section 2 to nominate Gerald R. Ford (1913–2006) as vice president following the resignation of Vice President Spiro Agnew (1918–1996) in October 1973. When Nixon resigned from office the following year, Ford succeeded him immediately and was sworn in the same day as per the amendment. Ford then used the procedures in the amendment to nominate Nelson Rockefeller (1908–1979) as vice president.

When President Ronald Reagan (1911–2004) underwent surgery for cancer in July 1985, he handed over power to Vice President George H. W. Bush (1924–) for eight hours, though it is unclear whether Reagan formally invoked the Twenty-fifth Amendment. Similarly, President George W. Bush (1946–) signed presidential authority over to Vice President Dick Cheney (1941–) when he was preparing to undergo a colonoscopy. Cheney served as acting president from 7:09 to 9:24 a.m. on June 29, 2002.

Red Lion Broadcasting Co. v. Federal Communications Commission

The U.S. Supreme Court's decision in the landmark case *Red Lion Broadcasting Co. v. Federal Communications Commission* (1969) upheld as constitutional the Federal Communications Commission's (FCC) "fairness doctrine." The fairness doctrine is a policy aimed at making radio and television broadcasters present a fair and balanced account of public issues by requiring them to provide equal time for a response by those who have been personally attacked on the air in the context of political debate or editorializing. The key question of the case is whether the fairness doctrine violated broadcasters' constitutionally protected right to free speech by telling them what content they had to air. The Supreme Court ruled that the doctrine did not violate that right, and that companies broadcasting on the limited number of frequencies available—frequencies that theoretically belong to the public—are obligated to present a variety of viewpoints on all subjects their programming touches upon.

Background When commercial radio came into existence in the 1920s, the airwaves were unregulated. The available broadcast frequencies were up for grabs, their allocation left up to the business community. The result was a dysfunctional system that did not serve listeners well. To make sense of this chaotic situation, the federal government created the Federal Radio Commission (FRC; later renamed the Federal Communications Commission) in 1927. The FRC quickly asserted that radio stations were obligated to serve the public interest, and set about creating a broad range of regulations aimed at bringing order to the young broadcasting industry. As part of its congressionally mandated mission to protect the public interest, the FCC stated in 1929 that public interest "requires ample play for the free and fair competition of opposing views," applicable to "all discussions of issues of importance to the public." By the end of the 1940s this commitment had been distilled into the so-called fairness doctrine, which required broadcasters to offer free air time for response to anybody who represented views different from those being put forth via a station's programming.

The facts of the *Red Lion* case revolve around a November 27, 1964, broadcast by the Pennsylvania radio station WGCB. The show in question was a fifteen-minute program by the Reverend Billy James Hargis, part of an ongoing series called "Christian Crusade." In the broadcast, Hargis took issue with the beliefs of Fred J. Cook, who had written a book titled *Barry Goldwater: Extremist on the Right*. Hargis, a fan of the Republican politician Goldwater, launched a scathing personal attack on Cook, calling him a communist and stating that he had been fired from his newspaper job for fabricating a story.

Equal Time for Reply Cook heard the show, and quickly demanded free airtime for a rebuttal as per the fairness doctrine that had been official policy of the FCC for more than a decade. WGCB refused to honor Cook's request, however, and the matter was referred to the FCC. The FCC ruled that Hargis's broadcast was indeed a personal attack on Cook, and that WGCB, as a licensed broadcaster, was therefore obligated to provide Cook with free airtime to respond to the attack.

The station was unhappy with the FCC's ruling, and in 1967 they brought the case before the U.S. Court of Appeals for the District of Columbia Circuit. Their argument hinged upon the notion that the FCC was violating the station's First Amendment free speech rights by dictating how they must allocate their precious airtime. While the case was under consideration by the court of appeals, the FCC took the opportunity to clarify the parameters of the fairness doctrine with regard to personal attacks and political editorials. They came up with a new definition of "personal attack." Under the newly articulated policy, a personal attack has taken place "when, during the presentation of views on a controversial issue of public importance, an attack is made upon the honesty, character, integrity or like personal qualities of an identified person or group." The FCC also outlined specific remedies for when such an attack occurs. The policy provided that the broadcaster shall notify the person or group of the broadcast, provide them with a transcript or tape of the attack, and offer a reasonable opportunity to respond on the air.

The court of appeals upheld the FCC's *Red Lion* ruling, but at almost the same time the U.S. District Court of Appeals for the Seventh Circuit ruled the amended fairness doctrine unconstitutional in a separate case, *United States v. Radio Television News Directors Association*. With these two contradictory rulings on the books, the U.S. Supreme Court came into the picture, hearing arguments for the two cases on April 2 and 3, 1969.

Erosion of the Fairness Doctrine The Supreme Court ruled unanimously on June 9, 1969, that the fairness doctrine was consistent with the First Amendment, and actually enhanced rather than infringed upon the freedoms of speech protected by the Constitution. The Court's position was that a license to broadcast over the airwaves did not give a radio or television station the right to monopolize its licensed frequency with its own opinions on important issues, and that it was perfectly justifiable to impose regulations to ensure that broadcasters fulfill their public interest obligation to present diverse viewpoints on controversial matters.

Red Lion marked the high point for the fairness doctrine. Portions of the doctrine were chipped away through a variety of later decisions, including

Miami Herald Publishing Co. v. Tomillo (1974), in which the Supreme Court ruled that the right to reply did not extend to print media. The doctrine was dealt its deathblow in 1987, when President Ronald Reagan (1911–2004), a staunch opponent of most forms of industry regulation, vetoed legislation that would have written the fairness doctrine into the law of the land. The FCC gave up on the doctrine altogether shortly afterward.

BIBLIOGRAPHY

Books

Abernathy, Ralph. *And the Walls Came Tumbling Down.* New York: Harper and Row, 1989.

Ambrose, Stephen E. *Eisenhower.* 2 vols. New York: Simon and Schuster, 1983–1984.

Clark, Hunter R. *Justice Brennan: The Great Conciliator.* Secaucus, N.J.: Carol Publishing Group, 1995.

Collier, Peter, and David Horowitz. *The Kennedys: An American Drama.* New York: Summit Books, 1984.

Dallek, Robert. *Flawed Giant: Lyndon Johnson and His Times, 1961–1973.* New York: Oxford University Press, 1998.

Davis, Flora. *Moving the Mountain: The Women's Movement in America since 1960.* New York: Simon and Schuster, 1991.

Halberstam, David. *The Best and the Brightest.* New York: Random House, 1972.

Herring, George C. *America's Longest War: The United States and Vietnam, 1950–1975.* New York: Knopf, 1986.

LaFeber, Walter. *America, Russia, and the Cold War, 1945–1996.* 8th ed. New York: McGraw-Hill, 1996.

McCoy, Donald R. *The Presidency of Harry S. Truman.* Lawrence: University Press of Kansas, 1984.

Painter, David S. *The Cold War: An International History.* New York: Routledge, 1999.

Quirk, Robert E. *Fidel Castro.* New York: Norton, 1993.

Report of the President's Commission on the Assassination of President John F. Kennedy. Washington, DC: Government Printing Office, 1964.

Salmond, John A. *My Mind Set on Freedom: A History of the Civil Rights Movement, 1954–1968.* Chicago: Ivan R. Dee, 1997.

Schrecker, Ellen. *Many Are the Crimes: McCarthyism in America.* Boston: Little, Brown, 1998.

Schwartz, Bernard, ed. *The Warren Court: A Retrospective.* New York: Oxford University Press, 1996.

Sundquist, James L. *Politics and Policy: The Eisenhower, Kennedy, and Johnson Years.* Washington, D.C.: Brookings Institution, 1968.

Thompson, Robert Smith. *The Missiles of October: The Declassified Story of John F. Kennedy and the Cuban Missile Crisis.* New York: Simon and Schuster, 1992.

Tushnet, Mark V. *Making Constitutional Law: Thurgood Marshall and the Supreme Court, 1961–1991.* New York: Oxford University Press, 1997.

Unger, Irwin. *The Best of Intentions: The Triumphs and Failures of the Great Society under Kennedy, Johnson, and Nixon.* New York: Doubleday, 1996.

Young, Andrew. *An Easy Burden: The Civil Rights Movement and the Transformation of America.* New York: HarperCollins, 1996.

Periodicals

Calabresi, Guido. "The Exclusionary Rule." *Harvard Journal of Law and Public Policy* 26 (2003): 111.

MacDonald, Maurice. "Food Stamps: An Analytical History." *Social Service Review* 51 (December 1977): 642–658.

Web Sites

American Meteorological Society. "A Look at U.S. Air Pollution Laws and Their Amendments." http://www.ametsoc.org/sloan/cleanair/cleanairlegisl.html (accessed April 18, 2007).

U.S. Department of Veterans Affairs. "GI Bill Website." http://www.gibill.va.gov/GI_Bill_Info/benefits.htm (accessed April 19, 2007).

Introduction to the Watergate Era (1968–1979)

The Watergate era was a particularly troubled time in American history. In 1968 the U.S. war in Vietnam was at its worst, with more than five hundred thousand American soldiers deployed to the South Asian nation. Back home, protestors marched against the protracted war and the military draft that was pulling young people into its service. Despite the great civil rights achievements of just a few years earlier, riots erupted in segregated neighborhoods as racial tensions continued to simmer. The Reverend Martin Luther King Jr. (1929–1968) and Senator Robert F. Kennedy (1925–1968) were assassinated by gunmen within two months of one another. President Lyndon B. Johnson (1908–1973), undone by the quagmire in Vietnam, bowed out of pursuing a second term. His successor, Richard M. Nixon (1913–1994), was voted into office twice, but he resigned early in disgrace after details of the Watergate scandal came to light. The next two U.S. presidents—Gerald Ford (1913–2006) and Jimmy Carter (1924–)—would also depart under difficult circumstances.

Watergate revealed the inner workings of the Nixon administration, leaving Americans distrustful of government. The Vietnam War, which ended in ignominious defeat, left some fifty thousand Americans dead and thousands more maimed and emotionally scarred. Equal rights were finally guaranteed by law to African-Americans, but poverty and sociopolitical disenfranchisement continued to be scourges on their population. Women gained greater control over their personal lives, which gave rise to an angry antifeminist movement. Two energy crises caused oil shortages, forcing Americans to use less energy in their homes and wait in long lines to fill their gas tanks. Nuclear power, touted by many at the time as an alternative energy source, was believed to hold great promise in solving U.S. fuel problems, but in March 1979 a malfunction and radioactive leak at Pennsylvania's Three Mile Island nuclear plant caused widespread panic. Before the year was out, Muslim extremists in Iran raided the U.S. embassy in Iran, where they held more than fifty Americans hostage for 444 days.

While bad news dominated the front pages, many governmental reforms that passed during the 1970s actually improved the lives and safety of many Americans. Congress established regulations and standards to benefit American workers and automobile users. New crime-fighting and public safety agencies were launched. The nascent environmental movement convinced voters and politicians alike to be proactive in protecting the health of the planet. After Watergate, integrity and transparency became government priorities.

The reforms of the 1960s and 1970s continue to influence the United States, as do the anxieties caused by all that went wrong during the Watergate era. By 1979 the nation's ego was deflated and its confidence drained. In Vietnam, the Middle East, and its own cities, the United States experienced turmoil that threatened to turn Americans against each other and the rest of the world. Assumptions of power and privilege—by the federal government, the U.S. military, and segments of the American populace—were challenged as never before.

After more than a decade of being forced to see what was wrong with America, the nation wanted to hear what was right. In 1980 presidential candidate Ronald Reagan (1911–2004) ran a campaign that focused on the positive, ultimately winning the presidency.

The Watergate Era (1968–1979)

✪ How They Were Governed

The Drug Enforcement Administration

The Drug Enforcement Administration (DEA) is the lead federal agency in charge of enforcing the nation's narcotics and controlled substances laws, both domestically and abroad.

Origins of the DEA and the Controlled Substances Act The DEA was established in 1973 by President Richard Nixon (1913–1994) as a means of consolidating and coordinating the federal government's drug control efforts. While illicit drug use in the 1970s did not reach the high numbers experienced in the years following, the problem was considered significant enough for Nixon to declare "an all-out global war on the drug menace." According to Nixon, "Certainly, the cold-blooded underworld networks that funnel narcotics from suppliers all over the world are no respecters of the bureaucratic dividing lines that now complicate our anti-drug efforts."

At the time Nixon was making his arguments, the Department of Justice's Bureau of Narcotics and Dangerous Drugs (BNDD) was responsible for enforcing federal drug laws, as were the U.S. Customs Service and several other Department of Justice divisions (including the Office of National Narcotics Intelligence). Advocates for creating the DEA maintained that a single agency, housed within the Department of Justice, would put an end to interagency competition, better involve the Federal Bureau of Investigation (FBI), make a single agency accountable, and provide a focal point for coordinating federal drug enforcement efforts with those of state, local, and foreign police authorities.

Prior to the inception of the DEA, Congress passed the Controlled Substances Act (CSA), Title II of the Comprehensive Drug Abuse Prevention and Control Act of 1970, which established a single system of control for both narcotic and psychotropic drugs. The act also established five schedules that classify controlled substances according to how dangerous they are, their potential for abuse and addiction, and whether they possess legitimate medical value. Though amended on several occasions, the CSA's legal framework for drug classification remains in effect today, with the most dangerous drugs being classified as Schedule 1 narcotics.

The Rise of Cocaine Use When drug use began to escalate among Americans in the mid-1970s, President Gerald Ford (1913–2006) asked his vice president, Nelson Rockefeller (1908–1979), to assess the extent of drug abuse in the United States and to make recommendations for handling it. In his resulting report, Rockefeller maintained that "all drugs are not equally dangerous. Enforcement efforts should therefore concentrate on drugs which have a high addiction potential." The report described marijuana as a minor problem and declared that "cocaine is not physically addictive ... and usually does not result in serious social consequences such as crime, hospital emergency room admissions, or death." The report recommended that "priority in both supply and demand reduction" should focus on the more dangerous drugs of heroin, amphetamines, and mixed barbiturates. Several years later even the chief drug policy adviser to President Jimmy Carter (1924–) considered cocaine to be "probably the most benign of the illicit drugs currently in widespread use. At least as strong a case should be made for legalizing it as for legalizing marijuana."

As a result of Rockefeller's assertions, and the prevailing belief that cocaine was not addictive (an assumption that by the 1980s would be proved false), the DEA shifted its focus away from marijuana and cocaine and toward heroin and other opiates, most of which came from Mexico. The DEA's lack of emphasis on marijuana and cocaine laid the foundations for what would become by the 1980s the powerful Medellín and Cali Colombian drug cartels. In 1972, 5.4 million Americans admitted to having used cocaine at least once. By the early 1980s that figure had risen to 22 million.

DEA agents at the scene of a colleague's murder, 1998. © David Butow/CORBIS SABA

Drug Use Rates since the 1970s According to the annual *Monitoring the Future* drug use survey conducted by the U.S. National Institutes of Health (NIH), from the late 1970s to the early 1990s rates of marijuana use remained steady, but the use of other illicit drugs declined appreciably among young people. The NIH credits the improvements to "changes in attitudes about drug use, beliefs about the risks of drug use, and peer norms against drug use" and, as a result, a decrease in consumer demand for illicit narcotics.

While advocating the importance of social policies and educational efforts to encourage young people not to use drugs, the report also warns against taking declines in drug use for granted. "Relapse is always possible and, indeed, just such a 'relapse' in the longer term epidemic occurred during the early to mid-1990s, as the country let down its guard on many fronts. The drug problem is not an enemy that can be vanquished, as in a war. It is more a recurring and relapsing problem ... that requires an ongoing, dynamic response from our society."

In the decades that followed its founding, the DEA has been in pursuit of such narcotics as crack cocaine, Ecstasy (MDMA), methamphetamines, and even legal pharmaceuticals (such as the painkiller OxyContin) that are misused and abused. The DEA reports that in 1972 it employed 2,775 workers, including 1,470 special agents. In 2006 those numbers had increased to 10,891 total employees and 5,320 special agents. By the turn of the twenty-first century the DEA had offices throughout the United States and in more than fifty foreign countries.

U.S. Department of Energy

The U.S. Department of Energy (DOE) is responsible for energy policy and security in the United States. The department was established in 1977 by the Department of Energy Organization Act, which was signed by President Jimmy Carter (1924–) and consolidated many energy-related governmental functions into one umbrella organization. The secretary of the DOE is a member of the president's cabinet.

Background The origins of the DOE can be traced to World War II and the federal government's secret "Manhattan Project" to develop the atomic bomb. After the war the Atomic Energy Commission (AEC) was created to maintain civilian government control over the nation's atomic energy research and development, such as designing and producing nuclear weapons and reactors for naval propulsion.

In the mid-1970s the AEC was replaced by two new agencies: the Nuclear Regulatory Commission (NRC), charged with regulating the nuclear power industry, and the Energy Research and Development Administration, which managed the programs for nuclear weapons, naval reactors, and energy development. But the energy crisis of the 1970s—due to the Arab oil embargo of 1973–74 and later, during the presidency of Jimmy Carter, unrest in Iran—led the federal government to better coordinate its myriad energy efforts by consolidating them into a single department.

DOE Mission   The DOE's overall mission focuses on energy, national security, and technology. Its responsibilities include producing and destroying the nation's nuclear weapons; managing the U.S. Navy's nuclear reactors; pursuing fossil fuels and renewable energy sources; and sponsoring weapons and energy research and performing weapons cleanup programs. The DOE is also in charge of the U.S. Strategic Petroleum Reserve, which is the nation's backup oil supply.

During the late 1970s the DOE emphasized energy development, conservation, and regulation. When the oil shortages ended, the United States deemphasized its efforts to find alternative energy sources, and during the 1980s nuclear weapons research, development, and production took priority. Since the end of the cold war in the early 1990s, the DOE has focused on the environmental cleanups of nuclear weapons complexes, nonproliferation and stewardship of the nuclear stockpile, energy efficiency and conservation, and technology transfer and industrial competitiveness.

The Federal Emergency Management Administration

The Federal Emergency Management Administration (FEMA) is an agency within the federal government that is responsible for emergency planning and preparedness, as well as recovery assistance and coordination following natural or human-caused disasters. Depending on the situation, FEMA either provides direct assistance to those in need or works with various federal, state, local, and nonprofit agencies to coordinate responses to emergency situations.

FEMA's Founding   In response to a request from the National Governor's Association, FEMA was established by executive order on March 31, 1979, by President Jimmy Carter (1924–) as a means of consolidating the nation's emergency-related assistance programs. FEMA reported directly to the White House, and in 1993 its secretary was made a cabinet-level position. In March 2003 FEMA lost its cabinet stature when the agency was subsumed into the Department of Homeland Security, which was created by President George W. Bush (1946–) in reaction to the terrorist attacks of September 11, 2001.

The concept that the federal government should directly assist the citizenry in times of crisis stems from legislation called the Congressional Act of 1803, which provided aid to a New Hampshire town devastated by a huge fire. Subsequently, the federal government stepped in with assistance following hurricanes, floods, earthquakes, and similar natural disasters. But the efforts were often disorganized, with various federal agencies taking the lead at different times. The creation of FEMA coordinated all of these activities under one roof.

Among other agencies, FEMA absorbed the Federal Insurance Administration, the National Fire Prevention and Control Administration, the National Weather Service Community Preparedness Program, the Federal Disaster Assistance Administration, and the Defense Department's Defense Civil Preparedness Agency.

Disaster Responsiveness   Soon after its founding, FEMA had to manage the federal government's emergency response to the hazardous waste contamination of Love Canal, New York; a Cuban refugee crisis in Miami; and a nuclear reactor accident at the Three Mile Island nuclear power plant near Harrisburg, Pennsylvania. In 1992 the devastation wreaked upon South Florida by Hurricane Andrew was another high-profile disaster requiring FEMA's involvement.

FEMA was one of the many relief and recovery agencies to respond to the terrorist attacks of September 11, 2001. But nearly five years later, when Hurricane Katrina struck New Orleans and the Gulf Coast states of Mississippi and Alabama in August 2005, FEMA was revealed to be wholly unprepared for the task it was assigned. Experienced staff members who had been appointed by President Bill Clinton (1946–) had been replaced by less-qualified appointees named by President George W. Bush (1946–). The most notorious of these appointments was a new director, Michael Brown, an attorney and Republican fundraiser with no emergency management experience. Blame for FEMA's lack of preparedness in the aftermath of the storm was placed, at different times, on President Bush, Director Brown, and the usurpation of FEMA's authority by the newly created Department of Homeland Security.

The FEMA Bureaucracy   In defending its failures after Katrina, FEMA officials emphasized that the agency is not a "first responder." Instead, FEMA expects state and local emergency teams to handle most disasters, with the federal government principally serving as the rescuer of last resort. If requests cannot be fulfilled by state or local agencies, FEMA can then respond, but only by the direct request of a state's governor and on the recommendation of that FEMA region's director. Those requests are then passed to the director of FEMA, who makes recommendations to the secretary of the Department of Homeland Security, who then consults with the president. Even when FEMA is granted permission to assist, the agency defers to rather than directs the state government involved.

According to the agency, in 2007 FEMA employed roughly twenty-six hundred people as part of its

Incoming FEMA Director Joe Allbaugh addresses press after being sworn in by President George W. Bush, 2001. © *Reuters/CORBIS*

permanent staff and had access to more than four thousand reservists who could be deployed in an emergency. First responders at the local level, including firefighters, police officers, and emergency managers, often work with FEMA but are not employed by it.

⭐ Important Figures of the Day

Daniel Patrick Moynihan

Daniel Patrick Moynihan (1927–2003) was a social scientist, senator, college professor, and ambassador to the United Nations and to India. He is the only person to have served in the administrations of four consecutive presidents, Democrat as well as Republican.

Early Years Moynihan was born in Tulsa, Oklahoma, the eldest of three children born to John Henry (a journalist) and Margaret Ann Moynihan. By the time Moynihan was ten, his father had abandoned the family, and from then on he lived in relative poverty as his mother supported her three children by working as a nurse. Living in the slums of Manhattan, the Moynihans moved yearly because, as Moynihan later explained, the first month's rent was free if the tenant signed a one-year lease. Moynihan did well in school, graduating at the top of his high school class in Harlem in 1943. He then

worked as a longshoreman on the Hudson River docks until a friend persuaded him to take the entrance examination for the City College of New York. "I swaggered into the test room with my longshoreman's loading hook sticking out of my back pocket. I wasn't going to be mistaken for any sissy college kid. But I passed the test and decided to go to City—and that was the beginning of a lot of things in my life," he said.

Education and Early Career After a year in college, he enlisted in the Navy, which sent him to Tufts College for officer training and then to an assignment as a gunnery officer. He was seventeen. In 1947, after his discharge from the military, Moynihan enrolled in Tufts on the GI Bill and graduated cum laude a year later. He received a master's degree from the Fletcher School of International Law and Diplomacy at Tufts in 1949. Moynihan then won a Fulbright scholarship to the London School of Economics. He enjoyed England so much he stayed two more years, supporting himself by working at the U.S. Air Force base in Middlesex. He returned to the United States in 1953 and worked for Robert F. Wagner Jr. (1910–1991), the Democratic candidate for mayor of New York City. That effort led to work on the gubernatorial campaign of W. Averell Harriman (1891–1986) and a job as special assistant to Harriman after he

Daniel Patrick Moynihan at a press conference in 1969. © *Bettmann/CORBIS*

was elected governor of New York. In 1960 Moynihan worked on the presidential campaign of Democratic candidate John F. Kennedy (1917–1963) and became an assistant to Secretary of Labor Arthur Goldberg (1908–1990) in Kennedy's administration. While working at the White House he also completed work on a doctoral degree, awarded by Tufts University in 1961.

In March 1963 Moynihan became assistant secretary of labor for policy planning and research and collaborated that same year with sociologist Nathan Glazer (1923–) on the study *Beyond the Melting Pot: The Negroes, Puerto Ricans, Jews, Italians, and Irish of New York City.* Kennedy asked Moynihan to draft the government's first antipoverty legislation; after Kennedy's assassination, Moynihan stayed on with the project under President Lyndon Johnson (1908–1973). A year later Moynihan and others presented a draft of the Economic Opportunity Act of 1964, which led to the governmental programs known as the War on Poverty. Moynihan joined Johnson's 1964 presidential campaign, writing his speeches and helping to develop the Democratic platform.

The Moynihan Report In 1965 Moynihan's department produced "The Negro Family: The Case for National

Action." Commonly known as the Moynihan Report, it urged the federal government to adopt a national policy for the reconstruction of the black family. The report focused on the way government policies affected the stability of urban black families, noting that black children—boys in particular—who grew up in fatherless homes did not do well, particularly if their problems were complicated by racial prejudice and poverty. "From the wild Irish slums of the nineteenth-century Eastern seaboard, to the riot-torn suburbs of Los Angeles, there is one unmistakable lesson in American history: A community that allows large numbers of young men to grow up in broken families, dominated by women, never acquiring any stable relationship to male authority, never acquiring any set of rational expectations about the future—that community asks for and gets chaos. Crime, violence, unrest, disorder...are not only to be expected, they are very near to inevitable," explained Moynihan in a 1966 article in *America* magazine. The Moynihan report, which was supposed to be confidential, generated controversy at the time; however, many policy analysts have since come to see Moynihan's observations as prescient.

Later Career For three years he was director of the Joint Center for Urban Studies of Harvard University and the Massachusetts Institute of Technology. He then went to work for Republican President Richard Nixon (1913–1994) as an urban-affairs adviser. Moynihan returned to teaching at Harvard in 1970, but three years later accepted Nixon's appointment as U.S. ambassador to India, where he served for two years. President Gerald Ford (1913–2006) then appointed him as U.S. Permanent Representative to the United Nations.

In 1976 Moynihan was elected to the U.S. Senate from New York. A Democrat, in his four terms he became known for speaking his own mind. For example, he criticized the health-care plans proposed by Democratic President Bill Clinton (1946–) and surprised left-wing members of his party by supporting legislation to ban partial-birth abortion. In 2000 he decided not to run for re-election and retired to teach and write books. He wrote or edited eighteen books during his career and died following surgery in March 2003.

Richard M. Nixon

Richard Milhous Nixon (1913–1994), the thirty-seventh president of the United States, was the only president to resign from the office. His career is overshadowed by the Watergate scandal, which ended his political career. However, his presidency is also remembered for several important foreign policy decisions, including approval of a plan to bomb targets in Cambodia and Laos, which were neutral during the Vietnam War; reestablishment of relations with the People's Republic of China; and treaty negotiations to end the arms race with the Soviet Union.

Early Years and Education   Nixon, the son of a citrus farmer, was born in Yorba Linda, California, and taught himself to read before he went to first grade. When he was nine, the family moved to Whittier, California, where they regularly attended meetings of the Religious Society of Friends. Also known as Quakers, the Society of Friends is a pacifist religious sect that stresses the importance of a personal relationship with God and the equality of all people. Nixon's younger brother Arthur died of meningitis when Nixon was twelve, an experience that affected him profoundly. When Nixon graduated from high school he turned down a scholarship from Harvard because his parents could not afford the other expenses necessary to send him there. He saved money by attending Whittier College, graduating summa cum laude with a degree in government and history in 1934. Nixon then enrolled at Duke University Law School on a scholarship and graduated third in his class in 1937.

In 1942, with a recommendation from a former law school professor, Nixon went to work for the Office of Price Administration in Washington, D.C. When the Navy issued a call for lawyers during World War II, Nixon signed on and served in the Pacific, although he never saw combat. He resigned his commission as lieutenant commander in 1945 to run for Congress.

From Congress to the White House   Nixon's first public attention came during his work on the House Committee on Un-American Activities, where he helped bring about the conviction of Alger Hiss (1904–1996), a high-ranking State Department official, for being a Soviet spy. Nixon repeatedly used the fear that Communists had infiltrated the government—it was the era of the Red Scare—to his political advantage, often claiming that his opponents had Communist sympathies. After two terms in the House, he was elected to the Senate. In 1952 he was chosen by Dwight D. Eisenhower (1890–1969) as his vice presidential running mate. They won and served two terms in the White House.

Nixon ran for president against John F. Kennedy (1917–1963), a Democratic senator from Massachusetts, in 1960. In the first-ever televised debate Nixon, who was recovering from an illness and declined makeup to lighten his skin and cover the stubble on his face, stood out in stark contrast to a rested, clean-shaven, and tanned Kennedy. Kennedy also appeared to many viewers to be confident and competent, allaying fears that he was too young and did not have as much experience as Nixon. Many historians have considered the televised debate to be the deciding moment in the close race: Nixon lost the election.

Nixon returned to California, where he ran for governor and lost dramatically to Edmund G. "Pat" Brown Sr. (1905–1996). He thought the media had favored his opponent in their reporting, so the morning after the election he announced his "last press conference" and told the press, "[You] won't have Dick Nixon to kick around anymore."

In 1968 he surprised many by becoming a candidate for president again. With Maryland Governor Spiro Agnew (1918–1996) as his running mate, Nixon defeated the incumbent vice president, Democrat Hubert H. Humphrey (1911–1978), and the former Alabama governor, George C. Wallace (1919–1998), who ran as a third-party candidate.

President Nixon   Once in office Nixon initiated a program of "Vietnamization" that was designed to gradually withdraw U.S. troops from Vietnam. Their role was to be filled by South Vietnamese troops, bolstered by U.S. military supplies and aid. However, he also increased U.S.-led air attacks on North Vietnam and ordered secret bombing campaigns of North Vietnamese supply areas in politically neutral Laos and Cambodia. In 1970 those attacks led to public protest, which prompted Nixon to order government agencies to collect intelligence information on antiwar organizations and individuals who criticized his Vietnam tactics.

In February 1972 Nixon stunned his supporters, as well as the world, by reopening communications with the Communist leadership of the People's Republic of China and making an official visit. Tension between China and the Soviet Union had grown over the

Vice-President Richard Nixon (right) with Senator Barry Goldwater, 1960. © *Bettmann/CORBIS*

previous decade, especially along their mutual border. Nixon and his national security adviser, Henry Kissinger (1923–), decided to improve relations with China to gain a strategic advantage over the Soviet Union. The "China card," as it became known, increased pressure on the Soviets to improve relations with the West. In May Nixon became the first U.S. president to visit Moscow, where he and Soviet leader Leonid Brezhnev (1906–1982) signed the Strategic Arms Limitation Talks (SALT I) agreement, a treaty to halt the nuclear arms race. Nixon's visit also led to combined scientific and aeronautic ventures and bilateral trade accords.

The Watergate Scandal   Nixon was reelected in 1972, defeating George S. McGovern (1922–), a Democratic senator from South Dakota. His second term was marked by the scandal that became known as Watergate, which involved illegal activities by Nixon and his aides during his re-election campaign. Five men, who had been hired by the Republican Party's Committee to Reelect the President, were arrested for burglary on June 17, 1972, at Watergate, an office-apartment-hotel complex in Washington, D.C., where they had been attempting to wiretap the headquarters of the Democratic National Committee. Shortly after the break-in, Nixon asked White House counsel John Dean (1938–) to oversee a cover-up of the administration's involvement and

authorized secret payments to the Watergate burglars to discourage them from talking. In February 1973 a special Senate committee, chaired by Democratic Senator Sam Ervin (1896–1985) of North Carolina, was set up to investigate the situation. By April several White House aides had resigned, and Dean had been fired. In May a special prosecutor for Watergate-related matters was appointed.

During the Watergate committee's televised hearings, Dean linked Nixon to the cover-up, and staff members attested to illegal activities of both the Nixon administration and his campaign staff. On July 13 a former White House aide, Alexander Butterfield (1926–), told the committee that Nixon routinely taped conversations in the Oval Office, in the White House cabinet room, in his office in the Executive Office Building, and on four of his personal telephones. Five days later Nixon had the taping system disconnected. The special prosecutor ordered Nixon to turn the tapes over to the Senate Watergate Committee, but he refused, citing executive privilege. On July 24 the Supreme Court ordered Nixon to turn the tapes over to the committee. Three days later the House Judiciary Committee passed three articles of impeachment against Nixon. On August 9 he resigned, and Vice President Gerald R. Ford (1913–2006) took office.

President Richard Nixon announcing his resignation, 1974. © *Bettmann/CORBIS*

Citizen Nixon One month after Nixon left office, Ford pardoned him for his role in the Watergate scandal. In retirement Nixon wrote books about foreign policy and his experiences in public life and traveled to Asia, Africa, Europe, and the Middle East. He went to the Soviet Union in 1986 to meet with Mikhail Gorbachev (1931–), then its leader, and was later credited for helping to bring Soviet leaders and the administration of Ronald Reagan (1911–2004) to their arms limitation agreement.

> *See also* **Watergate**
> *See also* **United States v. Nixon**

Warren Burger

Warren Earl Burger (1907–1995) was the fifteenth chief justice of the United States, serving from 1969 to 1986. Under his leadership the court delivered landmark decisions on school desegregation, obscenity, abortion, and religious freedom. It also hastened the resignation of President Richard Nixon (1913–1994) in 1974, when the court ordered Nixon to submit audiotapes of White House meetings for Senate review during the Watergate scandal.

Early Years After high school, Burger was offered a scholarship to Princeton University, but he declined it because it did not cover enough of his educational expenses. Instead, he took a job at an insurance company and attended classes at the University of Minnesota at night. After two years he transferred to St. Paul College of Law (later renamed William Mitchell College of Law) and graduated magna cum laude in 1931.

Burger joined a leading law firm and during the 1930s became active in Republican Party politics. He helped to organize the Minnesota Young Republicans and managed the successful campaign for governor of another Minnesota lawyer, Harold Stassen (1907–2001). While serving as floor manager for Stassen at the 1948 Republican National Convention, Burger was first introduced to Nixon, then a freshman congressman.

In 1953 Burger was appointed assistant attorney general of the United States by President Dwight D. Eisenhower (1890–1969). Before long Burger gained public notice for his successful prosecution of Greek shipowner Stavros Niarchos (1909–1996) and others for illegally buying surplus U.S. war vessels. Burger resigned this position in 1956, planning to return to his law practice in St. Paul, but Eisenhower appointed him instead to the U.S. Court of Appeals for the District of Columbia. "I never have had a passion to be a judge," Burger once admitted to friends, but he accepted the position in part because he thought the East Coast climate was better for his wife's health.

During the thirteen years Burger served on the appeals court, he was critical of a number of decisions regarding criminal procedure that were made by the Supreme Court under the leadership of Chief Justice Earl Warren (1891–1974). He attracted Nixon's attention in 1967 when *U.S. News and World Report* reprinted a speech in which Burger insisted the U.S. criminal justice system needed to be changed because, he said, it was slanted toward the criminal. While a candidate for president, Nixon later told Burger, he used two points from the article in a campaign speech. Nixon was no fan of the Warren Court and was critical of it during his 1968 campaign. He thought justices should be strict constructionists—that is, jurists who believed in applying the text of the Constitution or law as written, inferring no additional meaning. Such a judicial philosophy opposes more interpretive approaches—for example, those that attempt to understand the original intentions of the authors of the Constitution or those that consider the social context of the decision. In 1969 Nixon nominated Burger to be chief justice when Warren retired. The honor both surprised and mystified Burger. "I hardly knew Nixon," he admitted.

The Burger Court Part of Burger's influence on the court was administrative. For example, he added staff librarians, clerks, and administrative assistants, and he upgraded the court's law library and technology. He established the Supreme Court Fellows Program, through which individuals from various professional and academic backgrounds work and study at the Supreme Court to see firsthand how the federal judiciary operates and how it relates to the other branches of government. Burger also helped develop the Federal Judicial Center, which is the education and research agency for the federal courts, and the National Center for State Courts, which provides research, education, and publications for lower courts. As important, he successfully lobbied Congress to limit the court's case docket, for he believed the court was overloaded.

During his seventeen years as chief justice Burger wrote 265 majority opinions in addition to dissenting or concurring opinions. As a Nixon appointee he was expected to follow a strict constructionist approach to constitutional law and guide the court in that direction. Social conservatives had been critical of the Warren court for its judicial activism—using the court's authority to extend or effect laws—and expected Burger to reverse this trend. However, the Burger court implemented a pragmatic, case-by-case approach rather than one adhering strictly to a single judicial philosophy.

Many of the cases decided by the Burger Court became landmarks. It upheld the 1966 *Miranda v. Arizona* decision, which said that individuals under arrest have the right to an attorney and the right to remain silent, and that nothing they say can be admitted in court or used against them unless they agreed to waive their rights. Burger wrote the unanimous opinion for *Swann v. Charlotte-Mecklenburg Board of Education* (1971), which upheld the use of busing or redistricting to integrate public schools, and for *Wisconsin v. Yoder* (1972), which defended freedom of religion and refused to force Amish parents to send their children to public schools. In *Lemon v. Kurtzman* (1971), which established the basic standard that courts should use to ensure the separation of church and state, Burger devised a three-part constitutional test: The government's action had to have a legitimate secular purpose; the action could not have the primary effect of either advancing or inhibiting religion; and it could not result in what Burger called "excessive government entanglement" with religion. He delivered the defining opinion in *Miller v. California* (1973), in which he said that local "contemporary community standards" must decide what is considered obscene for each community. He also voted with the majority in *Roe v. Wade* (1973), which said that most laws against abortion violated a constitutional right to privacy under the Due Process Clause of the Fourteenth Amendment.

Perhaps most memorably, in *United States v. Nixon* (1974), Burger showed a loyalty to constitutional law instead of to the president who had appointed him. On behalf of a unanimous court, he delivered the decision that ruled against President Nixon, who had insisted that executive privilege gave him the right to maintain the confidentiality of audiotaped recordings of White House conversations. A special prosecutor who was investigating the Watergate scandal wanted the tapes for evidence of criminal activity among Nixon and his associates, and the president was ordered to turn over the recordings "forthwith." Nixon admitted that he was "disappointed" by the decision, but said he would comply. He resigned seventeen days later. Burger retired from the Supreme Court in 1986.

See also **United States v. Nixon**
See also **Watergate**

Chief Justice Warren Burger swearing in Jimmy Carter as thirty-ninth president of the United States, 1977. *Bernard Gotfryd/Getty Images*

Gloria Steinem

Gloria Steinem (1934–) was one of the most important leaders of the women's movement in the late twentieth century. She cofounded *Ms.* magazine in 1972 and helped establish numerous feminist organizations beginning in the 1960s. A prominent media figure and public speaker, Steinem tirelessly lobbied for equality for women and for political action on the social and legal issues that most affect women's lives.

Early Life Steinem is the granddaughter of suffragist Pauline Perlmutter Steinem (1863–1940), who once addressed Congress about women's right to vote. Steinem's early years were spent traveling the country in a mobile home while her father bought and sold antiques. Because the family never stayed long in one place, she was home schooled by her mother, who had a teaching certificate. When Steinem graduated from Smith College in 1956 with a degree in government she embarked on a fellowship for two years of study in India.

Career as a Journalist In 1960 Steinem moved to New York City, where she worked as a freelance journalist writing for newspapers and magazines. An assignment from *Show* magazine was her first major investigative-reporting job. Armed with a diary she applied incognito for a position as a "bunny," or waitress, at the New York Playboy Club. After working there for three weeks, she produced a lengthy article that exposed the degrading treatment and poor wages of the young women hired to work as waitresses in a luxury club for wealthy men. Initially the story resulted in Steinem's not being taken seriously as a journalist, but it did help to improve the working conditions for the women at the club. In 1984 the story was turned into a film for television, *A Bunny's Tale.* Years later, after watching a rerun of the show, Steinem said she finally stopped regretting writing the article and "began to take pleasure in the connections it made with women who might not have picked up a feminist book or magazine, but who responded to the rare sight of realistic working conditions and a group of women who supported each other."

In 1968 Steinem became a founding member of *New York* magazine, where she worked as a political columnist until 1972. She covered a meeting of a feminist group and listened as women shared their experiences of having abortions, which at that time were in almost all cases illegal. "I heard women standing up and saying in public and taking serious something that only affected women. Up until then, I'd never heard that. If it didn't also affect men, it couldn't be serious," she said. For some time

Steinem had been politically active, working in political, civil-rights, and peace campaigns, but the women's event, she said, "was the beginning of the unraveling." Steinem turned her focus to women's causes.

Steinem, who is white, began speaking across the country with Dorothy Pitman Hughes (1938–), an African-American childcare activist, and later Florynce Kennedy (1916–2000), an African-American lawyer, and Margaret Sloan (1947–2004), an African-American civil-rights activist. "It was a time when even one feminist speaker was a novelty, and interracial teams of feminists seemed to be unheard of since the days of Sojourner Truth," said Steinem. The activists found dialogue with their audiences after their talks to be the most important. Women spoke honestly about their experiences, and both men and women in attendance heard their stories. "Most of all," said Steinem, "women in those audiences discovered they were neither crazy nor alone. And so did we."

Ms. Magazine   In 1971 Steinem helped start *Ms.* magazine, which began as an insert in *New York* magazine. When the magazine was launched in 1972, most magazines geared to women had articles about marriage, fashion, and beauty. *Ms.* had articles that challenged prevailing attitudes about women and their roles, examined stereotypes in child rearing, and questioned sexist language. It was intended, Steinem said, to be "a friend that comes into your house and is something that really tells the truth about your life and will help change life instead of just offering an escape." *Ms.* was the first mainstream national magazine to be completely run and managed by women. The three hundred thousand copies of the premiere issue sold out in eight days and elicited twenty-six thousand subscription orders.

A Legacy of Organizations   In 1971 Steinem, along with Shirley Chisholm (1924–2005), Bella Abzug (1920–1998), Myrlie Evers (1933–), and Betty Friedan (1921–2006), formed the National Women's Political Caucus, an organization dedicated to increasing women's participation in politics. Steinem helped found other organizations, including Voters for Choice, the Women's Action Alliance, the Coalition of Labor Union Women, and the Women's Media Center. She also participated in the creation of Take Our Daughters to Work Day in 1993, an effort to expose young women to the realities of the workplace and to help them determine future career goals.

Over the course of her career Steinem produced several books, including *Outrageous Acts and Everyday Rebellions* (1983) and *Revolution from Within: A Book of Self-Esteem* (1992). In 1993 she was inducted into the National Women's Hall of Fame.

On September 3, 2000, when she was sixty-seven, she surprised many observers by marrying David Bale (1941–2003), a South African pilot and entrepreneur, who had once been banned from South Africa because

Gloria Steinem marching at a women's rights rally in New York City, 1995. *Evan Agostini/Liaison/Getty Images*

of his antiapartheid work. Steinem herself was astonished by the public reaction to her marriage: "What surprised me was that no one saw how much marriage has changed since the '60s, when I would have had to give up most of my civil rights." In the ceremony, the word *partners* was used instead of *husband and wife*. Bale died three years later from brain lymphoma.

Gerald R. Ford

Gerald Rudolph Ford (1913–2006) was the thirty-eighth president of the United States and the first person to become president without having been elected either vice president or president. Ford had aspired to be speaker of the House; instead, as scandals caused the removal of first the vice president and then the president from office, Ford assumed the executive office in August 1974.

Early Years and Career   Ford was born Leslie Lynch King Jr. in Omaha, Nebraska. Two weeks later his mother separated from her husband and moved to Grand Rapids, Michigan, to live with her parents. She divorced King,

and two years later married Gerald R. Ford, a paint salesman. The Fords began calling her son Gerald Jr., but his
name was not legally changed until 1935. When he was
thirteen Ford learned that Gerald Sr. was not his biological father, and when he was seventeen he finally met
King, who casually stopped by on a road trip to Detroit.

Ford attended the University of Michigan, where he
played center on the football team and was voted Most
Valuable Player during the 1934 season. In 1935 he
played in the East-West college game in San Francisco
and the Chicago Charities College All-Star game against
the Chicago Bears of the National Football League. He
graduated with a bachelor's degree in economics and
political science in 1935. The Detroit Lions and the
Green Bay Packers offered him professional football contracts, but Ford declined both in order to take a coaching
job at Yale, where he hoped to attend law school. Initially
denied admission to Yale Law School because of his full-
time coaching jobs, Ford was accepted in the spring of
1938. He worked on the presidential campaign of
Republican Wendell Willkie (1892–1944) in 1940.

Ford returned to Grand Rapids after his graduation
from law school in 1941 and opened a practice with
Philip A. Buchen, a friend from his time at the University
of Michigan. Ford also became active in local politics and
helped launch a reform group of like-minded Republicans, called the Home Front, who were opposed to a
local political boss.

Military Career When the United States entered
World War II, Ford enlisted in the Navy and was sent
first to the naval academy in Annapolis, Maryland, as a
physical training instructor and later to Chapel Hill,
North Carolina, as an athletic training officer. He served
on the carrier USS *Monterey* as a gunnery officer and
athletic officer, later becoming an assistant navigator.
During Ford's tour of duty the ship was involved in
operations in the Pacific theater, including the Battle of
Makin in November 1943 and the Battle of the Philippine Sea in April 1944.

A Run for Congress Encouraged by his associates in
the Home Front; by his stepfather, who was county
Republican Party chair; and by Senator Arthur Vanden-
berg (1884–1951), Ford ran for the House of Representatives in 1948 and won. He was reelected twelve
times. During his first term he, along with former Navy
lieutenant commander Richard Nixon (1913–1994) and
a number of other young House Republicans, opposed
monthly bonuses for war veterans, which they deemed
too costly. In 1951 Ford was appointed to the House
Appropriations Committee, where he served for many
years. By 1961 he had become the ranking Republican
on the Defense Appropriations Subcommittee.

The Warren Commission On November 29, 1963,
one week after the assassination of President John F.
Kennedy (1917–1963), Ford was appointed by Presi-

dent Lyndon Johnson (1908–1973) to a commission
to investigate Kennedy's murder. In their report the
seven members of the commission—which became
known as the Warren Commission after its chair, Chief
Justice Earl Warren (1891–1974)—concluded that Lee
Harvey Oswald (1939–1963) acted alone in killing Kennedy and that there was no evidence of a conspiracy in
the assassination. They proposed the strengthening of
Secret Service protection for the president and legislation that would make it a federal offense to kill either the
president or vice president.

Rise to the Presidency In 1964 Ford was elected
House minority leader, the top position among Republicans in Congress. He held this position until 1973,
when he was appointed by Nixon to replace Vice President Spiro Agnew (1918–1996). Agnew had resigned in
a scandal that emanated from his earlier years as governor
of Maryland. Ford was the first vice president nominated
under the Twenty-fifth Amendment to the Constitution,
which clarified procedures for filling vacancies in the
offices of vice president and president. When Nixon
resigned the following year as a result of the Watergate
scandal, Ford became president.

The Chief Executive On August 9, 1974, Ford took
the oath of office, acknowledging "I have not sought
this enormous responsibility, but I will not shirk it." In a
reference to Watergate, he said, "My fellow Americans,
our long national nightmare is over. Our Constitution
works; our great Republic is a government of laws and
not of men.... As we bind up the internal wounds of
Watergate, more painful and more poisonous than those
of foreign wars, let us restore the golden rule to our
political process, and let brotherly love purge our hearts
of suspicion and of hate." He selected former New York
governor Nelson Rockefeller (1908–1979) to be vice
president.

Less than a month later Ford granted a full pardon
to Nixon, which resulted in public outcry and accusations of a prearranged deal. Ford maintained that no
arrangement had been made and that the pardon was
the right thing to do for the country. He feared that
ongoing legal proceedings against Nixon would intensify
partisan rancor, impede progress on other issues, and
damage U.S. credibility abroad. Ford wanted the Watergate era to end. In announcing Nixon's pardon, he
declared "My conscience tells me that only I, as President, have the constitutional power to firmly shut and
seal this book. My conscience tells me it is my duty, not
merely to proclaim domestic tranquility but to use every
means that I have to insure it."

During his administration Ford issued limited
amnesty for men who had evaded the draft during the
Vietnam War. Under Ford's plan, those who had resisted
service were to be pardoned in exchange for two years of
civilian service. In 1975 he announced the Vietnam War
was "finished as far as America is concerned" and ordered

President Gerald Ford, defending his pardon of former President Richard Nixon at a press conference, 1974.   *Keystone/Consolidated News Pictures/Getty Images*

the evacuation of U.S. personnel and high-risk South Vietnamese officials from Saigon. Soon afterward, in April 1975, Saigon fell to Communist forces.

Ford signed the Federal Election Campaign Act Amendments of 1974, which placed limits on political campaign contributions; the Privacy Act of 1974, which prohibited the unauthorized release by federal agencies of information about individual citizens; and the Government in the Sunshine Act, which required that meetings of government agencies be open to public view. Ford vetoed the Freedom of Information Act Amendments, which clarified procedures for public access to information from government agencies, but Congress overrode his veto and the bill became law.

In 1975 two assassination attempts were made on Ford's life, the first by Lynette "Squeaky" Fromme (1948–), a follower of cult leader Charles Manson (1934–), and the second, only a few weeks later, by Sara Jane Moore (1930–), a member of left-wing radical groups. He was not injured.

Ford was defeated by Jimmy Carter (1924–) in the 1976 presidential election. Many believe he lost because he had pardoned Nixon. However, Carter acknowledged Ford's role in getting the country past the Watergate scandal when he thanked Ford in his inaugural address "for all he has done to heal our land." In 2001 the John F. Kennedy Foundation presented Ford the Profiles in Courage Award for his pardon of Nixon, which "ended the national trauma of Watergate," according to Caroline Kennedy Schlossberg (1957–), the president's daughter. In doing so, she said, "he placed his love of country ahead of his own political future."

Jimmy Carter

James Earl "Jimmy" Carter Jr. (1924–), the thirty-ninth president of the United States and former governor of Georgia, is a human-rights activist and recipient of the Nobel Peace Prize for his accomplishments after leaving the White House. When he was elected president in 1976, he became the first chief executive from the Deep South since the election of Zachary Taylor (1784–1850) in 1848.

Early Years and Career Carter was born in Plains, Georgia, into a strongly religious family devoted to evangelical Christianity and Democratic politics. He graduated from the local public school in 1941 and attended Georgia Southwestern College and Georgia Institute of Technology before being accepted to the U.S. Naval Academy. Ranked in the top 10 percent of his class, he received a bachelor's degree in engineering in 1946, then went to submarine officer training school. He later served in both Atlantic and Pacific fleets and ultimately achieved the rank of lieutenant. Under Admiral Hyman Rickover (1900–1986) Carter served on the USS *Seawolf*, one of the nation's first nuclear submarines.

From State Senator to Governor In 1953 Carter resigned his naval commission and took over the family peanut farm after the death of his father. He began serving on local governing boards that oversaw education and hospital management and decided to run for state senator, an office his father had held a year before he died. Carter lost the primary by 139 votes, but was declared the winner after a recount that exposed corruption and racial discrimination in election administration. He subsequently won the seat and was sworn in as a Georgia state senator in 1963.

Three years later Carter joined the race for the governor's office. He lost the Democratic nomination to Lester Maddox (1915–2003), a restaurant owner and segregationist, who later won the general election. In response to this political disappointment, Carter turned to religious works. He served as a missionary in Pennsylvania and Massachusetts, taught Sunday school in Plains, and gave talks about Christianity.

In 1970 Carter again ran for governor, and a contentious debate on racial segregation raged throughout the campaign. Because he refused to condemn such segregationists as Governor George C. Wallace (1919–1998) of Alabama during his campaign appearances, voters inferred that Carter approved of policies that maintained separation of the races. Carter won the election. At his inauguration, the newly elected governor startled his constituents and garnered national attention when he declared, "[The] time for racial discrimination is over.... No poor, rural, weak, or black person should ever have to bear the additional burden of being deprived of the opportunity of an education, a job, or simple justice." Undeterred by criticism, Carter appointed blacks and women to state government positions and had portraits of Martin Luther King Jr. (1929–1968) and other notable black Georgians hung in the state capitol. *Time* magazine put him on its May 31, 1971, cover with the headline, "Dixie Whistles a Different Tune." Carter created biracial groups to manage racial tension, promoted prison reform, and developed new programs in health care and education. He instituted a governmental reorganization plan that combined some three hundred state agencies into twenty-two.

Two years into his term Carter decided to run for president against incumbent President Gerald Ford (1913–2006). While he had a network of Democratic Party leaders throughout the country, he still was not widely known to the vast majority of voters. With the words "Hi! My name is Jimmy Carter, and I'm going to be your next president" and his characteristic toothy grin, he achieved recognition. During the campaign he focused on his character, presenting himself as an honest man and not a Washington insider. He chose Minnesota Senator Walter F. Mondale (1928–) as his vice presidential running mate, and together they won the election. On Inauguration Day, in keeping with his folksy, approachable manner, Carter startled everyone by getting out of the presidential limousine and walking with his wife and daughter along Pennsylvania Avenue to the White House.

The Presidency The day after his inauguration Carter extended conditional amnesty to Vietnam draft resisters who had either not registered or had fled the country. The pardon, however, excluded deserters and soldiers who received dishonorable discharges. Response was mixed, mostly negative from veterans' groups, but, as Carter said later, "I thought the best thing to do was to pardon them and get the Vietnam War behind us." During his presidency Carter increased the number of women, blacks, and Hispanics appointed to government positions. He taught Sunday School classes in Washington, D.C., and sent his daughter to public school.

As an administrator he divided the Department of Health, Education, and Welfare into the Department of Health and Human Services and the Department of Education, and he created the Department of Energy. When a nuclear reactor at the Three Mile Island power plant in Pennsylvania experienced a partial meltdown, Carter personally went to the site and assessed the reactor in an effort to calm public anxiety. One month later, however, some sixty-five thousand demonstrators marched in Washington, demanding all U.S. nuclear plants be shut down. Carter held firm, saying that such a policy was "out of the question."

Many of Carter's most significant accomplishments were in foreign policy. In 1978 he invited Israeli Prime Minister Menachem Begin (1913–1992) and Egyptian President Anwar Sadat (1918–1981) to meet with him at Camp David, the presidential retreat in Maryland,

Democratic presidential candidate Jimmy Carter, 1976.
© *Bettmann/CORBIS*

where he brokered a peace accord between the two countries. A year later he watched as they signed the Egypt-Israel Peace Treaty at the White House. He instituted full diplomatic relations with the People's Republic of China, building on the work begun during the presidency of Richard M. Nixon (1913–1994), and obtained ratification of the Panama Canal treaty, which established a timetable for transferring the canal to Panamanian sovereignty. He also completed negotiation of the second Strategic Arms Limitation Treaty (SALT II), which he signed with Soviet leader Leonid Brezhnev (1906–1982); however, the Soviets' invasion of Afghanistan in 1979 forced Carter to ask the Senate to table the treaty.

The Iran Hostage Crisis Carter's foreign policy achievements are often overshadowed by a crisis that developed in 1979 after he allowed Mohammad Reza Pahlavi (1919–1980), the shah of Iran, to enter the United States for medical treatment. The shah had fled Iran after a year of public unrest led by Muslim cleric Ayatollah Ruhollah Khomeini (1902–1989) in response to alleged human rights abuses during Pahlavi's regime.

Angered by Carter's perceived support of the shah, militant Iranian students overtook the U.S. embassy in Tehran on November 4, 1979, seizing sixty-three hostages and demanding that the shah be returned to Iran for trial. Carter froze all Iranian financial assets in the United States. A few days later the Iranians freed thirteen African-American and female hostages, but continued to hold the others. On April 24, 1980, a U.S. military mission to rescue the hostages had to be aborted when a helicopter crash resulted in the deaths of eight servicemen and injuries to three. Days before, Secretary of State Cyrus Vance (1917–2002) had resigned over the decision to proceed with the mission. On July 11 the Iranians released one more prisoner who had developed a serious medical condition. On July 27 the shah died. Two months later the Iranian government indicated it was willing to discuss releasing the hostages.

Meanwhile, former California governor Ronald Reagan (1911–2004) was running against Carter for president. On November 2, the Iranian parliament issued a statement, saying the hostages would not be released before the election. Two days later Reagan won a landslide victory. Minutes after Reagan was inaugurated in January 1981, the Iranians released the hostages. On behalf of Reagan, Carter flew to Germany to meet the freed hostages. Although the ordeal had ended, many critics blamed Carter's inaction and lack of resolve in ending the hostage crisis with both prolonging the suffering for the hostages and ending his own political career.

Human Rights Activism After his presidency Carter established the Carter Center in Atlanta, Georgia, with the goal of advancing human rights and alleviating human suffering internationally. It offers a variety of programs to resolve conflicts and fight diseases in many parts of the world. He and his wife also became involved in Habitat for Humanity, an interfaith organization that helps people of limited means build their own homes. Each year the couple devotes one week to construction projects in the United States and elsewhere. In 2002 Carter was awarded the Nobel Peace Prize for "his decades of untiring efforts to find peaceful solutions to international conflict."

See also **The Iran Hostage Crisis**

✪ Political Parties, Platforms, and Key Issues

Polling and Public Opinion

Public opinion polling is used to assess the views of a specific segment of the population—or of the entire nation—by asking questions of a representative sample of people. Public opinion polling is used by marketers trying to sell services or products and by politicians to understand the will of the people and sell themselves and their policies to the electorate at large.

How Polls Are Conducted In the earliest days of public opinion polling—believed to have occurred in 1824 during the presidential election between Andrew Jackson (1767–1845) and John Quincy Adams (1867–1848)—the survey method was a "straw poll," which in many ways is like asking a group of people gathered in a particular place to indicate their views with a show of hands, and then counting and comparing those votes. Straw polls are not scientific and they are generally not representative of overall public opinion.

Later polling methods came to include mailings, in which one or many questions are sent to a selection of addresses and the results are tallied from the responses received. While these types of surveys can be sent to thousands of people at once, it is difficult to determine whether the results represent a true sampling of opinion. One potential problem, for example, is that the only people who respond might be those who were willing or able to spend the time and the cost of postage.

Public opinion polls can also be conducted face to face (either on the street or at people's homes), by tele-phone, or, since the late 1990s, via e-mail or the Internet.

The Gallup Methodology Although there are many outlets through which to conduct an opinion poll, only those that survey what has come to be called "a scientific sample" of the population are considered accurate. In the 1930s a sociologist named George Gallup (1901–1984) devised a polling method in which he could survey a small but scientifically selected sample of individuals that could accurately represent the population at large. For example, if it is known that 51 percent of the adult population in the United States is female and 49 percent is male, rather than survey every man and woman in the country, Gallup could survey just 1,000 people, making sure that 510 of the participants were female and 490 male. The results of Gallup's small survey could be extrapolated to what the citizenry at large is thinking.

Polls based on such scientific samples are subject to a "sampling error" or estimated level of imprecision; for example, a result may be considered accurate to within plus or minus three percentage points. What cannot be controlled by any polling method is the "bias" effect, which acknowledges that there may be people that polling just cannot reach, such as individuals who will not accept phone calls from strangers. Another variable is called "response bias," which is an acknowledgment that some respondents do not tell pollsters their true beliefs—perhaps out of embarrassment, fear, impatience, or because the questions asked were manipulative and written in a way meant to elicit a certain response.

George Gallup founded the American Institute of Public Opinion in 1936. Since then, his polling methodology has dominated marketing and political polling. Agencies similar to Gallup include the Roper Poll, the Harris Poll, and the National Opinion Research Center.

Political Polling Abraham Lincoln (1809–1865) once said, "What I want to get done is what the people desire to have done, and the question for me is how to find that out exactly." Since the 1930s and the fine-tuning of polling techniques by George Gallup, U.S. presidents and presidential candidates have used public opinion polls to take the pulse of the country. While both Franklin D. Roosevelt (1882–1945) and Dwight D. Eisenhower (1890–1969) sought the assistance of public opinion polling during their campaigns and administrations, Harry Truman (1884–1972) did not. John F. Kennedy (1917–1963) was the first presidential candidate to rely heavily on polling during the campaign, and every presidential candidate since has included poll-sters as members of the campaign team. Presidents Lyndon Johnson (1908–1973), Richard Nixon (1913–1994), Jimmy Carter (1924–), and George H. W. Bush (1924–) reached out to pollsters during their presiden-cies, and Ronald Reagan (1911–2004), Bill Clinton (1946–), and George W. Bush (1946–) routinely used

Political consultants such as James Carville use polling and public opinion data to shape politicians' campaigns and their policies while in office. © *Nancy Kaszerman/ZUMA/Corbis*

polling as a tool before and during their respective two terms in the White House.

Media polls conducted by news organizations and nonpartisan polling agencies such as Gallup and Roper are generally considered to provide fair and accurate assessments of the subject at hand, but beginning with Kennedy, presidents also hired their own pollsters. Such private polling has become increasingly political and partisan, with public opinion polls specifically commissioned and scripted to support certain policies and points of view.

✪ Current Events and Social Movements

The Black Panther Party

The Black Panther Party was a civil rights organization that espoused black nationalism and, if necessary, violent revolution as a means for African-Americans to achieve liberation from white oppression. Strongly socialist in nature, the Black Panthers sought to end police brutality, reduce the number of African-American men incarcer-

---

BLACK PANTHER PARTY FOR SELF-DEFENSE: *THE TEN-POINT PLAN*

Echoing the prose of Thomas Jefferson (1743–1826) in the *Declaration of Independence*, in 1966 Huey P. Newton (1942–1989) and Bobby Seale (1936–) issued the Black Panther Party's manifesto, which they titled *The Ten-Point Plan*. In 1972 the points were amended to expand the Panthers' mission to benefit "all oppressed people."

The cofounders of the Black Panther Party devised the plan while sitting in an Oakland, California, jail after an altercation with police. Their final text was a combination of both lofty and tangible demands. Great emphasis was placed on the principles of self-determination, liberty, peace, justice, and the "immediate end to police brutality" and "all wars of aggression." In addition, the Panthers called for full employment, decent housing, food, education, and "completely free health care" for all oppressed people inside the United States. They wanted blacks to be exempt from military service and called for the release of "all black and oppressed people now held in U.S. federal, state, city, and military prisons and jails."

Speaking to a college audience in 2006, four decades after issuing the *Ten-Point Plan*, Seale commented: "A lot of people thought the Black Panther Party started because we wanted to be macho with some guns, but we were readers and researchers.... We not only captured the imagination of the African-American community, we captured the imagination of everybody."

---

ated in American prisons, provide meals and education for African-American children and, ultimately, create a separate society for blacks in the United States.

The Origins of the Black Panther Party Originally called the Black Panther Party for Self Defense, the Black Panthers were founded by Huey P. Newton (1942–1989) and Bobby Seale (1936–) in Oakland, California, in 1965 after riots in the impoverished Watts neighborhood of Los Angeles and the assassination of Nation of Islam leader Malcolm X (1925–1965). Although by 1965 the federal government had codified equal rights and protections for people of all races into the law, actual improvements in the lives of poor African-Americans were minimal, if not nonexistent. To the Panthers, the guarantees of equality secured by the Civil Rights Act of 1964 were inadequate—especially when considered in the context of the country's long history of slavery, segregationist laws, and tolerance for the murderous actions of white supremacists in the Ku Klux Klan.

The Black Panther Movement Police brutality against African-Americans was the specific impetus for the organization of the Black Panthers. The Panthers considered the ghettos where poor African-Americans lived to be "occupied territories" brutalized by a racist government. Hence, they believed that jailed black men were "prisoners of war" and that convictions made by white juries were invalid because the defendants had not been tried by a jury of their peers. The Black Panther Party argued that African-Americans should not be drafted to serve in Vietnam because both African-Americans and the people of Vietnam were at war with the U.S. government.

Unlike the more mainstream activists of the civil rights movement—the National Association for Colored People (NAACP) and the Southern Christian Leadership Conference (SCLC) headed by the Reverend Martin Luther King Jr. (1929–1968)—the Black Panther Party did not seek as its ultimate goal equality and integration with whites. Nor did the Panthers' founders accept King's peaceful resistance and the NAACP's strategy of securing equality and a guarantee of Constitutional rights through the federal courts. Instead, the Black Panthers advocated violence, revolution, and armed resistance in order to gain complete black independence from whites or any other authority. Whereas King and other Southern civil rights activists dressed in business attire, the Panthers' wardrobe consisted of black leather jackets and black berets, often accessorized with shotguns. There were frequent confrontations between the Panthers and law enforcement officials, which resulted in shoot-outs, deaths on both sides, and the arrests of Panther members.

In the mid-1970s a rift developed between Black Panther members who wanted to scale back the violence and expand the party's mission to serve all oppressed people and those who wanted to maintain the "Black

---

Two members of the Black Panther Party on the steps of the California State Capitol, 1967. The police officer is informing them that they will be allowed to keep their weapons as long as they do not disturb the peace. © *Bettmann/CORBIS*

Power" focus. But the Panthers' stated mission did expand to include community service work, in part to quell its reputation for being solely a paramilitary organization. The Panthers started a free breakfast program for schoolchildren, founded free health clinics, distributed clothing to the needy, and established transportation programs for the elderly and the families of prisoners.

Public Enemy #1   Critics alleged that the goods and money distributed by the Panthers were attained by intimidating local businesses and individuals. The Panthers maintained that the Federal Bureau of Investigation (FBI) harassed the service program's volunteers and vandalized its facilities in order to undermine their good works. In the late 1960s the Black Panther Party was labeled "Public Enemy #1" by the FBI. The Panthers were the primary concern of the agency's counterintelligence program, commonly referred to as COINTEL-PRO. FBI Chief J. Edgar Hoover (1895–1972) even declared the Black Panthers to be "the greatest threat to the internal security of the United States."

In 1967 Huey P. Newton was shot in a gun battle with police and was charged with manslaughter in the death of a white police officer. He was convicted and served two years before his case was overturned on appeal. Two more trials ended in hung juries. In 1968 Bobby Seale was charged with trying to violently disrupt the Democratic National Convention in Chicago. He was convicted, but the verdict was later overturned. Both men resigned from the Black Panther Party in 1974. In 1980 Newton earned a Ph.D. in social philosophy from the University of California at Santa Cruz. He continued to have run-ins with the law, including prison time, before he was fatally shot at the age of forty-seven in Oakland in 1989. The Dr. Huey P. Newton Foundation keeps his name and the Black Panther history alive.

Lasting Impact   By the late 1970s the party's infighting and the FBI's pursuit of its members had weakened the organization. The Panthers are considered to have fully disbanded in 1982. Although the group's official membership is believed to have never exceeded five thousand, the Black Panthers had chapters around the country and achieved worldwide fame. Their efforts inspired militant movements among other minority groups, including Mexican Americans in Southern California (who formed the Brown Berets), Chinese Americans in San Francisco (the Red Guards), and even a band of disgruntled senior citizens (the Gray

Panthers). The Black Panther Party remains a symbol of Black Power and the counterculture movements of the 1960s.

The Environmental Movement

Concerns about the environment began to get attention in the 1960s, but the year 1970 marked a turning point in the public's awareness and concern about pollution and other environmental hazards. This acknowledgement of the problem, coupled with a building energy crisis, gave birth to the environmental movement.

Early Warnings In 1962 biologist Rachel Carson (1907–1964) published *Silent Spring*, a book about the potentially deadly effects of chemical fertilizers and pesticides on animals, plants, and humans. Carson's study alerted readers to the possibility that even eating a salad could have fatal consequences. The book became an unexpected bestseller and inspired President John F. Kennedy (1917–1963) to order an investigation into the author's claims. In May 1963 Kennedy's Science Advisory Committee supported Carson's findings. These efforts eventually led to a ban on DDT and other chemicals, as well as to legislation establishing auto emission reduction efforts and standards. For the first time, federal, state, and local governments were addressing environmental problems and concerns.

Environmentalism Takes Off The alarm raised by Carson's *Silent Spring* was only the first of many environmental concerns of the time. One tactic used by the United States in the Vietnam War was the dropping of herbicides from airplanes to defoliate the jungles in which the Vietcong and North Vietnamese were hiding. These chemicals—particularly the most notorious one, known as Agent Orange—degraded over time and released toxins into the environment that are believed to have caused cancers and genetic defects in the populations of the region as well as American war veterans who came into contact with them. Much was also made of the assertion that the United States, while comprising only 6 percent of the world's population, was responsible for consuming more than 30 percent of its resources.

At the time of the first Earth Day, on April 22, 1970, many of America's rivers and lakes were so polluted they were considered to be dying. Smog caused by industry and automobiles plagued cities. The bald eagle was on the verge of extinction, and communities such as Love Canal, in upstate New York's Niagara Falls region, were discovering that their homes had been built above toxic waste buried decades earlier, resulting in severe birth defects of many residents' children. The Love Canal crisis would lead to the 1980 passage of the Comprehensive Environmental Response, Compensation, and Liability Act, commonly called the Superfund Act.

Although largely hobbled by the quagmire of the Vietnam War and a stumbling economy, President Richard M. Nixon (1913–1994) responded to the rising environmental movement with numerous initiatives, the most significant of which was the establishment, in December 1970, of the Environmental Protection Agency (EPA), an independent federal agency charged with promoting, safeguarding, and enforcing environmental protection.

Less than two weeks later, the EPA's first administrator, William D. Ruckelshaus (1932–), told the mayors of the heavily polluted cities of Cleveland, Detroit, and Atlanta that if they did not come into compliance with water regulations, the EPA would take court action. Also that December, Congress passed the Clean Air Act of 1970, which brought substantive changes to the federal air quality program. The law set statutory deadlines for reducing automobile emission levels: 90 percent reductions in hydrocarbon and carbon monoxide levels by 1975 and a 90 percent reduction in nitrogen oxides by 1976.

The Movement's Lasting Impact Because environmentalism is a cause that has extreme supporters and equally extreme detractors, the EPA has often been in the middle of a tug-of-war, with the health and safety concerns of the citizenry and science communities on one side, and the corporate world and labor unions on the other. Looking back, the EPA's Ruckelshaus commented that although the EPA was to be the government's environmental advocate, the agency was typically forced into the position of a mediator "caught between two irresistible forces. [There] was one group, the environmental movement, pushing very hard to get emissions down no matter where they were—air, water, no matter what—almost regardless of the seriousness of emissions. There was another group ... pushing just as hard in the other direction and trying to stop all that stuff, again almost regardless of the seriousness of the problem."

Some presidential administrations have strengthened the EPA's authority, while others have diminished its credibility and impact. Economic issues, such as the energy crises in the 1970s, pitted the pursuit of nuclear energy and drilling for oil in Alaska against public fears about the safety of nuclear power and the objections of environmentalists concerned about destroying natural habitats.

Environmental legislation flowed steadily from the Nixon administration and those of his successors Gerald R. Ford (1913–2006) and Jimmy Carter (1924–). In addition to establishing regulations and standards for safety and clean-up, federal environmental efforts also included land preservation, whereby millions of acres throughout the United States were set aside as protected lands, never to be disturbed, exploited or developed. In 1980 the Alaska National Interests Lands Act set aside in perpetuity the preservation of one hundred million acres of wild lands.

Bob Woodward (left) and Carl Bernstein, the *Washington Post* staff writers who broke the Watergate story, 1973. © *Bettmann/CORBIS*

According to the EPA, between 1970 and 2004 total emissions of the six major air pollutants in the United States dropped by 54 percent. During the same period, through land restoration efforts, six hundred thousand acres of contaminated land were reclaimed. Although many environmental hazards and energy challenges remain (chief among them global warming and dwindling oil supplies), since the celebration of the first Earth Day, twice as many rivers and lakes are safe for fishing and swimming today as in 1970. Drinking water is safer and auto emissions and ozone-damaging gases have been reduced. Natural lands have been protected, toxic waste sites have been cleaned up, and the bald eagle has been removed from the Endangered Species List.

Watergate

A bungled 1972 break-in at the Democratic party's Washington, D.C., headquarters in the Watergate hotel complex lead to the resignation two years later of U.S. President Richard M. Nixon (1913–1994). The incident, which occurred five months before Nixon's landslide victory for a second term, had been executed by members of his administration and reelection commit-

tee. The scandal became a textbook example of how "the cover-up is worse than the crime." The Watergate scandal undermined the nation's trust in its leaders and raised lasting debates about the Constitution and the powers of the presidency. The repercussions of Watergate continued into the twenty-first century.

The Break-in and the Cover-up   At 2:30 a.m. on June 17, 1972, police caught five men attempting to break into and wiretap the offices of the Democratic National Committee (DNC). During court proceedings later that year, it was revealed that the burglars and two accomplices had connections to the Committee to Re-elect the President (CRP; commonly referred to as "Creep"). All seven men were convicted in January 1973, and two months later one of them, former CIA agent James McCord Jr. (1924–), wrote to trial judge John J. Sirica (1904–1992) that the burglary was in fact part of a larger, high-level political conspiracy and cover-up.

The Washington Post   During the summer of the June break-in, Bob Woodward (1943–) and Carl Bernstein (1944–), two reporters for the *Washington Post*, had begun their own investigation of the Watergate break-in and its political connections. Their efforts were helped

Former White House aide G. Gordon Liddy leaving U.S. District Court, where he pleaded not guilty to breaking into the Democratic National Headquarters at the Watergate Hotel, 1972. © *Bettmann/CORBIS*

by leads from a government source acquired by Woodward and identified only as "Deep Throat," who told them to "follow the money." In doing so, they uncovered connections between Nixon's attorney general, John Mitchell (1913–1998), and funds used to finance espionage operations against Democrats. Woodward and Bernstein's reporting helped unravel the Watergate conspiracy.

The Watergate Hearings During the June 1973 Senate hearings on the incident, John Dean (1938–), the former White House counsel who had been dismissed by Nixon two months earlier, testified that the Watergate break-in was approved by John Mitchell—who had resigned his post as attorney general in January 1972 to head CRP—with the involvement of White House advisers John Ehrlichman (1925–1999) and H. R. (Bob) Haldeman (1926–1993). Dean asserted that Nixon knew about and approved of the resulting cover-up. He also revealed that the Nixon White House routinely spied on political rivals.

Under pressure from Congress, Nixon's third attorney general, Elliot Richardson (1920–1999), appointed a special prosecutor, Archibald Cox (1912–2004), to investigate the Watergate affair. In doing so, Cox's staff

uncovered evidence of spying by CRP, the illegal wiretapping of citizens by the Nixon administration, and bribes from corporate contributors to the Republican Party. When Cox demanded in July 1973 that the White House turn over Oval Office tape recordings of the president's conversations, Nixon claimed "executive privilege." After a summer of court battles over the tapes, Nixon ordered his attorney general to fire the prosecutor. Both Richardson and his assistant, William Ruckelshaus (1932–), resigned their jobs rather than dismiss Cox. On October 20, 1973, in what was dubbed by the press the "Saturday Night Massacre," Robert Bork (1927–), the U.S. solicitor general who was serving as acting attorney general, succeeded in firing Cox.

Cox's dismissal backfired on Nixon. The citizenry, the press, and congressional leaders began calling for the president's impeachment. In November 1973 Nixon's Justice Department appointed a new special prosecutor, Leon Jaworski (1905–1982). At a November 17 press conference, Nixon defended himself against the growing accusations of his misdeeds by declaring, in what would become an iconic moment of his presidency, "I am not a crook." Within a week, two of the subpoenaed White House tapes were declared to be missing and another was revealed to contain an 18-½-minute-long erased gap. Investigators believed that the White House was destroying evidence.

Over the next several months Jaworski indicted and convicted several administration officials, including Ehrlichman and Haldeman. A grand jury investigation cited Nixon as an "unindicted conspirator," believing it was unconstitutional for a prosecutor to indict a sitting president. Jaworski referred any further inquiries into Nixon's actions to the Judiciary Committee of the House of Representatives.

Ignoring numerous subpoenas for the Oval Office tapes, in April 1974 Nixon provided edited transcripts of the recordings to the Judiciary Committee. On July 24 of that year, the U.S. Supreme Court rejected Nixon's "executive privilege" defense and unanimously affirmed a lower court ruling in *The United States v. Nixon* that the White House must turn over the subpoenaed tapes.

Articles of Impeachment and Resignation
During the last week of July 1974, the House Judiciary Committee adopted three articles of impeachment against Nixon, for obstructing the Watergate investigation; for misusing power and violating the oath of office; and for failing to comply with House subpoenas.

On August 5, 1974, Nixon released transcripts of conversations that had occurred between himself and H. R. Haldeman six days after the Watergate break-in. The transcripts, which become known as the "smoking gun," confirmed that Nixon both ordered the FBI to stop its Watergate break-in investigation and directed a cover-up of the White House's involvement.

On August 9, 1974, under threat of certain impeachment, Nixon resigned the presidency. Vice President Gerald Ford (1913–2006) succeeded him. (Nixon's original vice president, Spiro Agnew (1918–1996), had resigned in October 1973 due to federal tax evasion charges.)

On September 8, 1974, President Ford granted Nixon a "full free and absolute" pardon for "all offenses against the United States" committed between January 20, 1969, and August 9, 1974. In January 1975 Haldeman, Ehrlichman, and Mitchell, among others, were convicted for their roles in the Watergate scandal. Nearly forty officials in the Nixon administration were convicted for crimes involving Watergate or other offenses.

See also **United States v. Nixon**
See also **The Independent Counsel**

Three Mile Island

A reactor malfunction at the Three Mile Island nuclear power plant near Harrisburg, Pennsylvania, in March 1979 resulted in the release of radioactive materials, the panicked evacuation of nearby residents, and several days of uncertainty about the severity of the situation. Although no one was killed and the amount of leaked radioactivity into the surrounding environment was minimal, the Three Mile Island incident is considered to be the most serious mishap ever in the U.S. commercial nuclear power industry. It also alerted the nation to the potential hazards of nuclear energy, despite earlier assurances from the industry and its government regulators.

What Happened
Three Mile Island's second reactor had been in operation for less than a year when, at about 4 a.m. on March 28, 1979, a problem was detected in the turbine building. Soon after, as the alarm lights were flashing and the warning bells were ringing, technicians realized that the reactor had overheated, causing portions of the uranium core to melt and hydrogen gas to accumulate. The primary fear during the crisis was that such a severe core meltdown, the most dangerous kind of nuclear accident, would cause a steam explosion and the dispersal of deadly radioactivity.

The White House was notified of the incident at 9:15 in the morning. At 11 a.m. all nonessential staff was told to leave the power plant. Pennsylvania's governor, Richard Thornburgh (1932–), soon ordered the evacuation of all pregnant women and preschool-age children within a five-mile radius of the plant. Ultimately, some one hundred thousand residents of all ages would choose to evacuate. Reports about the situation at the plant and its threats to the surrounding area were often confused and contradictory, which further frightened people in the area. Adding to the panic was the odd coincidence of the motion picture *The China Syndrome*—about an accident at a nuclear power plant—opening in theaters just days before the Three Mile Island meltdown.

The overriding fear of an explosion at Three Mile Island diminished on Sunday, April 1, when scientists determined that a lack of oxygen in the reactor's pressure vessel meant a fire or explosion could not occur.

A federal investigation would later find that the Three Mile Island reactor meltdown was caused by human error as well as serious mechanical and design flaws. One of the key components leading to the crisis was a malfunctioning automatic release valve, which prevented the reactor from cooling itself and caused highly explosive hydrogen gases to accumulate.

Health Consequences of the Accident
Although the worst did not occur in the Three Mile Island incident, tests at the time and since did reveal that some radioactive water and gas was released. During the crisis, no plant workers or civilians suffered any injuries, and there were no deaths. Several long-term studies by both government and independent researchers have failed to link any deaths or disabilities to the crisis. Nor were any correlations made between radiation levels in the agricultural animals and products in the area and the incident at the plant.

Experts estimate an exposure dose of about 1 millirem for each of the two million people who were in the rural and agricultural areas near the power plant and the cities of York, Lancaster, and Harrisburg (the state's

The Three Mile Island nuclear plant, with the damaged reactor number two in the foreground, 1999. *John S. Zeedick/Getty Images*

capital, located ten miles south of Three Mile Island). By comparison, exposure from a full set of chest X-rays is about 6 millirem, and in that part of Pennsylvania residents were believed to be exposed to at least 100 millirem per year of naturally generated radioactivity.

In a study that took place from 1979 to 1998, researchers at the University of Pittsburgh stated there is "no consistent evidence" that radiation affected the mortality rates of people living within five miles of the reactor at the time of the accident.

Lasting Impact One of the lasting effects of the Three Mile Island accident is that the nation, which had spent much of the 1970s struggling through gas and oil shortages, stopped embracing nuclear power as an alternative energy source. The construction of new nuclear power plants was significantly reduced. But when the energy crisis ended, the United States no longer gave priority to weaning itself from fossil fuels.

As a result of the Three Mile Island incident, the federal government did revise its standards for nuclear power plant licensing, employee training, and emergency preparedness. It also revamped the structure and purpose of the Nuclear Regulatory Commission (NRC), which is responsible for licensing and regulating the nonmilitary use of nuclear energy. "What shook the public most," observed Victor Gilinsky (1934–), the commissioner of the NRC during the Three Mile Island event, "was seeing the men in the white lab coats standing around and scratching their heads because they didn't know what to do."

Clean-up and monitoring efforts of the Three Mile Island site lasted for fifteen years. After the accident, Reactor No. 2 was permanently shut down, defueled, and decontaminated. The Three Mile Island facility is expected to be decommissioned when the operating license for Reactor No. 1 expires in 2014.

The Iran Hostage Crisis

On November 4, 1979, Iranian militants in Iran's capital of Tehran stormed the United States Embassy, taking as hostages the Americans inside. The ordeal lasted 444 days, during which time Americans back home in the United States became acutely aware of their nation's vulnerability to the anger of extremists abroad and of the power foreign governments had over the country's energy needs. As U.S. President Jimmy Carter (1924–) struggled with both the hostage situation and a concurrent energy crisis, the American electorate chose Ronald Reagan (1911–2004) to be its next president in 1980.

A Brief History of U.S. Involvement in Iran The build-up to the hostage taking in 1979 began a generation earlier, in the 1950s, when the young shah of Iran, Mohammed Reza Pahlavi (1919–1980), faced a challenge to his throne, which he had inherited from his father in 1941. Fearing a loss of access to Iran's oil fields, the United States took the shah's side in the throne conflict, ousting his opponent, Prime Minister Mohammed Mossadegh (1882–1967), and providing the shah with economic and military aid. By the early 1960s Iranians had begun objecting to the cultural "westernizing" of their nation, the uneven distribution of wealth among its citizenry, and the shah's continued refusal to grant political freedoms to the people. During upheavals in 1963, the shah cracked down on protestors and suppressed his opposition, including the popular Muslim cleric Ayatollah Ruhollah Khomeini (1900–1989), whom he arrested and exiled. In addition to his opposition to the shah, Khomeini—who escaped to neighboring Iraq—despised the United States. With the rebellion quelled, the shah continued to spend Iran's oil revenues on the country's military and his own lavish lifestyle. Less-fortunate Iranians, meanwhile, were growing poorer and angrier. In January 1979 the shah and his family, claiming to be going on a vacation, fled from Iran, fearful for their lives. They temporarily settled in Egypt.

The Hostage Crisis Within weeks of the shah's exit from Iran, the exiled Ayatollah Khomeini returned. After the shah, who had eventually moved on to Mexico, was allowed to enter the United States for cancer treatment in October 1979, an angry mob stormed the U.S. Embassy compound on November 4, 1979. At the start of the siege, there were nearly one hundred captives. After the ringleaders released almost all the women, non-Americans, and blacks, sixty-six American captives remained at the embassy and in an Iranian ministry building nearby. The hostage-takers wanted the shah and his money returned to Iran so he could stand trial and his money distributed to poor Iranians. While Khomeini was not believed to be directly involved in the hostage taking, he did endorse the act.

Carter's Conflicts Deciding that military action against Iran was too risky, the Carter administration responded to the hostage drama with diplomatic efforts, freezing Iranian assets in the United States, and an embargo against the importation of Iranian oil. Rather than frighten the Iranians, the measures inspired further protests against the United States. Carter, who felt personal responsibility for the safety of the American

An American hostage being paraded before cameras by his Iranian captors, 1979. *MPI/Getty Images*

U.S. hostages in Iran, 1979. © *CORBIS SYGMA*

hostages, then severed all diplomatic relations with Iran and in April 1980 imposed a complete economic embargo on the country. Also in April, Carter approved of a secret U.S. mission, based out of the Iranian desert, to rescue the hostages. The effort failed miserably when mechanical problems plagued the U.S. aircraft involved, some of which collided and killed eight soldiers. The disastrous rescue attempt and ineffective diplomatic efforts damaged President Carter's political capital, causing him to be viewed as hesitant and weak.

The student militants holding the hostages stood firm despite the death in July 1980 of the exiled shah, who had returned to Egypt, and the invasion of Iran by Iraq on September 22, 1980, which resulted in a full-scale war between the nations. That fall, Iran, under the rule of the Ayatollah Khomeini, resumed negotiations with the United States. On inauguration day in January 1981, the United States agreed to return $8 billion in frozen Iranian assets and lift trade sanctions in exchange for the release of the hostages.

444 Days in Captivity Although the Carter administration and President Carter himself had agonized and

negotiated for more than a year over the safety and release of the hostages—up until and during the inauguration day drive to the U.S. Capitol—it was Reagan who got to make the announcement, moments after being sworn in, that the 444-day Iranian hostage crisis was over and the Americans, who had been blindfolded, isolated, and abused during their captivity, had been released. Of the sixty-six hostages taken, thirteen had been released a few weeks after the crisis began, one was returned the following July, and the remaining fifty-two were freed that inauguration day. The next day former President Carter flew to the U.S. Air Force base in Wiesbaden, West Germany, to greet the hostages on Reagan's behalf.

✪ Legislation, Court Cases, and Trials

The National Traffic and Motor Vehicle Safety Act and Highway Safety Act

The National Traffic and Motor Vehicle Safety Act and Highway Safety Act of 1966 established safety standards

Wreckage from a traffic accident, 1954.   © *Bettmann/CORBIS*

for motor vehicles in order to reduce accidents and the deaths and injuries caused by them.

The Purpose of the Legislation   Signed into law by President Lyndon B. Johnson (1908–1973) in 1966, the National Traffic and Motor Vehicle Safety Act and Highway Safety Act placed the federal government in the leadership role of a comprehensive national program to reduce the number of injuries and deaths on U.S. highways. The act created the first federally mandatory safety standards for motor vehicles. Starting with vehicles and tires built after the 1968 model year, the standards required manufacturers to protect the public against "unreasonable risk of accidents occurring as a result of the design, construction, or performance of motor vehicles" and also against "unreasonable risk of death or injury . . . in the event accidents do occur."

Authority for the act was first assigned to the Department of Commerce. In 1970 the Highway Safety Act was amended to establish the National Highway Traffic Safety Administration (NHTSA) to carry out the safety programs developed and mandated by the National Traffic and Motor Vehicle Safety Act.

After early opposition, the automobile industry worked to implement the standards required by the new law, which has undergone numerous revisions over the years. Speaking for many of his Detroit colleagues, Henry Ford II (1917–1987) had initially complained that the new auto safety standards were "unreasonable, arbitrary, and technically unfeasible." But in 1977 Ford conceded on the television news show *Meet the Press* that "we wouldn't have the kinds of safety built into automobiles that we have had unless there had been a federal law."

The Need for Auto Safety Standards   The impetus for the legislation was the growing evidence that auto accidents were caused by unsafe vehicles rather than just bad drivers. An influential proponent of this theory was Ralph Nader (1934–), a consumer advocate who detailed automobile safety issues in the book *Unsafe at Any Speed*, published in November 1965. In his book Nader charged that the automobile industry subordinated safety concerns to "power and styling." His chief target was the General Motors Corvair, a sports car prone to violent skidding and rollovers. According to Nader, many auto-related injuries were caused not by

ESTIMATED LIVES SAVED BY AUTO SAFETY TECHNOLOGIES, 1969–2002

When researchers with the National Traffic and Highway Safety Administration (NTHSA) compared the auto-related death rates in the United States before and after the enactment of the automobile and highway safety standards acts of 1966, the results showed that some 328,551 lives had been saved lifesaving technologies (Charles J. Kahane, *Lives Saved by the Federal Motor Vehicle Safety Standards and Other Vehicle Safety Technologies, 1960–2002—Passenger Cars and Light Trucks,* October 2004).

Dual master cylinders and front disc brakes were believed to have saved 13,053 lives. Energy absorbing steering columns, a 1960s technology, were credited with protecting 53,017 drivers. Improved door locks prevented 28,902 fatalities. Frontal air bags, a 1990s improvement, prevented 12,074 deaths. The most effective safety addition to the automobile was seat belts, especially the three-point belt with a chest restraint that was introduced in the 1970s. Over the course of twenty-two years, seat belts alone were believed to have saved 168,524 lives.

the "nut behind the wheel," but by the engineering and design flaws that made many vehicles high-speed death traps, regardless of a driver's skill. Traffic fatalities had increased by nearly 30 percent between 1960 and 1965, and experts predicted that by 1975 the nation could be looking at one hundred thousand motor vehicle–related deaths each year.

In signing the legislation on September 9, 1966, President Johnson remarked: "Over the Labor Day weekend, twenty-nine American servicemen died in Vietnam. During the same Labor Day weekend, 614 Americans died on our highways in automobile accidents.... In this century more than one-and-a-half million of our fellow citizens have died on our streets and highways: nearly three times as many Americans as we have lost in all our wars."

Provisions of the Act The National Traffic and Motor Vehicle Safety Act and Highway Safety Act lead regulators to issue more than a dozen standards for passenger cars, including seat belts for all occupants, impact-absorbing steering columns, padded dashboards, safety glass, and dual braking systems. Over time, requirements and standards were added for such items as windshield wipers, lights, rearview mirrors, door locks, and head restraints. Safety standards were also developed for trucks, buses, motorcycles, and other vehicles. In 1974 the act was amended to require manufacturers to remedy safety-related defects at no cost to consumers. After-

ward, auto manufacturers issued so many recalls to repair safety issues that the number of recalled cars between 1977 and 1980 exceeded the number of new cars sold.

Since the act's signing, traffic fatalities and the fatality rate (measured in fatalities per million vehicle miles traveled) declined 17 percent and 71 percent, respectively, between 1967 and 2001. While the new regulations and standards certainly deserve credit, additional factors have had an impact as well. Over the years, speed limits have been reduced, vehicle inspections have improved, driver education programs have become more comprehensive, road and traffic control systems have been improved, medical care has advanced, the use of child safety seats are required, and public attitudes generally condemn drunk driving and other risky behaviors.

See also **Ralph Nader**

The Racketeer Influenced and Corrupt Organizations Act

The Racketeer Influenced and Corrupt Organizations Act, commonly referred to as RICO, was signed into law on October 15, 1970. The specific purpose of RICO was "the elimination of the infiltration of organized crime and racketeering [extorting money] into legitimate organizations operating in interstate commerce." But because Congress mandated that the statute "be liberally construed to effectuate its remedial purposes," RICO has been used to prosecute a variety of illegal activities affecting interstate or foreign commerce. Under RICO, successful prosecutions result in extended sentences for crimes committed as part of an ongoing criminal organization.

In Pursuit of Organized Crime Congress passed the RICO as part of the Organized Crime Control Act of 1970. The intent was to go after criminal organizations that were using legitimate businesses as fronts for criminal activity. With the Organized Crime Control Act of 1970, law enforcement could pursue and prosecute individuals for *participating* in *organized* criminal acts. Previously, such criminals were pursued solely for the acts (such as gambling, loan sharking, etc.) themselves.

Congress's efforts to pursue organized crime via a RICO-type statute began in the 1950s with hearings conducted by Tennessee Senator Estes Kefauver. One of the original purposes of RICO was to eliminate organized crime families (specifically the Mafia). Because Congress could not legislate against specific persons or groups, it used far-reaching language in order to toss a broad net in which to pursue organized crime's racketeering activities.

The Act and its Penalties While RICO has very specific requirements for who can be charged under the statute, the menu of offenses is expansive. Under RICO, a person or group that commits any two of among thirty-five crimes within a ten-year period and, in the opinion of the U.S. attorney bringing the case, has committed those crimes with similar purpose or results, can be charged with racketeering; these crimes include murder, gambling, bribery, extortion, bankruptcy, mail fraud, prostitution, narcotics trafficking, and loan sharking.

A RICO-qualifying defendant must also be connected with an "enterprise," which is defined by the statute as "any individual, partnership, corporation, association, or other legal entity, and any union or group of individuals associated in fact although not a legal entity."

The punishment for violating the criminal provisions of RICO is intentionally harsh. If convicted, a defendant is fined and sentenced to not more than twenty years in prison for each offense. In addition, the racketeer must forfeit all monies acquired through a pattern of "racketeering activity." The act also contains a civil component that allows plaintiffs to sue for triple damages.

Uses of RICO In addition to prosecuting acts of extortion and blackmail, RICO has been used against individuals and corporations who intimidate or threaten witnesses, victims, and whistleblowers in retaliation for cooperating with law enforcement. RICO has also been used to prosecute the sexual abuse scandals involving the Catholic Archdioceses in the United States. RICO laws also were successfully cited in *National Organization for Women v. Scheidler*, a lawsuit that sought an injunction against antiabortion activists who physically blocked access to abortion clinics.

RICO has proven to be a powerful tool in the federal government's fight against organized crime. As a back-up to RICO, many states have enacted their own RICO-type statutes, which are used in the rare instances when the federal law does not apply.

Some critics charge that RICO's reach is too far, especially when it is used to convict nonviolent criminals who are sentenced to long prison stays. Advocates of RICO counter that crimes committed by organized networks of people are more dangerous, and more damaging, than crimes committed by individuals—in part because they are harder to stop. Because the crime is more serious, the theory goes, the punishments should be more severe.

When it comes to RICO's civil applications, however, many say the law is too easily abused. Because RICO's civil provisions, which allow for triple damages, can be a source of great profit, some civil attorneys have filed RICO suits on behalf of plaintiffs willing to sue accountants, bankers, insurance companies, securities firms, and major corporations, believing that the defendants might settle rather than risk having a judge or jury grant a triple-damages judgment.

As a tool of criminal prosecutions, however, RICO has been successful in securing convictions against organized crime leaders. In the mid-1980s the bosses of all five New York City Mafia families—

THE ACTS AND THREATS PROSECUTABLE UNDER RICO

Under the Racketeer Influenced and Corrupt Organizations Act (RICO), a person and/or group involved in committing any two of among thirty-five crimes within a ten-year period, with similar purpose or results, can be prosecuted under RICO. Such crimes include:

- Murder
- Kidnapping
- Gambling
- Arson
- Robbery
- Bribery
- Extortion
- Dealing in obscene materials
- Dealing in controlled substances
- Counterfeiting
- Embezzlement (particularly from pension, welfare, or union funds)
- Extortionate credit transactions
- Fraud (involving identification documents, mail fraud, wire fraud, financial fraud, securities fraud, passport, visa or citizenship fraud, financial fraud)
- Obstruction of justice
- Peonage (involving a debtor having to work for a creditor)
- Slavery
- Human trafficking
- Interference with commerce
- Transportation of wagering paraphernalia
- Money laundering
- Auto theft
- Sexual exploitation (including of children)
- Murder-for-hire involvement
- Possession of stolen property
- Electronic piracy
- Trafficking in contraband cigarettes
- Trafficking or using biological, nuclear, or chemical weapons
- The felonious manufacture, importation, receiving, concealment, buying, selling, or otherwise dealing in a controlled substance or listed chemical (as defined by the Controlled Substances Act)

among them the famed John Gotti, head of the Gambino crime family—were convicted under RICO, and each was sentenced to at least one hundred years in prison.

The Occupational Safety and Health Act

The Occupational Safety and Health Act (OSHA) was approved on December 30, 1970, and enacted three

Mafia boss John Gotti (center) was successfully prosecuted under the RICO Act in 1992.   © *Bettmann/CORBIS*

months later to help ensure the safety and health of workers in the U.S. labor force.

The Need for OSHA   The introduction to the Occupational Safety and Health Act states its intended purpose: "To assure safe and healthful working conditions for working men and women; by authorizing enforcement of the standards developed under the Act; by assisting and encouraging the States in their efforts to assure safe and healthful working conditions; by providing for research, information, education, and training in the field of occupational safety and health."

The hazards of the American workplace garnered attention in the 1960s due to the concerns of employees and labor unions seeking protection from the dangers of unsafe working conditions. Worker advocates found supporters in Congress and even in President Richard M. Nixon (1913–1994), who passed the legislation despite the opposition of influential business leaders. One theory for why Nixon sided with workers over management is that he wanted to curry favor with working-class voters and George Meany (1894–1980), the powerful president of the American Federation of Labor-Congress of Industrial Organizations (AFL-CIO). A concession made to

business interests is that OSHA described workplace safety as a responsibility shared by the employer *and* the employee.

At the time, congressional leaders noted that, annually, more than fourteen thousand workers were being killed and two million more disabled due to job-related accidents, most commonly in manufacturing. U.S. Representative William S. Broomfield (1922–) declared that "75 out of every 100 teenagers now entering the workforce can expect to suffer a disabling injury sometime in his working career." Representative William A. Steiger (1938–1978), the bill's chief advocate in the House, added: "In the last 25 years, more than 400,000 Americans were killed by work-related accidents and disease, and close to 50 million more suffered disabling injuries on the job."

Although some states had already established workplace safety standards, the protections were inconsistent. Invoking its powers to regulate interstate commerce, Congress decided to nationalize workplace protections and impose minimum safety standards for protecting the American workforce.

OSHA, NIOSH, and OSHRC   The Occupational Safety and Health Act of 1970 established three permanent agencies, and an expansive bureaucracy, charged with protecting worker safety and health:

- The Occupational Safety and Health Administration (OSHA) operates within the Labor Department. It creates and enforces workplace safety and health standards.

- The National Institute for Occupational Safety and Health (NIOSH) is part of the Department of Health and Human Services (then called the Department of Health, Education, and Welfare). NIOSH's mandate is to conduct research on occupational safety and health.

- The Occupational Safety and Health Review Commission (OSHRC) is an independent agency. Its role is to adjudicate enforcement actions challenged by employers.

Impact of OSHA According to the Occupational Safety and Health Administration, since OSHA's inception in 1971, workplace fatalities have decreased by more than 60 percent and occupational injury and illness rates by 40 percent. New cases of diseases such as brown lung and asbestosis are now extremely rare. Exposure levels to dangerous toxins such as cotton dust, lead, arsenic, beryllium metal, and vinyl chloride have been greatly reduced.

Observers do argue over whether or not OSHA should be credited with such successes. Advances in science, technology, and medicine may also explain the improvements. As was the case when the act was first signed, pro-business interests continue to feel that OSHA is unnecessarily restrictive and costly to companies, especially small ones.

While OSHA did set safety standards, its enforcement of such standards has been frequently criticized by worker advocates. By the agency's own admission, in the 1980s its focus was to reduce the regulatory burdens its standards had caused, and the OSHA inspection efforts were limited to "the most hazardous companies within the most hazardous industries." Under President Ronald Reagan (1911–2004) the agency's impact was lessened by the administration's policy of limited government, particularly where business interests were involved. During these years OSHA received no funding increases and lost 20 percent of its staff. Additionally, many of Reagan's appointees to the Department of Labor and OSHA had strong business connections and little interest in producing or enforcing federal safety standards.

Labor activists acknowledge that the existence of OSHA has raised awareness about workplace safety and health issues, but many consider the agency little more than a "paper tiger," whose bark is worse than its bite. In states that have Occupational Safety and Health agencies, local efforts have sometimes been more effective than federal ones.

THE "GENERAL DUTY CLAUSE" OF THE OCCUPATIONAL SAFETY AND HEALTH ACT

The "General Duty Clause" of the Occupational Safety and Health Act (OSHA) states in basic terms the overall responsibilities of employers to protect their workers.

(a) Each employer—

(1) shall furnish to each of his employees employment and a place of employment which are free from recognized hazards that are causing or are likely to cause death or serious physical harm to his employees;

(2) shall comply with occupational safety and health standards promulgated under this Act.

(b) Each employee shall comply with occupational safety and health standards and all rules, regulations, and orders issued pursuant to this Act which are applicable to his own actions and conduct.

SOURCE: Occupational Safety and Health Act of 1970, *Section 5, U.S. Department of Labor, Occupational Safety and Health Administration, http://www.osha.gov/ (accessed July 13, 2007).*

Lemon v. Kurtzman

In 1971 the Supreme Court found in *Lemon v. Kurtzman* that state laws that enabled payment of teachers of secular subjects in parochial schools from public funds were unconstitutional. Two state laws that permitted state government to supplement the salaries of teachers of nonreligious subjects in parochial schools were at issue: Rhode Island's Salary Supplement Act of 1969 and Pennsylvania's Nonpublic Elementary and Secondary Education Act of 1968. The Court found that both laws violated the establishment clause of the First Amendment, which guarantees that "Congress shall make no law respecting an establishment of religion."

The Laws Pennsylvania's Nonpublic Elementary and Secondary Education Act, passed in 1968, provided financial aid to private elementary and secondary schools—the overwhelming majority of which were parochial schools—by paying portions of teachers' salaries as well as the costs of textbooks and instructional materials used in nonreligious subjects. Rhode Island's law, the Salary Supplement Act, paid teachers of secular subjects in parochial schools a supplemental salary of up to 15 percent of their annual salaries, subject to maximum limits set by the state.

The Suit Alton J. Lemon, who gave his name to the case, was a resident and taxpayer in Pennsylvania and

THE PLEDGE OF ALLEGIANCE—IS ITS RECITATION IN PUBLIC SCHOOL CONSTITUTIONAL?

The Pledge of Allegiance was first published in *The Youth's Companion* in 1892 in this form: "I pledge allegiance to my Flag and the Republic for which it stands; one nation indivisible, with liberty and Justice for all." By 1924 the words "the flag of the United States of America" had been substituted for "my Flag." The U.S. government officially adopted the Pledge of Allegiance in 1942.

By the 1950s, however, many Americans believed that the Pledge did not reflect what they viewed as the singularly religious purpose of the United States. At the request of President Dwight D. Eisenhower (1890–1969), Congress added "under God" to the Pledge. Congress intended that students would recite the Pledge each day to "proclaim in every city and town, every village and rural schoolhouse, the dedication of our Nation and our people to the Almighty."

Several legal challenges to the practice of reciting the Pledge daily in public schools have been mounted in recent decades. In one case of note the Seventh Circuit Court upheld an Illinois law in 1992 that required teachers to lead the Pledge every day, as long as students could opt not to recite it themselves.

Later, Michael Newdow sued the Elk Grove Unified School District challenging its policy of having the Pledge recited every day to satisfy a California state law that every public school begin its day with "patriotic exercises," claiming that it violated his daughter's First Amendment rights. Newdow stated that his daughter was injured because she was forced to "watch and listen as her state-employed teacher in her state-run school leads her classmates in a ritual proclaiming that there is a God." While the district court had dismissed Newdow's case, the Ninth Circuit Court of Appeals agreed with him, ruling in 2003 that the phrase "under God" signified a government sanctioned religious purpose.

The Supreme Court agreed to hear the case on appeal. The central issue was whether daily recitation of the Pledge of Allegiance violated the establishment clause of the First Amendment. In the end, the Supreme Court sidestepped the issue. Rather, they challenged Newdow's right to sue because he did not have primary legal custody of his daughter. In a unanimous decision the justices reversed the lower-court decision that the daily recitation of the Pledge of Allegiance in public schools is unconstitutional.

While the path would seem to be clear for any parent with legal custody of his or her child to challenge the constitutionality of the daily recitation of the Pledge of Allegiance in public schools, several justices stated in their concurring opinions that the Pledge does not violate the Constitution. Justice William H. Rehnquist (1924–2005) went a step further. "To give the parent of such a child a sort of 'heckler's veto' over a patriotic ceremony willingly participated in by other students, simply because the Pledge of Allegiance contains the descriptive phrase 'under God' is an unwarranted extension of the establishment clause, an extension which would have the unfortunate effect of prohibiting a commendable patriotic observance," he wrote.

father of a student in the state public school system. Arguing that the Nonpublic Elementary and Secondary Education Act violated the establishment clause of the First Amendment, Lemon challenged the Pennsylvania law in federal court and filed suit against David Kurtzman, the state superintendent of schools. When the federal court dismissed his case, he appealed to the U.S. Supreme Court. The Rhode Island statute had been found unconstitutional by a district court and was then appealed by the appellants to the Supreme Court. The two cases were combined into one case in *Lemon*.

The Opinion Chief Justice Warren Burger (1907–1995) delivered the opinion of the Supreme Court. He outlined a three-part "Lemon Test" to determine whether the laws met the requirements of the First Amendment. For a law to be constitutional under the Lemon Test, it must not have a religious purpose; second, the law must neither advance nor inhibit religion; and third, the law must not foster entanglement of church and state to an excessive degree. The Court admitted that some relationship between religious organizations and the government was inevitable and in fact, required. Parochial schools, for example, were covered under compulsory school attendance laws. "In order to determine whether the government entanglement with religion is excessive," Burger stated in the opinion, "we must examine the character and purposes of the institutions that are benefited, the nature of the aid that the State provides, and the resulting relationship between the government and the religious authority."

The two state statutes at issue in the case were found in compliance with the first and second requirements; if anything, the state laws were meant to improve the quality of secular education offered at parochial schools. However, the laws failed the third requirement of no excessive entanglement. The Court found that the amount of oversight the state would be obliged to engage in to guarantee that the programs did not further a religious purpose involved an "excessive entanglement between government and religion." Burger wrote, "A comprehensive, discriminating, and continuing state surveillance will inevitably be required to ensure that these restrictions are obeyed and the First Amendment otherwise respected.... These ... contacts will involve excessive and enduring entanglement between state and church." Therefore, the Supreme Court struck down both state laws as unconstitutional violations of the establishment clause of the First Amendment.

The Court opinion in *Lemon v. Kurtzman* provided guidelines to legislators and courts—the "Lemon Test"—to ensure the constitutionality of laws. However, in the intervening years, the Court has since modified its understanding of the "Lemon Test." Since 1971, justices have shifted their understanding of the second criterion. In 1971 justices understood the test to be whether or not the law advanced or inhibited religion; today, justices understand the test to be whether or not the law conveys a message that the government endorses or disapproves of religion. In addition, the wording of the third criteria, "excessive government entanglement," leaves what constitutes excessive entanglement as a matter open for debate.

The Pentagon Papers

The Pentagon Papers detailed three decades of U.S. involvement in Vietnam and, when leaked to the press, caused a public outcry against the war that eventually led to the largest political scandal in U.S. history and the downfall of the administration of Richard M. Nixon (1913–1994). The Pentagon Papers had been commissioned by the administration of Lyndon B. Johnson (1908–1973) and consisted of forty-seven volumes analyzing the history of U.S. policy in Vietnam. The papers included four thousand pages of internal documents from four presidential administrations along with three thousand pages of analytical commentary. Among other things, the papers demonstrated that the government had deliberately obfuscated the nation's military actions in Vietnam. Daniel Ellsberg (1931–), a consultant at the Rand Corporation, whose analysts contributed to the report, leaked the Pentagon Papers to the *New York Times* in June 1971. President Nixon vainly tried to block their publication. His administration's illegal tactics in its attempts to discredit Ellsberg were early elements of the Watergate scandal.

The Contents of the Papers Secretary of Defense Robert S. McNamara (1916–) had ordered the compilation of the Pentagon Papers at a time when the Vietnam War seemed to be at an impasse. Three dozen Pentagon officials and civilian analysts gathered classified documents and wrote an additional three thousand pages of analysis. While the papers were by no means a complete record of American involvement in the Vietnam War—most significantly, they lacked internal White House memoranda—they did draw upon sealed files of the Defense of Department, presidential orders, and diplomatic files.

The Pentagon Papers showed that the government had taken definite steps to increase its involvement in the Vietnam conflict through four presidential administrations. Government leaders throughout the period believed that if one Asian nation "fell" to commu-

Defendents Daniel Ellsberg (left) and Anthony Russo speaking to the press after the opening session of their trial, 1973. *© Bettmann/ CORBIS*

nism, others would fall in turn, a philosophy called the "domino theory." However, civilian government leaders refused to authorize the commitment of troops and escalation of the war that military advisers urged was necessary in order to decisively defeat the Communist forces. Each presidential administration balanced the fear of being defeated by an inferior enemy without the commitment of a larger military force in Southeast Asia with the fear of drawing in Communist China or the Soviet Union if the war was drastically escalated.

Above all, the Pentagon Papers demonstrated that the government had deliberately and systematically misled the American people about the extent of U.S. involvement in Southeast Asia and the prospects for success in Vietnam. Daniel Ellsberg, who worked for the Rand Corporation and had served as a pro-war adviser to the administration of John F. Kennedy (1917–1963), had come to believe that U.S. policy in Vietnam was a grave mistake. He believed that the government actions detailed in the Pentagon Papers should be made public. He secretly copied the papers, with the

DANIEL ELLSBERG: FROM DETERMINED COLD WARRIOR TO ANTIWAR HERO

As a young man, Daniel Ellsberg (1931–) served for two years as an officer in the Marine Corps before receiving a Ph.D. in economics from Harvard University and becoming a consultant for the Rand Corporation, a conservative think tank located in California that did regular consulting work for the U.S. Department of Defense. In several published papers, Ellsberg recommended a military buildup in Vietnam in order to advance U.S. policy in Southeast Asia and halt the spread of communism there. In 1964 and 1965 the Pentagon hired Ellsberg as an adviser to the assistant secretary of defense, during which time he lobbied on Capitol Hill for continued and increased military involvement in Southeast Asia.

In 1965 Ellsberg traveled to Vietnam in order to be able to better recommend policy in the area; it was during this trip that his views on military policy in Vietnam changed. He accompanied army battalions in the Mekong Delta in order to assess the effectiveness of the U.S. policy of pacification, which involved painstakingly searching South Vietnamese communities to root out Communist insurgents. He saw firsthand the destruction of Vietnam's land and people as well as the corruption of the U.S.-supported regime in South Vietnam. His developed grave moral concerns about the nation's involvement in and perpetuation of the Vietnam conflict.

Upon his return to the United States, Ellsberg was asked, along with thirty-five other analysts, to produce the Pentagon Papers, the multivolume, top-secret analysis of the nation's policy in Vietnam. Ellsberg himself did not write much of the study. However, he was further disturbed by the pattern of deceiving of the American people and increasing involvement in Vietnam that the papers documented. Ellsberg believed that the U.S. government had deliberately misled the American public about the nation's involvement in Southeast Asia for twenty years. In his view the government practiced this deceit in order to ensure that public attention would not turn against the war and force a troop withdrawal and a humiliating military defeat.

Ellsberg photocopied the entire report, file by file, and began leaking the papers to the *New York Times* in 1971. After the Department of Justice received an injunction banning the publication of the papers in the *New York Times*, Ellsberg then leaked them to both the *Washington Post* and the *Boston Globe*. He later said of his actions, "I felt as an American citizen . . . I could no longer cooperate in concealing this information from the American people. I took this action on my own initiative, and I am prepared for all the consequences."

After Ellsberg's indictment on charges of conspiracy and espionage, his case became a cause célèbre. His conversion from "hawk" to "dove" provided inspiration for the antiwar movement, and he spoke to groups around the country. After charges against him were dismissed, Ellsberg continued his activism, supporting antinuclear demonstrations, advocating nuclear disarmament, and criticizing U.S. policy in Central America. He was arrested many times for acts of civil disobedience. He remains an activist and a popular lecturer.

help of Anthony J. Russo (1937–), and released them to the *New York Times*.

Publication of the Pentagon Papers The *New York Times* created an uproar when it began publication of the papers in June 1971. Antiwar protesters immediately seized upon the papers, arguing that they highlighted a "credibility gap" and demonstrated that the government had deliberately misled Congress and the American people in order to expand the country's involvement in a foreign conflict. President Nixon was enraged by the leak. He believed that the publication of the Pentagon Papers would undermine his administration's ability to wage war in Vietnam.

Court Actions The U.S. Department of Justice succeeded in obtaining an injunction halting the publication of the papers in the *New York Times*. Ellsberg, however, leaked the documents to other newspapers, and the *Washington Post* and the *Boston Globe* continued their publication. In an extraordinarily swift decision, the Supreme Court ruled in *New York Times v. United States* on June 30 that the government had violated the Constitution's guarantee of freedom of the press, rejecting the government's argument that the papers should be censored because of national security concerns.

Subsequently, Ellsberg was indicted for leaking the papers on charges of espionage, theft, and conspiracy. Russo was also charged. Determined to obtain a conviction, the Nixon administration organized a secret White House group called the "Plumbers" to try to discredit Ellsberg. To that end the Plumbers broke into the office of Ellsberg's psychiatrist, looking for information in the psychiatrist's files to use against Ellsberg. These illegal activities, once exposed, caused U.S. District Judge William M. Byrne Jr. to declare a mistrial because of gross government misconduct. The case was dropped.

The Pentagon Papers had a profound impact on American history. First, they offered an inside view of the government's actions in Vietnam. Once made public, the papers generated a huge public outcry and led to the eventual withdrawal of American troops from Vietnam. The government's illegal activities in pursuit of a conviction of Ellsberg on charges of espionage were early events in the Watergate scandal that soon led to the downfall of the Nixon administration and the resignation of the president himself.

See also **Richard M. Nixon**
See also **United States v. Nixon**
See also **Watergate**

Furman v. Georgia

Furman v. Georgia effectively abolished the death penalty as it was used in the United States prior to 1972. In a 5 to 4 decision handed down on June 29, 1972, the Supreme Court severely limited the death penalty's use based on the Eighth Amendment, which prohibits "cruel and unusual" punishment. The decision resulted in more than six hundred prisoners leaving death row while states rewrote their statutes to meet the constitutional requirements indicated in the decision.

The History of the Death Penalty The death penalty's use has been accepted practice in the United States since the nation's founding. Periodically, activists have attempted to abolish capital punishment. One such period was in the first half of the nineteenth century, when reformers worked to reduce the number of crimes punishable by death. After the Civil War these reform efforts diminished, and Americans generally accepted capital punishment. Before *Furman*, however, the death penalty's use had declined. Only 56 people were executed in 1960, compared to 155 persons in 1930.

The Legal Defense and Educational Fund Challenges Capital Punishment While the Supreme Court had affirmed a rapist's death sentence in a 1963 decision, lawyers in the Legal Defense and Educational Fund (known as the LDF), a branch of the National Association for the Advancement of Colored People (NAACP), were encouraged by the lone dissenting justice's statement in that case that the Supreme Court's task was to decide whether or not the death penalty was constitutional. LDF lawyers viewed the death penalty as a form of legally sanctioned lynching, especially when applied to African-American men who had been convicted of raping white women. By 1967, the Legal Defense Fund was representing all inmates on death row, who were disproportionately African-American men. The LDF brought several class action suits on behalf of these inmates, hoping the Supreme Court would eventually agree to hear a case and rule on the constitutionality of capital punishment.

An initial victory came in 1968, when the Supreme Court ruled in *Witherspoon v. Illinois* that a potential juror who had reservations about sentencing a convicted person to death could not be automatically dismissed in a capital case. This ruling resulted in many death row inmates receiving new trials. The LDF followed up this victory by mounting several challenges to the constitutionality of the death sentence itself, all of which failed. Finally, the LDF decided to challenge capital punishment on the grounds that it was cruel and unusual punishment prohibited by the Eighth Amendment.

William Henry Furman The Supreme Court agreed to hear this challenge in the case of *Furman v. Georgia*. This case combined the cases of three African-American men who had been sentenced to death, including two rapists as well as William Henry Furman, who had been convicted of murder. Furman, who gave his name to the case, had entered his victim's home intending to commit burglary. Furman tried to run when discovered, but his gun accidentally went off. The bullet hit and killed the victim. The victim's family called the police immediately; when police searched the neighborhood, they found Furman still carrying the murder weapon.

Before his trial Furman was committed to a state mental hospital and found to be both mentally deficient and prone to psychotic episodes. Nevertheless, the Superior Court of Chatham County, Georgia, found Furman competent to stand trial and denied his insanity plea. Furman had a court-appointed lawyer, and his trial, including jury selection, lasted just one day. The judge in the case made clear to the jury that Georgia's death penalty statute allowed capital punishment for any killings that occurred while the defendant was committing a criminal act. He instructed jurors to convict Furman of murder whether or not he had intended to kill his victim if they believed he had intended to break into and enter the victim's home. Furman was found guilty and sentenced to death, despite the fact that the shooting had been accidental.

The Supreme Court Decision On June 29, 1972, the Supreme Court handed down its decision that the death penalty, as it was currently applied in the United States, was cruel and unusual punishment prohibited by the Eighth Amendment to the Constitution. The justices, however, were deeply divided on the issue, and each justice took the unusual step of writing a separate opinion in the case. Justices William J. Brennan Jr. (1906–1997) and Thurgood Marshall (1908–1993) stated that the death penalty was unconstitutional in every case. Justices William O. Douglas (1898–1980), Potter Stewart (1915–1985), and Byron R. White (1917–2002) stated that capital punishment was unconstitutional because it was applied arbitrarily. These justices stated that Furman was sentenced to death unfairly because he was poor, African-American, had received a quick, one-day trial, and was uneducated and mentally ill. Douglas wrote: "It would seem to be incontestable that the death penalty inflicted on one defendant is 'unusual' if it discriminates against him by reason of his race, religion, wealth, social position, or class, or if it is imposed under a procedure that gives room for the play of such prejudices. . . . One searches our chronicles in vain for the execution of any member of the affluent strata of this society."

Four justices dissented from the majority view—Chief Justice Warren Burger (1907–1995), Harry A. Blackmun (1908–1999), William H. Rehnquist (1924–2005), and Lewis F. Powell Jr. (1907–1998). They argued that capital punishment had a long tradition and was implicitly authorized in the Constitution under the Fourteenth Amendment.

The Fate of Capital Punishment The wording of the opinions of Justices Douglas, Stewart, and White left

THE LEGAL FIGHT AGAINST DISCRIMINATION

The Legal Defense and Educational Fund (known as the LDF) was incorporated by the National Association for the Advancement of Colored People (NAACP) in 1940 to administer tax-exempt donations for legal defense work. Thurgood Marshall (1908–1993), who sat on the Supreme Court during the *Furman v. Georgia* case, led the LDF in its early years. Initially, the LDF defended African-Americans in cases where there was clear evidence of racial discrimination. Lawyers often put themselves in danger by traveling throughout the South to defend African-Americans in criminal cases in small southern towns. While the lawyers often lost these cases, they frequently won them on appeal to higher courts. In addition, the lawyers' presence at these trials helped bring some measure of fairness to the criminal procedures.

At the same time, the LDF fought for civil rights—especially in education—at the national level and won a variety of landmark cases before the Supreme Court. Throughout the American South, African-American children were segregated into schools with inferior buildings, scanty books and instructional materials, and poorly paid teachers. LDF focused on gradually dismantling this "separate but equal" doctrine in education that had been established in *Plessy v. Ferguson* in 1896.

Lawyers won a series of cases argued before the Supreme Court between 1948 and 1950 that ruled that segregation of graduate schools and law schools was discriminatory. The LDF then challenged segregation in public schools, which culminated in the landmark Supreme Court decision in *Brown v. Board of Education* (1954) in which the court ruled that schools must be desegregated "with all deliberate speed." In the years thereafter, the LDF concentrated on bringing lawsuits that would force southern states to desegregate their schools as ordered in *Brown*, a slow and frustrating process. Due to the continued litigation of the LDF, the Court finally did away with the "all deliberate speed" idea in 1968 and ordered immediate and total desegregation of all public schools in *Green v. County School Board of New Kent County*.

The LDF formally split from the NAACP in 1954 due to disagreements over the focus of the organization. While the LDF continued to pursue equality in education, it also took on other civil rights cases. By 1970, capital punishment had become a focus of the LDF's efforts. While *Furman* turned out to be a temporary victory, the LDF had more success in the fight against capital punishment in rape cases. A study funded by the LDF had found that 89 percent of convicted rapists sentenced to death between 1930 and 1962 were African-American. In a case represented by the LDF in 1977, *Coker v. Georgia*, the Supreme Court barred the death penalty for rape.

open for debate the question of whether the death penalty could ever be considered constitutional. As a result, thirty-five states responded to *Furman* by immediately beginning the process of rewriting their death penalty statutes to attempt to eliminate the arbitrary nature of capital punishment's application. By 1976 there were 450 inmates on death row, although none had been executed since 1967.

In 1976 the Supreme Court heard *Gregg v. Georgia* to determine if Georgia's new death penalty statute was constitutional. Georgia had overhauled its death penalty laws, instituting two separate trials in capital cases—one to determine guilt and one to determine punishment—to allow the accused to testify at the penalty phase without being forced to incriminate himself at the first trial. The statute also required the presence of aggravating circumstances (circumstances that increase the severity of the crime) and the absence of any mitigating circumstances (circumstances that do not excuse the crime but provide a reason for reducing the punishment for it) in order to impose the death penalty. And finally, any death sentence would be automatically appealed to the state's highest court. The Supreme Court found this statute constitutional, and in 1977 Gary Gilmore was the first person to be executed in the nation in ten years.

Most states followed the Court's findings in the *Gregg* decision and wrote death penalty statutes meant to protect the poor, minorities, mentally ill people, and members of other disenfranchised groups. Most states also repealed the death penalty for accidental killings, like the one in *Furman*. Subsequent Supreme Court decisions upheld the constitutionality of various rewritten death penalty statutes. In 1987 the Court found that the disproportionate number of African-Americans sentenced to death was not necessarily due to racial bias, and therefore capital punishment was not unconstitutional on the grounds of discrimination.

While executions did resume in 1977, *Furman v. Georgia* still had far-reaching effects. It had led immediately to the release of more than six hundred inmates from death row due to the "arbitrary and capricious" application of death penalty statutes. As a result of the Court's decision, states rewrote their death penalty statutes to place stringent requirements on the imposition of the death sentence in capital cases.

Title IX of the Education Amendments of 1972

Title IX of the Education Amendments of 1972, which were amendments to the Civil Rights Act of 1964, prohibits gender discrimination by institutions of higher education that receive federal funds (almost every educational institution receives at least some federal funding). The Office for Civil Rights within the U.S. Department of Education is charged with enforcing the rights and regulations detailed in the legislation.

The Need for Title IX With the women's rights movement of the late 1960s and early 1970s, the nation began to recognize the inequities and discriminatory practices that prevented women and girls from achievements in education and, ultimately, the workforce. For example, until a court order was issued in 1970, Virginia state law prohibited women from being admitted to the University of Virginia's College of Arts and Sciences, the top-rated public college in the state. In 1966 Georgetown University's School of Nursing refused to admit married women. Even Luci Baines Johnson (1947–), the daughter of President Lyndon Johnson (1908–1973), was refused readmission to the program after her marriage.

Congressional and White House recognition of the need for protective statutes was widespread by 1971, when several education bills included language disallowing gender discrimination. Because the proposals differed in their language and provisions, it took several months for the final legislation—with a provision against sex discrimination—to develop. President Richard M. Nixon (1913–1994) signed Title IX on June 23, 1972. The law went into effect on July 1.

Title IX was the first comprehensive federal law to prohibit gender discrimination against students, faculty, and staff of educational institutions, which are defined in the act as elementary and secondary schools, colleges and universities, and other educational programs that receive federal funds. The law dictated that males and females receive fair and equal treatment in all areas of publicly financed schooling, including recruitment, admissions, course offerings, counseling, financial aid, housing, scholarships, and protection from sexual harassment. Also, women could no longer be discriminated against based on marital status or maternity.

Title IX and Athletics Title IX has been most notably used to acquire increased financing from colleges and universities for women's collegiate sports. The statute provides specific criteria for determining whether or not a school's athletic programs are in compliance with Title IX. To be in compliance, the following criteria must be met:

- A school must demonstrate that it offers proportionate athletic opportunities for male and female athletes, has continued to expand opportunities for the underrepresented sex, or has effectively accommodated the interests and abilities of the underrepresented sex. In other words, schools do not have to offer identical sports—such as male and female football teams—yet they do need to provide an equal opportunity for males and females to play in sports of interest.

- The amount of money provided in athletic scholarships must be substantially proportionate to the ratio of female and male athletes. For example, at a college with forty female athletes and sixty male athletes and a scholarship budget of $1 million, an equitable distribution of the funds would provide $400,000 in scholarship aid to female athletes and $600,000 to males.

- Activities and staffing related to athletics must also be equal. In this category would be items such as coaching, equipment, facilities, medical services, travel allowances, and tutoring. For purposes of comparison, however, the compliance standard measures the quality of the services rather than the quantity of dollars spent. Spending more on men's basketball uniforms than women's is fine, as long as both teams are properly outfitted. Giving the men's basketball team its own luxury motorcoach bus with air conditioning, televisions, and toilet facilities while making female basketball players ride in a standard yellow school bus is not acceptable.

When Gender Distinctions Are Allowed There are certain situations in which a school provides separate instruction and activities based on gender. These include sex education classes at the elementary and secondary school levels, and physical education classes or after-school programs during which bodily contact sports, such as wrestling, boxing, rugby, or football, will be played. Similarly, choruses where a specific vocal range may be required can be single sex or disproportionate in terms of gender. Nor does the law apply to fraternities and sororities, youth service organizations (such as Boy Scouts and Girl Scouts), or activities such as school-based father-son, mother-daughter events.

The Impact of Title IX As with many policies involving mandates and gender issues, Title IX has its champions and its detractors. It has been credited with enhancing collegiate sports programs and blamed for undermining them (especially when it comes to men's athletics). Title IX has been supported by some presidential administrations and demeaned by others. Yet, a generation after its creation, Title IX is still law. What is not debated is that the 1972 legislation vastly expanded the opportunities for women in sports. In 1971 fewer than 100,000 girls played organized high school sports, accounting for about 5 percent of high school athletes. By the 2002–2003 school year, that number had increased to more than 2.8 million. In 1972 fewer than 30,000 women played intercollegiate athletics (compared with 170,000 men). By 2002, 151,000 women played on National Collegiate Athletic Association (NCAA) teams and thousands more participated at the intramural and community college level.

The Equal Rights Amendment

The equal rights amendment (ERA) sought to affirm that women and men are equally granted the rights guaranteed by the U.S. Constitution. Its passage would prevent gender discrimination against both women and men and give equal legal status to women for the first time in American history.

Congress approved the ERA in 1972, sending the proposed text to the states for ratification. When the ratification period expired in 1983, only thirty-five states had voted in support. The ERA fell three votes shy of the two-thirds—or thirty-eight states—required for an amendment to be added to the Constitution.

A Long History The equal rights amendment was drafted in 1923 by Alice Paul (1885–1977), founder of the National Woman's Party. Having achieved the passage of the Nineteenth Amendment, giving American women the right to vote, the next step, according to suffragists, was to secure for women the Constitutional protection of equal rights under the law. The amendment was introduced into Congress that year.

Many groups, especially labor and women's organizations, initially opposed the equal rights amendment because they feared it would end protective labor legislation for women. As the years passed, Congress had different concerns and priorities, including the stock market crash of 1929, the Great Depression, World War II, and the Vietnam War, which kept the ERA on the back burner. But as the women's rights movement gained momentum in the 1960s, several organizations, particularly the National Organization for Women (NOW), took up the amendment as one of their major issues. But by the time of the amendment's ratification deadline of June 30, 1982, the ERA was still three states short of the thirty-eight necessary to make it law.

Why Did the ERA Fail? There are many theories for why the ERA failed. Some say it was the timing and a weakening momentum due to the lengthy ratification process. A larger issue was American society's response to the changing roles and attitudes of women in the late 1960s and beyond. The ERA became subsumed by the tensions that existed toward and among feminists (those in support of women's rights) and traditionalists (those opposed to feminism). The essential principles of the amendment—securing the freedoms and rights afforded Americans regardless of gender—were thrown into a

Former New York Congresswoman Bella Abzug (second from right) at a pro-ERA rally, 1980. © *Bettmann/CORBIS*

large basket with hot-button issues such as abortion, birth control, homosexuality, and women in the workforce. There were concerns about what would happen to the traditional structure of the family (husband as breadwinner, wife as caregiver). Fears were expressed that official equality under the law would be used by men as a free pass to walk out on a marriage and not financially support the wife and children left behind.

Although national polls consistently showed that the majority of Americans favored the equal rights amendment, the extremism within both camps, as with many social issues, came to dominate the issue. The perception became that only women who rejected marriage and motherhood would support the ERA.

The most effective opposition to the ERA came from religious conservatives, the right-wing John Birch Society, and the activist group STOP ERA headed by Phyllis Schlafly (1924–), all of whom presented the ERA as an effort by radical feminists to undermine the worth of women as wives and mothers. Such opponents charged that supporters of the ERA were so vehement in their call for equality that, if the ERA passed, divorced women would no longer receive alimony, women would be drafted into the military, and males and females would have to share public bathrooms. Men who were threatened by women's equality applauded the anti-ERA lobby, whose strategies convinced women who did not aspire to a career that their way of life was at risk. ERA supporters, many of whom were, by comparison, more provocative in their appearance and lifestyle than more traditionalist women, were never able to overcome charges that women either did not need or should not want equal rights with men.

During the years the ERA was working its way through the states for ratification, the political winds changed in the United States. In 1980 Republican Ronald Reagan (1911–2004) was elected to the presidency with enormous support from conservatives and the religious right. That same year the equal rights amendment, which for decades had been supported by both political parties, was dropped from the Republican Party Platform.

The ERA, Today and Tomorrow The equal rights amendment continues to be introduced into each session of Congress, where it has typically languished in a committee or been otherwise set aside without a vote. The hope of supporters is that when or if the ERA finally passes, no deadline will be placed on the ratification process. Up for debate is whether the amendment will be allowed to keep the thirty-five states that already ratified it, or if the entire process will need to begin again. The fifteen states that have not ratified the equal rights amendment are Alabama, Arizona, Arkansas, Florida, Georgia, Illinois, Louisiana, Mississippi, Missouri, Nevada, North Carolina, Oklahoma, South Carolina, Utah, and Virginia.

FULL TEXT OF THE EQUAL RIGHTS AMENDMENT

First proposed in 1923, the equal rights amendment (ERA) was approved by Congress and sent to the states for ratification in 1972. Adding an amendment to the U.S. Constitution requires the affirmative vote of two-thirds of the nation's fifty states. When the ratification process expired in 1982, the ERA had only thirty-five of the necessary thirty-eight states. Below is the full text of the amendment:

Section 1. Equality of rights under the law shall not be denied or abridged by the United States or by any state on account of sex.

Section 2. The Congress shall have the power to enforce, by appropriate legislation, the provisions of this article.

Section 3. This amendment shall take effect two years after the date of ratification.

SOURCE: Equal Rights Amendment, *http://www.equalrightsamendment. org/overview.htm* (accessed April 15, 2007)

Roe v. Wade

Roe v. Wade, decided by the Supreme Court on January 22, 1973, struck down state laws that restricted women's access to abortions. Attorneys Linda Coffee (1942–) and Sarah Weddington (1945–) had brought the suit on behalf of the so-called Jane Roe, challenging antiabortion laws in Texas on the grounds that the statutes violated the due process clause of the Fourteenth Amendment as well as the Constitution's implied right to privacy in the Ninth Amendment. The Supreme Court agreed that the right to privacy encompassed a woman's right to terminate a pregnancy, striking down antiabortion laws throughout the nation. After *Roe v. Wade*, controversy and debate over women's reproductive choice raged for decades.

The History of the Movement to Legalize Abortion Antiabortion laws had been enacted throughout the United States since the late nineteenth century. By the 1960s the modern women's rights movement had begun in part because women had been politicized in other social movements of the era, including the student antiwar movement and the civil right movement.

As women joined the work force in larger and larger numbers, they called for more reproductive choices. Many women chose to obtain abortions illegally; estimates of the number of abortions performed in the 1960s range from 200,000 to 1,200,000 annually. Doctors publicized the dangers women faced with these "back alley" abortions, and public attitudes began to

Sarah Weddington, one of the attorneys who represented Jane Roe in the landmark *Roe v. Wade* case in the early 1970s, talking to reporters at a 1989 press conference. © *Bettmann/CORBIS*

change. By 1970 it was estimated that 60 percent of Americans believed that the choice to have an abortion should be a private decision. Women's rights activists began calling for reforms in the statutes regulating abortion and eventually the repeal of all antiabortion laws. Several states reformed their abortion laws in this public climate, including New York, California, Colorado, and Hawaii. Abortion rights activists were looking for a case with which they could challenge the laws that outlawed abortion.

Enter Norma McCorvey In 1969 Norma McCorvey (1947–), a twenty-one-year-old single woman, found out she was pregnant. She already had a five-year-old child who was being cared for by her mother. She had little money and worked as a waitress in a bar. She did not think she could care for another child and wanted an abortion, but Texas law prevented her from doing so legally unless her life was endangered by the pregnancy. Her search for an illegal abortion was fruitless.

Linda Coffee and Sarah Weddington, both lawyers in Dallas, wanted to challenge the Texas laws regulating abortion as unconstitutional. They believed that the time

was ripe because the Supreme Court had decided several cases in recent history that indicated that they might consider ruling against state abortion statutes. In the most important of these, *Griswold v. Connecticut* (1968), the Court found that states could not make the sale of contraceptives to married couples illegal, ruling that such laws violated the right to privacy. (Later, in *Eisenstadt v. Baird* (1971), the Court extended the right to buy birth control to unmarried people.)

McCorvey met Coffee and Weddington during her search for an illegal abortionist. McCorvey agreed to be the plaintiff representing all pregnant women in a class-action suit challenging the Texas laws, even though she knew the verdict would not come fast enough for her to be able to have an abortion (and, in fact, McCorvey ultimately gave birth to the baby). Her one condition for the case was that she remain anonymous; thus she became Jane Roe.

Filing suit against Dallas County District Attorney Henry B. Wade (1916–) representing the state of Texas, Coffee and Weddington attacked the Texas abortion statutes on the grounds that they violated the Fourteenth Amendment's due process clause, which guaranteed equal protection to all citizens under the law, and the Ninth Amendment, which had been used in the *Griswald v. Connecticut* case to show that rights not specifically discussed in the Constitution were retained by the people—specifically, the right to privacy. Coffee and Weddington argued that a woman should have the right to decide whether or not to become a mother, because that decision was protected by the right to privacy.

The Case The case was first argued in the Fifth Circuit Court in Dallas, Texas, on May 23, 1970. Coffee and Weddington represented McCorvey, the plaintiff, while Jay Floyd defended the Texas antiabortion law. Anticipating the state argument that the case should be dismissed because "Roe" must have already reached the point in her pregnancy when an abortion would be unsafe, Coffee argued that McCorvey did in fact have "standing to sue." The judges agreed with her. Weddington specifically argued against the state claim that a fetus had legal rights that should be protected. "Life is an ongoing process," she argued. "It is almost impossible to define a point at which life begins." When asked by the judges whether she believed the abortion statutes were weaker under the Fourteenth Amendment or Ninth Amendment, Weddington said she believed antiabortion laws were more vulnerable under the Ninth Amendment.

The judges of the Fifth Circuit Court agreed with Coffee and Weddington. The court issued its opinion on June 17, 1970: "The Texas abortion laws must be declared unconstitutional because they deprive single women and married couples, of their right, secured by the Ninth Amendment, to choose whether to have children." Because the Fifth Circuit Court, however, did not order the state to stop enforcement of the abortion law, Coffee and Weddington appealed to the Supreme Court. The Court agreed to hear the case.

Weddington and Floyd first argued the case before the Supreme Court on December 13, 1971, and again on October 10, 1972. Weddington argued that the Constitution declared people "citizens" at the moment of birth; at that moment persons were entitled to protection under the law. She contended that women who were compelled to bear children under the Texas law were left without control over their lives. Floyd repeated the state's argument that Roe could not represent pregnant women in a class action suit, because she had certainly given birth by then. When asked to define when life began according to the state of Texas, Floyd could not answer.

The Supreme Court Decision   Judge Harry A. Blackmun (1908–1999) authored the majority opinion in *Roe.* He stated that the choice to abort was protected by a fundamental right of privacy: "This right of privacy, whether it be founded in the Fourteenth Amendment's concept of personal liberty ... or ... in the Ninth Amendment's reservation of rights to the people, is broad enough to encompass a woman's decision to terminate her pregnancy." He disagreed with the state of Texas's claim that it

had the right to protect the fetus by infringing on the rights of pregnant women. According to the Court, the fetus was not a "person" under the Constitution.

The Court held that the state had a compelling interest in restricting a woman's right to choose an abortion in two instances—when a mother's health was at risk or when the well-being of a viable fetus was at risk. The decision relied on trimesters. During the first trimester, the Court ruled, choices must be left to the woman in consultation with her doctor. In the second trimester the state was given a very limited ability to restrict a woman's access to abortion—to protect maternal health. In the third trimester, when the fetus became viable, or able to live outside of the womb, the state's interest in regulating abortion became compelling. A state was allowed to regulate or prohibit abortion entirely in this trimester, except when an abortion was necessary to preserve the life of the mother.

Justice William H. Rehnquist (1924–2005) wrote a strong dissenting opinion to the Court's decision. He rejected the right to choose abortion as protected by the right to privacy. He also argued that abortion regulations should be decided locally and be respected by the Court.

Anti-abortion protesters marching past the U.S. Supreme Court in 1990.   © *Bettmann/CORBIS*

SARAH WEDDINGTON FIGHTS FOR THE RIGHTS OF WOMEN

The experience of Sarah Weddington (1945–) as a female in the male-dominated legal profession, as well as her personal experience of having an illegal abortion, served to politicize her and involve her in feminist causes. She had been one of only five women at the University of Texas School of Law in Austin. Although she graduated in the top 25 percent of her class in 1967, discrimination against women in law kept her from getting work in Texas. She eventually found work on the American Bar Association's project to standardize legal ethics.

In the meantime, Weddington became involved with a network of feminists in Austin who published an underground newspaper, *The Rag*. These women also counseled other women about birth control, including directing women to the safest abortion clinics in Mexico. Weddington took an interest in birth control work in part because she herself had had an illegal abortion in Mexico. She became convinced that women's reproductive rights were essential to women's equality.

Weddington enlisted the aid of a law school classmate, Linda Coffee (1942–), and the two began working on a case against the Texas antiabortion laws based on the constitutional right to privacy established in 1965 in the birth control case *Griswold v. Connecticut*. They began searching for a woman for whom they could file a class-action suit on behalf of all pregnant women in order to challenge the Texas laws.

Weddington was only twenty-five years old when she filed *Roe v. Wade* in federal court in Dallas, challenging the Texas antiabortion statute on behalf of Norma McCorvey (1947–). Young and inexperienced, she had never before tried a case. She is believed to be the youngest person to have ever won a case before the Supreme Court.

Weddington's success helped her win a seat in the Texas state legislature. She then served as general counsel for the Department of Agriculture during the administration of Jimmy Carter (1924–) for one year before becoming Carter's assistant on women's issues for the remainder of his presidency. In the early 1980s Weddington remained in Washington as a lobbyist for the state of Texas and remained active in women's issues and reproductive rights. In 1986 Weddington returned to Austin to practice law. In 1992 she wrote *A Question of Choice*, which tells the story of *Roe v. Wade* and details her position on women's reproductive rights. She remains a popular speaker and lecturer.

On the same day as the *Roe* decision, the Court handed down a decision in another abortion case, *Doe v. Bolton*, which challenged a Georgia law that regulated the procedures involved in getting an abortion, such as where abortions could be performed, residency requirements for women seeking abortions, and the need for approval of three physicians to procure an abortion. The Court struck down these restrictions.

Effects of the Decision *Roe v. Wade* had immediate and significant effects. Several states that had already reformed their abortion laws, including New York, Alaska, Hawaii, and Washington, were required to extend the period in which they allowed abortions by several weeks. Fifteen states had to completely overhaul their laws regulating abortion. In thirty-one states, including Texas, strict antiabortion laws immediately became invalid. Abortions became widely available in the United States, and the number of abortions performed yearly skyrocketed. By the late 1980s, 1.5 million legal abortions were performed annually in the country, and about three out of every ten pregnancies ended in abortions.

Roe v. Wade garnered more public controversy than perhaps any other decision in the Supreme Court's history. Supporters of state laws restricting women's access to abortions, drawn largely from the Catholic and Protestant fundamentalist religious right, were shocked by the Court's decisions in *Roe v. Wade* and *Doe v. Bolton*. These activists argued that abortion was tantamount to murder. They immediately mobilized into an antiabortion, or "pro-life," movement. Their initial demand for a "human rights amendment" to the Constitution that would ban abortion entirely failed. They did succeed, however, in getting some states to pass laws that would further restrict abortion, like requiring parental consent for minors or consent from fathers before an abortion. However, the Supreme Court struck these consent provisions down as too restrictive in *Planned Parenthood v. Danforth* in 1976. Other states reduced or eliminated public funding for abortions, which could limit a poor women's ability to procure an abortion. These restrictions were held up by the Supreme Court in several cases decided in 1977, including *Beal v. Doe*, *Maher v. Roe*, and *Poelker v. Doe*.

Ongoing Controversy Since the 1970s, the Republican Party has adopted the "pro-life" position as part of its party platform. This had the effect of gaining significant Catholic and fundamentalist support for the party while losing support of some women voters. The Democratic Party, on the other hand, adopted a "pro-choice" party platform and gained significant support from women voters, helping Democrat Bill Clinton (1946–) to be elected president in 1992.

That same year, the right of women to choose abortion was affirmed once again by the Court in *Planned Parenthood of Southeastern Pennsylvania v. Casey*. Women's groups, clinics, and doctors challenged Pennsylvania's Abortion Control Act, which required women to wait twenty-four hours after receiving abortion information mandated by the state before having an abortion. It also required minors to get consent from at least one parent and married women to notify their husbands that they were pregnant and intended to abort. The district court initially declared most provisions of the law unconstitutional, except for one that required physicians to notify women of the age of the embryo or fetus. The court of appeals, on the other hand, upheld all provisions of the law except the one requiring a woman to notify her spouse. The Supreme Court agreed to hear the appeals by both sides. Observers believed that *Roe v. Wade* might well be overturned by the conservative Court. However, conservative Justice Anthony M. Kennedy (1936–) changed his mind at the last minute, joining Justice Sandra Day O'Connor (1930–) and Justice David H. Souter (1939–) in a compromise meant to uphold *Roe.*

On June 29, 1992, Justices O'Connor, Kennedy, and Souter delivered the opinion of the Court, which upheld the essential holding of *Roe v. Wade* recognizing a woman's right to choose to have an abortion. However, the court upheld Pennsylvania's Abortion Control Act, except for the provision requiring spousal notification.

Roe v. Wade had a profound impact on the range of reproductive choices available to women. A large network of clinics was established where women could obtain safe and inexpensive abortions as well as counseling. The decision also proved an enduring and divisive issue in politics, and pro-choice and antiabortion forces quickly formed in the wake of the decision to fight the continuing battle over women's freedom to choose abortion. A number of acts of violence against clinics and doctors who perform abortions have been attributed to antiabortion groups. Legal restrictions on women's access to abortions continued to be litigated, and the Supreme Court continued to hear cases dealing with abortion matters in the following years.

United States v. Nixon

In *United States v. Nixon*, the Supreme Court ruled in 1974 that President Richard M. Nixon (1913–1994) must turn over to prosecutors tape recordings of conversations and other documents related to the break-in of the Democratic National Committee headquarters at the Watergate Hotel by members of Nixon's administration. Nixon argued that he should not be made to produce the tapes because conversations with aides and staff members needed to be conducted in a confidential environment. The Court rejected Nixon's claim that executive privilege made him immune to the judicial process, as well as his claim that White House documents must remain confidential to protect sensitive information.

Nixon Subpoenaed Several senior Nixon administration officials had been indicted on March 1, 1974, on charges of conspiracy to obstruct justice in *United States v. Mitchell*, including the U.S. Attorney General John N. Mitchell (1913–1988). Nixon was included as a coconspirator, but unindicted. On April 18 the special prosecutor conducting the investigation into Watergate asked for a subpoena ordering Nixon to turn over to the Court "certain tapes, memoranda, papers, transcripts, or other writings" related to specific meetings and conversations in the White House identified by the special prosecutor as of interest through the White House daily logs and records of appointments.

Nixon did not comply with the subpoena; instead, he handed over edited transcripts of conversations hoping he could avoid turning over the tapes. Nixon's attorney, James D. St. Clair (1920–2001), asked the judge to rescind the subpoena; the judge denied the request and ordered the tapes be turned over by the end of May.

The Case St. Clair filed an appeal with the U.S. Court of Appeals for the District of Columbia, but both sides were aware of the importance of the question at hand— whether the president could be subpoenaed or otherwise forced to take part in the judicial process. They were also aware of the political stakes in this particular case and unwilling to drag the public through a prolonged judicial process. On May 24 the special prosecutor asked the Supreme Court to take the case without waiting for the case to make it through the court of appeals. On June 6 St. Clair requested the same.

The Supreme Court granted the requests and took the case from the court of appeals on June 15, 1974. The case was argued before the Supreme Court on July 8. The Court issued its opinion a little more than two weeks later. The eight justices (Justice William H. Rehnquist [1924–2005] had served in the Nixon administration and excused himself from the case) wrote a unanimous decision in this case because of the important issues at stake—namely, the relationship between the judiciary branch and the executive branch.

The Court began by restating the principle of *Marbury v. Madison* (1803): It is the judicial branch's responsibility to interpret the law and the Constitution. Therefore, wrote the justices, "we reaffirm that it is the province and the duty of this Court to say what the law is with respect to the claim of privilege presented in this case."

The Court then addressed the two main arguments of Nixon's attorney: first, that presidential communications should be kept confidential so advisers would be able to speak freely; and second, that the separation of powers gives the president immunity from the judicial process. First, the Court stated that confidentiality, while a concern, could be protected by a judge reviewing evidence privately: "Absent a claim of need to protect military, diplomatic, or sensitive national security secrets, we find it difficult to accept the argument that even the very important interest in confidentiality of Presidential communications is significantly diminished by production of such material for in camera [private] inspection with all the protection that a District Court will be obliged to provide." Second, the Court said, a blanket executive privilege granting the president immunity from the judicial process would stand in the way of criminal prosecutions. "Unqualified privilege," the Court stated, "would place in the way of primary constitutional duty of the Judicial Branch to do justice in criminal prosecutions would plainly conflict with the function of the courts."

Aftermath The Court ordered Nixon to turn over the tapes to Judge John J. Sirica (1905–1992) for in camera inspection. The question remained whether Nixon would obey the court order. Within a day Nixon assured the public he would comply with the Court's decision: "While I am, of course, disappointed in the result, I respect and accept the court's decision, and I have instructed Mr. St. Clair to take whatever measures are necessary to comply with that decision in all respects."

Nixon turned over sixty-four tapes to Judge Sirica, including some containing highly incriminating conversations between Nixon and his aides shortly after the Watergate break-in. Realizing that Congress was poised to impeach him, Nixon resigned on August 8, 1974, and Gerald R. Ford (1913–2006) became president at noon the following day.

United States v. Nixon established that executive privilege did not provide the president with immunity from the judicial process. Furthermore, it established that the president does not have the power to ignore subpoenas or withhold evidence from the courts, except in cases where national security was in jeopardy.

See also **Richard M. Nixon**
See also **Watergate**

The Earned Income Tax Credit

The Earned Income Tax Credit (EITC) is a federal tax benefit that reduces taxes for low- to moderate-income workers. Even workers whose earnings are too low to owe any income tax can get the EITC, which for them will result in a payment from the government.

Origins of the Earned Income Tax Credit The EITC was established in 1975 as a way to decrease the tax burden of low-income workers with children. Since its inception, the qualifications for and the benefit of the EITC has been expanded in order to help raise the incomes of working families above the federal poverty level.

The EITC was formulated during the presidency of Richard M. Nixon (1913–1994) as a way to ensure a minimum income level for all Americans. The chief advocate for this effort was Senator Russell Long (1918–2003), a Louisiana Democrat who believed the government should provide a monetary benefit to poor people who held a job.

The credit was approved in 1975. Because it was part of a larger tax bill signed into law by President Gerald Ford (1913–2006), at the time of its inception the EITC received minimal media coverage or public attention. Qualifying persons who were aware of the benefit were able to claim the credit for 1975 with a

tax return filed in April 1976. For the 1975 tax year, the credit was claimed by 6.2 million households, at a cost of $1.25 billion. The tax credit was made permanent in 1978 and since then has been both increased in value and, after an expansion in 1986, indexed to inflation. (Additional expansions and changes have occurred during tax legislation passed in 1993 and 2001.) While the EITC was originally created solely to assist low-income earners with dependent children, the program has since been expanded to include certain childless households in which a person works but earns a minimal income.

How the Earned Income Tax Credit Works Unlike a tax deduction, which allows taxpayers to reduce their taxable income, a tax credit is subtracted from the actual tax a person is calculated to owe. Hence, a tax bill of $500 might be reduced or eliminated if a qualifying worker applies for the EITC. Under the EITC, the federal government reimburses families that do not earn enough to pay much, or any, federal income tax. The program is unique in that it requires people to file a return, even if they are not required to pay any taxes, in order to receive a benefit check. If the amount of the credit exceeds a filer's actual tax liability, the excess is paid directly to the applicant.

To qualify for the original EITC, an income earner must have been supporting a family that included at least one dependent child. In 1975 the benefit was available to households that earned less than $8,000 in annual income. At the time, the benefit was equal to 10 percent of the earned income, up to a maximum income of $4,000. For example, a worker earning $4,000 per year, who had a dependant child, would receive a $400 check, which was the maximum benefit available. Someone earning $5,000 would have his or her benefit reduced 10 percent by whatever portion of the earnings was above $4,000. Hence, applicants would qualify for the $400 on the first $4,000 of their earnings, but be reduced by 10 percent on that $1,000 extra, thus decreasing their $400 credit by $100, which would leave them with a reduced benefit check of $300. The average credit earned by families for the 1975 tax year was $201. By comparison, in 2003 it was $1,784.

Impact of the Earned Income Tax Credit Since its inception in 1975, the EITC has grown into the largest federally funded means-tested cash assistance program in the United States. It is one of several programs run by the federal government whose benefits are determined by recipients' income. Others include the Food Stamp program, Medicaid, and Temporary Assistance for Needy Families (TANF). A key difference is that the EITC requires that the qualifying person have income from gainful employment or other legal means. Because the tax credit received by applicants varies based on their earnings, the program is viewed to serve low-income families in three ways. As a "phase-in" benefit, the EITC acts as a wage subsidy for very low earners. In this range, as the family earns more, its EITC increases. In the "maximum credit range," the credit is constant regardless of earnings. In the "phase-out range," as the family earns more, the credit is reduced. In essence, the EITC can serve as an incentive for those with very low incomes to work. In other cases, such as with families whose incomes are close to disqualifying them for the benefit, the EITC can be viewed by some as a disincentive to increase one's earnings.

However, in its more than three-decade existence, the EITC has largely been viewed as a positive government benefit that helps both individuals and the labor force at large, because it encourages employment over traditional welfare by providing a benefit only available to low-income people who are trying to provide for themselves by working. According to the U.S. Congress, the EITC has lifted more children above the Federal Poverty Level than any other government assistance program. Some studies have indicated that the benefit is more useful than an increased minimum wage in raising the incomes of low earners. Because the EITC is a program that promotes work, family, and self-reliance over welfare, it has been widely supported by both Democratic and Republican politicians.

Buckley v. Valeo

In *Buckley v. Valeo*, handed down on January 30, 1976, the Supreme Court upheld limits on donations to political campaigns but declared limits on a campaign's expenditures unconstitutional, on the grounds that such limits violate the First Amendment's protection of political speech. In addition, the Court found that public funding of presidential campaigns through check-off boxes on tax returns did not violate the Constitution's free speech or due process clauses, as charged by the lawyers of Senator James Lane Buckley (1923–).

The Federal Election Campaign Act (FECA) of 1971 had reformed campaign financing by imposing limits on amounts political candidates could spend on campaigns as well as imposing limits on donations to political campaigns. It also legislated better recording of funding sources in an attempt to create greater accountability. After the Watergate scandal, which revealed political corruption that included campaign financing, Congress sought to further reduce the influence of money in political election through amendments to FECA.

The Case Hoping to keep the amendments from taking effect before the 1976 election, Buckley and other candidates for political office filed suit in the U.S. District Court for the District of Columbia against Francis R. Valeo, secretary of the Senate and member of the Federal Election Commission. When arguments that FECA restricted constitutional freedoms were rejected by the U.S. Court of Appeals, the U.S. Supreme Court agreed to hear the case.

"HARD" v. "SOFT" MONEY

The Supreme Court declared in *Buckley v. Valeo* (1976) that contributions to and expenditures of political action committees, or PACs, could not be limited by campaign finance laws because such laws violated the right to freedom of speech. This gave rise to, in the words of one commentator, a "freewheeling, money-driven dynamic" that has since been upheld in several Supreme Court cases, including *First National Bank of Boston v. Bellotti* (1978), *Federal Election Commission v. Massachusetts Citizens for Life* (1986), and *Colorado Republican Federal Campaign Committee v. Federal Election Commission* (1996).

The effect of these Court decisions has been to uphold limits on so-called "hard money." Hard money is regulated by the government through requirements that political campaigns keep good records of campaign donations and expenditures. Individuals can contribute no more than $1,000 to a political candidate's official campaign committee.

However, the law allowed "independent" individuals and groups to raise unlimited funds, called "soft money" because it is unregulated. Individuals and groups were considered independent as long as they are not the campaign committee itself. Consequently, the Democratic National Committee, for example, which is not affiliated with the campaign committee, was allowed to raise and spend unlimited money to support the Democratic candidate for president. Other "independent" groups included labor unions, corporations, conservative or religious organizations, and other political advocacy groups. These groups could spend any sum to advocate policy positions that would benefit their chosen candidates.

Soft money was regulated somewhat with the passage of the Bipartisan Campaign Reform Act of 2002. Popularly called the McCain-Feingold Law, it finally banned the national political parties from raising soft money. It also banned advertisements produced by PACS that mentioned a candidate by name within thirty days of a primary election or sixty days of a general election. These so called "issue ads," the Court found, could be regulated without impinging on freedom of speech. Unsurprisingly, these limits were immediately challenged in court; the Supreme Court, however, upheld the bans in *McConnell v. Federal Election Commission* (2003).

The Supreme Court Reshapes Campaign Finance Laws In its ruling the Supreme Court did uphold a limit of $1,000 that an individual could donate to a presidential or congressional campaign. But as long as no official tie existed between the donor and the election campaign proper, these "independent" individual and group donors were free to spend unlimited money to support political candidates. For example, an individual can only donate $1,000 to the official election campaign committee of either a Democratic or Republican candidate. But that same individual can donate any larger amount of money to, for example, either the Democratic

EXCEPTIONS TO THE GOVERNMENT IN THE SUNSHINE ACT

A meeting of a government agency, board, or commission that is covered by the Government in the Sunshine Act can be closed to the public if the release of such information is likely to do any of the following:

- Reveal national defense or foreign policy secrets
- Relate solely to the internal personnel rules and practices of an agency
- Disclose matters specifically exempted from disclosure by statute
- Disclose privileged or confidential trade secrets and commercial or financial information obtained from a particular person
- Involve formally censuring a person or accusing an individual of a crime
- Disclose information of a personal nature where disclosure would constitute a clearly unwarranted invasion of personal privacy
- Disclose investigatory records compiled for law enforcement purposes, or information that would interfere with enforcement proceedings by depriving a person of a right to a fair trial or an impartial adjudication, constituting an unwarranted invasion of personal privacy, disclosing the identity of a confidential source or confidential information furnished by such source, disclosing investigative techniques and procedures, or endangering the life or physical safety of law enforcement personnel
- Disclose information contained in or related to examination, operating, or condition reports by, for, or on behalf of an agency responsible for the regulation or supervision of financial institutions
- Disclose certain types of information that would lead to significant financial speculation in currencies, securities, or commodities, significantly endanger the stability of any financial institution and/or significantly frustrate the implementation of a proposed agency action
- Specifically concern an agency's issuance of a subpoena or the agency's participation in a legal proceeding in the United States or abroad

SOURCE: *The Government in the Sunshine Act, 5 U.S.C. § 552(b), U.S. Department of Justice, http://www.usdoj.gov/oip/gisastat.pdf (accessed on July 14, 2007).*

limits on expenditures violated the right of freedom of speech. Candidates themselves could also spend their own money, in any amount, on their campaigns to get elected to office.

The Court dismissed charges that public funding of presidential campaigns violated the First Amendment, saying that rather the First Amendment was actually furthered by the provision of funding political debates. It also dismissed challenges to the measure based on the due process clause of the Fifth Amendment. Appellants argued the measure favored major candidates and parties, but the Court disagreed. While the Court dismissed limits on campaign expenditures in general, it upheld the condition that candidates who accept public monies must agree to limits on campaign expenditures.

The Court decision in *Buckley v. Valeo* reshaped campaign finance laws and made it difficult to enact future legislation to limit the influence of "big money" in political campaigns. Because the Court ruled that individuals and groups may contribute freely as long as they are independent of official election campaigns, political units known as political action committees, or PACs, arose. PACs are legally allowed to raise huge amounts of money to help candidates get elected. Their influence on political campaigns has grown exponentially since *Buckley v. Valeo*.

The Government in the Sunshine Act

In an effort to promote openness to the public and among governmental agencies, Congress created the Government in the Sunshine Act in 1976. Sometimes referred to as the Open Meetings Act, the statute established regulations and guidelines directing the leaders of certain types of government agencies and committees to conduct the public's business in public—in other words, in the light of day, rather than in closed-door deal-making sessions.

The Need for Sunshine The Government in the Sunshine Act was the last in a series of four "open government" statutes that included the Freedom of Information Act in 1966, the Federal Advisory Committee Act in 1972, and the Privacy Act in 1974. The bill that evolved into the Government in the Sunshine Act was first introduced in 1972, by Senator Lawton Chiles (1930–1998). In the wake of the Watergate scandal, the bill was an effort by legislators to encourage Americans to understand the decision-making process in Washington and to again have confidence and trust in the federal government. President Gerald Ford (1913–2006) signed the bill into law on September 13, 1976.

The Government in the Sunshine Act is based on the policy that, as the act states, "the public is entitled to the fullest practicable information regarding the decision-making processes of the Federal Government." Its purpose is "to provide the public with such information

or Republican National Committees—independent groups not officially affiliated with candidates' campaigns—who in turn can spend unlimited amounts of money to promote a presidential candidate in ways either similar to or different from the ways in which the official campaign committee promotes the candidate. In addition, the Court stated that campaign committees could spend freely, finding that any

while protecting the rights of individuals and the ability of the Government to carry out its responsibilities."

The Sunshine Act requires that the policy-making deliberations and meetings of "collegially headed" federal agencies be open to public scrutiny. For purposes of the legislation, a collegially headed agency is one in which several members (a majority of whom were appointed by the president and approved by the Senate) make decisions collaboratively, through discussions and voting, such as is done on a board or commission. The more than fifty governmental organizations subject to the law are typically independent regulatory agencies, such as the Securities and Exchange Commission, the Federal Communications Commission, and the Federal Reserve Board. The statute does not apply to departments headed by one person, such as the Department of State, or to the president of the United States.

Closure of meetings covered by the Sunshine Act is allowed if the reason is in accordance with at least one of ten exemptions to the rule. For example, a meeting can be closed if it involves the discussion of classified information that would invade an individual's privacy or impact a law enforcement investigation or pending litigation.

As much as the law helps the public to be aware of what decisions are being made and why, the statute was also created for its benefit to other arms of the government—because there is no statutory requirement for one government agency to share its information with another. Congress and the judiciary can issue subpoenas for such information, but this can be time-consuming and costly. With the Sunshine Act, and the other public information acts, numerous deliberations were made part of the public record.

What Is a "Meeting"? Provisions similar to or the same as the act are currently in effect in all fifty states. And such laws often expand beyond government to include the meetings of organizations such as homeowner associations (HOAs). However, individuals who have wanted to circumvent the law have often managed to do so, primarily by avoiding adherence to the act's official definition of the term "meeting." Under the Sunshine Act, a meeting must:

- Include a quorum, which is the minimum number of members who need to be present in order to vote and take action on behalf of the board, agency, or committee, etc.

- Allow members to discuss the issues, which would not be the case if one member made a speech and the others were in attendance only to listen

- Consist of "deliberations [that] determine or result in the joint conduct or disposition of official agency business"

By this definition, it is possible to have meetings that are not officially meetings. When an organization does not want to have an open meeting, there are ways to keep it closed, such as by not having a quorum or not voting. Contemporary technology that did not exist at the time of the Sunshine Act's passage now leaves room for the circumvention of the rules by allowing gathering for discussions via telephone conference call or e-mail. In essence, a board can have its discussions behind closed doors but meet in public only for a formal vote.

In *FCC v. ITT World Communications* (1984), the U.S. Supreme Court determined that a meeting occurs only when a quorum of members actually conducts or resolves official business. Hence, member discussions about issues, or to implement policies already voted upon, are not necessarily "meetings."

Another unintended consequence of the act, according to some observers, is that it has heightened the influence of an agency's chairperson (who typically runs the public meetings) and lessened the inclination and ability of other board members to speak freely. However, the Sunshine Act has proven particularly beneficial to cable news and twenty-four-hour television programming. By opening the governmental meetings to the public, cable networks such as C-SPAN (and its spin-offs) can broadcast even the most routine meetings of Congress and numerous federal agencies.

City of Philadelphia v. New Jersey

In *City of Philadelphia v. New Jersey*, Philadelphia argued that a New Jersey law, passed in 1973, that prohibited waste disposal in New Jersey from out of state violated the commerce clause of the Constitution. In 1978 the Supreme Court handed down its decision that New Jersey did in fact violate the commerce clause by banning waste disposal from other states within its borders. The commerce clause grants Congress the power to enact legislation to control interstate commerce, and therefore limits individual states' ability to regulate interstate commerce and trade. The decision was a blow to the emerging environmental movement.

Environmental Protectionism Environmental concerns in the 1960s led to a proliferation of environmental protection laws in the 1970s in a number of states. New Jersey's law prohibiting the dumping of out-of-state wastes within its borders was especially notable because the large eastern seaboard cities of New York and Philadelphia had used New Jersey as a dump for decades. The cities took their case to court.

The New Jersey Supreme Court found that the economic burden imposed on New York and Philadelphia was "slight" and that the state had a legitimate interest in protecting its residents and environment from the hazards posed by the "cascade of rubbish."

The Supreme Court found that the state of New Jersey could not bar garbage from being imported from other states.   © *Bettmann/CORBIS*

Philadelphia appealed to the U.S. Supreme Court, citing *Cooley v. Board of Wardens* (1851), which had established that state laws could not regulate interstate trade. The Court had previously used that precedent to overturn state protectionist laws of all kinds, including laws designed to protect a state's jobs, industries, and other resources.

The Supreme Court Decision   The Supreme Court found the New Jersey law was an unconstitutional violation of the commerce clause. Justice Potter Stewart (1915–1985) wrote the majority opinion in the case. He stated that "whatever New Jersey's ultimate purpose, it may not be accomplished by discriminating against articles of commerce coming from outside the State, unless there is some reason, apart from their origin, to treat them differently." In other words, if New Jersey allowed its own trash to be landfilled in the state, and New Jersey trash was indistinguishable from out-of-state-trash, then New Jersey was obliged to permit garbage from other states to be landfilled within its borders.

The Fate of Environmental Protectionism   *City of Philadelphia v. New Jersey* was significant because the Supreme Court essentially found a state's desire to protect its environment from harm as not a legitimate rea-

son to regulate interstate commerce. State legislatures were no longer able to give residents of their state rights over other state residents, protect the natural environment, or guard against fears of "contagion." It was a major setback for the environmentalist movement.

See also **The Environmental Movement**

Tennessee Valley Authority v. Hiram G. Hill

In *Tennessee Valley Authority v. Hiram G. Hill*, the Supreme Court found in 1978 that the Endangered Species Act prohibited the Tennessee Valley Authority from closing the gates of the Tellico Dam on the Lower Tennessee River because the flooding ensuing from the closed dam would destroy a "critical habitat" of the snail darter fish, an endangered species. The snail darter was listed as endangered under the Endangered Species Act, which had been enacted in 1973. The case was filed to protect the fish's habitat, and it reached the Supreme Court in 1978. The Supreme Court decided that the Endangered Species Act applied to this case and that the Tellico Dam could not complete its mission of closing the dam's gates, despite the economic losses that would ensue from abandoning an almost completed dam. However, subsequent legislation allowed the dam project to be completed.

History of the Tellico Dam Project The Tennessee Valley Authority began constructing the Tellico Dam on the Little Tennessee River in 1967. Environmentalists opposed construction of the dam, which would create a flooded reservoir covering 16,500 acres of land and stretching over thirty miles, providing, environmentalists argued, very few economic benefits. Although they succeeded in obtaining an initial injunction against the dam's completion under the terms of the National Environmental Policy Act of 1969, environmentalists were unsuccessful in permanently shutting down the project until the discovery of the snail darter fish, whose habitat was believed to be limited to the Little Tennessee River.

The Endangered Species Act Concerns about humans damaging the environment had been rising and become a major political issue in the late 1960s. In response, Congress had passed the Endangered Species Act of 1973 in order to prevent human impacts on ecosystems to endanger or cause the extinction of animal species. Environmentalists (including Hiram G. Hill, a member of the Tennessee Endangered Species Committee) filed suit in 1976 seeking protection of the snail darter fish's habitat under the provisions of the Endangered Species Act, beginning a three-year court battle over the closing of the gates of the Tellico Dam.

The Case What was at issue in the case was whether the requirements of the Endangered Species Act, passed in 1973, applied to a federal project that had been authorized before the passage of the act and which was virtually completed. A district court initially affirmed that the snail darter's habitat would be destroyed by the completion of the dam but found that the economic losses involved in scrapping a project that was almost finished at the time the fish was discovered were too great to stop the project from completion.

Environmentalists took their case to the court of appeals, which ruled that the current project status had no bearing on whether the provisions of the Endangered Species Act applied. The court of appeals issued an injunction against the completion of the dam. "It is conceivable," the court wrote, "that the welfare of an endangered species may weigh more heavily upon the public conscience, as expressed by the final will of Congress, than the writeoff of those millions of dollars already expended for Tellico."

The Tennessee Valley Authority appealed, and in 1978 the Supreme Court agreed to hear the case. In a 6–3 decision the Court affirmed the injunction against the closing of the doors of the dam that had been issued by the court of appeals. The Court found that because the area of the Little Tennessee River that would be flooded by the closing of the dam doors was the snail darter's "critical habitat," construction on the dam could not continue. Despite the economic losses from abandoning the Tellico project, the Court found, no

exemptions included in the Endangered Species Act applied to the project, despite the fact that Congress had continued appropriating money for the completion of the project even after the Little Tennessee River was found to be a "critical habitat." Noted the Court, "Congress has spoken in the plainest words, making it clear that endangered species are to be accorded the highest priorities."

Chief Justice Warren Burger (1907–1995) wrote the majority opinion in the case. He addressed the apparent incongruity of halting a multimillion dollar government project to save a tiny fish. "It may seem curious to some that the survival of a relatively small number of three-inch fish among all the countless millions of species extant would require the permanent halting of a virtually completed dam for which Congress has expended more than $100 million," he wrote. "The paradox is not minimized by the fact that Congress continued to appropriate large sums of public money for the project, even after congressional Appropriations Committees were apprised of its apparent impact upon the survival of the snail darter. We conclude, however, that the explicit provisions of the Endangered Species Act require precisely that result."

Subsequent Political Maneuvering Allows the Dam's Completion One month after the Court handed down its decision, Congress passed an amendment to the Endangered Species Act that allowed projects to be exempted from its restrictions for certain economic reasons. The Tennessee Valley Authority immediately sought an exemption from the Endangered Species Committee but was denied because the Tennessee Valley Authority had not taken necessary action to avoid a negative impact on the snail darter's "critical habitat."

Subsequently, two legislators representing Tennessee, Senator Howard H. Baker (1925–) and Representative John James Duncan, Sr. (1919–1988), included an amendment to the Energy and Water Development Appropriations Act in 1979 that would exempt the Tellico Dam from the requirements of the Endangered Species Act. Once passed, the gates of the Tellico Dam were allowed to be closed and the reservoir filled, destroying the snail darter fish's habitat in the Lower Tennessee River. Fortunately, within the following years, snail darter fish were found in other areas of the Tennessee River watershed, and the classification of the species was changed from endangered to threatened.

Tennessee Valley Authority v. Hiram G. Hill came to signify both the obstacles faced by the environmental movement and the movement's supposed excesses. The 1978 ruling was the first Supreme Court decision interpreting the 1973 Endangered Species Act and remains an important case in environmental law. However, the political maneuvering that followed on the heels of the decision illustrated that economic considerations often trump over environmental ones, despite the requirements of the Endangered Species Act. Still, the Endangered Species Act has had far-reaching ramifications, protecting not just species of animals but also the ecosystems on which they depend.

See also **The Environmental Movement**

Regents of the University of California v. Bakke

In *Regents of the University of California v. Bakke*, the U.S. Supreme Court ruled in 1978 that the "reverse discrimination" embodied in some affirmative action programs using quota systems was unconstitutional. Alan Paul Bakke (1940–), a white student twice denied admission to the University of California, Davis, School of Medicine while several places reserved for minority students went unfilled, filed suit charging his civil rights had been violated because he had been discriminated against based on his race. Bakke won the case. The Supreme Court ordered Bakke be admitted and that the University of California's special admissions program for minority students be dismantled. In the decision, the Court generally affirmed the constitutionality of affirmative action programs but declared that policies designed to increase minority representation through quota systems were unconstitutional because they discriminated against white students.

Affirmative Action Affirmative action programs are intended to increase the representation of traditionally underrepresented groups in employment or educational institutions. These programs are rooted in the Civil Rights Act of 1964, which prohibited job discrimination and required employers to provide equal opportunities to all employees, empowering workers and job applicants who believed they had been discriminated against based on their race, religion, or national origin to sue in federal courts. Executive Order 11375, signed by President Lyndon B. Johnson (1908–1973) in 1967, added sex to that list.

Affirmative action programs can take many forms. A program might be designed to hire or admit members of underrepresented groups in proportions equal to their proportion in the applicant pool. Programs might target women and minorities to increase their number in an applicant pool. Or an affirmative action program might establish numerical goals, which are quotas. All of these programs attempt to mitigate discriminatory effects on underrepresented groups.

Criticism of Affirmative Action While advocates of preferential affirmative action programs argue that these are temporary programs designed to remedy a long history of discrimination against minority groups, critics of affirmative action argue that the "preferential treatment" given to members of disadvantaged groups is discriminatory. The law, they argue, should only remedy discrimination by protecting individuals, rather than trying to remedy historical discrimination against groups of people. These critics charge that giving preference to members of minority or other disadvantaged groups is "reverse discrimination," mainly against white men.

The Case That was the point at issue in *Regents of the University of California v. Bakke*: Did reserving a certain number of spots in the University of California, Davis, School of Medicine for members of disadvantaged groups discriminate against white males? The case was brought by Allan Bakke, a white male who had been denied admission to the school in 1973 and 1974 even though his admission scores were higher than several minority students who had been accepted and even though several places reserved for minorities remained unfilled. The University of California, Davis, School of Medicine had begun an affirmative action program in 1968 in an attempt to increase the proportion of minority students in the student body. The school had set aside sixteen of its one hundred annual admissions for minority students, who were admitted under a separate process than were the general pool of candidates.

Bakke filed suit, charging that the university had not admitted him because of his race. He argued that the special admission program maintained by the school was unconstitutional because it violated his rights under the equal protection clause of the Fourteenth Amendment, which states that the laws must treat all individuals in the same manner as other individuals in similar circumstances.

The Superior Court of California agreed with Bakke but refused to order the medical school to admit him. Bakke appealed. The California Supreme Court upheld the lower court's finding that the admissions program was unconstitutional and ordered Bakke be admitted. The University of California appealed this ruling to the U.S. Supreme Court.

Reverse Discrimination? In a 5–4 split decision, the Supreme Court ruled that in fact the California program violated Bakke's civil rights under the equal protection clause and the Civil Rights Act because he was discriminated against based on his race. They ordered the University of California's special admissions program for minority students be dismantled and that Bakke be admitted to the medical school.

Justice Lewis F. Powell Jr. (1907–1998), writing for the Court, stated that universities could take race into account as a "plus" factor when making admissions decisions, because the First Amendment allowed educational institutions to promote cultural diversity. However, universities could not set aside a quota of spots for minority students that excluded whites. Powell argued that affirmative action programs could successfully recruit minority students without relying on a quota system. He wrote, "The experience of other university admissions programs, which take race into account in achieving the educational diversity valued by the First Amendment, demonstrates that the assignment of a fixed number of places to a minority group is not a necessary means toward that end."

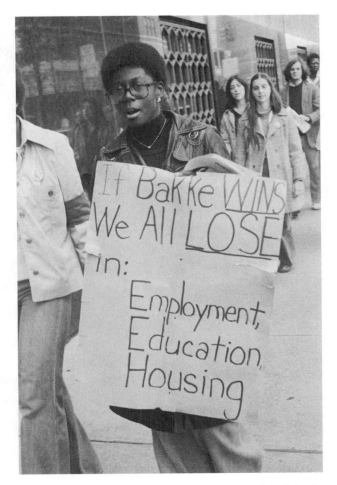

Pro–affirmative action protesters marching in front of the federal building in Detroit, 1977, while the Supreme Court deliberated the *Bakke* case. © *Bettmann/CORBIS*

Bakke was significant because it was the first time the Supreme Court had held that there could be such a thing as "reverse discrimination." The decision, while upholding the principle of affirmative action, effectively limited how those programs could operate in a university setting. Universities could no longer set aside a number of enrollment spots for minority groups, or, presumably for women, although they might consider race and gender as one factor in the admissions decision. A series of other decisions by the Supreme Court—for example, *United Steelworkers of America v. Weber* (1979), *United States v. Paradise* (1987), *Johnson v. Santa Clara County Transportation Agency* (1987), and *Watson v. Fort Worth Bank and Trust* (1988)—likewise accepted affirmative action plans that gave members of disadvantaged groups preference in the workplace but rejected outright quotas.

See also **Affirmative Action**

The Independent Counsel

An independent counsel is an attorney appointed by a panel of federal judges to investigate and prosecute crim-inal activity by high-level government officials. The independent counsel position, originally referred to as a "special prosecutor," was created to avoid the conflict of interest that could emerge if the U.S. Department of Justice, which is part of the executive branch of the government, had to investigate its own officials. The independent counsel as established by the 1978 Ethics in Government Act was inspired by the Watergate crisis. The legislation was in place for twenty-one years before Congress allowed it to lapse in 1999.

Watergate and the Independent Counsel When the Watergate scandal involving President Richard M. Nixon (1913–1994) erupted in the early 1970s, the initial investigation, authorized by Nixon, was conducted by the U.S. Department of Justice, under the supervision of the U.S. attorney general. But because the president appoints, and can dismiss, the attorney general, a possible conflict of interest existed—and in October 1973, it actually did exist. Angry about the questions being asked by Special Prosecutor Archibald Cox (1912–2004), Nixon had him fired, in an incident that came to be called the "Saturday Night Massacre" and led to the belief that the executive branch could not be trusted to enforce the law against itself.

After Watergate, legislators sought to develop a procedure by which the parameters of the special prosecutor's existence and purview would be defined: Who would appoint such a person? Under what circumstances? How could that person be dismissed? One reason for the independent counsel legislation was to restore public confidence in the government, particularly the Justice Department, by ensuring that the president and other powerful members of the government could not interfere with a high-level investigation or prosecution.

The Independent Counsel Statute Facing certain impeachment, Nixon resigned the presidency in August 1974. It took until 1978 for Congress to come up with the solution of having a judicial panel appoint an impartial, nonpartisan independent counsel to investigate and prosecute illegal acts by high-level government officials. The resulting Ethics in Government Act was signed into law by President Jimmy Carter (1924–) on October 26, 1978.

Under the Independent Counsel Act (as the reform was sometimes referred), if there was sufficient evidence of wrongdoing, the attorney general would refer the situation to a judicial panel, which would then appoint an independent attorney to investigate any allegations and, when appropriate, prosecute the case. Under the act, the attorney general was to request an outside prosecutor in cases involving high-level government officials where the "personal, financial, or political conflict of interest" is too great.

The act required reauthorization every five years. Because of Republican discontent with it, Congress allowed the act to lapse for eighteen months beginning in 1992. It was reenacted in 1994 and signed by President Bill Clinton (1946–), with the added authority of allowing independent counsels to investigate members of Congress.

When the evidence warranted doing so, the independent counsel had the authority to advise the House of Representatives of possible grounds for impeachment and, if such existed, be ordered by Congress to begin impeachment proceedings. While free from many of the supervisory constraints placed upon regular Justice Department attorneys, the independent counsel was bound by the same laws as all other prosecutors. As oversight, the independent counsel could be called to testify before Congress to explain his or her methods. The independent counsel was also audited twice per year by the General Accounting Office (now the Government Accountability Office). While the independent counsel did not report to the Justice Department, the attorney general, or the president, he or she could be ordered to close an investigation by the same judicial panel that made the appointment, or by the attorney general, provided there was "good cause."

Controversies At one time or another, both Democrats and Republicans have either favored or opposed the Independent Counsel Act. When independent counsel Lawrence E. Walsh (1912–) spent the late 1980s and early 1990s investigating the Iran-Contra affair and successfully prosecuted members of the administration of Ronald Reagan (1911–2004), Republicans were incensed and Democrats delighted. Outraged that Walsh's Iran-Contra report—which contained an unflattering portrayal of then-incumbent President George H. W. Bush (1924–)—was released just days before the 1992 election, Republicans in Congress let the law lapse.

When the presidency of Bill Clinton was bogged down by five years of investigations (involving alleged financial and sexual improprieties), led by independent counsel Kenneth Starr (1946–), it was the Democrats' turn to rail against the Independent Counsel Act, arguing that special investigations had no limits on cost, length, and scope. Starr, they said, was inappropriate and overzealous in his pursuit of Clinton.

Ironically, it was Clinton who had revitalized the expired independent counsel legislation that came to consume both terms of his presidency—and led to his November 1998 impeachment in the House of Representatives for committing perjury during the investigation of an extramarital affair with a White House intern. (Clinton was acquitted by the Senate in February 1999.)

In *Morrison v. Olson* (1988), the U.S. Supreme Court upheld the independent counsel statute, despite arguments that the legislation violated the constitutional separation of powers. Many felt the statute was too broad and should be redefined to apply to fewer executive branch positions and for only the most serious offenses.

Independent counsel Ken Starr reading from the Constitution during an impeachment inquiry against President Bill Clinton, 1998. © *Reuters/CORBIS*

Others feared that the broad powers and unlimited budget bestowed upon the independent counsel had the potential to be corrupted by partisan politics. Some claimed the statute was both overreaching and unnecessary, because Congress has always had the power to conduct hearings into executive branch conduct and impeach a president and members of his cabinet.

Expiration On June 30, 1999, the Independent Counsel Act was allowed to lapse. From 1978 through 1999, twenty-one independent counsels were appointed, with seven leading to convictions. The investigations cost a combined total of more than $160 million. The Whitewater-related investigations of Bill Clinton and Hillary Clinton (1947–) accounted for more than $64 million of that amount.

While the intent may have been noble, many considered the independent counsel legislation as it was actually applied to be flawed and in need of an overhaul. With the media and partisans eager for drama, independent counsel investigations had become political lightening rods. Even Kenneth Starr, who doggedly pursued allegations against the Clintons, testified before Congress that the act should expire, "for a cooling-off period, or perhaps more aptly, a cease fire."

With the independent counsel statute dissolved, the power to appoint (and remove) special counsels has reverted to the U.S. attorney general, who has sole discretion as to whether, and by whom, an investigation will be pursued. Hence, the responsibility for investigating official misconduct has gone back to where it was during and before Watergate.

BIBLIOGRAPHY

Books

Abrams, Floyd. *Speaking Freely: Trials of the First Amendment*. New York: Viking Penguin, 2005.

Ball, Howard. *The Bakke Case: Race, Education, and Affirmative Action*. Lawrence: University Press of Kansas, 2000.

Bernstein, Carl, and Bob Woodward. *All the President's Men*. New York: Simon and Schuster, 1974.

Bollier, David. *Citizen Action and Other Big Ideas: A History of Ralph Nader and the Modern Consumer Movement*. Washington, DC: Center for the Study of Responsive Law, 1991.

Carter, Jimmy. *An Hour Before Daylight*. New York: Simon and Schuster, 2001.

Dole, Robert, and George J. Mitchell, co-chairs. *Report & Recommendations for the Project on the Independent Counsel Statute*. Washington, DC: American Enterprise Institute and the Brookings Institution, May 1999.

Drew, Elizabeth. *Richard M. Nixon*. New York: Times Books, 2007.

Favre, David S. *Wildlife Law*. Detroit: Lupus Publications, 1991.

Fehner, Terrance R., and Jack M. Hall. *Department of Energy 1977–1994: A Summary History*. Washington, DC: U.S. Department of Energy/ Energy History Series, November 1994.

Garrow, David J. *Liberty and Sexuality: The Right to Privacy and the Making of "Roe v. Wade"*. New York: Macmillan, 1994.

Johnston, Lloyd D., et al. *Monitoring the Future: National Survey Results on Drug Use, 1975–2005. Volume II: College Students and Adults Ages 19–45* (NIH Publication No. 06-5884). Bethesda, MD: National Institute on Drug Abuse, 2006.

Karnow, Stanley. *Vietnam: A History, The First Complete Account of Vietnam at War*. New York: Viking Press, 1983.

Katzmann, Robert A., ed. *Daniel Patrick Moynihan: The Intellectual in Public Life*. Washington, DC: Woodrow Wilson Center Press, 1998.

Olson, Keith W. *Watergate: The Presidential Scandal That Shook America*. Lawrence: University Press of Kansas, 2003.

Shabecoff, Philip. *A Fierce Green Fire: The American Environmental Movement*. New York: Farrar, Straus & Giroux, 1993.

Steinem, Gloria. *Outrageous Acts and Everyday Rebellions*. New York: Henry Holt and Company, 1983.

Stoler, Peter. *Decline and Fall: The Ailing Nuclear Power Industry*. New York: Dodd, Mead & Company, 1985.

Urofsky, Melvin I. *Money and Free Speech: Campaign Finance Reform and the Courts*. Lawrence: University Press of Kansas, 2005.

Woodward, Bob, and Scott Armstrong. *The Brethren: Inside the Supreme Court*. New York: Avon Books, 1979.

Periodicals

Bailey, Lisa Pritchard, et al. "Racketeer Influenced and Corrupt Organizations." *American Criminal Law Review*, 36 (Summer 1999).

Baird, Benita S. "The Government in the Sunshine Act: An Overview." *Duke Law Journal*, 1977, no. 2, Eighth Annual Administrative Law Issue (May 1977): 565–92.

Hotz, V. Joseph, and John Karl Scholz. "The Earned Income Tax Credit." *National Bureau of Economics, Working Paper No. 8078* (January 2001).

Lain, Corinna Barrett. "Furman Fundamentals." *Washington Law Review* 82 (February 2007): 1–74.

Pomper, David. "Recycling *Philadelphia v. New Jersey*: The Dormant Commerce Clause, Post-Industrial 'Natural' Resources, and the Solid Waste Crisis." *University of Pennsylvania Law Review* 137 (April 1989): 1309–1349.

Staples, Shawn. "Nothing Sacred: In *Van Orden v. Perry*, the United States Supreme Court Erroneously Abandoned the Establishment Clause's Foundational Principles Outlined in *Lemon v. Kurtzman*." *Creighton Law Review* 39 (April 2006): 783–825.

Web Sites

American Experience, *Jimmy Carter: The Iran Hostage Crisis, November 1979–January 1981*, Public Broadcasting System, http://www.pbs.org/wgbh/ amex/carter/peopleevents/e_hostage.html (accessed April 14, 2007).

Black Panther Party/Huey P. Newton Foundation, *Ten-Point Plan*, http://www.blackpanther.org/ TenPoint.htm (accessed July 16, 2007).

Dickinson College, *Three Mile Island 1979 Emergency: Virtual Museum*, Dickinson College, Carlisle, PA, http://www.threemileisland.org (accessed April 3, 2007).

The Ford Museum, *The Watergate Files*, Gerald R. Ford Presidential Library & Museum, http:// www.ford.utexas.edu/museum/exhibits/ watergate_files/index.html (accessed April 2, 2007).

Introduction to the Internet Age (1980–Present)

The Internet Age profoundly changed the way the U.S. government conducted its business. Computer systems were expanded to provide citizens with vital information and to archive documents. Many transactions, such as payment of Social Security benefits, became paperless and quick. Nearly all politicians developed personal sites on the World Wide Web and used e-mail to communicate instantly and personally with voters; constituents could file complaints—or send campaign contributions—just as easily. Political activists, from individuals to corporations and special-interest groups, maintained Web sites that offered their own perspective on the issues.

For all its technology, the Internet Age faced many of the same challenges of earlier eras. The Cold War, a decades-long struggle over ideology and hegemony with the Soviet Union, finally ended, largely because the Soviet Union collapsed. However, that conflict was soon replaced by a battle against terrorism, manifested horrifically on U.S. soil on September 11, 2001, when hijacked commercial airliners were turned into weapons that killed thousands. U.S. troops retaliated with war in Afghanistan and Iraq, but the "war on terror," unlike previous conflicts, transcended geographical boundaries; the United States was opposed by clandestine paramilitary groups in many countries, rather than by national military entities. Fear of additional attacks in the United States lingered as the weight of security measures grew.

On the domestic front the economy evolved from a state of malaise in the 1980s to historic prosperity in the 1990s. The stock market bubbled—largely because of investors' faith in Internet companies—and then burst for those investors whose expectations were too great. The years of prosperity were also challenged by the expense of the antiterrorism war, by the effects of an aging population, and by new, aggressive competition in world markets. A previously unknown disease, acquired immune deficiency syndrome, or AIDS, became a serial killer. As the epidemic grew, so did a kind of public hysteria. Both were subdued, though not eliminated, by medical discoveries. Hurricane Katrina devastated the Gulf Coast and crushed Americans' illusions about the nation's preparedness for disaster. Global warming became the leading environmental issue of the era, and attempts by the government to regulate innovative technologies led to lawsuits to protect free speech, a fundamental constitutional right.

The presidency was dominated by Republicans. The popular, charismatic Ronald Reagan (1911–2004) took office in 1981 and was succeeded in 1989 by his vice president, George H. W. Bush (1924–). Both presidents pushed conservative political agendas. The more liberal Bill Clinton (1946–), a Democrat, was shadowed by financial investigations and sexual scandals, culminating in his impeachment by the House of Representatives, but acquittal by the Senate. Despite the scandals, he remained highly popular with the public. The hotly contested presidential race of 2000 sent Republican George W. Bush (1946–), the son of the former president, to the White House. The election was one of only four in U.S. history that hinged on electoral-college votes rather than the popular vote. Its outcome was ultimately decided in the courts. The enthusiastic poll ratings of Bush's first term plummeted in his second term as the public grew disillusioned with the lingering war in Iraq.

One political constant was fierce partisanship. Polarizing personalities and conflicting philosophies led to shutdown of the government on several occasions. Discontent with the two major parties focused new interest on third-party and independent candidates. The 2000 presidential election resulted in feelings of bitterness and suspicion. Not surprisingly, the intense partisanship of the era was fueled by a cacophony of voices emanating from many new communication outlets—from talk radio to opinion shows on TV to chat rooms and blogs on the Internet.

The Internet Age
(1980–Present)

✪ How They Were Governed

The Filibuster

A filibuster is a parliamentary tactic used in the U.S. Senate to delay a vote. It typically consists of a long speech-making session that brings other activity to a halt. Most often used by the minority party to thwart a measure with majority-party support, a filibuster can cause hard feelings between senators. The tactic has become more common in recent decades because of increased political partisanship.

The Filibuster's History The filibuster has a colorful history in U.S. politics. Derived from the sixteenth-century Spanish term *filibustero* (pirate), the word was first associated with U.S. legislators who obstructed the normal workings of the Senate in the 1800s. Filibustering is possible because Senate tradition allows unlimited debate on most matters—a vote cannot be taken until all debate is finished. The House followed the same tradition for a time, but abandoned it as too time-consuming.

By 1917 senators had wearied of limitless debates and adopted a rule—called cloture—that allowed a filibuster to be stopped if a two-thirds majority voted to end it. Because a two-thirds majority was difficult to obtain, the rule was changed in 1975 to allow a three-fifths majority—sixty votes—to stop a filibuster. However, since then the Senate has been fairly evenly split between the two major parties, making even a three-fifths majority hard to achieve.

Filibusters can be effective for a number of reasons. They hold up action on all other Senate matters, which can be very frustrating, particularly in the final days of the session when a backlog of legislation must be considered quickly. Unless cloture is invoked a filibuster can theoretically proceed forever. Because it is so troublesome to overcome, a filibuster often results in the bill under discussion being pulled from consideration.

Filibustering Becomes More Common Until the 1970s filibusters were infrequent, occurring on average less than once per year. They became much more common and polarizing during the following decades and came to represent the contentious relationship between the parties. In 1991, when George H. W. Bush (1924–) was president, the Democratic-controlled Senate wanted to investigate the role of Republicans—including Bush—in a decade-old controversy relating to Americans held hostage in Iran. Republicans filibustered the proposal, arguing that it was merely an attempt to embarrass Bush as he campaigned for president. The filibuster was successful, and the Democrats' planned investigation was not funded.

During the 1990s filibusters were employed frequently against presidential nominees and appointees. In 1993 George Mitchell (1933–), a Democratic senator from Maine and majority leader, complained that the filibuster had become a "political party device." During the administration of Democratic President Bill Clinton (1946–) Republican senators effectively waged a filibuster against Dr. Henry Foster Jr., who was Clinton's nominee for U.S. surgeon general. Other filibusters were launched against Clinton's judicial nominees. Democrats responded during the first term of President George W. Bush (1946–) with filibusters of their own against judicial nominees they deemed unsuitable. By that time the simple threat of a filibuster had become an often-used tactic.

Senator Zell Miller (1932–), a Democrat from Georgia, commented on the use of filibusters in a 2003 *Wall Street Journal* article, noting that "the Senate is the only place I know where 59 votes out of 100 cannot pass anything because 41 votes out of 100 can defeat it." In 2005 Republican Senator Bill Frist (1952–) of Tennessee claimed that frequent Democratic filibustering against Bush's judicial nominees amounted to "tyranny by the minority." While both parties argue that the filibuster allows a minority to thwart the will of the majority, neither party has made a serious effort to change Senate rules to stop the practice.

Senator Strom Thurmond after his record-breaking filibuster of 24 hours and 18 minutes, in which he attempted to prevent the passage of the Civil Rights Bill, 1957.   © *Bettmann/CORBIS*

The Fairness Doctrine

The Fairness Doctrine, adopted by the Federal Communications Commission (FCC) in 1949, required broadcasters to present contrasting points of view on issues of concern to the public. Following a court case in 1987, the FCC stopped enforcing the doctrine. Attempts to revive it have become controversial because of the effects it could have on broadcasts that present only one point of view, such as conservative talk-radio shows.

Development and History In the 1920s the government considered the electromagnetic frequencies over which radio was propagated to be a limited national resource because the number of frequencies is finite. A similar scarcity argument was used when commercial television first became available. The Radio Act of 1927 required broadcasters to provide equal opportunity for airtime to politicians seeking office. This provision was also included in the Communications Act of 1934.

In 1949 the FCC adopted the Fairness Doctrine, which required broadcasters to provide alternative viewpoints on issues of public importance. Although the rule was intended to ensure that broadcasts were balanced, it actually discouraged some stations from addressing controversial issues at all. Journalists began to believe that the rule was an unconstitutional infringement on their right to free speech. However, in *Red Lion Broadcasting v. FCC* (1969) the U.S. Supreme Court ruled unanimously that the Fairness Doctrine served to "enhance rather than abridge the freedoms of speech and press protected by the First Amendment."

Political and Technological Change In 1981 President Ronald Reagan (1911–2004) appointed a new FCC chairman, Mark Fowler, who—like the president—favored industry deregulation and decreased government oversight. By that time cable and satellite television had revolutionized the broadcasting industry and made the government's argument about the scarcity of broadcast

FAMOUS FILIBUSTERS

In 1917 Republican Senator Robert La Follette Sr. (1855–1925) of Wisconsin led a filibuster against a popular bill championed by President Woodrow Wilson (1856–1924) to allow U.S. merchant ships to be armed. Although the United States had not yet entered World War I, its merchant ships crossing the Atlantic Ocean were frequent targets of the German military. La Follette, a pacifist, and several other like-minded senators kept the bill from passing. An angry Wilson complained about "a little group of willful men, representing no opinion but their own," who were able to thwart the desire of the majority. Wilson got his way in the end, using his executive powers to arm the ships.

Louisiana Senator Huey Long Jr. (1893–1935), a Democrat, became famous for his creative filibustering during the Depression. He once spoke for more than fifteen hours, reading aloud the entire U.S. Constitution; answering questions from reporters; and reciting his favorite recipes. The filibuster finally ended at 4 A.M. when Long had to go to the bathroom.

During the 1920s and 1930s southern senators used the filibuster on many occasions to prevent passage of federal anti-lynching laws. In the 1950s and 1960s similar tactics were tried against civil-rights legislation. Strom Thurmond (1902–2003), a senator from South Carolina, spoke for twenty-four hours and eighteen minutes against the Civil Rights Act of 1957—the longest filibuster ever by a single senator. The bill passed anyway. Debate on the Civil Rights Act of 1964 was held up by a filibuster that lasted fifty-seven days. Cloture was finally invoked, and the bill passed.

Filibusters have also been used to thwart Senate confirmations of presidential nominees. In 1968 Republicans and conservative southern Democrats cooperated to filibuster against Abe Fortas (1910–1982), a Supreme Court justice who was nominated by President Lyndon Johnson (1908–1973) to be chief justice. Johnson bowed to the pressure and removed Fortas's name from consideration. It was the first filibuster in history regarding a Supreme Court nominee.

airwaves seem outdated. In 1985 the FCC released the *Fairness Report*, which declared that the Fairness Doctrine was obsolete and no longer served the public interest. However, the agency did not stop enforcing the rule because it believed the doctrine could only be repealed by Congress. This notion was dismissed by the District of Columbia Circuit Court, which ruled in *Meredith Corporation v. FCC* (1987) that the agency did not have to continue to enforce the Fairness Doctrine.

Calls for Reinstatement Even as the Fairness Doctrine was being eliminated, Congress sought to keep it alive through statutory action. A bill was passed by both houses of Congress in 1987; however, it was vetoed by Reagan. Since that time Congress has made several unsuccessful attempts to resurrect the measure.

To many industry analysts the elimination of the Fairness Doctrine in the 1980s led to the subsequent proliferation of conservative talk-radio programs, which became very popular in some markets. Absent the doctrine, the shows do not have to provide airtime to opposing viewpoints. Conservatives have complained that liberals opposed to the shows are behind the efforts to reinstate the Fairness Doctrine.

Computerized Voting Machines

The federal government began encouraging the use of computerized voting machines after the 2000 presidential election. That race revealed the shortcomings of paper ballots, especially during the vote recounts conducted in Florida. Advocates tout electronic voting as reliable and secure; opponents claim the machines are vulnerable to electronic attack and subject to hardware and software problems. Both camps also debate whether the machines should be required to produce paper records so that voting results can be easily verified.

Voting Methods Voting by paper ballot, marked by hand, was the norm in the first two hundred years of U.S. elections. Then, in the twentieth century, the standard became lever-operated voting machines—voters designate their choices by moving levers next to the names of their preferred candidates—and machines that incorporate punch cards—voters punch out prescored circles in paper cards using a stylus or other pointed instrument. In the 1980s they were replaced in some areas by optical-scanning systems, which incorporate paper ballots on which voters mark their choices by filling in circles or arrows with a marking device (often a simple pencil). The votes are "read" by an optical-scanning device. The technology is similar to that used by school systems to check the answers on standardized tests. In the 2000 presidential election optical systems were used by nearly a third of registered voters. The remainder used other voting systems, primarily punch cards.

The closeness of the 2000 presidential election prompted a recount by hand of votes cast by punch card in four Florida counties. The recount revealed many problems with punch-card ballots; for example, incompletely punched holes made it unclear if the voters had attempted to punch through them and were unable to do so or if the voters had changed their minds. Human counters had to examine each of the ballots rejected by the counting machines to determine the voter's intent. In one county the layout of the ballot was considered confusing by many voters, causing them to punch the hole next to the name of the wrong candidate. The controversy spurred calls for modernization of the U.S. voting system.

In 2002 Congress passed the Help America Vote Act, which provided nearly $4 billion for states to expand use of computerized voting machines. It also

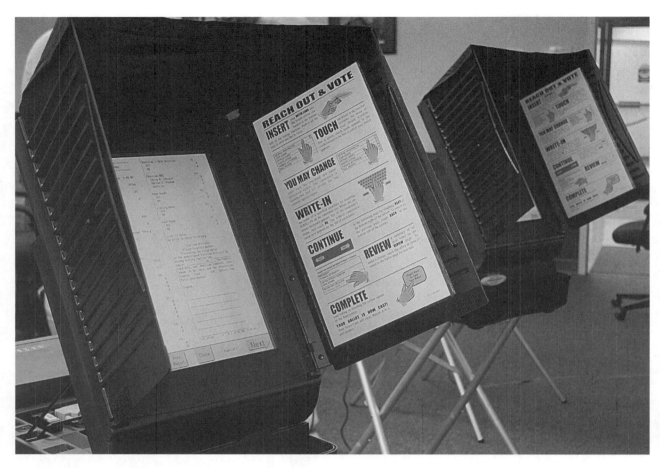

Electronic voting machines, 2006. *AFP/Getty Images © 2006 AFP*

established the Election Assistance Commission (EAC) to oversee disbursement of the funds and development of quality standards for the machines. The EAC, which began operating in January 2004, had little influence over the types of voting systems used in the November 2004 elections.

Direct Recording Electronic Systems Direct Recording Electronic Systems (DREs) are wholly computerized voting machines—similar to ATM machines—that allow voters to push buttons or use touch-screen controls to cast their votes. The votes are stored on computer chips within the machines and on removable disks that elections officials use to tabulate voting results. Although DREs were introduced in the 1970s, only 12 percent of voters used them in the 2000 election.

The government's push to expand the use of DREs spurred intense scrutiny of the technology. Reports about problems multiplied, many of them involving DREs manufactured by Diebold Corporation, an Ohio-based company that entered the voting-machine business in 2001. DRE software code was reportedly discovered on unsecured Diebold Web pages. Computer specialists demonstrated how easy it was to manipulate the software

to ignore votes cast for a specific candidate or to change votes. The controversy magnified when it was learned that in 2003 Diebold's CEO had sent a fund-raising letter to fellow Republicans in which he pledged "to help Ohio deliver its electoral votes" to President George W. Bush (1946–) in the upcoming 2004 election. Diebold subsequently changed its ethics policy to prevent top executives from engaging in political activities, but the damage to the company's reputation was severe. In 2004 the state of California settled a lawsuit against Diebold for $2.6 million. California counties had purchased Diebold voting machines, many of which failed during the 2004 primary election. The state alleged that the company had made false statements about the effectiveness and security of its DREs.

In the 2004 presidential election approximately 29 percent of voters used DREs. Reports of problems with the machines surfaced immediately. In North Carolina a DRE with a full memory card failed to record more than four thousand votes. Pennsylvania officials reported that DRE screens froze. One Florida county had difficulties with touch screens—it took up to an hour to activate them. More than two dozen DREs in Ohio transferred an unknown number of votes from one candidate to another. Although none of the problems reported were believed significant enough to have changed the outcome of the presidential election, activists worried about possible software glitches that went unnoticed.

A 2005 report from the Government Accountability Office (GAO) listed many concerns about the performance of DREs, including "weak security controls, system design flaws, inadequate system version control, inadequate security testing, incorrect system configuration, poor security management, and vague or incomplete voting system standards." Although the report acknowledged that many of the problems were specific to particular DRE models, the GAO noted that the overall security and reliability of electronic voting systems needed to be addressed by the EAC.

DREs and a Paper Trail Some DREs produce a paper copy of the completed ballot, which allows voters to verify that their selections were properly recorded. The paper copies are collected at the polls and provide a verifiable source if a vote recount is needed. Many election activists believe that all DREs should be equipped with paper-verification systems. Opponents claim that such systems make DREs more expensive and cause problems when paper jams or poll workers fail to reload the paper.

In 2003 David Dill, a computer science professor at Stanford University, began a movement calling for voter-verified paper records (VVPRs) for all DREs. Dill argued that paperless electronic voting poses too many security risks and possibilities for vote tampering and computer glitches that could go undetected. In 2004 Nevada and California became the first states to require VVPR capability for all DREs. California replaced forty thousand paperless machines in time for its primary elections in June 2006. Dill and his organization, Verified Voting Foundation, have called for federal legislation to mandate VVPRs nationwide. In April 2007 a lawsuit successfully challenged Pennsylvania's certification of DREs that do not include methods for voter verification or independent audit.

The Department of Homeland Security

The U.S. Department of Homeland Security (DHS), a federal agency established in response to the terrorist attacks of September 11, 2001, has three primary responsibilities: to prevent terrorist attacks inside the United States; to reduce the nation's vulnerability to terrorist attacks and the damage caused by them; and to coordinate quick and effective recovery if terrorist attacks occur.

DHS coordinates its activities with other federal entities devoted to national security, particularly intelligence agencies, such as the Central Intelligence Agency (CIA); the U.S. military; and the Federal Bureau of Investigation (FBI). In addition DHS works with state

Public employee changing a Homeland Security Advisory System flag from yellow, indicating elevated risk, to orange, indicating high risk, 2003. © FRANK POLICH/Reuters/Corbis

and local agencies that would provide the first government assistance following a terrorist attack.

The Components of DHS DHS, as established by President George W. Bush (1946–), combined dozens of agencies and offices that had previously operated separately. They were devoted to emergency preparedness; risk reduction; scientific and technological responses to terrorist attacks; assessment of threats and vulnerabilities; and intelligence gathering and analysis.

Specific agencies within the DHS include the Federal Emergency Management Agency (FEMA), which manages the federal response to disasters and emergencies; the Transportation Security Administration (TSA), which protects the nation's transportation systems; U.S. Customs and Border Protection (CBP), which protects the borders and points of entry; U.S. Immigration and Customs Enforcement (ICE), which enforces immigration and customs laws; the U.S. Citizenship and Immigration Services (USCIS), which adjudicates immigration and naturalization applications and petitions and establishes policies and priorities for immigration services; the U.S. Coast Guard (USCG), which patrols U.S. waters and provides rescue assistance; and the U.S. Secret Service, which protects high-ranking government officials and their families and investigates financial crimes.

DHS and National Security In July 2002 Bush issued *The National Strategy for Homeland Security*, which laid out the details of DHS. For example, DHS has its own intelligence agents who work with the CIA, FBI, and other organizations to collect and analyze information about terrorist plots and plans. DHS agents conduct detailed analyses of terrorist groups to learn about their motivations, structures, and fund-raising activities. DHS also assesses the vulnerability of likely targets of terrorist attacks and the consequences such attacks would have.

In addition DHS operates a national warning system that uses color codes to indicate the risk of terrorist attacks—green indicates low risk; blue, guarded risk; yellow, elevated risk; orange, high risk; and red, severe risk. For each risk level the DHS recommends actions for the public to take. Since the inception of the warning system, the risk level has been set at yellow most of the time, although orange alerts have been issued on several occasions. Red alerts have been issued for specific sectors, such as air transportation.

Four DHS agencies ensure that the nation's borders and transportation systems are safeguarded. The CBP assesses and processes travelers coming into the United States and inspects their belongings. It also screens incoming and outgoing cargo. ICE enforces immigration and customs laws and investigates the people who support terrorism and other criminal activities. The TSA is responsible for preflight screening of passengers and baggage at airports; provides air marshals on certain flights; and coordinates some security activities of the nation's air, rail, and mass transportation systems. The Coast Guard patrols the waters around the United States

Secretary of Homeland Security Michael Chertoff, 2005. *© Shaun Heasley/Reuters/Corbis*

to prevent illegal activities, such as smuggling and unauthorized entry.

The DHS Infrastructure Protection Program provides funds to secure a variety of facilities and systems that are considered critical to national security, including transit programs, intercity bus systems, and trucking lines. It also provides money to establish buffer zones around chemical facilities, financial institutions, nuclear and electric power plants, dams, stadiums, and other facilities deemed to be at high risk of terrorist attack. DHS grants also go to such preparedness activities as strengthening materials against explosives.

DHS works with federal, state, and local agencies to minimize the potential damage from terrorist attacks and to ensure they have the capabilities to respond when attacks occur. For example, it can provide funds to have professionals draw up building-evacuation plans. DHS also operates a public awareness program for nonterrorist emergencies, such as natural disasters.

FEMA dispatches personnel and provides financial aid to help people displaced by natural disasters and terrorist attacks. It also provides training programs for first responders, such as police officers, firefighters, and emergency medical technicians, and assists local and state emergency management agencies in preparing their disaster and response plans.

Controversy and Criticism Since its creation DHS has been heavily criticized for its performance—or lack of performance. Some of its difficulties stemmed from the massive reshuffling and blending of existing agencies that took place to form the agency. More than one hundred seventy-five thousand employees from diverse organizations were gathered under the DHS umbrella, causing considerable management challenges.

The FEMA arm of the agency came under intense fire for its emergency response in the aftermath of hurricanes Katrina and Rita, which hit the Gulf Coast in the summer of 2005. An independent audit later that year by the DHS inspector general revealed a host of management and financial problems that hampered the agency's relief efforts, including poor oversight of grant and contractor programs that resulted in overspending, fraud, and waste of funds intended to clean up and rebuild devastated areas.

Two other reports critical of DHS were released in December 2005. A report from House Democrats accused the agency of failing to deliver dozens of promised improvements for protecting the nation's borders

Illegal Mexican immigrants being detained by the U.S. Customs and Border Patrol in Calexico, California, 2006.   © Ken Cedeno/Corbis

and critical infrastructure. A "report card" issued by the independent commission that investigated the September 11, 2001, terrorist attacks was as critical. The so-called 9/11 Commission handed out C, D, and F grades to the government for its failure to implement specific recommendations on tasks related to vulnerability assessment, emergency preparedness, and transportation security—all areas under DHS oversight.

The Federal Budget Deficit

A federal budget deficit occurs when the government spends more money than it takes in during a fiscal year. This has been a frequent occurrence throughout U.S. history, but starting in 1970 it became the norm: the United States had a deficit each year for nearly three decades. Budget surpluses were achieved from 1998 through 2002—the federal government took in more money than it spent each year—but the budget deficit returned in 2003.

Budget Background Each year the president must submit a proposed budget to Congress by the first Monday in February prior to the start of the next fiscal year. (The federal fiscal year begins on October 1 and runs through September 30.) Congress considers the president's proposed budget and passes a series of appropriation acts, each of which authorizes funding for one or more federal agencies. This funding is known as discretionary spending, because the amounts can be changed at the discretion of the government. Mandatory spending, on the other hand, refers to money delegated to entitlement programs, such as Social Security, Medicare, Medicaid, and veterans' benefits. Mandatory spending is not covered by annual appropriations acts because entitlement programs are considered "permanently" funded.

Record Deficits Trigger Action Deficits have occurred most often because of wartime spending or economic disruptions, such as the Great Depression. During the 1970s the economy struggled because of energy problems and rising interest rates. Those challenges, which continued into the early 1980s, were made worse by a crisis in the savings and loan industry, which required a government bailout costing billions of dollars. At the same time rapidly rising expenditures on health-care programs—Medicare serves the elderly and Medicaid the very poor—strained the federal budget.

In fiscal year 1982 the federal deficit exceeded $100 billion—the largest in history up to that time. The following year it soared above $200 billion. In response, a coalition of senators—Phil Gramm (1942–), a Republican from Texas; Warren Rudman (1930–), a Republican from New Hampshire; and Ernest Hollings (1922–), a Democrat from South Carolina—drafted the Balanced Budget and Emergency Deficit Control Act of 1985.

The act, which was signed into law by President Ronald Reagan (1911–2004) in December 1985, set deficit targets for the next five years and mandated automatic spending cuts across a variety of programs if the targets were exceeded. Any new spending programs had to be financed by either reducing existing expenditures or raising new revenues—by raising taxes, for example. In 1986 the Supreme Court, ruling in *Bowsher v. Synar*, declared that the law was unconstitutional because it delegated major decisions about spending cuts to the comptroller general, who is the director of the Government Accountability Office, an agency of the legislative branch. The act was amended in 1987 to give that responsibility to the Office of Management and Budget, an agency of the executive branch.

Although budget deficits decreased following passage of the law, the targets were not met. In 1990 the Budget Enforcement Act (BEA) put annual limits on appropriation acts and included a pay-as-you-go (PAYGO) restriction to prevent new mandatory spending or new tax laws from increasing the deficit. Violations of the spending caps triggered automatic cuts in discretionary programs. Violations of the PAYGO restriction triggered automatic cuts in certain mandatory programs. The BEA provisions were extended several times, primarily in the Balanced Budget Act (BBA) of 1997. That goal of the law was to balance the federal budget by 2002—the year the law was to expire—primarily through reforming the Medicare program to reduce spending.

During the mid 1990s budget deficits began to decline. In 1998 there was a budget surplus for the first time in nearly thirty years. Annual surpluses occurred through fiscal year 2001. The turnaround has been attributed to a number of factors. For example, the nation spent much less on defense in the early 1990s because the Cold War ended when the Soviet Union dissolved. In addition the economy thrived throughout much of the 1990s, which led to more tax money for government coffers.

The Early Twenty-First Century Budget deficits returned in fiscal year 2002 and grew quickly during the ensuing years. Spending on national defense and homeland security increased dramatically following the September 11, 2001, terrorist attacks. Additional funds went to the wars and rebuilding in Afghanistan and Iraq. In fiscal year 2004 the deficit reached $413 billion, a new record. The government responded with the Deficit Reduction Act of 2005, which called for major cuts in spending on Medicare, Medicaid, and student loan programs. The act was signed into law only months after hurricanes Katrina and Rita devastated the Gulf Coast region, spurring an unexpected spike in federal spending.

In February 2007 President George W. Bush (1946–) proposed a long-term budget plan to reduce the deficit each successive year and achieve a balanced budget by fiscal year 2012. The plan assumed that Congress would slow

THE NATIONAL DEBT

The national debt—the total amount owed by the U.S. government—was relatively low until the early 1940s, when it rose in response to deficit spending for World War II. During the next three decades the debt increased at a slow pace. During the late 1970s the national debt began a steep climb that continued into the 2000s. The budget surpluses from 1998 through 2002 had a slight dampening effect on the growth of the debt, but did not actually decrease it. The budget deficits that have occurred since 2003 have increased the debt rapidly.

The national debt has two components—money that the federal government has borrowed from investors, which is called "debt held by the public," and money that the federal government has loaned itself, which is called "intragovernmental holdings."

The public loans money to the federal government by buying bonds and other securities. The government borrows the money with a promise to pay it back with interest after a set term.

When the federal government borrows from itself, the debt is owed by one Treasury Department account to another. Most of the so-called internal debt involves federal trust funds, such the one that supports Social Security. If a trust fund takes in more revenue in a year than it pays out, it loans the extra money to another federal account. In exchange, the loaning trust fund receives an interest-bearing security—basically an IOU—that is redeemable from the Treasury in the future. In other words, the government makes a promise to itself to pay itself back in the future.

As of January 1, 2007, the total national debt of $8.68 trillion was made up of $4.90 trillion in debt held by the public and $3.78 trillion in intragovernmental holdings.

U.S. government securities can be purchased by both domestic and foreign investors. Foreign investors may include individuals and businesses, such as banks, but also national governments. In January 2007 the United States owed foreigners $2.1 trillion, or 43 percent of the total amount of debt held by the public. The largest single foreign holder was Japan with $627 billion, followed by China with $400 billion. Collectively the major oil-producing countries—most of which are in the Middle East—held more than $100 billion in U.S. debt.

spending on both discretionary and mandatory programs and that U.S. expenses in Iraq would decline dramatically by 2010. Critics claimed that neither of those assumptions was likely to become fact.

Why Deficits Matter Deficits have important economic and political implications. Whenever the federal government has a budget deficit, the Treasury Department must borrow money. The total amount of money that the Treasury has borrowed over the years is called the national debt. On the first day of 2007 the national debt stood at $8.68 trillion. This is money that has to be paid back in the future and represents a burden upon future taxpayers. In addition, like any other debtor, the U.S. government pays interest on the money it borrows; interest payments consume billions of dollars each year. When the government borrows money it competes with the private sector—both businesses and individuals—for investment funds, leaving less money for businesses to spend on new factories, for example, which could provide new jobs and benefit the economy overall.

Politicians who engage in deficit spending risk incurring the wrath of the public. For some voters it is a matter of principle, believing that balanced budgets demonstrate restraint and common-sense money management. Others worry about the economic consequences of the national debt, particularly upon future generations of Americans. However, reducing deficits, either through increased taxes or reductions in government programs, can anger voters as well. As the population ages, payouts will increase dramatically for programs such as Social Security and Medicare. That will put even greater stress on the federal budget and make the politicians' job even more difficult.

✪ Important Figures of the Day

Ronald Reagan

When Ronald Reagan (1911–2004) became the fortieth president of the United States, the nation's economy was ailing, and its foreign policy was consumed by the Cold War with the Soviet Union. He responded with an economic policy so unique it was dubbed Reaganomics. Its chief components were huge tax cuts, deregulation of industry, and removing barriers to foreign trade. Critics claimed that Reaganomics benefited the wealthy, burdened the poor, and saddled the nation with record-setting federal deficits. Much of the deficit spending was caused by his main foreign-policy initiative: a more aggressive stance toward the Soviet Union, bolstered by a massive buildup of U.S. military forces. In the early 1990s when the Soviet empire splintered into smaller, less powerful republics, Reagan received much of the political credit. He was hugely popular while in office and afterward, despite a major arms scandal that plagued his administration.

Early Life and Public Service Reagan, who got the nickname Dutch from his father, a shoe salesman, excelled at sports, performed in plays, and worked part time while attending tiny Eureka College, in Eureka, Illinois. He studied economics and sociology and was student body president. After graduating in 1932, in the midst of the Great Depression, he worked as a sports radio announcer. A Hollywood screen test in 1937 earned him a contract with the motion-picture company Warner Brothers. During the following two decades he appeared in more than fifty movies, but never attained the fame of a Hollywood

President Ronald Reagan presenting his tax plan, 1981. © *Bettmann/CORBIS*

star. Reagan did not go into combat during World War II because of nearsightedness, but did produce military training films.

Following the war Reagan served as president of the Screen Actors Guild and became an outspoken anticommunist and political activist. Although he was a Democrat in his early years, he shifted to the Republican Party in the 1960s and grew increasingly more conservative in his views. By that time he had become a prolific public speaker and made important political connections in California. He ran for governor in 1966 and won easily, partly because of his folksy manner and emphasis on traditional values.

The Presidency In 1980 Reagan ran for president with his running mate George H. W. Bush (1924–). Reagan faced incumbent President Jimmy Carter (1924–), a Democrat, whose popularity had plunged because of a weak economy and because he had failed to achieve the release of Americans held hostage in Iran for more than a year. The Reagan-Bush team won 51 percent of the popular vote and captured 489 out of 538 electoral votes. Republican senators swept into office on Reagan's coattails, giving the party majority control of the Senate for the first time in decades. Democrats maintained majority control of the House in 1980, but by a smaller margin than before.

Just two months after taking office Reagan was wounded in an assassination attempt. His good humor and perseverance during his recovery earned him public praise. That kind of reaction to adversity—a down-to-earth manner and wit—served him well throughout his presidency.

When Reagan and Bush ran for re-election in 1984, their Democratic challengers were former vice president Walter Mondale (1928–) and Geraldine Ferraro (1935–), a representative from New York. Reagan and Bush won more decisively than before, capturing 59 percent of the popular vote and 525 of the 538 electoral votes. The Republican Party held onto majority control of the Senate but, despite significant gains, remained the minority party in the House.

Reaganomics The most pressing issue when Reagan took office was the economy. The 1970s had seen unemployment and inflation rates at historic highs and energy shortages caused by oil embargoes in the Middle East. Oil producers refused to ship petroleum to countries that supported Israel in its war with Egypt and Syria. In addition they curtailed production, which raised oil prices and affected the economies of all nations. Reagan embraced a remedy called supply-side economics, which targeted the supply, or production,

President Ronald Reagan making his famous challenge to Soviet Premier Mikhail Gorbachev to tear down the Berlin Wall, 1987. © *Bettmann/CORBIS*

side of the supply-and-demand equation. It focused on easing the tax and regulatory burden on entrepreneurs and businesses—generally the wealthiest sector of the populace—so they could invest and produce more. The benefits of that investment were supposed to "trickle down" to the lower-income sectors. Opponents branded it a Republican ploy to help the rich get richer while the poor got poorer. The Economic Recovery Tax Act of 1981 reduced tax rates across the board. The Tax Reform Act of 1986 lowered the top rate, but increased the bottom rate.

Reagan embraced two other components of supply-side economics. Deregulation, which had started under Carter, is the removal of governmental restraints on private industries. Reagan expanded deregulation to cover more businesses, particularly in the financial and telecommunications industries. In addition trade barriers, such as high tariffs on imported goods, were reduced or eliminated to encourage business with other countries.

By the end of Reagan's second term the economy was in much better shape. Although the administration got most of the credit, some economists argued that the improvement was due largely to the efforts of the Federal Reserve, the nation's central bank. The Fed, as it is called, had a new chairman, Paul Volcker (1927–)—he had been appointed by Carter in 1979—who implemented fiscal policy that tightened the nation's money supply, making credit more difficult to obtain and eventually lowering inflation rates.

The Deficits In fiscal year 1980, when Reagan ran for president, the federal budget deficit totaled $59 billion. By 1982 it exceeded $100 billion—the largest in history to that time. The next year it soared above $200 billion. A group of senators—Phil Gramm (1942–), a Republican from Texas; Warren Rudman (1930–), a Republican from New Hampshire; and Ernest Hollings (1922–), a Democrat from South Carolina—drafted the Balanced Budget and Emergency Deficit Control Act of 1985. Signed into law by Reagan, it set deficit targets for upcoming budgets and required automatic spending cuts if the targets were exceeded. In addition new spending programs had to be financed by reducing existing expenditures or raising new revenues—by raising taxes, for example. Despite these controls, deficits continued to occur.

The deficits of the mid 1980s were more than twice what they had been during the mid 1970s for several reasons. Reagan pushed for greater spending on national defense as a tactic in the Cold War with the Soviet Union. Although his administration made selective cuts in spending on social services, the largest and most expensive of these programs—such as Medicare, which provides assistance to the elderly—were not substantially decreased. At the same time tax cuts meant that less revenue went into government coffers. The federal deficit in Reagan's last year in office exceeded $150 billion.

Reagan's Cold War For years the cornerstone of U.S. policy in the Cold War with the Soviet Union was "containment" of communism—to keep it from spreading into noncommunist countries. Reagan quickly took a more aggressive stance, referring to the Soviet Union as "the evil empire." He pushed a massive—and expensive—buildup of the military, which Reagan called a "peace through strength" approach. By the end of the decade the Soviet Union, partly because it had followed suit and built up its military forces, developed serious economic problems. Political opposition and unrest precipitated a breakup of the Soviet Union into individually governed republics. Reagan was championed by many in the West as the president who "stared down the Soviet Union" and ended the Cold War.

The Iran-Contra Affair Ironically it was Reagan's fierce anticommunism that led to his administration's greatest challenge—the Iran-Contra scandal. In 1986 the public learned that high-ranking U.S. officials had been engaged in two secret and illegal programs: one provided money and military aid to counterrevolutionaries, known as Contras, seeking to overthrow Nicaragua's leftist government, and the other sold arms to Iran. Some money from the arms sales was funneled to the Contra operation. An independent counsel investigated and issued a scathing report critical of the Reagan administration, noting that Reagan had shown "disregard for civil laws enacted to limit presidential actions abroad" and created a climate in which some of his officials felt emboldened to break those laws to implement his policies.

Several of the officials were indicted by a grand jury. Two convictions were overturned on appeal, and many of the charges against others were dismissed because the administration refused to turn over classified documents considered crucial to the case. Other indicted officials were pardoned in 1992 by George H. W. Bush as his term as president was about to end.

Throughout the scandal Reagan denied knowing that the operations were illegal and attributed them to rogue elements within his administration. The independent counsel was skeptical of his claims, noting "the governmental problems presented by Iran-Contra are not those of rogue operations, but rather those of Executive Branch efforts to evade congressional oversight."

Lebanon and Libya Reagan faced two other major foreign-policy challenges. In 1983 terrorists detonated a bomb at a barracks in Lebanon that housed United Nations peacekeeping forces. More than two hundred U.S. Marines were killed. Responsibility for the bombing could not be determined conclusively; therefore, no U.S. retaliatory action was taken. Several months

STAR WARS

In 1983 President Ronald Reagan (1911–2004) proposed a Space Defense Initiative (SDI) to develop space-based weapons to protect the United States from incoming Soviet nuclear missiles. The proposal increased tensions between the United States and the Soviet Union, which Reagan had already described as the "focus of evil in the modern world." Soviet officials responded that Reagan was full of "bellicose lunatic anticommunism."

The media dubbed SDI the "Star Wars" program after the 1977 hit movie. SDI had many detractors, including scientists who doubted that it was technically feasible and politicians who feared it would be extremely expensive and start an arms race in space. Despite these criticisms, Reagan continued to push the SDI program. In 1984 the U.S. Army successfully tested an interceptor missile that flew above the atmosphere, located, tracked, and destroyed a missile launched from another location. More than $1 billion was spent on SDI in 1985.

SDI became a major point of contention between Reagan and Soviet leader Mikhail Gorbachev (1931–). During arms talks in 1986 Gorbachev offered to make huge cuts in Soviet stockpiles of nuclear missiles if the U.S. would abandon SDI. Reagan refused, unwilling to give up a project he deemed crucial to the nation's future security. In 1989 Congress made drastic cuts in the SDI budget. By that time the Soviet Union had started to break up into smaller republics. The Cold War soon ended.

SDI, however, lingered on. Largely ignored for more than a decade, the program found renewed interest after the terrorist attacks on the United States in 2001. Advocates saw it as a defense against ballistic missiles launched by rogue governments or terrorists.

later U.S. troops were removed from Lebanon. During the 1980s Libya was linked to terrorist acts in which Americans were killed, particularly a bombing at a disco in Germany in 1986. Reagan ordered military strikes on Libyan targets in response, destroying several facilities that were believed to be used for training terrorists. In addition Libyan leader Muammar al-Gadhafi (1942–) was wounded and his infant daughter was killed.

Post Presidential Life The Ronald Reagan Presidential Library opened in Simi Valley, California, in 1991. Three years later his family released a letter from the president announcing that he had been diagnosed with Alzheimer's disease, a degenerative disease of the neurological system. He rarely appeared in public after that time. Reagan died on June 5, 2004, at age 93.

See also **Supply-Side Economics**

Sandra Day O'Connor

Sandra Day O'Connor (1930–) was the first woman to serve on the U.S. Supreme Court. Nominated in 1981

SOFT MONEY

One of the most partisan issues in politics is campaign finance reform. In 2002 John McCain (1936–), a Republican senator from Arizona, and Russ Feingold (1953–), a Democratic senator from Wisconsin, sponsored the Bipartisan Campaign Finance Reform Act (BCRA). The act banned campaign donations to the political parties of "soft money"—monetary contributions not regulated by the federal election laws, which were passed in the 1970s and are enforced by the Federal Election Commission.

So-called hard-money contributions are regulated and go directly to the campaign funds of individual candidates. Soft-money donations go to the political parties, which are supposed to spend them on generic purposes, such as get-out-the-vote drives or advertisements about party platforms and issues. During the 1990s both of the major parties began stretching the rules, targeting the soft money to help individual candidates in races. The BCRA put an end to that practice.

In 2003 the act was challenged in court by Mitch McConnell (1942–), a Republican senator from Kentucky, and dozens of special interest groups. Historically, campaign donations have been considered expressions of free speech guaranteed by the U.S. Constitution because they reflect political values. By a vote of 5 to 4 the court upheld the law as constitutional. Writing for the court, Justices Sandra Day O'Connor (1930–) and John Paul Stevens (1920–) reasoned that the soft-money restrictions resulted in a minimal restraint on free speech because soft money was supposed to be devoted to generic purposes, not specific candidates' campaigns. They noted, "We are under no illusion that BCRA will be the last congressional statement on the matter. Money, like water, will always find an outlet. What problems will arise, and how Congress will respond, are concerns for another day."

As the justices predicted, during the 2004 presidential election tax-exempt political organizations—named "527s" after a section of the tax code—took in large contributions of soft money and used it in highly targeted campaign advertisements. Critics complained loudly that 527s, which legally cannot endorse specific candidates, had used a loophole so they could get awfully close to doing so.

by President Ronald Reagan (1911–2004), O'Connor at first took a conservative stance on many issues—as Reagan had hoped—but gradually adopted a centrist position and was often the swing vote on closely contested cases. She retired from the court in 2005.

Background Sandra Day, born into a Texas ranching family, earned a law degree from Stanford University. She married John Jay O'Connor, who was also a student at Stanford, in 1953. They had three sons. O'Connor worked as a deputy county attorney and in private practice before being appointed an Arizona state senator in 1969. She was reelected to that position several times, finishing her last term in 1975. She then served as a county judge and as a member of the Arizona Court of Appeals.

During the 1980 presidential campaign Reagan promised that, if elected, he would name a woman to the Supreme Court. In 1981 the new president nominated O'Connor to take the place of Justice Potter Stewart (1915–1985), who had retired. Neither conservatives nor liberals were particularly pleased by O'Connor's credentials. Conservatives were dismayed to find out that, as an Arizona state senator, she had voted for a bill to decriminalize abortion in that state. Liberals were hoping for a female jurist more supportive of feminist causes. Nevertheless, O'Connor was confirmed unanimously by the U.S. Senate.

O'Connor's Decisions During her twenty-four years on the court O'Connor gradually earned a reputation as a moderate coalition-builder whose decision on a particular issue was difficult to predict. For example, in 1992 she coauthored the decision in *Planned Parenthood v. Casey*, which reaffirmed a woman's right to an abortion, which had been guaranteed by the court's decision in *Roe v. Wade* (1973). However, the 1992 ruling also upheld as constitutional the rights of a state to regulate abortion as long as the regulations do not place an "undue burden" on women seeking abortions. The case involved a Pennsylvania law that required, among other conditions, a waiting period of twenty-four hours before an abortion could be obtained. That particular provision was upheld as constitutional by the court because it did not meet their "undue burden" test.

During her tenure O'Connor considered a number of cases that dealt with affirmative action. In the 1980s she typically dissented from court rulings that upheld remedial hiring preferences for women and minorities, such as cases brought under Title VII of the Civil Rights Act of 1964. Gradually she came to rule that affirmative action was acceptable when "narrowly tailored" to a "compelling interest." In *Grutter v. Bollinger* (2003) the court considered the case of a white woman who alleged she had been denied admittance to the University of Michigan Law School because school officials, to produce a diverse student body, had used race as a factor in making admissions decisions. The court ruled in favor of the school 5 to 4. Writing for the majority, O'Connor said the university's actions were constitutional because they fit the "narrowly tailored" and "compelling interest" criteria.

In a pair of notable cases O'Connor showed a change of opinion regarding the death penalty for mentally retarded defendants. In her opinion for the majority in *Penry v. Lynaugh* (1989), she wrote that the court upheld such executions as constitutional because a "national consensus" had not developed regarding the practice. However, in *Atkins v. Virginia* (2002) she joined the majority in ruling that execution of mentally retarded criminals was "cruel and unusual punishment" and prohibited by the

Eighth Amendment to the U.S. Constitution. By that time more than fifteen states had outlawed the execution of the mentally retarded. O'Connor considered that to be adequate to determine "national consensus" on the issue.

Alan Greenspan

Alan Greenspan (1926–) was chairman of the nation's central banking system, the Federal Reserve—known as the "Fed"—from 1987 to 2006. He is widely credited with implementing monetary policy that helped the U.S. economy to prosper during the 1990s and early 2000s. Greenspan wielded so much influence that he was often referred to as the second most powerful man in the United States. His high-profile tenure brought great public attention to the Fed and the important role it plays in the economy.

Early Life and Career Greenspan, who was born into a middle-class family in New York, became an accomplished musician at an early age, playing both the clarinet and the saxophone. He alternately toured with a jazz band and attended New York University, where he earned a bachelor's, a master's, and a doctorate in eco-

nomics. He eventually became chairman and president of an economic consulting firm.

In the mid 1970s President Gerald Ford (1913–2006) chose Greenspan to chair the President's Council of Economic Advisers. In the early 1980s he chaired the National Commission on Social Security Reform. President Ronald Reagan (1911–2004) appointed Greenspan to a number of advisory boards.

Greenspan's first marriage in 1952 to painter Joan Mitchell lasted less than a year. In 1997 he married Andrea Mitchell (1946–), a correspondent for NBC news.

Chairman Greenspan In 1987 Greenspan was appointed chairman of the Board of Governors of the Federal Reserve System. The Fed influences the overall economy by controlling both the amount of money in circulation and the interest rates that banks charge their customers. During his long tenure as chairman Greenspan was reappointed by presidents Reagan; George H. W. Bush (1924–), Bill Clinton (1946–); and George W. Bush (1946–).

Under Greenspan's leadership the Fed made decisions that helped to keep unemployment low and production high during the 1990s and to keep inflation

Economist Alan Greenspan, 1983. © *Bettmann/CORBIS*

THE FED

The Federal Reserve, which is usually called the Fed, was created in 1913 to be the nation's central bank, to furnish currency, and to supervise banking in the United States. Eventually it assumed additional authority, influencing the amount U.S. currency in circulation and the interest rates charged by banks to their customers. The Federal Reserve System is made up of twelve banks across the country and is overseen by a seven-member board headquartered in Washington, D.C.

The Fed was designed to be an independent entity, immune to pressure from the president and Congress to impose politically popular but short-term solutions to economic problems. It was supposed to take a big-picture, long-range view of the nation's economic policy.

The Fed affects the state and growth of the economy by influencing interest rates on loans. When interest rates go down, people and businesses are more likely to borrow money and spend it or invest it. That can provide a boost to a lackluster economy. However, the Fed's work is a delicate balancing act. If it puts too much money into circulation, demand for goods and services can grow faster than the supply of goods and services, which can lead to excessive price increases, or inflation. To curb inflation the Fed raises interest rates to make borrowing less appealing.

The Fed also plays a major role in the nation's money supply—the total amount of coins and paper currency in circulation and held by financial institutions. When the money supply increases, banks make more loans, which puts more money into the hands of consumers and pushes up demand for goods and services. If that practice becomes too inflationary, the Fed may decide to decrease the amount of money that banks can loan to the public. When borrowing decreases, demand for goods and services slows down and is better matched with supply.

under control. Inflation occurs when prices of goods and services increase over time. A small amount of inflation is considered acceptable, but excessive inflation discourages people and businesses from spending and investing.

During the late 1980s the Fed began making interest-rate cuts that prompted a boom in the real-estate market that lasted into the early 2000s. Although some economists argued that it was a good move for the economy, others said Greenspan and the Fed made it too easy for people to take on more debt than they could afford. In 2004 the Fed began raising interest rates in response to signs that inflation was rising.

The nation prospered during the 1990s and early 2000s, and Greenspan received much of the credit. In 2005 he was awarded the Presidential Medal of Freedom, the highest award given to a civilian by the U.S. government. The following year he retired from the Fed and became a prolific public speaker.

George H. W. Bush

George H. W. Bush (1924–), the forty-first president of the United States, faced two major issues when he was in office: the Persian Gulf War, in which a U.S.-led military coalition ousted Iraqi forces from Kuwait, and the state of the U.S. economy. Despite achieving an overwhelming military victory against Iraq, Bush lost favor at home because of an economic slowdown, large federal budget deficits, and his decision to raise taxes after promising not to do so.

Early Life Born into a well-to-do New England political family, Bush joined the U.S. Navy immediately after graduating from high school. He became a pilot and was on active duty in the Pacific during the latter years of World War II. He was awarded the Distinguished Flying Cross for his service. In 1945 he married Barbara Pierce (1925–) of New York. They had five children, one of whom died of leukemia at a young age. Their two oldest sons went on to careers in public service: George W. (1946–) as governor of Texas and president of the United States and Jeb (1953–) as governor of Florida.

The senior Bush graduated from Yale University in 1948 with a degree in economics. The family then moved to Texas, where he worked in the oil business and eventually founded his own oil company.

Public Service In 1964 Bush, a Republican, ran unsuccessfully for a Texas seat in the U.S. Senate. Two years later he was elected to the U.S. House of Representatives. Bush was reelected to the House in 1968, then was defeated in a second run for the U.S. Senate in 1970. In 1971 President Richard Nixon (1913–1994) appointed Bush U.S. ambassador to the United Nations, a post he held for two years. He then became chairman of the Republican National Committee. In 1976 President Gerald Ford (1913–2006) named Bush director of the Central Intelligence Agency. Bush was replaced a year later when Democrat Jimmy Carter (1924–) became president.

During the 1980 presidential primaries Bush's main rival for the Republican nomination was the former California governor Ronald Reagan (1911–2004). Reagan advocated supply-side economics, a policy that favored incentives, such as tax cuts, to spur entrepreneurs and investors. Bush famously denounced Reagan's plan as "voodoo economics." Although Bush performed well in some of the early primaries, he was soon eclipsed by the charismatic Reagan, who became the party's nominee. Reagan at first sought former president Ford as his running mate. When a political deal between the two could not be reached, Reagan chose Bush instead. Bush was considered a moderate Republican who brought foreign-affairs experience to the ticket.

The Reagan-Bush team won the election over Carter, the incumbent, in a landslide, garnering 489 out of

President George H. W. Bush speaking at a press conference, 1990. © *Wally McNamee/CORBIS*

538 electoral votes. In 1984 Reagan and Bush had an even more impressive win—525 electoral votes—against their Democratic challengers, former vice president Walter Mondale (1928–) and Geraldine Ferraro (1935–), a representative from New York. During his years as vice president Bush focused on such administration priorities as deregulation and the war on illegal drugs.

The 1988 Election As Reagan approached the end of his second term, Bush became the Republican frontrunner for president. He benefited from the enormous popularity that Reagan had enjoyed, but presented a quieter and more deliberate personality. When he accepted his party's nomination, he said, "I want a kinder and gentler nation." It was an attempt to quell criticism that the Reagan administration had been insensitive to the needs of the poor and disadvantaged. Bush also spoke of the importance of the nation's many social and religious organizations and compared them to "a thousand points of light in a broad and peaceful sky." But perhaps his most famous remark (and one that came back to haunt him) was a promise: "Congress will push me to raise taxes, and I'll say no, and they'll push, and

I'll say no, and they'll push again, and I'll say to them, 'Read my lips: no new taxes.'"

As his running mate Bush chose Senator Dan Quayle (1947–) of Indiana. The choice invoked some criticism because Quayle was a relatively unknown and inexperienced legislator. However, the Bush-Quayle ticket easily won the election with 53 percent of the popular vote and 426 electoral votes. Their main opponents were Democrats Michael Dukakis (1933–), the governor of Massachusetts, and Lloyd Bentsen (1921–2006), a senator from Texas.

Domestic Policy Issues Bush worked with Congress to enact legislation on a variety of domestic issues. The Whistleblower Protection Act (1989) encouraged and protected government employees who disclosed instances of waste, corruption, or illegal behavior by federal agencies. The Americans with Disabilities Act (1990), a civil-rights law, provided legal protections for disabled persons against discrimination in employment; state and local government programs and services; public accommodations; commercial facilities; transportation; and telecommunications. Bush supported an amendment to the U.S. Constitution to ban desecration of the American flag, but a joint resolution to that effect was voted down in Congress. Instead, Congress passed the Flag Protection Act of 1989, which Bush did not sign, but allowed to become law. It was subsequently ruled unconstitutional by the U.S. Supreme Court in *United States v. Eichman* (1990).

Among the most important pieces of legislation passed during the Bush administration were the Clean Air Act Amendments (CAAA) of 1990, which addressed three issues of growing concern: acid rain, urban air pollution—particularly smog—and emissions of toxic air pollutants. They strengthened enforcement and compliance procedures and established emissions allowances that could be bought and sold at auction—a market-based way for businesses to meet their pollution-reduction goals.

Foreign Affairs Bush's foreign policy was dominated by two events. U.S. forces invaded Panama in December 1989 to oust that nation's military leader, Manuel Noriega (1938–), who had invalidated the results of recent elections and was considered a threat to U.S. interests, particularly the Panama Canal, a major shipping channel connecting the Atlantic and Pacific oceans. The United States also accused Noriega of engaging in drug trafficking and money laundering. The U.S. military captured Noriega within days and took him to the United States, where he was convicted and sentenced to forty years (later reduced to thirty years) in prison.

Another event had a more profound effect on Bush's legacy: in August 1990 Iraqi military forces invaded neighboring Kuwait, ostensibly because of a dispute over oil rights. Iraq's leader, Saddam Hussein (1937–2006), ignored demands from the international community to leave Kuwait. The United Nations imposed strict economic sanctions on Iraq, and the Security Council set a deadline of January 15, 1991, for Iraq's withdrawal from Kuwait. Bush assembled an international coalition to use military force to enforce the resolution. On January 12 the U.S. House and Senate authorized the use of U.S. troops. Four days later the coalition began bombing targets within Iraq. In late February coalition ground forces swept into Kuwait and pushed the Iraqis back across the border within days. Bush declared a cease-fire and chose not to expand the war against Iraq. More than 2 million U.S. military personnel served in the Persian Gulf War; 382 died, 147 of them in combat.

After the war the Security Council imposed additional sanctions on Iraq, restricting its development of nuclear and other weapons. Iraq was ordered to work with inspectors from the International Atomic Energy Agency to ensure that all materials related to nuclear weapons were destroyed. During the following decade Hussein allowed inspections at some times but not at others.

The nation's initial reaction to the Persian Gulf War was relief and a surge of patriotic pride. Bush's approval ratings soared.

Bush and the Economy Although Reagan's tax cuts had pleased many voters, they had meant reduced revenue for the federal government. He had also pushed for greater national defense spending as part of his "peace through strength" policy toward the Soviet Union. The combination of these factors resulted in high federal deficits. In 1981 the national debt passed $1 trillion.

When Bush entered the White House he faced political pressure to reduce the federal deficit without raising taxes, a difficult task. The prospect became even more bleak when the savings and loan industry, which had recently been deregulated, nearly collapsed. A series of unwise loans and poor business decisions left most of the industry in shambles and a subsequent government bailout exceeded $500 billion. At the same time the administration faced rapidly growing costs for Medicare, the health-care program for the elderly, and Medicaid, which serves the very poor. Despite his "read my lips" pledge, Bush reluctantly agreed with Congress that taxes had to be raised. The Omnibus Budget Reconciliation Act of 1990 included spending caps on government programs, but also enacted a significant tax increase. Raising taxes proved to be damaging politically for Bush.

In late 1990 and early 1991—at the time of the Persian Gulf War—the U.S. economy went into recession, with unemployment increasing and production decreasing. The economy was slow to recover, which became an issue in the 1992 presidential election. Bush and Quayle were defeated by Democrats Bill Clinton (1946–), the governor of Arkansas, and Al Gore Jr. (1948–), a senator from Tennessee.

Post-Presidential Life After leaving the White House Bush maintained a relatively low public profile for several years, concentrating on speaking engagements and business ventures. His foundation built the George Bush Presidential Library Center on the campus of Texas A&M University. It includes the George Bush Presidential Library and Museum and the George Bush School of Government and Public Service. In 2004 Bush teamed with Clinton to lead an international fund-raising drive for victims of a tsunami that devastated Indonesia and other countries along the Indian Ocean. The next year the two men collaborated again to raise money for those who lost their homes and businesses when Hurricane Katrina hit the U.S. Gulf Coast.

Bill Clinton

Bill Clinton (1946–), the forty-second president of the United States, led the nation during a time of relative peace and economic prosperity. The federal government achieved a budget surplus for the first time in decades. However, Clinton's presidency was plagued by scandals, including his extramarital affair with a White House intern. Clinton lied about the affair to the public; he also lied during court testimony, which led to impeachment (indictment) by the House of Representatives. He was acquitted of the charges by the Senate. Clinton was a

Future president Bill Clinton (left) meeting John F. Kennedy (right) at a ceremony in the White House Rose Garden, 1963. *© Getty Images*

popular president despite the scandals and maintained a high-profile role in public life after leaving the White House in January 2001.

Early Life and Public Service Three months before William (Bill) Jefferson Blythe III was born, his father died in a traffic accident. His mother later remarried, and he began using his stepfather's last name. He was an excellent student and became interested in politics after meeting President John F. Kennedy (1917–1963) during a White House visit. After graduating from Georgetown University, Clinton won a prestigious Rhodes Scholarship to Oxford University in England. While other young men were being drafted for service during the Vietnam War, Clinton obtained a deferment from being drafted by making a verbal commitment to join the ROTC program at the University of Arkansas. Later he changed his mind. By that time the draft rules had changed, and he was not called for military service.

During the early 1970s he attended Yale University, where he met his future wife—Hillary Rodham (1947–). Both graduated with law degrees. They married in 1975.

In 1974 Clinton ran for Congress as a Democrat in his home state of Arkansas, but was defeated. Two years later he was elected the state's attorney general. In 1978 Clinton ran for governor and, after promising to improve the state's schools and road system, won by a wide margin. In 1980 he was defeated in his bid for re-election, but tried again two years later and was elected. His second stint as governor lasted from 1983 until his successful bid for the presidency in 1992.

Clinton Wins the White House Clinton's primary competitors for the presidential election of 1992 were the incumbent president, George H. W. Bush (1924–), a Republican, and Ross Perot (1930–), a Texas businessman running as an independent. A recession during the Bush administration and the high federal budget deficit made the economy a key issue during the campaign. Clinton's opponents tried to use his past against him—chiefly his draft deferment during the Vietnam War; his admission that he smoked marijuana as a young man; and allegations of sexual affairs. However, Clinton's personal charm and promises of economic reform resonated with the voters. He and his running mate, Al Gore Jr. (1948–), a senator from Tennessee, were relatively young candidates and capitalized on the nation's yearning for change. Clinton won the election easily, capturing 370 of the 538 electoral votes. He won 43 percent of the popular vote, while Bush won 37 percent and Perot won 19 percent.

Clinton's Rocky Start During his first years in office Clinton had some successes—notably the Family and Medical Leave Act (1993); the Brady Handgun Violence Prevention Act (1993); and the Violent Crime Control and Law Enforcement Act (1994). However, most other domestic legislation he championed struggled for survival. His foreign-policy efforts included implementation

Former president Bill Clinton, 2003.   *© B MATHUR/Reuters/CORBIS*

of the North American Free Trade Agreement (1993), but he was hurt politically by a failed humanitarian mission in Somalia in which several U.S. soldiers were killed.

When Clinton took office Congress was controlled by his party, the Democrats, so the public expected that he would have little trouble gaining passage of economic and social reforms. That expectation proved to be overly optimistic. The president's proposed economic stimulus and jobs program prompted a Republican filibuster and complaints from centrist members of his own party. Critics grumbled that Clinton had campaigned as a populist reformer, but behaved like a "tax-and-spend liberal" once he was in office. Bickering over the program went on for months, which damaged Clinton's standing in public-opinion polls. Ultimately Congress passed the Omnibus Budget Reconciliation Act of 1993, which combined tax increases and spending cuts in an effort to end a string of high federal budget deficits.

The president also had trouble implementing a campaign promise to allow gays and lesbians to serve in the military. After it became clear that Congress would not support such a measure, Clinton backed down. A policy called "don't ask, don't tell" was instituted: commanders are not to ask service members about their sexual orientation, and gay service members are not to volunteer information about

HOW IMPEACHMENT WORKS

Impeachment is a procedure for removing a public official from office because of misconduct. The U.S. Constitution provides for impeachment in Article 2, Section 4, which reads, "The President, Vice President and all civil Officers of the United States, shall be removed from Office on Impeachment for, and Conviction of, Treason, Bribery, or other high Crimes and Misdemeanors." Although impeachment is commonly associated with presidents, it also applies to other officials, such as federal judges and cabinet members. The procedure is not applicable to members of Congress; the House and Senate have their own rules for dealing with misconduct by their members.

Impeachment begins in the House of Representatives. According to Article 1, Section 3 of the Constitution, "The House of Representatives shall choose their Speaker and other Officers; and shall have the sole Power of Impeachment." It is considered the power to indict, similar to what a grand jury does in criminal law. The House Judiciary Committee examines the charges and evidence and draws up specific indictments called Articles of Impeachment. All House members then vote on each individual article; a simple majority—more than 50 percent—is required to obtain impeachment.

If the House votes for impeachment, the U.S. Senate then becomes the courtroom. According to Article 1, Section 3, Clause 6 of the U.S. Constitution, "The Senate shall have the sole Power to try all Impeachments. When sitting for that Purpose, they shall be on Oath or Affirmation. When the President of the United States is tried, the Chief Justice shall preside: And no Person shall be convicted without the Concurrence of two thirds of the Members present."

The penalty for conviction is prescribed in Article 1, Section 3, Clause 7 of the Constitution: "Judgment in Cases of Impeachment shall not extend further than to removal from Office, and disqualification to hold and enjoy any Office of honor, Trust or Profit under the United States: but the Party convicted shall nevertheless be liable and subject to Indictment, Trial, Judgment and Punishment, according to Law." In other words, impeached officials can still face criminal trial for their wrongdoings.

their sexual orientation. Those service members who divulge their homosexuality can be discharged from the military.

Clinton had also promised reforms of the country's welfare and health systems. Welfare reform had broad public appeal, but Clinton was slow to develop a policy. In mid 1994 he proposed a plan that satisfied neither Democrats nor Republicans in Congress and was soon abandoned. Early in his administration he placed health-care reform under the direction of his wife, a radical break with tradition regarding the role of a first lady. She chaired the President's Task Force on National Health Care Reform, which several months later released a health-care plan that was more than a thousand pages long. Although it was supposed to be secret, portions were leaked to the press. Republicans, moderate Democrats, and key interest groups harshly criticized the plan for its complexity, cost, and bureaucratic nature. Congressional leaders of both parties proposed alternative plans, but no consensus was ever reached.

In the 1994 midterm elections Republican candidates took advantage of public discontent over Clinton's perceived shortcomings. The so-called Republican Revolution gave the party majority control over the House and Senate.

Congressional Conflict and Economic Prosperity

The remaining years of Clinton's presidency were characterized by conflict with Congress, particularly over financial matters. On two occasions in 1995 and 1996 many operations of federal agencies were forced to cease when he and Congress could not agree on spending priorities. The Republicans wanted to balance the federal budget by cutting expenditures for Medicare, Medicaid, and welfare programs and by implementing tax cuts. The president opposed the plan, arguing that their proposed cuts in social programs were too deep. The two sides waged a very public feud in the media. In general, Clinton won the public-opinion battle, as congressional Republicans got most of the blame for government shutdowns.

Despite all of the bickering, the resulting economic policy proved highly effective. During the mid 1990s federal budget deficits began to decline. In 1998 there was a budget surplus for the first time in nearly thirty years. Annual surpluses occurred throughout the remainder of Clinton's presidency. The economy flourished, with both low unemployment and low inflation rates. The prosperous economy was a major factor in Clinton's re-election in 1996. He won easily, garnering 49 percent of the popular vote and 379 out of 538 electoral votes. His major competitors were Bob Dole (1923–), a Republican senator from Kansas, and Perot, running on the ticket of the newly formed Reform Party.

In 1996 long-awaited welfare reform was finally achieved in the Personal Responsibility and Work Opportunity Reconciliation Act. This act, which was drafted largely by congressional Republicans, established new time limits for federal assistance and included work requirements for recipients. That same year Clinton persuaded Congress to increase the minimum wage and to pass a law granting the president the authority to veto specific items in spending bills. The law, the Line-Item Veto Act, was later ruled unconstitutional by the U.S. Supreme Court. In 1997 the booming economy prompted passage of the Taxpayer Relief Act, which included incentives for Americans to save and invest more and pay for college education. However, the tax cuts were relatively small compared with the tax increases that had been implemented in 1993.

Scandal and Impeachment During his second year in office a special prosecutor began investigating the Clintons' involvement in a failed real-estate venture dating back decades. In 1978 the Clintons, along with their business partners, Jim (1940–1998) and Susan McDougal (1955–), invested in an Arkansas real-estate development called Whitewater. The McDougals later operated a savings and loan institution while Bill Clinton was governor and hired Hillary Clinton to do legal work. During the 1980s and 1990s the McDougals' business deals became the subject of federal investigations. In 1994 Attorney General Janet Reno (1938–) appointed the first of several independent counsels who investigated the Clintons' involvement in the Whitewater venture. The investigation, which lasted until 2000, found no evidence of wrongdoing by the Clintons. The McDougals and a dozen of their business associates were convicted of federal crimes.

In 1994 Paula Jones (1966–) filed a civil lawsuit against the president, alleging that he had sexually harassed and assaulted her when he was governor of Arkansas. The president's lawyers tried unsuccessfully to get the case delayed until he was out of office. Meanwhile, in the ongoing Whitewater probe, independent counsel Kenneth Starr (1946–) began investigating allegations that Clinton had engaged in extramarital affairs. Jones's lawyers received anonymous tips that Clinton had been having an affair with Monica Lewinsky (1973–), a White House intern. Starr also learned about Lewinsky and suspected that the president had asked her to lie when she was subpoenaed to testify in the Jones case. In January 1998 during a pretrial deposition Jones's lawyers questioned Clinton about Lewinsky; he denied under oath having had an affair with her.

The Lewinsky allegations soon became international news. On January 26, 1998, Clinton appeared on television and stated "I did not have sexual relations with that woman, Miss Lewinsky. I never told anybody to lie, not a single time, never. These allegations are false." Several months later the Jones case was dismissed without going to trial. In July 1998 Starr obtained DNA evidence that proved a sexual encounter had occurred between Lewinsky and Clinton. In exchange for immunity from prosecution Lewinsky testified before a federal grand jury and revealed details about her affair with the president. However, she denied that he had asked her to lie under oath in the Jones case. In August Clinton testified before the same jury via videotape, but refused to answer many of the questions. He appeared again on television and this time admitted that he had had a relationship with Lewinsky that was "not appropriate."

In September 1998 Starr presented his report to the House of Representatives, which released it to the public. The report included graphic details about the Clinton-Lewinsky affair. In December the House began considering articles of impeachment, accusing Clinton of lying under oath; obstruction of justice by encouraging witnesses to give false testimony; and abuse of power. On December 19, 1998, the president was impeached for perjury and obstruction of justice. Clinton became only the second president in history, after Andrew Johnson (1808–1875), to be impeached by the House. Meanwhile, Clinton continued to enjoy high approval ratings from the public.

The impeachment trial in the Senate began on January 7, 1999, with Chief Justice William Rehnquist (1924–2005) presiding. The trial lasted for more than a month and included videotaped testimony from Lewinsky. On February 12, 1999, the final vote was taken. The president was found not guilty by a vote of 55 to 45 of perjury. The vote on the obstruction charge was 50 to 50. Because the required two-thirds majority was not obtained for impeachment, the president was acquitted.

After the Presidency Clinton left office in January 2001 with relatively high job-approval ratings from the public. He established the William J. Clinton Foundation at the Clinton Presidential Center in Little Rock, Arkansas. The foundation focuses on health issues, particularly HIV and AIDS; economic empowerment; leadership development and citizen service; and reconciliation of racial, ethnic, and religious differences. In 2004, following the tsunami that devastated Indonesia and other countries along the Indian Ocean, Clinton teamed with former president George H. W. Bush in an international fund-raising drive. In 2005 Clinton established the Clinton Global Initiative, which brings together governments, private corporations, and nonprofit organizations to address such problems as poverty and pollution. That same year he and Bush teamed up again to raise money for the victims of Hurricane Katrina, which ravaged the Gulf Coast of the United States.

Ross Perot

Ross Perot (1930–), a Texas businessman and billionaire, ran for president in 1992 and 1996 as an independent, third-party candidate. His image as a straight-talking, no-nonsense, political outsider proved popular with voters who were disenchanted with the two major parties. He garnered 19 percent of the popular vote in 1992 and about 9 percent in 1996, but received no electoral-college votes in either election. He founded a new party—the Reform Party—for his second campaign.

Early Life and Career Henry Ross Perot, born into a middle-class family in Texarkana, Texas, graduated from the Naval Academy in 1953 and served in the Navy for four years. He married Margot Birmingham, and they had five children. After leaving the Navy, Perot had a successful career as a salesman for IBM Corporation. In 1962 he started his own company, Electronic Data

Ross Perot at a press conference, 1992.   © *Reuters/CORBIS*

Systems (EDS), which he built into a highly profitable technology-services firm. Perot sold the company in 1984 for $2.5 billion. Several years later he founded a similar—and successful—company called Perot Systems Corporation.

During the early 1970s EDS acquired a multimillion-dollar contract in Iran. By the end of the decade that country was torn by revolution, and most EDS personnel had been evacuated. Two EDS executives who remained behind were seized and imprisoned by the Iranian government. When diplomatic efforts failed to free the men, Perot secretly financed a multimillion-dollar rescue attempt led by a retired military officer and staffed by EDS volunteers. The team entered Iran illegally and joined with revolutionaries to storm the jail and release all the prisoners. The U.S. contingent managed to get out of the country undetected. The event was dramatized in a 1983 book "On the Wings of Eagles," which was made into a television miniseries in 1986. Both helped make Ross Perot a household name and a popular hero.

Political Experience   Although he would later claim to be a political outsider, Perot met with President Richard Nixon (1913–1994) on several occasions and enjoyed close ties with his administration. Depending on

the situation, Nixon's aides viewed Perot as a useful and wealthy ally or an unpredictable pest. He funded some projects deemed helpful to Nixon's image, but often defied directives from his White House contacts and demanded favors from them to further his business interests.

In 1969 Perot formed a citizens' action group called United We Stand, which was devoted to soldiers who were prisoners of war (POWs) in Vietnam or considered missing in action (MIAs). With the secret blessing of the White House, he funded and led a humanitarian mission in which several planes were loaded with food, medicines, and presents for POWs held in North Vietnam. The North Vietnamese refused to let the planes land in their country or accept the shipments. Perot hop-scotched around Asia, using the trip to get international press coverage for the POWs. On several occasions he paid the expenses of wives of POWs who traveled to Paris, the site of ongoing peace talks. After the war ended, POWs maintained that Perot's widely publicized efforts helped achieve better treatment for them while they were in captivity. Perot became very popular with military and veterans' groups. In 1979 Perot privately funded several unsuccessful covert operations to rescue Americans held hostage in Iran.

During the 1980s Perot earned praise for heading Texas committees that overhauled the state's drug-abuse laws and school system. He was also a trusted adviser to President Ronald Reagan (1911–2004), who appointed Perot to the Foreign Intelligence Advisory Board. In 1988 Vice President George H. W. Bush (1924–) was elected president. Perot had known Bush for many years and reportedly disliked him very much. He often criticized the new president's policies, particularly his decision to wage the Persian Gulf War in 1991. Although Perot had been a political insider during the Republican administrations of Nixon and Reagan, he turned against the party while Bush was president.

Perot's Presidential Bids   In 1991 Perot began quietly preparing to run for president as an independent, finally announcing his intentions in February 1992 on the CNN program "Larry King Live." It was the first of many appearances on the show, which Perot used to share his platform with the public. He cast himself as a political outsider with a common-sense plan for reform. He focused primarily on economic and foreign-trade issues, avoiding sensitive social issues that tended to polarize voters. Perot spent more than $50 million of his own money on his campaign, using such unconventional means as televised infomercials to spread his message. He got high marks in public-opinion polls—sometimes higher than his two main challengers, Bush, the Republican, and Arkansas Governor Bill Clinton (1946–), the Democrat.

During the summer his campaign stumbled. Remarks he made about gays and African-Americans caused

THIRD-PARTY POLITICS

Since the 1800s American politics have been dominated by two parties, the Republicans and the Democrats. However, many other parties—all of which are called "third" parties—have appeared from time to time.

States make it difficult for third parties to compete, imposing stringent requirements for being listed on ballots. Typically candidates must get a certain number of verifiable signatures on petitions within a certain amount of time. For example, Georgia's procedure is considered one of the most restrictive in the nation. It requires that a petition be signed by at least 5 percent of the number of people who were eligible to vote in the previous election, and all signatures must be obtained in a 180-day period. Georgia's requirements were upheld as constitutional by the U.S. Supreme Court in *Jenness v. Fortson* (1971).

Another roadblock for third-party presidential candidates involves "federal matching funds"—money provided from public funds that matches a certain amount of the money raised by candidates from private donors. The program, which is administered by the Federal Election Commission (FEC), is funded on a voluntary basis by U.S. taxpayers. Federal income-tax returns include a box that taxpayers can check to indicate they want $3 of their federal tax payment to go to the program.

The FEC designates funds for the Republican and Democratic national conventions and for the nominees of those two parties in the general presidential election. All candidates in the primary elections can request public funds to match the contributions they have received from individuals (up to $250 from each donor). However, the FEC imposes strict eligibility requirements. A candidate must first raise $100,000 in private donations, including at least $5,000 contributed from people in at least twenty different states, to become eligible for federal matching funds.

Third parties that received at least 5 percent of the popular vote in the previous general election are eligible for public funds for the next general election. New third parties—those participating for the first time in a general election—are not eligible. However, the FEC ruled in 1996 that even though the Reform Party did not exist in 1992, the performance by independent candidate Ross Perot (1930–) in that election qualified him for matching federal funds in 1996. The FEC did not address the issue of whether a different Reform Party candidate in 1996 would have been eligible.

Another major obstacle for third-party candidates is participation in the presidential debates held several weeks before the general election. The private Commission on Presidential Debates determines which candidates are eligible, using fairly rigorous criteria. For example, a candidate must be listed on the ballot in enough states to have a mathematically possible chance of winning the electoral-college vote. A candidate must also receive the support of at least 15 percent of the people interviewed for five public-opinion polls selected by the commission—that requirement effectively eliminated Perot from the 1996 presidential debates.

---

controversy. Stories in the press painted him as a difficult and paranoid egomaniac. He accused the Republican Party of waging a "dirty tricks" campaign against him and his family. In July 1992 Perot suddenly quit the race. His stunned followers continued to work on his behalf, however, conducting petition drives that succeeded in placing his name on ballots in all fifty states.

In October 1992 Perot reentered the presidential race and performed well in televised debates with the other candidates. He garnered more than 19 million votes in the 1992 election, capturing 18.9 percent of the popular vote. It was the best showing by an independent candidate in nearly eighty years. Because he got more than 5 percent of the popular vote, Perot became eligible for matching federal campaign funds for the next presidential election. He adopted a new issue—opposition to passage of the North American Free Trade Agreement (NAFTA). NAFTA was passed by a Democrat-controlled Congress in November 1993, prompting Perot to encourage Americans to vote Republican in the 1994 midterm elections.

In 1995 Perot created the Reform Party and, in August 1996, accepted its nomination for president. His core issues were reducing the federal deficit; reforming campaign-finance laws; and opposing NAFTA. The economy was booming, and Perot's popularity had fallen since 1992. He got approximately 9 percent of the popular vote in 1996. Perot won no electoral college votes in either presidential election.

Fading from the Political Stage Perot's performance in the 1996 election weakened his position in the Reform Party. Internal conflicts arose, and many of his followers left the party. In June 2000 he announced that he did not intend to run for president that year. Shortly before the election he endorsed George W. Bush (1946–), the son of his former campaign opponent. Perot then faded from the political stage, turning his attention to his business ventures and continuing his public campaign on behalf of veterans.

See also **The Reform Party**

Hillary Clinton

Hillary Rodham Clinton (1947–) was first lady from 1993 to 2001 and was elected U.S. senator from New York in 2000 and 2006. In 2007 she announced she was a candidate for president in the 2008 election. As first lady she had unprecedented political duties. Almost immediately after he was inaugurated, her husband, President Bill Clinton (1946–), put her in charge of a task force that developed a plan for universal health insurance for the country. Although that particular plan did not pass Congress, the goal of health-care reform remained a cornerstone of her political agenda.

Early Life and Career Hillary Rodham, the oldest child of a middle-class Chicago family, was active in student government during her high school and college years. After graduating from Wellesley College in Massachusetts she earned a law degree from Yale University, where she met her future husband. After graduation they moved to her husband's native Arkansas. They had a daughter, Chelsea, in 1980.

Clinton worked for a law firm while her husband began his political career. In 1976 he was elected attorney general; two years later he ran for governor and won. Although defeated for re-election in 1980, he ran again in 1982 and was elected. His tenure as Arkansas governor ultimately lasted from 1983 until his successful run for president in 1992. While she was first lady of Arkansas, she focused on issues important to women and children, primarily in education and health care.

First Lady of the United States As first lady of the United States, Clinton played an unprecedented role in her husband's administration. Days after the president took office he placed health-care reform under her direction. She chaired the President's Task Force on National Health Care Reform, which developed a plan for universal government-sponsored health insurance. The effort took several months and was largely conducted in secret, although many people contributed to the project. The resulting plan was more than a thousand pages long. After portions of the plan were leaked to the press, it was roundly condemned by Republicans, moderate Democrats, and key interest groups for its complexity, cost, and bureaucratic nature. Hillary Clinton was blamed for its failure to garner public or political support. Although congressional leaders of both parties proposed alternative health-insurance plans, no consensus was ever reached. For her role in the debacle, she got poor marks in public-opinion polls. Some of her critics, particularly conservative Republicans, branded her an unrealistic far-left radical.

During their second year in the White House the Clintons came under investigation for their involvement in the so-called Whitewater affair—a failed real-estate investment in Arkansas dating back to the 1970s. The Clintons had entered the business venture with Jim (1940–1998) and Susan McDougal (1955–), a couple who became the focus of federal investigations into financial crimes. The McDougals had operated a savings and loan institution during Bill Clinton's years as governor. They were legal clients of Hillary Clinton. In 1994 Attorney General Janet Reno (1938–) appointed the first of several independent counsels to examine the Clintons' involvement in the Whitewater venture. The investigation lasted until 2000, but found no evidence of wrong-

Senator Hillary Clinton at a press conference in 2006. © *Brooks Kraft/Corbis*

doing by the Clintons. The McDougals and a dozen of their business associates were convicted of federal crimes.

Before and during his presidency, Bill Clinton was accused by several women of having made unwanted sexual advances toward them when he was governor of Arkansas. The Whitewater investigation inadvertently turned up evidence that the president had engaged in an extramarital affair with Monica Lewinsky (1973–), a White House intern. The first lady defended her husband against the accusations and blamed a "vast right-wing conspiracy" for plotting against him. Eventually the president admitted that he had had an "inappropriate" relationship with Lewinsky. In December 1998 he was impeached (indicted) by the U.S. House of Representatives for lying under oath and obstruction of justice. However, he was acquitted by the U.S. Senate. Hillary Clinton publicly stood by her husband throughout these scandals, which raised her stature in public-opinion polls.

Senator Clinton In 2000 Hillary Clinton ran for the U.S. Senate from New York, winning 55 percent of the vote. During her first term she surprised political observers by taking a centrist stand on many issues. She even collaborated on legislation with Republican senators who had been among her husband's most vocal critics when he was in the White House. In 2002 she voted in support of the proposal by President George W. Bush (1946–) to use military force against Iraq. Her vote was criticized by many liberal Democrats. In 2005 she introduced legislation known as the Count Every Vote Act, which called for several election reforms, such as requiring electronic voting machines to create verifiable paper records and making election day a national holiday. The bill died in committee; she reintroduced it two years later.

In 2006 Clinton was reelected easily, capturing 67 percent of the vote. She served on the powerful Senate Armed Services Committee, the Senate Committee on Environment and Public Works, the Senate Committee on Health, Education, Labor and Pensions, and the Senate Special Committee on Aging. She championed expansion of the Children's Health Insurance Program (CHIP), a joint federal-state initiative that provides health insurance to children in families that make too much money to qualify for Medicaid, but not enough money to afford private health insurance. She has described CHIP as "a step" toward universal health care.

In January 2007 she announced her candidacy for president in 2008. Universal health care, removing U.S. troops from Iraq, and energy independence were among her major campaign themes.

George W. Bush

George W. Bush (1946–), the forty-third president of the United States, faced one overriding issue after his inauguration: terrorism. The terrorist attacks of September 11, 2001, set off an unprecedented chain of events, including wars in which the United States invaded Afghanistan and Iraq. Although the country rallied around Bush at first, his popularity plummeted as the death toll of U.S. troops serving in Iraq increased. Americans were shocked by military and political scandals during his administration, including the mistreatment and torture of prisoners captured during the wars.

Early Life and Public Service
Bush was born into a well-to-do family with a distinguished record in public service and the Republican Party. Bush's grandfather represented Connecticut in the U.S. Senate during the 1950s and early 1960s. His father, George H. W. Bush (1924–), was the forty-first president of the United States.

George W. Bush attended Yale University, graduating in 1968 with a degree in history. He was a pilot in the Texas Air National Guard and then earned a master's degree in business administration from Harvard Business School in 1975. After graduating he returned to Texas to work in the energy industry and was part owner of a professional baseball team. In 1994 he was elected governor of Texas; he was reelected four years later. As governor Bush developed a reputation as a consensus-builder, able to work with Democrats in a bipartisan fashion to achieve desired legislation.

The 2000 Election
In the 2000 presidential campaign Bush espoused a political philosophy called "compassionate conservatism" and—because he thought the presidency had been tainted by scandals during the Clinton administration—promised to bring dignity and respect back to the White House. Bush defined compassionate conservatism as follows: "It is compassionate to actively help our fellow citizens in need. It is conservative to insist on responsibility and results." He chose as his running mate former secretary of defense Dick Cheney (1941–). Their main opponents were Democratic Vice President Al Gore Jr. (1948–) and Senator Joseph Lieberman of Connecticut (1942–).

The election proved to be extremely close and contentious. Bush was eventually declared the winner, but only after a month of legal wrangling over a vote recount in Florida. Bush received less of the popular vote (47.9 percent) than did Gore (48.4 percent), but won the election by capturing 271 electoral votes—only one more than was required. Congressional outcomes in that election were close as well. U.S. Senate elections resulted in a 50-50 split between Democrats and Republicans. The Republican Party lost seats in the U.S. House, but maintained a slim majority.

Some Democrats were bitter about the outcome of the presidential election—they believed that Gore had been denied victory unfairly—so Bush entered office in a highly partisan political climate.

9/11 and Afghanistan
Bush's agenda changed on September 11, 2001, when terrorists commandeered four commercial airliners in the United States. Two of the planes were crashed into the twin towers of the World Trade Center in New York, leading to their collapse. A third plane struck the Pentagon. The fourth hijacked plane crashed in rural Pennsylvania after passengers stormed the cockpit. More than two thousand nine hundred people were killed. In a televised address that evening Bush promised to bring the terrorists to justice, noting "we will make no distinction between the terrorists who committed these acts and those who harbor them."

Intelligence revealed that the hijackers were associated with the terrorist organization al-Qaeda, led by Osama bin Laden (1957–), the son of a wealthy Saudi family, and aided by the Taliban government of Afghanistan. In an address to Congress on September 20 Bush publicly demanded that the Taliban hand over bin Laden and his top lieutenants or the United States would strike. "Every nation, in every region now has a decision to

President George W. Bush, 2006. © *Brooks Kraft/Corbis*

make," he said. "Either you are with us, or you are with the terrorists."

The Taliban did not comply with Bush's demands, so the U.S. military invaded Afghanistan to oust its government and capture bin Laden. U.S. forces encountered little organized resistance. A multinational military force organized by the United Nations and including a significant number of U.S. troops eventually took over security responsibilities for Afghanistan. They found themselves in a lingering guerrilla-type conflict with former Taliban supporters and al-Qaeda fighters. U.S. forces did not find bin Laden.

The Case against Iraq After the 9/11 attacks Bush called for a worldwide war against terrorism. His firm stance and quick action against Afghanistan earned the president high ratings in public-opinion polls—his approval rating soared to nearly 90 percent. However, support began to erode as bin Laden remained elusive, and the Bush administration turned its attention to Iraq.

Iraq and its leader Saddam Hussein (1937–2006) had worried the U.S. government for more than a decade. Following the Persian Gulf War in 1991 the UN Security Council called on Iraq not to acquire or develop nuclear weapons and to turn over any nuclear weapons or related equipment to the International Atomic Energy

Agency (IAEA). Hussein alternately denied IAEA inspectors access to the country and then let them in; he regularly refused to abide by UN resolutions. Bush and many of his inner circle—Cheney, Secretary of Defense Donald Rumsfeld (1932–), and Deputy Secretary of Defense Paul Wolfowitz (1943–)—became convinced that Iraq was developing weapons of mass destruction. During Bush's State of the Union address in 2002, he described Iraq as a member of an "axis of evil" in the world. In October 2002 Congress approved a resolution authorizing the use of force if Iraq failed to comply with UN Security Council resolutions regarding weapons inspections.

The Bush administration was spurred by intelligence reports (later found to be in error) that Iraq was developing nuclear weapons. Bush highlighted this intelligence in his 2003 State of the Union address. Soon afterward Secretary of State Colin Powell (1937–) tried unsuccessfully to persuade the United Nations that military action should be taken against Iraq. Only Britain pledged its full support for the U.S. war plan. In March 2003 Bush addressed the nation and presented his case for war against Iraq, noting that the intelligence gathered "leaves no doubt that the Iraq regime continues to possess and conceal some of the most lethal weapons ever devised." He gave Hussein and his sons forty-eight hours to leave Iraq or face military action. The president promised the Iraqi people that the United States would help them build "a new Iraq that is prosperous and free."

The War in Iraq On March 20, 2003, U.S.-led forces began with a massive bombing campaign against Iraq, followed by an invasion by ground troops. By early April U.S. troops had captured Baghdad, Iraq's capital, and British troops occupied much of southern Iraq. Initial jubilation by some Iraqi citizens turned to dismay when U.S. troops could not maintain order. However, massive looting and lawlessness were downplayed by Bush administration officials. On May 1, 2003, Bush announced that the major combat operations in Iraq were over. Before the end of the year most former members of Iraq's regime had been captured or killed. Hussein was found hiding in a pit and turned over to Iraq's new government to stand trial for war crimes. He was eventually convicted and hanged.

Bush's declaration of an official end of combat operations did not bring peace and security to Iraq. U.S. and British forces soon faced deadly attacks from insurgents determined to drive them from their country. Meanwhile, after a careful search of the country, no weapons of mass destruction were discovered.

In early 2004 reports began appearing in the media about the abuse of prisoners at the Abu Ghraib detention facility operated by the U.S. military in Iraq. These reports included digital photos taken by U.S. soldiers that showed prisoners enduring humiliating and abusive treatment. The news shocked Americans and resulted in apologies from Bush and Rumsfeld.

The 2004 Elections Bush began his 2004 election campaign in a relatively strong political position. The economy had weathered dips caused by the collapse of Internet stocks and by the 9/11 terrorist attacks. The Economic Growth and Tax Relief Reconciliation Act (2001) implemented the tax cuts he had promised. Education reform was also under way, led by the No Child Left Behind Act (2002). The Medicare Prescription Drug, Improvement and Modernization Act (2003) created a new prescription-drug plan for seniors. Foreign affairs and the war on terror dominated the 2004 campaign. Bush was subject to some criticism for his handling of the war as commander in chief, particularly regarding the growing insurgency in Iraq and the Abu Ghraib scandal, but he was able to counter with the fact that no new terrorist acts had occurred on U.S. soil.

Bush and Cheney were reelected with 51 percent of the popular vote, capturing 286 of the 538 electoral votes. Their Democratic opponents were Massachusetts Senator John Kerry (1943–) and North Carolina Senator John Edwards (1963–). Congressional Republicans built on gains they had made during the 2002 midterm elec-

tions. In 2004 they maintained their majorities in both houses of Congress.

The Second Term Bush's political fortunes fell quickly in his second term. In 2005 Tom DeLay (1947–), a Republican representative from Texas and a close Bush ally, was indicted by a grand jury for his role in funneling corporate contributions to Republican candidates for state office. One of DeLay's associates, lobbyist Jack Abramoff (1959–), was indicted for fraud in a separate investigation, which grew to expose a massive scandal involving influence peddling. Then in August Hurricane Katrina hit the Gulf Coast. Floodwater breached weakened levees, and the city of New Orleans was flooded. The federal government's response to the disaster was widely criticized as slow and inadequate.

In Iraq insurgent attacks increased dramatically between 2004 and 2006. Violence between Iraq's two major religious sects—Sunni Muslims and Shiite Muslims—threatened to escalate into civil war. U.S. military forces suffered increasing numbers of casualties from insurgent attacks as they trained Iraqi army and police forces. By mid 2007 more than three thousand U.S. military personnel had died in Iraq, and thousands more had been injured. Meanwhile there was an upswing in militant violence in Afghanistan, particularly in the southern part of the country.

In 2005 a commission created by Bush to investigate America's prewar intelligence about Iraq issued its final report, and it was extremely critical. The commission said that U.S. intelligence agents had relied on false information from unreliable informants and poor data sources, such as forged documents. As important, the commission said, was a reluctance among intelligence analysts to accept any evidence that challenged their preconceived notions about Iraq. The commission found that Iraq had had no active program to develop or acquire weapons of mass destruction since the Persian Gulf War. The findings embarrassed the administration, for it had used the intelligence extensively as it pressed for the invasion of Iraq in 2003. Bush's critics began to ask if the administration had knowingly used faulty intelligence to make its case for the war.

The 2006 Midterm Elections All of these issues had a dramatic effect on the 2006 midterm elections. Democratic candidates received widespread support from voters dissatisfied with the war in Iraq and government scandals. Democrats seized majority control in both houses of Congress (two of the newly elected senators were independents who aligned with the Democratic Party). California Representative Nancy Pelosi (1940–) became the first woman in history to be speaker of the House.

The day after the election Bush accepted Rumsfeld's resignation and appointed Robert Gates (1943–), who had earlier run the Central Intelligence Agency, to take his place as secretary of defense. Bush stated, "I recognize that many Americans voted last night to register their displeasure with the lack of progress being made in Iraq." Democratic leaders began calling for a timetable for withdrawal of U.S. troops from Iraq.

The Bush Presidency   As of mid 2007, the Bush presidency had been defined by lingering problems in Iraq and relatively good economic conditions at home. Deficit spending had soared, however—the war in Iraq had been particularly expensive, as had the new Medicare prescription-drug plan and emergency spending because of Hurricane Katrina. When Bush entered office the federal budget was in surplus; then, in each fiscal year from 2002 through 2005, the federal deficit exceeded $300 billion. It dipped below $250 billion for fiscal year 2006. (The fiscal year runs from October 1 through September 30). In February 2007 Bush proposed a long-term plan to reduce the federal deficit gradually each year and achieve a balanced budget by fiscal year 2012. The plan assumed that Congress would reduce spending on domestic programs and that U.S. expenses in Iraq would decline dramatically by 2010. Critics doubted that those two goals would be realized. Bush's approval rating dropped to near 30 percent, one of the lowest levels ever recorded for a second-term president.

Dick Cheney

Dick Cheney (1941–) was elected vice president on the 2000 Republican ticket with President George W. Bush (1946–). He played a prominent role in the administration, particularly in making the case for war with Iraq.

Early Life and Career   Cheney, who was raised in Casper, Wyoming, graduated from the University of Wyoming and began his political career with various positions in the administration of Republican President Richard Nixon (1913–1994). During the mid 1970s Cheney served as White House chief of staff for Republican President Gerald Ford (1913–2006). In 1978 he was elected to the U.S. House of Representatives from Wyoming; he was reelected five times. In 1988 he became minority whip, a House leadership position that made him responsible for mobilizing votes within the Republican Party on key issues.

Secretary of Defense   When President George H. W. Bush (1924–) named him secretary of defense in 1989, Cheney began streamlining the U.S. military into a smaller, more mobile force suitable for regional conflicts; the effort was precipitated partly by budget deficits but mostly by the breakup of the Soviet Union, which effectively ended the Cold War. Cheney recommended General Colin Powell (1937–) to be chairman of the Joint Chiefs of Staff, the first African-American to hold that position.

In 1990, when the Iraqi military invaded Kuwait, Cheney obtained permission from King Fahd (1921–2005) of Saudi Arabia to amass U.S. troops on Saudi

Vice-President Dick Cheney, 2005.   © *Matthew Cavanaugh/epa/ Corbis*

soil—an operation named Desert Shield. The United Nations Security Council subsequently set a deadline of January 15, 1991, for Iraq to withdraw from Kuwait or be forcibly expelled. Bush formed an international coalition of military forces to impose the Security Council resolution. Operation Desert Storm began two days after the deadline passed with air strikes on Iraqi forces in Kuwait and Iraq. A ground offensive followed and within days had pushed Iraqi troops out of Kuwait. Cheney and Powell were widely credited as the architects of the successful Persian Gulf War. In 1991 Cheney was awarded the Presidential Medal of Freedom for his role.

Vice President   In 1995 Cheney became president and chief executive officer of Halliburton Energy Services, a Texas-based company that specializes in oil and gas exploration, development, and production. In 2000 George W. Bush, then governor of Texas, chose Cheney as his vice presidential running mate. The two narrowly won the election against their Democratic challengers, Al Gore Jr. (1948–), a senator from Tennessee, and Joseph Lieberman (1942–), a senator from Connecticut.

The terrorist attacks of September 11, 2001, occurred less than a year later and thrust Cheney into a major role in administration strategy. According to some observers, he became obsessed with the idea that Iraq was involved in the attacks and was amassing weapons of mass destruction. Like Secretary of Defense Donald Rumsfeld (1932–) and Deputy Secretary of Defense Paul Wolfowitz (1943–)—the three had known each other for years—Cheney urged an aggressive military approach toward Iraq. The nation's first response to the terrorist attacks was a military operation in Afghanistan that ousted the Taliban government. That effort was followed by a push for an invasion of Iraq. Using reports by intelligence agencies, the administration claimed that Iraq was in collusion with terrorists and was amassing weapons of mass destruction. However, the head of the Central Intelligence Agency at the time, George Tenet (1953–), later claimed that the decision to invade Iraq was made without "serious debate" by the Bush administration. The allegation that Iraq colluded with terrorists was later found to be inaccurate, and the weapons of mass destruction were never found.

In 2003 the United States and a handful of allies—chiefly Britain—began an aerial and ground assault on Iraq. The operation was successful at first. Iraqi leader Saddam Hussein (1937–2006) was ousted from power and a new government was installed. However, as allied forces tried to rebuild the country a fierce insurgency erupted and widened into a deadly struggle between Iraqi factions divided by religious and political differences.

Americans who became disillusioned with the war placed much of the blame on Cheney for advocating the invasion so forcefully. In 2004 his chief of staff, I. Lewis "Scooter" Libby (1950–), was indicted by a federal grand jury for his involvement in leaking the identity of a CIA agent to the press. The leak was considered an attempt to undermine reports that the administration knowingly used faulty intelligence about Iraq's efforts to develop nuclear weapons. Libby was convicted in 2007 of perjury, making false statements, and obstruction of justice for his involvement in the leak. Cheney steadfastly denied knowing about the leak. At the same time questions of conflict of interest arose when Cheney's former employer, Halliburton, was awarded a multibillion dollar government contract to participate in the rebuilding of Iraq.

Cheney, who has had four heart attacks, said early in the Bush administration that he had no interest in running for president when Bush left office.

Tom DeLay

Tom DeLay (1947–) was a Republican representative from Texas from 1985 until 2006, when he gave up his post as majority leader and resigned from Congress after being indicted on federal charges related to campaign contributions.

Background DeLay had a long career in public service, starting in 1979 when he was elected to the Texas

House Majority Leader Tom DeLay presiding over a joint session of Congress, 2005. *© Shawen Thew/epa/Corbis*

House of Representatives. In 1984 he was elected to the U.S. House and reelected ten times. DeLay and Newt Gingrich (1943–), a Republican representative from Georgia, were the principal architects behind the so-called Republican Revolution of 1994, which gave the party majority control of the House for the first time in four decades. DeLay, who was nicknamed "the hammer," wielded great power in his party, serving as majority whip (1998–2000) and majority leader (2000–2006).

The Charges In 2005 Delay was indicted by a Texas grand jury for his role in a scheme to funnel corporate contributions to Republican candidates in his state. According to the indictment, an organization called Texans for the American Way Political Action Committee (TAWPAC) accepted nearly $200,000 in donations from corporate donors in 2002 and transferred it to the Republican National State Elections Committee—an arm of the Republican National Committee—which, in turn, distributed it among Republican candidates running for the Texas House. It is illegal in Texas to use corporate funds in state election campaigns.

DeLay helped organize and fund TAWPAC, served on its advisory board in 2001 and 2002, and participated in its fund-raisers. However, he denied being involved in

GERRYMANDERING?

At the heart of the indictments that led to the resignation of Republican representative Tom DeLay (1947–) of Texas lies a battle over congressional redistricting for partisan political gain—a practice known as gerrymandering.

As directed by the U.S. Constitution, the nation is divided into districts, each of which has one representative in the U.S. House. The number of congressional districts in each state is based on population (determined by the U.S. Census, which is conducted every ten years). As the nation's population grew, so did the number of congressional districts. In 1911 the U.S. Congress limited the number of districts to 435. That required apportionment—the distribution of those 435 seats among the fifty states according to population. States with smaller populations, such as Alaska and Delaware, have fewer House seats than states with large populations, such as California and Texas. Within each state the congressional districts are also apportioned according to population and are typically redrawn after each national census. Following the 2000 census each congressional district represented, on average, 646,952 people.

Most states allow their state legislatures to conduct redistricting; many observers say that practice encourages gerrymandering to benefit the party that controls the legislature. For example, politicians may choose to redraw districts so that most voters of the opposite party live in just a few of the state's districts. Alternatively they may spread their opponents across many districts to dilute their voting power. Yet another possibility is racial gerrymandering, in which congressional districts are redrawn to affect the voting power of minority populations within a state.

Redistricting to dilute or concentrate votes is unconstitutional because it violates the Equal Protection Clause of the Fourteenth Amendment. However, it is difficult to prove in court.

While the indictment gave few details, analysts believe that the purpose of the money-laundering scheme linked to DeLay was to elect enough Republicans to the Texas House in 2002 so the party would have majority control. It could then conduct a redistricting favorable to the Republican Party in Congress. In 2002 the Republicans did win majority control of the Texas House—for the first time in 130 years—and did perform a congressional redistricting. In the 2004 election the Republican Party gained six new seats in the U.S. House.

The redistricting was challenged in court. However, in *League of United Latin American Citizens v. Perry* (2006) the U.S. Supreme Court upheld the redistricting, except for one district in which the court believed racial gerrymandering had taken place. Approximately one hundred thousand Hispanic voters had been moved from a district with a Republican representative to a new district. The court also ruled that states can legally redistrict between national censuses, meaning that state legislatures could redistrict every time the majority party shifts.

TAWPAC's day-to-day operations and knowing about the transactions outlined in the indictment. As required by House rules, DeLay stepped down from his position as majority leader after he was indicted.

DeLay's Resignation DeLay ran for re-election in the 2006 and easily won the primary against his Republican competitors. By that time a number of his associates, including lobbyist Jack Abramoff (1959–), had been indicted in a separate corruption investigation. Only months before the general election, DeLay resigned from the House and abandoned his re-election campaign. However, DeLay's name remained on the ballot for the general election because state officials ruled it was too late to change the ballot. The Texas Republican Party challenged that decision in state and federal courts, but was unsuccessful. The party called upon Republicans in DeLay's congressional district to vote for a write-in Republican candidate, but she was defeated by a Democratic challenger, Nick Lampson (1945–).

After he resigned, DeLay wrote *No Retreat, No Surrender: One American's Fight*, which was released in early 2007. In the book he criticized many of his former allies in the Republican Party and continued to declare his innocence. As of mid 2007 he was still awaiting trial on charges of money laundering.

✪ Political Parties, Platforms, and Key Issues

Supply-Side Economics

Supply-side economics is a theory that advocates stimulating the efforts of businesses and entrepreneurs in order to achieve overall growth in the nation's economy. Embraced by the Reagan administration (1981–1989), supply-side policies contrasted with traditional economic practices, which tended to encourage consumer spending—the demand side. The methods used to implement the policy were reductions in tax rates, deregulation of industries, and lowered trade barriers.

Stagflation and "Reaganomics" When President Ronald Reagan (1911–2004) took office in January 1981 the economy was in a recession, or slowdown, and unemployment was high. Inflation was also very high, meaning that prices were rising quickly. This unusual combination of economic troubles is called stagflation. Reagan asserted that the cure for stagflation was an economic policy that directly helped entrepreneurs and producers of goods and services. In a 1988 speech he said, "God did give mankind virtually unlimited gifts to invent, produce, and create. And for that reason alone, it would be wrong for governments to devise a tax structure or economic system that

Economist Arthur Laffer with former California governor Ronald Reagan at a business conference in New York in 1978. Laffer's theories of supply-side economics later formed the basis of President Reagan's economic policies.   © *Bettmann/CORBIS*

suppresses and denies those gifts." Reagan's economic philosophy—it became known as "Reaganomics"—was influenced and aided by several of his contemporaries, including Jack Kemp (1935–), a Republican representative from New York; Bill Roth (1921–2003), a Republican senator from Delaware; economists Arthur Laffer (1940–) and Robert Mundell (1932–); and Jude Wanniski (1936–2005), a *Wall Street Journal* writer who is credited with coining the phrase "supply-side economics."

Reagan and his advisers argued that if entrepreneurs and producers—generally the wealthiest segment of the populace—were less burdened by taxes and regulations, they would produce and invest more. The benefits, they claimed, would "trickle down" to individuals in the lower income levels. Critics derided this theory as a political ploy to help the rich get richer while the poor got poorer.

Marginal Tax Rates   To implement the policy Reagan's team advocated a radical change in income tax

brackets. Income was—and is—taxed at different rates depending on its amount. The tax rate paid on the highest dollar earned is called the marginal tax rate. Supply-side economists of the 1980s believed that marginal tax rates should be lowered to encourage people to earn more. For a simplified example, consider a person making $50,000 per year in taxable income. Imagine the first $10,000 is taxed at 15 percent; income from $10,001 to $50,000 is taxed at 30 percent; and any income over $50,000 is taxed at 70 percent. A supply-side advocate would argue that this person has little incentive to earn more than $50,000 because the government will take seventy cents of every additional dollar earned.

In 1977 Kemp and Roth sponsored a bill to cut federal tax rates. It was rejected as inflationary by the Carter administration, but resurrected with Reagan's blessing in the Economic Recovery Tax Act (ERTA) of 1981. ERTA reduced the highest tax rate from 70 percent to 50 percent and lowered the other rates by varying percentage points. The lowest tax rate, 14 percent, was decreased to 10 percent.

ERTA was supposed to reduce the marginal tax rates without substantially reducing the amount of tax revenue taken in by the federal government. Supply-side proponents believed that people—particularly those in the highest tax brackets—would be inspired by cuts in the marginal tax rate to earn more income. In the most optimistic scenario enough "new" income would be earned at the lower tax rates to offset the loss to the government of income taxes that would have been paid at the higher tax rates.

Another consideration in the debate over tax brackets was the amount of money that people declared as income. Supply-side theorists asserted that the nation's wealthiest people were avoiding high marginal tax rates by putting some of their income into tax havens in other countries or by using tax loopholes. Lowering the marginal tax rates, they predicted, would encourage the wealthy to report—and pay taxes on—more of their income.

The capital-gains tax is a tax paid on the profit made from selling an investment, such as stocks, bonds, or real estate. At the federal level capital-gains taxes are tied to marginal tax rates, so lowering the marginal tax rates serves to lower capital-gains tax rates. Supply-side supporters knew that it was primarily the wealthy who incurred capital gains and paid taxes on them. Therefore, the economists argued that lowering the capital-gains tax rates would encourage more investing, which would provide a boost to the economy.

Another benefit of reducing the marginal tax rates, they said, was the elimination of "bracket creep." Wages and salaries had been increasing in response to rising prices during the 1970s, pushing many taxpayers into higher tax brackets. While their buying power had stayed about the same, taxpayers had less to spend because their income was taxed at a higher rate. A reduction of the marginal tax rates was expected to help taxpayers across the spectrum by correcting their shift into higher brackets.

ERTA phased in tax-rate changes gradually and included provisions that lowered corporate taxes and estate and gift taxes. The Tax Reform Act of 1986 lowered marginal tax rates even further—for example, the highest rate was decreased from 50 percent to 28 percent.

Deregulation and Free Trade

Deregulation and Free Trade Two other components of supply-side economics, deregulation and free trade, were also championed by the Reagan administration. President Jimmy Carter (1924–) had started deregulation, which removes or reduces governmental restraints on industry sectors. In the Reagan years it was expanded to cover more businesses, particularly in the financial and telecommunications industries. Supply-side theorists believed that reducing or eliminating

government regulations, which often required considerable expenditures by industries, would allow them to spend more on expanding their businesses. That, in turn, would help the economy overall. Likewise, trade barriers, such as high tariffs on imported goods, were viewed as excessive burdens on private industry. During his 1980 presidential campaign Reagan promoted free trade between the United States and Mexico. He signed the U.S.-Canada Free Trade Agreement in 1988 and supported the international talks that eventually produced the World Trade Organization, which has overseen multinational trade agreements since 1995. He also vetoed bills that would have impeded textile imports to the United States.

Praise and Criticism By 1989 the nation's economy was doing much better; unemployment and inflation were down substantially. Economists had mixed opinions on the role supply-side economics had played in this turnaround. Some believed that the cuts in marginal tax rates inspired investment by the wealthiest sectors, which helped jumpstart the economy. Others believed that a recovery was going to happen anyway and that the changes in the tax code unfairly burdened the poorest taxpayers. They pointed to data indicating that people in the lowest tax brackets wound up paying a higher, rather than a lower, percentage of their income in taxes after the tax code was changed. The new tax laws, they noted, not only changed the tax brackets but also reduced the tax exemptions and deductions that were most utilized by lower-income Americans. Other analysts pointed to actions by the Federal Reserve, the nation's central bank, which operates independently of congressional and presidential control. In the 1980s it had a new chairman, Paul Volcker (1927–), who had been appointed by Carter. Some economists thought his actions, which affected both the amount of money circulating in the United States and interest rates, may have been crucial factors in the economic upturn.

When the tax changes were first proposed, critics of supply-side economics claimed that the loss of tax revenue would force the government to borrow a lot of money, which would increase the budget deficit and the national debt. Deficit spending was high during the Reagan administration, which seemed to validate their opinion. However, other factors can be seen at work: for example, the government maintained a high defense budget as a tactic in the Cold War with the Soviet Union, which increased federal spending. Reagan also refused to make major cuts in some of the most expensive social programs, such as Social Security.

See also **Ronald Reagan**

The Contract with America

The Contract with America was a set of political promises made by the Republican Party six weeks before the 1994 elections. The party pledged to make specific

House Speaker Newt Gingrich holding a copy of the "Contract with America" in 1995. © *Reuters/CORBIS*

economic and social reforms if Republican candidates were elected in sufficient numbers to control Congress. The voters responded positively, and the Republican-dominated House followed through on nearly all of the contract's promises. Many of the reforms did not survive Senate scrutiny or presidential veto; nevertheless, the contract is remembered as a bold political move and a symbol of the Republican Party's resurgence during the 1990s.

Political Background In 1994 the Democratic Party had controlled the House of Representatives for forty years. A Democratic president—Bill Clinton (1946–)—had been in office for two years. Congressional scandals and public disenchantment with Clinton's early political agenda presented a positive climate for Republican candidates as the November 1994 elections approached. With great fanfare the party unveiled the Contract with America on the steps of the U.S. Capitol on September 28, 1994. Signed by 350 Republican candidates, the contract promised a balanced federal budget, numerous tax cuts, a crackdown on crime, greater government accountability, and many other reforms.

Republicans did well in the election, seizing majority control of both houses of Congress. Newt Gingrich (1943–), a Republican representative from Georgia, was elected speaker of the House. One of the coauthors of the contract, he was considered its chief champion.

The Terms of the Contract The Contract with America had two major components—eight reforms the Republican majority promised to launch on its first day in session and ten bills to be introduced during the first one hundred days.

The specific promises were:

1. Members of Congress would be subject to all laws applicable to the rest of the people.
2. A comprehensive audit of Congress would be conducted to detect "waste, fraud or abuse."
3. The number of House committees would be reduced, as would the number of people staffing the committees.
4. The terms of all committee chairs would be limited.
5. Committee members would be banned from casting proxy votes.
6. All committee meetings would be open to the public.
7. A three-fifths majority vote would be needed to pass a tax increase in the House.
8. The House would implement zero base-line budgeting to provide "an honest accounting" of the nation's finances.

The ten pieces of legislation in the Contract with America covered a variety of economic, social, and legal issues. The Fiscal Responsibility Act called for a balanced federal budget, tax limits, and a presidential line-item veto. The Taking Back Our Streets Act was a comprehensive crime-and-punishment package. The Personal Responsibility Act overhauled the welfare system. The Family Reinforcement Act covered child support, adoption, education, child pornography, and elderly dependents. The American Dream Restoration Act promised tax cuts and reforms. The National Security Restoration Act pledged that U.S. troops would not serve under the command of the United Nations and called for greater spending on national security. The Senior Citizens Fairness Act made changes in the Social Security program. The Job Creation and Wage Enhancement Act contained a variety of incentives for small businesses. The Common Sense Legal Reform Act put limits on lawsuits. The Citizen Legislature Act implemented term limits on certain "career politicians."

The Contract with America also included a promise that the budget would be cut sufficiently to ensure that implementation of these laws would not increase the federal deficit.

The Outcome The House delivered on all but one of the promises contained in the Contract with America. A vote to amend the U.S. Constitution to implement term limits on certain politicians did not pass. However, many of the specific measures passed by the House did not make it through the Senate unscathed or were vetoed by Clinton. The measures that eventually became law in some form included a tax credit for families that adopt children; tax cuts for businesses; a line-item veto (later ruled unconstitutional by the U.S. Supreme Court); congressional accountability; health insurance reforms; tax deductions for long-term care insurance; restrictions on lobbyists; and welfare reform.

Government Shutdowns

Many operations of federal agencies were forced to cease on two occasions in 1995 and 1996 because the Republican-controlled Congress and Democratic President Bill Clinton (1946–) failed to agree on spending legislation. These "government shutdowns" highlighted the deep division between the legislative majority and the executive branch on the financial priorities of the country—in particular, how best to deal with federal deficits, which occur when the government spends more money than it takes in.

Appropriations Acts By federal law the president must submit a proposed budget to Congress by the first Monday in February prior to the start of the next fiscal year. (The federal fiscal year begins on October 1 and runs through September 30.) Congress considers the president's proposed budget and passes a series of appropriation acts, each of which authorizes funding for one or more federal agencies. These acts must be passed by October 1 so the agencies can continue to operate. Since the late 1800s passage of all appropriations acts by the deadline has rarely been achieved. To provide funding past October 1, "continuing resolutions," have been passed by both houses of Congress and signed by the president.

A "funding gap" occurs if neither an appropriations act nor a continuing resolution is in place. A funding gap can also occur if a continuing resolution expires and is not replaced with a new one.

The History of Funding Gaps Funding gaps were first reported in the 1880s. For nearly a century they were very short affairs that were resolved quickly. This began to change during the 1970s as disagreements about spending priorities grew sharper. Between 1976 and 1979 there were several funding gaps, one of which exceeded two weeks. At that time funding gaps did not have a major effect on government operations: the affected federal agencies continued to operate—they minimized their spending activities—despite the presence in federal code of the Antideficiency Act. It began as a simple statute in 1870 and evolved into a complex law covering the government's actions during a funding gap.

In an opinion released in 1980 Benjamin Civiletti (1935–), who was attorney general in the Carter administration, said that the Antideficiency Act required "non-essential" government operations to cease completely when a funding gap occurs. This opinion achieved dramatic results: there was no funding gap that year. During the following decade the funding gaps that did occur lasted only a day or two. From 1991 through 1994 there were no funding gaps at all.

The 1995 and 1996 Funding Gaps When the elections of 1994 gave the Republican Party majority control of Congress, a contentious relationship quickly developed between powerful Republican lawmakers and the Democratic president, which hindered agreement on appropriations acts. In late September 1995 a continuing resolution was passed to fund the government from October 1 through November 13. A second continuing resolution passed Congress, but was vetoed by the president, triggering a funding gap that began on Tuesday, November 13, 1995, and lasted through the weekend. On November 20 a continuing resolution was enacted to fund the government through December 15. It expired and was not replaced. The funding gap that began on December 15 lasted for more than three weeks—the longest in history. It was resolved on January 6, 1996, by a new continuing resolution—the first of several passed in 1996 until a final budget agreement was reached.

During the two funding gaps, parts of the federal government closed down. Approximately eight hundred thousand employees were put on temporary furlough during the first shutdown. Far fewer people—around two hundred eighty thousand—were furloughed during the second shutdown because some funding bills did get passed. National parks, museums, and monuments around the country closed during the shutdowns, greatly affecting tourism. Thousands of applications for passports and visas were not processed. Many other government services were delayed or slowed. Operations deemed "essential" did not cease, however, including the military and federal law enforcement agencies, mail delivery, and the processing of payments to existing recipients of Social Security and Medicare.

The Budget Battle The Republican budget plan called for a balanced federal budget within seven years through cuts in the Medicare, Medicaid, and welfare programs. It also called for tax cuts. This approach was championed by Kansas Senator Bob Dole (1924–), the majority leader of the Senate, and Georgia Representative Newt Gingrich (1943–), the speaker of the House. The president refused to support the plan, claiming that it cut too much funding from social, educational, and environmental programs. A very public feud was conducted in the media, with each side blaming the other for the impasse.

The battle took an interesting twist after Clinton, Dole, and Gingrich traveled with many other U.S. politicians to Israel on November 6, 1995, for the funeral of

Israeli Prime Minister Yitzhak Rabin (1922–1995). Afterward Gingrich complained that he and Dole had been snubbed by Clinton during the trip—he said they had had to exit the plane by the rear door instead of the front door—and that Clinton could have engaged them in dialogue on the budget during the long flights to and from Israel, but chose not to do so. The incident, Gingrich told the press, caused him to take a harder line in his budget negotiations with the White House. Critics lambasted Gingrich, calling him a "crybaby." The event helped turn public opinion against the Republican position. Congressional phone lines were flooded with complaints. The budget impasse was resolved, and the government resumed normal operations.

The Reform Party

The Reform Party is a political organization created in 1995 by Texas billionaire Ross Perot (1930–) to further his campaign for president. Perot was unsuccessful in his bid in 1996, and the party was subsequently torn apart by conflicts between his followers and those of two party newcomers—Jesse Ventura (1951–), who won the Minnesota governorship in 1998, and Pat Buchanan (1938–), who ran unsuccessfully for president in 2000.

The Perot Years Perot made a surprisingly strong showing as an independent candidate in the 1992 presidential election, garnering about 19 percent of the popular vote to finish in third place. Three years later he inspired his followers to found a new political party. Hurried petition drives got the party certified and on the presidential ballot election in as many states as possible. In November 1995 the Reform Party received its first official recognition from the state of California. The following summer it held its first national convention.

On August 18, 1996, Perot accepted the party's nomination for president. Because of his performance in the 1992 race, he was eligible for millions of dollars in matching campaign funds from the federal government. Perot's 1996 platform called for reducing the federal deficit; campaign reforms; and opposition to the North American Free Trade Agreement (NAFTA). Perot captured about 9 percent of the vote in 1996—enough to secure matching campaign funds for the party for the next presidential election, but not enough to get on the ballot in some states (many states have a 10 percent threshold).

Deep Divisions Arise In 1998 the party's Minnesota chapter helped Ventura, a former professional wrestler and mayor of Brooklyn Park, Minnesota, win the governor's office. Ventura resented attempts by the national leadership to take credit for his victory and distanced himself from the party. He became more disillusioned in 1999 when Buchanan left the Republican Party for the Reform Party and made clear his intentions to run for president in 2000. Ventura and his followers left the Reform Party soon afterward. A court battle for party

Minnesota Governor Jesse Ventura testifying before Congress in 2001. Ventura was the first Reform Party candidate to win statewide office. © *Reuters/CORBIS*

leadership ensued between the Perot and Buchanan factions. When Buchanan's camp emerged victorious, Perot and his followers also abandoned the Reform Party.

In the 2000 presidential election Buchanan, as the Reform Party candidate, garnered 0.4 percent of the popular vote. His showing resulted in the loss of ballot access in many states and no chance for matching federal campaign funds for the 2004 election. In 2002 many of Buchanan's followers left the Reform Party for the Constitution Party and the newly formed America First Party. The Reform Party was severely crippled by these defections. In 2004 it did not field a candidate for president; instead, many of its remaining chapters endorsed independent candidate Ralph Nader (1934–).

See also **Ross Perot**

The Green Party

The Green Party is a political party that rose to national prominence by fielding consumer advocate Ralph Nader (1934–) as a candidate in the 1996 and 2000 presidential elections. The Green Party began in the United States as an informal offshoot of the European Greens, a federation of European political parties devoted to environmental issues and social justice. The Green Party of the United States made a respectable showing in the 2000 presidential election, but has concentrated since that time on local and state political contests.

RALPH NADER—SHADES OF GREEN

Early in his career Ralph Nader (1937–), a graduate of Princeton University and Harvard University Law School, became active in politics and developed an interest in public safety and health issues. In 1965 he wrote *Unsafe at Any Speed: The Designed-In Dangers of the American Automobile*, a book that catapulted him to fame and triggered major changes in federal oversight of the automobile industry. During the following decades Nader's outspoken activism earned him a reputation as a consumer advocate fighting corporate interests. In 1992 he ran for president as an independent write-in candidate. Nader was critical of both major political parties, claiming there was virtually no difference between them.

In early 1996 Green Party leaders persuaded Nader to run on their ticket in the California election for president. Greens in other states seized this opportunity to gain national recognition for the party. Although Nader never officially joined the Green Party, he identified with many of its political goals. Despite his late entry into the race and lack of campaigning, Nader garnered enough votes to encourage a second run on the Green ticket. His 2000 presidential campaign raised more than $4 million and received endorsements from Hollywood celebrities and other public figures. However, a furor arose among his liberal supporters because the final election result was so close: he was accused of siphoning votes away from Democrat Al Gore (1948–) and helping propel Republican George W. Bush (1946–) into the White House. Nader adamantly disagreed, saying that the Gore campaign had been lackluster and failed on its own.

In 2003 Nader chose Green activist Peter Camejo (1939–) as his vice presidential running mate and hoped to win the endorsement of the Green Party; however, he was disappointed at its national convention. The Green Party chose two of its members—attorney David Cobb (1962–) for president and businesswoman Pat LaMarche (1960–) for vice president. Nader ran as an independent, garnering slightly more than four hundred thousand votes—less than 0.4 percent of the popular vote. Nader did not receive any electoral votes in any of the presidential elections in which he participated.

A "Grassroots" Party The Green Party began in the United States with organizations at the local and state level. This "grassroots" origin became one of its greatest recruiting points. Gradually two factions emerged within the party—one moderate and one more leftist in its political philosophy. The latter faction began calling itself The Greens/Green Party USA and splintered away from the main group.

In 1996 the Association of State Green Parties (ASGP) formed to consolidate the power of the moderate state and local chapters and recruited Nader to run for president. The ASGP managed to get Nader on the ballot in twenty-two states, despite its raising only a few thousand dollars in campaign financing. Nader garnered slightly more than seven hundred thousand votes, representing less than 1 percent of the popular vote. The ASGP capitalized on its experiences in the first election and conducted a much more sophisticated campaign for Nader in 2000. He received nearly 2.9 million votes (2.7 percent of the popular vote) to come in third, after the Republican candidate, Texas Governor George W. Bush (1946–), and the Democratic candidate, Vice President Al Gore (1948–). Gore's camp complained bitterly that Nader's entry into the race diverted votes from their candidate and gave the win to Bush.

In 2001 the AGSP became the Green Party of the United States and was officially recognized by the Federal Election Commission. That recognition allowed the party to accept much higher campaign contributions from individual donors. After a split with Nader, the party fielded a virtually unknown candidate—David Cobb (1962–), a Texas lawyer—in the 2004 presidential election. Cobb received less than 0.1 percent of the popular vote.

The Green Party Platform At its convention in 2000 the Green Party ratified "ten key values" that represented its priorities and goals: grassroots democracy; social justice and equal opportunity; ecological wisdom; nonviolence; decentralization of wealth and power; community-based economics and economic justice; feminism and

Consumer rights advocate and Green Party presidential candidate Ralph Nader, 1996. © AP/Wide World Photos

gender equity; respect for diversity; personal and global responsibility; and future focus and sustainability, especially in regard to natural resources, economic development, and fiscal policies.

The Post-Nader Party Following Nader's split with the Green Party it faded on the national political scene. In 2007 the party reported that more than two hundred members held elected local offices in more than two dozen states, mostly in California, Pennsylvania, and Wisconsin. Because the Green Party failed to garner at least 5 percent of the popular vote in the 2004 presidential election, it was rendered ineligible for matching campaign funds from the federal government for the 2008 presidential election.

See also **Ralph Nader**

✪ Current Events and Social Movements

The AIDS Crisis

The AIDS (Acquired Immunodeficiency Syndrome) crisis began in the United States in 1981 when an unknown, potentially fatal disease was diagnosed in previously healthy people. Initially, AIDS was found mostly in gay men and those who injected illegal drugs, giving it a social and political stigma. The government's response in the early years was lackluster, reflecting indifference or ignorance about the seriousness of the threat. As the death rate from AIDS increased, a kind of public hysteria developed, particularly as the disease began to spread into more mainstream populations. By the mid 1990s new medications had turned AIDS into a chronic—and in many cases manageable—disease in the United States and other wealthy nations. Public concern shifted to the toll that AIDS was taking in Africa and other parts of the developing world. The U.S. government pledged billions of dollars worldwide in the fight against AIDS.

AIDS in the 1980s In 1981 doctors began reporting that they had diagnosed dozens of young, previously healthy, gay men with rare illnesses that usually afflict only people with severely weakened immune systems. Public health officials and medical specialists suspected that an unidentified infectious agent was to blame. They initially called it gay-related immune deficiency syndrome (GRIDS); the name was changed in 1982 to acquired immunodeficiency syndrome (AIDS) to reflect occurrences outside the gay community, primarily in people who injected drugs and recent Haitian immigrants to the United States. More than four hundred cases were reported in 1982, and more than one hundred fifty people died from the disease. Although media coverage made the public aware of the disease, its association with homosexuality and drug use limited concern about its spread in the general population. Some commentators claimed those infected with AIDS were to

blame because they engaged in what was seen as risky and immoral behavior.

Public concern rose dramatically when medical authorities began to report cases of AIDS in heterosexual women and people who had received blood transfusions. Fears grew about the safety of the nation's blood supply and about contracting the disease through casual contact. Although government researchers assured the public that the disease was spread through sexual activity, the sharing of needles, and blood transfers, public anxiety about AIDS and discrimination against those who had been diagnosed with AIDS became serious problems. By mid 1984 nearly five thousand Americans had been diagnosed with the disease, and more than 75 percent of them had died. That year brought the first major breakthrough when scientists identified the infectious agent that causes AIDS: the human immunodeficiency virus (HIV). The first drug specifically targeting AIDS was also developed that year. It did not provide a cure; however, it did slow the progress of the disease in those who were infected.

When actor Rock Hudson (1925–1985) died from AIDS in 1985—he was the first major public figure whose death was attributed to the disease—the news shocked the public and increased its anxiety. Then in Russiaville, Indiana, Ryan White (1971–1990), a thirteen-year-old boy, was barred from his school after he contracted AIDS from a tainted blood product. White suffered from hemophilia, a blood disease that is treated with frequent blood transfusions. The boy took classes via a special telephone hookup while his family fought the school's decision for more than a year. After officials relented and readmitted the boy, he attended school for only one day before being barred again because of a lawsuit filed by a group of parents. The suit was later dropped. In 1987 White's family relocated to another town where the boy attended school without incident. However, his cause had attracted widespread attention, and he became a symbol of the nation's fear and hostility toward people with AIDS. He was befriended by major celebrities, featured on the cover of national magazines, and spoke frequently on television news shows. White died from AIDS in 1990 at age eighteen. More than fifteen hundred people attended his funeral, including first lady Barbara Bush (1925–).

In 1989 the government reported that more than one hundred fourteen thousand Americans had been diagnosed with AIDS since the disease was first discovered. Nearly fifteen hundred of the cases were in infants younger than age five who had been infected while still in the womb or while being breastfed.

The Government's Initial Response The first medical reports about the mysterious new illness stirred action by the nation's public health professionals. At the federal level this effort was waged primarily by the National Institutes of Health (NIH) and the Centers for Disease

AIDS activists in San Francisco, 1983.   © *Bettmann/CORBIS*

Control and Prevention (CDC). Both are agencies of the Department of Health and Human Services (HHS). The NIH immediately accepted AIDS patients into its clinical center and began processing requests from researchers for public grant money to study the disease. The CDC took primary responsibility for investigating AIDS outbreaks for epidemiological factors (for example, factors that influence the spread and control of the disease). In 1981 HHS spent $200,000 on AIDS research; in 1989 expenditures exceeded $1 billion.

The AIDS crisis began during the first year of the presidency of Ronald Reagan (1911–2004). He had been elected in 1980 on a popular mandate of deregulation, lowered taxes, and less government intervention in the lives of Americans. Reagan was a conservative Republican, and many of his supporters were members of the Moral Majority, a religious/political movement that considered homosexuality and drug use to be sinful. The more vocal of its members publicly hinted that AIDS was God's punishment for immoral behavior. AIDS received little attention from the White House during the early years of the epidemic. The president did not speak publicly about AIDS during this time, and an official policy was not developed for dealing with the health crisis.

In 1981 Reagan appointed C. Everett Koop (1916–) to be the nation's surgeon general. Koop watched uneasily as the epidemic worsened with no reaction from the White House. He later claimed that he was prevented access to the president by Reagan's inner circle. Finally in 1985 Reagan asked Koop to write a report for the American people about AIDS. Three million copies of the sixteen-page report were distributed. The report was so frank in its discussion of sexuality and anatomical parts of the body that it caused outrage in conservative circles.

At a meeting of the president's cabinet in 1987 Koop played a major role in developing an official government policy on the AIDS crisis. He fought against mandatory testing, fearing that it would drive possible AIDS patients underground and out of reach of the public health system. In 1988 he convinced the Senate to fund the mailing of an AIDS brochure to more than one hundred million American households—the largest government mailing ever conducted. By that time it was estimated that more than one million Americans were infected with HIV. In 1989 Congress created the National Commission on AIDS to advise legislators and the president on national AIDS policy. The statute authorizing the commission expired in 1993.

THE CDC

The Centers for Disease Control and Prevention (CDC) in Atlanta, Georgia, plays a major role in the U.S. public health and security system. The CDC evolved from a World War II agency, Malaria Control in War Areas, which had been set up because malaria posed a considerable threat at military training bases in the southern United States and U.S. territories in tropical regions. On July 1, 1946, the Communicable Disease Center was created to continue and expand upon the work of the wartime agency. Its focus became the study of many diseases to determine their incidence and distribution and to find ways to control and prevent those diseases.

The center made a name for itself during the 1950s by training "disease detectives" who investigated mysterious illnesses and tracked down their causes. They also collected data leading to the development of national flu vaccines. Throughout the 1960s the center's responsibilities were expanded to cover chronic diseases; venereal diseases; tuberculosis; nutrition; occupational safety and health; immunizations; and family planning. It also recorded data on diseases that originated outside the United States. In 1970 its name was changed to the Centers for Disease Control. Over the following two decades the center played a key role in determining the causes of emerging health threats, including Legionnaire's Disease, a severe bacterial infection that usually leads to pneumonia—it got its name after an outbreak at an American Legion convention in 1976.

The CDC's image was severely damaged in the early 1970s when the media reported about the agency's role in a public health study, begun forty years earlier in Tuskegee, Alabama, which traced the progression of syphilis in hundreds of poor, uneducated African-American men. Government doctors did not treat the men with penicillin, even though it had become the drug of choice for curing the disease in the 1940s. The public was outraged when the details became public. The victims and their families received a $10 million settlement from the government. In 1997 President Bill Clinton (1946–) issued an official apology, noting "I am sorry that your federal government orchestrated a study so clearly racist."

The center's image was further tarnished in the 1970s when it orchestrated a nationwide effort to vaccinate Americans against swine flu. The agency acted after a soldier in New Jersey died from influenza. Government researchers believed the strain of influenza was very similar to the one that caused the flu epidemic of 1918 in which millions of people died worldwide. The vaccination effort proved counterproductive, however, when hundreds of people became ill and twenty-five died from a side-effect of the vaccine. The vaccination program was ended prematurely, and the swine flu epidemic never materialized.

Despite these lapses, the CDC remains a leading force in disease identification and containment. The CDC's techniques using public health networks and data to track and monitor the progress of diseases and epidemics—known as surveillance—are world-renowned, and played a key role in the eradication of smallpox in the 1960s and 1970s and the identification of AIDS in the early 1980s. Thanks to the CDC's efforts, many outbreaks of food-borne illness are traced back to their source within days of the initial infection. In 2006 the CDC celebrated its sixtieth anniversary in government service.

The AIDS Crisis in the 1990s Republican President George H. W. Bush (1924–) did not speak publicly about AIDS until early 1990, nearly two years into his term. In 1991 the National Commission on AIDS issued a report, "America Living with AIDS," that was sharply critical of the response of government and society to the health crisis. The commission complained that "the country has responded with indifference" and warned that "soon everyone will know someone who has died of AIDS." Only months after the report was issued, professional basketball player Earvin "Magic" Johnson announced that he was infected with HIV. The revelation from a popular sports hero and self-described heterosexual stunned the country. Johnson quit basketball and was named by Bush to the National Commission on AIDS. He resigned less than a year later, complaining that Bush had "dropped the ball" in the nation's fight against AIDS.

When Democrat Bill Clinton (1946–) became president in 1993, he promised to increase funding for AIDS research and make the epidemic a top priority of his administration. He held the first White House Conference on HIV and AIDS and created the White House Office of National AIDS Policy and the Presidential Advisory Council on HIV and AIDS. Government spending on AIDS research, prevention, and treatment exceeded $4 billion per year by the end of the decade.

Through the early 1990s the annual death toll from AIDS continued to rise. There were more than fifty thousand deaths per year by 1995. That same year the Food and Drug Administration approved newly developed drugs called protease inhibitors that had a dramatic effect on the AIDS epidemic. In 1996 the death rate dropped for the first time since the epidemic began and continued to decline as the decade progressed. A new AIDS drug regimen—nicknamed a "cocktail" because it mixes several potent drugs—slowed or even stopped multiplication of the virus within the body and strengthened the immune system so it could better fight off infection. The advent of the drug cocktails turned AIDS from a disease that was nearly always fatal into one that was survivable in many cases.

At the end of 1999 the CDC reported that more than four hundred thousand Americans were living with HIV or AIDS. During the 1990s the epidemic began to affect increasingly larger percentages of African-Americans, Hispanics, and women.

The AIDS Crisis in the 2000s During the early 2000s the number of people living with HIV or AIDS continued to increase, but the number of new cases reported each year decreased slightly. By 2005 the total number of Americans who had ever had HIV/AIDS was approaching one million. Approximately half of them had died. The number of HIV/AIDS deaths in 2005 (the most recent year for which data are available) was about seventeen thousand—approximately one-third of what it was a decade earlier.

The epidemic continues to spread in many developing nations, particularly in Africa, where life-saving drugs are not as widely available. In 2006 the United Nations estimated that as many as forty-seven million people worldwide were afflicted with AIDS and that between three million and six million more were becoming infected every year.

In 2003 President George W. Bush (1946–) pledged $15 billion over five years for the care and treatment of people with HIV/AIDS and prevention of the spread of the disease in developing countries. In 2007 he doubled the pledge. The initiative has been criticized because the money comes with strings attached: the prevention program relies on an "ABC strategy," in which *A*, *B*, and *C* stand for "abstinence," "be faithful," and "condom use." Strict requirements were established concerning the proportion of funds that can be allocated to each element of the program. Too much focus is placed on the A and B elements, critics say, when widespread and correct use of condoms could be much more effective in stopping the spread of HIV/AIDS.

The Iran-Contra Scandal

The Iran-Contra scandal, which erupted during the administration of Republican President Ronald Reagan (1911–2004), involved an elaborate, secret scheme in which administration officials sold weapons to Iran and used some of the profits to fund a counterrevolution in Nicaragua. The arms sales to Iran were intended to curry favor with moderate elements within the Iranian government in hopes that they could help secure the release of Americans held hostage in Lebanon. The counterrevolution in Nicaragua—led by forces known as Contras—worked to oust the communist-leaning government controlled by the Sandinistas, a leftist political party. The Sandinistas had earlier overthrown the government of Anastasio Somoza Debayle (1925–1980), whose family had ruled Nicaragua since the 1930s. Freeing American hostages and halting the spread of communism were both high priorities for Reagan; however, he denied having direct involvement in any illegal activities undertaken by high-ranking members of his government. Although criminal charges were lodged against more than a dozen officials, some were later dropped for technical reasons and others led to pardons granted by President George H. W. Bush (1924–), who was Reagan's successor.

The Scandal Unfolds The scandal first came to light in the fall of 1986 when two seemingly unrelated events occurred. The Nicaraguan government shot down a U.S. cargo plane filled with military supplies. The lone survivor of the crash admitted that he worked for the Central Intelligence Agency (CIA). Less than a month later a Lebanese publication claimed that the United States had been selling arms to Iran. U.S. Department of Justice officials learned that some of the money obtained from the Iranian arms sales had been diverted to support the Contras in Nicaragua. Attorney General Edwin Meese (1931–) appointed an independent counsel to investigate. Hearings into the matter, which lasted for nearly a year, revealed that the operation had been carried out by National Security Council (NSC) staff members who believed they had the blessing of the president. The NSC is part of the Executive Office of the President and provides advice on national security issues.

The independent counsel concluded that the arms sales to Iran certainly violated U.S. policy and possibly violated the Arms Export Control Act of 1976. U.S.-Iranian relations had been tense since the late 1970s, when U.S. embassy personnel in Iran were held hostage for more than a year. Many top officials, including Reagan, admitted knowing about the arms sales; however, legal experts disagreed about whether the sales violated U.S. law. Providing U.S. financial support to the Contras was expressly forbidden by the Boland Amendment, which Congress attached to a defense-appropriations bill. Reagan signed the law in December 1982.

The Convictions and Pardons The special counsel indicted and obtained convictions of eleven people on such charges as conspiracy, obstruction of justice, perjury, defrauding the government, and altering or destroying evidence. Among those convicted for their roles were NSC adviser John Poindexter (1936–); NSC staff member Oliver North (1943–), a lieutenant colonel in the U.S. Marine Corps; Richard Secord (1932–), a retired U.S. Air Force major general; Albert Hakim (1937–2003), an Iranian-born American citizen and business partner to Secord; NSC adviser Robert McFarlane (1937–); and Secretary of Defense Caspar Weinberger (1917–2006). The convictions of North and Poindexter were overturned on appeal because of technicalities. The charges against one defendant were dropped after the Reagan administration refused to release classified information relevant to the case.

On December 24, 1992, Bush—who had been vice president under Reagan—issued pardons for Weinberger, McFarlane, and three CIA officials. The pardons were controversial because Bush was in the last weeks of his presidency, having been defeated for re-election the month before. Only five of the original defendants were

Lieutenant Colonel Oliver North at the Iran-Contra hearings. © *UPI/Bettmann/Corbis*

sentenced for their crimes. Four of them (including Secord and Hakim) received probation and fines; the fifth served sixteen months in prison for income-tax fraud.

The Political Effect When it first became public the Iran-Contra scandal seemed to pose a serious threat to Reagan's presidency. However, Reagan weathered the controversy because he was not directly implicated in any criminal activity. The independent counsel did complain that Reagan had shown "disregard" for laws intended to curb his presidential powers and had given his advisers the impression that he tacitly approved of their actions in the affair.

The Savings and Loan Crisis

The savings and loan (S&L) crisis occurred during the late 1980s, shortly after the S&Ls were deregulated by the government. The companies made so many unwise loans and poor business decisions that the government had to supply billions of dollars to prevent the industry from collapsing.

The Crisis Develops S&Ls first appeared in the United States in the 1800s. Their original purpose was to provide mortgage loans to working-class people not typically served by conventional banks. U.S. government officials saw them as useful to the economy because S&Ls helped the housing industry and promoted home ownership. During the early 1980s the government began loosening regulations on the institutions so they could provide more services and expand their customer base. The S&Ls had been weakened by competition from banks and by the poor economy during the 1970s.

The Depository Institutions Deregulation and Monetary Control Act of 1980 and the Garn-St. Germain Act of 1982 were parts of an overall government move during the late 1970s and early 1980s to lessen regulatory oversight on major industries. Deregulation was championed by the administrations of Jimmy Carter (1924–), a Democrat, and Ronald Reagan (1911–2004), a Republican.

The Failures Begin In 1984 a large S&L in Texas failed. Authorities discovered that the institution had been making high-risk loans and engaging in criminal activities. The following year all S&Ls in Ohio had to be closed temporarily because of lack of funds. The state allowed a few to reopen after they obtained deposit insurance from the federal government. Months later a similar situation occurred with S&Ls in Maryland. During the late 1980s a number of financially troubled S&Ls around the country were allowed to continue operating despite reporting major losses. This problem was particularly acute in Texas, which was suffering a statewide recession because of low prices for crude oil.

Charles Keating, the owner of the failed Lincoln Savings and Loan Association of Irvine, CA, appearing before the House Banking Committee, 1989. © *Bettmann/CORBIS*

In January 1987 a government report showed that the Federal Savings and Loan Insurance Corporation (FSLIC), which insured deposits in S&Ls, was in severe financial stress. Months later the failure of an S&L in California resulted in losses of more than $2 billion. The institution was operated by Charles Keating (1923–), who had made substantial campaign contributions to five senators—Alan Cranston (1914–2000), a Democrat from California; Dennis DeConcini (1937—), a Democrat from Arizona; John Glenn (1921–), a Democrat from Ohio; John McCain (1936–), a Republican from Arizona; and Donald Riegle (1938–), a Democrat from Michigan. Congress investigated the senators—the so-called Keating Five—after it was learned that they had questioned the chairman of the Federal Home Loan Bank Board about the appropriateness of investigating Keating's S&L. Although the Keating Five were chastised by Congress for their actions, no criminal activity was uncovered.

When George H. W. Bush (1924–) took office in 1989, he crafted a bailout plan for the S&L industry.

The Financial Institutions Reform, Recovery and Enforcement Act of 1989 abolished the Federal Home Loan Bank Board and the FSLIC and gave regulatory authority for S&Ls to a newly created Office of Thrift Supervision. In addition, deposit insurance responsibility was shifted to the Federal Deposit Insurance Corporation, which provides deposit insurance for conventional banks.

More than one thousand S&Ls closed during the crisis. Because deposit-insurance reserves were insufficient to cover their losses, approximately $124 billion of taxpayer money was required to back up the commitments of the failed institutions.

The Persian Gulf War

The Persian Gulf War began in August 1990 with the invasion of Kuwait by Iraq and ended in February 1991 after a U.S.-led coalition sanctioned by the United Nations drove Iraqi forces out of Kuwait. As the first major war waged by the United States since the Vietnam era, the Persian Gulf War highlighted U.S. military strengths and the use of modern technology in warfare.

The March to War In August 1990 Iraqi military forces invaded Kuwait after a dispute arose over an oil field near the border between the two countries. Iraq's action was protested by other countries in the region and around the world. The UN Security Council responded with resolutions condemning the invasion and imposed economic sanctions on Iraq. In November 1990 the council adopted Resolution 678, which authorized nations to "use all necessary means" after January 15, 1991, if Iraq did not withdraw from Kuwait.

Meanwhile the administration of Republican President George H. W. Bush (1924–) assembled a coalition of dozens of nations willing to cooperate with the United States in the use of military force against Iraq. Some, like Britain and France, committed troops to the effort, while most others pledged money or equipment. The United States was concerned that Middle Eastern oil supplies would be disrupted and that Iraq might invade Saudi Arabia. The U.S. government obtained permission from King Fahd (1921–2005) of Saudi Arabia to amass U.S. troops on Saudi soil to prevent such an incursion.

On January 13, 1991, Congress authorized the use of U.S. military force against Iraq to enforce UN Resolution 678. The vote was not overwhelming: in the House, 250 to 183; in the Senate, 52 to 47.

The Air and Ground Offensive On January 17, 1991, Operation Desert Storm began with a massive bombing campaign by the coalition against Iraqi targets and forces. Iraq responded by launching Scud missiles into Israel and Saudi Arabia. Israel was anxious to strike back at Iraq for the Scud attacks, but was persuaded not to take action by Bush because the coalition included many Arab

General Colin Powell briefing the press on the Persian Gulf War, 1991. *Terry Ashe/Time Life Pictures/Getty Images*

countries whose leaders would have rebelled against participation by Israel.

On February 24, 1991, the ground offensive began. Coalition troops swept into Kuwait and within days had routed the Iraqi military and driven it back across the border into Iraq. As they retreated the Iraqis set fire to many of Kuwait's oil wells, creating huge clouds of noxious smoke, which became an environmental disaster. On February 28, 1991, Bush declared an end to Desert Storm. The United States lost 382 troops in the Persian Gulf War, of which 147 were killed in action.

Reflections on the War The Persian Gulf War was the largest operation conducted by U.S. troops since the early 1970s. The nation's military showed off its new capabilities with so-called "smart" weapons, such as laser-guided missiles and bombs. The war was followed closely by television viewers around the world, who watched much of the action unfold live before their eyes. The success of the military operation temporarily enhanced U.S. public opinion of Bush; however, questions would linger about the appropriateness of leaving Iraqi dictator Saddam Hussein (1937–2006) in power.

UN Security Council Resolution 687 set forth the terms of the cease-fire between Iraq and Kuwait. It required Iraq to destroy any chemical or biological weapons in its possession and prohibited Iraq from acquiring or developing nuclear weapons. It also required Iraq to allow international inspection teams into Iraq to enforce the resolution. Over the following decade those inspections were at times allowed and at other times abruptly stopped by Hussein. Experts repeatedly charged that he was attempting to build nuclear weapons and refused inspections so he could hide his clandestine efforts; ultimately those charges led to war with the United States in 2003.

The Internet

The Internet is a worldwide computer network infrastructure that has provided arguably the greatest advance in communications technology since the invention of the radio. The U.S. government spearheaded the creation of the Internet in the late 1960s, and by the mid-1990s it had made the transition from obscure government and academic research tool to full-fledged consumer utility. The Internet has changed the way that personal communications and commerce are transacted throughout the world. In the areas of government and politics it has facilitated grassroots organization of political causes, enhanced fundraising efforts, and expanded the dissemination of campaign literature and propaganda. In the United States, there has also been substantial debate about regulating the Internet, primarily focused on the balance between free speech and "indecent" words and images that are transmitted over this medium.

The History of the Internet

In 1957 the Soviet Union launched the unmanned satellite Sputnik into the Earth's orbit, bringing the Cold War to a new level. Many of the same technologies that were used to put Sputnik in orbit could be used to create an Intercontinental Ballistic Missile, which would allow the Soviets to launch a nuclear attack against any point on the globe—including the United States. Sputnik convinced the U.S. government that there was an urgent need to close the "science gap" between the two superpowers, and as a result the Advanced Research Projects Agency (ARPA) was formed within the Department of Defense.

J. C. R. Licklider (1915–1990), the first head of ARPA's Information Processing Office, proposed a system to interconnect the computer networks of various ARPA projects throughout the United States, and envisioned the creation of a massive network of computers, which would result in vast amounts of information being available at the fingertips of any person connected to the network. In the 1960s it was determined that this project, called ARPAnet, would use digital packet-switching technology, as opposed to circuit-switching technology then used for telephonic communication. In 1974 Vinton Cerf (1943–) and Robert E. Kahn (1938–) developed a new method for computers to connect to the packet-switched network, coining the term "Internet" in the process. Although commercial use of packet-switched network technology started that year, it would take almost twenty years—and the widespread prevalence of the personal computer—for the Internet to reach the mainstream.

The Role of the Internet in Political Campaigns and Grassroots Organization

While certain uses of the Internet, such as electronic mail and commerce, were adopted quickly by the population at large in the 1990s, political parties were slow to embrace the medium. The November 1999 World Trade Organization (WTO) conference in Seattle, Washington, offered a glimpse of the Internet's potential as a tool in grassroots organization, as protesters from different interest groups and countries coordinated the efforts of large groups of people in unexpectedly aggressive demonstrations against the WTO and globalization policies.

Full utilization of the Internet in major U.S. political campaigns did not occur until the 2004 presidential election, spurred by a new awareness of the Internet's capabilities as a fundraising tool. The prodigious fundraising of Vermont governor Howard Dean (1948–) in preparation for the 2004 Democratic Party primaries was ascribed to his campaign's efficient use of technology, including a personal blog—an Internet journal—maintained by the candidate himself. Dean's experience showed that the Internet was a good tool for collecting small donations from a large number of Americans.

Other candidates, including, John Kerry (1943–), the candidate who eventually beat Dean for the Democratic nomination, have since emulated Dean's example.

The emerging role of the Internet in politics has not been limited to official campaign activities. In September 2004 a network television report accusing President George W. Bush (1946–) of being absent without leave from his service with the Texas Air National Guard during the Viet Nam War, was retracted after multiple political bloggers contested the authenticity of documents presented in the course of the report. This was hailed as an example of new media, amateur reporters on the Internet, trumping the power of the established media—the news division of one of America's oldest and largest television networks.

The Internet has also decreased the cost of creating and disseminating political propaganda and advertising, often through the "viral video" phenomenon, in which a video clip hosted by a free public Web site is disseminated by the recommendations of viewers to their friends and contacts. In a nation where millions of people have the ability to record photos or video using their mobile phones, any embarrassing moment in public for a person in office or seeking office can easily be recorded and broadcast around the world. For example, Senator George Allen (1952–) of Virginia lost a closely contested election in 2006 after a video of him using a racial slur against an opposition campaign worker was widely viewed on the Internet. In addition to capturing spontaneous blunders such as Allen's for posterity, viral video is also being used to disseminate low-cost political attack ads, sometimes produced by private citizens, often without the "official" approval of a candidate or political campaign.

Regulating the Internet

Although the Internet started as a U.S. government project, it has long been a question to what extent—if any—the federal government should regulate expression and transactions online. Much of the legislation aimed at regulating the Internet has focused on security concerns, such as identity theft, fraud, and electronic terrorism (or "cyberterrorism"). A 2004 survey of 269 companies found that they had lost $144 million to computer security failures, the worst of which were computer viruses and worms, followed by "denial of service" attacks. One difficulty in enforcing the law online is the Internet's international nature—many computer crimes are carried out from overseas, particularly Asia and Eastern Europe, outside of the jurisdiction of American law enforcement.

A secondary focus of American attempts to regulate the Internet has been the attempt to curtail vice, particularly pornography and online gambling—two industries that quickly and vigorously established their presences on the Internet. Jurisdiction has played a role in attempts to regulate these industries, as Internet gambling operations, in particular, have taken care to establish themselves outside of U.S. jurisdiction. Nonetheless, the government has attempted to reduce the populace's access to indecent or pornographic material, through the use of blocking software in schools and libraries. While there is a general consensus in favor of protecting children from the online activities of sexual predators, there is considerable controversy about the use of blocking software, since many of the same programs which block access to pornographic Web sites also block students' access to medical information about birth control and abortion.

Global Warming

Global warming is the accelerated warming of the Earth's temperature over the past few decades. Most scientists agree that this warming trend is the result of human activities, such as the burning of coal and oil, that load the atmosphere with carbon dioxide and other heat-trapping gases. The temperature increase has caused changes in some ecosystems around the world and, if it is not reversed, is expected to lead to major climatic changes in the future. In response to global warming many of the world's nations have pledged to abide by the Kyoto Protocol—an international agreement that set target levels for emissions of heat-trapping gases. The U.S. government did not accept the Kyoto Protocol, arguing that it unfairly excuses developing countries, such as China and India, from meeting emissions limits and places an undue economic burden on the United States.

The Scientific Background　Radiation from the sun passes through Earth's atmosphere and warms the planet. The planet then releases some of that radiation, which does not escape into outer space but is trapped in the atmosphere. Atmospheric composition plays a major role in this phenomenon. Some gases, such as water vapor, carbon dioxide, and methane are naturally found in the atmosphere and act to trap heat in the same way that glass panels trap heat in a greenhouse. The glass panels allow sunlight into the greenhouse, but prevent heat from escaping.

The naturally occurring greenhouse effect is necessary to provide a warm atmosphere conducive to life on Earth. Many scientists believe that the natural effect has been, and is being, augmented by the release of large amounts of "greenhouse gases" from human activities, such as burning fossil fuels (mostly coal and oil).

Two U.S. government agencies—the National Climatic Data Center and the Goddard Institute for Space Studies, which is part of the National Aeronautics and Space Administration (NASA)—track temperature records. According to their data the 1990s was the warmest decade of the twentieth century and the warmest decade since humans began measuring temperatures in the mid nineteenth century. The 2000s are likely to break that record—2005 was the hottest year ever

reported. The next four hottest years on record have been 1998, 2002, 2003, and 2006.

Nations Respond　The first major warning about global warming came in 1979 from the World Meteorological Organization (WMO—a nongovernmental agency under the United Nations Environment Programme, or UNEP). The WMO warned that human activities "may" cause global climate changes. In 1988 the WMO and UNEP established the Intergovernmental Panel on Climate Change (IPCC) to assess available scientific information on climate change, estimate the expected impact of climate change, and formulate strategies for responding to the problem. The first IPCC assessment report, issued in 1990, noted several alarming trends that included rising Earth temperatures and faster melting of glaciers and sea ice. A second IPCC report, issued in 1995, said the scientific evidence suggested a human influence on global climate. Additional IPCC reports released in 2001 and 2007 reaffirmed the previous findings and predicted worldwide climate disruptions because of continued global warming.

The UN Framework Convention on Climate Change
In 1992 the United Nations crafted the United Nations Framework Convention on Climate Change—an international agreement in which countries agreed to voluntary, nonbinding reductions of greenhouse gases. The agreement was signed by more than one hundred countries, including the United States. Republican President George H. W. Bush (1924–) signed the document at the United Nations Conference on Environment and Development in Rio de Janeiro, Brazil. (The conference is often referred to as the Earth Summit or the Rio Summit.) The U.S. Senate voted to approve the agreement, and it was signed into law by Bush in October 1992. The agreement became effective internationally two years later.

In 1997 delegates from 166 countries met in Kyoto, Japan, to negotiate specific binding targets for greenhouse-gas emissions. Officials of some developed nations, including the United States, argued that all countries should abide by emissions limits. Representatives from developing countries said industrialized nations were responsible for most global warming and therefore should bear the brunt of economic sacrifices to control it.

The delegates developed an agreement known as the Kyoto Protocol to the United Nations Framework Convention on Climate Change (or Kyoto Protocol, for short). Different targets were set for different countries, depending on their economic and social circumstances. Developing countries, such as China and India, were not required to commit to limits, but did have to develop national programs for dealing with climate change. Overall, the Kyoto Protocol was intended to reduce total greenhouse-gas emissions by at least 5 percent by 2012 compared with 1990 levels.

HOW TREATIES ARE MADE

A treaty is an official agreement between two or more nations. In the United States treaties are negotiated by the executive branch—by the president, the vice president, or their designees, such as State Department officials. The U.S. Constitution describes the role of the president in regard to treaties in Article 2, Section 2: "He shall have Power, by and with the Advice and Consent of the Senate, to make Treaties, provided two thirds of the Senators present concur."

The requirement for a two-thirds majority in the Senate, instead of a simple majority (more than 50 percent of those voting), makes it less likely that one political party can push a treaty through the Senate. Historically the Senate has been fairly evenly split between Democratic and Republican senators, so a bipartisan effort has been necessary to gain concurrrence on treaties.

After the Senate receives a treaty from the president, the treaty is referred to the Committee on Foreign Relations for review. The committee can make recommendations about the treaty to the Senate at large. Technically the Senate does not vote to approve a treaty; instead it votes on a "resolution of ratification," in which it formally gives its advice and consent on the treaty and empowers the president to proceed with ratification.

Most legislation dies if it does not pass by the end of each two-year session of Congress. Treaties, however, can carry over from one congressional session to the next. If a treaty gets held up in committee, it can still be considered by Congress in the next session.

The Kyoto Protocol also established an emissions trading system, which allowed countries that exceeded their limits to purchase credits from countries that emitted less than they were allowed. This provision was added to satisfy members of the U.S. delegation.

In 2005 the Kyoto Protocol went into effect after being ratified by the required number of countries. Ratifying entities included Canada, China, the European Union, India, Japan, and Russia. Democratic Vice President Al Gore Jr. (1948–) had signed the Kyoto Protocol on behalf of the United States in 1998; however, because the administration believed the Republican Senate would not ratify the protocol, it never submitted the treaty for a vote. As of mid 2007 the United States had still not ratified the Kyoto Protocol.

The U.S. Viewpoint Republican President George H. W. Bush opposed precise deadlines for carbon-dioxide limits, arguing that the extent of global warming was too uncertain to justify painful economic measures. He did sign the Global Change Research Act of 1990, which authorized formation of the U.S. Global Change Research Program (USGCRP).

After Democratic President Bill Clinton (1946–) took office in 1993, the government issued *The Climate Change Action Plan*, which included measures to reduce emissions for all greenhouse gases to 1990 levels by 2000. However, the U.S. economy grew much faster than anticipated during the 1990s, so emissions levels increased instead of decreased. In addition Congress did not provide full funding for the plan. The Clinton administration implemented some policies that did not require congressional approval. It focused on energy efficiency and renewable energy technologies and required all federal government agencies to reduce their greenhouse-gas emissions below 1990 levels by 2010. Clinton also established the U.S. Climate Change Research Initiative (USCCRI) to study global climate change and to identify priorities for public funding.

In 1997 Robert Byrd (1917–), a Democratic senator from West Virginia, and Chuck Hagel (1946–), a Republican senator from Nebraska, sponsored a nonbinding resolution that stated the U.S. Senate would not ratify any environmental treaty that did not include all nations or that damaged U.S. economic interests. The resolution passed unanimously and effectively blocked Senate consideration of the Kyoto Protocol.

When Republican President George W. Bush (1946–) took office in 2001, he established a new cabinet-level structure to oversee government investments in climate-change science and technology. The USCCRI and USGCRP were placed under the oversight of the Interagency Climate Change Science Program (CCSP), which reports integrated research sponsored by thirteen federal agencies. The CCSP is overseen by the Office of Science and Technology Policy, the Council on Environmental Quality, and the Office of Management and Budget.

In 2002 the Bush administration released U.S. Climate Action Report–2002, which acknowledged that greenhouse gases resulting from human activities were accumulating in the atmosphere and that they were causing air and ocean temperatures to rise. However, it did not rule out the role of natural factors in global warming. Bush announced that the United States planned to reduce its greenhouse-gas emissions by 18 percent by 2012 through a combination of existing regulations and voluntary, incentive-based measures. Bush repeatedly said that he did not support U.S. ratification of the Kyoto Protocol because it does not require developing countries, mainly China and India, to commit to emissions reductions even though China and India are major emitters of greenhouse gases.

The Internet Stock Bubble

The Internet stock "bubble" refers to a phenomenon of the late 1990s and early 2000s when stocks of Internet-related businesses increased dramatically in price. For many investors, excitement about possible financial gains

Stock traders at the Chicago Mercantile Exchange trading frantically on April 3, 2000, as a massive sell-off of technology stocks caused the market to drop dramatically. © *Reuters Corbis*

overruled sober analysis of the stocks' real value. Those who got into the buying frenzy early profited handsomely if they sold their stocks while the bubble was still growing. However, predicting if a bubble exists and, if it does, when it will "burst" is extremely difficult. Many investors waited too long and lost much of their money when Internet stock prices collapsed.

The Bubble Grows During the 1990s access to the Internet became widespread, creating new market opportunities for entrepreneurs. Analysts called it the "new economy." Investors enthusiastically poured money into the stocks of "dot.com" businesses, such as online retailers and auction houses, travel services, and Internet search engines. All of these companies were relatively new and unproven, but many people were convinced that they would be extremely profitable. Investors relied on perceived potential, rather than business history to make investment decisions. As investors bought the stock of an Internet company, its price would rise, which encour-

aged other investors to buy in anticipation of further increases. The boom in Internet stocks also boosted such related sectors as computers, microchips, and information technology.

The Fed and the Bubble In a capitalist nation, such as the United States, the government does not manage the overall economy. However, the government does have some influence on the financial decisions made in the private sector. This is particularly true of the Federal Reserve (the Fed), which is the nation's central bank. Its decisions affect the amount of money circulating in the United States and the interest rates charged by banks to their customers.

In 1999 Alan Greenspan (1926–), the chairman of the Federal Reserve's Board of Governors, acknowledged that many goods and services were moving from traditional markets onto the Internet. "[U]ndoubtedly some of these small companies whose stock prices are going through the roof will succeed," Greenspan said.

"They may well justify even higher prices. The vast majority, however, are almost certain to fail. That is the way the markets tend to work in this regard." Greenspan's words failed to change investors' minds.

The Bubble Bursts   Very few of the new Internet businesses managed to turn much of a profit. Many lost money because of poor business planning, lack of experience, failure to build a customer base, or widespread competition. When enough investors realized their stocks had become overvalued—meaning that the stocks' increased prices could not be sustained by the companies' actual financial performance—a selling frenzy began. Stock prices for Internet companies plummeted. Affiliated businesses were hurt as well.

NASDAQ is a U.S.-based stock market on which the stocks of many technology companies are traded. The NASDAQ composite index is a measure of the performance of many of the stocks listed on NASDAQ. In 1990 the index was below 500. In early 2000 the index peaked above 4,000—the height of the Internet stock bubble. By late 2002 the NASDAQ composite index had dropped to about 1,200.

The 2000 Presidential Election

The 2000 presidential election was one of the closest and most contentious races in U.S. history. The two major-party candidates were Vice President Albert Gore Jr. (1948–), a Democrat from Tennessee, and Texas Governor George W. Bush (1946–), a Republican. The final outcome was delayed for more than a month after the election because of legal wrangling over a vote recount in Florida, where only a few hundred votes separated the two candidates.

The Race   Polling throughout most of the campaign indicated that the race was very close. One candidate would pull ahead temporarily and then lose the lead. Gallup polls conducted a month before the election indicated that prospective voters saw little difference between the two candidates in terms of their policies and leadership abilities. However, Bush outpolled Gore when respondents were asked to rate the two men on their honesty and trustworthiness. In the days leading up to the election, most polls gave Bush a very slight lead.

How the Outcome Is Determined   The president and vice president are actually elected indirectly: electors in each state who are pledged to specific candidates cast votes in state capitals forty-one days after the election. The candidate who wins the most popular votes in a state usually wins the electoral vote in that state. Since 1964 the number of electors has been set at 538, with the number in each state equal to the number of seats allocated to that state in the House of Representatives. To win an election, a candidate must get at least 270 electoral votes. Candidates often win many more popular votes in some states than in others, so the final out-

Vice-President Al Gore addressing the press on November 8, 2000, to discuss his decision to retract his election-night concession.   © *Reuters/CORBIS*

come is determined by which candidate carries which states. On election day interest is focused on the states with many electoral votes. In the 2000 presidential election, the states with the largest number of electoral college votes were California (fifty-four), New York (thirty-three), Texas (thirty-two), Florida (twenty-five), Pennsylvania (twenty-three), and Illinois (twenty-two).

As the votes were counted on November 7, 2000, it soon became apparent that Florida was going to be a "swing" state—its electoral votes could go to either candidate—and play a major role in the election's outcome. By the time the polls closed it was clear Gore had won in Illinois, New York and Pennsylvania. Shortly before 8 P.M. Eastern Standard Time all of the television networks projected a win for Gore in Florida. Two hours later the networks issued a retraction and declared the state for Bush. This gave Bush a sizable lead in electoral votes, as he had already won most of the Southeast and Midwest and his home state of Texas. Although Gore got a sizable jump late in the evening by winning California, most other western states went to Bush. Shortly after 2 A.M. the networks declared Bush the nationwide winner. Gore called Bush and conceded the election.

Less than an hour later vote counts still coming in from Florida revealed that Bush's lead there had shrunk dramatically. Gore retracted his concession. At 4:15 A.M.

Supporters of both presidential candidates demonstrating in front of the U.S. Supreme Court in Washington, D.C., on December 11, 2000. © *Reuters/CORBIS*

the networks retracted their projection of a Bush win, admitting that the Florida vote made the race too close to call. As Americans woke up on November 8 they discovered that neither candidate had captured the 270 electoral votes needed to win the election. The final tally in Florida was going to decide the presidency.

The Florida Recount   Because the vote was so close in Florida—less than half of one percent of votes separated the two candidates—a mechanical recount was automatically triggered. It was completed on November 10 and gave Bush a win by only a few hundred votes. However, the state was still waiting for absentee ballots to come in, so the final tally was not certain.

Soon after the mechanical recount began, Gore's lawyers requested a recount by hand of ballots cast in four hotly contested counties—Broward, Miami-Dade, Palm Beach, and Volusia. Bush's lawyers went to federal court to halt the manual recounts. Over the following days numerous lawsuits were filed by both parties. Florida was supposed to certify its final election results by November 14. It soon became obvious that the recounts would not be completed by that date. Katherine Harris

(1957–), a Republican who was then Florida's secretary of state, extended the deadline by one day. On November 15 she ordered the manual recounts to cease. The following day the Florida Supreme Court ordered the manual recounts to proceed. On November 18 a count of the absentee ballots revealed that Bush had won the state overall by 930 votes. The legal battle continued. On November 21 the Florida Supreme Court again ordered manual recounts to continue and a set a deadline of November 26 for certification of election results. On that date Harris certified the state's results minus the manual recount from Palm Beach County, because it was not completed by the deadline. She declared Bush the winner in Florida by 537 votes.

Two days before the certification date Bush's legal team was granted an appeal before the U.S. Supreme Court. The court decided on December 4 in *Bush v. Palm Beach County Canvassing Board* that the Florida Supreme Court should explain its decision to extend the deadline for the manual recounts. The legal battle returned to the Florida courts. On December 8 the Florida Supreme Court ordered recounts of contested ballots in every county. The Bush team appealed that decision to the U.S. Supreme Court. On December 12, the court ruled 7 to 2 in *Bush v. Gore* that the Florida Supreme Court's recount scheme was unconstitutional. The following day Gore conceded the election to Bush.

The final, official vote count in Florida was the one certified by Harris on November 26, which gave Bush the win by only 537 votes. Florida's 25 electoral votes gave Bush a total of 271 electoral votes, enough to clinch the presidency. Nationwide he received 50.5 million popular votes compared with 60 million cast for Gore. It was only the fourth time in U.S. history that the winner of the popular vote did not win the presidency. The previous occurrences were in 1824, 1876, and 1888.

The Disputed Florida Ballots The Gore campaign chose the four Florida counties for manual recounts largely because the counties used punch-card voting. In that system voters receive paper ballots printed with the names of the candidates. Next to each name is a pre-scored square or circle that the voters punch out with a stylus—a pointed instrument—to indicate their choices. The tiny pieces of punched-out paper are called "chads." Completed punch cards are fed through a machine that detects the punches and tallies the votes. Ballots with incompletely punched holes are rejected by the machines. Ballots that do not clearly indicate a selection are called "undervotes." Undervotes may or may not be counted manually at the county's discretion. Immediately after the polls closed thousands of undervotes were reported in the four counties that Gore targeted. He hoped that manual analysis of the punch cards in those counties would change many of the undervotes to votes for him.

The manual recount was covered extensively by the media. It soon became apparent that counting punch-card undervotes was fraught with problems. Television viewers watched as local elections officials with enormous magnifying glasses examined individual punch cards looking for hanging chads—chads that had not been completely dislodged from the punch cards—or even indentations in still intact chads. The latter were called "dimpled chads" or "pregnant chads." Officials assumed that voters had attempted to punch out the chads, but had been unsuccessful. Debate soon arose over the practices used by elections official to interpret voter intent on contested punch cards.

An additional controversy erupted over the layout of the punch-card ballot used in Palm Beach County.

DISENFRANCHISED VOTERS

Disenfranchised voters are those who have been denied their legal right to vote. In common usage, the word *disenfranchisement* is also used to describe any circumstance that discourages voters from voting. The 2000 presidential election in Florida was noteworthy not only for the closeness of the race and for disputed ballots, but also for generating thousands of complaints (mostly from minorities) about obstacles that kept people from voting. The Voting Rights Act of 1965 forbids discrimination against voters on account of race, color, religion, sex, age, disability, or national origin.

The U.S. Commission on Civil Rights (USCCR) is an independent bipartisan agency that investigates voting irregularities. In early 2001 the commission heard testimony from hundreds of witnesses regarding their Florida election experiences. The most common complaints came from voters who had been turned away from the polls because their names were not on precinct voter lists. Several poll workers testified that they tried to verify registration status in such cases, but the phone lines to their supervisors' offices were constantly busy or not answered. Most poll workers said they were unaware that Florida law allowed these people to vote as long as they signed an affidavit swearing that they were registered voters.

The USCCR also heard many complaints about polling places that closed early, moved without providing advanced notice to voters, or turned away voters who were waiting in line at closing time. Some African-American witnesses testified that they were turned away by poll workers who allowed white voters to enter.

Others complained about a Florida Highway Patrol roadblock set up on a major road near a polling place that served neighborhoods with large minority populations. Although the highway-patrol officials denied that the roadblock was intended to disenfranchise minority voters, the commission noted that its presence was perceived by some local residents as voter intimidation.

Florida's Voter Registration Act allows residents to register to vote in several places; for example, they can register at the Department of Highway Safety and Motor Vehicles when they apply for or renew a driver's license. The USCCR documented many instances in which the information for these "motor voters" was not filed with local elections offices.

The commission concluded that there had been "widespread denial of voting rights" in Florida because of "injustice, ineptitude, and inefficiency." It further stated that "disenfranchisement of Florida's voters fell most harshly on the shoulders of black voters." This statement was based in part on the high level of rejected ballots reported for African-American voters. The ballots were rejected primarily for overvoting (more than one candidate selected for a particular office). Overvoting can be caught by sophisticated voting equipment that allows voters to correct their mistakes. The USCCR found that minority communities were less likely to have this sophisticated equipment than white communities. As a result African-American voters were nearly ten times more likely than nonblack voters to have their ballots rejected.

Typically a punch card has two columns of candidate names with prescored chads to the right of the names. Palm Beach County officials had laid out their ballot as a "butterfly" with all the prescored chads in a single column down the middle of the card. The Republican and Democratic candidates for president were listed on the left side of the card and third-party candidates were listed on the right side. Voters had to be careful to match names to chads to prevent errors.

The day after the election several private citizens sued the Palm Beach County Canvassing Board, claiming that the butterfly design had confused many voters, particularly elderly ones, into voting for the wrong candidate. This allegation seemed to be supported by data which showed that third-party presidential candidate Patrick Buchanan (1938–) received more than three thousand four hundred votes in the county—more than three times the number reported in any other Florida county. Buchanan's name was on the right-hand side of the butterfly ballot; the prescored chad for Buchanan was positioned between those for Bush and Gore. Lawyers collected affidavits from local residents who claimed that the layout of the ballot had caused them to vote for Buchanan when they had meant to vote for Gore. They asked for a countywide revote. The Florida Sup-

reme Court ultimately vetoed a revote for constitutional reasons.

The Consequences The disputed 2000 presidential election had two major consequences in American politics. First, it aggravated partisan divisions. Many Gore supporters adamantly believed that the election had been "stolen" from their candidate. They blamed elections officials in Florida—a state whose governor was Republican Jeb Bush (1953–), the brother of the president-elect; the Supreme Court, which was dominated at the time by conservative justices who had been appointed by Republican presidents; and even Ralph Nader (1934–), who ran for president in 2000 on the Green Party ticket and captured nearly three million popular votes. Second, the election spurred widespread calls for reform and modernization of election methods, particularly development of computerized voting machines.

The Terrorist Attacks of September 11, 2001

On the morning of September 11, 2001, hijackers commandeered two U.S. commercial airliners—American Airlines Flight 11 and United Airlines Flight 175—and crashed them into the twin towers of the World Trade

The west-facing wall of the Pentagon after a hijacked commercial airliner crashed into this spot on September 11, 2001. *Mail/Time Life Pictures/Getty Images*

THE WAR IN AFGHANISTAN

On October 7, 2001, the United States and its coalition partners, including Britain, began Operation Enduring Freedom with an aerial bombardment of Afghanistan. The war plan—tailored to avoid a lengthy ground campaign against guerrilla-type fighters in the mountainous terrain—relied on covert intelligence agents; special forces trained in counterterrorist actions; air power; and opposition forces within Afghanistan, such as the Northern Alliance, a coalition of Afghani forces that had been fighting each other but united to rout the Taliban from the country. Only a relatively small number of U.S. ground troops were required. By the end of December 2001 the Taliban government had been removed from power.

Afghan opposition leaders met with officials of the United Nations in Bonn, Germany, to work out a plan for a new permanent government for Afghanistan and to ensure security, reconstruction, and political stability. UN officials called for a multinational military force, the International Security Assistance Force (ISAF), to secure Kabul, Afghanistan's capital. In 2003 the North Atlantic Treaty Organization (NATO) assumed control of ISAF and expanded its area of responsibility. In 2006 ISAF relieved U.S. and allied troops of security details in southern Afghanistan and assumed responsibility for the entire country. Nearly twelve thousand U.S. troops became part of ISAF, and thousands more continued to train and equip Afghani police and army forces.

As of mid 2007 more than two hundred U.S. military personnel had died in combat in Operation Enduring Freedom and more than one thousand two hundred had been wounded.

Center in New York. A short while later a third hijacked plane—American Airlines Flight 77—was crashed into the Pentagon outside Washington, D.C. A fourth plane—United Airlines Flight 93—crashed in a field in Pennsylvania after passengers decided to resist the hijackers who had taken control. Its intended target is unknown. Because the planes were laden with jet fuel, the crashes ignited massive fires. Both World Trade Center towers collapsed after burning for more than an hour. The attacks killed more than two thousand nine hundred people.

Within hours intelligence agencies had learned that the hijackers were associated with the militant Islamist group al-Qaeda, led by Osama bin Laden (1957–), the son of a wealthy Saudi family, and aided by the Taliban government of Afghanistan. The attacks—the most extensive and orchestrated terrorist attacks in U.S. history—led to an invasion of Afghanistan by U.S. and allied forces.

The Government Reacts President George W. Bush (1946–) was visiting a Florida school at the time the planes crashed. He spoke briefly on television, indicating that the country had experienced "an apparent terrorist attack," and then disappeared from public view for hours as he was flown from one military installation to another for security reasons. Meanwhile the White House, Capitol, and other government buildings were evacuated. The first lady, the vice president, and other top officials were taken to secure locations. The Federal Aviation Administration grounded all domestic air flights and diverted U.S.-bound transatlantic flights to Canada.

Bush returned to Washington, D.C., late in the afternoon. That evening, in a nationally televised address, he promised to bring the terrorists to justice and noted "we will make no distinction between the terrorists who committed these acts and those who harbor them."

Three days later Congress authorized the president to use "all necessary and appropriate force" against those found to have been involved in the terrorist attacks. On September 20, 2001, before a joint session of Congress, Bush issued an ultimatum to Afghanistan's Taliban government. He wanted all al-Qaeda leaders turned over to U.S. authorities; all terrorist training camps closed; and every terrorist handed over to the appropriate authorities. The demands were not open to negotiation: "The Taliban must act, and act immediately," Bush warned. "They will hand over the terrorists, or they will share in their fate." The Taliban rejected the ultimatum.

The United States and allied forces launched a war against Afghanistan and drove the Taliban from power in less than three months. A multinational peacekeeping force was assembled to help U.S. forces secure the country, while a new government was installed. Although the military operation was deemed a success, security was difficult to maintain in Afghanistan because of continued rebel uprisings. In addition the U.S. failed to locate bin Laden.

The Victims of September 11, 2001 The vast majority of casualties from the attacks were at the World Trade Center towers. More than two thousand seven hundred people died there; about two hundred died at the Pentagon; and forty-three at the Pennsylvania crash site. The area of wreckage and debris at the World Trade Center site became known as "ground zero." Rescue, recovery, and cleanup operations lasted for months. More than $1 billion in charitable contributions was raised for the victims and their families.

Within two weeks of the attacks Congress passed the Air Transportation Safety and System Stabilization Act to provide financial assistance to the airlines—lawmakers feared that lawsuits might bankrupt the industry—and to protect the U.S. economy. Congress also created the September 11th Victim Compensation Fund of 2001 to provide public compensation to victims (or their relatives) who had been killed or physically injured in the attacks. The fund, which was available to claimants who agreed not to sue the airline companies, paid out about $7 billion to the survivors of

The World Trade Center in New York after being hit by two hijacked commercial airliners in the terrorist attacks of September 11, 2001. *Helene Seligman/AFP/Getty Images*

2,880, or 97 percent, of the individuals killed in the attacks. Some 2,680 injured persons were also compensated by the fund. The average death award was in excess of $2 million per claim; the average injury award was approximately $400,000.

The 9/11 Commission Report In 2002 the president and Congress created the National Commission on Terrorist Attacks upon the United States to investigate all of the circumstances relating to the terrorist attacks. For nearly two years the commission reviewed relevant documents and interviewed more than one thousand people, including captured al-Qaeda operatives, to re-create the events leading up to and occurring on and after September 11, 2001. Its report, which became known as *The 9/11 Commission Report*, traces the plotting, execution, and aftermath of the attacks. The commission learned that all nineteen hijackers were from nations in the Middle East; sixteen of them were Saudis. Six of the men were "lead operatives"—the best trained of the team.

Four of these men, who piloted the hijacked planes, had studied for months at U.S. flight schools. The lead operatives lived in the United States for up to a year before the day of the attacks. Thirteen were "muscle hijackers" selected to assist in overpowering the flight crews and passengers. They came to the United States only months before the attacks after undergoing extensive training at al-Qaeda camps in Afghanistan.

According to the report, all of the hijackers were selected by al-Qaeda because of their willingness to martyr themselves for the Islamist cause espoused by bin Laden. However, the commission also discovered that very few people within al-Qaeda knew the details and scope of the hijack plan before it was carried out.

The War in Iraq

The war in Iraq is an extension of the "war on terror" that was initiated by the United States in the aftermath of the September 11, 2001, terrorist attacks on New York City and Washington, D.C. In March 2003 troops from the United States, Britain, and a handful of other countries, attacked Iraq in an effort to oust its dictator, Saddam Hussein (1937–2006). The military action was precipitated by claims from the intelligence community that Iraq was amassing weapons of mass destruction (WMD). These claims would later prove to be mistaken.

Military operations in Iraq were initially successful. Within weeks in 2003 long-time Iraqi dictator Hussein was removed from power, and before long a new government was installed. Reconstruction of Iraq and training of Iraqi forces to take over security duties got under way. However, a fierce insurgency erupted, driven by militant elements opposed to the occupation. Eventually the violence widened into a deadly civil struggle between Iraqi factions divided by religious and political differences. As of mid 2007 U.S. troops still occupied Iraq, and the effort to stabilize and rebuild Iraq continued. The rising toll of U.S. military casualties made the American public dissatisfied with the progress of the war and spurred calls for a timetable for withdrawal of U.S. troops.

The History of U.S.-Iraq Relations By the early 2000s the United States and Iraq had had a rocky relationship for decades. In 1967 Iraq severed diplomatic ties to protest U.S. support of Israel during the Arab-Israeli Six-Day War. In 1984 diplomatic ties were restored when the U.S. government favored Iraq in its war with neighboring Iran. However, the relationship cooled after U.S. officials condemned Hussein for using chemical weapons in that war and against the Kurds, a minority people in northern Iraq. In 1990 Iraq invaded neighboring Kuwait, ostensibly in a dispute over oil rights. Republican President George H. W. Bush (1924–) assembled an international military coalition to force Iraq to retreat. The Persian Gulf War, as it became known, quickly liberated Kuwait. It ended with UN resolutions that required

Secretary of Defense Donald Rumsfeld briefing reporters at the Pentagon in 2002.   © *Reuters/CORBIS*

Iraq to destroy any WMD that it possessed and to refrain from development of such weapons. In addition inspectors from the International Atomic Energy Agency were to be allowed into Iraq to verify that the government was abiding by the resolutions. During the next decade, however, Hussein behaved belligerently toward the United Nations, although at first he allowed inspectors into the country. In 1998 he expelled the inspectors. His continuing defiance convinced some observers that he was hiding a weapons program.

After the Persian Gulf War, U.S. and British military personnel began enforcing a "no-fly zone" over northern Iraq to prevent Hussein from attacking the Kurds from the air. Another no-fly zone was added in southern Iraq to protect the largely Shiite population from a crackdown by Hussein's government, which was predominantly Sunni. (Shiite and Sunni are two distinct sects within the religion of Islam.) Iraqi military forces often fired at U.S. and British warplanes enforcing the no-fly zones. In response, the coalition bombed Iraqi air-defense systems on the ground.

The Intelligence against Iraq   The terrorist attacks in the United States on September 11, 2001, drastically

changed the government's policy toward Iraq. President George W. Bush (1946–) disclosed later that he "wondered immediately after the attack whether Hussein's regime might have had a hand in it." Although U.S. intelligence agencies found no conclusive evidence that Iraq had been involved, suspicions lingered. Some members of the administration, including Secretary of Defense Donald Rumsfeld (1932–) and Deputy Secretary of Defense Paul Wolfowitz (1943–), advocated striking Iraq as part of Bush's "war on terror."

In early 2002 Bush described Iraq as a member of an "axis of evil" in the world. Later that year intelligence officials told the president they were certain Iraq had restarted its nuclear-weapons program and likely had new chemical and biological weapons as well. In October Congress voted to authorize the use of U.S. military force in Iraq if diplomatic efforts failed to get Iraq to submit to inspections by the IAEA.

The administration sought worldwide support for military action, but found very little. In February 2003 Secretary of State Colin Powell, in a speech before the United Nations General Assembly, asserted that the United States had evidence that Iraq had purchased uranium yellowcake, a nuclear material, from Niger. He pressed for a UN resolution that would allow the use of military force against Iraq. Although the United Nations was frustrated by Iraq's behavior toward international inspectors, it did not authorize military action.

On March 17, 2003, Bush presented his argument for war in a nationally televised address. He highlighted Iraq's failure to abide by UN resolutions regarding weapons inspections and noted that U.S. intelligence "leaves no doubt that the Iraq regime continues to possess and conceal some of the most lethal weapons ever devised." He expressed his fear that those weapons could be transferred to terrorists, who could use them against the United States. In the address he told Hussein and his sons they had forty-eight hours to leave Iraq or face military action. He promised the Iraqi people that the United States would help them build a prosperous and free country.

The War Unfolds The coalition that formed to fight the war was much smaller than the group that had joined together for the Persian Gulf War in 1991. Besides the United States, only Britain pledged large numbers of troops; some other countries contributed smaller numbers of troops—primarily Australia, Denmark, and Poland. Many traditional allies of the United States, especially France and Germany, were opposed to military action against Iraq and offered no assistance.

On March 20, 2003, the war effort—known as Operation Iraqi Freedom—began with a massive aerial bombardment followed by a ground invasion. Within three weeks U.S. troops had captured Baghdad, the capital, and British troops occupied much of southern Iraq. The nation's oil-field infrastructure had been secured with little damage, which was considered important: oil income was expected to pay for reconstruction of the country. Initially some Iraqis were jubilant about the toppling of Hussein's repressive government. However, the mood quickly evaporated as lawlessness and massive looting erupted. Coalition troops were unable to restore order in many areas. On May 1, 2003, Bush announced that major combat operations in Iraq were over. He promised that the coalition would begin securing and reconstructing Iraq.

During the summer L. Paul Bremmer (1941–), who was appointed the U.S. administrator of Iraq by Bush, created the Coalition Provisional Authority as a transitional government. Among its major tasks were establishment of an Iraqi Governing Council and oversight of the training of Iraq's Security Forces (ISF—both army and police). Bringing the ISF to full capacity and strength was considered essential to ending the coalition's occupation of Iraq.

As the summer progressed, however, insurgents began to disrupt all aspects of the reconstruction effort, including the training of Iraqi military and police officers; the rebuilding of damaged infrastructure; and production from Iraq's oil fields.

By the end of 2003 U.S. troops had killed or captured dozens of the most wanted members of Iraq's former regime, including Hussein. He was later tried for war crimes by the new Iraqi government, and was convicted and executed in 2006.

A Constitution and Elections In June 2004 UN Resolution 1546 transferred the sovereignty of Iraq from the Coalition Provisional Authority to the Iraqi Interim Government. Over the next year it hammered out a new constitution, which was approved by the Iraqi people in October 2005. Two months later Iraq held national elections.

The insurgents continued their efforts to disrupt reconstruction, however, using sniper fire, suicide bombings, and improvised explosive devices (IEDs)—usually planted along roads where they were struck by armored personnel carriers—to kill and wound Iraqi troops and civilians, as well as U.S. and British troops. The number of attacks increased dramatically in 2004, largely because of the leadership of Abu Musab al-Zarqawi (1966–2006), a Jordanian terrorist, who spearheaded an ultraviolent group, Tawhid and Jihad, that captured worldwide media attention by videotaping the beheadings of kidnapped Western civilians, primarily contractors working for the coalition. In 2005 the United States put a $25 million bounty on al-Zarqawi and accused him of waging attacks against Iraqi Shiites to spark a sectarian war. In June 2006 Zarqawi was killed in a U.S. bombing raid. However, sectarian violence continued and threatened to escalate into full-blown civil war.

No WMD After the invasion, U.S. forces searched thoroughly for weapons of mass destruction, but none were found. Bush established an investigatory commission to examine prewar intelligence about Iraq. After months of hearings, the Commission on the Intelligence Capabilities of the United States Regarding Weapons of Mass Destruction issued a report in 2005. It concluded that U.S. intelligence agencies were "dead wrong" in almost all of their prewar assessments regarding Iraq's weapons program. The commission noted that much of the U.S. intelligence was based on false information from unreliable informants and poor data sources. For example, the much-touted evidence that Iraq had purchased uranium yellowcake from Niger turned out to be based on forged documents. The commission also reported that intelligence agents had ignored information that did not fit their preconceived notions about Iraq. The report prompted Bush's critics to charge that he and his administration had used that intelligence to sustain their own preconceived notions. Some said the administration misled or lied to the American public—that it had used intelligence it knew was false—to make a convincing case for war.

The Repercussions Growing public discontent with the war caused Bush's poll ratings to plunge. In the 2006 congressional elections that dissatisfaction brought widespread success for Democratic candidates; Democrats and independents gained majority control of both the House and the Senate. The day after the election Bush accepted the resignation of his secretary of defense, Donald Rumsfeld, one of the chief architects of the war. Bush acknowledged that voters had shown their displeasure with the lack of progress in Iraq.

As of mid 2007 more than three thousand U.S. military personnel had died in Iraq, and thousands more had been wounded. Many were severely injured, with a considerable number returning to the United States as amputees. Many soldiers experienced brain trauma from the explosion of IEDs as well.

In Iraq reconstruction continued, although it was repeatedly interrupted by sectarian warfare. Thousands of Iraqis had fled to safety in neighboring countries.

More than one hundred fifty thousand U.S. troops remained in Iraq.

The Abramoff Scandal

Jack Abramoff (1959–), a highly paid lobbyist with political connections, pleaded guilty in 2006 to several criminal charges, including conspiracy to bribe public officials. The investigation of Abramoff resulted in the indictments of one former congressman and several staff members in other congressional offices. Because Abramoff agreed to cooperate with authorities as part of his plea arrangement, the scandal was still unfolding in mid 2007.

Background   A professional lobbyist is a person who is paid to influence legislation on behalf of a special-interest group, industry, or particular cause. In the early

Washington lobbyist Jack Abramoff, 2005.   © *CARLOS BARRIA/Reuters/Corbis*

1980s Abramoff made important political connections as a young man through his activities in the College Republicans, a student organization for supporters of the Republican Party. In 1994—the year he became a lobbyist for a Washington, D.C., firm—the so-called Republican Revolution swept many Republican candidates into national office and gave the party majority control in the U.S. House of Representatives for the first time in decades. Abramoff lobbied his Republican friends and associates in government on behalf of a number of high-paying clients, including several Native American tribes that operated gaming casinos.

In February 2004 the *Washington Post* published an article describing Abramoff's dealings with the tribes and the millions of dollars they paid him for his efforts on their behalf. The article noted Abramoff's ties to Michael Scanlon, who had been an aide to Tom DeLay (1947–), a Republican representative from Texas who was a powerful leader of the U.S. House. Scanlon, who operated a public relations firm, was also paid large sums of money by the tribes. Federal officials began investigating Abramoff and Scanlon because federal law places tight restrictions on how tribes that are engaged in gaming can spend their revenues.

The Scandal Erupts

In January 2006 Abramoff pleaded guilty to fraud, tax evasion, and conspiracy to bribe public officials. In exchange for his plea, he agreed to provide investigators with information about his dealings with high-ranking officials in Congress and the administration of President George W. Bush (1946–). Abramoff admitted that he had defrauded some of his tribal clients out of millions of dollars by persuading them to hire Scanlon's firm for their public-relations needs; Abramoff split the fees paid to Scanlon in a kickback scheme. Abramoff also provided investigators with details about trips, campaign contributions, and favors that he had lavished on politicians to influence their activities.

A 2006 investigation by the U.S. House Government Reform Committee showed that Abramoff had made hundreds of contacts with Bush administration officials, including Karl Rove (1950–), Bush's deputy chief of staff. As of mid 2007 the Abramoff scandal had resulted in criminal charges against several figures, including Bob Ney, a former Republican representative from Ohio, who was sentenced to more than two years in prison for conspiring to commit fraud; making false statements; and violating lobbying laws. As part of his deal with prosecutors, Scanlon pleaded guilty to conspiring to bribe a member of Congress and other public officials and agreed to pay back $19.6 million to Indian tribes that had been his clients. He also agreed to assist in the investigation and testify against Abramoff.

Hurricane Katrina

Hurricane Katrina was one of the most devastating natural disasters in the history of the United States. Hitting the Gulf Coast in August 2005, Katrina caused an estimated $81 billion in property damages and killed more than fifteen hundred people. The storm surge from the hurricane ravaged coastal areas in Mississippi and Louisiana and overwhelmed levees protecting the City of New Orleans. Low-lying areas of the city were flooded up to the rooftops of houses, stranding tens of thousands of people. A massive rescue effort was carried out by the U.S. Coast Guard. The Federal Emergency Management Agency (FEMA)—a federal agency responsible for disaster relief—was harshly criticized for its response to the disaster.

The Storm

As Hurricane Katrina approached the United States, forecasters warned that it could be one of the most powerful storms ever to hit the country. Hurricanes are rated on the Saffir-Simpson scale of intensity from Category 1 (the weakest) to Category 5 (the strongest). Katrina first crossed the southern tip of Florida as a Category 1 storm, killing seven people. Over the warm waters of the Gulf of Mexico it quickly gained strength to a Category 5 storm.

New Orleans residents carrying their belongings to shelter in the Superdome after Hurricane Katrina flooded the city, 2005. © *Michael Ainsworth/The Dallas Morning News/epa/Corbis*

Residents returning to Jefferson Parish, outside New Orleans, after Hurricane Katrina, 2005. © *Gary I. Rothstein/epa/Corbis*

Warnings were issued across the Gulf Coast, and more than one million people evacuated the area. More than seventy-five thousand people gathered at shelters. In New Orleans approximately ten thousand people sought shelter in the Superdome.

Hurricane Katrina was a strong Category 3 storm when it hit land again on the morning of August 29, 2005, just east of New Orleans near the border between Louisiana and Mississippi. The storm covered a wide area, and its winds pushed a powerful storm surge ashore. The Mississippi coastline was flooded for more than five miles inland, encompassing the cities of Gulfport and Biloxi. Structures were damaged or demolished by the combination of high winds and storm surge.

At first it appeared that New Orleans had been spared the worst of the hurricane. Damage was minimal, particularly in the downtown district. However, the Superdome lost power, leaving the people there with no air-conditioning in the sweltering summer heat and no working bathrooms. Around midday on August 29, some of the levees protecting New Orleans were breached by the enormous pressure of the water backed up behind them. More than half of New Orleans lies below sea level, so when the levees failed, water poured into the city, flooding to depths of twenty feet in some places. Desperate people climbed onto rooftops to escape

rising water. Coast Guard helicopters rescued more than a thousand people. Many of them went to the Superdome, which was already very crowded. Meanwhile, looting became a problem in downtown areas.

The FEMA Controversy Local officials claimed that FEMA acted too slowly to provide supplies and evacuate people. At first President George W. Bush (1946–) praised FEMA and its director, Michael Brown (1954–). As criticism grew Brown was relieved of his duties and returned to Washington, D.C. Days later he resigned his position. He defended his agency's actions, noting that local and state officials, not the federal government, are supposed to provide "first response" in emergencies.

In the following months more than a dozen congressional hearings investigated the government's response to the disaster. Brown complained that he received lackluster support from his superiors in the Department of Homeland Security. In February 2006 the U.S. Government Accountability Office published a report extremely critical of FEMA's handling of the Individuals and Household Program (IHP), which provides money directly to victims of natural disasters. The GAO complained that the agency's poor oversight of IHP payments, which had totaled more the $5 billion, resulted in "substantial fraud and abuse."

✪ Legislation, Court Cases, and Trials

Nixon v. Fitzgerald

In *Nixon v. Fitzgerald* (1982) the U.S. Supreme Court ruled that former president Richard Nixon (1913–1994) was immune from a civil lawsuit filed by a former Department of Defense employee who believed he had been wrongly dismissed from his job at Nixon's direction. The court found that absolute immunity is appropriate for presidents so they can act on behalf of the entire country without fear of incurring personal-damages claims from individuals aggrieved by public policy.

Background In 1968 A. Ernest Fitzgerald, a civilian analyst with the U.S. Air Force, testified before a congressional committee that cost overruns on a new C-5A transport plane could reach $2 billion, partly because of technical difficulties during development. The revelations were widely covered in the press and were considered embarrassing to Fitzgerald's superiors at the Department of Defense. The testimony occurred during the waning months of the presidency of Lyndon Johnson (1908–1973), who was succeeded by Nixon.

In January 1970 Fitzgerald lost his job, purportedly because of reorganization within the air force to cut costs and improve efficiency. His dismissal attracted press coverage and spurred calls for an official investigation. When asked publicly about the incident, Nixon promised to look into the matter. He subsequently made inquiries within his administration about transferring Fitzgerald to another position, but that idea was vetoed in writing by some of his aides who questioned Fitzgerald's loyalty. Fitzgerald protested to the Civil Service Commission (CSC) that he had been terminated unlawfully in retaliation for his 1968 testimony before the congressional committee. After a lengthy investigation a CSC examiner concluded in 1973 that no evidence supported Fitzgerald's claim that he had been dismissed as a retaliatory measure. However, the examiner did find that the dismissal violated CSC regulations because it was motivated by "reasons purely personal" and recommended that Fitzgerald be reinstated.

Fitzgerald promptly filed a civil lawsuit against several officials of the Defense Department and two White House aides. In 1978 he amended his lawsuit to include charges against Nixon. (Nixon had resigned the presidency in 1974.) Nixon's lawyers claimed their client could not be sued in a civil matter because historically immunity had been granted to high-ranking government officials in such cases. The U.S. Supreme Court agreed to consider the scope of immunity available to a president.

The Decision The court ruled 5 to 4 that a president is entitled to absolute immunity from liability for civil damages related to his official acts while in office. Justice

SEXUAL HARASSMENT AND THE PRESIDENT

During the mid 1990s the lawyers for President Bill Clinton (1946–) relied heavily on the court's decision in *Nixon v. Fitzgerald* to argue that a sexual harassment lawsuit against Clinton should be dismissed. The suit was filed by Paula Jones (1966–), a former Arkansas state employee who claimed that Clinton made unwanted sexual advances toward her when he was governor of Arkansas. She alleged that turning down his advances led to poor treatment of her by supervisors in state government.

In *Clinton v. Jones* (1997) the U.S. Supreme Court considered Clinton's claim to absolute immunity. In a unanimous decision the court ruled that absolute immunity did not apply in this case because the alleged misdeeds occurred before Clinton was president. Justice John Paul Stevens (1920–), in his opinion for the court, wrote that "immunities for acts clearly *within* official capacity are grounded in the nature of the function performed, not the identity of the actor who performed it." In addition the court noted that presidential immunity does not apply to "unofficial conduct."

In April 1998 a federal judge dismissed Jones's case against Clinton saying that it failed to meet the legal standards for proving sexual harassment and other charges made in the suit.

Lewis Powell (1907–1998), writing for the majority, noted that the court had long recognized that certain government officials are entitled to some form of immunity from suits for civil damages. The president, Powell concluded, occupies a "unique position in the constitutional scheme" and should be protected from private lawsuits that could risk "the effective functioning of government."

In a related and simultaneous case, *Harlow v. Fitzgerald*, the court ruled that Nixon's aides were not entitled to absolute immunity, but to qualified immunity. Powell's opinion describes qualified immunity as a shield from liability for civil damages so long as the conduct does not violate "clearly established statutory or constitutional rights of which a reasonable person would have known." In other words, conduct that does violate such rights is subject to civil litigation.

The Balanced-Budget Amendment

During the 1980s and 1990s several vigorous but unsuccessful attempts were made in Congress to pass an amendment to the U.S. Constitution that would force the U.S. government to balance the nation's budget each year. Republican lawmakers, in particular, made it a high political priority. When budget surpluses were achieved in the late 1990s and early 2000s the amendment movement faded.

AMENDING THE CONSTITUTION

As of mid 2007 there were twenty-seven amendments to the U.S. Constitution. Amendments 1 through 10—which are known as the Bill of Rights—were ratified by 1791. Five more amendments were added by the end of the 1800s, and the remaining dozen were ratified during the twentieth century.

The original framers of the Constitution purposely made it difficult to amend the document. Article V describes the two alternative processes that must be followed. The first requires a two-thirds majority vote in both the House of Representatives and the Senate. A two-thirds vote, rather than a simple majority (more than 50 percent), helps to ensure that an amendment enjoys broad support from the major political parties. Following congressional approval an amendment must then be ratified by at least three-fourths of the states. A second method for amending the Constitution requires the calling of a Constitutional Convention by at least two-thirds of the state legislatures. Any amendment resulting from the convention still must be ratified by three-fourths of the states. This method has never been used.

James Madison (1751–1836), one of the founding fathers and the fourth president of the United States, once wrote that the Constitution should only be amended on "certain great and extraordinary occasions." Despite this admonition more than eleven thousand amendments have been proposed in Congress over the years. In recent decades amendments have been offered on such topics as balancing the federal budget, criminalizing flag burning, imposing term limits on politicians, and protecting the rights of crime victims.

Advocates believe that a constitutional amendment, rather than conventional legislation, is the preferred way to commit the nation to a bedrock principle (such as the right of people of all races to vote, which was granted by the Fifteenth Amendment). However, many historians have argued that lawmakers often espouse amendments to gain political attention and are too quick to use them for fashionable causes that may not stand the test of time. The prime historical example is the prohibition of alcohol by the Eighteenth Amendment, which was ratified in 1919 and went into effect in 1920. It was repealed only fourteen years later by the Twenty-first Amendment.

Budget Deficits and Legislation A balanced budget occurs when the federal government spends the same amount of money that it takes in during a fiscal year. Balanced budgets have not been the norm in U.S. history. Budget deficits—when spending is greater than revenues—have occurred frequently, most often because of wartime spending or economic disruptions, such as the Great Depression. Beginning in 1970 a budget deficit occurred every year for nearly three decades.

The economy of the 1970s was plagued by energy problems, inflation, and high unemployment. These problems persisted into the early 1980s and were aggravated by growing expenses for national defense and domestic programs, such as Medicare, a health-care program for the elderly. During the 1980s the federal deficit regularly exceeded $100 billion each year. Lawmakers responded with legislation, including the Balanced Budget and Emergency Deficit Control Act of 1985 and the Budget Enforcement Act of 1990, but deficits continued to occur.

Each time a deficit occurs the Treasury Department must borrow money to cover the shortfall. Over time the government must pay back the borrowed money plus interest, diverting money from other uses. The borrowed money becomes part of the nation's debt, which represents a burden upon future taxpayers.

Pushing a Constitutional Amendment Some lawmakers have considered budget deficits so threatening to the nation's well-being that they advocated amending the U.S. Constitution to require Congress to balance the budget each year. Amending the Constitution is not easy: the measure must pass both the House of Representatives and the Senate with two-thirds majorities and then be ratified by three-fourths of the states. Only proposals with broad support from both major political parties and the public have a chance of succeeding.

Since the 1930s there have been many attempts to pass a balanced-budget amendment, but most attempts failed to make serious progress. Although the measures often found sufficient support in the House, they were stymied in the Senate. During the 1980s the political climate shifted when the newly dominant Republican Party, as part of its national platform, focused on elimination of federal deficits. Republican presidents Ronald Reagan (1911–2004) and George H. W. Bush (1924–) made a balanced-budget amendment a high priority. However, proposals were voted down in Congress in 1982, 1986, 1990, and 1992. In 1986 a balanced-budget amendment failed by only one vote in the Senate.

Democratic President Bill Clinton (1946–), who opposed a balanced-budget amendment, faced stiff opposition on the issue from the Republicans who took control of Congress in 1994. The so-called Republican Revolution was based on a platform called the Contract with America; among its prominent features was a balanced-budget amendment. Congressional votes between 1994 and 1997 did not obtain the majorities needed for passage. In 1997 a proposal failed by only one vote in the Senate.

By that time a booming U.S. economy had caused budget deficits to decline. In 1998 there was a budget surplus for the first time in nearly thirty years. Annual surpluses continued each year through fiscal year 2001. The debate about a constitutional amendment for a balanced budget faded from the political landscape.

The Return of Deficits Budget deficits returned in fiscal year 2002 during the presidency of George W.

Bush (1946–). The terrorist attacks of September 11, 2001, and subsequent wars in Afghanistan and Iraq dramatically increased government spending on national defense and homeland security. In fiscal year 2004 the deficit reached $413 billion, an all-time record. Congress passed the Deficit Reduction Act of 2005, which called for major cuts in spending on Medicare; Medicaid, the health-care program for the very poor; and student loan programs. However, hurricanes Katrina and Rita devastated the Gulf Coast region that year, causing a spike in federal spending.

In 2007 Bush proposed a long-term budget plan to achieve a balanced federal budget by fiscal year 2012. The plan assumed that Congress would slow spending on domestic programs and that U.S. expenses on the war and rebuilding in Iraq would decline dramatically. Bush's critics were doubtful that those reductions would occur.

Bob Jones University. v. United States

In *Bob Jones University v. United States* (1983) the U.S. Supreme Court ruled that private schools with racially discriminatory practices are not eligible for tax-exempt status. The case was decided along with *Goldsboro Chris-* *tian Schools, Inc. v. United States.* In both cases the private schools operated as nonprofit corporations and espoused fundamentalist Christian beliefs. Bob Jones University was opposed to interracial dating and marriage. Goldsboro Christian Schools, Inc., refused admittance to students who were not wholly or partially Caucasian. Both schools asserted that their school policies on these issues were biblically based and constitutionally protected. However, the court decided that the policies violated the public goal of eliminating racial discrimination in the schools and therefore invalidated the schools' claims to tax-exempt status.

Background In 1970 the Internal Revenue Service (IRS) ruled that it would no longer grant tax-exempt status under Section 501(c)(3) of the Internal Revenue Code to private schools that practiced racial discrimination. The ruling was prompted by a lawsuit filed earlier that year by parents of African-American children who attended public schools in Mississippi. The parents argued that the IRS should not grant tax-exempt status under 501(c)(3) to private schools in the state that discriminated against African-Americans.

Bob Jones University is a private Christian college and seminary located in Greenville, South Carolina. The

Bob Jones III, president of Bob Jones University, outside the U.S. Supreme Court on the day the university's tax exemption case was heard. © *Bettmann/CORBIS*

university had a policy, which it believed to be Bible-based, that forbade interracial dating and marriage by its students. Students who belonged to organizations that advocated interracial dating or marriage could be expelled as well. Goldsboro Christian Schools, Inc., operated a private Christian school in Goldsboro, North Carolina. Based on its interpretation of the Bible, the school refused admission to students who were not Caucasians, although it had made a few exceptions for racially mixed students with at least one Caucasian parent. Both schools fought the new IRS ruling in court, arguing that the IRS had exceeded its delegated powers and that the ruling infringed upon their rights under the religion clause of the First Amendment. That clause says "Congress shall make no law respecting an establishment of religion, or prohibiting the free exercise thereof."

The Supreme Court Decision By a vote of 8 to 1 the court ruled that the IRS had acted legally in denying tax-exempt status to the two schools. Chief Justice Warren Burger (1907–1995), in the majority opinion, wrote that the original purpose of Congress, when it created the tax benefits in Section 501(c)(3), was to encourage the development of private institutions "that serve a useful public purpose." He noted that racial discrimination in education had been found by the court in recent decades to violate national public policy and individual rights. Therefore, the discriminatory policies of Bob Jones University and Goldsboro Christian Schools, Inc., were deemed "contrary to public policy." Burger concluded that "the Government's fundamental overriding interest in eradicating racial discrimination in education substantially outweighs whatever burden denial of tax benefits places on petitioners' exercise of their religious belief."

The dissenting vote was cast by Justice William Rehnquist (1924–2005), who argued that the IRS had exceeded its authority because it interpreted Section 501(c)(3) in a manner that went beyond the original language used by Congress. Rehnquist agreed that the United States did have a "strong national policy" against racial discrimination, but noted that Congress had failed to specify this policy in Section 501(c)(3), and therefore "this Court should not legislate for Congress."

Texas v. Johnson

In *Texas v. Johnson* (1989) the U.S. Supreme Court ruled that burning the American flag is protected as free speech under the First Amendment to the U.S. Constitution. The case involved a Texas man who burned a flag during a political protest.

Background In 1984 Gregory Johnson participated in a protest march during the Republican National Convention in Dallas, Texas. He and approximately one hundred

In *Texas v. Johnson*, the Supreme Court held that flag burning is constitutionally protected expression. © *Bettmann/CORBIS*

other participants were protesting the policies of President Ronald Reagan (1911–2004). The march culminated outside the city hall, where Johnson doused an American flag with kerosene and set it afire. The protestors gathered around the burning flag and chanted, "America, the red, white, and blue, we spit on you." No one was physically injured during the incident, and the demonstrators dispersed.

Johnson was subsequently convicted of violating a Texas law that made "desecration of a venerated object" a misdemeanor offense. In particular that law defined desecrate to mean "deface, damage or otherwise physically mistreat in a way that the actor knows will seriously offend one or more persons likely to observe or discover his action." Several witnesses testified that Johnson's burning of the flag offended them. He was sentenced to a year in jail and fined $2,000. His sentence was first affirmed on appeal and then reversed by Texas courts. The U.S. Supreme Court agreed to hear the case and judge its constitutionality.

The Supreme Court Decision The court ruled 5 to 4 that Johnson's act of flag burning constituted expressive conduct protected as free speech under the First Amendment to the U.S. Constitution. Justice William Brennan (1906–1997), writing for the majority, noted that although the amendment specifically refers to "speech," the Supreme Court had long considered the protection to extend beyond the spoken and written word to conduct "with elements of communication."

The majority rejected claims from Texas authorities that Johnson's conviction was justified by the state's interest in preserving the peace. No evidence was offered that the flag burning incited a riot or would incite a riot. Furthermore, the majority said, Johnson's expressive conduct did not include "fighting words" that could have been interpreted by an onlooker as a direct personal insult or a dare to start a fight. Brennan noted that a separate Texas law prohibits disturbing the peace, but Johnson was not charged under that law. The court also rejected the state's argument that it had an interest in protecting the flag as "a symbol of nationhood and national unity." Brennan wrote that "if there is a bedrock principle underlying the First Amendment, it is that the government may not prohibit the expression of an idea simply because society finds the idea itself offensive or disagreeable."

The court's decision caused a storm of controversy. Congress responded with the Flag Protection Act of 1989, which the Supreme Court later struck down as unconstitutional. Efforts to obtain a constitutional amendment to prohibit flag burning also failed.

Cruzan v. Director, Missouri Department of Health

In *Cruzan v. Director, Missouri Department of Health* (1990) the U.S. Supreme Court upheld as constitutional the actions by the state of Missouri courts to maintain life-support for a woman in a persistent vegetative state. The woman's parents wanted the life-support removed, arguing that she would not have wanted to continue living in such a state. The court upheld the state's policy of insisting on "clear and convincing evidence" that a patient would have wanted life-support removed. The parents subsequently obtained that evidence and the tube was removed. She died shortly thereafter.

Background In 1983 Nancy Beth Cruzan, who was twenty-five years old, sustained serious injuries in an automobile accident. She was not breathing when paramedics reached her. Medical experts estimated she had been deprived of oxygen for at least twelve minutes; permanent brain damage is presumed to occur after approximately six minutes of oxygen deprivation. Cruzan was resuscitated and taken to a hospital, where doctors found she had suffered cerebral contusions. After being in a coma for several weeks, she progressed to a persistent vegetative state in which she showed some motor reflexes, but no indication of significant brain function. A feeding and hydration tube was implanted

PROTECTING THE FLAG

Many politicians expressed outrage at the U.S. Supreme Court decision in *Texas v. Johnson* that flag burning is protected free speech under the First Amendment to the U.S. Constitution. Congress passed a number of resolutions condemning the decision. President George H. W. Bush (1924–) called for passage of a constitutional amendment to make flag desecration a federal crime. At first that idea had widespread political backing, particularly with Republicans, but it quickly lost steam. Instead, legislators enacted an amendment to existing U.S. Code. It was called the Flag Protection Act of 1989 and went into effect on October 30, 1989. That very day two people were charged under the new law—Shawn Eichman in Washington, D.C., and Mark Haggerty in Seattle, Washington.

Their cases were combined and argued before the U.S. Supreme Court, which ruled 5 to 4 in *United States v. Eichman* (1990) that the new law was unconstitutional because it violated the First Amendment protections of freedom of speech. Justice William Brennan (1906–1994) wrote the majority decision, as he had in *Texas v. Johnson*. "Punishing desecration of the flag dilutes the very freedom that makes this emblem so revered, and worth revering," he wrote.

The decision spurred renewed efforts in the Bush administration to amend the Constitution to ban flag desecration. In the following years such an amendment was approved several times by the House of Representatives, but was always voted down by the Senate. Obtaining passage of a constitutional amendment is difficult: it requires a two-thirds majority vote in both houses of Congress and then ratification by at least thirty-eight states within seven years.

to provide nutrition and water. After it became apparent that Cruzan had virtually no chance of regaining her mental faculties, her parents asked the hospital to remove the tube and allow her to die. The hospital refused, and the parents obtained a court order to do so. That decision was overturned by the Supreme Court of Missouri.

The U.S. Supreme Court Decision The U.S. Supreme Court, voting 5 to 4, upheld the decision of the Missouri Supreme Court. At issue was the Fourteenth Amendment to the U.S. Constitution, which says that no state shall "deprive any person of life, liberty, or property, without due process of law." Justice William Rehnquist (1924–2005), writing for the majority, noted that the due process clause protects an individual's interest in life and in refusing life-sustaining medical treatment. However, the right is not extended to "incompetent" people because they are "unable to make an informed and voluntary choice."

The state of Missouri did have a procedure in place that allowed a surrogate—a person acting on behalf of

THE GOVERNMENT AND BIG TOBACCO

In the mid 1990s a number of state governments filed lawsuits against tobacco manufacturers to recoup Medicaid funds spent on tobacco-related illnesses. Medicaid is a health program for the poor that is funded by taxpayer money. In 1998 a "master settlement agreement" was reached between the major tobacco manufacturers and forty-six state attorneys general (Texas, Florida, Minnesota, and Mississippi settled independently). The tobacco companies accepted limitations on how they market and sell their products, including no more youth-targeted advertising, marketing, and promotion; limiting brand-name sponsorship of events with significant youth audiences; terminating outdoor advertising; banning youth access to free samples; and setting the minimum package size at twenty cigarettes. (The last requirement expired at the end of 2001.) In addition, the tobacco companies agreed to pay more than $200 billion to the states.

In his 1999 State of the Union address President Bill Clinton (1946–) promised to sue the tobacco industry to recover money spent by the federal government to treat illnesses caused by smoking. The U.S. Department of Justice filed suit, alleging that tobacco companies had misled and defrauded the public regarding the dangers of cigarette smoking. The federal government hoped to recover more than $200 billion from the companies under a federal racketeering law and force cigarette manufacturers to abide by new sales and marketing restrictions.

In 2005 a federal appeals court blocked the government's claim for monetary damages. In August 2006 a federal judge ruled that the tobacco companies had engaged in a conspiracy for decades to deceive the public about the health risks of cigarette smoking. However, she refused to impose the multi-billion-dollar damages that the government had requested. Instead, she ordered the cigarette companies to cease using labels such as "light" or "low tar" on certain brands, arguing that these labels are deceptive. She also ordered the companies to conduct an advertising campaign to warn people about the adverse health effects of smoking.

bers will necessarily be the same as the patient's would have been had she been confronted with the prospect of her situation while competent."

After the Supreme Court decision made national news, three people who had known Cruzan contacted her parents and told them about conversations in which she had said she would not want to be kept alive in a vegetative state. This evidence was presented to a Missouri court and deemed to be "clear and convincing." On December 14, 1990, the feeding and hydration tube was removed. Cruzan died on December 26, 1990, at age thirty-three.

Cipollone v. Liggett Group, Inc.

In *Cipollone v. Liggett Group, Inc.* (1992) the U.S. Supreme Court ruled that the federally mandated health warnings that appear on cigarette packages do not protect cigarette manufacturers from being sued under state personal-injury laws. The case involved a smoker who sued three cigarette manufacturers after she contracted lung cancer from smoking for more than forty years. The court ruled on the specific types of lawsuits that can be filed—mainly those involving claims of fraudulent advertising or conspiracy to mislead the public about the adverse health effects of cigarette smoking.

Background In 1983 New Jersey residents Rose Cipollone and her husband filed a lawsuit against three cigarette companies—Liggett Group, Philip Morris, and Lorillard—alleging that she had contracted lung cancer because of the harmful effects of smoking. She died in 1984. Her son, acting on behalf of her estate, filed an amended lawsuit. It alleged that the cigarettes were defective; that the manufacturers had failed to provide adequate warnings on the packages; and that the cigarette companies had been negligent in the way they researched, advertised, and promoted their product. In addition the lawsuit alleged that the companies had warranted that smoking did not have significant health consequences; had used advertising to neutralize the federally required warning labels; had failed to act upon data in their possession indicating that cigarette smoking was hazardous; and had conspired to withhold that data from the public.

The manufacturers contended that the warning label required by the Federal Cigarette Labeling and Advertising Act of 1965—"Warning: The Surgeon General has determined that cigarette smoking is dangerous to your health"—protected them from liability incurred after 1965. A jury rejected most of Cipollone's claims but found that Liggett Group had "breached its duty to warn and its express warranties" prior to 1966. However, the jury noted that Cipollone had voluntarily incurred "a known danger" by smoking cigarettes and was 80 percent responsible for her injuries. Her husband was awarded $400,000 as compensation for the breach

another—in certain cases to make life-or-death decisions for a patient deemed incompetent. The procedure required that the surrogate's actions meet as best as possible the wishes expressed by the patient while still competent. Cruzan's parents had presented the testimony of one of their daughter's roommates, who recalled that Cruzan had once said she would not wish to be kept alive in such circumstances. The Missouri Supreme Court had ruled that this was not "clear and convincing evidence" that Cruzan would want the feeding and hydration tube removed. The U.S. Supreme Court agreed. Rehnquist concluded that "there is no automatic assurance that the view of close family mem-

of warranty claim. He died after the trial. The case was appealed to the U.S. Supreme Court.

The Supreme Court Decision The Supreme Court delivered a complicated decision, in which it reversed parts of the previous judgment and affirmed other parts. Justice John Paul Stevens (1920–) wrote that the federal government's 1965 law did not preempt lawsuits seeking damages at the state level. However, the court said that such lawsuits could not claim that cigarette manufacturers failed to warn about the dangers of cigarette smoking. However, such lawsuits could claim that the manufacturers used fraudulent advertising or conspired to mislead people about the dangers of cigarette smoking.

The Supreme Court decision prompted many lawsuits against major tobacco companies. Although juries awarded a few settlements, most legal actions against "Big Tobacco" were unsuccessful because they were filed as class-action suits, in which large numbers of complainants unite to sue. Court rulings found that class-action status was not appropriate because individual issues predominated over common issues in these cases.

The Brady Handgun Violence Prevention Act of 1993

The Brady Handgun Violence Protection Act of 1993 created a national system to check the backgrounds of people who want to purchase handguns. At the time it was anticipated that a computerized system, which would provide almost instantaneous background checks, would become available in five years. In the meantime, an interim system was set up that required local law-enforcement agencies to perform background checks on prospective handgun buyers. The interim system was subsequently struck down as unconstitutional by the U.S. Supreme Court. In 1998 a federally operated computerized system for background checks went into effect to satisfy the intent of the original legislation.

President Bill Clinton signing the Brady Bill with former White House Press Secretary James S. Brady, the bill's namesake, looking on.
© *Reuters/CORBIS*

Background The act is named for James Brady (1940–), who was the White House press secretary under President Ronald Reagan (1911–2004). In 1981 Reagan and Brady were both shot during an assassination attempt. Reagan fully recovered from his injuries, but Brady was left permanently disabled from a brain injury. In the years following the shooting, he and his wife devoted themselves to the cause of gun control. This was not a popular cause with Republican leaders. Despite a groundswell of public support for gun control, legislative efforts waged during the administrations of Reagan and his successor, George H. W. Bush (1924–), were not successful. Much of the pressure against such legislation was exerted by the National Rifle Association, which promotes the rights of gun owners and provides gun-safety education.

In 1993 the political climate changed with the inauguration of Democratic President Bill Clinton (1946–), who made passage of a new gun-control bill a prominent goal of his administration. The result was the Brady Act, which passed the House of Representatives 238 to 189 and the Senate 63 to 36. The bill was essentially an amendment to the Gun Control Act of 1968, which included prohibitions on the sale of handguns by dealers to many people, including convicted felons, the mentally impaired, and people under age twenty-one. However, that legislation relied on the honesty of the buyers in providing accurate information at the time of purchase. Critics called it the "lie and buy" system.

The Brady Act required the federal government to establish a national instant background-check system by November 30, 1998. In the interim it established a temporary system that required firearms dealers to submit applications from prospective gun buyers to their local "chief law-enforcement officer" for a background check to be completed within five business days. Sheriffs in Arizona and Montana challenged the law in court, arguing that it was unconstitutional for the federal government to mandate federal duties to local law-enforcement officers. A U.S. District Court agreed, but its finding was reversed on appeal to the U.S. Circuit Court. The case then went before the U.S. Supreme Court.

The Supreme Court Decision In *Printz v. United States* the Supreme Court ruled 5 to 4 that the interim background-check system was unconstitutional. The majority decision, written by Justice Antonin Scalia (1936–), noted that the "federal government's power would be augmented immeasurably and impermissibly if it were able to impress into its service—and at no cost to itself—the police officers of the 50 states." The ruling ended mandatory background checks; however, local law-enforcement officers were free to conduct background checks voluntarily.

A Brady Act Update In 1998 the Federal Bureau of Investigation's computerized National Instant Criminal Background Check System went into effect, fulfilling the original intent of the Brady Act. Meanwhile, Brady and his wife formed the Brady Center to Prevent Gun Violence and its affiliate, the Brady Campaign, to promote stronger gun-control laws.

Universal Health Insurance

Universal health insurance is a system in which everyone is covered by some type of health insurance, whether private or public. Such plans became a high priority in the late twentieth and early twenty-first centuries: as the cost of medical care skyrocketed, and fewer workers were covered by employer-funded health plans, millions of people could not afford to buy private medical insurance. Most of them did not qualify for the government-funded insurance plans that already existed—Medicare for the elderly and Medicaid for the very poor. When uninsured people require treatment for illness or injury and cannot pay their bills, the costs are ultimately passed on to other consumers in the health-care system. Most of the advocates for universal health insurance see it has a matter of social justice—they believe that affordable health care should be a right guaranteed to all Americans.

Background Several systems have been proposed for implementing universal health insurance. In the most centralized system—often called "socialized medicine"—the doctors and other medical workers are government employees and the hospitals are owned by the government. That type of system is used in some European countries, notably the United Kingdom, and by the U.S. Veterans Administration. In another model, known as single-payer national health care, doctors have their own private practices but their fees are paid directly from a single government fund. Health-care providers and hospitals negotiate with the government to determine fees. Medicare is an example of a single-payer system. The least-centralized type of universal health care is market-based: everyone is covered, by either public or private insurance, and the costs are divided up among the consumers of health care, the government, and employers.

Two States Try It In 2006 Massachusetts lawmakers approved a comprehensive market-based system for universal health coverage that was endorsed by Republican Governor Mitt Romney (1947–). The plan required all state residents to be covered by a public or private health insurance plan by July 2007. Businesses with at least ten employees had to pay for health insurance for their employees or pay a fee to the government. The state subsidized—on a sliding scale—the cost of insurance for those residents who did not get it from their employers and could not afford it on their own. Massachusetts officials expected that the plan would reduce some costs. For example, uninsured people often go to hospital emergency rooms when they are sick because they cannot be refused treatment there; providing health insurance for those people would give them an incentive to visit doctors' offices or clinics instead, which would be much cheaper.

In January 2007 Arnold Schwarzenegger (1947–), the Republican governor of California, announced a similar proposal for insuring all of that state's thirty-six million residents.

The National Level Universal health insurance is not a new political issue at the national level. It was advocated by Democratic presidents Franklin Roosevelt (1882–1945) and Harry Truman (1884–1972) in the 1940s. Neither could muster enough public and congressional support for a program, however. In the 1990s it played a prominent role in the political agenda of Democratic President Bill Clinton (1946–). He placed health-care reform under the direction of his wife, Hillary Clinton (1947–). She chaired the President's Task Force on National Health Care Reform, which developed a plan for universal government-sponsored health-care insurance. The plan was roundly condemned for its complexity, cost, and bureaucratic nature and did not proceed further. Other proposals were offered in the following years, but, as of mid 2007, none had made headway on the national level.

The North American Free Trade Agreement

The North American Free Trade Agreement (NAFTA) is an agreement implemented in 1994 between the United States, Canada, and Mexico to lower trade barriers between the three nations. NAFTA was politically controversial when it was first introduced and passed. Criticism faded, but did not disappear, in the following years. Historically, free-trade agreements have been embraced by Republican leaders because of their commitment to lowering government impediments to business; NAFTA was politically unique, however, because it also enjoyed strong support from a Democratic president—Bill Clinton (1946–), who was instrumental in securing its passage.

Trade Barriers A tariff is a duty, or tax, imposed on imported goods by a government. Tariffs have economic, foreign-relations, and political effects. High tariffs imposed by the U.S. government on incoming products raise government revenues and give U.S. producers of the same goods a price advantage in the United States. However, the tariffs typically increase prices for the imported products, which displeases American consumers and cause foreign nations to retaliate by imposing high tariffs on American goods. Maintaining an appropriate balance between these competing interests is a challenge; the goal of the U.S. government, starting in the 1980s, was to reduce or eliminate tariffs and other trade barriers to allow easier flow of goods, services, and money between nations. This effort was called trade liberalization or free trade.

Ross Perot addressing an anti-NAFTA rally, 1993. © *Reuters/ CORBIS*

Modern Trade Agreements Following World War II the United States and the United Kingdom pushed for creation of an international trade organization to negotiate trade rules and tariff reductions between countries. The result was the General Agreement on Tariffs and Trade (GATT), which was established in 1947. In 1995 the World Trade Organization (WTO) was formed to oversee GATT and monitor other trade rules. The WTO also provides a framework for trade negotiations.

The United States forged a free-trade agreement with Israel in 1985 during the presidency of Republican Ronald Reagan (1911–2004), a staunch advocate of free trade as part of his overall economic philosophy of reducing government regulation of business. The U.S.-Israel Free Trade Area agreement gradually eliminated duties on Israeli merchandise entering the United States. It did not prevent the two countries from using other trade barriers, such as quotas, to protect certain agricultural commodities.

In 1988 the Reagan administration negotiated the U.S.-Canada Free Trade Agreement (FTA), which targeted trade in such sectors as agriculture, automobiles, energy, and financial services. It also established procedures for resolving trade disputes. The FTA received little attention in the United States, but became a major political issue in Canada. Its opponents feared the

ON THE FAST TRACK

NAFTA, like many other trade agreements adopted by the United States, came about through a legislative procedure known as "expedited consideration" or "fast track." The president or other members of the executive branch negotiate foreign agreements. However, the U.S. Constitution requires all bills raising revenue to originate in the House of Representatives and gives the Senate the opportunity to propose or concur with amendments. Because tariffs are revenues, free-trade agreements require congressional approval. However, this makes it difficult for a president to conduct negotiations in good faith, not knowing if the agreements will meet with subsequent congressional approval.

The Tariff Act of 1890 delegated tariff-bargaining authority to the president and allowed him to change or remove existing duties on particular items. This law was challenged in the U.S. Supreme Court, but upheld as constitutional. The Reciprocal Trade Agreements Act of 1934 granted the president temporary authority to enter into tariff agreements and, within certain limits, to set tariffs without obtaining subsequent congressional approval. That authority was used when the United States joined the General Agreement on Tariffs and Trade (GATT) in 1947.

The Trade Act of 1974 allowed the president to negotiate multiparty trade agreements during a set period of time and permitted him to make certain tariff reductions and modifications. It also included procedures for expedited consideration of bills resulting from trade negotiations. The fast-track provision meant that Congress could only vote yes or no on the bills—no revisions were allowed—and had to conduct the vote within a specific time period—typically ninety days.

The Trade and Tariff Act of 1984 gave the president temporary statutory authority to make bilateral (two-country) free-trade agreements. The Omnibus Trade and Competitiveness Act of 1988 extended presidential authority to enter free-trade agreements until 1993. (It was later extended to 1994). That authority and the fast track were used to negotiate NAFTA and get it passed into law.

The presidential fast-track authority expired in 1994 and was not reinstated until passage of the Trade Act of 2002, during the administration of George W. Bush (1946–). That law set a new expiration date of June 2007.

the details of NAFTA were first revealed, they drew congressional opposition, mostly from Democratic lawmakers who expressed concerns about the impact of the agreement on American workers and the environment. Bush signed NAFTA on December 17, 1992, shortly before he left office; however, the agreement still had to receive congressional approval to go into effect. Under federal law NAFTA was a congressional-executive agreement, rather than a treaty. A treaty requires a two-thirds majority in the Senate for passage; NAFTA required a simple majority (over 50 percent) in both the House and the Senate.

When he became president in 1993, Clinton pledged to continue U.S. support for NAFTA. He faced an uphill battle with members of his own party who had majority control of the U.S. House and U.S. Senate for the first two years of his presidency. Democrats were under intense pressure from their historical allies—labor unions—not to support NAFTA for fear it would drive wages down in the United States and encourage industries to move manufacturing jobs to Mexico to take advantage of cheaper, nonunionized labor. Some environmental groups also opposed NAFTA, fearing that industrial expansion in Mexico would be loosely regulated, leading to pollution problems.

Politicians at the left end of the political spectrum, including Ralph Nader (1935–) and foes of globalization, believed NAFTA would benefit only large multinational corporations and hurt middle- and working-class people. On the right, politicians such as Pat Buchanan (1938–) argued that NAFTA would weaken the nation's sovereignty and increase foreign influence over the U.S. government. Ross Perot (1930–), a Texas billionaire who had made a respectable showing as an independent candidate for president against Clinton in the 1992 presidential election, famously said that Americans would "hear a giant sucking sound" as their jobs went south into Mexico.

Despite well-funded opposition to NAFTA, Clinton managed to gain its passage with strong support from Republican lawmakers. On November 17, 1993, the North American Free Trade Agreement Implementation Act passed the House 234 to 200. Three days later it passed the Senate 61 to 38.

NAFTA Is Implemented NAFTA, which went into effect on January 1, 1994, gradually eliminated nearly all tariffs between the United States and Canada by 1998 and between the U.S. and Mexico by 2008. NAFTA also removed many nontariff barriers that helped to exclude U.S. goods from the other two markets. The agreement ended restrictive government policies on investors; included provisions to protect intellectual property rights, such as trademarks and patents; and ensured that industries and businesses in all three countries would have access to government procurement contracts.

agreement would weaken Canada's economy—and even undermine the nation's sovereignty—in the face of the much larger and stronger U.S. economy. FTA advocates prevailed, however, and the agreement went into effect in 1989. Plans for a larger free-trade area were already under way.

NAFTA Politics In 1990 newly elected President George H. W. Bush (1924–), a Republican, informed Congress that his administration intended to negotiate a free-trade agreement with Mexico. Canada soon joined the negotiations, which proceeded through 1992. When

Despite its tumultuous beginnings, NAFTA became largely a political nonissue during the prosperous decade that followed its passage. Perot tried, but failed, to make it a major concern during the 1996 presidential campaign. Opposition to NAFTA did not fade completely—it was regularly criticized as detrimental to labor standards and workers' rights and blamed for the transfer of jobs from the United States to Mexico, particularly in the manufacturing sector. This movement of jobs was part of a broader economic phenomenon known as offshoring, in which U.S. businesses relocate all or portions of their work to foreign countries, primarily developing countries where labor costs are much cheaper. Although offshoring is decried by politicians, some economists argue that it ultimately leads to lower prices for U.S. consumers, which, they say, benefits the overall economy.

Advocates of NAFTA point to data indicating increases in trade among the three nations and growth in the U.S. economy since the agreement was passed. Opponents believe the gains were the result of many factors and might have occurred without NAFTA. The administration of Republican President George W. Bush (1946–) continued the nation's strong support of NAFTA and secured passage of free-trade agreements between the United States and other countries.

United States v. Lopez

In *United States v. Lopez* (1995) the U.S. Supreme Court ruled that a federal law criminalizing the possession of a firearm in a school zone was unconstitutional because Congress had overstepped its power under the U.S. Constitution. A student in Texas, who had been arrested at school for carrying a firearm, was charged under the law. The court found that the law did not fall under the powers granted by the U.S. Constitution to the legislative branch of the federal government to regulate interstate commerce.

Background In 1992 Alfonzo Lopez, a twelfth-grader at Edison High School in San Antonio, Texas, was arrested at school for carrying a concealed .38-caliber handgun and five bullets. He was charged with violating a state law that prohibits the carrying of firearms on school grounds. The following day the state charges were dropped, and Lopez was charged under the federal Gun-Free School Zones Act of 1990. That law made it a federal offense "for any individual knowingly to possess a firearm at a place that the individual knows, or has reasonable cause to believe, is a school zone." A U.S. District Court found Lopez guilty and sentenced him to six months in prison and two years of supervision upon release. His lawyers appealed the conviction, arguing that Congress had exceeded its power in passing the federal law. The U.S. Court of Appeals agreed and reversed the conviction. The case was then brought before the U.S. Supreme Court.

Provisions of the Communications Decency Act focused on children's access to indecent material over the Internet, particularly in libraries and schools. © *O'Brien Productions/CORBIS*

The Court's Decision The court decided 5 to 4 that the reversal by the court of appeals was correct because the Gun-Free School Zones Act of 1990 was unconstitutional. Chief Justice William Rehnquist (1924–2005), who wrote for the majority, noted that Article 1, Section 8 of the U.S. Constitution says that Congress shall have power "to regulate commerce with foreign nations, and among the several states, and with the Indian Tribes." The Supreme Court has historically identified three broad categories of activities that Congress may regulate under the commerce clauses: the use of the channels of interstate commerce; the instrumentalities of interstate commerce or persons or things in interstate commerce; and activities that substantially affect interstate commerce. While the states have primary authority for defining and enforcing criminal law, Congress can pass criminal laws as long as they fall into at least one of the three categories.

The federal government argued that the law being considered fell under the last category—activities that substantially affect interstate commerce—for two

THE LIBRARY WARS

In 2000 Congress passed the Children's Internet Protection Act (CIPA), which requires public schools and libraries that receive certain types of federal funding to implement measures to keep children from viewing some content on the Internet. According to Federal Communications Commission rules implemented in 2001, schools subject to CIPA must adopt and enforce a policy to monitor the online activities of minors. Schools and libraries subject to CIPA must ensure that minors cannot access inappropriate materials, and they must protect the safety of minors using e-mail, chat rooms, and other forms of electronic communications. CIPA includes a provision that allows blocking or filtering measures to be disabled when adults want to use the computers for research or other purposes.

In 2001 the American Library Association and American Civil Liberties Union challenged the new law in federal court. The court ruled unanimously that CIPA violated the First Amendment; that Congress had exceeded its authority; and that the use of software filters was not an action sufficiently tailored to the government's interest in preventing the dissemination of harmful materials to minors.

The government appealed the ruling to the U.S. Supreme Court. In *U.S. v. American Library Association* (2003) the court, by 6 to 3, overturned the lower court's ruling. It found CIPA to be constitutional because the blocking and filtering mechanisms can be easily disabled to allow adult access to online content. Chief Justice William Rehnquist (1924–2005), writing for the court, noted, "Because public libraries' use of Internet filtering software does not violate their patrons' First Amendment rights, CIPA does not induce libraries to violate the Constitution, and is a valid exercise of Congress' spending power. Congress has wide latitude to attach conditions to the receipt of federal assistance to further its policy objectives."

reasons: first, because possession of a firearm in a school zone can result in violent crime, which has detrimental effects on the nation's economy; and second, because firearms in the schools impair the educational process, which ultimately is bad for the economy. The court rejected the validity of both claims and affirmed the decision of the court of appeals to reverse Lopez's conviction.

Democratic President Bill Clinton (1946–) publicly expressed his disappointment at the court's decision and urged lawmakers to amend the law to make it constitutionally acceptable. In the amendment Congress used new language, saying "it shall be unlawful for any individual knowingly to possess a firearm that has moved in or that otherwise affects interstate or foreign commerce at a place that the individual knows, or has reasonable cause to believe, is a school zone." In other words, the new law focuses on the firearm itself and its relationship to commerce to demonstrate Congress's authority over

the crime. The amendment was tacked on to a budget bill, the Omnibus Consolidated Appropriations Act of 1997, which was enacted as Public Law 104-208. As of mid 2007 the constitutionality of the amendment had not been challenged.

Communications Decency Act of 1996

The Communications Decency Act of 1996 prohibited the use of telecommunications equipment for obscene or harassing purposes. Its primary target was the Internet. In 1997 two provisions of the law were declared unconstitutional by the U.S. Supreme Court. Both provisions criminalized the knowing transmission of obscene or indecent materials to people younger than age eighteen. The court ruled that these provisions were overly broad and suppressed materials that adults have a constitutional right to send and receive under the First Amendment of the U.S. Constitution. In addition it ruled that some of the language used in the provisions was vague and undefined. In 1998 Congress tried again with the Child Online Protection Act. It too was declared unconstitutional by the Supreme Court.

Background The 1996 telecommunications act was the first major reform in this field since the original telecommunications act was passed in 1934. The new law dealt primarily with economic and market issues related to the telecommunications industry. However, legislators added a section, Title V: Obscenity and Violence, that was called the Communications Decency Act (CDA) of 1996. It prohibited a variety of actions, including the transmission of obscene or indecent materials to persons known to be younger than age eighteen.

The act was immediately challenged in court by a large group of petitioners, including online service providers; library and media associations; civil-liberty groups, such as the American Civil Liberties Union (ACLU); and thousands of individual Internet users. After a U.S. District Court in Pennsylvania ruled in favor of the petitioners, the federal government appealed the case to the Supreme Court.

The Supreme Court Decision The Supreme Court upheld the lower court's decision in *Reno v. American Civil Liberties Union*. Specifically, the court considered two disputed provisions of the law: Section 223(a)(1) prohibited the use of telecommunications devices to knowingly transmit any language or image communication "which is obscene or indecent" to a recipient younger than age eighteen. Section 223(d) prohibited the use of any interactive computer service to display to a person younger than age eighteen any language or image communication that "depicts or describes, in terms patently offensive as measured by contemporary community standards, sexual or excretory activities or organs."

The court ruled that the provisions violated the right of freedom of speech guaranteed by the First Amendment. In particular, the court complained that "the CDA lacks the precision that the First Amendment requires when a statute regulates the content of speech." Although the court acknowledged that the law had "legitimate purposes," it thought the provisions placed an unacceptable burden on adult speech. It pointed to other alternatives that would be as effective, such as computer software that parents could use to prevent their children from accessing material the parents considered inappropriate. In addition the court noted that the terms "indecent" and "patently offensive" were undefined in federal law. (The term "obscene" is already defined in federal law.)

Congress Tries Again In 1998 Congress passed the Child Online Protection Act in an attempt to remedy the constitutional problems with the CDA. The new law prohibited "communication for commercial purposes that is available to any minor and that includes any material that is harmful to minors." The law was immediately challenged in federal court; a temporary injunction was issued to prevent implementation of the law. Eventually, in *Ashcroft v. American Civil Liberties Union* (2004), the Supreme Court upheld the injunction as constitutional. In 2007 a federal court in Pennsylvania issued a final ruling that struck down the law for interfering with First Amendment rights.

Clinton v. City of New York

In *Clinton v. City of New York* (1998) the U.S. Supreme Court ruled that the Line Item Veto Act of 1996 was unconstitutional. The line-item veto allows a president to veto particular items in the federal budget bills passed by Congress and submitted for the president's signature. While advocates tout the presidential tool as a way to cut out wasteful federal spending, critics believe it grants too much power to the president.

Background The line-item veto, which has been sought by presidents since the Civil War, would allow a president to veto particular items in spending bills, which often contain provisions inserted by lawmakers to fund "pet projects," such as roads and bridges, in their home districts. The projects are also called "pork" because legislators can take credit for "bringing home the bacon." Advocates of the line-item veto believe that presidents should be able to eliminate expensive pet projects and pork from budget bills to save taxpayers money.

The push for the line-item veto gained momentum during the administrations of Republican presidents Richard Nixon (1913–1994), Gerald Ford (1913–2006), Ronald Reagan (1911–2004), and George H. W. Bush (1924–). It was also a prominent feature of the Contract with America, the Republican Party platform for the midterm election campaign of 1994.

In 1996 Congress passed the Line Item Veto Act. Clinton, the first president to have the authority, used the line-item veto on the Balanced Budget Act of 1997 and the

PORK

Bills crafted by Congress generally target matters of broad concern to the American people. However, members of Congress often slip in provisions, particularly in spending bills, that are beneficial only to their own constituents. Examples include funding for bridges, roads, and parks. Over the years these provisions have earned the nickname "pork." In general, a specific piece of pork is considered wasteful by everyone except those people it benefits directly. Legislators are highly motivated to get pork projects passed because the projects can earn them votes. This is particularly true for members of the House of Representatives, who face re-election every two years. The most successful purveyors of pork are said to "bring home the bacon" for their constituents.

Some projects are loudly—and quickly—branded as pork. In 2005, for example, Congress passed a $286 billion federal highway and mass transportation bill. It included about $200 million for construction of a bridge to connect the small town of Ketchikan, Alaska, to nearby Gravina Island. Ketchikan has a population of around nine thousand and the island has fewer than one hundred residents. The bridge was intended to replace the ferry to the island—the ferry trip takes about ten minutes. Critics called it "the bridge to nowhere." The bridge was championed by two powerful Alaskan lawmakers—Representative Don Young (1933–) and Senator Ted Stevens (1923–). Both are senior Republican legislators with decades of experience and positions on key congressional committees that make major funding decisions. The bridge sparked widespread criticism in the media and won the Golden Fleece Award from Taxpayers for Common Sense, an organization that calls itself a "nonpartisan budget watchdog." While Republican leaders agreed to take the bridge out of the spending bill, they provided the same amount of money for Alaska, which the state government could spend as it wished—even on the bridge. Young was reelected easily in 2006, proving that bringing home the bacon has its political rewards.

Taxpayer Relief Act of 1997. Both items he vetoed, which affected a variety of jurisdictions, including New York City, were then returned to Congress for reconsideration. After the law was ruled unconstitutional by a U.S. District Court, it ended up before the U.S. Supreme Court.

The Supreme Court Ruling The court, by 6 to 3, upheld the lower court's ruling that the line-item veto law was unconstitutional. Justice John Paul Stevens (1920–), writing for the court, noted that the law violated the presentment clauses, set out in Article I, Section 7 of the U.S. Constitution, which prescribe how a bill becomes a law. The presentment clauses say that every bill passed by Congress "shall, before it become a law, be presented to the President of the United States; if he approve he shall sign it, but if not he shall return it…" and that all orders, resolutions, or votes in which the concurrence of Congress is necessary (excluding adjournments) "shall be presented to the President of the United States; and before the same shall take effect, shall be approved by him, or being disapproved by him, shall be repassed by two thirds of the Senate and House of Representatives. . ." In other words, Stevens said, the president has only two choices—to approve or to disapprove of a bill in its entirety.

Stevens noted that if Congress wanted to implement a new procedure for presentments, such a change would have to come through an amendment to the Constitution.

The court's ruling was hailed by strict constitutionalists, but disappointed the Clinton administration as well as Republican leaders. In February 2006 Clinton's successor, Republican President George W. Bush (1946–), asked Congress for line-item veto authority in a new bill that he believed would pass constitutional muster. The bill passed the Republican-controlled House several months later but never made it to the Senate floor for a vote.

Nixon v. Shrink Missouri Government PAC

In *Nixon v. Shrink Missouri Government PAC* (2000) the U.S. Supreme Court declared constitutional a Missouri law that placed limits on the amount of money that individuals and groups could contribute to candidates running for state office. The case was initiated by a candidate for Missouri office and a political action committee (PAC) that supported him. They claimed that contribution limits violated constitutional guarantees of free speech, free association, and equal protection. The court disputed these claims and found Missouri's contribution limits to be justifiable to prevent corruption and the appearance of corruption in government.

Background In 1994 the Missouri legislature passed a law that imposed limits on campaign contributions to candidates running for state offices. The amount that each contributor was allowed to give to each candidate ranged from $250 to $1,000, depending on the size of the population represented by the office. The law allowed the limits to be raised slightly every two years to compensate for inflation. The contribution limit in 1998 for the office of Missouri state auditor was $1,075.

In 1998 Zev David Feldman, a Republican candidate for that office, received the maximum donation allowed from a PAC named Shrink Missouri Government. PACs are private organizations that raise money to support candidates who share their political interests. Feldman and the PAC alleged in court that the contribution limits violated their rights under the First and Fourteenth Amendments to the U.S. Constitution. Campaign contributions have historically been considered a form of free speech. In addition Feldman argued that the limits severely impeded his campaign efforts and that the effects of inflation were not properly accounted for in the state's limits. After a U.S. District Court ruled

against Feldman and the PAC, the case was appealed and the judgment reversed.

The U.S. Appeals Court found that Missouri had improperly based its law on the U.S. Supreme Court's decision in *Buckley v. Valeo* (1976). That case set the legal precedent for limiting campaign contributions to candidates for national office and declared the limits necessary for "avoiding the corruption or the perception of corruption caused by candidates' acceptance of large campaign contributions." The appeals court ruled that Missouri had to show "demonstrable evidence" that "genuine problems" resulted from allowing contributions greater than the limits.

The Court's Decision The Supreme Court reversed the appeals court decision, ruling 6 to 3 that *Buckley v. Valeo* was sufficient authority to impose contribution limits on candidates for state offices and for the same reasons. Justice David Souter (1939–), writing for the majority, noted "the cynical assumption that large donors call the tune could jeopardize the willingness of voters to take part in democratic governance." The court found that a showing of "demonstrable evidence" by the state was not necessary to prove a correlation between large campaign contributions and corruption or the appearance of corruption. The court also ruled that the state law did not have to match the contribution limit specified in *Buckley v. Valeo* ($1,000 per donor).

The Patriot Act

The Patriot Act, passed only weeks after the September 11, 2001, terrorist attacks on the United States, included a number of provisions intended to improve the country's security, strengthen and coordinate intelligence and law-enforcement actions against terrorists, and provide aid for people victimized by terrorism. Although considered relatively benign at first, the law soon became controversial for its implications for civil liberties, particularly with respect to surveillance procedures. The Patriot Act was renewed in 2006, but with new safeguards designed to better protect the civil rights of Americans.

Overwhelming Support The Uniting and Strengthening America by Providing Appropriate Tools Required to Intercept and Obstruct Terrorism (USA PATRIOT) Act of 2001 is known simply as the Patriot Act. It passed the House of Representatives by a vote of 357 to 66. In the Senate, only one senator voted against it—Russ Feingold (1953–), a Democrat from Wisconsin. He stated that he supported most of the law, but was deeply troubled by the civil-liberty implications of a handful of provisions.

The U.S. Department of Justice claimed that the Patriot Act made only "modest, incremental changes" to existing law related to criminal activities and made tools available in the "war on terror" that had been used for decades against other kinds of crimes, particularly organized crime and drug trafficking. These tools include surveillance techniques, such as wiretapping, and legal maneuvers, such as streamlining procedures to obtain search warrants. The law also allows federal agents to obtain business records relevant to national-security investigations without obtaining a subpoena from a grand jury. Agents make such requests to a special federal court, the Foreign Intelligence Surveillance Court (FISC), which can grant permission if the government meets certain criteria.

Criticism of the Act The Patriot Act was quickly criticized by private organizations concerned with protecting civil liberties, including the American Civil Liberties Union (ACLU) and the Electronic Privacy Information Center (EPIC). Civil libertarians worried that the law was passed so quickly in the aftermath of the September 11, 2001, terrorist attacks that few safeguards afforded by the U.S. Constitution were included.

Controversy over the FISC The FISC is made up of eleven federal district court judges. The court convenes only when needed. Much of its work is conducted in secret because of the sensitive nature of national-security matters and because it relies on classified information. According to public records, the FISC has approved thousands of applications from the government to conduct electronic surveillance as part of national-security investigations.

In 2005 the *New York Times* reported that the administration of President George W. Bush (1946–) had been conducting wiretap operations without FISC approval. The newspaper alleged that in early 2002 Bush issued a secret executive order authorizing the National Security Agency (NSA) to bypass FISC procedures for conducting domestic surveillance. The NSA oversees signals intelligence operations for the U.S. intelligence community.

The *New York Times* estimated that the international phone calls and e-mails of "hundreds, and perhaps thousands" of Americans had been monitored to search for links to international terrorism. It also acknowledged that the surveillance program helped uncover several terrorist plots against targets in the United States and Britain. According to the newspaper's account, the president based his order on his belief that a September 2001 congressional resolution granted him "broad powers" in the war on terror to protect U.S. interests. The program was reportedly suspended in mid 2004 because of a complaint from the federal judge overseeing the FISC. The program was "revamped" and continued to operate.

Repercussions The ACLU filed a lawsuit against the NSA, claiming that the surveillance program violated the First and Fourth Amendments to the U.S. Constitution and that Bush had exceeded his authority under the separation of powers outlined in the Constitution. The ACLU asked for the program to be dismantled. In August 2006 a federal judge ruled in the group's favor on grounds that the surveillance program violated the Fourth Amendment. She also found that Bush had exceeded his authority under the Constitution. Two months later a Court of Appeals panel stayed the ruling while the government appealed the decision. Top government officials continued to defend the program as necessary to combat terrorism.

Renewing the Patriot Act The original Patriot Act called for sixteen of its sections to sunset—that is, automatically expire–after four years unless they were renewed by Congress. In 2005 intense debate began about whether those sections should be renewed. Ultimately the House voted 251 to 174 to renew the provisions with some modifications. In March 2006 the USA PATRIOT Act Improvement and Reauthorization Act of 2005 passed the Senate by a vote of 89 to 10. The modified Patriot Act makes permanent fourteen of the original sixteen sunset provisions and places new four-year sunset periods on the other two provisions, which concern surveillance techniques and the acquisition of business records. The Department of Justice stated that "dozens of additional safeguards to protect Americans' privacy and civil liberties" were included as part of the reauthorization.

BIBLIOGRAPHY

Books

Binder, Sarah A., and Steven S. Smith. *Politics or Principle?: Filibustering in the United States Senate.* Washington, DC: The Brookings Institution, 1997.

Periodicals

Bartlett, Bruce. "How Supply-Side Economics Trickled Down." *New York Times*, April 6, 2007. http://select.nytimes.com/search/restricted/article?res=F60C14FC3C5B0C758CDDAD0894DF404482 (accessed April 20, 2007).

Curry, Timothy, and Lynn Shibut. "The Cost of the Savings and Loan Crisis: Truth and Consequences." *FDIC Banking Review* 13, no. 2 (2000). http://www.fdic.gov/bank/analytical/banking/2000dec/brv13n2_2.pdf (accessed May 3, 2007).

Farrell, Maureen. "The Future of Universal Health Care." *Forbes*, March 28, 2007. http://www.forbes.com/2007/03/28/unitedhealth-walmart-medicaid-ent-hr-cx_mf_0328outlookuniversal.html (accessed May 24, 2007).

Kosar, Kevin R. "Shutdown of the Federal Government: Causes, Effects, and Process." *CRS Report for Congress* (Congressional Research Service), September 20, 2004. http://www.rules.house.gov/archives/98-844.pdf (accessed May 2, 2007).

San Francisco Chronicle. "Special Section: U.S. vs. Iraq; The 1991 Gulf War" (September 24, 2002). http://www.sfgate.com/cgi-bin/article.cgi?f=/c/a/2002/09/24/MN168392.DTL&hw=The+1991+Gulf+War&sn=002&sc=713 (accessed May 2, 2007).

Schmidt, Susan, and James V. Grimaldi. "Abramoff Pleads Guilty to 3 Counts." *Washington Post,* January 4, 2006. http://www.washingtonpost.com/wp-dyn/content/article/2006/01/03/AR2006010300474_pf.html (accessed May 19, 2007).

Stanford Report. "Computerized Voting Lacks Paper Trail, Scholar Warns" (February 4, 2003). http://news-service.stanford.edu/news/2003/february5/dillsr-25.html (accessed April 28, 2007).

Wallis, Claudia. "AIDS: A Growing Threat." *Time,* April 18, 2005. http://www.time.com/time/magazine/article/0,9171,1050441,00.html (accessed May 3, 2007).

Web sites

CNN. "A Chronology: Key Moments in the Clinton-Lewinsky Saga." http://www.cnn.com/ALLPOLITICS/1998/resources/lewinsky/timeline/ (accessed May 4, 2007).

CNN. "September 11: Chronology of Terror." http://archives.cnn.com/2001/US/09/11/chronology.attack/ (accessed May 19, 2007).

Government Printing Office. "Citizen's Guide to the Federal Budget: Fiscal Year 1999." http://www.gpoaccess.gov/usbudget/fy99/guide/guide.html (accessed April 23, 2007).

Library of Congress. "H.R. 1025 (The Brady Handgun Bill)." http://thomas.loc.gov/cgi-bin/bdquery/z?d103:HR01025:&D&summ2=m& (accessed May 24, 2007).

Limburg, Val E. "U.S. Broadcasting Policy." The Museum of Broadcast Communications. http://www.museum.tv/archives/etv/F/htmlF/fairnessdoct/fairnessdoct.htm (accessed April 20, 2007).

McCarthy, Leslie. "2006 Was Earth's Fifth Warmest Year." Goddard Institute for Space Studies, National Aeronautics and Space Administration. February 8, 2007. http://www.nasa.gov/centers/goddard/news/topstory/2006/2006_warm_prt.htm (accessed May 17, 2007).

National Commission on Terrorist Attacks Upon the United States. "The 9/11 Commission Report." July 22, 2004. http://www.9-11commission.gov/report/911Report.pdf (accessed May 24, 2007).

Office of the United States Trade Representative. "NAFTA: A Strong Record of Success." *Trade Facts,* 2006. http://www.ustr.gov/assets/Document_Library/Fact_Sheets/2006/asset_upload_file242_9156.pdf (accessed May 21, 2007).

The Oyez Project. *Reno v. ACLU.* 521 U.S. 844 (1997). http://www.oyez.org/cases/1990-1999/1996/1996_96_511/ (accessed May 21, 2007).

Public Broadcasting Service. "Once upon a Time in Arkansas." *Frontline,* October 7, 1997. http://www.pbs.org/wgbh/pages/frontline/shows/arkansas/ (accessed May 4, 2007).

Public Broadcasting Service. "The Presidents: Ronald Reagan." *American Experience.* http://www.pbs.org/wgbh/amex/presidents/40_reagan/index.html (accessed May 4, 2007).

Public Broadcasting Service. "Reforming the Reform Party." *Online NewsHour,* July 26, 1999. http://www.pbs.org/newshour/bb/election/july-dec99/reform_7-26.html (accessed April 17, 2007).

The White House. "Presidents of the United States." http://www.whitehouse.gov/history/presidents/chronological.html (accessed April 9, 2007).

U.S. Commission on Civil Rights. "Voting Irregularities in Florida during the 2000 Presidential Election." *The 2000 Vote and Election Reform,* June 2001. http://www.usccr.gov/pubs/vote2000/report/main.htm (accessed May 1, 2007).

U.S. Supreme Court Center. *Texas v. Johnson,* 491 U.S. 397 (1989). http://supreme.justia.com/us/491/397/case.html (accessed May 21, 2007).

Further Reading

Alchon, Guy. *The Invisible Hand of Planning: Capitalism, Social Science, and the State in the 1920s*. Princeton, NJ: Princeton University Press, 1985.

Amar, Akhil Reed. *America's Constitution: A Biography*. New York: Random House, 2005.

Bailyn, Bernard. *The Ideological Origins of the American Revolution*. Rev. ed. Cambridge, MA: Harvard University Press, Belknap Press, 1992.

Barber, William J., ed. *The Development of the National Economy: The United States from the Civil War through the 1890s*. London: Pickering and Chatto, 2004.

Berardi, Gigi M., and Charles C. Geisler, eds. *The Social Consequences and Challenges of New Agricultural Technologies*. Boulder, CO: Westview Press, 1984.

Berkowitz, Edward, and Kim McQuaid. *Creating the Welfare State: The Political Economy of Twentieth-Century Reform*. Rev. ed. Lawrence: University Press of Kansas, 1992.

Berwanger, Eugene H. *The Frontier against Slavery: Western Anti-Negro Prejudice and the Slavery Extension Controversy*. Urbana: University of Illinois Press, 2002.

Bolger, Daniel P. *Americans at War, 1975–1986: An Era of Violent Peace*. Novato, CA: Presidio, 1988.

Bonomi, Patricia U. *Under the Cope of Heaven: Religion, Society, and Politics in Colonial America*. Rev. ed. Oxford: Oxford University Press, 2003.

Boot, Max. *The Savage Wars of Peace: Small Wars and the Rise of American Power*. New York: Basic Books, 2003.

Brinkley, Alan. *The End of Reform: New Deal Liberalism in Recession and War*. New York: Knopf, 1995.

Bruchey, Stuart. *Enterprise: The Dynamic Economy of a Free People*. Cambridge, MA: Harvard University Press, 1990.

Catton, Bruce, and William B. Catton. *The Bold and Magnificent Dream: America's Founding Years, 1492–1815*. Garden City, NY: Doubleday, 1978.

Chudacoff, Howard P., and Judith E. Smith. *The Evolution of American Urban Society*. 6th ed. Upper Saddle River, NJ: Pearson/Prentice Hall, 2005.

Curtis, Susan. *A Consuming Faith: The Social Gospel and Modern American Culture*. Baltimore, MD: Johns Hopkins University Press, 1991.

Dippie, Brian W. *The Vanishing American: White Attitudes and U.S. Indian Policy*. Middletown, CT: Wesleyan University Press, 1982.

Donaldson, Gary A. *America at War since 1945: Politics and Diplomacy in Korea, Vietnam, and the Gulf War*. Westport, CT: Praeger, 1996.

Dorrien, Gary. *The Neoconservative Mind: Politics, Culture, and the War of Ideology*. Philadelphia: Temple University Press, 1993.

Draper, Theodore. *A Struggle for Power: The American Revolution*. New York: Times Books, 1996.

Dunar, Andrew J. *America in the Fifties*. Syracuse, NY: Syracuse University Press, 2006.

Ellis, Joseph J. *After the Revolution: Profiles of Early American Culture*. New York: Norton, 1979.

Farber, David. *The Age of Great Dreams: America in the 1960s*. New York: Hill and Wang, 1994.

Foster, Gaines M. *Ghosts of the Confederacy: Defeat, the Lost Cause, and the Emergence of the New South, 1865 to 1913*. New York: Oxford University Press, 1987.

Fried, Richard M. *Nightmare in Red: The McCarthy Era in Perspective*. New York: Oxford University Press, 1990.

Gallagher, Gary W. *The Confederate War*. Cambridge, MA: Harvard University Press, 1997.

Greenberg, Jack. *Crusaders in the Courts: How a Dedicated Band of Lawyers Fought for the Civil Rights Revolution*. New York: Basic Books, 1994.

Grossberg, Lawrence. *Caught in the Crossfire: Kids, Politics, and America's Future*. Boulder, CO: Paradigm, 2005.

Grossman, Mark. *Political Corruption in America: An Encyclopedia of Scandals, Power, and Greed*. Santa Barbara, CA: ABC-CLIO, 2003.

Hawley, Ellis W. *The Great War and the Search for a Modern Order: A History of the American People and Their Institutions, 1917–1933*. 2nd ed. New York: St. Martin's Press, 1992.

Hirshson, Stanley P. *Farewell to the Bloody Shirt: Northern Republicans and the Southern Negro, 1877–1893*. Gloucester, MA: P. Smith, 1968.

Hoffman, Paul E. *A New Andalucia and a Way to the Orient: The American Southeast during the Sixteenth Century*. Baton Rouge: Louisiana State University Press, 1990.

Hoogenboom, Ari. *Outlawing the Spoils: A History of the Civil Service Reform Movement, 1865–1883*. Urbana: University of Illinois Press, 1961.

Janin, Hunt. *Claiming the American Wilderness: International Rivalry in the Trans-Mississippi West, 1528–1803*. Jefferson, NC: McFarland, 2006.

John, Elizabeth A. H. *Storms Brewed in Other Men's Worlds: The Confrontation of Indians, Spanish, and French in the Southwest, 1540–1795*. 2nd ed. Norman: University of Oklahoma Press, 1996.

Johnson, Barry L. *Environmental Policy and Public Health*. Boca Raton, FL: CRC Press, 2007.

Kagan, Robert. *Dangerous Nation*. New York: Knopf, 2006.

Kennedy, David M. *Freedom from Fear: The American People in Depression and War, 1929–1945*. New York: Oxford University Press, 1999.

Maddock, Shane J., ed. *The Nuclear Age*. Boston: Houghton Mifflin, 2001.

Matson, Cathy, ed. *The Economy of Early America: Historical Perspectives and New Directions*. University Park: Pennsylvania State University Press, 2006.

Matthews, Jean V. *Women's Struggle for Equality: The First Phase, 1828–1876*. Chicago: Ivan R. Dee, 1997.

McCullough, David. *1776*. New York: Simon and Schuster, 2005.

Morrison, Michael A. *Slavery and the American West: The Eclipse of Manifest Destiny and the Coming of the Civil War*. Chapel Hill: University of North Carolina Press, 1997.

Nye, Russel Blaine. *Society and Culture in America, 1830–1860*. New York: Harper and Row, 1974.

Pagden, Anthony. *Spanish Imperialism and the Political Imagination: Studies in European and Spanish-American Social and Political Theory, 1513–1830*. New Haven, CT: Yale University Press, 1990.

Pletcher, David M. *Diplomacy of Annexation: Texas, Oregon, and the Mexican War*. Columbia: University of Missouri Press, 1973.

Potter, David M. *The Impending Crisis, 1848–1861*. Edited and completed by Don E. Fehrenbacher. New York: Harper and Row, 1976.

Powaski, Ronald E. *Toward an Entangling Alliance: American Isolationism, Internationalism, and Europe, 1901–1950*. New York: Greenwood Press, 1991.

Prucha, Francis Paul. *The Great Father: The United States Government and the American Indians*. Lincoln: University of Nebraska Press, 1984.

Rodgers, Daniel T. *The Work Ethic in Industrial America, 1850–1920*. Chicago: University of Chicago Press, 1978.

Rosen, Ruth. *The World Split Open: How the Modern Women's Movement Changed America*. New York: Viking, 2000.

Rothman, David J. *Politics and Power: The United States Senate, 1869–1901*. Cambridge, MA: Harvard University Press, 1966.

Scammell, G. V. *The First Imperial Age: European Overseas Expansion c. 1475–1715*. London: Unwin Hyman, 1989.

Shilts, Randy. *And the Band Played On: Politics, People, and the AIDS Epidemic*. New York: St. Martin's Press, 1987.

Sigler, Jay A. *Civil Rights in America: 1500 to the Present*. Detroit: Gale, 1998.

Silber, Nina. *The Romance of Reunion: Northerners and the South, 1865–1900*. Chapel Hill: University of North Carolina Press, 1993.

Solow, Barbara L., ed. *Slavery and the Rise of the Atlantic System*. Cambridge, U.K.: Cambridge University Press, 1991.

Steele, Ian K. *Warpaths: Invasions of North America*. New York: Oxford University Press, 1994.

Toobin, Jeffrey. *The Nine: Inside the Secret World of the Supreme Court*. New York: Doubleday, 2007.

Traxel, David. *Crusader Nation: The United States in Peace and the Great War, 1898–1920*. New York: Knopf, 2006.

Watkins, T. H. *The Hungry Years: A Narrative History of the Great Depression in America*. New York: Henry Holt, 1999.

Weisbrot, Robert. *Freedom Bound: A History of America's Civil Rights Movement*. New York: Norton, 1990.

Index

E